Using 1-2-3 Release 2.2

Special Edition

Developed by
Que Corporation

que®
CORPORATION
LEADING COMPUTER KNOWLEDGE

Using 1-2-3® Release 2.2

Copyright © 1989 by Que® Corporation

Library of Congress Catalog No.: LC 89-62443
ISBN 0-88022-501-7

92 91 90 89   5 4 3 2

Interpretation of the printing code: the rightmost double-digit number is the year of the book's printing; the rightmost single-digit number, the number of the book's printing. For example, a printing code of 89-4 shows that the fourth printing of the book occurred in 1989.

Using 1-2-3 Release 2.2, Special Edition, is based on 1-2-3 Releases 2.01 and 2.2.

ABOUT THE AUTHORS

David P. Ewing is publishing director for Que Corporation. He is the author of Que's *1-2-3 Macro Library*, *Using 1-2-3 Workbook and Disk*, and *Using 1-2-3 Workbook and Instructor's Guide*; coauthor of Que's *Using Symphony*, *Using Q&A*, *Using Javelin*, and *1-2-3 Macro Workbook*; and contributing author to *Using 1-2-3 Release 3*, *Using 1-2-3*, Special Edition, *1-2-3 QuickStart*, and *Upgrading to 1-2-3 Release 3*. Over the past five years, in addition to authoring and coauthoring a number of Que titles, Ewing has served as product development director for many of Que's application software and DOS titles. He has directed the development of such series as the Que workbooks and instructor's guides, QueCards, and QuickStart books.

Joseph Desposito is a free-lance writer who was recently the senior project leader at PC Labs for *PC Magazine*. He has been the technical editor for several other leading publications. He worked as editor-in-chief and publisher of *PC Clones* magazine. He has also worked for several publications, including *Creative Computing* and *Computers and Electronics*.

Rebecca Bridges has a degree from Stanford in economics. She owns her own microcomputer training and consulting business. Her specialty is developing computer training materials. She is technical editor for *Absolute Reference: The Journal for 1-2-3 and Symphony Users* and the revision author for Que's *1-2-3 Release 2.2 Quick Reference*; *1-2-3 QueCards*, 2nd Edition; and *Using Symphony*, 2nd Edition.

Timothy S. Stanley has worked for Que since 1985 as a technical editor. In addition to technical editing a number of Que's books, he has contributed to *Using 1-2-3 Release 3*, *Upgrading to 1-2-3 Release 3*, and *Absolute Reference: The Journal for 1-2-3 and Symphony Users*.

Bill Weil works extensively with 1-2-3 and Symphony, and has contributed to Que's *Using 1-2-3 Release 3*; *Using 1-2-3*, Special Edition; and *1-2-3 Tips, Tricks, and Traps*, 2nd Edition. Weil, who has 20 years of experience with computers of all sizes, formed Pacific Micro Group in 1987 to provide consulting services to large businesses.

Marianne B. Fox, CPA, holds a full-time faculty position with Butler University where she teaches a variety of accounting and computer-related courses. She is co-owner of A & M Services, Inc., a firm specializing in microcomputer systems design, requirement analysis, and training. She is coauthor of *1-2-3 Release 3 Workbook and Disk*, *1-2-3 Release 2.2 Workbook and Disk*, *dBASE IV QuickStart*, and *WordPerfect 5 Workbook and Disk*. She is a contributing author to *Using 1-2-3*, Special Edition.

Lawrence C. Metzelaar lectures at Vincennes University and Ohio State University. He is co-owner of A & M Services, Inc., a firm specializing in microcomputer systems design, requirement analysis, and training. He is coauthor of *1-2-3 Release 3 Workbook and Disk*, *1-2-3 Release 2.2 Workbook and Disk*, *dBASE IV QuickStart*, and *WordPerfect 5 Workbook and Disk*. He is contributing author to *Using 1-2-3*, Special Edition.

Publishing Director

David P. Ewing

Product Line Director

David P. Ewing

Acquisitions Editor

Terrie Lynn Solomon

Editors

Shelley O'Hara   Kathie-Jo Arnoff
Lisa Hunt   Virginia Noble
Alice Martina Smith   Martin E. Brown

Acquisitions Aide

Stacey Beheler

Technical Editors

Bob Breedlove   David A. Knispel
Larry D. Lynch   Lynda Fox-Robling

Book Design and Production

Dan Armstrong   Jon Ogle
Brad Chinn   Cindy L. Phipps
Gail Francis   Joe Ramon
David Kline   Dennis Sheehan
Lori A. Lyons   Mae Louise Shinault
John Malloy   Peter Tocco
Jennifer Matthews

Indexer

reVisions Plus, Inc.

Composed in Garamond and Excellent No. 47
by Que Corporation

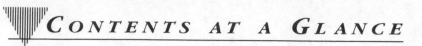

CONTENTS AT A GLANCE

TABLE OF CONTENTS

II   **Creating 1-2-3 Reports and Graphs**

14   Introducing the Advanced Macro Commands............................... 517

IV   Quick Reference Guide to 1-2-3

ACKNOWLEDGMENTS

Using 1-2-3 Release 2.2, Special Edition, is the result of the immense efforts of many dedicated people. Que Corporation thanks the following individuals for their contributions to the development of this book.

Shelley O'Hara, for her direction and coordination of the many editors working on this project and for her determination to produce the highest quality 1-2-3 Release 2.2 book available.

Lisa Hunt, for her excellent editing of the Command Reference, for the many long days and nights she devoted to completing the final stages of the book project, and for being a constant reminder to all of us how to handle pressure gracefully.

Alice Martina Smith, for the tremendous effort she put forth as a new editor taking on full responsibility for the production edit of many of the book's chapters and for her attention to improving the content of Chapters 9, 10, and 13 and the Troubleshooting Section.

Terrie Lynn Solomon, for her incredible organizational skills and for masterminding and managing the flow of materials between authors and editors. Also, thanks to Terrie for being sensitive to keeping all of us calm during the last days of working on this book.

Tim Stanley, for many technical and developmental contributions he made to this book, for providing support to editors and technical editors, and for his willingness to take on more than most people can handle, yet respond to every request and respond well.

Kathie-Jo Arnoff and Ginny Noble, for their versatility and outstanding editing skills that enabled them to "pinch hit" during the final days of this book project.

Lynda Fox-Robling and David Solomon, for pitching in during the final days of this book project to assist with the development and technical review of chapters and appendixes in this book.

Stacey Beheler, for handling the flow of materials between authors, editors, and production staff and for providing editorial assistance on the manuscript.

Doug Dunn, Joe Ramon, and Lori Lyons, for their extraordinary cooperation, the excellent communication they provided to the editing department, and for being key team players working on this book.

Brad Chinn, Jon Ogle, Dan Armstrong, Dennis Sheehan, Jennifer Matthews, Gail Francis, Louise Shinault, Cindy Phipps, and John Malloy for making this project a top priority for the Que typesetting and paste-up department and for being dedicated to producing the quality final pages for this book.

David Kline and Peter Tocco, for the excellent proofing they did of this book.

Kathy Murray, for the complete index she developed for this book.

Last, but not least, Que thanks Lotus Development Corporation for the tremendous support provided during the development of *Using 1-2-3 Release 2.2*, Special Edition:

Chris Noble, Product Design Manager, for his time and interest in providing Que with up-to-date information on the development of Release 2.2.

Mary-Beth Rettger, Beta Test Administrator, for providing technical assistance throughout the development of *Using 1-2-3 Release 2.2*, Special Edition.

Alexandria Trevelyan, Public Relations Specialist, and Mary Ann Singleton, Public Relations Assistant, for their constant support, for assistance in answering questions and solving problems as they arose while authors and editors were developing *Using 1-2-3 Release 2.2*, Special Edition.

TRADEMARK
ACKNOWLEDGMENTS

Que Corporation has made every effort to supply trademark information about company names, products, and services mentioned in this book. Trademarks indicated below were derived from various sources. Que Corporation cannot attest to the accuracy of this information.

A number of conventions are used in *Using 1-2-3 Release 2.2*, Special Edition, to help you learn the program. One example is provided for each convention to help you distinguish among the different elements in 1-2-3.

References to keys are as they appear on the keyboard of the IBM personal computer. The function keys, F1 through F10, are used for special situations in 1-2-3. In the text, the key name is usually followed by the number in parentheses: Graph (F10).

Direct quotations of words that appear on-screen are printed in a special typeface. Information you are asked to type is printed in **boldface**. The first letter of each command from 1-2-3's menu system also appears in **boldface**: **/R**ange Format Currency.

Elements printed in uppercase include range names (SALES), functions (@PMT), modes (READY), and cell references (A1..G5).

Conventions that pertain to macros deserve special mention here:

1. Macro names appear with the backslash (Alt-character combinations) and single-character names in lowercase: \a. In this example, the \ indicates that you press the Alt key and hold it down while you also press the A key.

2. All /x macro commands, such as /xm or /xn, appear in lowercase.

3. Representations of cursor-movement keys {RIGHT}, function keys {CALC}, and editing keys {DEL} appear in uppercase and in braces.

4. Advanced macro commands appear in uppercase: MENUBRANCH. In the command syntax, the command is enclosed in braces: {MENUBRANCH location}.

5. 1-2-3 menu keystrokes in a macro line appear in lowercase; range names within macros appear in uppercase: /rncTEST.

6. Enter is represented by the tilde (~).

Introduction

Since 1983, Que has helped more than two million spreadsheet users learn the commands, features, and functions of Lotus 1-2-3. *Using 1-2-3*—through three editions—has become the standard guide to 1-2-3 for both new and experienced 1-2-3 users worldwide. Now with the publication of *Using 1-2-3 Release 2.2*, Special Edition, Que builds on those six years of experience to bring you the most comprehensive tutorial and reference available for the new Release 2.2, as well as Release 2.01.

Que's unprecedented experience with 1-2-3—and 1-2-3 users—has resulted in this high-quality, informative book. But a book like *Using 1-2-3 Release 2.2*, Special Edition, does not develop overnight. This book is the result of long hours of work from a team of expert authors and dedicated editors.

The experts who developed *Using 1-2-3 Release 2.2*, Special Edition, are experienced with many of the ways 1-2-3 is used every day. As consultants, trainers, and 1-2-3 users, the authors of *Using 1-2-3 Release 2.2*, Special Edition, have used 1-2-3 and have taught others how to use 1-2-3 to build many types of applications—from accounting and general business applications to scientific applications. This experience, combined with the editorial expertise of the world's leading 1-2-3 publisher, brings you outstanding tutorial and reference information.

Using 1-2-3 Release 2.2, Special Edition, is the best available guide to 1-2-3 Releases 2.2 and 2.01. Whether you are using 1-2-3 for inventory control, statistical analysis, or portfolio management, this book is designed for you. Like previous editions of this title, *Using 1-2-3 Release 2.2*, Special Edition, leads you step-by-step from spreadsheet basics to the advanced features of 1-2-3. Whether you are a new user or an experienced user upgrading to Release 2.2, this book will occupy a prominent place next to your computer, as a tried and valued reference to your most-used spreadsheet program.

Who Should Read This Book

Using 1-2-3 Release 2.2, Special Edition, is written and organized to meet the needs of a wide range of readers, from first-time users of 1-2-3 Release 2.01 and 2.2, to experienced Release 2.01 users who are still using Release 2.01 or who are upgrading to Release 2.2, to experienced Release 2.2 users.

If Release 2.01 or 2.2 is your first 1-2-3 package, this book will help you learn all the basics so that you can quickly begin using 1-2-3. The first five chapters in particular teach you basic concepts for understanding 1-2-3—commands, special uses of the keyboard, features of the 1-2-3 screen, and methods for creating and modifying 1-2-3 worksheets.

If you are an experienced 1-2-3 Release 2.01 user and have upgraded to Release 2.2, this book describes all the new features in Release 2.2 and explains how to apply them as you develop worksheet applications, create graphs, and print reports and graphs. The special Release 2.2 icon in the margin marks those places in the text where a Release 2.2 feature is described.

If you are an experienced Release 2.01 user who intends to continue to use that release, you will find a wealth of information pertinent to 1-2-3 Release 2.01 included in this book. Clear references in the text and icons in the margin indicate those features not included in your particular release.

Whether you are new to either release of 1-2-3, are upgrading to Release 2.2, or are using Release 2.01, *Using 1-2-3 Release 2.2*, Special Edition, provides tips and techniques to help you get the most from 1-2-3. As you continue to use 1-2-3, you'll find that you turn time and again to the 1-2-3 Command Reference with its easy-to-use format. The Command Reference reminds you of the steps, tips, and cautions for using 1-2-3 commands.

The Details of This Book

If you flip quickly through this book, you can get a better sense of its organization and layout. The book is organized to follow the natural flow of learning and using 1-2-3.

Part I—Building the 1-2-3 Worksheet

Chapter 1, "An Overview of 1-2-3 Releases 2.2 and 2.01," presents an overview of 1-2-3, including the uses, features, and commands in both Release 2.01 and 2.2, along with new Release 2.2 features. Also, this chapter introduces the general concepts of 1-2-3 as a spreadsheet program and introduces the program's major uses—creating worksheets, databases, graphics, and macros.

Chapter 2, "Getting Started," helps you begin using 1-2-3 Release 2.01 or 2.2 for the first time, including starting and exiting from the program, learning special uses of the keyboard, understanding features of the 1-2-3 screen display, getting on-screen help, and using the 1-2-3 tutorials.

Chapter 3, "Learning Worksheet Basics," introduces the concepts of worksheets and files and teaches you how to move the cell pointer around the worksheet, enter and edit data, and, for Release 2.2 users, use the new Undo feature. 1-2-3 Release 2.2 users also learn how to create formulas that link cells of different worksheets.

Chapter 4, "Using Fundamental 1-2-3 Commands," teaches you how to use the 1-2-3 command menus to access the fundamental commands for building worksheets. You also learn how to save your worksheet files and leave 1-2-3 temporarily to return to the operating system.

Chapter 5, "Formatting Cell Contents," shows you how to change the way data appears on-screen, including the way values, formulas, and text are displayed. You also learn how to suppress the display of zeros.

Chapter 6, "Using Functions in the Worksheet," covers the following functions available in Releases 2.2 and 2.01: mathematical, trigonometric, statistical, financial, accounting, logical, special, date, time, and string functions.

Chapter 7, "Managing Files," explains those commands related to saving, erasing, and listing files as well as commands for combining data from several files and extracting data from one file to another. In addition to introducing these commands, Chapter 7 teaches you how to transfer files between different programs and how to use 1-2-3 Release 2.2 in a multiuser environment.

Part II—Creating 1-2-3 Reports and Graphs

Chapter 8, "Printing Reports," shows you how to print a report immediately or create a file to be read by another program. You learn how to create a basic report as well as enhance a report by using commands to add such elements as headers and footers, to change margins, and to use setup strings for changing type size or font.

Chapter 9, "Using Allways: The Spreadsheet Publisher," is meant for users of 1-2-3 Release 2.2 who receive Allways as part of their 1-2-3 package, and also for users of 1-2-3 Release 2.01 who already have a copy or will purchase the Allways add-in program. You learn how to use this program to produce presentation-quality output directly from 1-2-3, to include 1-2-3 graphs in the same printouts as worksheet data, and to vary fonts, shading, and text attributes, among other things.

Chapter 10, "Creating and Displaying Graphs," shows you how to take advantage of 1-2-3's considerable graphics capabilities by creating basic line, bar, stack-bar, XY, and pie graphs. The chapter also shows you how to enhance basic graphs in a variety of ways including adding legends and titles, changing scale, and displaying graphs in color.

Chapter 11, "Printing Graphs," teaches you how to use the PrintGraph utility program to print graphs and to improve the appearance of printed graphs. The chapter also shows you how to tailor PrintGraph to your particular hardware setup.

Part III—Customizing 1-2-3

Chapter 12, "Managing Data," introduces the advantages and limitations of 1-2-3's database capabilities and shows you how to create, modify, and maintain data records, including sorting, locating, and extracting data. Chapter 12 also covers the special commands and features of 1-2-3 data management, such as database statistical functions, parsing data to use in the worksheet, and regression analysis.

Chapter 13, "Using Macros To Customize Your Worksheet," is an introduction to the powerful macro capability in both Release 2.2 and 2.01. This chapter teaches you how to create, name, and run macros and build a macro library. Also, the chapter covers macro features specific to Release 2.2, such as creating a macro by automatically recording keystrokes, naming macros with descriptive names, invoking macros from a menu, and using the Macro Library Manager.

Chapter 14, "Introducing the Advanced Macro Commands," explains the powerful advanced macro commands in Releases 2.2 and 2.01, and includes a complete reference of all advanced macro commands with numerous examples of their use.

Part IV—Quick Reference Guide to 1-2-3

"Troubleshooting" is an easy-to-use problem-solving section that can help everyone from the novice user to the most advanced "power user." You can use the section both as a reference when you have problems and as a source of practical advice and tips as you browse through the book.

"1-2-3 Command Reference" is a quick, easy-to-use, and comprehensive guide to the procedures for using almost every command on the command menus. This section also gives numerous reminders, important cues, and cautions that will greatly simplify and expedite your day-to-day use of 1-2-3.

Appendixes

Appendix A of this book shows you how to install 1-2-3 Release 2.2 for your hardware and operating system.

Appendix B provides a summary of the features specific to Release 2.2.

Other Titles To Enhance Your Personal Computing

Although *Using 1-2-3 Release 2.2*, Special Edition, is a comprehensive guide to both Release 2.2 and Release 2.01, no single book can fill all your 1-2-3 and personal computing needs. Que Corporation publishes a full line of microcomputer books that complement this best seller.

Several Que books can help you learn and master your operating system. *Using PC DOS*, 3rd Edition, is an excellent guide to the IBM-specific PC DOS operating system. Its counterpart—written for all DOS users—is *MS-DOS User's Guide*, 3rd Edition. Both books provide the same type of strong tutorial and complete command reference found in *Using 1-2-3 Release 2.2*, Special Edition. If you prefer to get up and running with DOS fundamentals in a quick manner, try Que's *MS-DOS QuickStart*. This graphics-based tutorial helps you teach yourself the fundamentals of DOS. If you plan to run 1-2-3 Release 2.2 or 2.01 under OS/2, you will want the information and suggestions in *Using OS/2*.

You are probably using 1-2-3 on a personal computer equipped with a hard disk drive. The key to efficient computer use is effective hard-disk management. Que's *Managing Your Hard Disk*, 2nd Edition, shows you how to get the most from your hard disk by streamlining your use of directories, creating batch files, and more. This well-written text will be an invaluable addition to your library of personal computer books.

As you may be aware, 1-2-3 Releases 2.2 and 2.01 will run faster on more powerful computing equipment. If you find that your current computer hardware does not give you the level of performance you want, examine Que's *Upgrading and Repairing PCs*. This informative text shows you how to get the most from your current hardware and how to upgrade your system to get the most from high-powered software—such as 1-2-3 Releases 2.2 and 2.01. Mark Brownstein called this book "one of the best books about the workings of personal computers I've ever seen; it will be a useful, easy-to-read, and interesting addition to most anyone's library."

Learning More about 1-2-3

If *Using 1-2-3 Release 2.2*, Special Edition, whets your appetite for more information about 1-2-3, you're in good company. More than one million *Using 1-2-3* readers have gone on to purchase one or more additional Que books about 1-2-3.

1-2-3 Release 2.2 Business Applications is a book and disk set that provides you with a series of business models in ready-to-run form. This book is a time-saver for the dedicated 1-2-3 user.

1-2-3 Database Techniques contains concepts and techniques to help you create complex 1-2-3 database application. Also valuable to users of Release 3, this book introduces database fundamentals, compares 1-2-3 with traditional database programs, offers numerous application tips, and discusses add-in programs.

1-2-3 Release 2.2 Quick Reference is an affordable, compact reference to the most commonly used Release 2.01 and 2.2 commands and functions. This book is a great book to keep near your computer when you need fast information on proper 1-2-3 procedures.

1-2-3 Tips, Tricks, and Traps, 3rd Edition, covers all releases of 1-2-3 and presents hundreds of tips and techniques to help you get the most from the program. This book covers all the new features of Release 2.2, including the Allways program.

1-2-3 Graphics Techniques is designed specifically to help you increase the quality of your 1-2-3 output. Written for all 1-2-3 releases, this book shows you how to create more effective graphs and charts, and provides you with tips and techniques to get the most out of Allways.

1-2-3 Macro Library, 3rd Edition, is a comprehensive guide to 1-2-3 macros and advanced macro commands. A complete library of useful macros is included on the bound-in disk.

In addition to these books, Que publishes several books for new Release 2.2 users: *1-2-3 Release 2.2 QuickStart* and *1-2-3 Release 2.2 Workbook and Disk*. Que also publishes a complete line of books for users of 1-2-3 Release 3, including *Using 1-2-3 Release 3* and *1-2-3 Release 3 QuickStart*. Of interest to all 1-2-3 users is the book *Upgrading to 1-2-3 Release 3*. If you have any questions about Release 3, this book has the answers.

Also from Que is a book on Lotus's newest program, Magellan. *Using Lotus Magellan* guides you through the operations and applications of Magellan, an advanced file-management program of particular value to 1-2-3 users.

Finally, *Absolute Reference* is Que's monthly journal for 1-2-3 and Symphony power users. Now in its sixth year of publication, *Absolute Reference* is read by thousands of users eager to get new 1-2-3 information, applications, and tips every month.

All these books can be found in better bookstores worldwide. In the United States, you can call Que at 1-800-428-5331 to order books or obtain further information.

Summary

Using 1-2-3 Release 2.2, Special Edition, for Releases 2.2 and 2.01 follows the Que tradition of providing quality text that is targeted appropriately for the 1-2-3 user. Because of the dedication to this goal, Que ultimately has only one way of improving—by hearing from you. Let Que know how you feel about this book or any other Que title. Que wants to keep improving its books, and you are the best source of information.

Part I

Building the 1-2-3 Worksheet

Includes

An Overview of 1-2-3 Releases 2.01 and 2.2

Getting Started

Learning Worksheet Basics

Using Fundamental 1-2-3 Commands

Formatting Cell Contents

Using Functions in the Worksheet

Managing Files

1

An Overview of 1-2-3
Releases 2.01 and 2.2

For more than five years, 1-2-3 has been the dominant spreadsheet software product used in businesses worldwide. Today, 1-2-3 is used by five million people and continues to be the standard.

When first introduced in 1983, 1-2-3 revolutionized microcomputing by replacing the dominant spreadsheet product at the time, VisiCalc, and soon became the program identified with the IBM PC and the established tool for financial analysis. Designed for 16-bit computers like the IBM personal computer, the first release of 1-2-3 took full advantage of the computer's speed and memory capacity. As computer hardware advanced, providing power far beyond the original IBM PC, 1-2-3 kept in step by taking advantage of the newer machines' expanded capabilities. With the availability (and lower costs) of more memory, faster speed, and hard disk drives, Lotus developed Release 2.

With the introduction of Release 2.2 in 1989, 1-2-3 remains the leader in microcomputer spreadsheet software by maintaining the overall functionality, command structure, and screen and keyboard features of Release 2.01. At the same time, however, Release 2.2 provides many significant improvements over Release 2.01: the capability to link worksheet files, improved printed worksheets and graphs, improved graphics, and enhanced macro capabilities.

Why is 1-2-3 so popular? 1-2-3 provides users with three fundamental applications integrated in one program. Without having to learn three separate kinds of software, you can perform financial analysis with the 1-2-3 worksheet, create database applications, and create graphs. Commands for all

Reminder:
You can use 1-2-3 to create three kinds of applications: worksheets, databases, and graphs.

11

three applications are combined in one main menu and are accessed easily. When a command is selected, prompts guide you through each step needed to perform a task.

This chapter presents an overview of 1-2-3 Releases 2.2 and 2.01, including the uses, features, and commands in each release that are the same. This chapter also points out what's new in 1-2-3 Release 2.2. If you are upgrading from 1-2-3 Release 2.01, this chapter provides a general introduction to the differences between Releases 2.2 and 2.01 and identifies many of the features and commands that are unique to Release 2.2. Specifically, in this chapter you learn about the following topics:

- The general capabilities of 1-2-3 (presented especially for those readers who are new to 1-2-3)

- An overview of the features that are special to Release 2.2 (developed for readers who are planning to or have just upgraded from Release 2.0 or 2.01)

- Features that identify 1-2-3 as a spreadsheet program, including creating, modifying, and using 1-2-3 worksheets

- File-management capabilities and worksheet and file protection

- The creation of 1-2-3 reports, graphs, and databases

- Keyboard macros and advanced macro commands

- The hardware and operating system requirements for running 1-2-3 Releases 2.2 and 2.01

Introducing 1-2-3 Release 2.2

Because 1-2-3 Release 2.2 is one of Lotus Development Corporation's newest products, let's take a moment to examine some of the ways it differs from 1-2-3 Release 2.01. If you have used a previous version of 1-2-3, you will find the program unchanged in its primary functions. You still can use 1-2-3 Release 2.2 for creating simple to complex financial applications; for organizing, sorting, extracting, and finding information; and for creating graphs.

Reminder:
Release 2.2 adds several new features to 1-2-3, including the capability to link files.

What makes Release 2.2 different from 2.01 and other versions of 1-2-3? The major enhancements to Release 2.2 over Releases 2.01, 2.0, 1A, and 1 include the following:

- The capability to link the cells of one worksheet to another worksheet

- Enhancements that make Release 2.2 easier to use than earlier versions, such as the capabilities to adjust the widths of several columns in a range at once; to search for and replace labels and strings in formulas; to check graph, print, worksheet, and other settings; and to create a graph without having to enter each separate range manually

- Improved report and graph printing through the add-in program All-ways

- The capability to undo a worksheet change or command operation

- A minimal recalculation capability that lets 1-2-3 Release 2.2 recalculate only those cells affected by a change in the worksheet

- New macro commands, the capability to create macros automatically, and the capability to store and access macros in an area of memory separate from the worksheet

A more specific discussion of these features is provided in the following sections and in chapters throughout the book.

Using 1-2-3 as an "Electronic" Accountant's Pad

Although Release 2.2 provides many new capabilities, it also retains the familiar command menu, structure, and uses of previous releases of 1-2-3. Releases 2.2 and 2.01, as well as earlier versions, can be described as an electronic accountant's pad or electronic spreadsheet. Whenever you start 1-2-3 Release 2.2 or 2.01, your computer screen displays a column-and-row area into which you can enter text, numbers, or formulas as an accountant would on one sheet of a columnar pad and with the help of a calculator (see fig. 1.1).

With Releases 2.2 and 2.01, as with earlier versions of 1-2-3, the worksheet is the basis for the whole product. Whether you are working with a database application or creating graphs, you complete both operations within the structure of the worksheet. Graphs are created from data entered in the worksheet; database operations are performed on data organized into the worksheet's column-and-row format, and macro programs are stored down a column of the worksheet.

In addition to performing operations within the worksheet, you also initiate all commands the same, from the main menu (see fig. 1.2). And you enter data in the same way for all operations. All data—text, numbers, or formulas—are stored in individual cells in the worksheet. 1-2-3 sets aside a rectangular area—a single cell, its location indicated by the intersection of a particular column and row on the worksheet. If you type a number in the cell two rows down from the top border and three columns to the left of the left border, you are entering the number in cell C2 (see fig. 1.3). Columns in the worksheet are marked by letters from A to IV; rows are marked by numbers 1 to 8,192.

Fig. 1.1.
1-2-3 as an accountant's columnar pad.

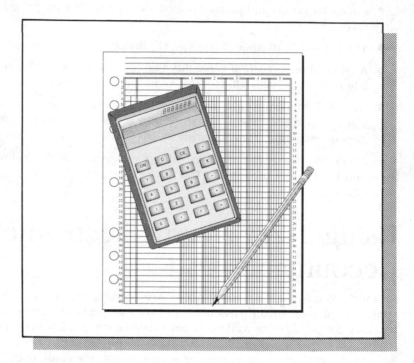

Fig. 1.2.
The main 1-2-3 command menu.

```
A20: [W9]                                                              MENU
Worksheet Range Copy Move File Print Graph Data System Add-In Quit
Global  Insert  Delete  Column  Erase  Titles  Window  Status  Page  Learn
          A         B         C         D         E         F         G
1   1989 CASH FLOW DATA
2
3   =========================================================================
4   WORKING CAPITAL ACCOUNTS          Jan       Feb       Mar       Apr
5   =========================================================================
6   Current Assets:
7     Cash                          $31,643   $34,333   $36,657   $35,614
8     Accounts Receivable           510,780   533,597   551,287   577,314
9     Inventory                     169,209   176,671   189,246   206,788
10                                  --------  --------  --------  --------
11      Total Current Assets        711,632   744,601   777,189   819,715
12
13  Current Liabilities:
14    Accounts Payable              130,754   139,851   150,186   163,731
15    Other Short-term Debt               0         0         0         0
16                                  --------  --------  --------  --------
17      Total Current Liabilities   130,754   139,851   150,186   163,731
18
19  Net Working Capital            $580,878  $604,750  $627,003  $655,984
20                                  ========  ========  ========  ========
14-Jul-89  05:05 PM
```

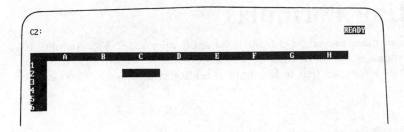

Fig. 1.3.
A 1-2-3
worksheet cell.

Potentially, you could fill more than 2,000,000 cells in a single worksheet. Most likely, few users will need or have computer equipment to handle this much data. At the minimum, though, Release 2.01 requires 256 kilobytes (K) of memory, and Release 2.2 requires 320K of memory. To use the Allways add-in program, you need 512K of memory. See table 1.1 for a complete list of 1-2-3 Releases 2.2 and 2.01 specifications. Also, see the section "Understanding 1-2-3 Hardware Requirements and Options" later in this chapter.

Reminder:
Release 2.01
requires 256K
memory; Release
2.2 requires 320K.

Table 1.1
1-2-3 Releases 2.2 and 2.01 at a Glance

Published by:	Lotus Development Corporation 55 Cambridge Parkway Cambridge, Massachusetts 02142
System Requirements:	IBM PC or IBM PS/2 compatible
Display:	VGA, EGA, or CGA color or monochrome
Disk Drives:	Two floppy disk drives or one hard disk drive and one floppy disk drive
Memory:	320K RAM (Release 2.2) (512K with Allways) 256K RAM (Release 2.01)
Maximum usable memory:	640K conventional memory 4M expanded memory
Operating System:	DOS V2.0 or later
Other hardware:	Color/graphics adapter, printer, plotter, expanded memory card, 8087, 80287, or 80387 math coprocessor
Price:	$495

Creating Formulas

Because the primary use of 1-2-3 is financial applications, 1-2-3's capability to develop formulas is one of its most sophisticated and yet easy-to-use features. You can create a formula that is as simple as adding the values in two cells of a worksheet:

+A1+B1

This formula entered in another cell, such as C1, indicates that the value stored in cell A1 will be added to the value stored in B1. The formula does not depend on the specific values contained in A1 and B1, but adds whatever values are entered. If A1 contains the value 4 and B1 the value 3, the formula computes to 7. If you change the value in A1 to 5, the formula automatically recalculates to 8. You can create formulas with the following operators: addition (+), subtraction (−), multiplication (*), and division (/).

RELEASE

2.2

Reminder:
Release 2.2 allows
you to link files.

In addition to entering formulas that calculate numeric results, you can access data from one worksheet file in another worksheet file and then create a formula that calculates the data from the outside file. A significant change between Release 2.2 and prior versions of 1-2-3 is its file-linking capabilities. Previous releases of 1-2-3 do not allow you to access information from worksheets saved on disk from the worksheet in memory. But Release 2.2 provides this capability. By referencing cells in other worksheets, formulas can calculate results from numerous, separate worksheet applications.

When you access data from another worksheet, you first indicate what worksheet the data is located in (indicated by the file name of the worksheet); then you follow this file name with a cell reference. The following example shows an entry that links data between two worksheets:

+<<SALES.WK1>>C5

What are the advantages of linking files? First of all, it's ideal for consolidations—consolidations of regional sales, of department budgets, of product forecasts, and so on. You easily can create formulas that consolidate data from other worksheets saved to disk. And these formulas are updated automatically anytime you change the data in the other file.

You might, for example, receive data from separate departments (in separate files) to consolidate. Your consolidation file can use formulas to combine the data from each separate file. The process also works in reverse. You can have a central database file as well as separate files to distribute to each department. The individual department files can contain formulas that refer to data in the central database file. See Chapter 3 for more information on creating formulas that link data across files.

Recalculating Formulas in Release 2.2

As you create formulas, 1-2-3 recalculates and updates the worksheet. Normally, 1-2-3 recalculates the file whenever any cell changes. This feature is called automatic recalculation. With versions of 1-2-3 previous to Release 2.2, large worksheets could take a long time to recalculate, slowing work greatly. With Release 2.2, however, recalculation is now optimal.

Optimal recalculation means that only cells that contain formulas that refer to the changed cell are recalculated. If you change a cell in a large file and that cell is used in only one formula, only that one formula is recalculated. Recalculation is therefore fast.

Playing "What If" with 1-2-3

Because 1-2-3 remembers the relationships between cells and does not simply calculate values, you can change a value in a cell and see what happens when your formulas automatically recalculate. This "what if" capability makes 1-2-3 an incredibly powerful tool for many types of analysis. You can, for example, analyze the effect of an expected increase in the cost of goods and determine what kind of price increase may be needed to maintain your current profit margins. Creating formulas is discussed in Chapters 3 and 4.

Using Release 2.2 and 2.01 Functions

Without the capabilities to calculate complex mathematical, statistical, logical, financial, and other types of formulas, building applications in 1-2-3 would be difficult. 1-2-3 Releases 2.2 and 2.01, however, provide 88 and 90 functions, respectively, that let you create complex formulas for a wide range of applications, including business, scientific, and engineering applications. Instead of entering complicated formulas containing operators and parentheses, you can use functions as a shortcut to creating such formulas.

Reminder:
Releases 2.01 and 2.2 provide 88 and 90 functions, respectively.

All functions in 1-2-3 begin with the @ sign followed by the name of the function—for example, @SUM, @RAND, @ROUND. Many functions require that you enter an argument, the specifications of the functions needed to calculate the formula, after the function name.

Releases 2.2 and 2.01 include seven categories of functions: (1) mathematical and trigonometric, (2) statistical, (3) financial and accounting, (4) logical, (5) special, (6) date and time, and (7) string.

Mathematical Functions

The mathematical functions, which include logarithmic and trigonometric functions, provide convenient tools that let you easily perform a variety of standard arithmetical operations such as adding and rounding values or calculating square roots. For engineering and scientific applications, 1-2-3 includes all standard trigonometric functions, such as those to calculate sine (@SIN), cosine (@COS), and tangent (@TAN).

Statistical Functions

1-2-3 Releases 2.2 and 2.01 include a set of seven statistical and seven database statistical functions that allow you to perform all the standard statistical calculations on your worksheet data or in a 1-2-3 database. You can find minimum and maximum values (@MIN and @MAX), calculate averages (@AVG), and compute standard deviations and variances (@STD and @VAR). Database statistical functions are specialized versions of the statistical functions; these functions apply only to 1-2-3 databases.

Financial Functions

Financial functions allow you to perform a series of discounted cash flow, depreciation, and compound-interest calculations that ease considerably the burden and tediousness of investment analysis and accounting or budgeting for depreciable assets. Specifically, the 1-2-3 Release 2.2 and 2.01 functions include two that calculate returns on investments (@IRR and @RATE), one that calculates loan investments (@PMT), two that calculate present values (@NPV and @PV), one that calculates future values (@FV), two that perform compound-growth calculations (@TERM and @CTERM), and three functions that calculate asset depreciation (@SLN, @DDB, and @SYD).

Logical Functions

The logical functions let you add standard Boolean logic to your worksheet and use the logic either alone or as part of other worksheet formulas. Essentially, each of the logical functions allows you to test whether a condition—either one you've defined or one of 1-2-3's predefined conditions—is true or false. The @IF function, for example, tests a condition and returns one result if the condition is true and another if the condition is false.

RELEASE

2.2

New to 1-2-3 Release 2.2 are two functions that help you check the status of add-in functions and programs. The @ISAFF function checks the status of an add-in function and also discriminates between add-in and built-in functions.

The @ISAPP function checks whether a particular add-in program has been installed or attached with the Add-In Manager.

Special Functions

Special functions are tools for dealing with the worksheet itself. For example, one special function returns information about specific cells. Others count the number of rows or columns in a range. @CELL and @CELLPOINTER can return up to 10 different characteristics of a cell, including the type of address and prefix, format, and width of a cell. The special functions are often used in macro programs.

Date and Time Functions

The date and time functions allow you to convert dates, such as June 7, 1989, and times, such as 11:00 a.m., to serial numbers and then use these serial numbers to perform date and time arithmetic. These functions are a valuable aid when dates and times affect worksheet calculations and logic. Date and time functions are also useful for documenting your worksheets and reports. For example, you can enter date and time functions that display the current date and time in your worksheet. If you include the cells that contain these functions in your print range when you print a report, the report will show the date and time you prepared the report.

String Functions

String functions help you manipulate text. You can use string functions to repeat text characters, to convert letters in a string to upper- or lowercase, and to change strings to numbers and numbers to strings. You also can use string functions to locate or extract characters and replace characters.

Using the 1-2-3 Command Menu

The worksheet is the basis for all applications you create, modify, and print in 1-2-3. You enter data in the form of text, numbers, and formulas into your worksheet; one single main command menu lets you format, copy, move, print, create a graph, and perform database operations on this data. In addition to the activities accessed by the main command menu, 1-2-3 provides menu commands that allow you to save and retrieve your worksheet as a file on disk, manage and change files, and read files in formats different from a 1-2-3 worksheet file format.

The commands in the main menu lead to many sublevels of commands, in total more than 400 commands. Some commands you will use frequently whenever you create or modify a worksheet application. Other commands, such as specialized database commands, you may rarely or never use. Certain commands are new with 1-2-3 Release 2.2—for instance, the /Worksheet Column-Width Column-Range command. Throughout this book, new commands are highlighted and discussed. The following sections briefly introduce the commands you will probably use most frequently—those commands related to creating and modifying worksheet applications.

RELEASE

2.2

As you explore 1-2-3 Release 2.2's command menu, you will find that many menus offer settings sheets. A settings sheet is a screenful of information showing you the default or current settings for a particular menu or operation. For example, when you select /Worksheet Global Default, you see the Default Settings sheet (see fig. 1.4).

Fig. 1.4.
The Default
Settings sheet.

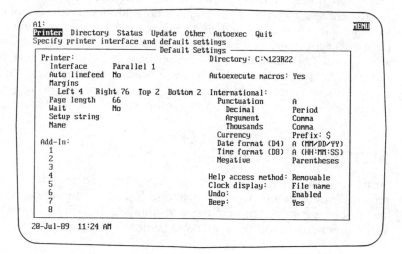

This settings sheet shows you the current settings for 1-2-3. At a glance, you can tell the current printer, the margins set for the printer, the current directory, among other options. As you make a change to the global defaults, the changes are reflected in the settings sheets. You find other settings sheets in the Print, Graph, and Data menus as well.

Using /Worksheet and /Range Commands

Understanding the 1-2-3 worksheet structure and the effect of certain commands on the worksheet is the first step in using 1-2-3 successfully for your applications. When you begin to investigate the 1-2-3 command menu, you will find that some commands affect the whole worksheet, while other commands affect only a portion or block of cells in the worksheet, referred to as a *range*.

As a beginning 1-2-3 user, you'll need to keep in mind whether you want a command to affect the entire worksheet or just a specific range. The following sections discuss both /Worksheet and /Range commands.

Using /Worksheet Commands

/Worksheet, the first command on the main 1-2-3 command menu, allows you to make changes to either the whole worksheet or columns and rows in the worksheet. With /Worksheet commands, you can specify the way numbers and formulas appear in a worksheet—in Percentage format, Currency format, comma format, and so on. Other commands that affect the overall worksheet include those for inserting and deleting columns and rows.

Cue:
Use /Worksheet commands to affect the entire worksheet or rows and columns.

Some /Worksheet commands let you change the way data and graphs appear on-screen. You can, for example, freeze certain columns or rows so that they remain on-screen even though you move the cell pointer to other areas of the worksheet. You also can split your screen and display two areas of the worksheet at one time. Another /Worksheet command displays a status report showing such information as how much memory is available and what settings are in effect for the worksheet.

Using /Range Commands

Rather than making changes to the entire worksheet, sometimes you will want to affect a smaller section of the worksheet. The /Range command can affect a single cell or a range of cells.

Cue:
Use /Range commands to change one cell or a range of cells.

One of the most useful /Range commands is a command that lets you attach a name to a single cell or a range of cells. By naming a column of numbers, for example, you can create a formula that totals these numbers by simply entering the function @SUM followed in parentheses by its range name— @SUM(QTR1). Range names are also useful for printing. Rather than defining the exact cell boundaries for an area you want to print, you can give that area a name and enter the name when you are prompted for a print range. Other uses for range names include naming parts of a worksheet so that you

Reminder:
Naming ranges offers many advantages.

can easily move the cell pointer from one area to another. As you become accustomed to using range names, you'll find many occasions when range names simplify and save time as you create and use worksheet applications.

/Range commands offer many other capabilities. For instance, you can use /Range commands to control the way data in one cell or a range of cells appears on-screen and prints. You can, for example, change the way numbers and formulas are displayed; indicate whether you want text to be aligned to the left, right, or center of the cell; and justify the right margin of a block of text that spans down many rows of the worksheet. You also can change data from displaying in column format to row format and vice versa.

You also use /Range commands to protect certain areas of your worksheet so that you or other users do not accidentally change, erase, or overwrite data. If you do want to erase data in one cell or a range of cells, you can use the /Range Erase command.

RELEASE

2.2

The /Range Search command in Release 2.2 lets you search a range of cells to find a string of characters in labels and formulas. This feature works much like the search-and-replace feature in many word processors. You can, for example, search for and replace range names in formulas or macros. You can even change arguments in formulas with /Range Search. You can, for example, change the formula @ROUND(A1*B1,2) to @ROUND(A1*B1,4) by simply searching for ,2 and replacing it with ,4.

Copying and Moving Cell Entries

As indicated in the previous sections, /Worksheet and /Range are two of the most frequently used commands. Two other commands, however, are also commonly used for creating and modifying worksheet applications. These commands, /Copy and /Move, allow you to copy and move data from one cell or a range of cells to another in the worksheet.

Cue:
Use the /Copy command to copy text, numbers, formatting, and formulas.

The /Copy command will save you hours of time by letting you duplicate text, numbers, formatting lines, and formulas. Copying formulas is one of the most important functions of this command. You can create a few key formulas and then copy these formulas to other parts of the worksheet.

When you use /Move, you can move not only the contents of one cell to another but the contents of a large range of cells to another area of the worksheet.

Reminder:
The file extension for Releases 2.01 and 2.2 worksheets is .WK1.

Managing Files with 1-2-3

The type of file you will create most often when using 1-2-3 Releases 2.2 and 2.01 is a worksheet file. This type of file saves all the data, formulas, and text you've entered into a worksheet and also saves such things as the format of cells, the alignment of text, names of ranges, and protection status. Saved as Release 2.2 or 2.01 files, these files are stored with a .WK1 extension. You can create and save two other types of files in 1-2-3 Releases 2.2 and 2.01: text files denoted with a .PRN extension and graph-image files denoted with a .PIC extension. And in 1-2-3 Release 2.2, you can save a backup file (with a .BAK extension) on disk.

The **/File** commands provide a wide range of file management, modifications, and protection capabilities. Some **/File** commands are similar to your operating system commands, such as those that enable you to erase or list files. Other commands relate to specific 1-2-3 tasks and applications. You can, for example, combine data from several files and extract data from one file to another file. In 1-2-3 Release 2.2, you also can "reserve" a file so that only one user is permitted to write information to and update the file. This **/File** command is particularly important for those who are using 1-2-3 Release 2.2 on a network.

In addition to options for managing, modifying, and protecting files, the Translate utility on the Access System menu lets you translate several file formats that differ from the 1-2-3 worksheet file format. You can, for example, convert files from the following programs and read them into 1-2-3 Release 2.2 or 2.01: dBASE II, dBASE III, dBASE III Plus, Multiplan, VisiCalc, and files in DIF format. You also can convert Releases 2.2 and 2.01 files to formats that can be read by 1-2-3 Release 1A, dBASE II, dBASE III, dBASE III Plus, Multiplan, VisiCalc, and programs that use the DIF format. You do not need to use the Translate utility to read worksheet files created by 1-2-3 Releases 1A, 2, and 3 and Symphony 1, 1.01, 1.1, 1.2, and 2. See Chapter 7 for a complete discussion of **/File** commands.

Creating a Backup File in Release 2.2

RELEASE
2.2

One of the most important **/File** commands is **/File Save**. This command allows you to save your file in memory to disk so that you can retrieve and use the file again. In 1-2-3 Release 2.2, you also can save a backup file by choosing **Backup** from the **File Save** menu. Backup renames the previous file with a .BAK extension and then saves the new file under the same file name with a .WK1 extension. You then have both files on disk.

Using 1-2-3 Release 2.2 in a Multiuser Environment

RELEASE
2.2

Entire
Section

If you use 1-2-3 Release 2.2 in a network or other multiuser environment, you should be aware that two or more people can try to access or update the same file at the same time. The network administrator sets up shared disks so that some files can be shared and some cannot. You do not have to worry about those files on a network server that you alone can read.

Release 2.2 has a "reservation" system to avoid multiple updates of the same shared file. When you read a file that no one else is using, 1-2-3 gives you the reservation for that file. When you have the reservation, you can update the file and save it under the same name. Chapter 7 discusses using 1-2-3 in a multiuser environment.

Protecting Files and Worksheets

In addition to Release 2.2's command that lets you assign a reservation status to a file, both 1-2-3 Release 2.2 and 2.01 allow you to assign a password to a file so that file retrieval is restricted to only those with that password. You may, however, want to give other users access to a file but restrict their ability to make changes or delete, intentionally or unintentionally, data in the application. The /**W**orksheet **G**lobal **P**rotection and /**R**ange **P**rot (in Release 2.2) or /**R**ange **P**rotect (in Release 2.01) commands allow you to protect any area of your worksheet from change. See Chapter 4 for more information on /**W**orksheet **G**lobal **P**rotection and /**R**ange **P**rot (or /**R**ange **P**rotect).

Printing Reports

After you create your worksheets, you often will need to create reports from the data you have entered. By using 1-2-3's /**P**rint command, you can print an entire worksheet or any part of the worksheet. In addition to sending data files directly from 1-2-3 to the printer, you can save worksheet data in a text file so that the data can be incorporated in another program, such as a word processing program.

The **P**rint menu in 1-2-3 provides options for developing page-layout features—setting margins, indicating text for headers and footers, telling 1-2-3 to print certain column or row data on every page, setting the length of the page, or telling 1-2-3 whether you want data printed as displayed on-screen or printed in formula notation.

RELEASE

2.2

Reminder:
Release 2.2
includes the
spreadsheet
publishing add-in
program Allways.

1-2-3 Release 2.2 includes Allways, a spreadsheet publishing add-in program, as a standard feature. (If you have Release 2.01 and you did not receive the program bundled with your software, you must purchase this program separately.) Allways lets you produce presentation quality output from 1-2-3. With Allways, you can use up to eight fonts in one printout, create boldface or underlined text, shade areas of the worksheet, draw lines either horizontally or vertically, box cells or ranges, double-underline data, integrate graphs with worksheet data, and print in color (if you have a color printer).

In addition to enhanced text formatting, Allways enables you to embed 1-2-3 graphs in your printouts, add enhanced text to your printed graphs, and print 1-2-3 graphs and associated worksheet data directly from Allways. For more information on Allways, see Chapter 9.

Creating and Printing 1-2-3 Graphs

When 1-2-3 was first introduced, business users quickly recognized the advantages of being able to recognize worksheet data as graphs produced by the same worksheet program. 1-2-3 Releases 2.2 and 2.01 let you create four types of graphs: line, bar, stack-bar, and pie graphs.

Depending on how data is organized in your worksheet, 1-2-3 Release 2.2 can create a graph automatically. You can create a graph automatically by using Release 2.2's /Graph Group command and highlighting a range of data.

Beyond creating a simple graph, 1-2-3 /Graph commands let you enhance and customize graphs for your needs. You can, for example, add titles to label data points, change the format of values displayed on a graph, create a grid, and change the scaling along the x- or y-axis. By naming the settings you have entered to create a graph and saving this name, you can redisplay the graph whenever you access the file in the future.

1-2-3 Releases 2.2 and 2.01 also give you the option of saving the graph for printing on a printer or plotter. When you save a graph, 1-2-3 gives the file a special .PIC extension. You later can print this file by using 1-2-3's separate PrintGraph program.

To print graphs in 1-2-3 Releases 2.2 and 2.01, you must exit 1-2-3 and invoke the PrintGraph program. The PrintGraph program offers several formatting options. For example, you can change the size of the graph, choose two fonts from among a selection of seven different styles, and select colors for the graph (if you have a color printer or plotter). You can find more information about PrintGraph in Chapter 11.

Managing Data with 1-2-3

The column-and-row structure used to store data in the 1-2-3 worksheet is similar to the structure of a relational database. 1-2-3 provides true database management commands and functions so that you can sort, query, extract, and perform statistical analysis on data. One important advantage of 1-2-3's database manager over independent database programs is that its commands are similar to the other commands used in the 1-2-3 program. You can, therefore, learn how to use the 1-2-3 database manager along with the rest of the 1-2-3 program.

RELEASE

2.2

Reminder:
With Release 2.2,
you can create a
graph
automatically.

Using /Data Commands and Functions

After you build a database in 1-2-3 (which is no different from building any other worksheet application), you can perform a variety of functions on the database. You can accomplish some of these tasks with standard 1-2-3 commands. For example, you can add records to a database with the /Worksheet Insert Row command. You can add fields with the /Worksheet Insert Column command. Editing the contents of a database cell is as easy as editing any other cell; you simply move the cursor to that location, press Edit (F2), and type the new entry.

Cue:
*Use database
functions to
analyze your
database records.*

You also can sort data, on a primary and secondary key, in ascending or descending order, using alphabetic or numeric keys. In addition, you can perform various kinds of mathematical analyses on a field of data over a specified range of records using database functions. For example, you can count the number of times database records match a set of criteria (@DCOUNT); compute a mean (@DAVG), variance (@DVAR), or standard deviation (@DSTD); and find the maximum or minimum value in the range (@DMAX and @DMIN). The capacity to perform a statistical analysis on a database is an advanced feature of database management systems on any microcomputer.

Other database operations require database commands, such as /Data Query Unique and /Data Query Find. You can query a 1-2-3 database in several ways. After specifying the criteria on which you are basing your search, you can ask the program to point to each selected record in turn, or to extract the selected records to a separate area of the worksheet. You also can ask the program to delete records that fit your specified criteria.

The /Data Query commands require that you specify one or more criteria for searching the database. The criteria refer to a field in the database and set the conditions that data must meet in order to be selected. 1-2-3 allows a great deal of latitude in defining criteria. You can include in the criteria range as many as 256 cells across, each containing multiple criteria. Criteria can include complex formulas as well as simple numbers and text entries. You can use the AND and OR operators to join two or more criteria. You also can include wild-card characters that stand for other characters in the criteria.

The combination of database functions and 1-2-3's database commands make this program a capable data manager. 1-2-3's data management capabilities, however, do not put the program in competition with more sophisticated database languages such as dBASE III Plus, dBASE IV, or R:BASE. These programs use a database language to translate the user's requests to the computer. By comparison, 1-2-3's data management is fairly simple. (1-2-3's data management capabilities are covered in detail in Chapter 12.)

Using the /Data Table Command

One of the most useful, but most misunderstood, /Data commands is /Data Table. A data table is simply a way to look at all the outcomes of a set of conditions without having to enter each set into the equation manually. The command allows you to build a table that defines the formula you want to evaluate and contains all the values you want to test. A data table is similar to the X-Y decision grids you probably built as a math student in high school.

You can use the /Data Table command to structure a variety of "what if" problems. You also can combine this command with 1-2-3's database and statistical functions to solve far more complex problems. (Chapter 12 explains in detail the /Data Table command and gives examples that will help you master this powerful tool.)

Figuring Multiple Regression and Simultaneous Equations

1-2-3's multiple regression command significantly expands the program's capabilities for statistical analysis. If you use regression analysis, the regression command could save you the cost of a stand-alone statistical package. For business applications, the /Data Regression command probably will meet all your regression analysis needs.

You can use a /Data Matrix command to solve systems of simultaneous equations. This capability, although likely to be of greater interest to scientific and engineering users, is available if needed.

Creating Keyboard Macros and Using Advanced Macro Commands

One of 1-2-3's most exciting features is its macro capability, which allows you to automate and customize 1-2-3 for your special applications. 1-2-3's macro capability and advanced macro commands allow you to create, inside the 1-2-3 worksheet, user-defined programs that you can use for a variety of purposes. At the simplest level, these programs are keystroke-alternative programs that reduce, from many to two, the number of keystrokes for a 1-2-3 operation. At a more complex level, 1-2-3's advanced macro commands provide a full-featured programming capability.

RELEASE

2.2

Reminder:
You can record
macros
automatically with
Release 2.2.

Release 2.2 makes creating macros much easier than creating macros in Release 2.01. With Release 2.2, you can use LEARN mode to record automatically a series of keystrokes. These keystrokes then are copied to the worksheet as macros. In addition to naming a macro with the backslash (\ ) key and a single letter as in Release 2.01, Release 2.2 lets you name a macro with a name consisting of up to 15 characters.

Whether you use 1-2-3's programming capability for keystroke-alternative macros or for a programming language, you'll find that it can simplify and automate many of your 1-2-3 applications. When you create a macro, you can activate its series of commands by pressing two keys—the Alt key and a letter key. Additionally in Release 2.2, you can select a macro from a menu.

The implications for such keystroke-alternative macros are limited only by 1-2-3's capabilities. For example, typing the names of months as column headings is a task frequently performed in budget building. You easily can turn this task into a 1-2-3 macro, thereby reducing keystrokes. You can structure a macro program in 1-2-3 to make decisions when the program is executed. These decisions can be based either on values found in the worksheet or on input from the user. By combining the keystroke-alternative features of 1-2-3's macro capability with the advanced macro commands, you can automate many tasks.

When you begin to use 1-2-3's sophisticated advanced macro commands, you'll discover the power available for your special applications of 1-2-3. For the applications developer, the advanced macro commands are much like a programming language (such as BASIC), but the programming process is simplified significantly by all the powerful features of 1-2-3's worksheet, database, and graphics commands. Whether you want to use 1-2-3 to create keystroke-alternative macros or to program, Chapters 13 and 14 give you the information you need to get started.

RELEASE

2.2

Entire
Section

Adding In Features

1-2-3 Release 2.2 contains commands that assist you in enhancing the features of the 1-2-3 program. To access this set of commands, called the Add-In Manager, select the Add-In command from the main menu or press Alt-F10. One of the Add-In Manager's commands allows you to "attach" an add-in program, such as Allways or the Macro Library Manager, to 1-2-3. After you attach an add-in program, another command lets you invoke it at any time. Add-in programs such as Allways enhance the power of 1-2-3, yet are easy to learn and use because they work like 1-2-3.

You can find more information about Allways and the Macro Library Manager in Chapters 9 and 13, respectively. Many other add-in programs for 1-2-3 Release 2.2 are available from third-party sources.

1-2-3 Release 2.01 lacks an integrated Add-In Manager. However, if you purchase an add-in program for 1-2-3 Release 2.01, such as Allways, the add-in program includes the Add-In Manager.

Understanding 1-2-3 Hardware Requirements and Options

Both 1-2-3 Releases 2.2 and 2.01 are capable of running on computer systems configured with just two floppy disks, a monochrome monitor, and 320 kilobytes (K) of random access memory (RAM). However, if you use 1-2-3 for serious business purposes, you are likely to have much more sophisticated hardware. In the following sections, the minimum requirements are described as well as some of the more useful options.

Operating System and Hardware Requirements

1-2-3 Releases 2.2 and 2.01 will run on any 8088-, 8086-, 80286-, or 80386-based personal computer compatible with the IBM personal computer. Your system must have at least two floppy disk drives, or one floppy disk drive and one hard disk drive. You also need a monochrome or color monitor and a keyboard. If you intend to use Allways, you must have a hard disk—Allways cannot be used with a two-disk system.

Reminder:
To use Allways, you must have a hard disk.

The minimum amount of memory required by Release 2.01 is 256K; the minimum amount required by Release 2.2 is 320K. Either version supports up to 640K of conventional memory and 4 megabytes of expanded memory. When using Allways, you need a minimum of 512K.

1-2-3 runs under PC DOS V2.0 to V4.01 or MS-DOS V2.0 and higher.

Hardware Options

1-2-3 Releases 2.2 and 2.01 support a variety of video displays and printers. 1-2-3 supports the majority of display systems available on the market today. These systems include the following:

Monochrome Display Adapter (MDA)
Color Graphics Adapter (CGA)

Multicolor Graphics Array (MCGA)
Enhanced Graphics Adapter (EGA)
Video Graphics Array (VGA)

In addition, Releases 2.2 and 2.01 support the following graphics products:

Hercules Graphics Card
Hercules Mono Graphics Display Adapter Plus with Ram Font

Although Releases 2.2 and 2.01 run on a monochrome display adapter (MDA), you cannot display graphics with such a system.

1-2-3 Releases 2.2 and 2.01 support popular dot-matrix, laser, and other types of printers as well as plotters. When you run 1-2-3's install program, you are given a complete list of the printers that 1-2-3 supports.

Appropriate hardware will help you maximize the capabilities of 1-2-3. If your computer has less than 640K RAM, you should consider upgrading to that amount. If your worksheets tend to be large and you find yourself running out of memory, you should consider adding an expanded memory board to your computer. The board should be compatible with the LIM V4.0 standard (Lotus/Intel/Microsoft). If you perform calculations that are math intensive, consider adding a math coprocessor to your computer. If you have an 8088- or 8086-based computer, you should add an 8087 coprocessor; if you have an 80286-based computer, you should add an 80287 coprocessor; if you have an 80386-based computer, you should add an 80387 coprocessor.

These hardware extras greatly increase the practical size of 1-2-3's spreadsheet and speed calculations.

Chapter Summary

Both 1-2-3 Releases 2.2 and 2.01 are flexible, powerful spreadsheet programs. Release 2.2, however, goes a step further than its predecessor with features such as file linking and automatic macro development.

This chapter has described, in general terms, the capabilities that make 1-2-3 Releases 2.2 and 2.01 impressive programs. Turn now to the remaining chapters of this book and learn how to use 1-2-3's features quickly and productively.

2

Getting Started

This chapter helps you get started using 1-2-3 for the first time. If you are new to computers, several books published by Que Corporation can give you a basic introduction to your operating system. If you are using DOS, the *MS-DOS QuickStart* provides a visually oriented approach to learning MS-DOS. Other Que titles that can serve as a reference when learning DOS include *Using PC DOS*, 3rd Edition, and *MS-DOS User's Guide*, 3rd Edition, both by Chris DeVoney. If you are using the OS/2 operating system, refer to *Using OS/2* by Caroline Halliday, David Gobel, and Mark Minasi.

If you are familiar with 1-2-3 but new to Release 2.2, you may find the introductory material too basic. If you want to begin using 1-2-3 immediately, first read through the tables in this chapter, and then skip to Chapter 3. The tables include important reference information new with Release 2.2.

This chapter covers the following topics:

- Starting and exiting 1-2-3
- Using the 1-2-3 Access System
- Understanding the computer keyboard and the 1-2-3 screen display
- Finding on-screen help
- Using the 1-2-3 Tutorial

Many first-time users find the Tutorial a helpful introduction to 1-2-3. If you are new to 1-2-3, you can use the Tutorial as you read through this book. If you have worked with 1-2-3, but are new to Release 2.2 or 2.01, parts of the Tutorial will be useful for you as well. (The Tutorial is on disk in Release 2.01 and part of the manual in Release 2.2.)

Before you begin, be sure that 1-2-3 is installed on your computer system. Follow the instructions in Appendix A to complete the installation for your system.

Starting 1-2-3 from the Operating System

You can use one of two different methods of starting 1-2-3. You can start from within the 1-2-3 Access System or directly from the operating system. Most users start directly from the operating system because this method is easier, faster, and uses less memory. Starting from the operating system is covered in the following sections. Starting from the Access System is covered later in the chapter.

Starting 1-2-3

If you have installed 1-2-3 according to the directions in Appendix A, the 1-2-3 program is stored in a subdirectory named 123. To start 1-2-3 directly from the operating system, use the following steps:

1. Change to the drive on which you installed 1-2-3. On most systems, this is drive C, but you may have installed 1-2-3 on drive D, E, or another drive. If 1-2-3 is installed on drive C and drive C is not the current drive, type **C:** and press Enter.

2. Type **CD \123** and press Enter to change to the 123 directory.

3. Type **123** and press Enter to start 1-2-3.

To simplify this process, you can create a start-up batch file or add 1-2-3 to a start-up menu. You can use a text editor or word processor to create a batch file. The specific instructions depend on the program and operating system you use. If you are using OS/2, follow the instructions in the documentation or in *Using OS/2* to add a program to the Start Programs window.

The following steps illustrate one way to create a start-up batch file by using the DOS COPY command. The following example assumes that your batch files are kept in the BATCH directory.

1. Change to the directory in which you keep your batch files. Type **CD \BATCH** and press Enter.

2. Type **COPY CON 123.BAT** and press Enter.

3. Type **C:** (or the name of the drive on which you have installed 1-2-3) and then press Enter.

4. Type **CD \123** and press Enter.

5. Type **123** and press Enter.

6. Type **CD** and press Enter.

7. Press Ctrl-Z (hold down the Ctrl key and press Z).

After creating this batch file, you need only type **123** and press Enter to start 1-2-3. If you also include C:\BATCH in your PATH command, you can start 1-2-3 from any subdirectory.

After you start 1-2-3, the registration screen appears for a few seconds while the program loads. Then a blank worksheet appears, and you are ready to start using 1-2-3.

Exiting 1-2-3

To exit 1-2-3, you must use the 1-2-3 command menu. 1-2-3 commands and their menus are explained extensively throughout this book. At this point, however, you need to know only how to access the main menu and to use one command.

To access the 1-2-3 command menu, press the slash (/) key. A menu that contains 11 options appears across the top line of the worksheet (see fig. 2.1). The /Quit option exits the worksheet and returns you to the operating system.

Cue:
Press the slash key (/) to access the command menu.

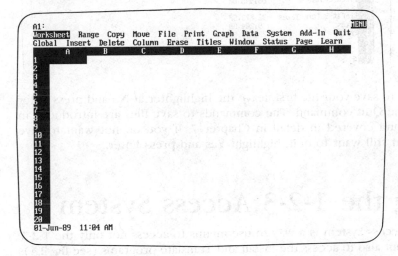

Fig. 2.1.
The 1-2-3 main command menu.

To select /Quit, use the right- or left-arrow keys to move the menu highlighter to **Quit** and then press Enter. You must verify your choice before you exit 1-2-3. Unless you have saved it, your worksheet file and temporary settings are lost when you /Quit 1-2-3. To verify you want to exit, move the highlighter to **Yes** and press Enter (see fig. 2.2). In 1-2-3 Release 2.2, if you made changes to your worksheet and did not save it, 1-2-3 prompts you a second time to verify this choice before you exit (see fig. 2.3).

Caution:
Save your work before you /Quit the worksheet.

Fig. 2.2.
The
confirmation
prompt to quit
1-2-3.

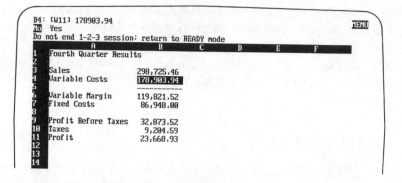

Fig. 2.3.
In 1-2-3
Release 2.2, the
second
confirmation
prompt to quit
1-2-3.

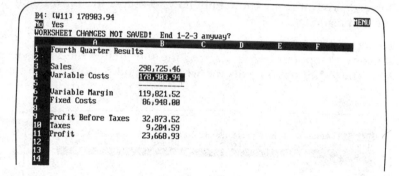

If you want to save your file first, leave the highlighter at **No** and press Enter to cancel the **Quit** command. The commands to save files are introduced in Chapter 4 and covered in detail in Chapter 7. If you do not want to save your file but still want to quit, highlight **Yes** and press Enter.

Using the 1-2-3 Access System

Cue:
Appendix A
contains complete
installation
instructions.

The 1-2-3 Access System is a way to use menus to access not only the 1-2-3 worksheet but also to access the Install and Translate programs (see fig. 2.4). Use the Install program to change any installation settings, such as the type of printer and display. (See Appendix A for a complete discussion of the Install program.) You use the Translate program to transfer files between 1-2-3 and other programs, and previous versions of 1-2-3 and Symphony. (See Chapter 7 for more information on the Translate program.)

```
┌─────────────────────────────────────────────────────────────┐
│ ┌───────────────────────────────────────────────────────┐   │
│ │ 1-2-3  PrintGraph  Translate  Install  Exit            │   │
│ │ Use 1-2-3                                              │   │
│ └───────────────────────────────────────────────────────┘   │
│ ┌───────────────────────────────────────────────────────┐   │
│ │                  1-2-3 Access System                   │   │
│ │                  Copyright 1986, 1989                  │   │
│ │               Lotus Development Corporation            │   │
│ │                   All Rights Reserved                  │   │
│ │                      Release 2.2                       │   │
│ │                                                        │   │
│ │  The Access system lets you choose 1-2-3, PrintGraph, the Translate utility, │
│ │  and the Install program, from the menu at the top of this screen.  If │
│ │  you're using a two-diskette system, the Access system may prompt you to │
│ │  change disks.  Follow the instructions below to start a program. │
│ │                                                        │   │
│ │  o  Use → or ← to move the menu pointer (the highlighted rectangle │
│ │     at the top of the screen) to the program you want to use. │
│ │                                                        │   │
│ │  o  Press ENTER to start the program.                  │   │
│ │                                                        │   │
│ │  You can also start a program by typing the first character of its name. │
│ │                                                        │   │
│ │  Press HELP (F1) for more information.                 │   │
│ └───────────────────────────────────────────────────────┘   │
└─────────────────────────────────────────────────────────────┘
```

Fig. 2.4.
The 1-2-3
Access System
menu.

If you have installed 1-2-3 according to the directions in Appendix A, the 1-2-3 Access System is in a subdirectory named 123. Use the following steps to start the 1-2-3 Access System:

1. Change to the drive on which you installed 1-2-3. On most systems, this is drive C. If 1-2-3 is installed on drive C and drive C is not the current drive, type **C:** and press Enter.

2. Type **CD \123** and press Enter to change to the 123 directory.

3. Type **LOTUS** and press Enter to start 1-2-3.

Notice that you type **LOTUS**, not **123**, even though the 1-2-3 Access System provides access only to 1-2-3 programs, not to other Lotus products. (Originally, this feature was called the Lotus Access System.)

Reminder:
*Type **LOTUS** to*
start the 1-2-3
Access System.

To simplify this process, you can create a start-up batch file or add 1-2-3 to a start-up menu. You can use a text editor or word processor to create a batch file. The specific instructions depend on the program and operating system you use. If you are using OS/2, follow the instructions in the documentation or in *Using OS/2* to add a program to the Start Programs window.

The following steps illustrate one way to create a start-up batch file by using the DOS COPY command. The following example assumes that your batch files are kept in the BATCH directory.

1. Change to the directory in which you keep your batch files. Type **CD \BATCH** and press Enter.

2. Type **COPY CON LOTUS.BAT** and press Enter to name the batch file LOTUS.BAT. To name the batch file ACCESS.BAT, type **COPY CON ACCESS.BAT** and press Enter.

3. Type **C:** (or the name of the drive on which you installed 1-2-3) and press Enter.

4. Type **CD \123** and press Enter.

5. Type **LOTUS** and press Enter.

6. Type **CD** and press Enter.

7. Press Ctrl-Z (hold down the Ctrl key and press Z).

After creating this batch file, type **LOTUS** and press Enter from the DOS level to start the 1-2-3 Access System. If you have changed the batch file name to **ACCESS.BAT** in Step 2, type **ACCESS** to start the 1-2-3 Access System. The 1-2-3 Access System command menu appears:

> **1-2-3** **PrintGraph** **Translate** **Install** **Exit**

To select any of these options, highlight the menu entry and press Enter, or type the first letter of the menu entry.

Starting and Exiting 1-2-3 from the 1-2-3 Access System

The first option in the 1-2-3 Access System menu, **1-2-3**, starts 1-2-3. When the menu appears, the highlighter is on this option. To select the option, press Enter. If you have moved the highlighter to another option, use the right- or left-arrow keys to return to the first option and then press Enter. After you start 1-2-3, the registration screen appears for a few seconds while the program loads. A blank worksheet appears, and you are ready to start using 1-2-3.

To exit the 1-2-3 program, press the slash (/) key to access the 1-2-3 main command menu. Use the right- and left-arrow keys to move the highlighter to the **/Quit** option and then press Enter. You must verify this choice before you exit 1-2-3; when you **/Quit** 1-2-3, your worksheet and temporary settings are lost unless you have saved them. To verify you want to exit, move the highlighter to **Yes** and press Enter. In Release 2.2 if you made changes to any worksheet and did not save it, 1-2-3 prompts you a second time to verify this choice before you exit. To verify you want to exit, move the highlighter to **Yes** again and press Enter.

If you start 1-2-3 by using the Access System, you return to the 1-2-3 Access System menu when you choose **Quit**. To exit the 1-2-3 Access System and return to the operating system, choose **Exit**.

Using the Install Program

Choose Install from the 1-2-3 Access Menu to access the Install program. You can use this program to change the options you set during the initial installation. Complete installation instructions are found in Appendix A. You can run Install to prepare 1-2-3 for a different display or printer.

You can access up to two displays and up to four printers and plotters from within 1-2-3, but you must first use Install to tell 1-2-3 that these devices are available.

When you choose the Install option, you may be asked to place one or more of the driver or font disks into drive A to continue. Follow the prompts and insert any disks requested; then press Enter to continue the Install process.

You can go directly from the operating system to Install without using the 1-2-3 Access System. To start Install directly from the operating system, follow these steps:

Cue:
Type **INSTALL** *to start the Install program directly from the operating system.*

1. Change to the drive on which you installed 1-2-3. On most systems, this is drive C. If 1-2-3 is installed on drive C and drive C is not the current drive, type C: and press Enter.

2. Type **CD \123** and press Enter.

3. Type **INSTALL** and press Enter.

Using the Translate Program

Choose Translate from the 1-2-3 Access Menu to access the Translate program. The Translate utility provides a method to convert files so that they can be read by a different program. To execute Translate, you must copy the Translate file onto your hard disk by using the Install program. (See Appendix A for details.)

Cue:
Use Translate to exchange data among many different programs.

You can use files in 1-2-3 Release 2.2 and 2.01 from the following programs:

1-2-3 Releases 1A and 2
Symphony Releases 1.0, 1.1, 1.2, or 2.0
dBASE II and III
Multiplan
Products that use the DIF format

You do not have to convert files from previous releases of 1-2-3 or Symphony. Releases 2.2 and 2.01 can retrieve these files directly, though in the case of Symphony you may lose some of the unique features of these files. See Chapter 7 for information about translating and accessing files from previous versions of 1-2-3 and Symphony.

Warning:
When you translate data from one program to another, you can lose some information.

You can save a 1-2-3 Release 3 file in 1-2-3 Release 2.2 or 2.01 format as long as the file does not include features unique to 1-2-3 Release 3. You can do so by naming the file with the .WK1 extension when you select **/File Save**. If the file does include unique features, you must use the 1-2-3 Release 3 Translate utility to translate it.

You can convert files *from* 1-2-3 Release 2.2 and 2.01 to the following programs:

    1-2-3 Releases 1A and 3
    Symphony Releases 1, 1.1, 1.2, 2
    dBASE II and III
    Products that use the DIF format

Cue:
Type **TRANS** *to start the Translate program directly from the operating system.*

You can go directly from the operating system to the Translate program. To do so, follow these steps:

1. Change to the drive on which you installed 1-2-3. On most systems, this is drive C. If 1-2-3 is installed on drive C and drive C is not the current drive, type **C:** and press Enter.

2. Type **CD \123** and press Enter.

3. Type **TRANS** and press Enter.

Understanding the 1-2-3 Keyboard

The most common configurations for keyboards on IBM and IBM-compatible personal computers are shown in figures 2.5, 2.6, and 2.7. The Enhanced Keyboard, shown in figure 2.7, is now the standard keyboard on all new IBM personal computers and most compatibles. Some compatibles, especially laptops, have different keyboards.

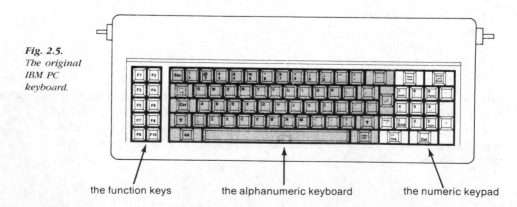

Fig. 2.5.
The original IBM PC keyboard.

the function keys   the alphanumeric keyboard   the numeric keypad

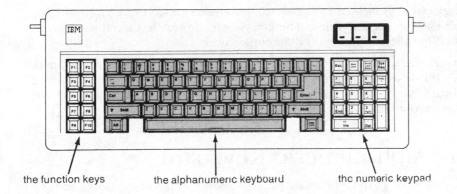

Fig. 2.6.
The original
IBM AT
keyboard.

the function keys   the alphanumeric keyboard   the numeric keypad

the function keys

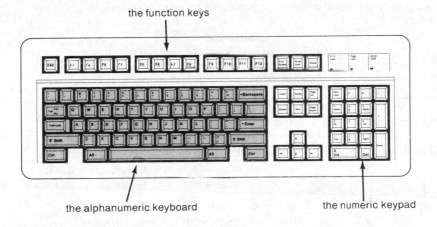

Fig. 2.7.
The Enhanced
Keyboard.

the alphanumeric keyboard   the numeric keypad

The keyboards are divided into three sections: the alphanumeric keyboard in the center, the numeric keypad on the right, and the function keys on the left or across the top. In addition to these sections, the special keys are found in various locations. The cursor-movement keys are found in a separate section on the Enhanced Keyboard only.

Most keys in the alphanumeric section match the keys on a typewriter, and most maintain their normal functions in 1-2-3. Several keys, however, take on new and unique functions or are not found on typewriter keyboards.

You use the keys on the numeric keypad (on the right side of the keyboard) to enter numbers or to move the cell pointer around the screen.

The function keys provide special actions. For example, you can use these keys to access 1-2-3's editing functions, display graphs, and call up help messages. These keys are located across the top of the Enhanced Keyboard and on the left side of the other two keyboards.

The special keys include Del (Delete), Ins (Insert), Esc (Escape), Num Lock, Scroll Lock, Break, and Pause. These keys, which provide special actions, are located in different places on different keyboards.

Reminder:
With the Enhanced Keyboard, you can use the numeric keypad to enter numbers and the separate arrow keys to move around the worksheet.

Only the Enhanced Keyboard has a separate section for cursor-movement keys—the keys with up, down, left, and right arrows. With the Enhanced Keyboard, you can use the numeric keypad to enter numbers and use the cursor-movement keys to move easily around the worksheet.

The Alphanumeric Keyboard

Although most of the alphanumeric keys shown in figures 2.5, 2.6, and 2.7 have the same functions as on a typewriter, several keys have special functions in 1-2-3. These keys and their functions are listed in table 2.1. The meaning of these keys will become clearer in later chapters.

Table 2.1
Alphanumeric Key Operation

Key	Function
⟶| (Tab)	Moves cell pointer one screen to the right.
|⟵ (Shift-Tab)	Moves cell pointer one screen to the left.
Caps Lock	Shifts the letter keys to uppercase. Unlike the Shift-Lock key on a typewriter, Caps Lock has no effect on numbers and symbols.
↑ (Shift)	Used with another key, shifts the character produced. Used with a letter, produces an uppercase letter. Used with a number or symbol, produces the shifted character on that key. Used with the numeric keypad, produces a number. Used with Caps Lock and a letter, produces a lowercase letter. Used with Num Lock and the numeric keypad, produces a cursor-movement key.
Ctrl	A special type of shift key. Used with several keys to change their functions.
Alt	A different type of shift key. Used with the function keys, provides different functions. Used with letter keys, invokes macros.

Key	Function
Backspace	During cell definition or editing, erases the preceding character. Cancels a range during some prompts that display the previous range. Displays the previous help screen while using Help.
/ (slash)	Starts a command from READY mode. Used as the division sign while entering data or editing a formula in a cell.
< (less than sign)	Used as an alternative to the slash key (/) to start a command from READY mode.
. (period)	When used in a range address, separates the address of the cell at the beginning of the range from the address of the cell at the end of the range. In POINT mode, moves the anchor cell to another corner of the range.

The Numeric Keypad and the Cursor-Movement Keys

The keys in the numeric keypad on the right side of the IBM PC- and AT-style keyboards are used mainly for cursor-movement (see figs. 2.5 and 2.6). With Num Lock off, you use these keys as movement keys. With Num Lock on, these keys serve as number keys. You can reverse the setting of Num Lock by holding down a Shift key before you press one of the numeric keys. The Enhanced Keyboard has separate keys for cursor-movement (see fig. 2.7). The functions of the cursor-movement keys are explained in Chapter 3; the other special keys on the numeric keypad are discussed later in this chapter.

The Function Keys

The 10 function keys, F1 through F10, are used for special actions in 1-2-3 (see figs. 2.5, 2.6, and 2.7). These keys are located across the top of the Enhanced Keyboard and on the left side on the other two keyboards. The Enhanced Keyboard has 12 function keys, but 1-2-3 uses only the first 10. You can use these keys alone or with the Alt key. Table 2.2 lists the function keys and an explanation of each key's action.

Table 2.2
Function Key Operation

Key	Function
F1 (Help)	Accesses the on-line help facility.
F2 (Edit)	Puts 1-2-3 into EDIT mode to change the current cell.
F3 (Name)	Displays a list of names any time a command (or formula in Release 2.2) can accept a range name or a file name.
F4 (Abs)	Changes a cell or range address from relative to absolute to mixed.
F5 (GoTo)	Moves the cell pointer to a cell address or range name.
F6 (Window)	Moves the cell pointer to another window when the screen is split. Turns off settings sheets.
F7 (Query)	In READY mode, repeats the last /Data Query command. During a /Data Query Find, switches between FIND and READY mode.
F8 (Table)	Repeats the last /Data Table command.
F9 (Calc)	In READY mode, recalculates all worksheets in memory. If entering or editing a formula, converts the formula to its current value.
F10 (Graph)	Displays the current graph if one exists. If no current graph exists, displays the data around the cell pointer.
Alt-F1 (Compose)	Creates international characters that cannot be typed directly using the keyboard.
Alt-F2 (Step)	Used for debugging macros. When turned on, you can execute macros one step at a time. To turn off Step mode, press Alt-F2 again.
Alt-F3 (Run)	In Release 2.2, runs a macro.
Alt-F4 (Undo)	In Release 2.2, reverses the last action.

RELEASE

2.2

Key	Function
Alt-F5(Learn)	In Release 2.2, allows you to save up to the last 512 keystrokes in a cell or to repeat a series of commands. Pressing Learn (Alt-F5) again turns off the feature.
Alt-F7 (App1)	In Release 2.2, starts an LDE (Lotus Development Environment) application assigned to this key.
Alt-F8 (App2)	In Release 2.2, starts an LDE application assigned to this key.
Alt-F9 (App3)	In Release 2.2, starts an LDE application assigned to this key.
Alt-F10 (Addin)	In Release 2.2, accesses LDE applications.

RELEASE

2.2

Entire
Section

The Special Keys

The special keys provide some important 1-2-3 functions. For example, certain special keys cancel an action. Both Esc and Break cancel a menu. Esc also cancels an entry, and Break also cancels a macro. The Del key deletes a character while editing a cell.

Some special keys change the actions of other keys. When you edit data in a cell, you can use the Ins key to change the mode from insert to overtype. Num Lock changes the action of the keys on the numeric keypad from movement keys to number keys. Scroll Lock changes how the arrow keys move the display. The functions and locations of the special keys on the different keyboards are listed in table 2.3.

Table 2.3
Special Key Operation

Key	Function
Break	Cancels a macro or cancels menu choices and returns to READY mode.
	On the PC and AT keyboards, Break is Ctrl-Scroll Lock. On the Enhanced Keyboard, Break is Ctrl-Pause.

Table 2.3—*continued*

Key	Function
Del	While editing a cell, deletes one character at the cursor. In the Install program, reverses the selection of the highlighted display or printer choice.
Esc	When accessing the command menus, cancels the current menu and backs up to the previous menu. At the main menu, returns to READY mode. When entering or editing data in a cell, clears the edit line. Cancels a range during some prompts that display the previous range. Returns from the on-line help facility.
Ins	While editing a cell, changes mode to overtype. Any keystrokes replace whatever is at that cursor position in the cell. You toggle Ins to return to insert mode, and any keystrokes are inserted at the cursor position.
Num Lock	Shifts the actions of the numeric keypad from cursor-movement keys to numbers. On the PC and AT keyboards, Ctrl-Num Lock serves as the Pause key.
Pause	Pauses a macro, a recalculation, and some commands until you press any key. On the PC and AT keyboards, Pause is Ctrl-Num Lock. On the Enhanced Keyboard, Pause is a separate key to the right of Scroll Lock.
Scroll Lock	Scrolls the entire window when you use the arrow keys. On the PC and AT keyboards, Ctrl-Scroll Lock serves as the Break key.

Understanding the 1-2-3 Screen Display

The main 1-2-3 display is divided into three parts: the control panel at the top of the screen, the worksheet area itself, and the status line at the bottom of the screen (see fig. 2.8). The reverse-video border marks the worksheet area. This border contains the letters and numbers that mark columns and rows.

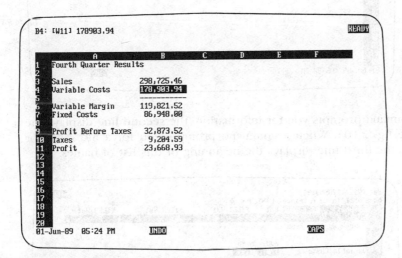

Fig. 2.8.
The control panel at the top of the display and the status line at the bottom.

The *cell pointer* marks the location of the current cell in the worksheet area. This is the intersection of a column and a row. When you enter data into the worksheet, the data goes into the location marked by the cell pointer.

The Control Panel

The three-line control panel is the area above the reverse-video border. The first line contains information about the current cell (see fig. 2.8). This information can include the address of the cell, the cell's contents, and the protection status (U if unprotected or PR if protected). The cell's address is the column and the row in the form B4 for column B, row 4. The format and column width ([Wxx]) are included if different from the default; these attributes are explained in later chapters.

When you use the command menus, the second line displays the menu choices, and the third line contains explanations of the current command menu item or the next hierarchical menu (see fig. 2.9). As you move the pointer from one item to the next in a command menu, the explanation in the third line of the control panel changes.

Cue:
The third line of the command menu displays an explanation of the highlighted command or a preview of the next menu.

Fig. 2.9.
The main
menu with the
Worksheet
menu option
highlighted.

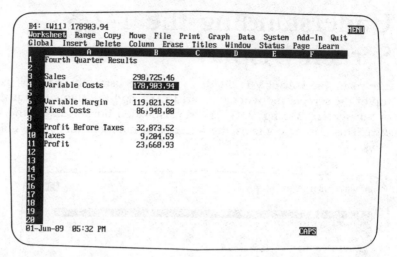

When a command prompts you for information, the second line displays the prompt (see fig. 2.10). When a command prompts you for a file range or graph name, the third line displays the beginning of this list of names.

Fig. 2.10.
The display
showing
command
prompts on the
second line and
lists of files on
the third line.

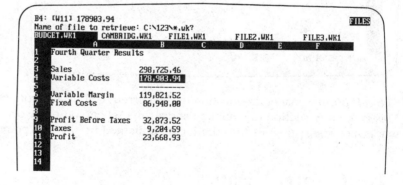

The Mode Indicators

The *mode indicator* is located in the upper right corner of the control panel. This indicator tells you what mode 1-2-3 is in and what you can do next (see fig. 2.11). Table 2.4 lists the mode indicators and their meanings.

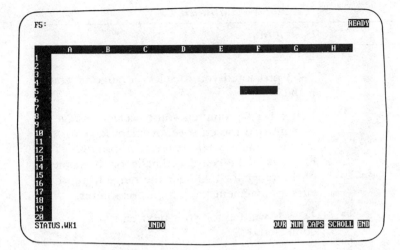

Fig. 2.11.
A worksheet in
READY mode
with several
status
indicators on
the bottom line
of the 1-2-3
display.

Table 2.4
Mode Indicators

Mode	Description
EDIT	You are editing a cell entry.
ERROR	1-2-3 encountered an error, or you used Break to cancel a macro. Press Enter or Esc to clear the error message (located in the lower left corner of the screen) and return to READY mode.
FILES	1-2-3 prompted you to select a file name from a list of files. Either type a file name or point to an existing file and press Enter.
FIND	1-2-3 is in the middle of a /Data Query Find operation.
FRMT	You selected /Data Parse Format-Line Edit to edit a format line.
HELP	You are in the Help facility. Press Esc to return to the worksheet.
LABEL	You are entering a label into a cell.
MENU	You are selecting command options from one of the command menus.

Table 2.4—*continued*

Mode	Description
NAMES	1-2-3 prompted you to select a range or graph name.
POINT	Either 1-2-3 prompted you to select a range, or you used the cursor-movement keys to specify a range while entering a formula. Either type the cell coordinates or the name of the range, or highlight the range using the cursor-movement keys; then press Enter.
READY	1-2-3 is waiting for your next entry or command.
STAT	1-2-3 is displaying a status screen.
VALUE	You are entering a number or a formula into a cell.
WAIT	1-2-3 is in the middle of some activity. Do not proceed until the activity finishes and the WAIT indicator disappears.

The Status Indicators

1-2-3 displays the *status indicators* in the middle and right side of the status line at the bottom of the display. These indicators give you various information about the state of the system. Each indicator displays in reverse video in a specific area (see fig. 2.11). These indicators and their meanings are listed in table 2.5.

Table 2.5
Status Indicators

Indicator	Description
CALC	If the CALC indicator appears on-screen, the file is set to **M**anual **R**ecalculation, and there has been a change since the last recalculation. This warns you that parts of the file may not be current. Press Calc (F9) to force a recalculation and clear this indicator.

Indicator	Description
	When CALC appears, you do not have to recalculate immediately. Finish making all entries, and before printing, press Calc (F9). The CALC indicator will not appear if recalculation is set to **Automatic**.
CAPS	You pressed Caps Lock. All letters are entered as uppercase. Press Caps Lock again to turn off.
CIRC	You have a circular reference in the worksheet. Use the **/W**orksheet Status command to find one of the cell addresses in the circular reference.
CMD	You are running a macro that has paused for input.
END	You pressed the End key to use with an arrow key to move across the worksheet.
MEM	You have fewer than 4,096 characters of memory left.
NUM	You pressed Num Lock. The keys on the numeric keypad now act as number keys. To use them as cursor-movement keys, press Num Lock again or hold down the Shift key.
OVR	You pressed Ins while editing a cell to change to overtype mode. Any keystrokes replace whatever is at that cursor position. Press Ins again to return to insert mode. Keystrokes are then inserted at the cursor position.
RO	In Release 2.2, the current file is read-only. The file can be saved only with a different name. Applies to files used on a network or multiuser system. Sometimes occurs if you run out of memory while reading a file.
SCROLL	You pressed Scroll Lock. Whenever you use an arrow key, the entire window moves in the direction of the arrow. To use the arrow keys to move the cursor from cell to cell, press Scroll Lock again.

RELEASE

2.2

Table 2.5—*continued*

Indicator	Description
SST	You are executing a macro in single-step mode.
STEP	You turned on single-step mode for macros, but you are not currently running a macro. When you start a macro, this indicator changes to SST.
UNDO	In Release 2.2, you may cancel the most recent entry or the results of a command by pressing Alt-F4 (Undo) when 1-2-3 is in READY mode.

RELEASE

2.2

The File and Clock Indicator

RELEASE

2.2

The lower left corner of the screen displays the date and time, which is the default setting. In 1-2-3 Release 2.2, if you prefer to show the file name instead, you can change the default setting. Changing the date and time display is explained in Chapter 3.

The Error Messages Area

Cue:
If the mode indicator changes to ERROR, look at the lower left corner of the screen for an error message.

When 1-2-3 encounters an error, the mode indicator changes to ERROR, and an error message replaces the clock or file message in the lower left corner of the screen (see fig. 2.12). Errors can be caused by many different situations. For example, you may have specified an invalid cell address or range name in response to a prompt or tried to retrieve a file that does not exist. Press Esc or Enter to clear the error and return to READY mode.

Using the 1-2-3 Help Features

1-2-3 includes features that provide help to users: the keyboard help facility and the 1-2-3 Tutorial. 1-2-3 provides on-line help at the touch of a key. You can be in the middle of any operation and press the Help (F1) key at any time to view information on what to do next.

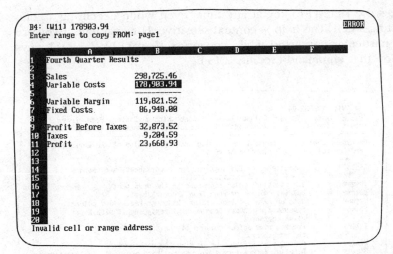

B4: [W11] 178903.94   ERROR
Enter range to copy FROM: page1

```
        A          B      C      D      E      F
1  Fourth Quarter Results
2
3  Sales               298,725.46
4  Variable Costs      178,903.94
5                      ──────────
6  Variable Margin     119,821.52
7  Fixed Costs          86,948.00
8
9  Profit Before Taxes  32,873.52
10 Taxes                 9,204.59
11 Profit               23,668.93
12
13
14
15
16
17
18
19
20
```

Invalid cell or range address

Fig. 2.12.
An error message displayed in the lower left corner of the screen.

Lotus also includes in its documentation a printed Tutorial to help you learn 1-2-3. This self-paced instructional manual leads you through a series of actual 1-2-3 worksheets that use the important features of the program.

For users of 1-2-3 Release 2.01, you can access an on-line introduction to the features and business applications of 1-2-3 called *A View of 1-2-3*.

Finding On-Screen Help

Press Help (F1) at any time to call the on-line help facility. If you press Help while in READY mode, the Help Index appears (see fig. 2.13). Choose any of the topics in the Help Index to move to other help screens.

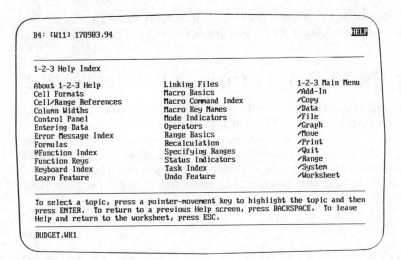

B4: [W11] 178903.94   HELP

1-2-3 Help Index

About 1-2-3 Help	Linking Files	1-2-3 Main Menu
Cell Formats	Macro Basics	/Add-In
Cell/Range References	Macro Command Index	/Copy
Column Widths	Macro Key Names	/Data
Control Panel	Mode Indicators	/File
Entering Data	Operators	/Graph
Error Message Index	Range Basics	/Move
Formulas	Recalculation	/Print
@Function Index	Specifying Ranges	/Quit
Function Keys	Status Indicators	/Range
Keyboard Index	Task Index	/System
Learn Feature	Undo Feature	/Worksheet

To select a topic, press a pointer-movement key to highlight the topic and then
press ENTER. To return to a previous Help screen, press BACKSPACE. To leave
Help and return to the worksheet, press ESC.

BUDGET.WK1

Fig. 2.13.
The Help Index screen.

You can press the Help (F1) key at any time, even while executing a command or editing a cell. The help is context-sensitive. For example, if you are executing a particular command when you press Help (F1), 1-2-3 displays information on that command (see fig. 2.14).

Fig. 2.14.
A context-
sensitive help
screen that
explains the
/Worksheet
commands.

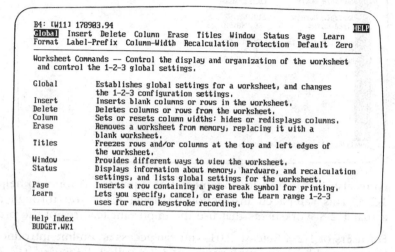

```
B4: [W11] 178903.94                                                    HELP
Global  Insert  Delete  Column  Erase  Titles  Window  Status  Page  Learn
Format  Label-Prefix  Column-Width  Recalculation  Protection  Default  Zero

Worksheet Commands -- Control the display and organization of the worksheet
 and control the 1-2-3 global settings.

Global      Establishes global settings for a worksheet, and changes
            the 1-2-3 configuration settings.
Insert      Inserts blank columns or rows in the worksheet.
Delete      Deletes columns or rows from the worksheet.
Column      Sets or resets column widths; hides or redisplays columns.
Erase       Removes a worksheet from memory, replacing it with a
            blank worksheet.
Titles      Freezes rows and/or columns at the top and left edges of
            the worksheet.
Window      Provides different ways to view the worksheet.
Status      Displays information about memory, hardware, and recalculation
            settings, and lists global settings for the worksheet.
Page        Inserts a row containing a page break symbol for printing.
Learn       Lets you specify, cancel, or erase the Learn range 1-2-3
            uses for macro keystroke recording.

Help Index
BUDGET.WK1
```

Certain parts of the help screen identify additional help topics. These topics are displayed in boldface on a monochrome monitor or in a different color on a color monitor. To get more information about a topic, move the high-lighter to that topic and press Enter. One or more additional topics are always located at the bottom of the screen. One of these is always the option to return to the Help Index.

Press the Backspace key to view a previous help screen. Press the Esc key to return to the 1-2-3 worksheet when you are finished with the help facility.

Taking the 1-2-3 Tutorial in Release 2.2

Another learning resource from Lotus is the Tutorial manual, a book that comes with the documentation. The Tutorial provides a self-paced series of lessons on 1-2-3. The lessons are arranged in order of increasing difficulty and build on each other. The Tutorial does not cover all of 1-2-3's functions and commands but covers enough to give you a basic understanding of the program. Before you use the Tutorial, you must install 1-2-3 on your hard disk.

The 1-2-3 Release 2.2 Tutorial is divided into 5 chapters with 20 lessons. Chapter 1 covers the basics of starting 1-2-3; entering and editing data; using command menus, formulas, functions, and ranges; formatting; and printing. Chapter 2 discusses graphs, and Chapter 3 shows how to link files. Chapter 4 covers databases; Chapter 5 introduces macros.

If you are new to 1-2-3, the best approach is to do one or two lessons at a time until you complete Chapter 1. After each lesson, work with 1-2-3 for a while before you tackle the more advanced topics. Only after you feel comfortable with all the material in Chapter 1 of the Tutorial should you try the other chapters. You can learn about the more specialized topics, such as databases or macros, without going through all the preceding lessons. If you are familiar with 1-2-3, but are new to Release 2.2, you should read the entire Tutorial and try out the new features.

For further details on 1-2-3 functions and commands, you can refer to the Command Reference section or other appropriate sections of this book or to the 1-2-3 documentation.

Chapter Summary

This chapter presents the information you need to use 1-2-3 for the first time. You learn how to start and exit 1-2-3 from either the operating system or the 1-2-3 Access System and how to implement the Install and Translate programs. The features provided in the 1-2-3 display and the keyboard are discussed also. And you learn how to use the on-line help facility and the Tutorial.

This chapter sets the stage so that you can begin to use 1-2-3. The next chapter presents information on entering and editing data and moving around worksheets. Chapter 3 also introduces a feature new with Release 2.2—linking worksheets.

3

Learning Worksheet Basics

This chapter presents the skills needed to use 1-2-3, the powerful electronic spreadsheet. If this is your first experience with spreadsheet software, you learn how to use a spreadsheet for data analysis. If you are familiar with electronic spreadsheets but are new to 1-2-3 or to Release 2.01 or 2.2, you find information in this chapter to help you understand the conventions and features of the program.

In this chapter, you learn the basics for using 1-2-3 presented in an order best suited for those learning to create spreadsheet applications for the first time. The chapter begins by showing you how to move around the worksheet so that you can easily perform such actions as entering, changing, moving, and copying data. You also learn how to move the cell pointer to and display any part of the large 256-column-by-8,192-row worksheet area.

In addition to teaching you the different ways of moving around the 1-2-3 worksheet, this chapter introduces entering and editing data. Specifically, you learn how to make the data in your worksheets understandable by you and others by entering titles, headings, names, comments, descriptions, and a variety of other entries, called labels. You also learn how to undo a change you've made by using the Release 2.2 Undo feature.

Cue:
Release 2.2 adds a new Undo (Alt-F4) key that enables you to undo changes.

Finally, this chapter teaches you how to tap the real power of 1-2-3 by creating formulas—formulas that link data in a single worksheet as well as formulas that link a cell in one worksheet to a cell in another worksheet. This file-linking capability, unavailable in releases of 1-2-3 prior to Release 2.2, will enable you to create many types of consolidations.

In this chapter, you learn how to do the following:

- Work with worksheets and files
- Move the cell pointer around the worksheet
- Enter data
- Edit data
- Use the Undo feature
- Use the linking features

Understanding Worksheets and Files

When you first start 1-2-3, you start with a blank worksheet file and build a worksheet in the computer's memory. To keep your worksheet, you save it in a file on disk with a file name. (Chapter 7 covers files in detail.) In 1-2-3 Release 2.2, 2.01, 2, and 1A, a file consists of one worksheet. (In Release 3, a file can contain many worksheets.)

Whenever you enter data into the worksheet, the entry goes into the cell at the location of the cell pointer. This location is called the *current cell*. To move around the worksheet, you move the cell pointer. By moving the cell pointer, you control where you place data in the worksheet. In figure 3.1, for example, any data you type goes into cell B6 until you move the cell pointer.

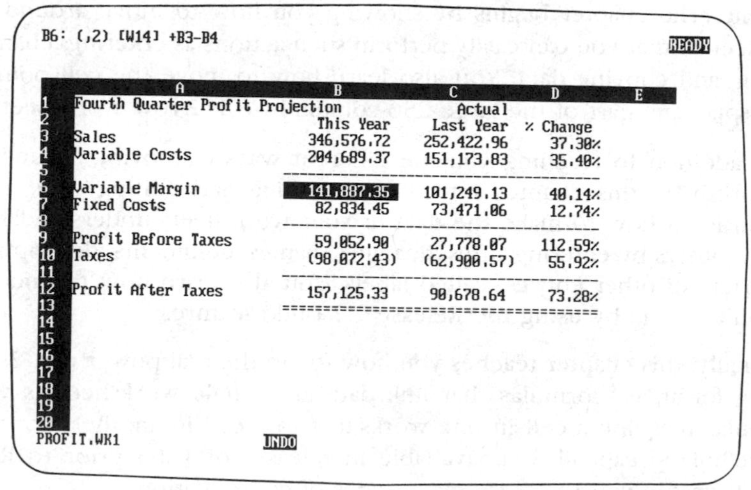

Fig. 3.1.
A sample worksheet with numbers, labels, and formulas.

```
B6: (,2) [W14] +B3-B4                                              READY

             A                B              C           D          E
 1  Fourth Quarter Profit Projection        Actual
 2                        This Year      Last Year   % Change
 3  Sales                346,576.72     252,422.96     37.38%
 4  Variable Costs       204,689.37     151,173.83     35.40%
 5
 6  Variable Margin      141,887.35     101,249.13     40.14%
 7  Fixed Costs           82,834.45      73,471.06     12.74%
 8
 9  Profit Before Taxes   59,052.90      27,778.07    112.59%
10  Taxes                (98,072.43)    (62,900.57)    55.92%
11
12  Profit After Taxes   157,125.33      90,678.64     73.28%
13
14
15
16
17
18
19
20
PROFIT.WK1                     UNDO
```

Usually the current time and date are displayed in the lower left corner of the screen. But if you are using Release 2.2, you can change this default display to the current file name. To do so, execute the **/Worksheet Global Default Other Clock Filename** command. In figure 3.1, the current file is PROFIT.WK1. The worksheet itself is displayed on-screen.

RELEASE

2.2

Formulas are operations or calculations you want 1-2-3 to perform on the data. Formulas make 1-2-3 an electronic worksheet, not just a computerized method of displaying data. You enter the numbers and formulas, and 1-2-3 performs the calculations. When you change a number, 1-2-3 changes the results of all the formulas that use that number. When you change the number in C3 or C4 in figure 3.1, the results of all the cells that contain formulas that depend on these cells change automatically.

Reminder:
The name of the current file may be displayed in the lower left corner of the screen with Release 2.2.

Introducing Linked Files

RELEASE

2.2

Entire
Section

1-2-3 Release 2.2 enables you to put a formula in a cell in one worksheet (the one currently in memory) that refers to cells in other worksheets stored on disk. This action is called *file linking*.

File linking lets you consolidate data in separate files easily. You might, for example, receive data from separate departments to consolidate. Each department's data is in a separate file. Your consolidation file can use formulas to combine the data from each separate file. The process also works in reverse. You can have a central database file as well as separate files to distribute to each department. The individual department files can contain formulas that refer to data in the central database file. See "Using Linked Worksheets in Release 2.2" later in this chapter.

Reminder:
1-2-3 Release 2.2 lets you put a formula in one worksheet that refers to a cell in another worksheet.

Using linked files instead of one large file has several advantages:

- You can use file linking to build large worksheet systems that are too large to fit into memory all at once.

- You can link files that come from different sources.

Using the Workspace

The workspace is the space available in your worksheet. The potential size of your workspace is formidable—256 columns and 8,192 rows. This large work area gives you flexibility when you design your worksheets. You do not have to crowd everything together to save space. You can lay out different parts of the worksheet in different places to make the data easier to use and understand.

If you try to build a worksheet that uses all possible rows and columns, you will have produced a worksheet that is complex, difficult to use, and possibly too large for your computer's memory. A typical large worksheet might contain information about thousands of employees or inventory items. This type of worksheet uses a few columns and many rows. Another worksheet might contain a series of related reports; this worksheet may use many columns but just a few rows.

You start out building small, simple worksheets. As you increase your skills using 1-2-3, you will feel comfortable building larger, more complex worksheets. The generous workspace lets you build your worksheets without worrying about running out of room.

Moving around the Worksheet

Cue:
You can use one of several methods to move the cell pointer quickly around the worksheet.

You can use several methods to move the cell pointer quickly anywhere in the worksheet. Remember that moving around the worksheet means moving the cell pointer, the bright rectangle that highlights—and identifies—an entire cell. Characters within the cell pointer appear in reverse video on the highlighted background. Any data typed into the worksheet goes into the cell at the location of the cell pointer. The *cursor*—the blinking line in the control panel when you enter or edit data in a cell—shows you the position of the next character typed. Within a menu, the *menu pointer* is the highlighter used to select a command.

Because you can enter data only at the location of the cell pointer, you must know how to move the cell pointer to the location you want. Because you can display only a small part of the worksheet at any one time, you also must know how to move the cell pointer so that you can see different parts of the worksheet at different times.

Reminder:
The same keys are used to move the cell pointer and the cursor, depending on the current mode.

Table 3.1 lists the keys that move the cell pointer. Table 3.2 (included later in this chapter) lists the movement keys that move the cursor in EDIT mode. Many of the same keys move either the cell pointer or the cursor, depending on the current mode. These keys are often called *pointer-movement* keys when they move the cell pointer and *cursor keys* when they move the cursor. This terminology can be confusing if you do not realize that these terms refer to the same keys.

Table 3.1
Worksheet Movement Keys

Key	Description
→	Moves the cell pointer one cell to the right
←	Moves the cell pointer one cell to the left
↑	Moves the cell pointer one cell up
↓	Moves the cell pointer one cell down
Ctrl→ or Tab	Moves the cell pointer right one screen
Ctrl← or Shift-Tab	Moves the cell pointer left one screen
PgUp	Moves the cell pointer up one screen
PgDn	Moves the cell pointer down one screen
Home	Moves the cell pointer to the home position (usually cell A1)
End Home	Moves the cell pointer to the lower right corner of the active area
End→, End↓, End←, End↑	Moves the cell pointer in the direction of the arrow to the next cell that contains data (the intersection between a blank cell and a cell that contains data)
F5 (GoTo)	Prompts for a cell address or range name and then moves the cell pointer directly to that cell
F6 (Window)	If the window has been split, moves the cell pointer to the next window
Scroll Lock	Toggles the scroll function on and off; when on, moves the entire window when you press one of the four arrow keys

The function of movement keys varies depending on the mode that is currently active:

Mode	Function of Movement Keys
READY or POINT	The movement keys move the cell pointer.
LABEL or VALUE	The movement keys end the entry, return to READY mode, and move the cell pointer.
EDIT	Some movement keys move the cursor in the control panel; other movement keys end the edit, return to READY mode, and move the cell pointer.
MENU	The movement keys move the menu pointer to menu choices.

This section discusses the movement of the cell pointer. Cursor movement is covered later in this chapter during the discussion of editing data in the worksheet.

The current cell address is displayed in the upper left corner of the display in a format that indicates the column and row locations. In figure 3.1, B6 represents the column letter (B) and the row number (6).

Using the Basic Movement Keys

The four directional arrow keys that move the cell pointer are located on the numeric keypad and on the separate pad of the Enhanced Keyboard. The cell pointer moves in the direction of the arrow on the key. When you hold down the arrow key, the cell pointer continues to move in that direction. When the pointer reaches the edge of the screen, the worksheet continues to scroll in the direction of the arrow. When you try to move past the edge of the worksheet, 1-2-3 beeps a warning.

You can use several other keys to page through the worksheet. Press the PgUp and PgDn keys to move up or down one screenful. Press Ctrl-right arrow (hold down the Ctrl key and press the right-arrow key) or Tab to move one screenful to the right; press Ctrl-left arrow (hold down the Ctrl key and press the left-arrow key) or Shift-Tab (hold down the Shift key and press Tab) to move one screenful to the left. The size of one screenful depends on the type of display driver in your system and whether a window is present on-screen. (Windows are discussed in Chapter 4.)

Table 3.1 summarizes the action of the movement keys. Press the Home key to move the cell pointer directly to the home position—usually cell A1. In Chapter 4, you learn how to lock titles on-screen. Locked titles can change the home position. The other keys listed in table 3.1 are covered in the following sections.

Using the Scroll Lock Key

The Scroll Lock key toggles the scroll function on and off. When you press the Scroll Lock key, you activate the scroll function, and the SCROLL status indicator appears at the bottom of the screen. When you press an arrow key with Scroll Lock on, the cell pointer stays in the current cell, and the entire window moves in the direction of the arrow key. If the cell pointer reaches the end of the display and you continue to press the same arrow key, the cell pointer moves to the next cell as the entire window scrolls. If the SCROLL status indicator is on, press the Scroll Lock key again to turn it off.

Use the scroll function when you want to see part of the worksheet that is off the screen without moving the cell pointer from the current cell. Suppose that the cell pointer is in B6, and you want to see the data in column F before you change the contents of B6. If you turn on the scroll function and press the right-arrow key once, the entire window moves to the right. You can see column F, and the cell pointer stays in B6 (see fig. 3.2). To get the same result without using Scroll Lock, you press the right-arrow key four times to display column F, and then press the left-arrow key four times to return to B6.

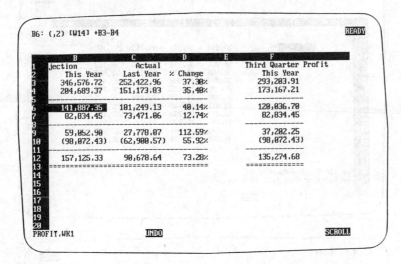

Fig. 3.2.
The Scroll Lock
key used to
move an entire
window.

Scroll Lock has no effect on the other movement keys. When the cell pointer does not move the way you expect, check to see whether Scroll Lock has been accidentally turned on. Check for the SCROLL indicator in the lower right corner of the screen, as shown in figure 3.2. Press Scroll Lock again to turn it off.

Reminder:
Check the SCROLL indicator when the cell pointer does not move the way you expect.

Using the End Key

The End key is used in a special way in 1-2-3. When you press and release the End key, the END status indicator appears in the last line of the display. If you then press one of the arrow keys, the cell pointer moves in the direction of the arrow key to the next intersection of a blank cell and a cell that contains data. The cell pointer always stops on a cell that contains data if possible. When there are no cells that contain data in the direction of the arrow key, the cell pointer stops at the edge of the worksheet.

For example, figure 3.3 shows the cell pointer in cell B3. The END status indicator at the bottom right corner of the screen shows that the End key has been pressed. If you now press the right-arrow key, the cell pointer moves right to the first cell that contains data. In this case, the cell pointer moves to D3, as shown in figure 3.4. If you press the End key and then the right-arrow key again, the cell pointer moves to the last cell that contains data before a blank cell. In this case, the cell pointer moves to G3, as shown in figure 3.5.

Fig. 3.3.
The END key
status
indicator.

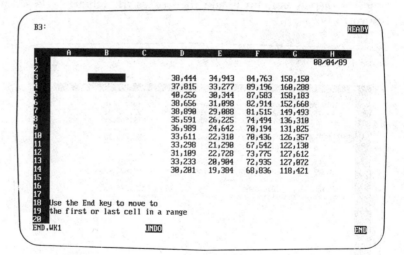

Fig. 3.4.
Using End-right
arrow to move
the cell pointer
to the first cell
that contains
data.

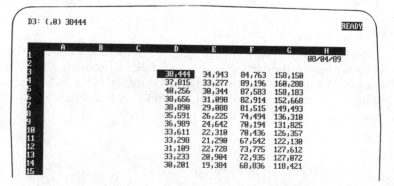

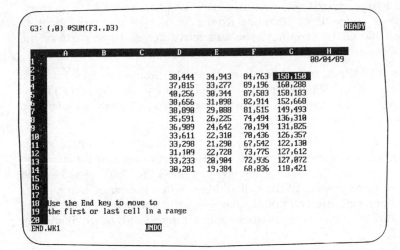

Fig. 3.5.
Using End-right
arrow to move
the cell pointer
to the last cell
that contains
data.

When no other data is in the worksheet and you press the End key and then the right-arrow key again, the cell pointer moves to the end of the worksheet to cell IV3. If you press End and then press the down-arrow key from G3, the cell pointer moves to G14.

Cue:
Use the End key to move directly to the end of a list of data.

The End key works the same way with the left- and up-arrow keys. In figure 3.5, End-left arrow takes you to D3. From D3, End-up arrow takes you to D1 (the edge of the worksheet). After you press the End key, the END indicator stays on until you press an arrow key or the End key again. If you press End in error, just press End again to turn off the END status indicator.

When you press the End key and then the Home key, the cell pointer moves to the lower right corner of the active area. The active area includes all rows and all columns that have data or cell formats. When you press End and then Home in figure 3.5, the cell pointer moves to H19. This cell is the end of the active area even though it is a blank cell. There is an entry in column H (in H1) and an entry in row 19 (in A19). Use End and then Home to find the end of the active area when you want to add a section to your worksheet and not interfere with any existing data.

Cue:
Press End and then Home to find the end of the active area when you want to add a section to your worksheet.

Using the GoTo Key To Jump Directly to a Cell

You can use the GoTo (F5) key to jump directly to any cell in the worksheet. When you press the GoTo (F5) key, 1-2-3 prompts you for a cell address. When you type the cell address, the cell pointer moves directly to that address. The address is in the format of the column letter from A to IV and the row number from 1 to 8,192.

If you have a large worksheet, you may have to press one of the pointer-movement keys many times to move from one part of the worksheet to another. With the GoTo (F5) key, you can move across large parts of the worksheet at once.

With a large worksheet, it is difficult to remember the addresses for each part of the worksheet. This can make it difficult to use the GoTo (F5) key. You can, however, use range names with the GoTo (F5) key so that you don't have to remember cell addresses.

Cue:
You can use range names with the GoTo (F5) key.

You can assign a range name to a cell or a rectangular group of cells. A *range name* is an English synonym for a cell address; for example, you can assign cell B56 the range name PROFIT. Then you can press the GoTo (F5) key and type the range name instead of the cell address. When the range name refers to more than one cell, the cell pointer moves to the upper left corner of the range. You can find more information about ranges and range names in Chapter 4.

Entering Data into the Worksheet

To enter data into a cell, move the cell pointer to that cell, type the entry, and then press Enter. As you type, the entry appears on the second line of the control panel. When you press Enter, the entry appears in the current cell and on the first line of the control panel. If you enter data into a cell that already contains information, the new data replaces the earlier entry.

Cue:
Use the movement keys to complete an entry and move to the next cell.

If you plan to enter data into more than one cell, you do not need to press Enter and then move the cell pointer to the next cell. You can type the entry and move the cell pointer with one keystroke; just press one of the pointer-movement keys (such as the arrow keys, Tab, or PgDn) after typing the entry.

The two types of cell entries are labels and values. A *label* is a text entry. A *value* is either a number or a formula. 1-2-3 determines the type of cell entry from the first character you enter. 1-2-3 treats your entry as a value (a number or a formula) if you begin with one of the following numeric characters:

0 1 2 3 4 5 6 7 8 9 + − . (@ # $

When you begin by entering any other character, 1-2-3 treats your entry as a label. As soon as you type the first character, the mode indicator changes from READY to either VALUE or LABEL.

Entering Labels

Labels make the numbers and formulas in your worksheets understandable. The labels in figure 3.1 tell you what the data means. In figures 3.3 through 3.5, the numbers and formulas have no labels, and you have no idea what this data represents.

Because a label is a text entry, it can contain any string of characters and can be up to 240 characters long. Labels can include titles, headings, explanations, and notes, all of which can help make your worksheet more understandable.

When you enter a label, 1-2-3 adds a label prefix to the beginning of the cell entry. The label prefix is not visible in the worksheet, but is visible in the control panel (see fig. 3.6). 1-2-3 uses the label prefix to identify the entry as a label and to determine how it is displayed and printed.

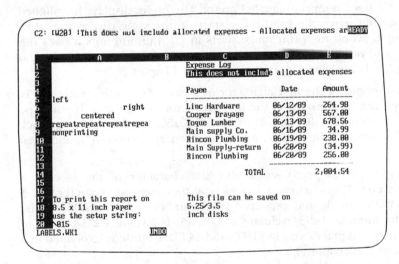

Fig. 3.6.
Examples of different label prefixes.

You can assign one of the following five label prefixes:

'	Left-aligned (default)
"	Right-aligned
^	Centered
\	Repeating
|	Left-aligned and nonprinting

When you enter a label, 1-2-3 by default adds the apostrophe (') for a left-aligned label. To use a different label prefix, you type the prefix as the first character of the label.

In figure 3.6, column A shows examples of the different label prefixes so that you can compare how they display. Columns C through E show how to use these label prefixes in a typical worksheet. A column of descriptions such as C6..C11 usually looks best when left-aligned—the normal way to line up text. Column headings should align with the data below. The heading in C4 is left-aligned to match the Payee descriptions.

When the entries fill the cell width, as do the dates in column D, the column heading can be aligned either left, right, or center. In this example, the date heading is centered. A centered label is best when the column heading is shorter than the data below it. Because numbers and numeric formulas are always right-aligned, the amount column heading in E4 is right-aligned.

The dashed lines in rows 5 and 13 are repeating labels. The repeating labels fill the entire width of the cell. When you change the column width, the label length changes to fill the new column width.

The note in C2 has a nonprinting label prefix. The prefix displays left-aligned but does not print when the print range starts in the same row as the label. In this example, when the print range starts in C1, the note in C2 does not print. When the print range starts in A1, the note does print. Printing and nonprinting labels are covered in more detail in Chapter 8.

To use a label prefix as the first character of a label, first type a label prefix and then type the label prefix as the first character of the label. If you type **\015** into A20, the cell displays 015015015015015015 as a repeating label. You must first type a label prefix, in this case an apostrophe ('), and then **\015**.

You must type a label prefix when the first character of the label is a numeric character. If not, as soon as you type the numeric character, 1-2-3 switches to VALUE mode and expects a valid number or formula. When the label is a valid formula, 1-2-3 evaluates it. When it is invalid, 1-2-3 refuses to accept the entry and places you in EDIT mode. (EDIT mode is explained in a later section of this chapter.)

In C18 in figure 3.6, you must type a label prefix to precede the label 5.25/3.5. If you do not, 1-2-3 treats the entry as a formula and displays the result of 5.25 divided by 3.5, which is 1.5.

In A18 in figure 3.6, you must type a label prefix to precede the label 8.5 × 11 inch paper, or 1-2-3 treats it as an invalid formula. You often encounter this problem when you enter an address such as 11711 N. College Ave.

When a label is longer than the cell width, the label displays across the cells to the right as long as these cells are blank (see cells B17..B19 in fig. 3.6). The cell display can even continue into the next window to the right as long as all these cells are blank.

The label in C2 in figure 3.6 is longer than what can be displayed in the window. You can see the continuation of the label in the next window to the right (see fig. 3.7)

Reminder:
A long label displays across blank cells to its right.

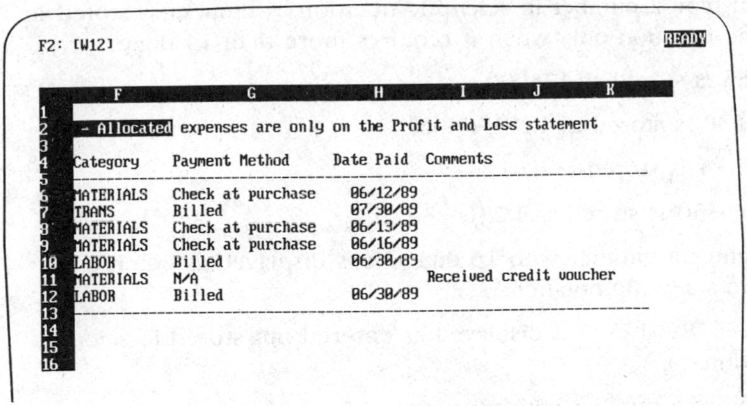

```
F2: [W12]                                                    READY

          F          G           H          I       J       K
1
2      - Allocated expenses are only on the Profit and Loss statement
3
4    Category     Payment Method    Date Paid  Comments
5    ─────────────────────────────────────────────────────────────
6    MATERIALS    Check at purchase  06/12/89
7    TRANS        Billed             07/30/89
8    MATERIALS    Check at purchase  06/13/89
9    MATERIALS    Check at purchase  06/16/89
10   LABOR        Billed             06/30/89
11   MATERIALS    N/A                          Received credit voucher
12   LABOR        Billed             06/30/89
13   ─────────────────────────────────────────────────────────────
14
15
16
```

Fig. 3.7.
A long label continuing into the next window.

1-2-3 includes several commands that can change many label prefixes at one time. This subject is covered in Chapter 5.

Entering Numbers

To enter a valid number, you can type any of the 10 digits (0 through 9) and certain other characters according to the following rules:

1. You can start the number with a plus sign (+); the sign is not stored when you press Enter.

   + 123 is stored as 123.

2. You can begin the number with a minus sign (−); the number is stored as a negative number.

   − 123 is stored as − 123.

3. You can place the number within parentheses ( ); the parentheses are dropped when the number is displayed.

   (123) is stored as 123.

4. You can begin the number with a dollar sign ($); the sign is not stored when you press Enter.

   $123 is stored as 123.

5. You can include one decimal point (.).

   .123 is stored as 0.123.

6. The number can end with a percent sign (%); the number is divided by 100, and the percent sign is dropped.

   123% is stored as 1.23.

7. You can type a number in scientific notation. A number is stored in scientific notation only when it requires more than 14 digits.

   123E3 is stored as 123000.

   1.23E30 is stored as 1.23E + 30.

   123E − 4 is stored as 0.0123.

   1.23E − 30 is stored as 1.23E − 30.

8. If you enter a number with 15 digits, it is displayed as entered but stored in scientific notation.

   123456789012345 is displayed as entered but stored in scientific notation.

9. If you enter a number with more than 15 digits, it is stored and displayed in scientific notation.

   1234567890123456 is stored and displayed in scientific notation.

When the number is too long to display normally in the cell, 1-2-3 tries to display what it can. If the cell uses the default **General** format and the integer part of the number can fit in the cell width, 1-2-3 truncates any part of the decimal part of the number that does not fit. In figure 3.8, the numbers in all three columns (C–E) are the same; only the column widths are different. In cell E5, 25.54321 displays truncated to 25. In cell C6, 1675.12345678 displays truncated to 1675.123. Cell formats are described in detail in Chapter 5.

Fig. 3.8.
Asterisks displayed in place of a number too long for the cell width.

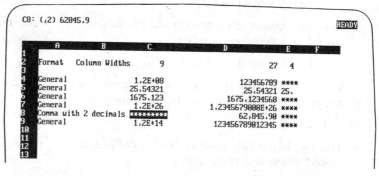

Reminder:
When the column width is too narrow to display a number, 1-2-3 displays asterisks (*).

When the cell uses the default **General** format and the integer part of the number does not fit in the cell, 1-2-3 displays the number using scientific notation. Examples are shown in cells C4, C7, and C9 in figure 3.8. When the cell uses a format other than **General** or the cell width is too narrow to display in scientific notation, and the number cannot fit into the cell width, 1-2-3 displays asterisks (*) as shown in figure 3.8.

Entering Formulas

The real power of 1-2-3 comes from its capability to perform calculations on formulas you enter. In fact, formulas make 1-2-3 an electronic worksheet—not just a computerized way to assemble data for reports. You enter the numbers and formulas into the worksheet; 1-2-3 calculates the results of all the formulas. As you add or change data, you never have to recalculate the effects of the changes; 1-2-3 does it automatically. In figure 3.1, if you change the sales or variable costs, 1-2-3 automatically recalculates the variable margin. In figure 3.6, the total expense in cell E14 is recalculated each time you add or change an expense amount.

You can enter formulas that operate on numbers, labels, and other cells in the worksheet. Like labels, a formula can be up to 240 characters long.

You can use one of three different types of formulas: numeric, string, and logical. *Numeric formulas* work with numbers, other numeric formulas, and numeric functions. *String formulas* work with labels, other string formulas, and string functions. *Logical formulas* are TRUE/FALSE tests that can test either numeric or string values. Functions are covered in Chapter 6. This chapter covers each type of formula.

Formulas can operate on numbers in the cell, such as $8+26$. This formula uses 1-2-3 just as a calculator. A more useful formula uses cell references in the calculation. The formula in cell F1 in figure 3.9 is $+B1+C1+D1+E1$. The control panel shows the formula, and the worksheet shows the result of the calculation—in this case, 183. The power and usefulness of this formula is that the result in cell F1 changes automatically any time you change any of the numbers in the other cells. This single fact is behind the power of the 1-2-3 electronic worksheet.

Reminder:
The formula displays in the control panel; the result of the calculation displays in the worksheet.

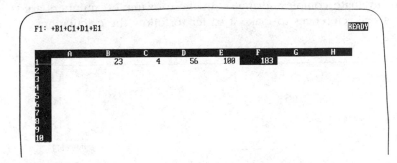

F1: +B1+C1+D1+E1   READY

A	B	C	D	E	F	G	H
1	23	4	56	100	183		

Fig. 3.9.
A formula displayed in the control panel; the result of the calculation displayed in the worksheet.

Note that the formula begins with a plus sign ($+B1$). When a formula begins with B1, 1-2-3 assumes that you are entering a label and does not perform a calculation.

Using Operators in Numeric Formulas

A *formula* is an instruction to 1-2-3 to perform a calculation. You use *operators* to specify the calculations to perform. The *numeric operators* include addition, subtraction, multiplication, division, and exponentiation (raising a number to a power). The formula in figure 3.9 uses the plus sign, the addition operator. The simplest numeric formula uses just the plus sign (+) to repeat the value in another cell. In figure 3.8, cells D4 and E4 both contain the formula +C4. The other cells in columns D and E are also formulas that refer to the cell in column C. In each case, the values of the cells in column C are repeated in columns D and E.

When 1-2-3 evaluates a formula, it calculates terms within the formula in a specified sequence. The following numeric operators are listed in *order of precedence*:

Operator	Meaning
^	Exponentiation
+, −	Positive, Negative
*, /	Multiplication, Division
+, −	Addition, Subtraction

Cue:
Use parentheses in a formula to change the order of precedence of the calculations.

When a formula uses all these operators, 1-2-3 calculates the exponentials first and then works down the list. If two operators are equal in precedence, it makes no difference which is calculated first. This order of precedence has a definite effect on the result of many formulas. To override the order, use parentheses. Operations inside a set of parentheses are always evaluated first.

The following examples show how 1-2-3 uses parentheses and the order of precedence to evaluate complex formulas. In these examples, numbers are used instead of cell references to make it easier to follow the calculations.

Formula	Evaluation	Result
5+3*2	5+(3*2)	11
(5+3)*2	(5+3)*2	16
−3^2*2	−(3^2)*2	−18
−3^(2*2)	−(3^(2*2))	−81
5+4*8/4−3	5+(4*(8/4))−3	10
5+4*8/(4−3)	5+((4*8)/(4−3))	37
(5+4)*8/(4−3)	(5+4)*8/(4−3)	72
(5+4)*8/4−3	(5+4)*(8/4)−3	15
5+3*4^2/6−2*3^4	5+(3*(4^2)/6)−(2*(3^4))	−149

Using Operators in String Formulas

String formulas have different rules than numeric formulas. A *string* is either a label or a *string formula*. You can use only two string formula operators. You can repeat another string, or you can join (concatenate) two or more strings.

The simplest string formula uses only the plus sign (+) to repeat the string in another cell. In figure 3.10, the formula in cell A6 is +A3. The formula to repeat a numeric cell and to repeat a string cell is the same.

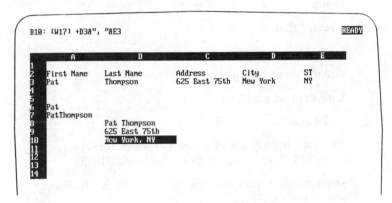

Fig. 3.10.
String formulas used to repeat or concatenate strings.

The string concatenation operator is the ampersand (&). The formula in cell A7 in figure 3.10 is +A3&B3. The first operator in a string formula must be a plus (+) sign; any other operators in the formula must be ampersands (&). If you do not use the ampersand, but use any of the numeric operators, 1-2-3 treats the formula as a numeric formula. A cell that contains a label has a numeric value of zero. The formula +A3+B3 in the worksheet in figure 3.10 is treated as a numeric formula and evaluates to zero.

When you use an ampersand (&) in a formula, 1-2-3 treats it as a string formula. If you also use any numeric operators (after the plus sign at the beginning), 1-2-3 considers it an invalid formula. The formulas +A3&B3+C3 and +A3+B3&C3 are invalid. When you enter an invalid formula, 1-2-3 puts you into EDIT mode. EDIT mode is covered later in this chapter.

In figure 3.10, the names run together in cell A7. Suppose that you want to put a space between the first and last names. You can insert a string directly into a string formula by enclosing the string in quotation marks ("). The formula in cell B8 is +A3&" "&B3. The formula in cell B10 is +D3", "&E3.

You can write more complex string formulas with string functions (see Chapter 6).

Using Operators in Logical Functions

Logical formulas are TRUE/FALSE tests. They compare two values and evaluate to 1 if the test is TRUE and 0 if the test is FALSE. Logical formulas are used mainly in database criteria ranges. Logical formulas are covered in more detail in Chapters 6 and 12.

The *logical operators* include the following:

Operator	Meaning
=	Equal
>	Greater than
<	Less than
>=	Greater than or equal to
<=	Less than or equal to
<>	Not equal
#NOT#	Reverses the results of a test (changes the result from TRUE to FALSE or from FALSE to TRUE)
#OR#	Logical OR to join two tests; the result is TRUE if *either* test is TRUE
#AND#	Logical AND to join two tests; the result is TRUE if *both* tests are TRUE

Figure 3.11 shows examples of logical formulas. For example, the formula in D4 compares A4 (1) to B4 (1) to see whether they are equal. The result of the formula is displayed in E4. In this case, the formula is TRUE (1).

Fig. 3.11. Logical formulas evaluated to 1 if TRUE or 0 if FALSE.

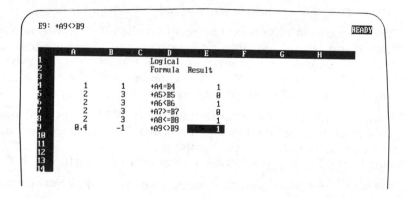

Pointing to Cell References

Formulas consist mainly of operators and cell references. The formula in figure 3.9 has four cell references. You can type each address, or you can use a better way. Whenever 1-2-3 expects a cell address, you can use the movement keys to point to the cell. As soon as you move the cell pointer, 1-2-3 changes to POINT mode, and the address of the cell pointer appears in the formula in the control panel.

Move the cell pointer until it is on the correct cell address in the formula. If this location marks the end of the formula, press Enter. If the formula contains more terms, type the next operator and continue the process until you are finished; then press Enter. If you want, you can type some addresses and point to others.

Because you can easily type an incorrect address in a formula, pointing to cells is more accurate than typing—and also much faster. The only time it is easier to type an address than point to the cell is when the cell reference is far from the current cell and you happen to remember the cell address. For example, if you enter a formula in Z238 and want to refer to cell I23, it may be faster to just type I23 than point to it. Experienced 1-2-3 users rarely type addresses. Specifying ranges is covered in Chapter 4.

Cue:
For speed and accuracy, use POINT mode to enter cell references in formulas.

Correcting Errors in Formulas

If, in error, you enter a formula that 1-2-3 cannot evaluate, the program beeps, changes to EDIT mode, and moves the cursor to the place in the formula where it encountered an error. You cannot enter an invalid formula into a worksheet. For more information about changing a cell in EDIT mode, see "Editing Data in the Worksheet" later in this chapter.

Common errors that make a formula invalid are missing or extra parentheses and mixing numeric and string operators. Other sources of errors are misspelled function names and incorrect arguments in functions (covered in Chapter 6) The following examples show some common simple errors:

+A1+A2&A3	Mixing numeric and string operators
+A1/(A2−A3	Missing right parenthesis
@SIM(A1..A3)	Misspelled @SUM function

If you do not know what is wrong or how to fix a formula, use the Help facility to check the format of a function. If you decide to switch from EDIT to READY mode by pressing Esc, remember that you will erase the entire formula you've entered. Rather than leaving EDIT mode when 1-2-3 indicates that a formula contains an error, it's usually best to correct the error in EDIT mode.

Cue:
To fix a formula that is in error, temporarily convert it to a label and move it to another cell.

When you know what is wrong with the formula, follow the procedures in "Editing Data in the Worksheet" later in this chapter. If you do not know how to correct the formula, convert it to a label. Because all labels are valid entries, this technique clears the error and lets you continue working. Follow these steps to convert a formula to a label, clear EDIT mode, and return to READY mode:

1. Press Home to move to the beginning of the formula.

2. Type an apostrophe (') as the label prefix. (1-2-3 accepts anything preceded by an apostrophe as a label.)

3. Press Enter.

You now can use the Help facility or look at another part of the worksheet that has a similar formula. When you find the error, correct the formula and remove the apostrophe. (Refer to the Troubleshooting section in this book for more details.)

Addressing Cells

A cell address in a formula is known as a cell reference. The formula in cell F1 in figure 3.9 has four cell references (+B1+C1+D1+E1). Normally, when you copy a formula from one cell to another cell, the cell references adjust automatically. If you copy the formula in cell F1 of figure 3.9 to cell F2, the cell references change to +B2+C2+D2+E2. This type of cell referencing is called *relative addressing*.

You can use cell references in formulas that are absolute instead of relative. An *absolute address* in a formula does not change when you copy the formula to another cell. You specify an absolute address by preceding the column and row address with a dollar sign ($). For example, $A$1 is an absolute address. If this address were in cell C9 and you copied it to cell E19, the cell reference would still be $A$1. To specify an absolute cell address in POINT mode, press the Abs (F4) key.

In addition to relative and absolute cell addresses, you can specify a mixed cell address. In a *mixed cell address*, part of the address is relative and part is fixed. For example, +A$1 is a mixed address.

Whether a cell reference is relative, absolute, or mixed has no effect on the how the formula is calculated. This type of addressing matters only when you copy the formula to another cell. Copying and cell addressing are covered in detail in Chapter 4.

Changing Cell Formats

Several commands change the way numbers and formulas display in the worksheet. These commands, /Worksheet Global Format and /Range Format, are covered in detail in Chapter 5.

For example, you can specify a fixed number of decimal digits so that the numbers in a column line up; add commas and currency symbols; show numbers as percents; and even hide the contents of the cell.

In addition, 1-2-3 includes special formats and functions to handle dates and times. These topics are explained in Chapters 5 and 6.

Editing Data in the Worksheet

After you make an entry in a cell, you may want to change it. You may have misspelled a word in a label or created an incorrect formula. You can change an existing entry in two ways.

You can replace the contents of a cell by typing a new entry. The new entry completely replaces the original entry.

You also can change (edit) the contents of the cell. To edit a cell's contents, move the cell pointer to the cell and press the Edit (F2) key to go into EDIT mode. You also can press the Edit (F2) key while you are typing an entry. When you make an error entering a formula, 1-2-3 forces you into EDIT mode.

The entry is displayed on the second line in the control panel. If the entry is too long to display completely on the control panel line, the latter 79 characters appear when you go into EDIT mode. You can display the remaining characters by pressing the left-arrow key until the entry begins to scroll in the display.

Table 3.2 describes the action of keys in EDIT mode. You use the keys in table 3.2 to move the cursor in the control panel. While you edit the cell, the contents of the cell as displayed in the first line of the control panel and in the worksheet do not change. The cell's contents change only when you press Enter to complete the edit. If you press any key that moves the cell pointer, but has no meaning in EDIT mode, such as the up-arrow key, 1-2-3 first completes the entry and then moves the cell pointer in its usual way.

Table 3.2
Key Actions in EDIT Mode

Key	Action
←	Moves the cursor one character to the left
→	Moves the cursor one character to the right
↑	Completes the edit and moves the cell pointer up one row
↓	Completes the edit and moves the cell pointer down one row
Ctrl← or Shift-Tab	Moves the cursor left five characters
Ctrl→ or Tab	Moves the cursor right five characters
Home	Moves the cursor to the beginning of the entry
End	Moves the cursor to the end of the entry
Backspace	Deletes the character to the left of the cursor
Del	Deletes the character at the cursor
Ins	Toggles between insert and overtype mode
Esc	Clears the edit line
Esc Esc	Cancels the edit and makes no change to the cell
F2 (Edit)	Switches to VALUE or LABEL mode
Enter	Completes the edit

Cue:
Press Esc twice to cancel the edit and restore the cell to its original contents.

If you press Esc while in EDIT mode, you clear the edit area. With a blank edit area, if you then press Esc, Enter, or one of the arrow keys that normally ends editing, you do not erase the cell. Instead, you cancel the edit, and the cell reverts back to the way it was before you pressed the Edit (F2) key.

RELEASE

2.2

Entire
Section

Using the Undo Feature

When you type an entry or edit a cell, you change the worksheet. If you change the worksheet in error, you can press the Undo (Alt-F4) key to reverse the last change in Release 2.2. For example, if you type over an existing entry, you can undo the new entry and restore the previous one.

Initially, the Undo feature is enabled, but you can use commands to disable Undo. To turn off the Undo feature, choose **/W**orksheet **G**lobal **D**efault **O**ther **U**ndo **D**isable. To make this change permanent, choose **/W**orksheet **G**lobal **D**efault **U**pdate. When Undo is enabled, 1-2-3 "remembers" the last action that changed the worksheet. This action requires memory. How much memory Undo requires changes with different actions. You should disable Undo only if you get low on memory.

Reminder:
You can disable
Undo.

Remember that you can undo only the last change. When you make an error, undo it immediately; otherwise, the previous data may be lost. Also, if you press Undo at the wrong time, just press Undo again to restore the correct entry.

Caution:
You can undo only
the last change.

Undo is useful, powerful, and tricky; you must use this feature carefully. 1-2-3 remembers the last change to the worksheet and reverses this change when you press Undo. You must understand what 1-2-3 considers a change.

A change occurs between the time 1-2-3 is in READY mode and the next time it is in READY mode. Suppose that you press the Edit (F2) key to go into EDIT mode to change a cell. You can make any number of changes to the cell and then press Enter to save the changes and return to READY mode. If you press Undo now, 1-2-3 returns the worksheet to the way it was at the last READY mode. In this case, it returns the cell to the way it was before you edited it.

You can change many cells at one time or even erase everything in memory with one command. If you press Undo after a command, you undo all the effects of the command.

With some commands, such as **/P**rint, **/G**raph, and **/D**ata, you can execute many commands before you return to READY mode. If you press Undo then, you reverse all the commands executed since the last time 1-2-3 was in READY mode.

Suppose that you type an entry into cell K33, press Enter, and then press Home. The cell pointer moves to cell A1. If you press Undo now, you not only undo the movement to A1, but also the entry in cell K33 as well.

A change can refer to either a change to one or more cells or a change to command settings. For example, to print a report, you must specify a print range. This action does not change any data in the worksheet, but it changes a setting. If you press Undo the next time you are in READY mode, you undo the print range.

Some commands do not change any cells or settings. Examples of such commands include **/F**ile **S**ave, **/F**ile **X**tract, **/F**ile **E**rase, and **/P**rint **P**rinter **P**age. When you make an entry in a cell, then save the file, then press Undo, you cannot restore the original cell entry. Because **/F**ile **S**ave was the last operation before pressing Undo, Undo has no effect.

Caution:
What 1-2-3
considers the last
change may not be
just the last action
you performed.

The more extensive a change, the more memory 1-2-3 needs to remember the status of the worksheet before the change. When there is not enough memory to save the status before the change, 1-2-3 pauses and presents you with the following prompt and a menu:

    You will not be able to undo this action--do you wish to proceed?

Choose **Yes** to disable Undo temporarily and complete the command. You will not be able to undo this command, but Undo is reenabled as soon as the command completes.

Caution:
When 1-2-3 runs out of memory in the middle of a command, part of the command may have been completed.

Choose **No** to cancel the command in progress. You do not quit 1-2-3; you return to READY mode. The command may have been partially completed before 1-2-3 ran out of memory. For example, if you copy a range multiple times, run out of memory, and choose **No**, the range may have been copied to part of the specified range. Check your work carefully to determine the effects of the last command.

In most cases, choose **Yes**. Be sure, however, that you want to perform the command—you cannot undo it. If you executed the command in error, choose **No** and then immediately undo whatever the command changed. If you get this prompt repeatedly and it slows you down, disable Undo. You won't be stopped by the prompt again, but you won't be able to use Undo.

Using Linked Worksheets in Release 2.2

RELEASE

2.2

Entire
Section

Linked worksheets make it easier to organize large, complex files. If you are new to 1-2-3, get comfortable with the basics by concentrating on one worksheet. When you are ready to design more complex worksheets, you can use the file-linking capability of 1-2-3 Release 2.2.

The commands related to linking worksheets include the following:

- **/File Admin Link-Refresh** updates the values of all cells in the current worksheet linked to cells in other worksheet files.

- **/File List Linked** displays a list of all source files referred to by linking formulas in the current worksheet.

- **/File Admin Table Linked** creates a table in the worksheet that lists linked files from a specified directory.

A formula can refer to cells in other files. This type of referencing is called *file linking*. Figures 3.12, 3.13, and 3.14 show three separate worksheet files. The formula in cell B4 of CONSOL in figure 3.14 refers to cell B3 in REGION1 in figure 3.12.

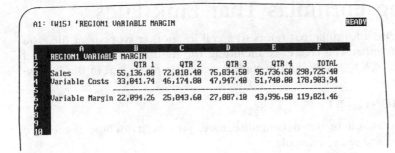

Fig. 3.12.
A worksheet that contains regional data to be used in fig. 3.14.

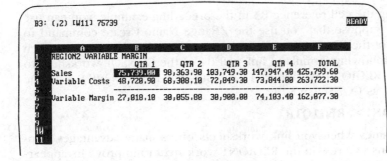

Fig. 3.13.
A second worksheet that contains regional data to be used in fig. 3.14.

```
B4: (,2) [W11] +<<REGION1.WK1>>B3                                READY
```

	A	B	C	D	E	F
1	CONSOLIDATED VARIABLE MARGIN					
2		QTR 1	QTR 2	QTR 3	QTR 4	TOTAL
3	Sales					
4	REGION1	55,136.00	72,018.40	75,834.50	95,736.50	298,725.40
5	REGION2	75,739.00	98,363.90	103,749.30	147,947.40	425,799.60
6	Variable Costs					
7	REGION1	33,041.74	46,174.80	47,947.40	51,740.00	178,903.94
8	REGION2	40,720.90	68,308.10	72,849.30	73,844.00	263,722.30
9						
10	Variable Margin	49,112.36	55,899.40	58,787.10	118,099.90	281,898.76
11						
12						
13						

Fig. 3.14.
A worksheet that contains formulas that link it to the worksheets in figs. 3.12 and 3.13.

This powerful feature lets you consolidate data from separate files automatically. Thus, cells B4 through E4 and cells B7 through E7 in the CONSOL worksheet refer to cells B3 through E3 and cells B4 through E4, respectively, in the REGION1 worksheet (see fig. 3.12). And cells B5 through E5 and cells B8 through E8 in the CONSOL worksheet refer to cells B3 though E3 and cells B4 through E4, respectively, in the REGION2 worksheet (see fig. 3.13).

You can use file linking on a network or other multiuser environment. If you think that one or more of these linked files has been updated since you read the file that contained the links, use /File Admin Link-Refresh to update these formulas.

Cue:
Use file links for consolidations.

Entering Formulas That Link Files

When you write a formula that refers to a cell in another worksheet file, you must type the entire cell reference including the file name (and extension if different from .WK1) inside double-angle brackets ($<<$ $>>$), as in the following example:

+$<<$REGION1$>>$B3

When the file is not in the default directory, you must include the entire path, as in the following example:

+$<<$C:\123\DATA\REGION1$>>$B3

Instead of using the cell reference B3 in the preceding example, you can use a range name. Suppose that you use the **/R**ange Name Create command to assign cell B3 of the REGION1 worksheet the range name REG1QTR1. Then you'd use the following formula to link cell B4 of the CONSOL worksheet to cell B3 of the REGION1 worksheet (assuming that REGION.WK1 is in the same directory as CONSOL.WK1):

+$<<$REGION1$>>$REG1QTR1

Cue:
Use range names in your linking formulas.

Using range names when you link worksheets offers many advantages. Suppose that you insert a row in the REGION1 worksheet to improve its appearance (see fig. 3.15). This moves REGION1's first quarter sales data to cell B4. By moving data in the source worksheet (the one that supplies the data), the target worksheet (the one that receives the data) no longer receives the correct data (see fig. 3.16). To correct the problem, you have to change the formula in the target worksheet to reflect the change made in the source worksheet. In other words, you have to change B3 to B4 in the linking formula. You don't have to make this change if you use a range name in the linking formula—range names automatically adjust to new locations.

Fig. 3.15.
Inserting a row in the REGION1 worksheet.

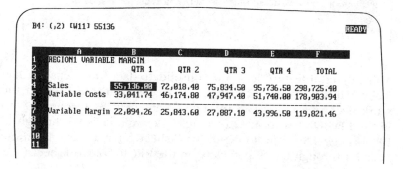

```
B4: (,2) [W11] 55136                                              READY

        A              B         C          D          E          F
 1 REGION1 VARIABLE MARGIN
 2                   QTR 1      QTR 2      QTR 3      QTR 4       TOTAL
 3
 4 Sales          55,136.00  72,018.40  75,834.50  95,736.50 298,725.40
 5 Variable Costs 33,041.74  46,174.80  47,947.40  51,740.80 178,903.94
 6                ----------------------------------------------------
 7 Variable Margin 22,094.26  25,843.60  27,887.10  43,996.50 119,821.46
 8
 9
10
11
```

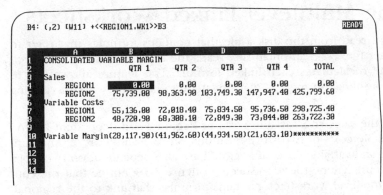

Fig. 3.16.
Incorrect results in the consolidated worksheet after inserting a row in the REGION1 worksheet.

In the CONSOL worksheet, the TOTAL column (column F) contains formulas that sum the values in columns B through E. For example, the formula in cell F4 in figure 3.17 is @SUM(B4..E4), the correct way to write the formula. You do not write the formula as

@SUM(<<REGION1>>B3..<<REGION1>>E3)

1-2-3 will not accept linking formulas as components of another formula.

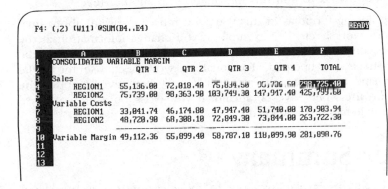

Fig. 3.17.
A correct SUM formula.

When you create a linking formula, you can copy the formula to other cells in the worksheet, just like any other formula. If the cell reference is a relative reference, it adjusts the way any relative cell reference does. For example, if you copy the formula <<REGION1>>B3 in cell B4 to cell C4, the formula changes to <<REGION1>>C3. If the cell reference in the linking formula is absolute ($B$3) or mixed ($B3 or B$3) and you copy the formula to another part of the worksheet, the cell reference copies as it normally does.

Cue:
You can copy linking formulas.

Creating Multilevel Linked Worksheets

Whenever you read from the disk a file that contains formulas that refer to cells in another file, 1-2-3 automatically reads the referenced cells from each linked file and recalculates each linked formula. This feature allows you to build large consolidation models that update automatically without running out of memory.

Suppose that the sales and variable costs of Region 1 are dependent on the sales and variable costs of two store locations, Store 1 and Store 2. And suppose the sales and variable costs of Region 2 are also dependent on two store locations. If you examine the worksheets in figure 3.18, notice that the consolidated, or top-level worksheet, contains formulas that link to the regional, or second level, worksheets. These regional worksheets, in turn, contain formulas that link to the store, or third-level, worksheets.

You enter the sales and variable cost figures at the lowest level in worksheets R1STORE1, R1STORE2, R2STORE1, and R2STORE2 (see fig. 3.18). The regional worksheets REGION1S and REGION2S contain linking formulas to access this information. Finally, the consolidated worksheet, CONSOL_S, contains linking formulas to pull this information up another level.

When you use linking formulas in this way, you must be careful about how you update your worksheets. For example, if you change information at the store level, the consolidated worksheet will not reflect the change until the regional worksheets are updated. To update a worksheet, use the **/File Retrieve** command to retrieve the worksheet and then save it under the same name with the **/File Save** command. If you work on a network, use /File Admin Link-Refresh to update the files.

Chapter Summary

This chapter begins by explaining how to move around worksheets and enter and edit data. You learn how to build different types of formulas, including formulas that refer to other worksheet files. In addition, pointing to cells in formulas and using the various operators are covered. The new Release 2.2 Undo feature, which you can use to undo a change made in error, is introduced. Another new Release 2.2 feature, file linking, is covered in this chapter also.

This chapter provides the basic skills to use 1-2-3. In the next chapter, you learn basic commands that provide the tools to build and use worksheets effectively.

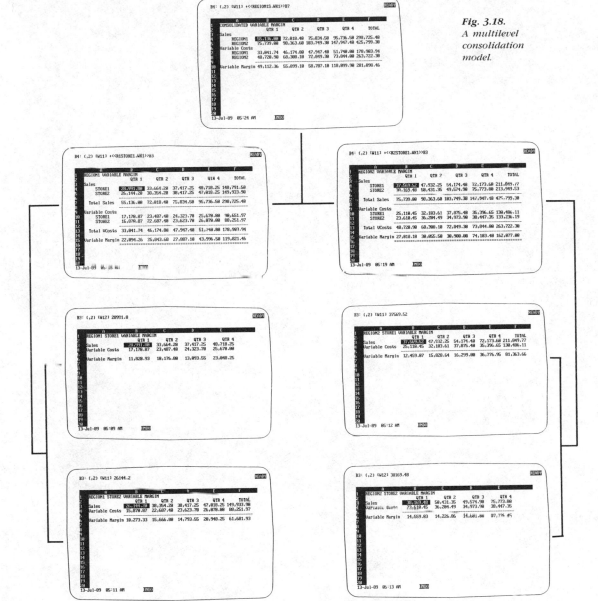

Fig. 3.18.
A multilevel
consolidation
model.

4

Using Fundamental
1-2-3 Commands

Much of the power of 1-2-3 comes from your use of its commands. You use commands to tell 1-2-3 to perform a specified task or sequence of tasks. Commands can change the operation of the 1-2-3 program itself, or they can operate on a file, a worksheet, or a range. You use commands to change how data displays in the cell, to arrange the display of the worksheet in one or more windows on-screen, to print reports, to graph data, to save and retrieve files, to copy and move cells, and to perform many other tasks.

1-2-3 includes over 500 commands (including the commands in the Print-Graph program). Certain commands are used every time you use the program; others are used rarely, if ever. Some commands perform general tasks that apply to all worksheets; other specialized commands apply only to certain circumstances. This chapter covers using command menus and the most fundamental 1-2-3 commands. Later chapters cover more specialized commands.

You also learn the limitations of these commands. Certain actions, such as formatting a backup diskette, you cannot do within 1-2-3. In this chapter, you learn how to access the operating system and return to 1-2-3.

In addition to the detailed explanation of the most important commands in this chapter, this book includes a separate command reference that lists and describes all the commands. A tear-out command menu map at the back of the book shows all the menus.

This chapter shows you how to do the following:

- Use command menus

- Save your files

- Use ranges and range names

- Set column widths

- Clear data from rows, columns, and worksheets

- Insert rows and columns

- Protect and hide data

- Move and copy data

- Reference cells with relative and absolute addressing

- Find and replace particular data

- Control recalculation

- Use window options

- Freeze titles on-screen

- Access the operating system without quitting 1-2-3

Selecting Commands from Command Menus

Reminder:
You can access the command menu from READY mode only.

You execute 1-2-3 commands through a series of menus. To access the main menu, which displays in the second line of the control panel, press the slash (/) key from READY mode. The mode indicator changes to MENU (see fig. 4.1). This menu gives you access to over 400 commands.

Fig. 4.1.
The main command menu.

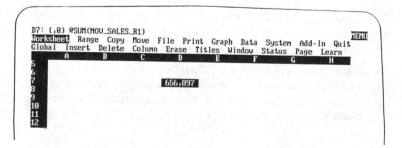

Throughout this chapter, the figures shown are from 1-2-3 Release 2.2. If you have 1-2-3 Release 2.01, you will sometimes notice minor differences between the figures in this book and the screens that appear on your computer. For example, in figure 4.1 Add-In is the next to last choice on the main menu. This choice does not appear in 1-2-3 Release 2.01. Differences such as these are noted as they occur.

When you access a menu, one command is highlighted. When you first press the slash key (/), Worksheet is highlighted. Below the menu options, on the third line, is either an explanation of the highlighted menu option or a list of the options in the next menu. In figure 4.1, the third line lists the Worksheet menu options.

To select a menu option, point to the choice and press Enter. Table 4.1 shows the keys that move the menu pointer, also called the highlighter. As you highlight each menu item, the next set of commands displays on the screen's third line. Figure 4.2 shows the menu after you select Worksheet. Notice that the third line in figure 4.1 has moved up to become the menu line in figure 4.2. (Users of 1-2-3 Release 2.01 do not see the Learn choice.) Continue to make menu selections until you get to the command you want. With some commands, you are prompted to specify ranges, file names, values, or other information.

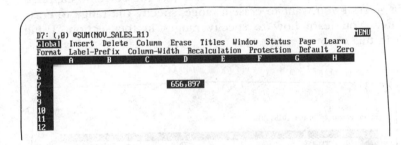

Fig. 4.2.
The Worksheet menu.

Table 4.1
Menu Pointer Movement Keys

Key	Function
→	Moves the pointer one command to the right. If at the last command, wraps to the first command.
←	Moves the pointer one command to the left. If at the first command, wraps to the last command.
Home	Moves the pointer to the first command.

Table 4.1—*continued*

Key	Function
End	Moves the pointer to the last command.
Enter	Selects the command highlighted by the menu pointer.
Esc	Cancels the current menu and moves to the previous menu. If at the main menu, cancels the menu and returns to READY mode.
Ctrl-Break	Cancels the menu and returns to READY mode.

Cue:
Type the first character of a command name to select the command from a menu.

Once you become familiar with the command menus, you can use a faster method to select commands. Just type the first letter of each command. This is the same as highlighting the command and pressing Enter. Every option on a menu begins with a different character; therefore, 1-2-3 always knows which menu option you want. Most users type the first letter of the commands they know and point to commands they don't use often.

One of the first commands you use when you begin working in 1-2-3 is **/R**ange **E**rase. To erase a cell or a range of cells, first press **/** from READY mode. Select **R**ange and then select **E**rase. The prompt Enter range to erase: appears (see fig. 4.3). If you want to erase just the current cell, press Enter (see fig. 4.4). If you want to erase a range, specify the range to erase and press Enter. You learn how to specify ranges in the section "Using Ranges" later in this chapter.

Fig. 4.3.
The /Range Erase prompt.

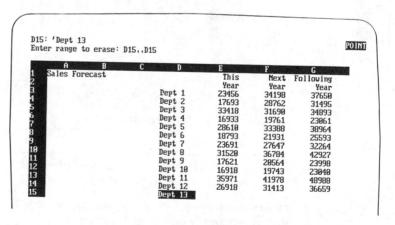

```
D15: 'Dept 13
Enter range to erase: D15..D15                                    POINT
        A         B         C         D         E        F         G
1  Sales Forecast
2                                                This      Next    Following
3                                                Year      Year      Year
4                                    Dept 1     23456     34198     37650
5                                    Dept 2     17693     28762     31495
6                                    Dept 3     33418     31690     34893
7                                    Dept 4     16933     19761     23061
8                                    Dept 5     28610     33308     38964
9                                    Dept 6     18793     21931     25593
10                                   Dept 7     23691     27647     32264
11                                   Dept 8     31520     36784     42927
12                                   Dept 9     17621     20564     23998
13                                   Dept 10    16918     19743     23040
14                                   Dept 11    35971     41978     48988
15                                   Dept 12    26918     31413     36659
                                     Dept 13
```

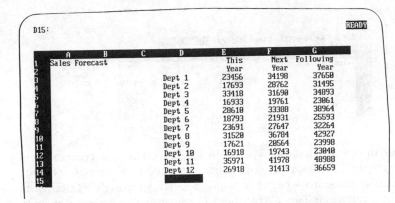

Fig. 4.4.
The current cell
erased with
/Range Erase.

You can point to each menu option or type the first letter of the option. In this book, the entire command name is shown; the first letter is in boldface. You type only the first letter. For example, to erase a range, you type **/re** (**/R**ange **E**rase).

As you select menu options, you can make an occasional error. If this happens, press Esc to return to the previous menu. If you press Esc at the main menu, you clear the menu and return to READY mode. If you press Ctrl-Break from any menu, you return directly to READY mode.

You can explore the command menus without actually executing the commands. Highlight each menu option in the main menu and read the third line in the control panel to find out more about the option or to see the next menu. Then select each menu option to get to the next menu. Continue to select the menu options you want to explore. Use the command menu map at the back of this book to help guide you through the menus.

Use the Esc key to back out of a menu to the next higher menu without actually executing the command. Figure 4.5 shows the **W**orksheet **C**olumn **C**olumn-Range menu available in 1-2-3 Release 2.2. Figure 4.6 shows the result of pressing Esc at this menu. You now can explore other **/W**orksheet **C**olumn commands.

Reminder:
Press Esc to return to the previous command menu; press Ctrl-Break to return to READY mode.

Cue:
Use the arrow keys and the Esc key to explore the command menus.

D15:   MENU
Set-Width Reset-Width
Specify the width of a range of columns
      A   B   C   D   E   F   G
1 Sales Forecast   This   Next Following
2   Year   Year   Year
3   Dept 1   23456 34198   37650
4   Dept 2   17693 28762   31495
5   Dept 3   33418 31690   34893
6   Dept 4   16933 19761   23061
7   Dept 5   28610 33388   38964

Fig. 4.5.
The Worksheet
Column
Column-Range
menu from
1-2-3 Release
2.2.

Fig. 4.6.
The Worksheet
Column menu.

```
D15:
Set-Width  Reset-Width  Hide  Display  Column-Range                    MENU
Change the width of a range of columns
        A         B         C        D        E        F        G
1  Sales Forecast
2                                            This     Next   Following
3                                            Year     Year     Year
4                                  Dept 1   23456    34198    37650
5                                  Dept 2   17693    28762    31495
6                                  Dept 3   33418    31690    34893
7                                  Dept 4   16933    19761    23061
                                   Dept 5   28610    33388    38964
```

Reminder:
A /Worksheet
command may
refer to an
individual
worksheet or 1-2-3
as a whole.

The names of the main menu choices help guide you to the correct command. For example, all the graph commands are accessed through /Graph, and all the data-management commands are accessed through /Data. Note one important exception: The /Worksheet commands can refer to an individual worksheet or to 1-2-3 as a whole. For example, you use /Worksheet Global Default to change overall 1-2-3 defaults, such as the choice of printer.

In 1-2-3 Release 2.2, if you execute a command in error, you can undo it. For example, if you erase a range in error, you can press Undo (Alt-F4) to recover the erased range. See Chapter 3 for a complete discussion of Undo.

Many different menus in 1-2-3 Release 2.2 offer settings sheets. A *settings sheet* is a screenful of information showing you the default or current settings for a particular menu or operation. For example, when you select /Worksheet Global Default, you see the Default Settings sheet (see fig. 4.7).

Fig. 4.7.
The Default
Settings sheet.

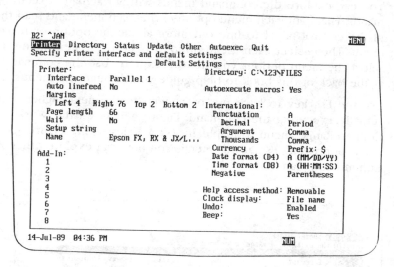

```
B2: ^JAN
Printer  Directory  Status  Update  Other  Autoexec  Quit              MENU
Specify printer interface and default settings
                          ─── Default Settings ───
  Printer:                              Directory: C:\123\FILES
    Interface      Parallel 1
    Auto linefeed  No                   Autoexecute macros: Yes
    Margins
      Left 4   Right 76  Top 2  Bottom 2  International:
    Page length    66                     Punctuation      A
    Wait           No                       Decimal        Period
    Setup string                            Argument       Comma
    Name           Epson FX, RX & JX/L...   Thousands      Comma
                                            Currency       Prefix: $
  Add-In:                                 Date format (D4) A (MM/DD/YY)
    1                                     Time format (D8) A (HH:MM:SS)
    2                                       Negative       Parentheses
    3
    4                                   Help access method: Removable
    5                                   Clock display:      File name
    6                                   Undo:               Enabled
    7                                   Beep:               Yes
    8
  14-Jul-89  04:36 PM                                          NUM
```

This settings sheet shows you the current settings for 1-2-3. At a glance, you can tell the printer to be used, the margins set for the printer, and the current directory, among other options. As you make a change to the global defaults, the changes are reflected on the settings sheets. You find other settings sheets in the Print, Graph, and Data menus as well.

To turn off the settings sheet to view your worksheet, press the Window (F6) key. This key acts as a toggle to display the settings sheet and the work-sheet while in MENU mode.

Saving Your Files

A worksheet you build exists only in the computer's memory. When you use /Quit to exit 1-2-3 and return to the operating system, you lose your work if you did not first save the file to disk. When you save a file, you copy the worksheet in memory to the disk and assign a file name. The file remains on disk after you quit 1-2-3 or turn off the computer. When you make changes to a worksheet, these changes are made only in the computer's memory. You must save the file again with the changes.

More information on file operations is included in Chapter 7. In that chapter, you learn how to read, use, and save files. For now, you learn to save your work by using the /File Save command.

First, choose /File Save from the command menu. 1-2-3 prompts for the name of the file to save and displays a default path name for the file. If you have not saved the file before, 1-2-3 displays the names of files already saved (if any) on the third line of the control panel (see fig. 4.8). You should type a meaningful file name, such as **DEPT1BUD** (a budget file for Depart-ment 1).

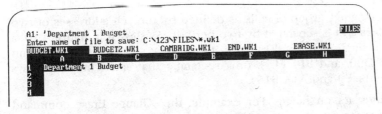

Fig. 4.8.
The default path name displayed when you issue the /File Save command.

Once you save a file, a default file name is supplied the next time you save it. The default file name is the name you supplied the last time you saved the file—DEPT1BUD in figure 4.9. To save the file again and keep the same name, just press Enter.

Fig. 4.9.
The default file name supplied.

RELEASE
2.2

To save the file with a different name, type the file name. The file name you type replaces the existing name. If the file already exists on the disk, 1-2-3 Release 2.2 displays a menu with the following options (1-2-3 Release 2.01 has only the first two options):

Cancel   **R**eplace   **B**ackup

Caution:
If you choose Replace from the File Save menu, the previous file with that name is lost.

Choose **R**eplace to write over the previous file. Once you choose **R**eplace, you lose the previous file. If you make an error in a file, save it with the same name, and choose **R**eplace, you cannot read the previous file. Choose **C**ancel to cancel the /File Save command. If you mistakenly type a file name that matches another file name, cancel the command so that you do not lose the other file.

If you choose **B**ackup, 1-2-3 renames the existing file on disk with a .BAK extension and then saves the new file. Suppose that, for example, you retrieve a sales forecast and change the original file. If you save the file by choosing **B**ackup, 1-2-3 saves the original forecast (before changes) as the backup and saves the changed forecast as the .WK1 file. With this choice, you have both the new file and the previous file on disk.

Cue:
In 1-2-3 Release 2.2, you can choose Backup to keep a backup copy of your file before you save a new version.

If you want to retrieve a backup file, you can type the file name with its .BAK extension at the file-to-retrieve prompt. You also can type ***.BAK** to list all .BAK files in the directory.

Using Ranges

A *range*, a rectangular group of cells, is defined by the cell addresses of two opposite corners and is separated by two periods. As shown in figure 4.10, a range can be a single cell (E1..E1), part of a row (A1..C1), part of a column (G1..G5, D13..D20, and F14..F15), or a rectangle that spans multiple rows and columns (B4..E9 and A13..B15).

Many commands act on ranges. For example, the /**R**ange Erase command prompts you for the range to erase. You can respond to a prompt for a range in three different ways. At different times, each one of these methods may be the most convenient. To specify a range, you can use any of the following methods:

- Type the addresses of the corners of the range.

- Highlight the cells in the range in POINT mode.

- Type the range name or press Name (F3) and point to the range name if one has been assigned.

Each method is covered in the following sections.

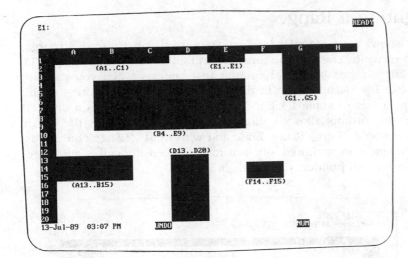

Fig. 4.10.
A sample of
1-2-3 ranges.

Typing Range Addresses

The first method, typing the addresses of the range, is used the least because it is the most prone to error. With this method, you type the addresses of any two opposite corners of the range.

You specify a range by typing the address of the upper left and lower right corners; separate the two addresses with one or two periods. 1-2-3 always stores a range with two periods, but you need to type only one period. For example, to specify the range B4..E9 in figure 4.10, you can type **B4..E9**, **B4.E9**, **E9..B4**, or **E9.B4**. You also can use the other two opposite corners: **E4..B9** or **B9..E4**. In all cases, 1-2-3 stores the range containing B4, B9, E4, and E9 as the four corners of the range.

You type cell addresses to specify a range in several situations: when the range does not have a range name; when the range you want to specify is far from the current cell and it is not convenient to use POINT mode; and when you happen to know the cell addresses of the range. Experienced 1-2-3 users rarely type cell addresses. Instead, they use one of the other two methods: specifying a range in POINT mode or using range names.

Specifying a Range in POINT mode

The second method, highlighting the cells in the range in POINT mode, is the most common. You can point to and highlight a range in commands and functions just as you can point to a single cell in a formula.

Highlighting a Range

Figure 4.11 shows a sample sales forecast. Suppose that because of a reorganization, you have to erase all the forecasts and enter new data. Figure 4.11 shows the Enter range to erase: prompt that appears when you execute **/R**ange **E**rase. The default range in the control panel is the address of the cell pointer, in this example E3..E3. The single cell is shown as a one-cell range. When the prompt shows a single cell as a one-cell range, the cell is said to be *anchored*. With **/R**ange **E**rase and with most **/R**ange commands, the default range is an anchored, one-cell range. When the cell is anchored, as you move the cell pointer, you highlight a range.

Fig. 4.11.
A one-cell range.

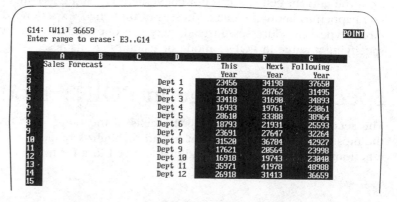

Cue:
Check the control panel to see whether the cell is anchored.

Figure 4.12 shows the screen after you press End-down arrow and then End-right arrow. Because G14 is the last cell in the worksheet, you can press End-Home, which is quicker and uses fewer keystrokes, to highlight the range. As you move the cell pointer, the highlighting expands from the anchored cell. The highlighted range becomes E3..G14; this is the range that appears in the control panel. When you press Enter, 1-2-3 executes the command using the highlighted range (see fig. 4.13). Notice that the cell pointer returns to the originating cell—E3.

Fig. 4.12.
A highlighted range.

```
G14: [W11] 36659                                                POINT
Enter range to erase: E3..G14

         A        B        C        D        E        F        G
 1  Sales Forecast                               This     Next   Following
 2                                               Year     Year     Year
 3                                   Dept 1      23456    34198    37650
 4                                   Dept 2      17693    28762    31495
 5                                   Dept 3      33418    31690    34893
 6                                   Dept 4      16933    19761    23061
 7                                   Dept 5      28610    33388    38964
 8                                   Dept 6      18793    21931    25593
 9                                   Dept 7      23691    27647    32264
10                                   Dept 8      31520    36784    42927
11                                   Dept 9      17621    28564    23998
12                                   Dept 10     16918    19743    23040
13                                   Dept 11     35971    41978    48988
14                                   Dept 12     26918    31413    36659
15
```

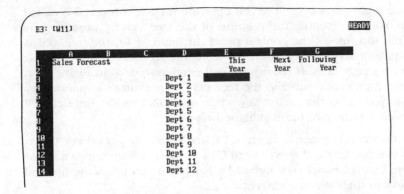

Fig. 4.13.
The highlighted range erased.

Pointing and highlighting in this typical example is faster and easier than typing the range addresses E3..G14. Also, because you can see the range as you specify it, you make fewer errors pointing than you do typing.

Use the End key when you highlight ranges. The End key moves to the end of a range of occupied cells. To highlight the range from E3..G14 in figure 4.12, you can press End-down arrow and End-right arrow, as in the previous example. Without the End key, you have to press the right-arrow key twice and the down-arrow key 11 times.

With some commands, such as /Range Erase, the anchored cell starts at the position of the cell pointer. You should move the cell pointer to the upper left corner of the range before you start the command. In figure 4.11, the cell pointer started at E3, the upper left corner of the range to erase.

Figure 4.14 shows what happens if the cell pointer is in the wrong cell when you use /Range Erase. The cell pointer is in F4; after you press End-down arrow and End-right arrow, the range F4..G14 is highlighted.

Cue:
Use the End key to highlight ranges quickly.

Cue:
Move to the upper left corner of the range you want before starting a /Range command.

```
G11: [W11] 36659                                                POINT
Enter range to erase: F4..G14
        A        B        C        D        E       F        G
1   Sales Forecast                              This    Next   Following
2                                               Year    Year     Year
3                                     Dept 1    23456   34198    37650
4                                     Dept 2    17693   28762    31495
5                                     Dept 3    33418   31690    34893
6                                     Dept 4    16933   19761    23061
7                                     Dept 5    28610   33388    38964
8                                     Dept 6    18793   21931    25593
9                                     Dept 7    23691   27647    32264
10                                    Dept 8    31520   36704    42927
11                                    Dept 9    17621   28564    23998
12                                    Dept 10   16918   19743    23040
13                                    Dept 11   35971   41978    40988
14                                    Dept 12   26918   31413    36659
15
```

Fig. 4.14.
The wrong range highlighted.

Whenever you highlight a range, the cell opposite the anchored cell is called the *free cell*. You can identify the position of the free cell by observing its address on the top line of the control panel. In figure 4.14, the free cell is G14. The highlight expands or contracts from the free cell when you use one of the movement keys. If the wrong cell is anchored, as in figure 4.14, you can move the anchor cell and the free cell by pressing the period key (.). Each time you press the period key while in POINT mode, the free cell moves to another corner of the highlighted range.

Cue:
Press the period key to move the free cell to another corner of the range.

To highlight the correct range in figure 4.14, first press the period key twice. You can tell that the free cell moves from G14 to F4 by observing its address change in the control panel (see fig. 4.15). Now you can press the up- and left-arrow keys to highlight the correct range.

Fig. 4.15.
The free cell moved to F4.

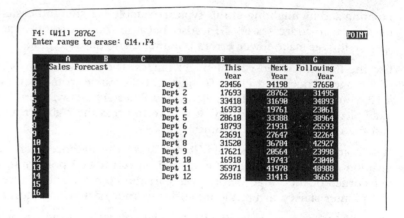

With **/R**ange Erase, 1-2-3 expects the range to start at the current location of the cell pointer. This is true of other commands, including all the **/R**ange commands (except **/R**ange Search) and **/C**opy and **/M**ove.

With other commands (including **/D**ata, **/G**raph, **/P**rint, and **/R**ange Search) at the Enter range: prompt, 1-2-3 does not expect the range to start at the current location of the cell pointer. The control panel shows the current cell address, M1, as a single address (see fig. 4.16). This means that the cell pointer is not anchored. When you use the movement keys, the address in the control panel changes to the single address of the current location of the cell pointer. To anchor the first corner of the range, press the period key. Figure 4.17 shows the screen after moving the cell pointer to M3 and pressing the period key. The address in the control panel changes to a one-cell range. If you want a larger range, move the cell pointer to highlight the range and press Enter.

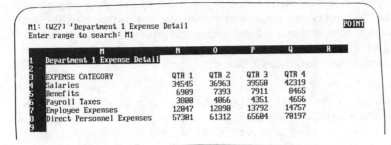

Fig. 4.16.
An unanchored
current cell.

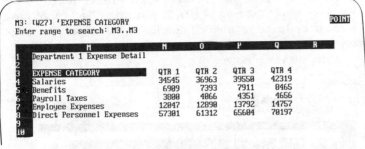

Fig. 4.17.
An anchored
cell after the
period key is
pressed.

You can press Esc or Backspace to clear an incorrectly highlighted range. The highlight collapses to the anchored cell only, and the anchor is removed. If you press Esc or Backspace in figure 4.14, the highlight becomes just F4 and the cell becomes unanchored (see fig. 4.18). Observe that the cell address in the control panel in figure 4.18 is the single address F4, not the one-cell range F4..F4.

```
F4: [W11] 28762                                    POINT
Enter range to erase: F4
      A       B     C     D      E       F       G
1  Sales Forecast                    This    Next  Following
2                                     Year    Year    Year
3                          Dept 1    23456   34198   37650
4                          Dept 2    17693   28762   31495
5                          Dept 3    33418   31690   34893
6                          Dept 4    16933   19761   23061
7                          Dept 5    28610   33300   38964
8                          Dept 6    18793   21931   25593
9                          Dept 7    23691   27647   32264
10                         Dept 8    31520   36784   42927
11                         Dept 9    17621   28564   23998
12                         Dept 10   16918   19743   23040
13                         Dept 11   35971   41978   48988
14                         Dept 12   26918   31413   36659
15
16
```

Fig. 4.18.
Clearing the
highlighted
range and the
anchor.

Dealing with Remembered Ranges

When you specify a range with some commands, such as **/Data**, **/Graph**, **/Print**, and **/R**ange Search, 1-2-3 remembers the range. When you repeat the command, 1-2-3 highlights the previous range.

If this is what you need, just press Enter. If you want to specify a new range, press Backspace to cancel the range and return the cell pointer to the cell that was current before you started the command. Move the cell pointer to the beginning of the new range, press the period key to anchor the cell, highlight the new range, and press Enter.

You also can use Esc to cancel a previous range. When you press Esc, the cell pointer moves to the upper left corner of the previous range, not the current cell in the worksheet. For example, suppose that the cell pointer is in M1, and you want to print this part of the worksheet. The range previously printed was A2..G18. When you choose **/P**rint **P**rinter **R**ange, 1-2-3 remembers the previous range (see fig. 4.19). If you press Backspace now, 1-2-3 cancels this range and returns the cell pointer to M1. If you press Esc now, 1-2-3 cancels the previous range but moves the cell pointer to A2, the upper left corner of the previous range.

Fig. 4.19.
A previously remembered range.

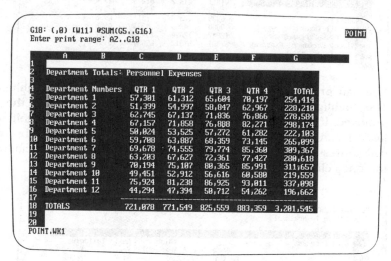

Specifying a Range with Range Names

As another method for specifying a range at the prompt, you can assign a range name. Range names, which should be descriptive, can include up to 15 characters and can be used in formulas and commands.

Using range names has a number of advantages. Range names are easier to remember than addresses. It is sometimes faster to use a range name rather than point to a range in another part of the worksheet. Range names also make formulas easier to understand. For example, if you see the range name NOV_SALES_R1 rather than D7..D10 in a formula, you have a better chance of remembering that the entry represents "November Sales for Region 1."

Whenever 1-2-3 expects a cell or range address, you can specify a range name, using one of two ways. You can type the range name, or you can press the Name (F3) key and point to the range name. When you press the Name (F3) key, the third line of the control panel lists the first five range names in alphabetical order. Use the movement keys to point to the correct range name and press Enter. If you have many range names, press the Name (F3) key again; 1-2-3 displays a full-screen list of range names (see fig. 4.20).

Cue:
You can use the Name (F3) key in commands and functions in conjunction with the GoTo (F5) key.

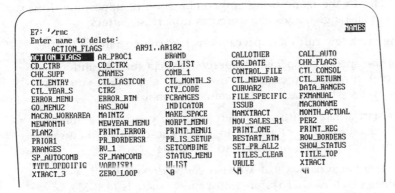

Fig. 4.20.
A full-screen display of range names.

If the command calls for a single-cell address, such as with **/D**ata **S**ort **P**rimary-Key or GoTo (F5), 1-2-3 can specify a range whether you type an English name or a cell address. If the prompt calls for a single-cell address and you type a range name that applies to a multiple-cell range, 1-2-3 uses the upper left corner of the range. If you type a nonexistent range name, 1-2-3 displays an error message. Press Esc or Enter to clear the error and try again.

Cue:
You can use a range name any time 1-2-3 expects a range or cell address.

Because a single cell is considered a valid range, you can name a single cell as a range. Whenever 1-2-3 expects a cell address, you can type the address, point to the cell, or type the single-cell range name.

Creating Range Names

To create range names, you use the **/R**ange **N**ame **C**reate or **/R**ange **N**ame **L**abels command to assign names to individual cells or ranges. Follow these steps to create range names with the **/R**ange **N**ame **C**reate command:

1. Move to the top left corner of the range you want to name.

2. Choose **/R**ange **N**ame **C**reate.

3. Type the name and then press Enter at the Enter name: prompt. 1-2-3 displays the Enter range: prompt.

If you type a new range name, 1-2-3 shows the current cell as an anchored range. Highlight the range or type the address or addresses of the cell or range; then press Enter.

If you type an existing range name, 1-2-3 highlights the existing range. Use the arrow keys to extend the range or press Esc to cancel the range and specify a new range. Press Enter.

Cue:
You can specify range names using any combination of upper- and lowercase letters.

Range names can include up to 15 characters and are not case-sensitive. You can type or refer to the name using any combination of upper- and lower-case letters, but all range names are stored as uppercase letters.

The following are a few rules and precautions for naming ranges:

1. Do not use spaces or special characters (except for the underscore character) in range names. If you use special characters, you can confuse 1-2-3 when you use the name in formulas.

2. Do not start a name with a number, although you can use numbers within names. Because of a quirk in 1-2-3, you cannot type a range name that starts with a number into a formula.

3. Do not use range names that are also cell addresses (such as P2), key names (such as GoTo), function names (such as @SUM), or advanced macro command keyword names (such as BRANCH). If you use a cell address as a range name, when you type the range name, 1-2-3 uses the cell address instead.

You also can create range names with the **/R**ange Name **L**abels command. With this command, you can assign range names to many individual cells at one time. You can use **/R**ange Name **L**abels to assign range names only to single-cell ranges. With this command, you use labels already typed into the worksheet as range names for adjacent cells. In figure 4.21, for example, you can use the labels in cells B5..B8 to name the cells with sales data in C5..C8. Because you want to name the cells to the right of the labels, use **/R**ange Name **L**abels **R**ight. Specify a range of B5..B8 and press Enter. Now C5 has the range name Dept_1.

Fig. 4.21.
Labels that can be used for range names.

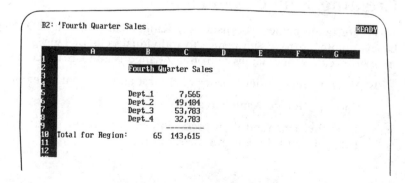

The other options with /**R**ange Name **L**abels include **L**eft, **D**own, and **U**p. These commands assign range names to labels only in the range you specify. If you specified a range of B2..B10 in figure 4.21, the blank cells in B3, B4, B9, and the number in B10 are ignored. The first 15 characters in the label in B2 become the range name for C2: Fourth Quarter. You do no harm if you include cells that are blank or include numbers or formulas in a /**R**ange Name **L**abels range, but do not include other labels. If you do, you end up with unwanted range names.

Listing All Range Names

You can use /**R**ange Name **T**able to create a list of range names and addresses. Using this command is the only way you can see your range-name addresses (see fig 4.22). A range name table can provide you with a directory of the locations of macros you've entered in your worksheet. (See Chapter 13 for information on naming macros with /**R**ange Name.)

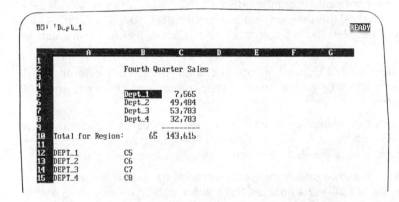

Fig. 4.22.
A table of range names and addresses created with /Range Name Table.

To delete an unwanted range name, use /**R**ange Name **D**elete. To delete all range names, use the /**R**ange Name **R**eset command. Be careful with this command; it immediately deletes all the range names in the file.

Caution:
The /Range Name Reset command deletes all range names.

Setting Column Widths

When you start a new worksheet, all columns are 9 characters wide. You can change this default column width and the width of each individual column or a group of columns to accommodate your data. If columns are too narrow, numbers display as asterisks, and labels are truncated if the adjacent cell is full. If columns are too wide, you cannot see as much on-screen or print as much on one page. Figure 4.23 shows a worksheet with a global column width of 5 characters and an individual column width of 13 for column A. The number in cell J8 is too wide for the column and displays as a row of asterisks. The label in A5 is too long for the column width and is truncated.

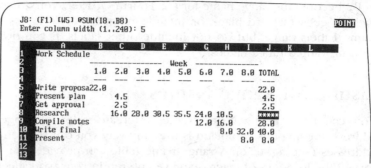

Fig. 4.23.
A worksheet with a global column width of 5 and individual column widths.

Whether a number can fit into a cell depends on both the column width and the format. In general, a number's width must be one character less than the column width. If a negative number displays with parentheses, which take two extra characters, the number width must be even less. If a number displays as a row of asterisks, change either the column width, the format, or both.

Use **/W**orksheet **G**lobal **C**olumn-Width to change the default column width for the entire worksheet. At the prompt, type a number between 1 and 240 and press Enter.

To set the width of one column, move the cell pointer to the column you want to change and use **/W**orksheet **C**olumn **S**et-Width. At the Enter column width: prompt, type a number between 1 and 240 and press Enter.

RELEASE
2.2

Often, when setting column widths, you may need to set more than one column width—but not all—at a time. In 1-2-3 Release 2.2, you can change multiple column widths in a range at the same time by using **/W**orksheet **C**olumn **C**olumn-Range **S**et-Width. For instance, to increase the width of columns B through F in your worksheet, follow these steps:

1. Select **/W**orksheet **C**olumn **C**olumn-Range **S**et-Width.

2. Highlight the columns to widen as shown in figure 4.24 and press Enter.

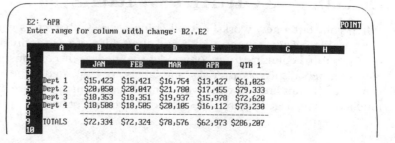

Fig. 4.24.
Highlighting a range of columns to change their width.

3. Use the right-arrow key to increase the column widths and press Enter (see fig. 4.25).

```
B2: [W11] ^JAN                                              POINT
Select a width for range of columns (1..240): 11

        A        B         C         D         E         F
1
2                 JAN       FEB       MAR       APR      QTR 1
3                --------  --------  --------  --------  --------
4    Dept 1      $15,423   $15,421   $16,754   $13,427   $61,025
5    Dept 2      $20,050   $20,047   $21,780   $17,455   $79,333
6    Dept 3      $18,353   $18,351   $19,937   $15,978   $72,620
7    Dept 4      $18,508   $18,505   $20,105   $16,112   $73,230
8                --------  --------  --------  --------  --------
9    TOTALS      $72,334   $72,324   $78,576   $62,973  $286,207
```

Fig. 4.25. Setting the width for a range of columns.

Use /**W**orksheet **C**olumn **R**eset-Width and /**W**orksheet **C**olumn **C**olumn-Range **R**eset-Width (1-2-3 Release 2.2 only) to remove an individual column width and reset the width to the global default.

An individual column width overrides the global column width and the column width of a range that has been set with /**W**orksheet **C**olumn **C**olumn-Range. Likewise, column widths set for a range of columns with /**W**orksheet **C**olumn **C**olumn-Range override the global column width. If you change the global column width shown in figure 4.23, the width of column A does not change.

If you are not sure of the exact column width you want, use the left- and right-arrow keys instead of typing a number. Each time you press the left-arrow key, the column width decreases by one. Each time you press the right-arrow key, the column width increases by one. When the display looks the way you want, press Enter. This technique works for both individual, column-range, and global column widths.

If the window is split when you change column widths, the column width applies only to the current window. When you clear a split window, the column widths in the upper or left window are saved. Any column widths in the lower or right window are lost.

RELEASE

2.2

*Cue:
Use the arrow keys to set column widths.*

Erasing and Deleting Rows and Columns

You can clear parts or all of your work in several ways. Any data you clear is removed from the workspace in memory, but does not affect the files on disk until you use the /**F**ile commands (see Chapter 7). You can use one of two ways to clear part of your work in memory. If you erase the work, you remove all the contents of the cells. If you delete the work, you remove the cells themselves.

Erasing Ranges

Use the **/R**ange **E**rase command to erase sections of a worksheet in memory. You can erase a single cell or a range of cells. When you erase a range, only the contents are lost. Characteristics, such as format, protection status, and column width, remain.

After you choose **/R**ange **E**rase, 1-2-3 prompts you for the range to erase. You highlight a range or type a range name and press Enter. You can also press the Name (F3) key for a list of range names. To erase only the current cell, press Enter.

Deleting Rows and Columns

After you erase a range, the cells remain but are now blank. In contrast, when you delete rows or columns, 1-2-3 deletes the entire row or column and updates the addresses in the rest of the worksheet. To delete a row, use **/W**orksheet **D**elete **R**ow. You then are prompted for the range of rows to delete. To delete one row, press Enter. To delete more than one row, use the movement keys to highlight the rows you want to delete; then press Enter. You need to highlight only one cell in each row—not the entire row (see fig. 4.26).

Fig. 4.26.
One cell in
each row
highlighted for
deletion.

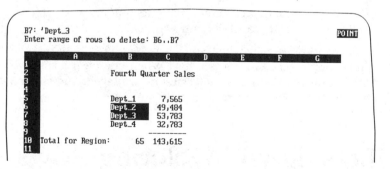

When you press Enter, the rows that contain highlighted cells are deleted. The rest of the worksheet then moves up (see fig. 4.27). 1-2-3 automatically adjusts all addresses, range names, and formulas. You can follow the same procedure to delete columns.

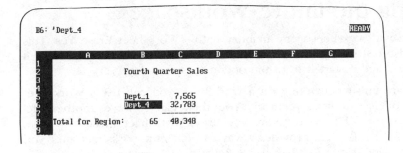

Fig. 4.27.
The worksheet
after rows are
deleted.

If you delete rows or columns that are part of a range name or a range in a formula, 1-2-3 automatically adjusts the range. If the deleted rows or columns contain data that is referenced by a formula or formulas in other cells, the reference changes to ERR, and the formulas become invalid (see fig. 4.28). This action can be a serious consequence of deleting rows and columns. These formulas do not have to be visible on-screen; they can be anywhere in the worksheet.

Caution:
When you delete
rows and columns,
ERR can occur
anywhere in the file
if the file contains
formulas that refer
to deleted cells.

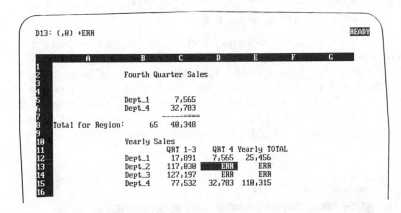

Fig. 4.28.
ERR replacing
cell addresses
in formulas
referring to
deleted cells.

Using 1-2-3 Release 2.01 to remedy this problem, you must either retype the formula or retrieve from the disk the model before the changes were made. If you have made significant changes to the model since you last saved it, you may find it more convenient to retype the formula. If you are using Release 2.2 and have Undo enabled, you can press Undo (Alt-F4) to restore the deleted columns or rows. Then make necessary changes to your formulas before deleting the rows or columns again. If Undo is disabled, however, you must follow the advice for Release 2.01 users.

RELEASE

2.2

Clearing the Entire Workspace

You can clear a worksheet from memory with /Worksheet Erase Yes. This command also restores all the default global settings. The effect is the same if you quit 1-2-3 and restart it from the operating system.

When you are finished working on a worksheet, you can use /Worksheet Erase Yes to clear it from memory. You then can retrieve another file. Remember to use /File Save before you use /Worksheet Erase Yes. Also, note that 1-2-3 Release 2.2 provides a way to reclaim a worksheet after you use this command: Undo (Alt-F4). 1-2-3 Release 2.01 does not.

Inserting Rows and Columns

You can delete rows and columns; you also can insert them anywhere in the worksheet. You insert rows with /Worksheet Insert Row and columns with /Worksheet Insert Column. You can insert one or more rows or columns at one time. At the Enter insert range: prompt, highlight the numbers of rows or columns you want to insert and press Enter.

Reminder:
When you insert
columns, all
addresses in
formulas and range
names adjust
automatically.

When you insert rows, all rows including and below the cell pointer are pushed down. When you insert columns, all columns including and to the right of the cell pointer are pushed to the right. All addresses in formulas and range names adjust automatically. Suppose that you want to insert a column between columns E and F in the worksheet in figure 4.29. Place your cell pointer in column F and use /Worksheet Insert Column. Figure 4.30 shows the result of this operation.

Fig. 4.29.
Inserting a
column
between
columns E
and F.

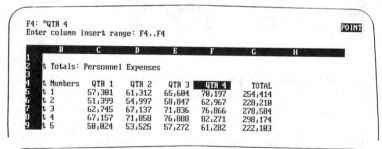

Fig. 4.30.
Addresses
automatically
adjusted after
inserting a
column.

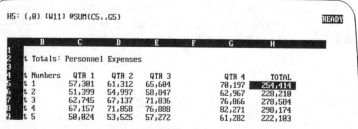

If you insert a row or column in the middle of a range, the range expands to accommodate the new rows or columns. In figure 4.29, the formula in G5 is @SUM(C5..F5). In figure 4.30, the formula is pushed to H5 and becomes @SUM(C5..G5). This range includes the columns in the previous range as well as the inserted column.

Protecting and Hiding Worksheet Data

A typical 1-2-3 worksheet contains numbers, labels, formulas, and macros. When you first build a worksheet, you may lay out the worksheets for an entire year (see fig. 4.31). The budget model in figure 4.31 contains all the labels and formulas for a yearly budget. Once you build this file, you do not want the labels and formulas to change. However, the detailed budget figures may change many times as different versions are submitted for approval or submitted to different departments for revision.

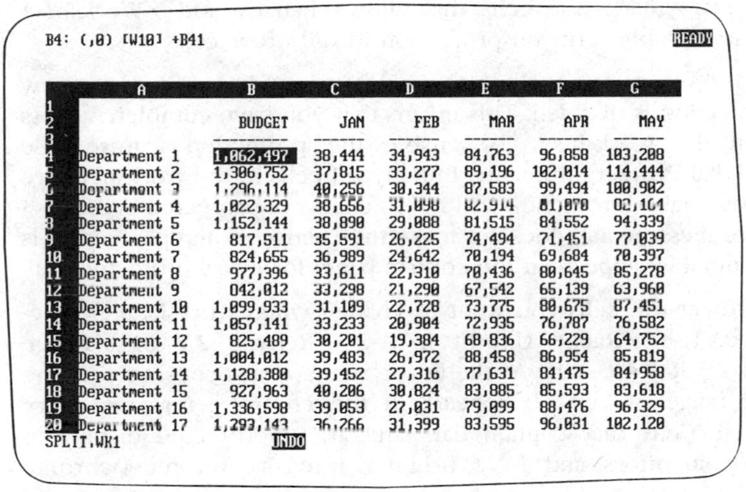

B4: (,0) [W10] +B41 READY

	A	B	C	D	E	F	G
1							
2		BUDGET	JAN	FEB	MAR	APR	MAY
3		---------	------	------	------	------	------
4	Department 1	1,062,497	38,444	34,943	84,763	96,858	103,208
5	Department 2	1,306,752	37,815	33,277	89,196	102,014	114,444
6	Department 3	1,296,114	40,256	30,344	87,583	99,494	100,902
7	Department 4	1,022,329	38,656	31,098	82,914	81,070	82,161
8	Department 5	1,152,144	38,890	29,088	81,515	84,552	94,339
9	Department 6	817,511	35,591	26,225	74,494	71,451	77,039
10	Department 7	824,655	36,989	24,642	70,194	69,684	70,397
11	Department 8	977,396	33,611	22,310	70,436	80,645	85,278
12	Department 9	042,012	33,298	21,290	67,542	65,139	63,960
13	Department 10	1,099,933	31,109	22,728	73,775	80,675	87,451
14	Department 11	1,057,141	33,233	20,904	72,935	76,787	76,582
15	Department 12	825,489	30,201	19,384	68,836	66,229	64,752
16	Department 13	1,004,012	39,483	26,972	88,458	86,954	85,819
17	Department 14	1,128,380	39,452	27,316	77,631	84,475	84,958
18	Department 15	927,963	40,206	30,824	83,885	85,593	83,618
19	Department 16	1,336,598	39,053	27,031	79,099	88,476	96,329
20	Department 17	1,293,143	36,266	31,399	83,595	96,031	102,120

SPLIT.WK1 UNDO

Fig. 4.31. A large worksheet.

Once the budget is approved, you may add actual expense data each month. Each time someone changes the detailed data, you run the risk of accidentally changing a formula or a label. If a formula is changed, all the totals can be wrong.

If different people add data to the file, an individual may want to change a formula that seems incorrect. For example, a model may use factors for inflation, growth, or foreign exchange rates. These factors may be decided by the finance department and should apply equally to all departments. Some department heads, however, may want to use their own factors. This can invalidate the overall budget that is submitted for approval.

1-2-3 includes a number of features that protect data from accidental or deliberate change. For example, parts of a file might contain confidential data such as salaries or cost factors. 1-2-3 includes features that let someone use the file but not see certain areas of the file. Unfortunately, none of these features can stop persons from finding this hidden information if they know enough about 1-2-3.

You also can password-protect a file that contains confidential data when you save it. This process completely prevents access to the file by anyone who does not know the password.

Protecting Cells from Change

Every worksheet has areas containing formulas and labels that do not change over time. Other areas of the worksheet contain data that can change. You can protect the cells that should not change and still allow changes to other cells by using two related commands: /Range Unprot (/Range Unprotect in 1-2-3 Release 2.01) marks the cells that allow changes, and /Worksheet Global Protection Enable turns on protection for all other cells.

You must tell 1-2-3 to use the cell-protection feature. When you start a new worksheet, protection is disabled. This means that you have complete access to all cells in the worksheet. To enable the protection feature, use /Worksheet Global Protection Enable. Initially, all cells in the worksheet are protected. If you enable protection and try to change a protected cell, 1-2-3 displays an error message and does not make the change. When protection is enabled, the symbol PR appears in the control panel for every protected cell.

You must unprotect the cells you want to change when worksheet protection is enabled. Use /Range Unprot in 1-2-3 Release 2.2 or /Range Unprotect in 1-2-3 Release 2.01. At the Enter range to unprotect: prompt, highlight each range of cells. U appears in the control panel for every unprotected cell. Cells that contain data and are unprotected display in green on color monitors and in a brighter intensity on monochrome monitors.

Once you unprotect a range of cells, you can protect them again with /Range Prot (/Range Protect in 1-2-3 Release 2.01). You can protect or unprotect ranges with global protection either enabled or disabled.

Typically, when you build a new worksheet, you leave global protection disabled. When you finish the worksheet, and you feel that all the formulas and labels are correct, you can unprotect the data input areas and enable global protection.

If you need to change a protected cell for any reason, you can unprotect the cell, change it, and then protect it again. You also can disable global protection, change the cell or cells, and then enable protection again. Because of this, 1-2-3's protection features protect against only accidental change, not from deliberate alteration of the worksheet by an unauthorized person.

Using /Range Input

When you use **/W**orksheet **G**lobal **P**rotection **E**nable, you restrict changes to cells that are unprotected. You can go one step further and restrict the cell pointer to unprotected cells in a specified range by using the **/R**ange **I**nput command.

You use **/R**ange **I**nput with data-entry areas or forms, such as the one in figure 4.32. The range K28..K33 is unprotected; the other cells are protected. Typically, you use **/R**ange **I**nput when you build worksheets for others to use for data entry. In this case, you want whoever will do the data entry to see the entire range I21..L34 but to be able to move the cell pointer only in the range K28..K33.

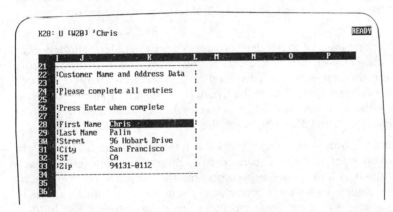

Fig. 4.32.
An input form used with
/Range Input.

When you choose **/R**ange **I**nput, the `Enter data input range:` prompt appears. You specify the input range and press Enter. In figure 4.32, the data-input range is I21..L34. 1-2-3 positions the display at the beginning of the data-input range and moves the cell pointer to the first unprotected cell in the range, in this case K28.

While **/R**ange **I**nput is active, you can move the cell pointer only to unprotected cells in the input range. If you press Home, the cell pointer moves to K28; press End to go to K33. If you are in K33 and press the down-arrow key, you "wrap" to K28. If you are in K29 and press the right-arrow key, the cell pointer moves to K30.

While /Range Input is active, you can type entries and edit any unprotected cells. You cannot, however, execute commands. If you press the slash key, you enter the slash character into a cell. To deactivate /Range Input, press Enter or Esc in READY mode. The cell pointer moves to its position before you selected /Range Input.

You can use /Range Input for convenience as well as security. You can use /Range Input if you work with novice users who know little about 1-2-3. Because these users can move the cell pointer to only unprotected cells while /Range Input is in effect, they will not accidentally try to change protected cells. /Range Input is almost always executed by a macro as part of a data-entry system. (Macros are covered in Chapters 13 and 14.)

Hiding Data

Sometimes you want to do more than just stop someone from changing data or formulas; you want to prevent others from even seeing the information. To do this, you can hide cells and ranges of cells.

You can hide data so that the data is not easily visible, but you cannot hide data to prevent someone from seeing it if that person knows how to use 1-2-3.

To hide a cell or range of cells, use /Range Format Hidden. Hidden cells display as blank cells in the worksheet. If you move the cell pointer to a hidden cell and the cell is protected with global protection enabled, the cell contents will not display in the control panel. To display the cell contents again in the worksheet, use any other range format as described in Chapter 5. Or use /Range Format Reset to reset the cell to the global format.

To hide columns completely, use /Worksheet Column Hide and highlight the columns you want to hide. You need to highlight only one cell in each column. A hidden column does not display in the window but retains its column letter. Figure 4.33 shows a worksheet with some columns about to be hidden. Figure 4.34 shows the worksheet after the columns are hidden. Note that in the column border, the letters D..F are skipped. The columns are still there, but they do not display, and you cannot move the cell pointer to them.

When you print a range with hidden columns, the hidden columns will not print. Note that hiding columns is not an effective way to hide sensitive information. Whenever you are in POINT mode, 1-2-3 displays the hidden columns so that you can include cells in the hidden columns in the range.

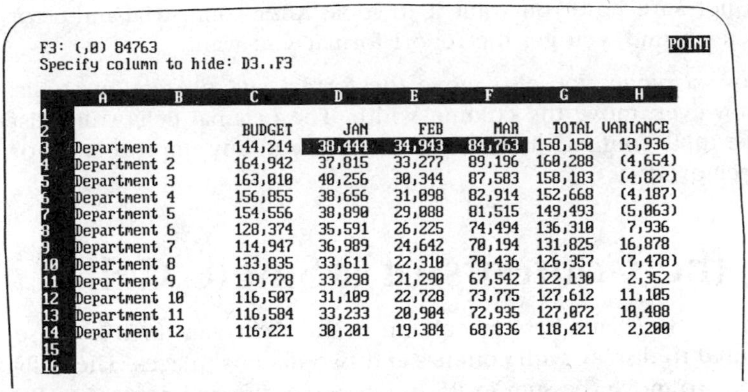

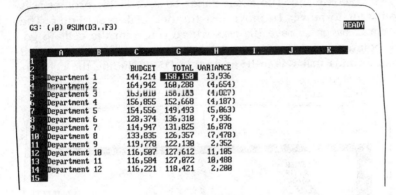

```
F3: (,0) 84763                                          POINT
Specify column to hide: D3..F3

      A       B      C       D       E       F      G       H
 1
 2                        BUDGET    JAN     FEB     MAR    TOTAL UARIANCE
 3 Department 1           144,214  38,444  34,943  84,763 158,150  13,936
 4 Department 2           164,942  37,815  33,277  89,196 160,288  (4,654)
 5 Department 3           163,810  40,256  30,344  87,583 158,183  (4,827)
 6 Department 4           156,855  38,656  31,098  82,914 152,668  (4,187)
 7 Department 5           154,556  38,890  29,088  81,515 149,493  (5,063)
 8 Department 6           128,374  35,591  26,225  74,494 136,310   7,936
 9 Department 7           114,947  36,989  24,642  70,194 131,825  16,878
10 Department 8           133,835  33,611  22,310  70,436 126,357  (7,478)
11 Department 9           119,778  33,298  21,290  67,542 122,130   2,352
12 Department 10          116,507  31,109  22,728  73,775 127,612  11,105
13 Department 11          116,584  33,233  20,904  72,935 127,872  18,488
14 Department 12          116,221  30,201  19,384  68,836 118,421   2,200
15
16
```

Fig. 4.33.
/Worksheet Column Hide used to hide columns.

```
G3: (,0) @SUM(D3..F3)                                   READY

      A       B      C       G       H      I.       J       K
 1
 2                        BUDGET  TOTAL UARIANCE
 3 Department 1           144,214 158,150  13,936
 4 Department 2           164,942 160,288  (4,654)
 5 Department 3           163,810 158,183  (4,027)
 6 Department 4           156,855 152,668  (4,187)
 7 Department 5           154,556 149,493  (5,063)
 8 Department 6           128,374 136,310   7,936
 9 Department 7           114,947 131,825  16,878
10 Department 8           133,835 126,357  (7,478)
11 Department 9           119,778 122,130   2,352
12 Department 10          116,507 127,612  11,105
13 Department 11          116,584 127,872  18,488
14 Department 12          116,221 118,421   2,200
15
```

Fig. 4.34.
The worksheet with hidden columns.

Saving a File with a Password

To prevent access to a file completely, you can save the file with a password. Without the password, no one can read the file or retrieve any information from the file. If you lose the password, you cannot access the file. You can find more information on protecting files with passwords in Chapter 7.

Reminder:
Save the file with a password to prevent access to a file completely.

Moving the Contents of Cells

When you build worksheets, you often enter data and formulas in one part of the worksheet and later want to move them somewhere else. Use the /Move command to move the contents of a cell or range from one part of a worksheet to another.

Use /Move to move other data out of the way so that you can add to a list, a report, or a database. You also use /Move to rearrange a report so that it prints in the exact format you want. When you first start to lay out a report, you are often not sure how you want it to look. After some trial-and-error moving the data around, you get the report format you want.

When you move a range, you also move the format and protection status. You do not, however, move the column width. The original cells still exist after you move their contents, but they are blank, and any unprotection or formatting is removed.

Moving the Contents of a Single Cell

Figure 4.35 shows three numbers in column B and their sum in B5. These cells are formatted to display with commas and two decimal places. The cells are unprotected. To move the sum in B5 to D5, move the cell pointer to B5 and use the /Move command. The Enter range to move FROM: prompt asks what cells you want to move. To move just the one cell, press Enter. The next prompt, Enter range to move TO: asks where you want the cells to go. Move the cell pointer to D5 and press Enter. The result is shown in figure 4.36. The exact formula that was in B5 is now in D5, including the cell for-mat and protection status.

Fig. 4.35.
A formula
before being
moved.

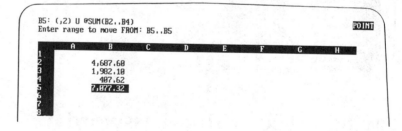

Fig. 4.36.
The formula
after being
moved.

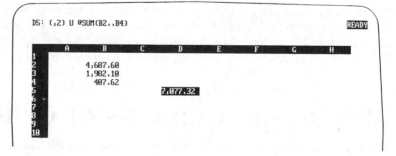

Moving the Contents of a Range

To move a range, move the cell pointer to the upper left corner of the range and start the /Move command. At the Enter range to move FROM: prompt, highlight the range of cells to move as in figure 4.37. Press Enter to lock in the FROM range. At the Enter range to move TO: prompt, move the cell pointer to the upper left corner of the new location and press Enter. This prompt's address is not anchored. In figure 4.38, the range was moved to C1. Like all commands that prompt for ranges, you can type addresses, point and highlight, or use range names.

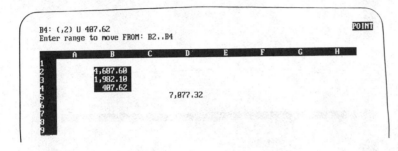

Fig. 4.37.
A range of numbers before being moved.

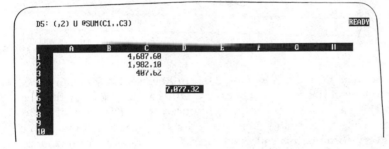

Fig. 4.38.
The formula adjusted after the numbers are moved.

In figure 4.38, not only were the contents moved, but also the formats and protection. The original cells in column B are still there, but they no longer contain data, formatting, or unprotected status.

Note one important feature of **/M**ove. The formula in D5 still shows the sum of the three numbers. When you move data, all formulas that refer to that data adjust their cell references to refer to the new location. The formula in D5 is now @SUM(C1..C3).

When you move a range, you completely eliminate anything that was in the destination range before the move. You lose the data, the format, and the protection status. If any formulas refer to those cells, the references change to ERR.

Suppose that in figure 4.39 you want to replace the numbers in C1..C3 with the numbers in H1..H3. Figure 4.40 shows the result if you move H1..H3 to C1..C3. The formula in D5 changes from @SUM(C1..C3) to @SUM(ERR).

Caution:
When you move cells, ERR can occur anywhere in the file if there are formulas that refer to the range you moved.

Fig. 4.39.
The worksheet before data is moved into cells already used in a formula.

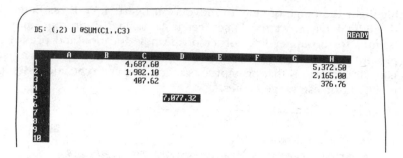

Fig. 4.40.
A formula changed to ERR when data is moved into cells already used in formulas.

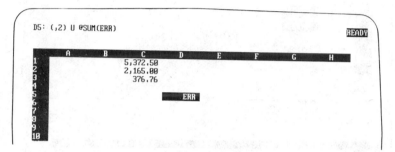

This change is permanent in 1-2-3 Release 2.01. In Release 2.2, you can press Undo (Alt-F4) to cancel the move, if necessary. Otherwise, you must reenter the formula in D5 manually. You can have hundreds of formulas in the file that refer to the cells C1..C3, and you must correct every one. (You don't have to type every formula; instead, you can use the /Copy command as explained in the next sections.) Be careful with the /Move command; you can destroy a worksheet if you use /Move incorrectly. The correct way to replace the data in C1..C3 with the data in H1..H3 is to copy H1..H3 to C1..C3 and then use /Range Erase on H1..H3.

The FROM and TO ranges can overlap, and the /Move command still works correctly. If you move just one corner of a range used in a formula, the range expands or contracts. Figure 4.41 shows what happens after you move F2..H6 to G2. The overlapping range caused no problems. A common use of /Move is to make room for a new row or column in a range of data.

Fig. 4.41.
The range expanded and formulas adjusted automatically as one corner of the range is moved out.

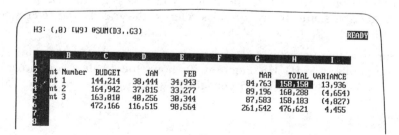

Originally, the formula in G3 in figure 4.41 was @SUM(D3..F3). After the move, the formula moved to H3 and is now @SUM(D3..G3). Notice that the @SUM in both formulas starts with cell D3. This cell did not move. But F3 in figure 4.41 moved to G3; therefore, the @SUM range expanded to D3..G3.

If you move the range G2..I6 in figure 4.41 back to F2, the formulas revert to the original ones (see fig. 4.42). ERR does not display even though part of the range was eliminated. ERR occurs only if you move a range on top of one of the corner cells in a range. In figure 4.40, a range was moved on top of the corner cells in the range in the formula in row D5; therefore, the formulas changed to ERR. In figure 4.42, the range was not moved on top of corner cells; therefore, the formulas do not change to ERR but just contract the range.

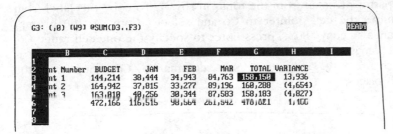

Fig. 4.42.
The range contracted and the formulas adjusted automatically as one corner of the range is moved in.

The cell pointer does not need to be at the top of the range when you start the /Move command. Sometimes it's easier to start at the destination range. At the Enter range to move FROM: prompt, press Esc to unanchor the range. Move the cell pointer to the range you want to move; press the period key to anchor the range; highlight the range to move; and then press Enter. At the Enter range to move TO: prompt, 1-2-3 moves back to the original location of the cell pointer. Press Enter to complete the move operation.

Copying the Contents of Cells

You use /Move to rearrange data in a file. You use /Copy to make duplicate copies of a range in a file. In a typical file, most formulas are duplicated many times. For example, in figure 4.42, the formula in G3 is duplicated in G4..G6. The same is true for the formulas in column H. This list could include hundreds of rows. It is long and tedious to type each formula separately. Fortunately, if you need the same number, label, or formula in a number of places in a file, you can enter them once and copy them.

You use /Copy more than any other 1-2-3 command. Copying can be simple or complicated. This section begins with simple examples and progresses to more complex examples.

You can copy a single cell or a range to another part of the worksheet. When you copy, you can make a single copy or many copies at the same time. When you copy a range, you also copy the format and protection status. You do not, however, copy the column width. The original cells are unchanged after you copy them. When you copy, the duplicate cells overwrite anything that was in the destination range before the copy. You lose the data as well as the format and protection status.

Copying the Contents of a Single Cell

The simplest example is to copy a label from one cell to another. Figure 4.43 shows the beginning of a budget application. A repeating label in C6 separates the department detail from the totals in row 7. To copy this label from C6 to D6, move the cell pointer to C6 and select /Copy. At the prompt Enter the range to copy FROM:, press Enter to specify the one-cell range C6. At Enter the range to copy TO:, move to D6 and press Enter. The result is displayed in figure 4.44. Unlike the /Move command, /Copy duplicates the label in both places.

Fig. 4.43.
A worksheet
before a label
is copied.

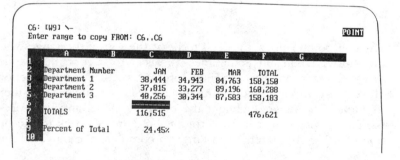

Fig. 4.44.
The worksheet
after a label is
copied.

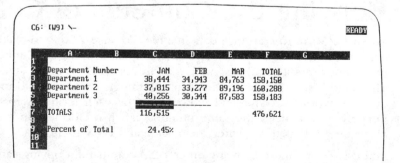

Copying a Formula with Relative Addressing

The real power of /Copy shows up when you copy a formula. The formula in C7 in figure 4.43 is @SUM(C3..C5). When you copy C7 to D7, the formula in D7 is @SUM(D3..D5), as shown in figure 4.45. This concept, *relative addressing*, is one of the most important concepts in 1-2-3. When you copy a formula, 1-2-3 adjusts the new formula so that its cell references are in the same relative location as they were in the original formula.

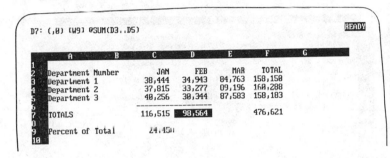

Fig. 4.45.
The addresses adjusted automatically when a formula is copied.

The best way to understand relative addressing is to understand how 1-2-3 actually stores addresses in formulas. The formula in C7 is @SUM(C3..C5). In other words, this formula means "sum the contents of all the cells in the range from C3 to C5." But that is not the way 1-2-3 really stores this formula. To 1-2-3, the formula is "sum the contents of all the cells in the range from the cell 4 rows above this cell to the cell 2 rows above this cell." When you copy this formula to D7, 1-2-3 uses the same relative formula but displays it as D3..D5.

In most cases, when you copy a formula, you want the addresses to adjust automatically. Sometimes, however, you do not want addresses to adjust, or you want part of an address to adjust. These situations are examined separately in the following sections.

Copying a Formula with Absolute Addressing

The formula in C9 in figure 4.45 is +C7/F7. This figure represents January's sales as a percent of the total. If you copy this formula to D9, you get +D7/G7. The D7, the sales for February, is correct. G7, however, is incorrect; G7 is a blank cell. When you copy the formula in C9, you want the address F7 to copy as an *absolute address*. This means that you do not want it to change after you copy it to D9.

Cue:
Specify absolute addresses when you write the formula, not when you copy it.

To specify an absolute address, type a dollar sign ($) before each part of the address you want to remain "absolutely" the same. The formula in C9 should be +C7/$F$7. When you copy this formula to D9, the formula becomes +D7/$F$7.

Instead of typing the dollar signs, you can type the address and press the Abs (F4) key. The address changes to absolute. In this case, the complete formula becomes +D7/$F$7 (see fig. 4.46).

Fig. 4.46.
An absolute address that remains unchanged when copied.

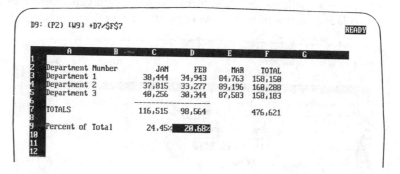

You can enter dollar signs while pointing to addresses in a formula. As you point to a cell, press the Abs (F4) key to make the address absolute. If you make an error and forget to make an address absolute, just press Edit (F2) to go into EDIT mode, move the cursor to the address you want to make absolute, and then press Abs (F4).

If you want to change an absolute reference (with dollar signs) back to a relative reference, press Edit, move the cursor to the reference, and then press Abs multiple times until there are no dollar signs. Press Enter to reenter the formula.

Another kind of addressing is called *mixed addressing*. Mixed addressing is covered later in this chapter.

Copying One Cell's Contents a Number of Times

In figure 4.45, one cell was copied one time. The idea, however, is to copy the formula in C7 to D7 and E7. You can do this in one copy operation. The FROM range is still C7, but at the Enter range to copy TO: prompt, move the cell pointer to D7, press the period to anchor the cell, highlight E7 as well, and then press Enter. The formula in C7 is copied to both cells (see fig. 4.47).

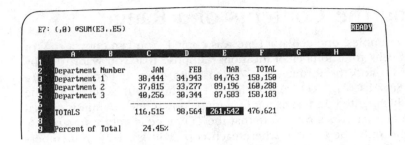

Fig. 4.47.
A cell copied to
a number of
cells in one
copy.

Copying One Cell's Contents to a Range of Cells

You can copy a single cell to a range in the worksheet. Figure 4.48 shows a simple price-forecasting model. The current prices are in column B. The formula in C3 increases the price by the amount in B1. To copy this formula through the table in the worksheet, copy FROM C3 TO C3..G10. The result is displayed in figure 4.49.

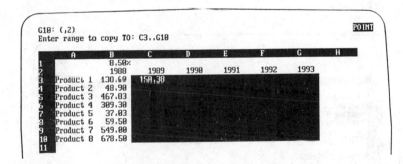

Fig. 4.48.
A cell copied to
a number of
rows and
columns in one
copy.

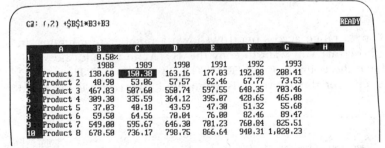

Fig. 4.49.
The worksheet
after the copy.

When you copy a single cell, you can include the FROM cell in the TO range, as in figure 4.48. As a general rule, the first cell in the FROM range can be the same cell as the first cell in the TO range. In most other cases, an overlapping FROM and TO range can destroy the data before it is copied.

Caution:
Avoid overlapping FROM and TO ranges. Unless the overlapping cell is the first cell of both the FROM and TO ranges, you can destroy the data before you copy it.

Copying the Contents of a Range

In previous examples, one cell at a time was copied. You can copy a row or a column of cells to a number of locations. Suppose that you want to copy the label in C6 and the formula in C7 across the other columns in figure 4.50. Copy FROM C6..C7 TO D6..F6. Figure 4.50 shows the screen after the TO range is highlighted. In this example, a range down one column is copied a number of times across a row. Note that the TO range is only across row 6. This highlights only the top cell where each copy will go. 1-2-3 remembers the size of each copy and fills in the lower cells of the copy accordingly. The result is displayed in figure 4.51.

Fig. 4.50.
A range copied a number of times across a row in one copy.

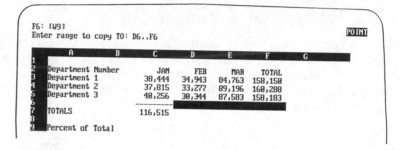

Fig. 4.51.
The worksheet after the copy.

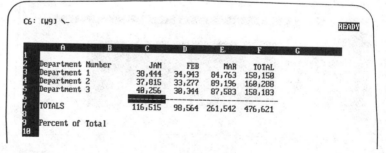

You also can copy a range across one row down a number of columns. In figure 4.52, suppose that you want to copy the TOTAL in G3 and the VARIANCE in H3 down the column. Copy FROM G3..H3 TO G4..G6. Figure 4.52 displays the screen after the TO range is highlighted. The result is displayed in figure 4.53.

Fig. 4.52.
A range copied a number of times down a column in one copy.

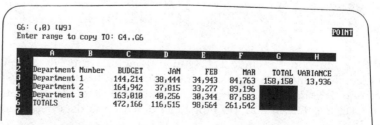

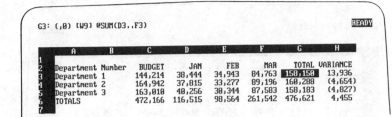

Fig. 4.53.
*The worksheet
after the copy.*

Copying a range a number of times is useful. When you build worksheets, you will use this technique often. The technique, however, does have limitations. In general, if the FROM range is only one cell wide in dimension, you can copy it a number of times in that dimension. A single cell is part of one row and one column. You can copy a single cell across a row and down a column.

Cue:
*If the FROM range
is only one cell
wide, you can copy
it a number of
times both down
rows and across
columns.*

Because the FROM range in figure 4.50 (C6..C7) occupies 2 rows, you can copy this range across columns. You cannot copy this range down rows. If you specified a TO range in figure 4.50 of D6..F7 or even D6..F100, you will get the same result as in figure 4.51. The rows are ignored in the TO range because they are fixed in the FROM range.

You can copy a two-dimensional range only once to a different area of the worksheet. For example, you can copy the range C3..G10 in figure 4.49 anywhere on the worksheet one time. If you highlight more than a single cell as the TO range, 1-2-3 uses the upper left corner and ignores the rest.

Copying with Mixed Addressing

In some cases, you must use formulas with a mix of both absolute and relative references if you want the formula to copy correctly. The following example shows you how to keep a row reference absolute while letting the column reference change during the copy.

Figure 4.54 shows a price-forecast worksheet similar to the one in figure 4.49, but this time the price increase percentage differs for each year. The formula in C3 is more complex. When you copy this formula down column C, you do not want the reference to C1 to change, but when you copy the formula across row 3, you want the reference to change for each column. The mixed reference is relative for the column and absolute for the row. The formula in C3 is +B3*(1+C$1). When you copy this down one row to C4, the formula becomes +B4*(1+C$1). The relative address B3 became B4, but the mixed address C$1 is unchanged. When you copy this formula to D3, the formula becomes +C3*(1+D$1). The relative address B3 becomes C3, and the mixed address becomes D$1. You can copy FROM C3 TO C3..G10 and create the correct formula throughout the worksheet.

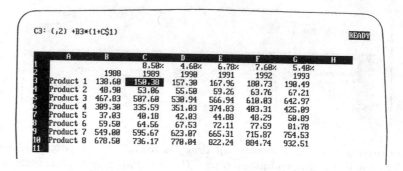

Fig. 4.54.
An adjusted
mixed address
in a formula.

To make an address mixed without typing the dollar signs, use the Abs (F4) key. The first time you press Abs, the address becomes absolute. As you continue to press Abs, the address cycles through all the possible mixed addresses and returns to relative. The complete list of relative, absolute, and mixed addresses is found in table 4.2. To obtain the address in figure 4.54, press Abs twice.

Table 4.2
Using Abs (F4) To Change Address Type

Number of Times Needed To Press Abs (F4):	Result	Explanation
1	$D$1	Absolute row and column
2	D$1	Absolute row
3	$D1	Absolute column
4	D1	Returned to relative

Using Range Names with /Copy

With all commands that prompt for a range, you can use range names for the FROM range, the TO range, or both. Just type the range name or press the Name (F3) key and point to the range name. Unfortunately, 1-2-3 makes it impossible to use range names with mixed addresses.

To specify an absolute address, you must type the dollar sign before the range name. To use the range name SALES in a formula as an absolute address, you type **$SALES**. You cannot use Abs (F4) with range names. And you cannot specify a range name and make it a mixed address. You must use the actual cell addresses.

Using /Range Value To Convert Formulas to Values

/Range Value is a special type of copy command. When you use **/Range Value** on a cell that contains a label or a number, this command works exactly like **/Copy**. When you use **/Range Value** on a cell that contains a formula, the current value, not the formula, is copied. You use **/Range Value** to freeze the value of formulas so that they won't change. Figure 4.55 shows a model that forecasts profits for future years. You update the forecasts each quarter, but you want to keep track of the forecasts from the previous quarter for comparison. You can do this by converting the formula results in row 16 into values in row 18. In this way, next quarter's changes won't affect row 18.

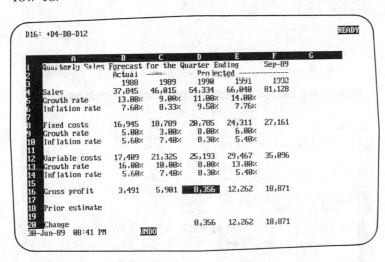

Fig. 4.55.
A worksheet before using /Range Value.

The profit figures in figure 4.55 are formulas. To obtain the previous estimate in row 18, use **/Range Value** FROM B16..F16 TO B18. The previous estimate is a copy of the gross profit converted to numbers. The result is shown in figure 4.56. The numbers in row 18 are the current values of the formulas in row 16.

In figure 4.57, the various rates were updated, and 1-2-3 calculated new gross profits. Because the previous estimates in row 18 did not change, you can compare the newest estimate with the previous one and calculate the difference in row 20.

```
D18: 8356                                                          READY

          A         B         C         D         E         F         G
 1 Quarterly Sales Forecast for the Quarter Ending        Sep-89
 2               Actual    ---------- Projected ----------
 3               1988      1989      1990      1991      1992
 4 Sales         37,845    46,015    54,334    66,040    81,128
 5 Growth rate   13.00%    9.00%     11.00%    14.00%
 6 Inflation rate 7.60%    8.33%     9.50%     7.76%
 7
 8 Fixed costs   16,945    18,789    20,785    24,311    27,161
 9 Growth rate   5.00%     3.00%     8.00%     6.00%
10 Inflation rate 5.60%    7.40%     8.30%     5.40%
11
12 Variable costs 17,409   21,325    25,193    29,467    35,096
13 Growth rate   16.00%    10.00%    8.00%     13.00%
14 Inflation rate 5.60%    7.40%     8.30%     5.40%
15
16 Gross profit  3,491     5,901     8,356     12,262    18,871
17
18 Prior estimate 3,491    5,901     8,356     12,262    18,871
19
20 Change                            0         0         0
30-Jun-89  08:42 PM         UNDO
```

```
D16: +D4-D8-D12                                                    READY

          A         B         C         D         E         F         G
 1 Quarterly Sales Forecast for the Quarter Ending        Sep-89
 2               Actual    ---------- Projected ----------
 3               1988      1989      1990      1991      1992
 4 Sales         37,845    46,015    54,534    64,492    77,836
 5 Growth rate   13.00%    8.30%     8.00%     12.00%
 6 Inflation rate 7.60%    9.43%     9.50%     7.76%
 7
 8 Fixed costs   16,945    18,789    21,007    25,701    28,985
 9 Growth rate   5.00%     4.50%     12.54%    7.00%
10 Inflation rate 5.60%    7.40%     8.30%     5.40%
11
12 Variable costs 17,409   21,325    24,873    29,550    34,572
13 Growth rate   16.00%    8.60%     9.70%     11.00%
14 Inflation rate 5.60%    7.40%     8.30%     5.40%
15
16 Gross profit  3,491     5,901     8,574     9,241     14,279
17
18 Prior estimate 3,491    5,901     8,356     12,262    18,871
19
20 Change                            218       (3,821)   (4,592)
30-Jun-89  08:48 PM         UNDO
```

Formulas take more memory than numbers; they also take time to recalculate. You can convert to numbers formulas that will never change. For example, the years for projections in row 3 in figure 4.57 are formulas that add 1 to the previous year. The formula in C3 is +B3+1. To convert these formulas to numbers, use **/R**ange **V**alue FROM C3..F3 TO C3.

You may encounter problems with **/R**ange **V**alue if you have recalculation set to **M**anual. If you use **/R**ange **V**alue on a formula that is not current, you freeze an inaccurate value. This problem is even worse if you convert formulas to numbers and the formulas are not current. You lose the formulas, and the resulting numbers are wrong. In figure 4.58, the CALC indicator shows that the worksheet is not current. If you use **/R**ange Value on the formula in B5, you freeze an incorrect value. If your worksheet is set to manual recalculation and the CALC indicator is on, press Calc (F9) before you use **/R**ange Value.

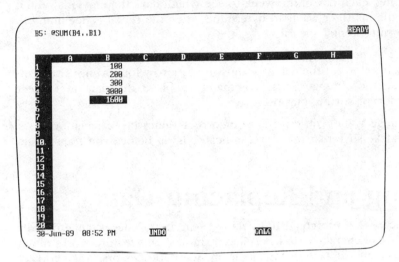

Fig. 4.58.
An incorrect value locked in when /Range Value is issued while the CALC indicator is on.

Using /Range Trans

/Range Trans is another special type of copy command. (In Release 2.01, the command is Transpose.) This command converts rows to columns, converts columns to rows, and changes formulas to values at the same time. In figure 4.59, the range F12..N19 is the result of the command **/R**ange Trans FROM A2..H10 TO F12. The rows and columns are transposed, and the formulas in row 10 become numbers in column N.

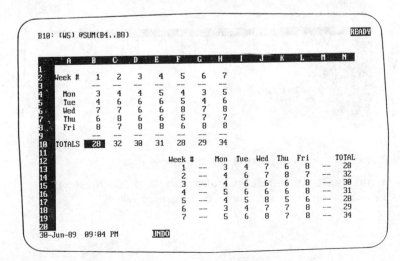

Fig. 4.59.
Using /Range Trans to transpose a table.

/**R**ange **T**rans is often used to change data in a database (see Chapter 12 for a discussion of databases). For example, suppose that the information in figure 4.59 is rental information on a VCR movie from a local movie rental store. The manager of the store wants to track how many times a particular movie is rented each day of the week to see which days the movie is rented most. Also, the manager wants to determine when the rental is beginning to taper off to run a rental special.

The database is not set up properly for 1-2-3 to be able to sort by day or week, as each record of the database must be in a row for sorting. The manager can use the /**R**ange **T**rans command to place the data in correct database order for sorting purposes.

Caution:
Make sure that the CALC indicator is off before you transpose a range.

As with /**R**ange **V**alue, you can freeze incorrect values if recalculation is set to **M**anual. Make sure that the CALC indicator is off before you transpose a range.

RELEASE
2.2
Entire
Section

Finding and Replacing Data

In 1-2-3 Release 2.2, the command /**R**ange **S**earch searches a range of cells to find a string of characters in labels and formulas. This feature works much like the search-and-replace feature in many word processors. An incorrect search and replace can destroy a file; therefore, always save the file first.

Suppose that you have a list of department names as labels, and you want to shorten the labels from "Department" to "Dept" (see fig. 4.60). To search and replace a label, choose /**R**ange **S**earch, and then follow these steps:

1. At the prompt, highlight the range to search, A3..A10, and then press Enter (see fig. 4.60).

Fig. 4.60.
A column of labels before a replace operation.

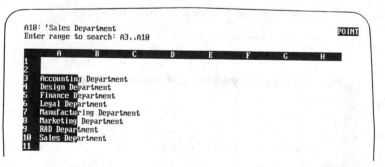

```
A10: 'Sales Department                                    POINT
Enter range to search: A3..A10

        A       B       C       D       E       F       G       H
1
2
3   Accounting Department
4   Design Department
5   Finance Department
6   Legal Department
7   Manufacturing Department
8   Marketing Department
9   R&D Department
10  Sales Department
11
```

2. Type the search string (**department**) and press Enter.

3. At the menu, choose to search **F**ormulas, **L**abels, or **B**oth (see fig. 4.61). Choose **L**abels to replace cells that contain labels.

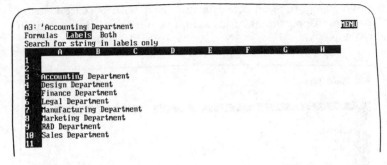

Fig. 4.61.
The Range
Search menu
with Labels
selected.

4. At the menu, choose to either **F**ind or **R**eplace (see fig. 4.62). Choose **R**eplace.

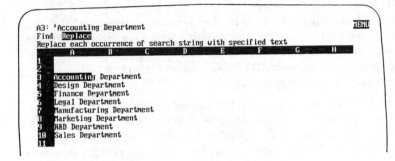

Fig. 4.62.
The Range
Search menu
with Replace
selected.

5. At the prompt, type the replacement string (**"Dept"**) and press Enter.

   The cell pointer moves to the first cell with a matching string (A3), and the following menu is displayed:

   Replace   **A**ll   **N**ext   **Q**uit

6. Choose **R**eplace to replace "Department" with "Dept" in this one cell and move to the next matching cell. Choose **A**ll to replace "Department" with "Dept" in all cells in the range. Choose **N**ext to skip the current cell without changing it and move to the next matching cell. Choose **Q**uit to stop the search and replace and return to READY mode.

A good idea is to choose **R**eplace for the first cell and make sure that the change is correct. If it is correct, choose **A**ll to replace the rest. If you made an error on the first replace, choose **Q**uit and redo the command. Remember that if something was replaced in error, press Undo (Alt-F4) to undo the change in Release 2.2.

Caution:
Always save the
file before using
the /Range Search
command in 1-2-3
Release 2.2.

The result is shown in figure 4.63. Case is not used with a search string ("department" matches "Department," for example), but case is important in the replacement string.

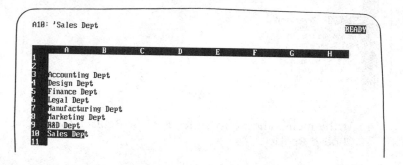

Fig. 4.63.
The replaced
labels.

If you choose **F**ind instead of **R**eplace in the menu in figure 4.61, the cell pointer moves to the first cell in the range with a matching string and gives you a menu with the options **N**ext or **Q**uit. Choose **N**ext to find the next occurrence or **Q**uit to return to READY mode. If there are no more matching strings, 1-2-3 stops with an error message.

You also can use **/R**ange **S**earch to modify formulas. If you have many formulas that round to 2 decimal places, such as @ROUND(A1*B1,2), you can change the formulas to round to 4 decimal places with a search string of ,2) and a replace string of ,4). You must be careful when you replace numbers in formulas. If you try to replace 2 with 4 in the last example, the formula @ROUND(A2*B2,2) becomes @ROUND(A4*B4,4).

You also can search both formulas and labels to find or replace text. Perhaps you want to replace the range name BUDGET_89 with BUDGET_90. If BUDGET_89 occurs in both formulas and macros (a macro is a list of label entries), then you would select **B**oth to search both formulas and labels for occurrences of BUDGET_89.

If your replacement makes a formula invalid, 1-2-3 cancels the replacement and returns to READY mode with the cell pointer at the cell that contains the formula it could not replace. At the end of a replace, the cell pointer is at the last cell replaced.

Controlling Recalculation

The commands discussed so far have shown you how to clear, protect, copy, and move data in worksheets. This section shows how you can control how 1-2-3 updates the worksheet as you change it.

Whenever a value in a worksheet changes, 1-2-3 recalculates all other cells that depend on the changed value. This is the essence of an electronic worksheet. 1-2-3 provides a number of recalculation options for different circumstances.

Understanding Recalculation Methods

Normally, 1-2-3 recalculates the file whenever any cell changes. This feature is called automatic recalculation. With versions of 1-2-3 previous to Release 2.2, large worksheets could take a long time to recalculate, slowing work greatly. With Release 2.2, however, recalculation is now optimal.

RELEASE

2.2

Optimal recalculation means that only cells that contain formulas that refer to the changed cell are recalculated. If you change a cell in a large file and that cell is used in only one formula, only that one formula is recalculated. Recalculation is therefore fast.

Recalculation is best left in the default **Automatic** mode most of the time. You can tell 1-2-3 not to recalculate the worksheet when there is a change by using **/W**orksheet **G**lobal **R**ecalculation **M**anual. To force a recalculation, press the Calc (F9) key. Until the recalculation is complete, the mode indicator is set to WAIT, and you cannot use 1-2-3. Many Release 2.01 users, who do not have optimal recalculation, will find that manual calculation will save time when working with a large worksheet.

Automatic recalculation can slow macro execution. If you use macros, you may prefer to have the macro set the recalculation to **Manual** while the macro executes, and then reset recalculation to **Automatic** before the macro ends. Special considerations for macros when recalculation is **Manual** are covered in Chapter 13.

During recalculation, 1-2-3 determines which formulas depend on which cells and sets up a recalculation order to ensure the correct answer. This process is called the natural order of recalculation. Spreadsheet programs before 1-2-3 could not do this and sometimes required many successive recalculations before they arrived at the right answer in all cells.

These early spreadsheet programs could recalculate only columnwise or rowwise. Columnwise recalculation starts in cell A1 and calculates the cells down column A, then down column B, and so on. Rowwise recalculation starts in cell A1 and calculates the cells across row 1, then across row 2, and so on. **C**olumnwise and **R**owwise are options in the **W**orksheet **G**lobal **R**ecalculation menu, but you, unless your model relies on this specific type of calculation, should ignore them and leave recalculation on **N**atural.

Using Iteration To Solve Circular References

In one situation, the circular reference, the natural order of recalculation does not ensure the correct answer for all cells. A circular reference is a formula that depends, either directly or indirectly, on its own value. Usually a circular reference is an error, and you should eliminate it immediately. Whenever 1-2-3 performs a recalculation and finds a circular reference, the CIRC indicator appears in the status line at the bottom of the display. Figure 4.64 shows a typical erroneous circular reference in which the @SUM function includes itself.

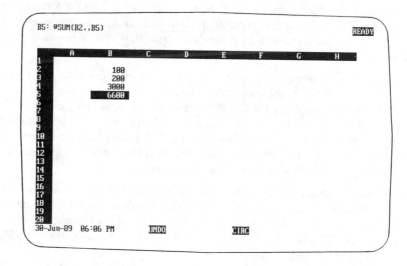

Fig. 4.64.
A circular reference.

Cue:
Use / Worksheet Status to find the location of a circular reference.

If you are not sure why the CIRC indicator appears, use /**W**orksheet **S**tatus for a basic status display (see fig. 4.65). This display points out one of the cells that caused the circular reference. (The cell that is displayed is always the lowest, rightmost circular reference in the worksheet. When you fix that formula, select /**W**orksheet **S**tatus again for the next circular reference.) In this case, you can fix the error by changing the formula to @SUM(B2..B4). In other cases, the source of the problem may be less obvious, and you may have to check every cell referred to in the cell that contains the formula.

In some special cases, a circular reference is deliberate. Figure 4.66 shows a worksheet with a deliberate circular reference. In this example, a company sets aside 10 percent of its net profit for employee bonuses. The bonuses themselves, however, represent an expense that reduces net profit. The formula in C5 shows that the amount of bonuses is net profit in D5*.1, or 10 percent. But net profit is profit before bonuses − bonuses (B5 − C5). The

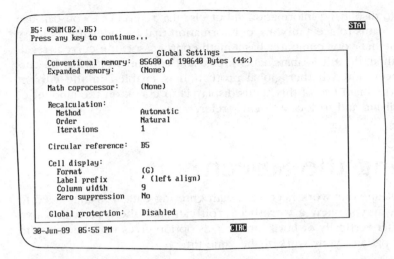

Fig. 4.65.
The circular reference displayed with the /Worksheet Status command.

value of employee bonuses depends on the value of net profit and the value of net profit depends on the value of employee bonuses. In figure 4.66, C5 depends on D5 and D5 depends on C5. This is a classic circular reference.

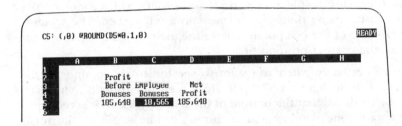

Fig. 4.66.
A worksheet with a deliberate circular reference.

Each time you recalculate the worksheet, the answers change by a smaller amount with a legitimate circular reference. Eventually, the changes become insignificant. This is called convergence. Note that the erroneous circular reference never converges, and the @SUM gets bigger every time you recalculate.

The worksheet in figure 4.66 needs five recalculations before the changes become less than one dollar. To determine the number of calculations needed, make an entry in cell B5 and press Enter. Because recalculation is set to **A**utomatic, the worksheet has calculated one time. Press Calc (F9) until C5 and D5 quit changing. You must press Calc (F9) four more times; this makes five calculations or iterations.

Once you establish this number, you can tell 1-2-3 to recalculate the worksheet 5 times every time it recalculates with /**W**orksheet **G**lobal **R**ecalculation **I**teration. Type the number **5** and then press Enter. In most cases, you can handle a converging circular reference with a macro (see Chapter 14).

In addition to displaying information about circular references, you can use /**W**orksheet **S**tatus to see a mixture of information that includes the memory available, whether your computer has a math coprocessor, the current recalculation method, default formats, label prefix and column width for the current worksheet, and whether global protection is enabled in the current worksheet. The main use of this status display is to check on the amount of memory available and to locate circular references.

Splitting the Screen

Once you set up your worksheet and begin entering data, you may need to change the way you view a worksheet. You can split the screen into two windows either vertically or horizontally. This option gives you the ability to see different parts of your work at the same time.

Reminder:
Move the cell
pointer to the
position where you
want the screen to
split.

You can split the screen either horizontally or vertically into two windows with /**W**orksheet **W**indow **H**orizontal or /**W**orksheet **W**indow **V**ertical. These commands are useful when you are using large worksheet applications because the commands enable you to see different parts of the worksheet at the same time. Because a split screen has two borders, you cannot display quite as much data at one time as you can with a full screen. The window splits at the position of the cell pointer; therefore, be sure that you move the cell pointer to the correct position first.

Split the screen vertically when you want to see the totals columns to the right of the data, as in figure 4.67. Split the screen horizontally when you want to see the totals rows at the bottom of the data. With a split screen, you can change data in one window and at the same time see how the totals change in the other window. This capability is handy for "what if" analysis.

Fig. 4.67.
The screen split
vertically.

```
D4: (,0) +D41                                                    READY

         A            B          C        D        O          P
1                                                1
2                   BUDGET      JAN      FEB     2   TOTAL    VARIANCE
3                   ------      ---      ---     3   -----    --------
4  Department 1    1,062,497   38,444   34,943  4 1,157,196   94,699
5  Department 2    1,306,752   37,815   33,277  5 1,317,651   10,899
6  Department 3    1,296,114   40,256   30,344  6 1,222,283  (73,831)
7  Department 4    1,022,329   38,656   31,098  7   992,506  (29,023)
8  Department 5    1,152,144   38,890   29,008  8 1,136,984  (15,160)
9  Department 6      817,511   35,591   26,225  9   899,477   81,966
10 Department 7      824,655   36,909   24,642  10  860,856   36,201
11 Department 8      977,396   33,611   22,310  11 1,015,467   38,071
12 Department 9      842,012   33,298   21,290  12  774,610  (67,402)
13 Department 10   1,099,933   31,109   22,728  13 1,005,255  (94,678)
14 Department 11   1,057,141   33,233   20,904  14 1,016,785  (40,356)
15 Department 12     825,409   30,201   19,384  15  824,043   (1,446)
16 Department 13   1,004,012   39,483   26,972  16 1,044,210   40,198
17 Department 14   1,128,380   39,452   27,316  17 1,167,000   38,620
18 Department 15     927,963   40,206   30,824  18 1,023,768   95,805
19 Department 16   1,336,598   39,053   27,031  19 1,283,445  (53,153)
20 Department 17   1,293,143   36,266   31,399  20 1,180,154 (112,989)
SPLIT.WK1                     UNDO
```

A split screen also comes in handy when you write macros. You can write the macro in one window and see the data that the macro operates on in the other window. Macros are covered in Chapter 13.

When you split the screen vertically, the left window includes the columns to the left of the cell pointer. In figure 4.67, the cell pointer was in column E when the window was split. Columns A–D (the columns to the left of the cell pointer) became the left window. The right window was then scrolled to display the TOTAL and VARIANCE in columns O and P. These columns are always visible as you scroll the left window.

When you split the screen horizontally, the top window includes the rows above the cell pointer. To display rows 10–20 in the upper window, scroll the display so that row 10 is at the top of the display. Then move the cell pointer to row 21 and select /Worksheet Window Horizontal.

As you move down the worksheet in figure 4.67, both windows scroll together. If you move the cell pointer below row 20, both windows scroll up so that you can see row 21. In this case, this is what you want. No matter where the cell pointer is in the left window, you can see the total for that department in the right window. This is called synchronized scrolling.

At other times, you may want to see two unrelated views of the worksheet, for example, when one window contains data and the other window contains macros. In this case, you want the two windows to scroll separately. Use /Worksheet Window Unsync to stop the synchronized scrolling and /Worksheet Window Sync to restore it.

When the two windows display different types of data, as in figure 4.68, you want unsynchronized scrolling. Notice that if you scroll down to row 50 in the left window in figure 4.68, you do not want to scroll down to row 50 in the right window.

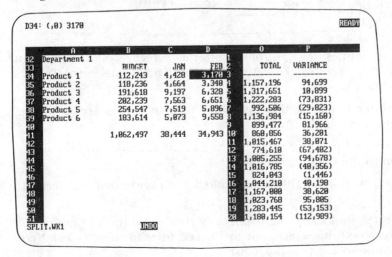

Fig. 4.68.
Different parts of a worksheet displayed in a split window.

To move between windows, use the Window (F6) key. To clear a split screen, use **/W**orksheet **W**indow **C**lear. No matter what window you are in, the cell pointer moves to the left or upper window when you clear a split screen.

Freezing Titles On-Screen

Most worksheets are much larger than can be displayed on-screen at any one time. As you move the cell pointer, you scroll the display. New data appears at one edge of the display while the data at the other edge scrolls out of sight. This scrolling can be a problem when titles at the top of the worksheet and descriptions at the left also scroll off the screen (see fig. 4.69). You can no longer tell what month and what departments the worksheet contains.

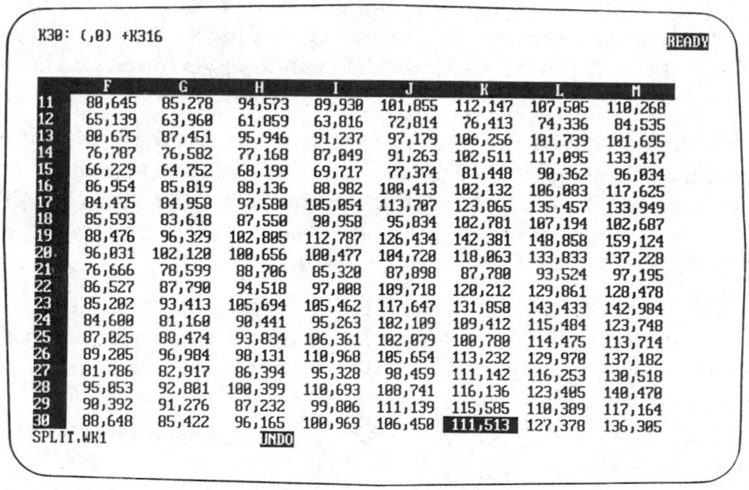

K30: (,0) +K316 READY

	F	G	H	I	J	K	L	M
11	80,645	85,278	94,573	89,930	101,855	112,147	107,505	110,268
12	65,139	63,960	61,859	63,816	72,814	76,413	74,336	84,535
13	80,675	87,451	95,946	91,237	97,179	106,256	101,739	101,695
14	76,787	76,582	77,168	87,049	91,263	102,511	117,095	133,417
15	66,229	64,752	68,199	69,717	77,374	81,448	90,362	96,034
16	86,954	85,819	88,136	88,982	100,413	102,132	106,083	117,625
17	84,475	84,958	97,580	105,054	113,707	123,865	135,457	133,949
18	85,593	83,618	87,550	90,958	95,834	102,781	107,194	102,687
19	88,476	96,329	102,805	112,787	126,434	142,381	148,858	159,124
20	96,031	102,120	100,656	100,477	104,720	118,063	133,833	137,228
21	76,666	78,599	88,706	85,320	87,898	87,780	93,524	97,195
22	86,527	87,790	94,518	97,008	109,718	120,212	129,861	128,478
23	85,202	93,413	105,694	105,462	117,647	131,858	143,433	142,984
24	84,600	81,160	90,441	95,263	102,109	109,412	115,484	123,748
25	87,025	88,474	93,834	106,361	102,079	100,780	114,475	113,714
26	89,205	96,984	98,131	110,968	105,654	113,232	129,970	137,182
27	81,786	82,917	86,394	95,328	98,459	111,142	116,253	130,518
28	95,053	92,801	100,399	110,693	108,741	116,136	123,405	140,470
29	90,392	91,276	87,232	99,806	111,139	115,585	110,389	117,164
30	88,648	85,422	96,165	100,969	106,450	111,513	127,378	136,305

SPLIT.WK1 UNDO

Fig. 4.69.
Titles scrolled off the worksheet.

Cue:
*Use the **/W**orksheet **T**itles command to prevent titles from scrolling off the screen.*

To prevent the titles from scrolling off the screen, you can use the **/W**orksheet **T**itles command to freeze, or lock, titles on-screen. To lock titles, follow these steps:

1. Position the display so that the titles you want to lock are at the top and left of the display.

2. Move the cell pointer to the first row below the titles and the first column to the right of the titles.

3. Choose **/W**orksheet **T**itles **B**oth to lock both horizontal and vertical titles.

Once these titles are locked, the data below row 3 and to the right of column A can scroll off the screen, but the locked titles in rows 2–3 and column A remain on-screen (see fig. 4.70).

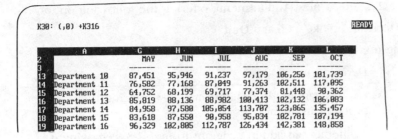

Fig. 4.70.
Locked titles
on-screen.

With locked titles, pressing Home moves the cell pointer to the position following the titles rather than to A1. In this case, the Home position is B4. You cannot use the movement keys to move into the titles area, but you can use the GoTo (F5) key. When you use GoTo to move to a cell in the titles area, the title rows and/or columns display twice (see fig. 4.71). You also can move into the titles area in POINT mode and see the same doubled display.

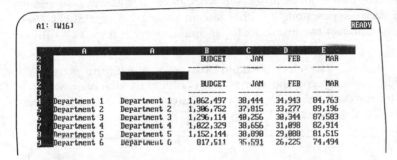

Fig. 4.71.
A doubled
display with
the cell pointer
in the titles
area.

Use /Worksheet Titles Clear to cancel the locked titles so that you can move freely in the titles area. You also can lock just the rows at the top of the screen with /Worksheet Titles Horizontal or just the columns at the left with /Worksheet Titles Vertical. To change the locked titles, you must use /Worksheet Titles Clear first and then specify the new locked titles. With a split screen, locking titles affects only the current window.

Adding In Capabilities to 1-2-3

1-2-3 Release 2 paved the way to add more functions to 1-2-3 by using add-ins. An *add-in* is a program you could add to 1-2-3 to provide capabilities that 1-2-3 was not initially designed to do. For example, add-ins have been developed to make 1-2-3 perform word processing, enhanced database management, and enhanced graphics. Yet, the add-in capability had to be "added-in."

RELEASE

2.2

Entire
Section

1-2-3 Release 2.2 adds a new **Add-in** menu, offering the following options:

Attach Detach Invoke Clear Quit

The following text describes each menu item:

Menu Item	*Description*
Attach	"Hooks" an add-in program to 1-2-3, placing the program in memory
Detach	"Unhooks" an add-in program from 1-2-3, removing it from memory
Invoke	Starts an add-in that has been attached to 1-2-3
Clear	Removes all add-in programs from memory, unhooking them from 1-2-3

Two add-in programs come with 1-2-3: a macro manager, which allows you to manage macros in memory outside the worksheet, and Allways, an add-in that lets you create typeset-quality reports from your 1-2-3 worksheet. (See Chapter 13 for more on the macro manager and Chapter 9 for a description of Allways.)

To install an add-in, first select **/Add-in Attach**. At the `Enter add-in to attach:` prompt, either type the name of the add-in to attach or select a name from the list (see fig. 4.72); then press Enter. In this example, notice that MACROMGR.ADN is selected.

Fig. 4.72.
Attaching an
add-in.

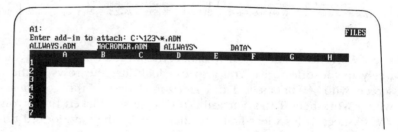

When you select the add-in to attach, the following menu is displayed:

No-Key 7 8 9 10

Once you select the add-in to attach, you can select to start the add-in by pressing Alt with either the F7, F8, F9, or F10 keys, or no key. If you choose **No-Key**, you must select **/Add-In Invoke** each time you want to start the add-in. Select **7** to assign the macro manager to Alt-F7. You return to the **Add-In** menu.

Select **Quit** to leave the **Add-in** menu. From READY mode, hold down the Alt key and then press F7. The macro manager add-in starts, displaying a menu (see fig. 4.73). Notice that the menu works just like a 1-2-3 menu.

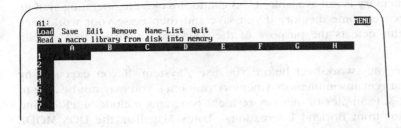

```
A1:                                                    MENU
Load  Save  Edit  Remove  Name-List  Quit
Read a macro library from disk into memory
      A       B       C       D       E       F       G       H
1
2
3
4
5
6
7
```

Fig. 4.73.
The macro
manager menu.

Because an add-in takes memory, you may want to remove it from memory if you have a worksheet that is large, or you notice that you are running low on memory. Select /**A**dd-In **D**etach to remove an add-in from memory. You see the prompt Enter add-in to detach and a list of add-ins. Type the name of the add-in or select it with the highlighter and press Enter. Only the one add-in will be removed from memory.

If you have several add-ins attached to 1-2-3 and need to remove them from memory, select **C**lear. All add-ins will be removed from memory, freeing up memory for the worksheet.

Accessing the Operating System

In this chapter, you learn how to use many different 1-2-3 commands to build and modify your worksheet files. At times, however, you may need to perform a function you cannot do in 1-2-3—one that requires you to use the operating system or another program. For example, suppose that you want to save a file on a disk, but you do not have a formatted disk available. In this case, you want to use the DOS FORMAT command. Or suppose that while you are working in 1-2-3, someone asks you to print a copy of a letter you created with a word processor.

In these situations, you can save your files and quit 1-2-3. Then, when you are finished with the other task, you can restart 1-2-3 and read the files again. However, you do not have to quit 1-2-3. You can use a faster way.

Use /**S**ystem to suspend 1-2-3 temporarily and access the operating system. Once in the operating system, you can copy files, format disks, execute other system functions, or even execute another program such as a word processor, if you have enough memory available. To return to 1-2-3, type **exit** and then press Enter. You return to 1-2-3 with the exact same status that you left. The same worksheet is in memory, and the cell pointer is in the same place. Window settings and any other defaults are exactly as you left them.

If enough memory is not available, 1-2-3 cannot invoke the operating system. You can recover some memory if you save and then erase your worksheet. However, this defeats the purpose of the /System command to a certain degree.

Caution:
Save your work before you use /System. You might not be able to return to 1-2-3.

Always save your worksheet before you use /System. If you execute any program that remains in memory (memory-resident), you may not be able to reenter 1-2-3. Examples of memory-resident programs include SideKick and SideKick Plus from Borland International, Lotus Magellan, the DOS MODE and PRINT commands, print spoolers, and many other programs. If you do not save your files and you cannot reenter 1-2-3, all your work will be lost.

Chapter Summary

In this chapter, you learn to use fundamental 1-2-3 commands. You learn how to use command menus, how to specify and name ranges, and how to save files. Erasing ranges and inserting and deleting rows and columns are presented as means of changing the layout of your worksheet. In addition, you learn how to protect and hide data. Just as important, you learn the limitations of these techniques and how they can be overridden.

Using /Move and /Copy, two basic commands used when you rearrange data and build worksheets, are explained. And you also learn how to use 1-2-3 Release 2.2's search and replace feature to find or find and change data.

The process of controlling how the worksheet is recalculated and how data is displayed on-screen is discussed, and you see how to split the screen into windows and lock titles. Finally, you learn how to suspend 1-2-3 so that you can perform actions that you cannot do in 1-2-3, and then return to the program just as you left it.

Learning all the commands in 1-2-3 is a formidable task. Fortunately, many commands perform specialized tasks; you can learn them as needed to perform these tasks. These more specialized commands are covered in the following chapters.

5

Formatting Cell Contents

Using 1-2-3 to manipulate data is only the first step in using an electronic worksheet. Making the results clear and easy to understand can be as important as calculating the correct answer. In this chapter, you learn to use the tools that control how data within cells is displayed on-screen. Changing how data displays is called *formatting*.

You can use two types of formatting commands. The /**R**ange commands, such as /**R**ange Format, affect the display of individual cells. The /**W**orksheet **G**lobal commands affect the display of an entire worksheet or file. You use both types of commands to customize the display of data.

When you format data, you change only the way the data displays. You do not change the value of the data itself. Other advanced formatting capabilities that apply only when you print reports are also available. Those printing capabilities are covered in Chapter 8.

This chapter shows you how to do the following:

- Set range and worksheet global formats
- Use the format commands to change how cells display
- Change label alignment in the cell
- Justify long labels across columns
- Suppress the display of zeros within cells

Setting Worksheet Global Defaults

1-2-3 includes a number of overall settings that define how 1-2-3 operates or how the screen looks. You can change these settings. You must select some settings with the Install program (see Appendix A). For example, you use Install to specify the type of display and the printers that are connected to your computer. You can change other settings as you work in 1-2-3. The main command to change these settings while you are in 1-2-3 is /Worksheet Global Default (see fig. 5.1).

Fig. 5.1.
The Worksheet Global Default menu of 1-2-3 Release 2.2.

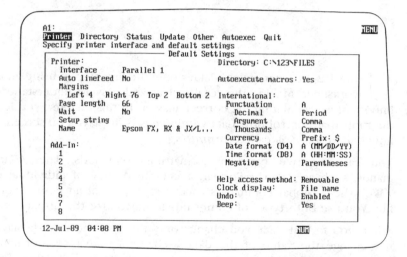

A Default Settings screen appears when you are using 1-2-3 Release 2.2. If you are using 1-2-3 Release 2.01, the screen appears as shown in figure 5.2. With either release, you choose **P**rinter from the menu to change the printer defaults, as described in Chapter 8. Choose **D**irectory to change the defaults for directories (see Chapter 7). Users of 1-2-3 Release 2.2 can choose **A**utoexec to control the automatic execution macros (see Chapter 13).

Choose **O**ther from the menu for additional choices (see fig. 5.3 for 1-2-3 Release 2.2 and fig. 5.4 for 1-2-3 Release 2.01). Choose the first command, **I**nternational, to display and select additional formatting options (see the section on international formats later in this chapter). The second command, **H**elp, is an obsolete command and should be ignored.

RELEASE
2.2

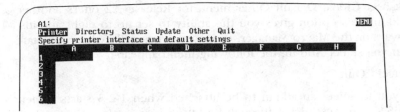

Fig. 5.2.
The Worksheet
Global Default
menu of 1-2-3
Release 2.01.

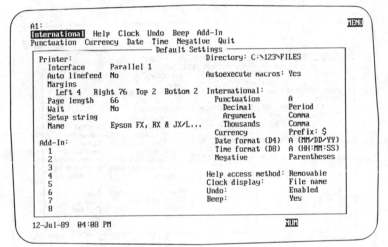

Fig. 5.3.
The Worksheet
Global Default
Other menu
of 1-2-3
Release 2.2.

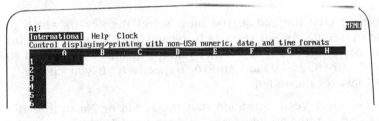

Fig. 5.4.
The Worksheet
Global Default
Other menu
of 1-2-3
Release 2.01.

Users of 1-2-3 Release 2.2 can choose Clock to change the default date and time indicator to display the file name at the lower left corner of the screen. Release 2.2 users also can choose Undo to disable Undo as explained in Chapter 3.

Normally, 1-2-3 beeps when you make an error. With 1-2-3 Release 2.2, you can turn off the beep with the /Worksheet Global Default Other Beep No command and turn the beep back on with the /Worksheet Global Default Other Beep Yes command. You might want to turn off the beep when you work in an area where the beep would disturb others, such as on an airplane. You also might turn off the beep when you demonstrate a 1-2-3 system to others so that it's not so obvious if you press a key in error.

RELEASE

2.2

Entire
Section

RELEASE
2.2

The /**W**orksheet **G**lobal **D**efault **O**ther menu for Release 2.2 offers another option—**Add-In**. This option gives you the ability to set up to eight add-ins, such as Allways or the Macro Manager, to load automatically when you start 1-2-3. When you select **Add-In**, the following menu appears:

Set   Cancel   Quit

Set allows you to select an add-in to be attached when 1-2-3 starts. When you choose **Set**, you must pick 1 through 8 as the add-in setting. Next, select the add-in to attach, as shown in figure 5.5.

Fig. 5.5.
Selecting an
add-in.

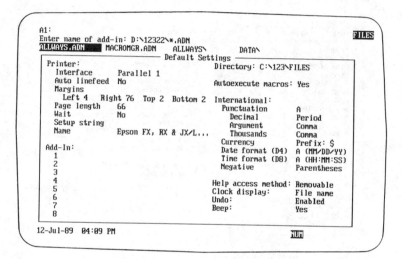

```
A1:
Enter name of add-in: D:\12322\*.ADN                                   FILES
ALLWAYS.ADN    MACROMGR.ADN    ALLWAYS\        DATA\
                        ── Default Settings ──
  Printer:                              Directory: C:\123\FILES
    Interface     Parallel 1
    Auto linefeed No                    Autoexecute macros: Yes
    Margins
      Left 4   Right 76  Top 2  Bottom 2  International:
    Page length   66                    Punctuation      A
    Wait          No                      Decimal        Period
    Setup string                          Argument       Comma
    Name          Epson FX, RX & JX/L...  Thousands      Comma
                                          Currency       Prefix: $
  Add-In:                               Date format (D4) A (MM/DD/YY)
    1                                   Time format (D8) A (HH:MM:SS)
    2                                     Negative       Parentheses
    3
    4                                   Help access method: Removable
    5                                   Clock display:     File name
    6                                   Undo:              Enabled
    7                                   Beep:              Yes
    8

12-Jul-89  04:09 PM                                            NUM
```

After you have selected the add-in, you must select the key to which to attach the add-in (see fig. 5.6). If you attach the add-in to **No-Key**, you must invoke it with the App (Alt-F10) key. Notice that the numbers 7, 8, 9, and 10 represent Alt-F7, Alt-F8, Alt-F9, and Alt-F10, respectively. If you choose 7, pressing Alt-F7 invokes the add-in.

Finally, you must select **Yes** to load and start the add-in or **No** to load the add-in, but not start it automatically. Once all the other selections are made, the name of the add-in appears in the settings sheet, as shown in figure 5.7.

Canceling an add-in is much easier than setting the add-in. To deselect an add-in, choose **Cancel**. Next, choose which one of the eight add-in options to cancel. The add-in name disappears from the settings sheet.

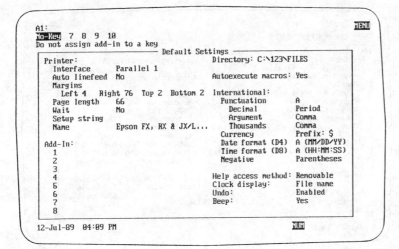

Fig. 5.6.
Selecting the
add-in key.

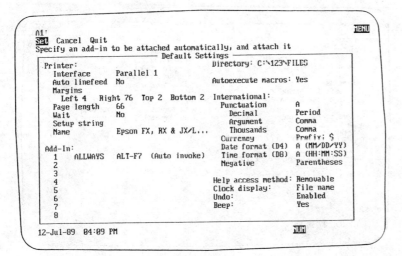

Fig. 5.7.
The name of
the add-in
displayed in
the settings
sheet.

To see the current status of all these settings, use the /Worksheet Global Default Status command (see fig. 5.8 for 1-2-3 Release 2.2 and fig. 5.9 for 1-2-3 Release 2.01). Notice that when you choose Status in Release 2.2, you are instructed to press any key to continue. Because the status is always shown, this option really has no purpose.

Cue:
Use the /Worksheet
Global Default
Status command to
see all the global
defaults at one
time.

Fig. 5.8.
The /*Worksheet
Global Default
Status screen
of 1-2-3
Release 2.2.*

Fig. 5.8.
The /Worksheet
Global Default
Status screen
of 1-2-3
Release 2.2.

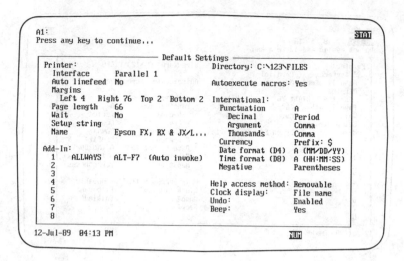

```
A1:                                                            STAT
Press any key to continue...
                      ┌──────── Default Settings ────────┐
    Printer:                          Directory: C:\123\FILES
      Interface      Parallel 1
      Auto linefeed  No               Autoexecute macros: Yes
      Margins
        Left 4   Right 76  Top 2  Bottom 2    International:
      Page length    66                 Punctuation       A
      Wait           No                   Decimal         Period
      Setup string                        Argument        Comma
      Name           Epson FX, RX & JX/L...  Thousands     Comma
                                            Currency       Prefix: $
    Add-In:                                 Date format (D4)  A (MM/DD/YY)
      1    ALLWAYS    ALT-F7  (Auto invoke)  Time format (D8)  A (HH:MM:SS)
      2                                      Negative       Parentheses
      3
      4                              Help access method: Removable
      5                              Clock display:      File name
      6                              Undo:               Enabled
      7                              Beep:               Yes
      8

 12-Jul-89  04:13 PM                                           NUM
```

Fig. 5.9.
The /Worksheet
Global Default
Status screen
of 1-2-3
Release 2.01.

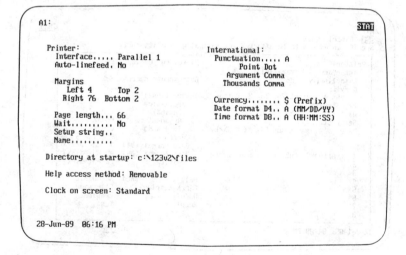

```
A1:                                                            STAT


    Printer:                         International:
      Interface..... Parallel 1        Punctuation..... A
      Auto-linefeed. No                  Point Dot
                                         Argument Comma
      Margins                            Thousands Comma
        Left 4       Top 2
        Right 76   Bottom 2           Currency........ $ (Prefix)
                                      Date format D4.. A (MM/DD/YY)
      Page length... 66               Time format D8.. A (HH:MM:SS)
      Wait.......... No
      Setup string..
      Name..........

    Directory at startup: c:\123v2\files

    Help access method: Removable

    Clock on screen: Standard



 28-Jun-89  06:16 PM
```

Caution:
Update the global
defaults; otherwise,
all changes are lost
when you quit
1-2-3.

Any setting changes you make are effective only until you quit 1-2-3. The next time you start 1-2-3, these settings revert to their original values. To update the changed settings permanently, execute the /Worksheet Global Default Update command. This command updates a configuration file called 123.CNF. 1-2-3 uses this file to determine the default for these settings.

Use the /Worksheet Status command to display global settings, such as the memory available; whether you have a math coprocessor in your computer; the current recalculation method; default formats, label prefix, and column width for the current worksheet; and whether global protection is enabled in the current worksheet. The main use of this status display is to check the amount of memory available and to find circular references (see fig. 5.10). See Chapter 4 for more information on circular references.

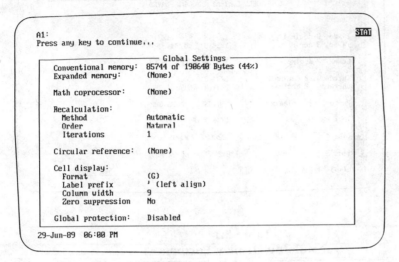

```
A1:                                                           STAT
Press any key to continue...
                      ─── Global Settings ───
   Conventional memory:  85744 of 190640 Bytes (44%)
   Expanded memory:      (None)

   Math coprocessor:     (None)

   Recalculation:
    Method               Automatic
    Order                Natural
    Iterations           1

   Circular reference:   (None)

   Cell display:
    Format               (G)
    Label prefix         ' (left align)
    Column width         9
    Zero suppression     No

   Global protection:    Disabled

29-Jun-89  06:00 PM
```

Fig. 5.10.
The /Worksheet
Status screen.

Setting Range and Worksheet Global Formats

Data in a cell has two characteristics: its contents and how it displays. These two characteristics are related, but they are not the same. The contents of the current cell are shown in the control panel; the formatted display of the contents appears in the worksheet (see fig. 5.11). A cell may contain a formula, but the current value of the formula displays in the cell. Other factors, such as the column width, can affect how a cell displays, but the cell format is the most important factor.

The Available Formats

You can display data in a cell in a number of different formats, listed in table 5.1.

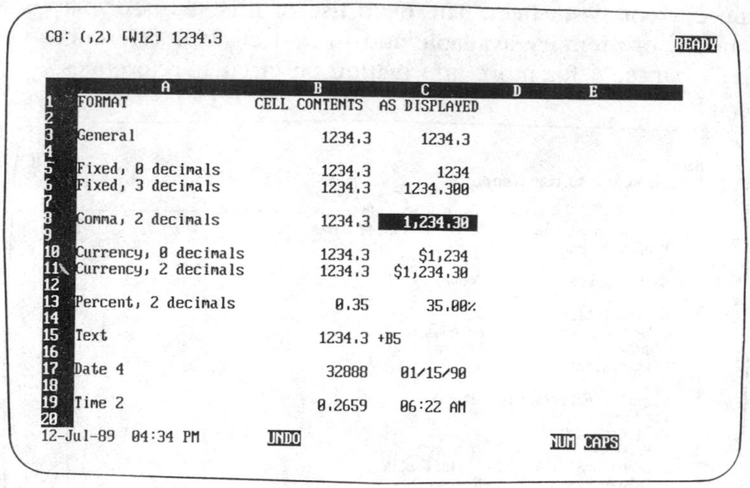

Fig. 5.11.
A worksheet
demonstrating
various
formats.

```
C8: (,2) [W12] 1234.3                                          READY

        A               B              C           D          E
1  FORMAT           CELL CONTENTS  AS DISPLAYED
2
3  General              1234.3        1234.3
4
5  Fixed, 0 decimals    1234.3          1234
6  Fixed, 3 decimals    1234.3       1234.300
7
8  Comma, 2 decimals    1234.3      1,234.30
9
10 Currency, 0 decimals 1234.3        $1,234
11 Currency, 2 decimals 1234.3     $1,234.30
12
13 Percent, 2 decimals    0.35        35.00%
14
15 Text               1234.3 +B5
16
17 Date 4               32888      01/15/90
18
19 Time 2              0.2659      06:22 AM
20
12-Jul-89  04:34 PM        UNDO                      NUM CAPS
```

Table 5.1
Available Display Formats

Format	Example	Application
General	1234.5	Numeric data
Fixed	1234.50	Numeric data
Comma (,)	1,234.50	Numeric data
Currency	$1,234.50	Numeric data
Percent	35.4%	Numeric data
Scientific	1.2345E+03	Numeric data
+/−	+ + + + +	Numeric data
Date	10/10/89	Special date serial numbers
Time	06:23 AM	Special time fractions
Text	+C6	All formulas
Hidden	No display	All data

Most formats apply only to numeric data (numeric formulas and numbers). If you format a label as Fixed or Currency, for example, the format has no effect on how the label displays. One format, Hidden, can apply to labels and string formulas. Figure 5.11 shows examples of some of the possible formats.

No matter what the format, numeric data is right-aligned. The rightmost digit always displays in the second position from the right. The extreme right position is reserved for a percent sign or right parenthesis. The result of string (text) formulas is always left-aligned, even if the formula refers to a label with another alignment.

The width of a cell is controlled by the column width setting, as described in Chapter 4. If the column is not wide enough to display a numeric entry, asterisks (*) fill the cell. To display the data, you must either change the format or change the column width.

Cue:
If numeric data displays as asterisks, change the format or the column width.

Because the extreme right position is reserved for a percent sign or right parenthesis, a number must fit into the cell using one character less than the column width. If the column width is 9, for example, the formatted number must fit into 8 positions not counting a percent sign or right parenthesis. Negative numbers display with either a minus sign or parentheses. This means that a negative number requires an extra character to display. With a column width of 9, then, a negative number must fit into 7 positions.

The Contents Versus the Format of a Cell

Remember that formatting changes how the data displays, not the data itself. For example, the number 1234 can display as 1,234, $1,234.00, 123400%, and in many other ways. No matter how the number displays, it remains the same number.

Some formats display a number as if it were rounded. If you format 1234.5 in Fixed format with zero decimal places, the number displays as 1235, but the actual value (1234.5) is used in formulas. In figure 5.12, the sales total in C8 looks as if an addition error has been made. Actually, the formula in C6 is +B6 * 1.1, projecting 10 percent higher sales next year. The value of the formula in C6 is 95.7. The display, however, shows 96 with a Fixed format and zero decimal places. The value of the formula in C7 is 83.6, but the display shows 84. The value of the sum in C8 is 179.3, but the display shows 179. The value appears as 96 + 84 = 179. This is an apparent rounding error produced by rounding the display.

Caution:
The number that displays in a cell may not be the exact value of the cell because of apparent rounding errors.

To avoid rounding errors, you need to round the actual value of the formulas, not just the display. To round the value of a formula, use the @ROUND function, as explained in Chapter 6.

Cue:
Use formats to change how a number displays; use @ROUND to round the decimal precision of the value in the cell.

Fig. 5.12.
An apparent
rounding error
caused by
formatting.

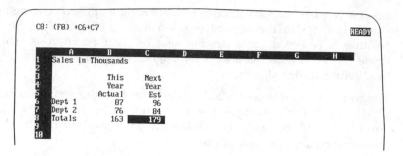

Using the Format Commands

You change the format of a cell or range of cells with the /Range Format command (see fig. 5.13). You then pick one of the formats from the menu. For comma format, you press the comma (,) key.

Fig. 5.13.
The Range
Format menu.

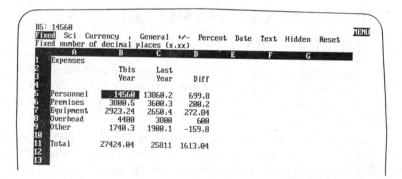

If you choose Fixed, Sci, , (comma), Currency, or Percent, you are prompted for the number of decimal places (see fig. 5.14). Whenever this prompt appears, 1-2-3 shows a default of 2 decimal places. Press Enter to accept the default, or type another number between 0 and 15 and press Enter. The Date and Time formats have additional menus that are covered later in this chapter. (The Time format is an option in the Date menu.)

After you select a format and any options, you are prompted for the range to format. Highlight the range and press Enter. Figure 5.15 shows the result after you use the /Range Format Fixed command with 2 decimal places on the range B5..B11. An abbreviation of the format appears in the control panel when the current cell has a range format. In figure 5.15, (F2) displayed in the control panel indicates that B5 has been range formatted as Fixed with 2 decimal places. If the cell has no range format, no format indicator appears in the control panel.

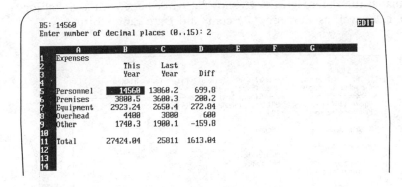

Fig. 5.14.
The prompt to enter the number of decimal places.

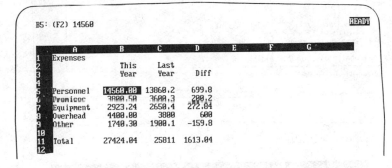

Fig. 5.15.
A range formatted as Fixed with 2 decimal places.

When you start a new file, none of the cells have a range format. For example, in figure 5.14, none of the cells have a range format. In figure 5.15, only the cells in the range B5..B11 have a range format. When a cell does not have a range format, the cell takes the format specified with the **/W**orksheet **G**lobal **F**ormat command.

When you start a new file, the global format is **G**eneral. To change the global format, use the **/W**orksheet **G**lobal **F**ormat command (see fig. 5.16). Figure 5.17 shows the worksheet after changing to comma format with 2 decimal places. Notice that the format in B5..B11 did not change. These cells have a range format; the global format affects only the cells with no range format.

Reminder:
A range format overrides the global format.

If you want a cell or range that has a range format to have the same format as the global format, you can remove range formatting with the **/R**ange **F**ormat **R**eset command. If you want a cell or range with a range format to have a different range format, execute the **/R**ange **F**ormat command again and choose a different format.

Use the global format for the format you expect to use the most in the worksheet. Then use the **/R**ange **F**ormat command to format ranges you want to display with other formats. Most worksheets look best if you use a variety of

Cue:
Choose the global format you will use most in the worksheet.

formats to match the data. Figure 5.18 shows a worksheet with a global format of comma, as well as **C**urrency, **P**ercent, and **D**ate range formats.

Fig. 5.16.
The Worksheet
Global Format
menu of 1-2-3
Release 2.2.

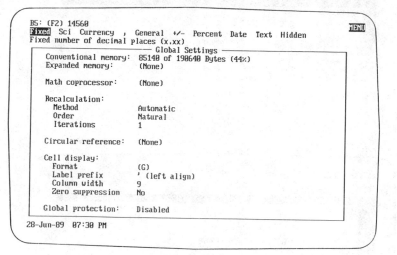

Fig. 5.17.
The worksheet
with a global
format of
comma (,)
with 2 decimal
places.

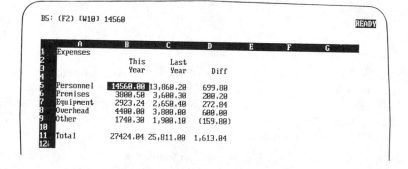

Fig. 5.18.
A worksheet
with a variety
of formats.

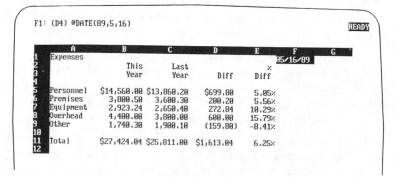

The following sections describe each format in detail. You can access each format command with /**W**orksheet **G**lobal **F**ormat or /**R**ange **F**ormat.

General Format

General format, the default for all new worksheets, displays only the number. If the number is negative, it is preceded by a minus sign. If the number contains decimal digits, it can contain a decimal point. If the number contains too many digits to the right of the decimal point to fit within the column width, the decimal portion that does not fit in the cell is truncated. If the number is too large to display normally, it displays in Scientific format (abbreviated **Sci** in Release 2.2). In a cell with a column width of 9, 123400000 displays as 1.2E+08. In the same cell, a very small number, such as 0.0000000012, is truncated and displays as 0.000000. Negative numbers in Scientific format display with a leading minus sign.

Reminder:
When you start a new file, the global format is General.

Following are several examples of General format in cells that have a column width of 9:

Typed Entry	Display Result
123.46	123.46
−123.36	−123.36
1.2345678912	1.234567
150000000	1.5E+08
−.00000002638	−0.00000

(G) appears in the control panel of cells that have been formatted with the /**R**ange **F**ormat **G**eneral command.

Fixed Format

Use the Fixed format when you want a column of numbers to line up on the decimal point. 1-2-3 displays the fixed number of decimal places, from 0 to 15, you specify. If the number has more decimal digits than the number you specify in the format, the number is rounded in the display, but not in the value used for calculations.

Cue:
Use Fixed format when you want a column of numbers to line up on the decimal point.

Following are several examples of Fixed format in cells that have a column width of 9:

Typed Entry	Cell Format	Display Result
123.46	(F0)	123
123.46	(F1)	123.5
−123.46	(F2)	−123.46
123.46	(F4)	123.4600
−123.46	(F4)	*********
12345678	(F2)	*********

In all cases, the full number in the cell is used in calculations. Negative numbers display with a leading minus sign.

(Fn) appears in the control panel of cells that have been formatted with the /Range Format Fixed command. n represents the number of decimal places.

Comma Format

Like the Fixed format, the comma format (,) displays data with a fixed number of decimal places (from 0 to 15). In addition, the comma format separates the thousands, millions, and so on with commas. Positive numbers less than 1,000 display the same way in Fixed format and comma format. The comma format is used most often for financial data.

If the number has more decimal digits than the number you specify in the format, the number is rounded in the display. The full value in the cell is used in calculations.

Cue:
Use comma format to make large numbers easier to read.

Use the comma format instead of Fixed format for large numbers. It is easier to read 12,300,000.00 than 12300000.00. With comma format in Release 2.01, negative numbers display in parentheses. −1234 displays as (1,234) with 0 decimal places.

RELEASE

2.2

Users of 1-2-3 Release 2.2 can change the setting so that negative numbers display with a leading minus sign by using the /Worksheet Global Default Other International Negative Sign command. −1234 then displays as -1,234 rather than (1234). To return to parentheses for negative numbers, use the /Worksheet Global Default Other International Negative Parentheses command. This default applies to 1-2-3 as a whole, not to any one worksheet.

(,n) appears in the control panel of cells that have been formatted with the /Range Format , command. n represents the number of decimal places.

Following are examples of comma (,) format in cells that have a column width of 9:

Typed Entry	Cell Format	Display Result
123.46	(,0)	123
1234.6	(,2)	1,234.60
−1234.6	(,0)	(1,235)
−1234	(,2)	*********

Currency Format

Currency format works much like comma format but includes a leading dollar sign ($). Because of the dollar sign, an extra position in the column width is needed to display a number in Currency format. Negative numbers are handled the same as with comma format.

You can change the dollar sign, the default currency symbol, if you are using a different currency. Use the /Worksheet Global Default Other International Currency command to specify a different currency symbol and to specify whether the symbol is a prefix or a suffix. The currency symbol can be up to 15 characters long—for example, $US and $CAN—and can include any of the characters in the Lotus International Character Set (LICS). You can find more about LICS characters in Chapter 6. The currency default applies to 1-2-3 as a whole, not to any one worksheet.

Cue:
You can change
the default
currency symbol.

Suppose that you create a file using Currency format for U.S. dollars and save the file. You later create a file that uses the British pound (£). You can change the /Worksheet Global Default Other International Currency to the British pound by typing the LICS character for this symbol. You do this by pressing Alt-F1 (Compose) and then typing L=. When you later retrieve another file, any cells formatted as Currency display the pound as the currency symbol.

Caution:
If you change the
currency symbol,
the change affects
the entire file and
all subsequent files
you retrieve.

(Cn) appears in the control panel of cells formatted with the /Range Format Currency command. n represents the number of decimal places.

Following are examples of Currency format in cells that have a column width of 9:

Typed Entry	Cell Format	Display Result
123	(C2)	$123.00
−123.124	(C2)	($123.12)
1234.12	(C0)	$1,234
1234.12	(C2)	*********

Percent Format

Use the **Percent** format to display percentages. You specify the number of decimal places from 0 to 15. The number displayed is the value of the cell multiplied by 100, followed by a percent sign. If the number has more decimal digits than the number you specify in the format, the number is rounded in the display.

Note that the number of decimal places you specify is for the number as a percent, not as a whole number. For example, only 2 decimal places are needed to display 0.2456 as a percent.

Reminder:
Enter percentages as decimal fractions, not as whole numbers.

The number displays as multiplied by 100, but the value of the cell is unchanged. To display 50% in a cell, type **.5** and format for percent. If you type **50** and format for **Percent** with zero decimal places, 5000% displays.

(Pn) appears in the control panel of cells formatted with the **/R**ange Format Percent command. n represents the number of decimal places.

Following are examples of **Percent** format in cells that have a column width of 9:

Typed Entry	Cell Format	Display Result
.2	(P2)	20.00%
−1.3528	(P2)	−35.28%
30	(P0)	3000%
30	(P4)	*********

Scientific Format

Cue:
Use Scientific format to display very large or very small numbers.

Use **Scientific** format to display very large or very small numbers. Very large and very small numbers usually have a few significant digits and many zeros as place holders to tell you how large or how small the number is.

A number in scientific notation has two parts; a mantissa and an exponent. The *mantissa* is a number from 1 to 10 that contains the significant digits. The *exponent* tells you how many places to move the decimal point to get the actual value of the number. You specify the number of decimal places from 0 to 15. If the number has more significant digits than the number you specify in the format, the number is rounded in the display.

1230000000000 displays as 1.23E+12 in **Scientific** format with 2 decimal places. E+12 signifies that you must move the decimal point 12 places to the right to get the actual number. 0.000000000237 displays as 2.4E-10 in Scientific format with 1 decimal place. E-10 means that you must move the decimal point 10 places to the left to get the actual number.

A number too large to display in a cell in **General** format automatically displays in scientific format.

(Sn) appears in the control panel of cells formatted with the **/Range Format Sci** command. n represents the number of decimal places.

Following are examples of **Scientific** format in cells that have a column width of 9:

Typed Entry	Cell Format	Display Result
1632116750000	(S2)	1.63E + 12
1632116750000	(S0)	2E + 12
− 1632116750000	(S1)	− 1.6E + 12
− 1632116750000	(S2)	********
.00000000012	(S2)	1.20E − 10
−.00000000012	(S0)	− 1E − 10

The + / − Format

The **+/−** format creates a horizontal bar graph based on the number in the cell. A positive number displays as a row of plus (+) signs; a negative number displays as a row of minus (−) signs; a zero displays as a period (.). The number of pluses or minuses can be no wider than the cell.

This format was originally devised to create imitation bar graphs in spreadsheets that had no graphing capability. The format has little practical use today.

(+) appears in the control panel of cells formatted with the **/Range Format +/−** command.

Following are several examples of **+/−** format in cells that have a column width of 9:

Typed Entry	Cell Format	Display Result
6	(+)	+ + + + + +
4.9	(+)	+ + + +
−3	(+)	− − −
0	(+)	.
17.2	(+)	********

Date and Time Formats

All the formats mentioned so far deal with regular numeric values. Use **Date** and **Time** formats when you deal with date and time calculations or time functions. These functions are covered in Chapter 6.

Choose the **/R**ange Format **D**ate or **/W**orksheet **G**lobal Format **D**ate commands to select from the five **Date** format options or to choose a **Time** format. Choose the **/R**ange Format **D**ate **T**ime or **/W**orksheet **G**lobal Format **Date Time** commands for the four **Time** format options.

Date Formats

When you use date functions, 1-2-3 stores the date as a serial number representing the number of days since December 31, 1899. The serial date number for January 1, 1900, is 1. The serial date number for January 15, 1990, is 32888. The latest date that 1-2-3 can handle is December 31, 2099, with a serial number of 73050. If the number is less than 0 or greater than 73050, a **Date** format displays as asterisks (*). **Date** formats ignore any fraction. 32888.99 with format **D4** (long international) displays as 01/15/90. The fraction represents the time, a fractional portion of a 24-hour clock.

Don't be concerned about which serial date number refers to which date. Let 1-2-3 format the serial date number to appear as a textual date.

Caution:
1-2-3 is one day off in serial-number calculations starting with March 1, 1900.

Actually, all the date serial numbers starting with March 1, 1900, are off by one day. The calendar inside 1-2-3 treats 1900 as a leap year, but it was not. A date serial number of 60 displays as 02/29/00—a date that does not exist. Unless you compare dates before February 28, 1900, to dates after February 28, 1900, this error has no effect on your worksheets. However, dates can be off by one day if you export data to a database.

Cue:
Change the default international date format with the /Worksheet Global Default Other International Date command.

When you choose the **/R**ange Format **D**ate command, the **Date** menu appears (see fig. 5.19). You can use the five **Date** formats listed in table 5.2 to format numbers to look like dates. Long International (**4**) and Short International (**5**) each have four different possible formats. The defaults are those that are most common in the United States. If you prefer one of the other international date formats, use **/W**orksheet **G**lobal **D**efault **O**ther International **D**ate and choose from formats A–D.

Fig. 5.19.
The Range
Format Date
menu.

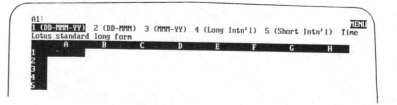

A1:
1 **(DD-MMM-YY)** 2 (DD-MMM) 3 (MMM-YY) 4 (Long Intn'l) 5 (Short Intn'l) Time ▮MENU
Lotus standard long form

Table 5.2
Date Formats

Menu Choice	Format	Description	Example
1	(D1)	Day-Month-Year DD-MMM-YY	01-Jan-90
2	(D2)	Day-Month DD-MMM	01-Jan
3	(D3)	Month-Year MMM-YY	Jan-90
4	(D4)	Long International *	
A		MM/DD/YY	01/15/90
B		DD/MM/YY	15/01/90
C		DD.MM.YY	15.01.90
D		YY-MM-DD	90-01-15
5	(D5)	Short International *	
A		MM/DD	01/15
B		DD/MM	15/01
C		DD.MM	15.01
D		MM-DD	01-15

* Use the **/W**orksheet **G**lobal **D**efault **O**ther International **D**ate command to select one of the international formats (A, B, C, or D).

(Dn) appears in the control panel of cells formatted with the **/R**ange **F**ormat **D**ate command. n represents the **D**ate format selection (1–5) in the Format Date menu.

Following are examples of **D**ate 4 format in cells that have a column width of 9:

Typed Entry	Cell Format	Display Result	Cell Contents
15	(D4)	01/15/00	15
32888	(D4)	01/15/90	32888
32888.4538	(D4)	01/15/90	32888.4538
– 32888	any date	*********	– 32888

You also enter dates into a worksheet using one of the date functions: @DATE, @DATEVALUE, or @NOW. You can find explanations of these functions in Chapter 6.

Time Formats

Reminder:
1-2-3 stores the time as a decimal fraction that represents the fraction of the 24-hour clock.

1-2-3 maintains times in a special format called time fractions. You then can format these time fractions so that they look like a time of day. When you enter a time function, 1-2-3 stores the time as a decimal fraction (from 0 to 1) that represents the fraction of the 24-hour clock. The time fraction for 3 a.m. is 0.125; the time fraction for noon is 0.5; and the time fraction for 6 p.m. is 0.75. You do not have to deal with the fractions—just let 1-2-3 display the fraction as a time.

When you choose the **/R**ange Format **D**ate **T**ime command, the **T**ime menu appears (see fig. 5.20). Use one of the four **T**ime formats, listed in table 5.3, to display fractions as times. Long International (**3**) and Short International (**4**) each have four different possible formats. The defaults are those most common in the United States. If you prefer one of the other international time formats, use the **/W**orksheet **G**lobal **D**efault **O**ther **I**nternational **T**ime command and choose from formats A–D.

Fig. 5.20.
The Range Format Date Time menu.

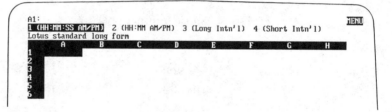

Table 5.3
Time Formats

Menu Choice	Format	Description	Example
1	(D6)	Hour:Minute:Second HH:MM:SS AM/PM	06:23:57 PM
2	(D7)	Hour:Minute HH:MM AM/PM	06:23 PM
3	(D8)	Long International *	
A		HH:MM:SS	18:23:57
B		HH.MM.SS	18.23.57
C		HH,MM,SS	18,23,57
D		HHhMMmSSs	18h23m57s
4	(D9)	Short International *	

Menu Choice	Format	Description	Example
A		HH:MM	18:23
B		HH.MM	18.23
C		HH,MM	18,23
D		HHhMMm	18h23m

* Use the **/W**orksheet **G**lobal **D**efault **O**ther International **T**ime command to select one of the international formats (A, B, C, or D).

If the number is greater than 1, **Time** formats ignore the integer portion. 32888.75 with format **D7** (**Time 2** or Lotus standard short form) displays as 06:00 PM. Negative numbers are not translated into time and are displayed as asterisks.

(Dn) appears in the control panel of cells formatted with the **/R**ange **F**ormat **D**ate **T**ime command. n represents the **Time** format selection (6–9). Note that 1-2-3 identifies **Time** formats in a confusing way. If you choose **Date Time 1**, 1-2-3 displays (D6) in the control panel, not (D1). **Date Time 2** displays as (D7), **Date Time 3** displays as (D8), and **Date Time 4** displays as (D9).

Following are several examples of **Time 2** format in cells that have a column width of 9:

Typed Entry	Cell Format	Display Result	Cell Contents
2	(D7)	12:00 AM	2
.25	(D7)	06:00 AM	0.25
−.25	(D7)	*********	−0.25

You also enter times into a worksheet using one of the time functions: @TIME, @TIMEVALUE, or @NOW. Explanations of these functions can be found in Chapter 6.

Text Format

Use the **Text** format to display in a cell both numeric and string formulas instead of their current value. Numbers formatted for **Text** display in the **General** format. If the formula is too long to display in the column width, it is truncated; the formula does not display across blank cells to the right like a long label.

All the entries in figure 5.21 are formatted as **Text**. The labels are unaffected. The numbers in B3..B5 display in **General** format. The formula B7 displays instead of the current value of the formula.

Fig. 5.21.
Samples of Text
format.

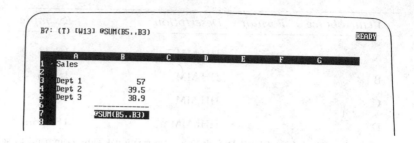

Cue:
*Use Text format to
enter and debug
complex formulas.*

One use of the **Text** format is for criteria ranges with **/Data Query** commands (covered in Chapter 12). You also can use **Text** format when you enter or debug complex formulas or to see formulas with **/Data Table**. You can change the format of a formula to **Text** temporarily so that you can see the formula in one cell while you build a similar formula in another cell. (You may need to widen the column temporarily while you do this.)

(T) appears in the control panel of cells formatted with **/Range Format Text**.

Hidden Format

A cell formatted as **Hidden** displays as blank no matter what the cell contains. Use this format for intermediate calculations you don't want to display or for sensitive formulas you want to hide. Using Release 2.2, if the cell is protected and global protection is enabled, the contents of a hidden cell do not display in the control panel when you move the cell pointer to that cell. In other cases, you can see the contents of the cell in the control panel. In Release 2.01, however, you can see the contents of the cell in the control panel even though the worksheet is protected. **Hidden** format is discussed in Chapter 4 also.

The worksheet in figure 5.22 has **/Worksheet Global Protection Enabled**. **/Range Prot** and **/Range Format Hidden** have been used on cell A1. The range C1..C5 is unprotected. The formula in C1 is +A1. This simple formula shows you the value of the hidden cell.

Caution:
*Don't rely on
Hidden formats to
hide sensitive
information.*

To determine the formula in A1, you need a macro. The {CONTENTS} macro in C3 puts the contents of A1 into C5 in **Text** format. The macro is named \a; press Alt-A to run the macro. See Chapter 13 for more about {CONTENTS}.

(H) appears in the control panel of cells formatted with the **/Range Format Hidden** command.

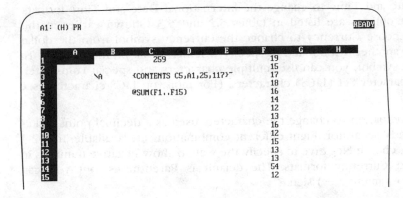

Fig. 5.22.
Using the
Hidden format.

International Formats

You can change some **D**ate and **T**ime formats and the characters 1-2-3 uses
for currency, the decimal point, and the thousands' separator. Because different countries have different formatting standards, these are called international formatting options. If you work with U.S. dollars in the United States,
you can keep the defaults and ignore these options. Or you can use the
/Worksheet **G**lobal **D**efault **O**ther **I**nternational command to access the
menu to change the defaults (see fig. 5.23). The menu for 1-2-3 Release 2.01
includes all choices shown except **N**egative. Also, a settings sheet is displayed in Release 2.2, but not in Release 2.01. Use the **/W**orksheet **G**lobal
Default **U**pdate command to make the change permanent.

RELEASE

2.2

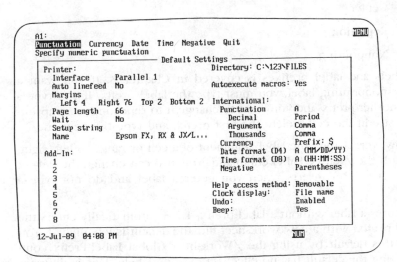

Fig. 5.23.
The Worksheet
Global Default
Other
International
menu for 1-2-3
Release 2.2.

Choose **D**ate and **T**ime to change the international **D**ate and **T**ime formats. The format options are listed in tables 5.2 and 5.3 (shown earlier in this chapter). Choose **C**urrency to change the currency symbol from the dollar sign ($) to another symbol and to specify whether it is a prefix or suffix. To change the symbol, you can use multiple characters and special Lotus International Character Set (LICS) characters. (For more on LICS characters, see Chapter 6.)

Choose **P**unctuation to change the characters used as a decimal point and as the thousands' separator. Eight different combinations are available. In 1-2-3 Release 2.2, choose **N**egative to specify the way to show negative numbers in comma and **C**urrency formats. The default is **P**arentheses, but you can change it to a minus (−) sign.

Changing Label Prefixes

Most formats apply to numeric data. Almost all numeric data formats have one thing in common: the numbers display right-aligned in the cell. With labels or text entries, however, you can align the text in different ways. Label alignment is based on the label prefix. The label prefixes include the following:

Prefix	Alignment
'	Left
"	Right
^	Center
\	Repeating
|	Nonprinting

Entering labels and label prefixes is covered in Chapter 3. If you want a repeating or nonprinting label, you must type the label prefix. If you type a label with another prefix and you want to change it to repeating or nonprinting, you must edit the cell, delete the first prefix, and type the new one.

You can, however, change the label alignment of a cell or range to left, right, or center with the **/R**ange **L**abel command. You also can change the default label prefix that 1-2-3 inserts when you enter a label and do not type a prefix.

Reminder:
When you enter a label without a label prefix, 1-2-3 automatically enters the default label prefix.

When you enter a label without a label prefix, 1-2-3 automatically enters the default label prefix. With a new worksheet file, the default is left-aligned. You can change this default by using the **/W**orksheet **G**lobal **L**abel-Prefix command. Changing the default has no effect on existing labels. This is different from the way 1-2-3 handles formats. When you change the global format, you change all cells that have not been range formatted. When you enter a label, 1-2-3 inserts a label prefix; the prefix does not change with the global default.

To change the label prefix of existing labels, use the **/R**ange Label command. Choose **Left**, **Right**, or **Center**; then specify the range. This method is usually faster than typing individual label prefixes as you enter labels.

Figure 5.24 shows left-aligned column headings that do not line up with the data. Figure 5.25 shows the headings after selecting the **/R**ange Label **Right** option. Right alignment starts one position from the extreme right. Right-aligned labels match the alignment of numeric data.

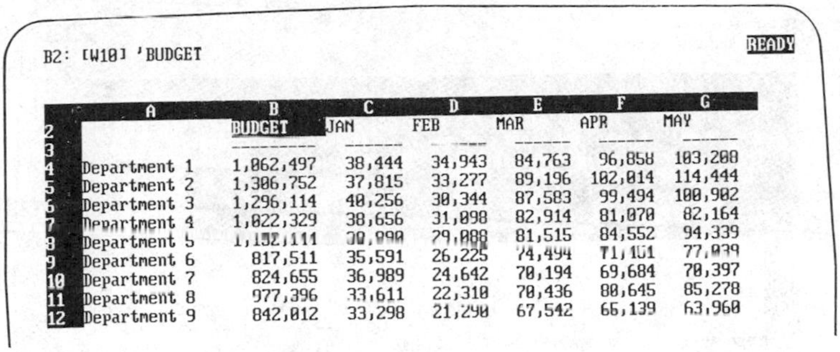

Fig. 5.24.
Left-aligned column headings that do not line up with numeric data.

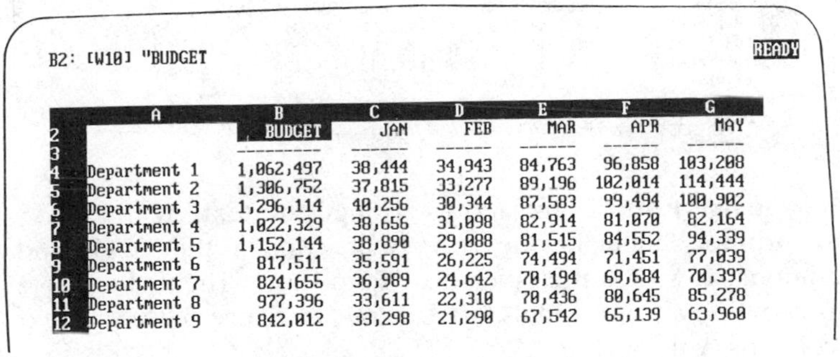

Fig. 5.25.
Using the /Range Label Right command to align headings.

Justifying Text

At times, you want to include in a worksheet several lines, or even a paragraph, that explain a table, graph, or report. 1-2-3 does not include word wrap like a word processor. Everything you type goes into one cell. You can use the **/R**ange Justify command to justify labels.

To justify labels, follow these steps:

1. Move the cell pointer to the first cell in the range of text.

2. Choose **/R**ange Justify.

3. Highlight the rows that contain labels; allow enough extra rows for the labels to expand into when they are justified.

4. Highlight the number of columns to show how wide each label can be.

You can perform Steps 3 and 4 in either order.

You can type one line of text into each cell, but entering and editing paragraphs in this way is slow and imprecise. You might get something like the ragged text shown in figure 5.26; some of the text is off the screen.

Fig. 5.26.
A column of long labels.

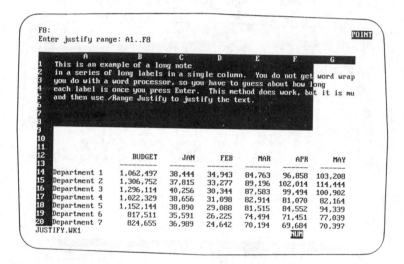

```
F8:
Enter justify range: A1..F8                                      POINT

          A          B          C         D         E         F        G
1    This is an example of a long note
2    in a series of long labels in a single column.  You do not get word wrap
3    you do with a word processor, so you have to guess about how long
4    each label is once you press Enter.  This method does work, but it is mu
5    and then use /Range Justify to justify the text.
6
7
8
9
10
11
12                    BUDGET     JAN       FEB       MAR       APR      MAY
13                    -------    -------   -------   -------   -------  -------
14   Department 1    1,062,497   38,444    34,943    84,763    96,858   103,208
15   Department 2    1,306,752   37,815    33,277    89,196   102,014   114,444
16   Department 3    1,296,114   40,256    30,344    87,583    99,494   100,902
17   Department 4    1,022,329   38,656    31,098    82,914    81,070    82,164
18   Department 5    1,152,144   38,890    29,088    81,515    84,552    94,339
19   Department 6      817,511   35,591    26,225    74,494    71,451    77,039
20   Department 7      824,655   36,989    24,642    70,194    69,684    70,397
JUSTIFY.WK1                                                    NUM
```

You can use the **/R**ange Justify command to arrange the text. At the Enter justify range: prompt, highlight the rows that contain the labels and include any additional rows for the labels to expand into. Highlight across the columns to show how wide each label can be. In figure 5.26, the text displays from columns A through F.

When you press Enter, 1-2-3 rearranges the text to fit the area you highlighted (see fig. 5.27). Labels are wrapped only at spaces. Where 1-2-3 breaks a label, it eliminates the space. Where 1-2-3 combines all or parts of two labels into one label, it adds a space.

Caution:
Don't use the
/Range Justify
command with a
one-row range if
data is present
below the labels.

If you add text in the middle, use the **/R**ange Justify command again to rejustify the text. If you specify a one-row range, 1-2-3 justifies the entire "paragraph." Figure 5.28 shows the data in figure 5.27 after you add text and then use the **/R**ange Justify command on the range A1..F1. This practice, however, is dangerous. 1-2-3 justifies the labels and uses as many rows as it needs, but it moves any data in column A down to make room. If fewer rows

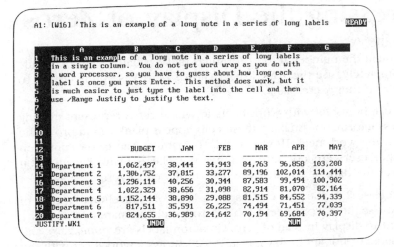

```
A1: [W16] 'This is an example of a long note in a series of long labels     READY

        A       B       C       D       E       F       G
1   This is an example of a long note in a series of long labels
2   in a single column.  You do not get word wrap as you do with
3   a word processor, so you have to guess about how long each
4   label is once you press Enter.  This method does work, but it
5   is much easier to just type the label into the cell and then
6   use /Range Justify to justify the text.
7
8
9
10
11
12              BUDGET    JAN     FEB     MAR     APR     MAY
13              --------  ------  ------  ------  -------  -------
14  Department 1  1,062,497  38,444  34,943  84,763   96,858  103,200
15  Department 2  1,306,752  37,815  33,277  89,196  102,014  114,444
16  Department 3  1,296,114  40,256  30,344  87,583   99,494  100,902
17  Department 4  1,022,329  38,656  31,098  82,914   81,070   82,164
18  Department 5  1,152,144  38,890  29,088  81,515   84,552   94,339
19  Department 6    817,511  35,591  26,225  74,494   71,451   77,039
20  Department 7    824,655  36,989  24,642  70,194   69,684   70,397
JUSTIFY.WK1        UNDO                              NUM
```

Fig. 5.27.
A series of long labels after executing a /Range Justify command.

```
A1: [W16] 'This is an example of some extra text that has been added to     READY

        A       B       C       D       E       F       G
1   This is an example of some extra text that has been added to
2   a long note in a series of long labels in a single column.
3   You do not get word wrap as you do with a word processor, so
4   you have to guess about how long each label is once you press
5   Enter.  This method does work, but it is much easier to just
6   type the label into the cell and then use /Range Justify to
7   justify the text.
8
9
10
11
12              BUDGET    JAN     FEB     MAR     APR     MAY
13              --------  ------  ------  ------  -------  -------
14              1,062,497  38,444  34,943  84,763   96,858  103,200
15  Department 1  1,306,752  37,815  33,277  89,196  102,014  114,444
16  Department 2  1,296,114  40,256  30,344  87,583   99,494  100,902
17  Department 3  1,022,329  38,656  31,098  82,914   81,070   82,164
18  Department 4  1,152,144  38,890  29,088  81,515   84,552   94,339
19  Department 5    817,511  35,591  26,225  74,494   71,451   77,039
20  Department 6    824,655  36,989  24,642  70,194   69,684   70,397
JUSTIFY.WK1        UNDO                              NUM
```

Fig. 5.28.
Using the /Range Justify command on one row.

are needed, it moves any data in column A up. In figure 5.28, the department numbers no longer line up with each department's data.

You cannot justify more than one column of labels at one time. When 1-2-3 reaches a blank or numeric cell in the first column, it stops. The labels must all be in the first column of the highlighted range. In figure 5.26, all the labels are in column A. Any labels in column B would be ignored.

Suppressing the Display of Zeros

You can use the /Worksheet Global Zero command to change the display of cells that contain the number zero or formulas that evaluate to zero. To hide the zeros completely, use the /Worksheet Global Zero Yes option. The zero cells display as if they were blank.

This feature can be useful with worksheets in which zeros represent missing or meaningless information. Making these cells appear blank can improve the appearance of the worksheet. However, this format also can cause confusion if you or other users are not sure whether the cell is blank because you forgot to enter the data or whether the cell results equal zero.

RELEASE

2.2

Cue:
You can type a label you want to display instead of zero—NA, for example.

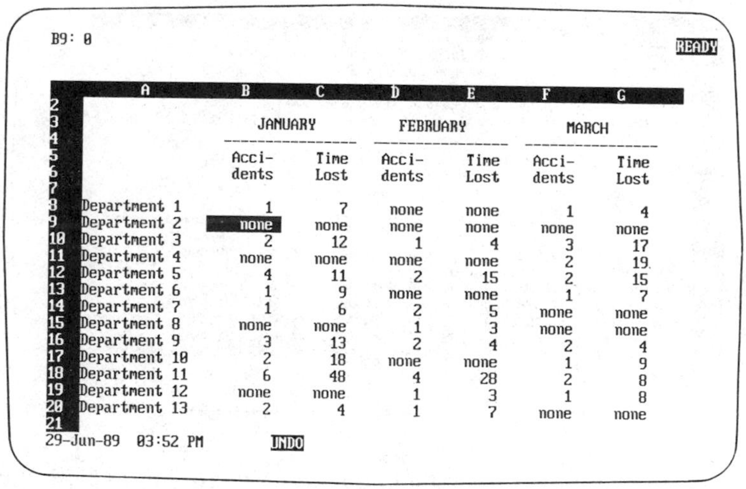

With 1-2-3 Release 2.2, you also can display a label of your choice instead of zero or blank. Use the /Worksheet Global Zero Label command and type the label you want to display instead of zero. Common labels are *none, zero,* and *NA* (not available or not applicable). Figure 5.29 shows a worksheet with the /Worksheet Global Zero Label option set to *none.* Use the /Worksheet Global Zero No option to cancel the option and display zeros as zeros.

Fig. 5.29.
A worksheet with zero values set to display as none.

```
B9: 0                                                              READY

           A          B        C        D        E        F        G
  2
  3                         JANUARY          FEBRUARY           MARCH
  4                     ----------------  ----------------  ----------------
  5                      Acci-    Time     Acci-    Time     Acci-    Time
  6                      dents    Lost     dents    Lost     dents    Lost
  7
  8   Department 1         1        7      none     none       1        4
  9   Department 2        none     none    none     none      none     none
 10   Department 3         2       12       1        4         3       17
 11   Department 4        none     none    none     none       2       19
 12   Department 5         4       11       2       15         2       15
 13   Department 6         1        9      none     none       1        7
 14   Department 7         1        6       2        5        none     none
 15   Department 8        none     none     1        3        none     none
 16   Department 9         3       13       2        4         2        4
 17   Department 10        2       18      none     none       1        9
 18   Department 11        6       48       4       28         2        8
 19   Department 12       none     none     1        3         1        8
 20   Department 13        2        4       1        7        none     none
 21
 29-Jun-89  03:52 PM           UNDO
```

Chapter Summary

In this chapter, you learned how to display numeric data in a variety of different formats, to display formulas as text, and to hide the contents of cells. Entering and formatting dates and times and changing the international date and time formats were discussed also. You learned how to change the alignment of labels and justify blocks of text.

You now can build and format worksheets. The next chapter extends your skills to perform data analysis. Chapter 6 covers the extensive library of functions you use to manipulate data beyond simple formulas, and opens up the vast analytical power of 1-2-3.

6

Using Functions
in the Worksheet

In addition to worksheet formulas you construct, you can take advantage of a variety of preconstructed formulas that 1-2-3 provides. These built-in formulas—called *functions*—are a welcome substitute to constructing your own formulas.

In total, 1-2-3 provides 92 functions that can be broken down roughly into seven categories:

- Mathematical
- Statistical
- Financial and accounting
- Logical
- Special
- Date and time
- String

The mathematical functions, which include logarithmic and trigonometric functions, should prove a necessity for engineering and scientific applications. These functions also provide convenient tools to perform a variety of standard arithmetic operations such as rounding values or calculating square roots.

A set of 7 statistical and 7 database statistical functions allow you to perform standard statistical calculations either on data in your worksheet or in a 1-2-3 database. (The database statistical functions are described in Chapter 12.)

The financial and accounting functions allow you to perform a series of discounted cash flow, depreciation, and compound interest calculations for investment analysis, and accounting or budgeting for depreciable assets.

The logical functions let you add standard Boolean logic to your worksheet and use the logic either alone or as part of other worksheet formulas. Each logical function allows you to test whether a condition is TRUE or FALSE.

1-2-3 also provides a set of special functions for dealing with the worksheet itself. For example, one special function returns information about specific cells. Others count the number of rows or columns in a range.

The date and time functions allow you to convert dates and times to serial numbers and then use these serial numbers to perform date and time arithmetic.

The final set of functions are string functions, which manipulate text. You can use string functions to repeat text characters, convert letters in a string to upper- or lowercase, and change strings into numbers and numbers into strings.

This chapter describes the steps for using 1-2-3 functions in general and then provides the steps for using specific functions. Each function description is accompanied by examples of its use.

How To Enter a 1-2-3 Function

Entering a 1-2-3 function is a three-step process:

1. Type the @ sign to tell 1-2-3 that you want to enter a function.

2. Type the function name.

3. Enter any information, or *arguments*, the function needs to make its calculations.

An example of a function is @AVG. If you enter the function @AVG(1,2,3), 1-2-3 returns the calculated result 2, which is the average of 1, 2, and 3.

Reminder:
All functions begin with—and are identified by—the @ character.

All functions begin with—and are identified by—the @ character. By typing @, you tell 1-2-3 you are entering a function.

With more than 90 functions, you probably will not be able to remember every name. Fortunately, 1-2-3 uses short, three-to-five character abbreviations for functions. These abbreviations allow you to identify and remember those you use most frequently. For example, the function name to calculate the internal rate of return is IRR, and the function name to round numbers is ROUND.

You enter a function's arguments inside parentheses that immediately follow the function's name. If the function has multiple arguments, you separate them with commas, semicolons, or periods. (Use **/W**orksheet **G**lobal **D**efault **O**ther **I**nternational **P**unctuation to change the default from commas to semicolons or periods.)

Functions provide an extremely powerful and timesaving set of tools. Suppose that you want to calculate the average sales of four salespersons: 10,000, 50,000, 60,000, and 80,000. If you remember that the function name to calculate an average is AVG, you easily can write the 1-2-3 function to make the calculation. To perform the calculation, enter the following:

@AVG(10000,50000,60000,80000)

1-2-3 returns the result, 50000, which is the average of the numbers entered as arguments. Notice that the function begins with the @ character, followed by the function name AVG. Also note that the function's arguments are included inside parentheses and separated by commas.

You also can use cell addresses and range names as arguments. For example, if you store the sales totals in worksheet cells B1, B2, B3, and B4, you can enter the function as the following:

@AVG(B1,B2,B3,B4)

Or, if you name each of the four cells that contain the sales amounts with the salesperson's first name, you could enter the function as this:

@AVG(Robert,Sarah,Emil,Maria)

A few functions don't require arguments, or inputs. Therefore, you don't need to use parentheses. For example, the function to return π is entered simply as

@PI

And the function to produce a random number is entered as

@RAND

Nevertheless, the first two steps—identify the function with an @ symbol and type the function's name—are the same for each of the 92 functions. In addition, you enter any required arguments inside parentheses. You will discover some variations when you use some of the functions. Those variations in particular functions are described in the text that follows.

Reminder:
A few of the functions don't require arguments.

Mathematical Functions

1-2-3 provides 17 mathematical functions that allow you to perform most of the common—and some specialized—mathematical operations. The operations you can perform include general, logarithmic, and trigonometric calculations.

General Mathematical Functions

1-2-3 offers six general mathematical functions. Table 6.1 lists these functions and provides brief descriptions of what they do. The text that follows provides the information you need to use these functions.

Table 6.1
General Mathematical Functions

Function	Description
@ABS(number or cell reference)	Computes the absolute value of the argument
@INT(number or cell reference)	Computes the integer portion of a specified number
@MOD(number,divisor)	Computes the remainder, or modulus, of a division operation
@RAND	Generates a random number
@ROUND(number or cell reference,precision)	Rounds a number to a specified precision
@SQRT(number or cell reference)	Computes the square root of a number

@ABS—Computing Absolute Value

The @ABS function calculates the absolute value of a number, using the following format:

@ABS(number or cell reference)

The function has one argument, which can be either a numeric value or a cell reference to a numeric value. @ABS converts a negative value into its equivalent positive value. @ABS has no effect on positive values. Some examples using @ABS are shown in figure 6.1.

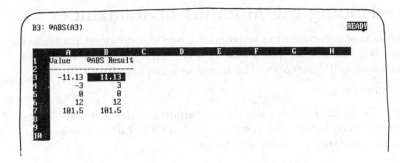

Fig. 6.1.
The results of using @ABS with positive and negative numbers.

@INT—Computing the Integer

The @INT function is used to convert a decimal number into an integer or whole number by truncating the decimal portion of a number. The function follows this format:

@INT(number or cell reference)

The function has one argument, which can be either a numerical value or a cell reference to a numerical value. The result of applying @INT to the value 3.1 yields an integer value of 3.

@INT is useful for computations where the decimal portion of a number is irrelevant or insignificant. Suppose that you have $1,000 to invest in XYZ company and that shares of XYZ sell for $17 each. You divide 1,000 by 17 to compute the number of shares you can purchase. Because you cannot purchase a fractional share, you can use @INT to truncate the decimal portion as shown in figure 6.2.

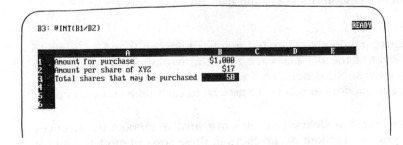

Fig. 6.2.
The @INT function used to calculate the number of shares that can be purchased.

@MOD—Finding the Modulus or Remainder

Cue:
The @MOD function computes the remainder when the dividend is divided by the divisor.

The @MOD function computes the remainder when the dividend is divided by the divisor. The function is called with two arguments that can be either numerical values or cell references. The function syntax of @MOD is

@MOD(number,divisor)

Because you can't divide by zero, the *divisor* argument needs to be something other than a zero value. The result of @MOD will be a value greater than or equal to zero, and less than the divisor.

Although you can use the @INT function to calculate the number of shares of XYZ, you also can use the @MOD function to make the same calculation, as shown in figure 6.3. Using @MOD, your result also determines the remainder or amount left over after the purchase.

Fig. 6.3.
The @MOD function used to return the remainder, or modulus, from a division.

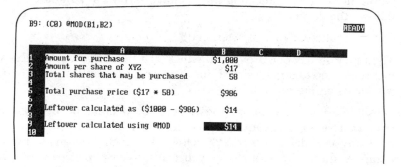

@RAND—Producing Random Numbers

@RAND generates random numbers and uses no arguments:

@RAND

@RAND returns a randomly generated number between 0 and 1, using 15 digits to the right of the decimal each time the worksheet is recalculated. Figure 6.4 shows @RAND generating 5 random numbers in cells A5 through A9. Note that new random numbers are generated each time you recalculate.

Reminder:
Use @RAND for modeling problems that involve random occurrences.

@RAND is helpful for modeling problems that involve random occurrences. Generally, to simulate random occurrences in these sorts of models, you use random numbers as model inputs.

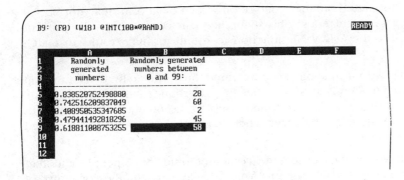

Fig. 6.4.
The @RAND
function used
to produce
random
numbers.

@ROUND—Rounding Numbers

The @ROUND function performs a rounding function using two arguments: the value you want to round, and the precision you want to use in the rounding. The function format of @ROUND is

@ROUND(number or cell reference,precision)

The *precision* argument determines the number of decimal places and can be a numeric value between −15 and + 15. You use positive precision values to specify places to the right of the decimal place and negative values to specify places to the left of the decimal. A precision value of 0 rounds decimal values to the nearest integer. Figure 6.5 demonstrates the use of @ROUND.

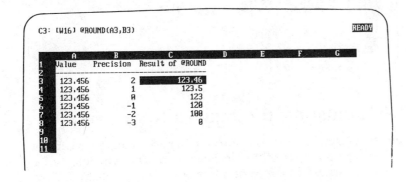

Fig. 6.5.
The @ROUND
function used
to round
values.

Note that the @ROUND function and the **/R**ange **F**ormat command perform differently. @ROUND actually changes the contents of a cell, where **/R**ange Format only alters how the cell's content is displayed.

In 1-2-3, the formatted number you see on-screen or in print may not be the number used in calculations. This difference can cause errors. To prevent such errors, use the @ROUND function to round formula results to match the display.

As you work with rounding, keep in mind how the @ROUND function works: if the number is less than 0.5, it gets rounded down to 0; if the number is 0.5 or more, it gets rounded up to 1. Sometimes, you want to round down to the nearest integer. Then again, at times, you want to round up to nearest integer.

Suppose that you need to schedule computer time for 9 people and that each person needs 1/4 of an hour. You calculate the number of hours of computer time to schedule as 1/4 times 9, or 2 1/4 hours of computer time. If you use the @ROUND function, 2 1/4 gets rounded down to 2. If you schedule only 2 hours, however, you end up being short by 1/4 hour. By scheduling 3 hours, you end up having 3/4 of an hour left over, but everybody gets the time they need. What you really want to do is round up.

If you need to round up to the nearest integer, you can do so by adding 0.5 to the number you need to round. Figure 6.6 illustrates this technique.

Fig. 6.6.
A result "rounded up" by adding 0.5 to the rounded number.

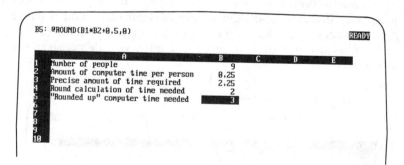

@SQRT—Calculating the Square Root

The @SQRT function calculates the square root of a positive number with an accuracy of 15 digits to the right of the decimal point. The function uses 1 argument, the number whose square root you want to find, and the following format:

@SQRT(value or cell reference)

The *value* squared must be a non-negative numeric value or a cell reference to such a value. If @SQRT is called with a negative value, the function returns ERR. Figure 6.7 shows examples of @SQRT. Note that the value of the displayed square root is calculated to 10 decimal places when the default

General format is used (and the width of the column is expanded to accommodate the number). If you want to display the value to 15 decimal places, you can change the format to **F15** and expand the width of the column to accommodate the number.

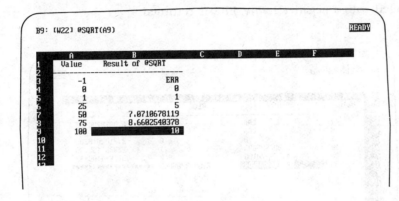

Fig. 6.7.
The @SQRT function used to find the square root of numbers.

Logarithmic Functions

1-2-3 has three logarithmic functions, described in table 6.2. Each function is called with one argument, which can be a numeric value or a cell reference to a numeric value. Figure 6.8 shows some examples.

Table 6.2
Logarithmic Functions

Function	Description
@EXP(value or cell reference)	Computes the number e raised to power of the argument
@LN(value or cell reference)	Calculates the natural logarithm of a specified number
@LOG(value or cell reference)	Calculates the common, or base 10, logarithm of a specified number

@EXP—Finding Powers of e

The @EXP function computes the power of e, using this format:

@EXP(value or cell reference)

With @EXP, you quickly can create large numbers. If the function's resulting value is too large to be displayed, asterisks are displayed instead.

@LN—Computing Natural Logarithms

The @LN function computes the natural, or base e, logarithm:

@LN(value or cell reference)

If @LN is called with a negative *value*, ERR is returned.

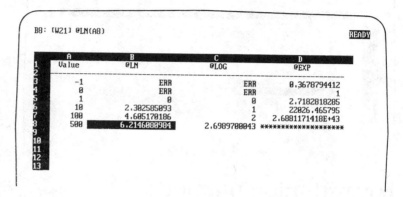

Fig. 6.8.
Examples of
1-2-3's
logarithmic
functions—
@LN, @LOG,
and @EXP.

@LOG—Computing Logarithms

The @LOG function computes the base 10 logarithm, using this format:

@LOG(value or cell reference)

If @LOG is called with a negative *value*, ERR is returned.

Trigonometric Functions

1-2-3 provides 8 trigonometric functions for engineering applications. All 8 functions have accuracy to 15 digits to the right of the decimal point. Table 6.3 lists the functions and their use.

Table 6.3
Trigonometric Functions

Function	Description
@PI	Calculates the value of π
@SIN(angle)	Calculates the sine given an angle in radians
@COS(angle)	Calculates the cosine given an angle in radians

Function	Description
@TAN(angle)	Calculates the tangent given an angle in radians
@ACOS(angle)	Calculates the arccosine given an angle in radians
@ASIN(angle)	Calculates the arcsine given an angle in radians
@ATAN(angle)	Calculates the arctangent given an angle in radians
@ATAN2(number1,number2)	Calculates the four-quadrant arctangent

@PI—Computing Pi

The @PI function computes the value of π. The function is called with no arguments:

Reminder:
@PI returns
the value
3.141592653589794.

@PI

@PI returns the value 3.141592653589794. You use @PI in calculating the area of circles and the volume of spheres. In addition, @PI is needed to convert from angle measurements in degrees to angle measurements in radians. Because 2*π radians are in 360 degrees, you can multiply the number of degrees by (2*π)/360, and the result represents radians as shown in figure 6.9.

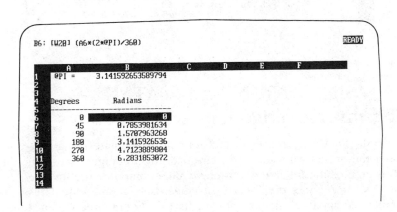

Fig. 6.9.
The @PI
function used
to convert
angles from
degrees to
radians.

@COS, @SIN, and @TAN—Computing Trigonometric Functions

The @COS, @SIN, and @TAN functions calculate the cosine, sine, and tangent, respectively, for an angle. Each function is called with one argument —an angle calibrated in radians.

@COS(angle in radians)

@SIN(angle in radians)

@TAN(angle in radians)

Cue:
Convert angle measurements into radians before using @COS, @SIN, and @TAN.

Be sure to convert angle measurements into radians before using these functions.

Figure 6.10 illustrates these three functions. Notice that in cells C5, C9, D7, and D11, the numbers returned are small, but not exactly zero, which they should be. This causes large numbers to be displayed in cells E5 and E9, which should be showing ERR (division by zero), and small numbers in cells E7 and E11, which should also be zero. These errors occur because of problems with 1-2-3's floating point driver. Keep this in mind when using these functions.

Fig. 6.10.
Examples of the @COS, @SIN, and @TAN functions.

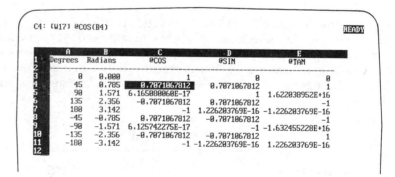

@ACOS, @ASIN, @ATAN, and @ATAN2— Computing Inverse Trigonometric Functions

The @ACOS, @ASIN, @ATAN, and @ATAN2 functions calculate the arccosine, the arcsine, the arctangent, and the four-quadrant arctangent, respectively. @ACOS computes the inverse of cosine; @ASIN computes the inverse of sine; and @ATAN computes the inverse of tangent. @ATAN2 calculates the four-quadrant arctangent using the ratio of its two arguments. Given a number, the @ASIN function calculates a radian angle that would produce that number from the @SIN function.

Both @ACOS and @ASIN are called with one argument:

@ACOS(value or cell reference)

@ASIN(value or cell reference)

Because all cosine and sine values lie between −1 and 1, you can use @ACOS and @ASIN only with values between −1 and 1. Each function returns ERR if you use a value outside this range. @ASIN returns angles between −π/2 and +π/2, while @ACOS returns angles between 0 and π/2. Figure 6.11 shows examples of the @ACOS, @ASIN, and @ATAN functions.

Reminder:
Because all cosine and sine values lie between −1 and 1, @ACOS and @ASIN can be called only with values between −1 and 1.

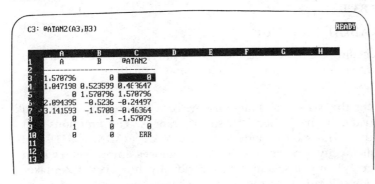

Fig. 6.11.
Examples of the @ACOS, @ASIN, and @ATAN functions.

For the @ATAN function, you again use one argument. You can call @ATAN with any number; this function returns a value between −π/2 and +π/2. The format of the @ATAN function is

@ATAN(value or cell reference)

@ATAN2 computes the angle whose tangent is specified by the ratio number2/number1, the two arguments. At least one of the arguments must be other than zero. @ATAN2 returns angles between −π and +π. The format of the @ATAN2 function is

@ATAN2(number1,number2)

Figure 6.12 gives examples of the @ATAN2 function.

Fig. 6.12.
Examples of the @ATAN2 function.

Statistical Functions

1-2-3 provides 7 statistical functions. (Additional statistical functions, specifically for databases, are described in Chapter 12.) Table 6.4 lists the functions, their arguments, and the statistical operations they perform.

Table 6.4
Statistical Functions

Function	Description
@AVG(list)	Calculates the arithmetic mean of a list of values
@COUNT(list)	Counts the number of cells that contain entries
@MAX(list)	Returns the maximum value in a list of values
@MIN(list)	Returns the minimum value in a list of values
@STD(list)	Calculates the population standard deviation of a list of values
@SUM(list)	Sums a list of values
@VAR(list)	Calculates the population variance of a list of values

Reminder:
Every statistical function uses the argument list.

Each of the statistical functions uses the argument *list*. List can be either individually specified values or cell addresses, a range of cells, or multiple ranges of cells. For example, each of the following formats (or any combination) works:

@SUM(1,2,3,4)

@SUM(B1,B2,B3,B4)

@SUM(B1..B4)

@SUM(B1..B2,B3..B4)

@SUM(A1,A3..A10,B11,C13..C20)

Although the preceding examples use the @SUM function (which totals the values included as arguments), the principles apply equally to each of the statistical functions.

Note that some of the statistical functions perform differently when you specify cells individually than when you specify ranges. The functions that perform differently in this case include @AVG, @MAX, @MIN, @STD, and @VAR. When you specify a range of cells, 1-2-3 ignores empty cells within the specified range. When you specify cells individually, however, 1-2-3 takes empty cells into consideration for the particular functions mentioned.

Suppose that, for example, you are looking for the minimum value in a range that includes an empty cell and cells that contain the entries 1, 2, and 3. In this case, 1-2-3 returns the value 1 as the minimum value. Suppose, however, that you instead specify individually a cell that is empty along with cells containing the entries 1, 2, and 3. In this case, 1-2-3 returns the value 0 as the minimum.

The reason is that empty cells actually contain invisible zeros. Accordingly, 1-2-3 assumes that if you specify an individual cell—even if it is empty—you must want it included in the statistical calculation.

When you specify cells, keep in mind also that 1-2-3 treats cells holding labels as zeros. This is the case both when you include the cell as part of a range and when you specify the cell individually.

@AVG—Computing the Arithmetic Mean

To calculate the average of a set of values, you add all the values and then divide the sum by the number of values. You will find the @AVG function a helpful tool for calculating the arithmetic mean—a commonly used measure of a set of values' average. Use the following format with the @AVG function.

@AVG(list)

As noted earlier, the *list* argument can be values, cell addresses, cell names, cell ranges, range names, or combinations of these.

Figure 6.13 shows the @AVG function argument as B3..B11. As long as cells B8 and B9 are empty and are included in the list argument only as part of a range, the values of these cells—actually zero—are ignored in the average calculation.

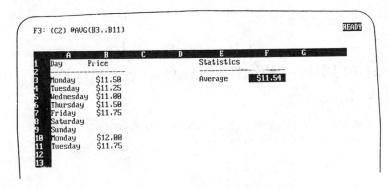

Fig. 6.13.
The @AVG
function used
to calculate the
mean price per
share.

@COUNT—Counting Cell Entries

The @COUNT function totals the number of cells that contain entries using the following format:

@COUNT(list)

The *list* argument can be values, cell addresses, cell names, cell ranges, range names, or combinations of these.

For example, you could use the @COUNT function to show the number of share prices included in the @AVG calculation made in figure 6.13. Figure 6.14 shows this calculation made in cell F4.

You should include only ranges as the arguments in the @COUNT function. If you specify a cell individually, 1-2-3 counts that cell as if it had an entry even if the cell is empty. If you must specify a cell individually, but want it counted only if it actually contains an entry, you need to use the @@ function described later in this chapter.

Fig. 6.14.
The @COUNT function used to calculate the number of prices per share in the average calculation.

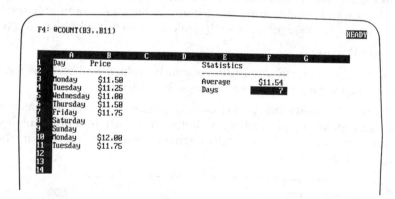

@MAX and @MIN—Finding Maximum and Minimum Values

The @MAX function finds the largest value included in your list argument, while the @MIN function finds the smallest value. The formats for these functions are as follows:

@MAX(list)

@MIN(list)

Figure 6.15 shows information concerning prices per share of an imaginary company. Using the @MAX and @MIN functions can help you easily find the lowest and the highest prices, respectively. You can see the argument of the @MAX function in the control panel as B3..B11. Although the example shows only seven values, the true power of these functions is most evident when your *list* consists of several dozen or several hundred items.

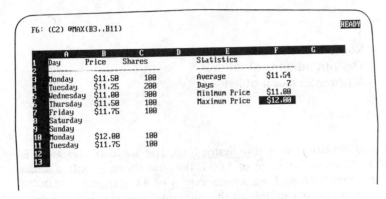

Fig. 6.15.
The @MIN and @MAX functions used to show low and high prices per share.

If you are familiar with statistics, you recognize that these two functions also provide the two pieces of data you need to calculate a range. A range, which is one measure of variability in a list of values, is the difference between the highest value and the lowest value in a list of values. (This is not the same as a worksheet range, which is a rectangular block of cells.)

@STD—Calculating the Standard Deviation

The @STD function calculates the standard deviation of a population. The format for the @STD function is as follows:

@STD(list)

The standard deviation is a measure of dispersion about or around an average. A smaller standard deviation indicates less dispersion, while a larger standard deviation indicates greater dispersion. A standard deviation of 0 indicates that there is no dispersion—meaning that every value in the list of values is the same.

The precise definition of the standard deviation formula is best shown by the formula 1-2-3 uses to calculate it. This formula is

$$STD = \sqrt{\frac{\displaystyle\sum_{n=1}^{N} (X_n - avg)^2}{N}}$$

where

N = Number of items in list
X_n = The *n*th item in list
avg = Arithmetic mean of list

Notice the standard deviation shown in figure 6.16. The standard deviation is small, only 0.3113 from the average of 11.54, because there is only a small variation from the minimum and maximum values of $11.00 and $12.00. If the values were greater—for example, if the minimum and maximum values were $110.00 and $120.00—the standard deviation would be larger. In this case, the deviation would be 3.113.

Fig. 6.16.
The @STD
function used
to calculate
standard
deviation.

```
F7: (F4) @STD(B3..B11)                                          READY

        A         B        C      D        E            F        G
   1  Day        Price    Shares         Statistics
   2
   3  Monday     $11.50     100          Average       $11.54
   4  Tuesday    $11.25     200          Days               7
   5  Wednesday  $11.00     300          Minimum Price $11.00
   6  Thursday   $11.50     100          Maximum Price $12.00
   7  Friday     $11.75     100          Std.Deviation  0.3113
   8  Saturday
   9  Sunday
  10  Monday     $12.00     100
  11  Tuesday    $11.75     100
  12                       ------
  13  Total Shares          1000
  14
  15
```

@SUM—Totaling Values

The @SUM function provides a convenient way to add a list of values that you specify as the *list* argument in the following format:

@SUM(list)

Further extending the stock price data example, assume that you have purchased the shares recorded in column C, as shown in figure 6.17. You could create a formula that adds these values with this calculation:

+C3+C4+C5+C6+C7+C10+C11

Or you could use @SUM(C2..C12) as shown in the control panel in figure 6.17.

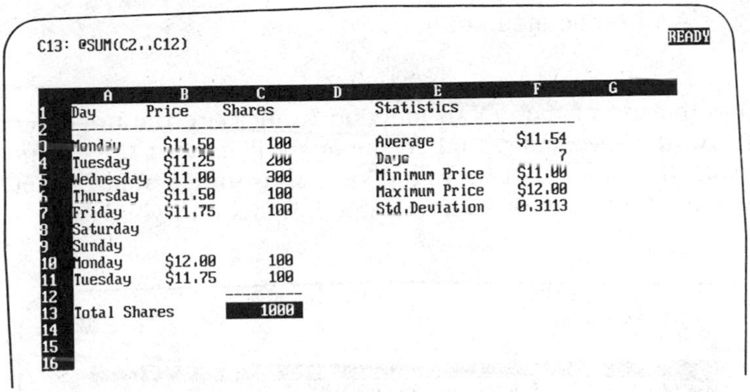

```
C13: @SUM(C2..C12)                                            READY

         A        B       C       D        E            F         G
   1  Day      Price   Shares             Statistics
   2
   3  Monday   $11.50    100              Average       $11.54
   4  Tuesday  $11.25    200              Days             7
   5  Wednesday $11.00   300              Minimum Price $11.00
   6  Thursday $11.50    100              Maximum Price $12.00
   7  Friday   $11.75    100              Std.Deviation  0.3113
   8  Saturday
   9  Sunday
  10  Monday   $12.00    100
  11  Tuesday  $11.75    100
  12
  13  Total Shares      1000
  14
  15
  16
```

Fig. 6.17.
The @SUM function used to calculate the total shares purchased.

Of all the statistical functions, @SUM is the one you probably will use most because it provides a shorthand way of constructing formulas. Because labels are included in statistical functions as zeros, you should include a cell at both ends of ranges you are summing with the @SUM function. That way, if rows or columns are inserted in the range, the range included as the function's list argument expands as part of the insertion. For instance, if you insert a row at rows 3 and 11 in the example, the list argument included in the @SUM function expands to become @SUM(C2..C14). If you do not include text placeholders at either end of an @SUM range, you might accidentally insert a value that appears to be in the total, when it is not.

@VAR—Calculating the Variance

The variance, like the standard deviation, is a measure of dispersion about, or around, an average. The @VAR function calculates the variance of a population. The format for the @VAR function is

@VAR(list)

Actually, calculating a statistical variance is an intermediate step in calculating the standard deviation described in the discussion of the @STD function. By comparing the two formulas that follow, you can see that the standard deviation is simply the square root of the variance.

$$VAR = \frac{\sum_{n=1}^{N} (X_n - avg)^2}{N}$$

where

N = Number of items in list
X_n = The nth item in list
avg = Arithmetic mean of list

Figure 6.18 shows the use of the @VAR function to measure the price per share variability over the specified period. As the figure illustrates, the @VAR function, along with the other statistical functions, constitute a valuable set of analytical tools that often will provide valuable insights into your data.

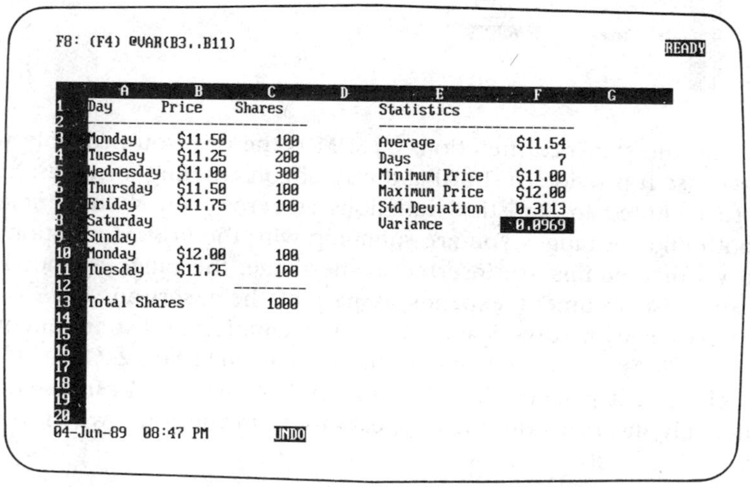

Fig. 6.18.
The @VAR
function used
to calculate
variance.

```
F8: (F4) @VAR(B3..B11)                                              READY

      A          B         C        D         E             F         G
1  Day        Price     Shares              Statistics
2  ---------------------------------       ------------------------------
3  Monday     $11.50      100              Average         $11.54
4  Tuesday    $11.25      200              Days                 7
5  Wednesday  $11.00      300              Mininum Price   $11.00
6  Thursday   $11.50      100              Maximum Price   $12.00
7  Friday     $11.75      100              Std.Deviation    0.3113
8  Saturday                                Variance         0.0969
9  Sunday
10 Monday     $12.00      100
11 Tuesday    $11.75      100
12                      ---------
13 Total Shares         1000
14
15
16
17
18
19
20
04-Jun-89  08:47 PM        UNDO
```

Financial and Accounting Functions

Release 2.2 of 1-2-3 provides 11 financial and accounting functions that perform discounted cash flow, loan amortization, and asset depreciation calculations. Table 6.5 summarizes the financial and accounting functions available with 1-2-3 Release 2.2.

Table 6.5
Financial and Accounting Functions

Investment Function	Description
@IRR(guess,cashflows)	Calculates the internal rate of return on an investment
@RATE(future value, present value,term)	Calculates the return on an investment given the present value and the future value
@PMT(principal, interest,term)	Calculates the loan payment amount
@NPV(interest, cashflows)	Calculates the present value of a stream of periodic cash flows—even if the cash flows are not even
@PV(payment,interest, term)	Calculates the present value of a stream of periodic cash flows if the cash flows are even
@FV(payment,interest, term)	Calculates the future value of a stream of periodic cash flows
@TERM(payment,interest, future value)	Calculates the number of times a loan payment is made
@CTERM(interest,future value,present value)	Calculates the number of periods for present value to grow to future value

Table 6.5—*continued*

Depreciation Function	Description
@SLN(cost,salvage,life)	Calculates straight-line depreciation
@DDB(cost,salvage, life,period)	Calculates 200% declining balance depreciation
@SYD(cost,salvage, life,period)	Calculates sum-of-the-years'-digits depreciation

@IRR—Internal Rate of Return

The @IRR function measures the percentage return on an investment. The format for the @IRR function is as follows:

@IRR(guess,cashflows)

Cue:
The guess argument should be a percent between 0 and 1.

The *guess* argument typically should be a percent between 0 and 1, and the first cash flow must be a negative amount. 1-2-3 uses the guess argument as the interest rate in the following formula and tests whether the result equals 0:

$$0 = \sum_{n=0}^{N} \frac{C_n}{(1+IRR)^n}$$

where C_n = Cash flow at *n*th period

If the result does not equal 0, 1-2-3 tries different interest rates in an attempt to make the equation TRUE—that is, the left side of the equation, 0, equals the right side of the equation. (Notice that the right side of the equation is the formula for calculating the profit measure called the net present value.) 1-2-3 attempts to converge to a correct interest, or discount rate, with .0000001 precision within 20 attempts or iterations. If the program cannot do so, the @IRR function returns an ERR value.

You may need to try several guesses to get one that's close enough for 1-2-3 to converge on the correct internal rate of return. Because the @IRR function finds an internal rate of return below the initial guess easier than one above the initial guess, guessing high is the best practice.

Figure 6.19 illustrates the @IRR function calculating the internal rate of return on a certificate of deposit. The purchase amount, a negative cash flow, is made at time 0. Other cash flows occur at the end of equally spaced periods. Notice that the monthly internal rate of return is converted to an annual rate by multiplying the monthly amount by 12.

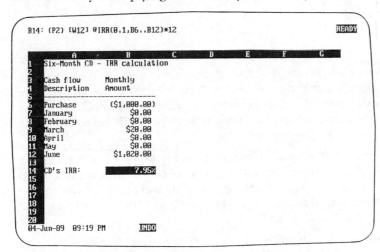

B14: (P2) [W12] @IRR(0.1,B6..B12)*12   READY

	A	B	C	D	E	F	G
1	Six-Month CD - IRR calculation						
2							
3	Cash flow	Monthly					
4	Description	Amount					
5							
6	Purchase	($1,000.00)					
7	January	$0.00					
8	February	$0.00					
9	March	$20.00					
10	April	$0.00					
11	May	$0.00					
12	June	$1,020.00					
13							
14	CD's IRR:	7.95%					

04-Jun-89   09:19 PM   UNDO

Fig. 6.19.
The internal rate of return calculated with the @IRR function.

Although the internal rate of return profit measure is widely used, you should be aware that the formula is currently being disputed. Note that the problem is with the internal rate of return formula itself, not with the @IRR function, which simply makes using the formula easier.

One problem is evident when you use the internal rate of return measure on an investment that has multiple internal rates of return. In theory, for example, the formula for calculating the internal rate of return for an investment with cash flows over 10 years is a 10th root polynomial equation with up to 10 correct solutions. In practice, an investment will have as many correct internal rates of return as there are sign changes in the cash flows.

Cue:
An investment may have multiple internal rates of return.

A sign change occurs when the previous period's cash flow is a negative amount while the current period's is a positive amount—or vice versa. Accordingly, even if you get the @IRR function to return an internal rate of return with your first guess, try other guesses to see that there's not another correct internal rate of return answer; you probably don't want to use the measure when it delivers multiple solutions. Figure 6.20 shows two mathematically correct internal rates of return being calculated based on the same set of cash flows shown.

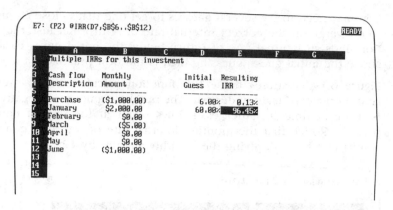

Fig. 6.20.
The @IRR
function
returning two
correct
solutions.

A second problem with the internal rate of return measure relates to ranking investments by their internal rates of return. Remember that the internal rate of return measure calculates the percentage profit per period. Typically, however, you are interested in the actual dollars of profit rather than the percentage.

Using the @IRR function measure blindly, for example, you might pick a $1 investment delivering a 50-percent internal rate of return over a $1,000,000 investment delivering a 49-percent return; and you might pick a $100 investment that delivers 25 percent for 1 year over a $100 investment that delivers 24.5 percent for 25 years.

In both of these examples, the internal rate of return possibly may direct you to the correct course of action. However, if you focus exclusively on the internal rate of return percentage, you may miss the better investment opportunity. Again, this isn't the fault of the 1-2-3 function @IRR, but rather a result of the internal rate of return formula itself.

@RATE—Compound Growth Rate

Reminder:
@RATE calculates the compound growth rate for an initial investment that grows to a future value over a number of periods.

The @RATE function calculates the compound growth rate for an initial investment that grows to a specified future value over a specified number of periods. The *rate* is the periodic interest rate and not necessarily an annual rate. The format of the @RATE function, where *term* equals the number of periods, is as follows:

@RATE(future value,present value,term)

This function's basic formula calculates the future value of an initial investment given the interest rate and the number of periods. For the @RATE calculation, the formula is rearranged to compute the interest rate in terms of the initial investment, the future value, and the number of periods.

Interest rate = (future value/present value)$^{1/term}$ − 1

You could use the @RATE function, for example, to determine the yield of a zero-coupon bond that is sold at a discount from its face value. Suppose that for $350 you can purchase a zero-coupon bond with a $1,000 face value, maturing in 10 years. The implied annual interest rate, shown in figure 6.21, is 11.07 percent.

Cue:
Use the @RATE function to determine the yield of a zero-coupon bond.

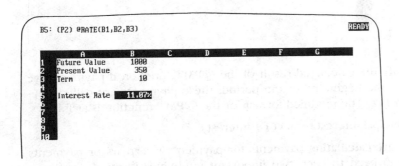

Fig. 6.21.
The @RATE function used to calculate the zero-coupon bond yield.

The @RATE function is also useful in forecasting applications to calculate the compound growth rate between current and projected future revenues, earnings, and so on.

@PMT—Loan Payment Amounts

You can use the @PMT function to calculate the periodic payments necessary to pay the entire principal on an amortizing loan. All you need to know is the loan amount (or the principal, periodic interest rate, and term) or the number of payment periods. You enter three arguments with the @PMT function:

@PMT(principal,interest,term)

The @PMT function assumes that payments are to be made at the end of each period; these payments are called *payments in arrears*. The function uses the following formula to make the payment calculation:

$$PMT = principal * \frac{interest}{1-(1+interest)^{-n}}$$

where n = Number of payments

Figure 6.22 shows the @PMT function being used to calculate the monthly payment on a $12,000 car loan. The loan is repaid over 60 months and accrues interest at the monthly rate of 1 percent.

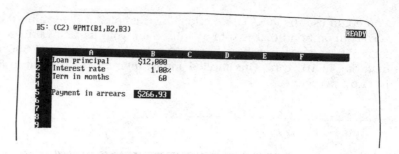

Fig. 6.22.
The @PMT
function used
to calculate
loan payments.

You can modify the calculated result of the @PMT function if payments are to be made at the beginning of the period; these payments are called *payments in advance*. The modified format for the @PMT function is as follows:

@PMT(principal,interest,term)/(1 + interest)

Whether you are calculating payments for payments in arrears or payments in advance, you need to keep two important guidelines in mind. First, you calibrate the interest rate as the rate per payment period. Second, you express the loan term in payment periods. Accordingly, if you make monthly payments, you should enter the interest rate as the monthly interest rate and the term as the number of months you will be making payments.

@NPV—Net Present Value

Cue:
The @NPV
function closely
resembles the
@PV function.

The @NPV function closely resembles the @PV function except that @NPV can calculate the present value of a varying, or changing, stream of cash flows. The format of the @NPV function is

@NPV(interest,cashflows)

The function calculates the following formula:

$$NPV = \sum_{n=1}^{N} \frac{C_n}{(1+i)^n}$$

where
C_n = Cash flow at *n*th period
i = Discount rate

Figure 6.23 shows how you can use the @NPV function to calculate the present value of a stream of varying cash flows.

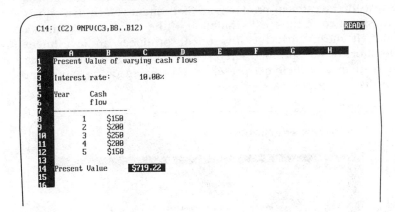

```
C14: (C2) @NPV(C3,B8..B12)                                    READY

      A        B         C         D     E     F     G     H
1  Present Value of varying cash flows
2
3  Interest rate:      10.00%
4
5  Year     Cash
6           flow
7  ----------------------------
8      1     $150
9      2     $200
10     3     $250
11     4     $200
12     5     $150
13
14 Present Value       $719.22
15
16
```

Fig. 6.23.
The @NPV function used to calculate the present value of varying cash flows.

Note that what 1-2-3 labels as the net present value function is not what accountants and financial analysts define as the *net present value profit measure*. 1-2-3's @NPV assumes that the first cash flow occurs at the end of the first period; therefore, the function actually is only a flexible present value function. In any situation where you might use the @PV function, therefore, you also can use the @NPV function to obtain the same result.

Accountants and financial analysts use the term *net present value* to refer to a measure of an investment's profitability using the following formula:

$$NPV = \sum_{n=0}^{N} \frac{C_n}{(1+i)^n}$$

where

C_n = Cash flow at *n*th period
i = Discount rate

To calculate the actual profitability measure called *net present value*, you need to subtract the initial investment from the results of the @NPV function. When you construct a formula using the @NPV function this way, you are testing whether the investment meets, beats, or falls short of the interest rate specified in the @NPV function.

Cue:
To calculate the actual profitability measure called net present value, subtract the initial investment.

If the calculated result of the preceding formula is a positive amount, it means that the investment produces an investment return that beats the interest rate specified in the @NPV function. If the calculated result equals zero, it means that the investment produces an investment return that equals the interest rate specified in the @NPV function. If the calculated result is a negative amount, it means that the investment produces an investment return that falls short of the specified interest rate. Figure 6.24 shows three investment alternatives and their net present values based on a 10-percent interest rate, or discount rate.

Fig. 6.24.
The @NPV
function used
to calculate the
net present
value profit
measure.

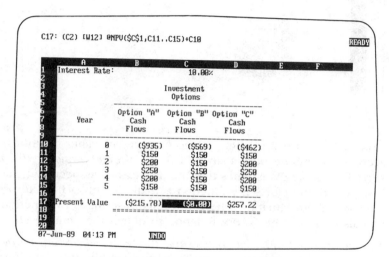

@PV—Present Value of an Annuity

The @PV function closely resembles the @NPV function in that @PV calculates the present value of a stream of cash flows. The difference is that the @PV function calculates the present value of a stream of equal cash flows occurring at the end of the period. This stream of equal cash flows is called an *ordinary annuity*, or payments in arrears. The @PV function uses the following format:

@PV(payments,interest,term)

The formula used in the function is

$$PV = payment * \frac{1-(1+interest)^{-term}}{interest}$$

Figure 6.25 shows the result of using the @PV function to calculate the present value of ten $1,000 payments.

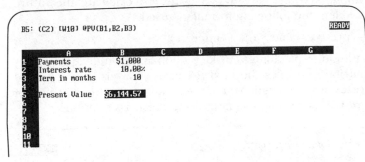

Fig. 6.25.
The @PV
function used
to calculate the
present value
of ten $1,000
payments.

Keep in mind that the @PV function assumes that the equal-amount cash flows, or payments, occur at the end of the period. If the cash flows occur at the beginning of the period—called an *annuity due* or *payments in advance*, use the following variation of the function:

@PV(payments,interest,term)*(1 + interest)

@FV—Future Value

The @FV function calculates to what amount a stated amount will grow based on a specified interest rate and number of years. The function is helpful for estimating the future balances into which current savings and investments will grow. The @FV function uses the following format:

@FV(payment,interest,term)

And the function uses the following formula:

$$\text{Future value} = \text{payment} * \frac{(1 + \text{interest})^{\text{term}} - 1}{\text{interest}}$$

You might, for example, use the future value function to calculate the estimated value of your individual retirement account 25 years from now. Figure 6.26 shows such a calculation assuming annual contributions of $2,000 and annual interest rates of 9 percent.

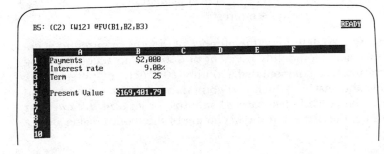

Fig. 6.26.
The @FV
function used
to calculate a
future IRA
balance.

In addition to calculating the future value of a stream of periodic cash flow payments (using the @FV function), you also may want to calculate the future value of amounts you've already set aside. To calculate the future value of a present value, the following formula is used:

Future value = present value * (1 + interest)^{term}

Suppose that in addition to planning to make $2,000 annual individual retirement account contributions over the next 25 years, you also have $5,000 dollars you've already accumulated. You want to know the future value of this amount. Figure 6.27 shows an example using these assumptions.

Fig. 6.27.
A formula used to calculate the future value of a present value amount.

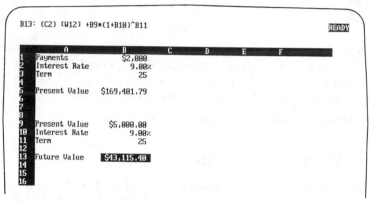

@TERM—Term of an Investment

The @TERM function calculates the number of periods required to accumulate a specified future value by making equal payments into an interest-bearing account at the end of each period. The format of the @TERM function is as follows:

@TERM(payment,interest,future value)

Reminder:
The @TERM function finds the number of periods required to reach the given future value.

The @TERM function is similar to the @FV function except that instead of finding the future value of a stream of payments over a specified period, the @TERM function finds the number of periods required to reach the given future value. The equation for calculating the number of periods is

$$\text{Term} = \frac{@\text{LN}(1 + (\text{interest*future value})/\text{payment})}{@\text{LN}(1 + \text{interest})}$$

Suppose that you want to determine the number of months required to accumulate $5,000 by making a monthly payment of $50 into an account paying 6 percent annual interest compounded monthly (0.5 percent per month). Figure 6.28 shows the answer, which is slightly more than 81 months for an *ordinary annuity*, but slightly less than 81 months for an *annuity due*. For this account, making the deposit at the beginning of the month makes only a little difference.

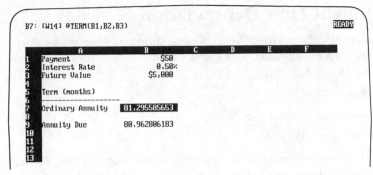

Fig. 6.28.
The @TERM function used to calculate the number of months to reach a specified future value.

To calculate the term for an annuity due, use the following equation:

Term for an annuity due = @TERM(payment,interest,future value/(1 + interest))

@CTERM—Compound Term of an Investment

The @CTERM function calculates the number of periods required for an initial investment earning a specified interest rate to grow to a specified future value. While the @TERM function calculates the number of periods needed for a series of payments to grow to a future value at a specified interest rate, the @CTERM function calculates the required number of periods based on the specified present value, future value, and interest rate. The format of the @CTERM function is as follows:

@CTERM(interest,future value,present value)

This equation is used to calculate @CTERM:

$$\text{Term} = \frac{\text{@LN(future value/present value)}}{\text{@LN(1 + interest)}}$$

The @CTERM function is useful for determining the term of an investment necessary to achieve a specific future value. Suppose that you want to determine how many years it will take for $2,000 invested in an IRA account at 10 percent interest to grow to $10,000. Figure 6.29 shows how to use the @CTERM function to determine the answer (just over 16 years and 10 months).

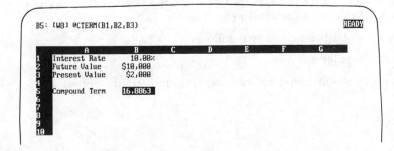

Fig. 6.29.
The @CTERM function used to calculate the number of years for $2,000 to grow to $10,000 at 10 percent.

@SLN—Straight-Line Depreciation

The @SLN function calculates straight-line depreciation given an asset's cost, salvage value, and depreciable life. The format of the @SLN function is as follows:

@SLN(cost,salvage value,life)

This formula is used to calculate @SLN:

SLN = (cost−salvage value)/life

The @SLN function conveniently calculates straight-line depreciation for an asset. Suppose that you have purchased a machine for $1,000 that has a useful life of 3 years and a salvage value estimated to be 10 percent of the purchase price ($100) at the end of its useful life. Figure 6.30 shows how to use the @SLN function to determine the straight-line depreciation for the machine, which is $300 per year.

Fig. 6.30.
The @SLN
function used
to calculate
straight-line
depreciation.

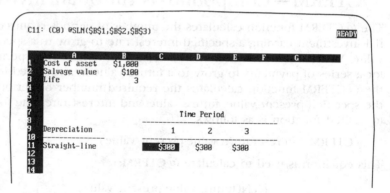

@DDB—Double-Declining Balance Depreciation

The @DDB function calculates depreciation using the double-declining balance method, with depreciation ceasing when the book value reaches the salvage value. Double-declining balance depreciation is a method of accelerating depreciation so that greater depreciation expense occurs in the earlier periods rather than the later ones. Book value in any period is the purchase price less the total depreciation in all prior periods.

The format of the @DDB function is as follows:

@DDB(cost,salvage,life,period)

In general, the double-declining balance depreciation in any period is the following:

book value*2/n

In this formula, *book value* is the book value in the period, and *n* is the depreciable life of the asset. 1-2-3 adjusts the results of this formula in later periods to ensure that total depreciation does not exceed the purchase price less the salvage value.

Figure 6.31 shows how the @DDB function can calculate depreciation on an asset purchased for $1,000, with a depreciable life of 3 years and an estimated salvage value of $100.

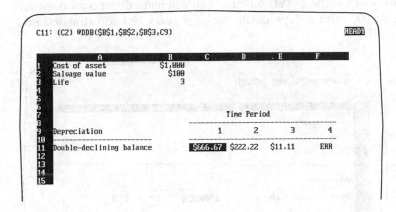

Fig. 6.31.
The @DDB function used to calculate a 200% declining balance depreciation.

Keep in mind that when you use the double-declining balance depreciation method for an asset with a small salvage value, the asset will not be fully depreciated in the final year.

@SYD—Sum-of-the-Years'-Digits Depreciation

The @SYD function calculates depreciation by the sum-of-the-years'-digits method. This method accelerates depreciation so that earlier periods of the item's life reflect greater depreciation than later periods. The @SYD function uses the following format:

@SYD(cost,salvage,life,period)

The *cost* is the purchase cost of the asset. The *salvage* is the estimated value of the asset at the end of the depreciable life. The *life* is the depreciable life of the asset. And the *period* is the period for which depreciation is to be computed.

@SYD calculates depreciation with the following formula:

$$SYD = \frac{(cost-salvage)*(life\ period+1)}{life*(life+1)/2}$$

The expression *life period + 1* in the numerator shows the life of the depreciation in the first period, increased by 1 in each subsequent period. This expression reflects the declining pattern of depreciation over time. The expression in the denominator, *life*(life + 1)/2*, is equal to the sum of the digits, as follows:

$$1 + 2 + ... + life$$

The name sum-of-the-years'-digits originated from this expression.

Figure 6.32 shows how the @SYD function can calculate depreciation for an asset costing $1,000 with a depreciable life of 3 years and an estimated salvage value of $100.

Fig. 6.32.
The @SYD
function used
to calculate
sum-of-the-
years'-digits
depreciation.

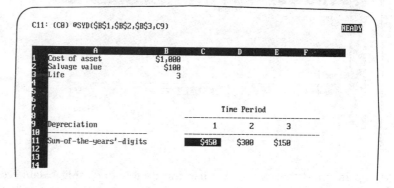

Logical Functions

Cue:
Logical functions
add Boolean logic
to your worksheet.

The logical functions allow you to add standard Boolean logic to your worksheet and use the logic either alone or as part of other worksheet formulas. Essentially, each of the logical functions allows you to test whether a *condition* is TRUE or FALSE.

For some of the logical functions, you describe the test and what the function should do based on the test. For example, the @IF function tests any condition you include as an argument and then returns one value or label if the test is TRUE, and another value or label if the test is FALSE. For other logical functions, both the test and what the function returns based on the test are built into the function itself. The @ISSTRING function is an example of this because it simply tests whether the argument is a string and returns 1 if the test is TRUE and 0 if the test is FALSE.

The nine logical functions that 1-2-3 provides are summarized in table 6.6. Rather than describe the logical functions in alphabetical order, the following text describes the logical functions in order of complexity. Therefore, you probably will want to read the description of the first function and progress from there.

Table 6.6
Logical Functions

Function	Description
@FALSE	Equals 0, the logical value for FALSE
@IF(test,TRUE,FALSE)	Tests the condition and then returns one result if the condition is TRUE and another if the condition is FALSE
@ISAAF(name)	Tests whether the argument is a defined add-in function
@ISAPP(name)	Tests the argument for an attached add-in
@ISERR(cell reference)	Tests whether the argument equals ERR
@ISNA(cell reference)	Tests whether the argument equals NA
@ISNUMBER(cell reference)	Tests whether the argument is a number
@ISSTRING(cell reference)	Tests whether the argument is a string
@TRUE	Equals 1, the logical value for TRUE

RELEASE

2.2

@IF—Creating Conditional Tests

The @IF function represents a powerful tool—one you can use both to manipulate text within your worksheets and to affect calculations. For example, you could use the @IF statement to test the condition "Is the inventory on-hand below 1,000 units?" and then return one value or string if the answer is TRUE, and another if the answer is FALSE. The @IF function uses the format

@IF(test,TRUE,FALSE)

Figure 6.33 shows several examples of the @IF function. To show clearly the functions, their arguments, and their results, the first column displays the function (formatted as text so that you can read it), and the second column shows the calculated results of the function.

*Fig. 6.33.
Examples of
the @IF
function using
strings and
values.*

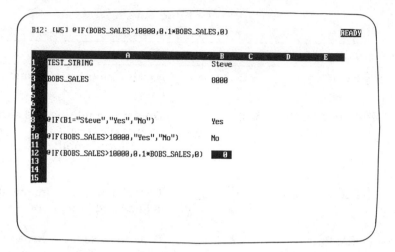

The first @IF function checks whether the contents of a cell equals a string and produces one of two strings based on whether the test is TRUE or FALSE. Notice that when you include a string in the @IF statement test, you include it in quotation marks. You use the equal sign (=) to compare the two strings.

The second @IF function tests whether the contents of the cell named BOBS_SALES exceed 10,000 and returns one string if the test is TRUE and another if the test is FALSE. The third @IF function again tests whether the contents of BOBS_SALES exceed 10,000 and then calculates the commission that the salesperson is entitled to if sales exceed 10,000. To test for BOBS_SALES exceeding 10,000, the function uses the greater than sign (>).

The @IF function performs six logical tests, summarized in table 6.7.

**Table 6.7
Logical Test Symbols**

Symbol	Description
<	Less than
<=	Less than or equal to
=	Equal to
>=	Greater than or equal to
>	Greater than
<>	Not equal to

As figure 6.33 illustrates, the @IF function allows you to add decision-making logic to your worksheets. That logic can be based on strings or numeric values, and the function can return either strings or numeric values. You can further expand the power of @IF functions by using compound tests.

Cue:
The @IF function allows you to add decision-making logic to your worksheets.

If you think about the conditions you test in your worksheet formulas, probably many are made up of two or more individual tests. For example, the following statement illustrates a compound condition:

IF	
(test 1)	Company revenues increase and
(test 2)	Company expenses decrease
THEN	
TRUE	Company profits will increase.

You will find occasion to use three complex operators in your worksheets. These are summarized in table 6.8.

Table 6.8
Complex Operators

Operator	Description
#AND#	Used to test two conditions that both must be TRUE in order for the entire test to be TRUE
#NOT#	Used to test that a condition is not TRUE
#OR#	Used to test two conditions; if either condition is TRUE, the entire test condition is TRUE

Figure 6.34 illustrates how you might use these three complex operators. In the figure, REVS89 is the name of the cell that contains the 1989 gross revenues, and REVS88 is the name that contains the 1988 gross revenues. MARG89 is the cell that contains the 1989 gross margin, and MARG88 is the name that contains the 1988 gross margin.

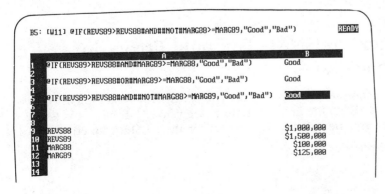

Fig. 6.34.
Compound @IF conditions being tested.

The first complex @IF condition tests whether both the conditions REVS89>REVS88 and MARG89>=MARG88 are TRUE. If both tests are TRUE, the function returns the string "Good"; otherwise, the function returns the string "Bad".

The second complex @IF function tests whether either one of the two conditions, REVS89>REVS88 or MARG89>=MARG88 is TRUE. If either test is TRUE, the function again returns the string "Good"; if both are FALSE, the function returns the string "Bad".

The third complex @IF condition tests whether the condition REVS89>REVS88 is TRUE and the condition MARG88>=MARG89 is FALSE. When both tests are passed, the function returns the string "Good"; when either of the two tests is FALSE, the function returns the string "Bad".

You also can specify the TRUE or the FALSE argument within an @IF function as another @IF function. Putting @IF functions inside other @IF functions is a common and powerful logical tool. This technique, called *nesting*, gives you the ability to construct sophisticated logical tests and operations in your 1-2-3 worksheets.

For example, figure 6.35 shows an @IF statement with nested IFs that calculates a sales commission where the salesperson receives a $500 commission if he or she books $10,000 or more in sales and also receives 10% of amounts exceeding $12,000.

Fig. 6.35.
Nested @IF
statements used
to calculate
sales
commissions.

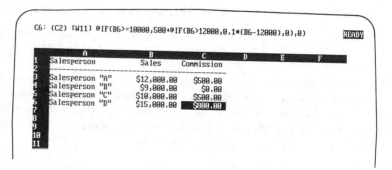

@ISERR and @ISNA—Trapping Errors in Conditional Tests

The @ISERR function tests whether what you specify as the argument equals ERR. If the test is TRUE, the function returns the value 1; if the test is FALSE, the function returns the value 0. The format for the @ISERR function is

@ISERR(cell reference)

You can use the @ISERR function to trap errors and thereby keep them from causing other, dependent formulas and functions from also returning an ERR value. Figure 6.36 illustrates the mechanics of the @ISERR function and the returned values both when the test condition is TRUE and when the test condition is FALSE.

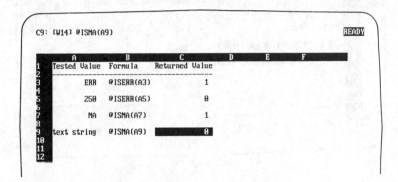

Fig. 6.36.
The @ISERR and @ISNA functions used to test arguments.

Figure 6.36 also shows the mechanics of the @ISNA function. The @ISNA function tests whether the argument you include is equal to NA. If the test is TRUE, the function returns the value 1; if the test is FALSE, the function returns the value 0. The format for the @ISNA function is

@ISNA(cell reference)

You use the @ISNA function to trap NA values in worksheets that use the @NA function. The @NA function, which represents "Not Available," is discussed in the "Special Functions" section of this chapter.

@TRUE and @FALSE—Checking for Errors

You use the @TRUE and @FALSE functions to check for errors. Neither function requires an argument. These functions are useful for providing formula and advanced macro command documentation. The @TRUE function returns the value 1, the Boolean logical value for TRUE. The @FALSE function returns the value 0, the Boolean logical value for FALSE.

Figure 6.37 uses an undocumented feature of 1-2-3 Release 2.2—its capability to perform Boolean logic—along with @TRUE and @FALSE statements to provide easy-to-read @IF functions. The Boolean formulas shown as text in cells B3 and B5 perform logical tests just like the @IF statement does. However, rather than returning a user-specified value if the test is TRUE (or FALSE), these formulas return the logical values for TRUE and FALSE shown in cells C3 and C5: 1 and 0.

RELEASE

2.2

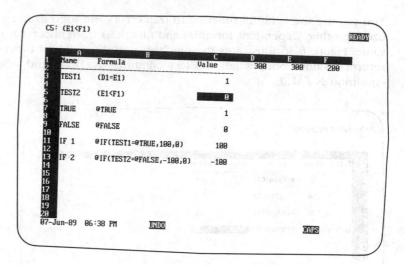

Fig. 6.37.
The @TRUE
and @FALSE
functions used
with Boolean
logic in @IF
statements.

Cells B7 and B9 show the @TRUE and @FALSE functions, and cells C7 and C9 show the logical values these two functions produce. The @IF functions in cells B11 and B13 compare the results of the Boolean logic in TEST1 to @TRUE and TEST2 to @FALSE and return values based on the outcome of these tests. Boolean logic allows you to construct logical tests using any of the logical operators, but without using the @IF statement—or, as in this case, a nested IF statement with only one @IF function.

@ISSTRING and @ISNUMBER—Checking the Cell's Aspect

Before using the contents of a cell, you may want to use functions to test the cell's *aspect*—what type of cell it is, whether the cell contains a number or a label, or whether the cell is empty. A cell's aspect also includes the cell's address, the row and column the cell resides in, the cell's label prefix (if any), the width of the cell, and the cell's format. Depending on the characteristics of a cell's aspect, you may need to use different cell-processing methods.

Two functions that help you determine the type of value stored in a cell are @ISSTRING and @ISNUMBER. Although these functions are used most often with the @IF function, you can use them with other types of functions as well. The @ISNUMBER function helps to verify whether a cell entry is a number. The format of the @ISNUMBER function is

@ISNUMBER(cell reference)

If the argument is a number, the numeric value of the function is 1 (TRUE). If the argument is a string, including the null string (""), the numeric value of the function is 0 (FALSE).

Suppose that you want to test whether the value entered in cell B3 is a number. If the value is a number, you want to show the label "number" in the current cell; otherwise, you want to show the label "string". To do so, use the following formula:

@IF(@ISNUMBER(B3),"number","string")

With this statement, you can be fairly certain that the appropriate label will appear in the current cell. The @ISNUMBER function, however, gives the numeric value of 1 to empty cells as well as to numbers, because blank cells actually contain invisible zeros. Obviously, the function itself is incomplete because the function will assign the label "number" to the current cell if cell B3 is empty. For complete reliability, you must modify the function to handle empty cells.

You can distinguish between a number and an empty cell by using the formula that follows. Note that cell AA3 must contain the range B3..B3.

@IF(@ISNUMBER(B3),@IF(@COUNT(@@(AA3)),"number","blank"),
    "string")

This function first tests whether the cell contains a number or a blank. If it does, the function then uses the @COUNT function to test whether the range B3..B3 contains an entry. (Recall that @COUNT assigns a value of 0 to blank cells and a value of 1 to cells with an entry when the argument used is a range rather than a cell reference. See this chapter's discussion of the @COUNT function for a detailed explanation.)

If the cell contains an entry, the label "number" is displayed. Otherwise, the label "blank" is displayed. If the cell does not contain a number or a blank, the cell must contain a string with the "string" label displayed.

As an alternative, you may consider using the @ISSTRING function. @ISSTRING works in nearly the same way as @ISNUMBER. @ISSTRING, however, determines whether a cell entry is a string value. The format of the @ISSTRING function is

@ISSTRING(cell reference)

If the argument for the @ISSTRING function is a string, the value of the function is 1 (TRUE). If the argument is a number or blank, however, the value of the function is 0 (FALSE). You can use this function to stop what Lotus calls the "ripple-through" effect of NA and ERR in cells that should have a string value. 1-2-3 considers both NA and ERR as numeric values.

Returning to the earlier example about distinguishing between a number and an empty cell, you also can complete the function with @ISSTRING by using the following formula. Note that cell AA3 must contain the range B3..B3.

@IF(@ISSTRING(B3),"string",@IF(@COUNT(@@(AA3))>0,
    "number","blank"))

This function first tests whether string data is present. If it is, the function assigns the label "string". Otherwise, the @COUNT function is used to determine whether the range B3..B3 contains a number or is empty. If the data is a number, the label "number" is assigned. Otherwise, the label "blank" is assigned.

@ISNUMBER provides the capability to test for a number, although the function's inability to distinguish between numbers and blank cells is its principal weakness. In many applications, however, @ISNUMBER provides sufficient testing of values, especially when you are certain that a cell is not blank. @ISSTRING provides the capability to test for a string. When used with the @COUNT function, @ISSTRING can distinguish blank cells from strings. The @COUNT function combined with both @ISNUMBER and @ISSTRING can help you distinguish between blank cells and numbers.

RELEASE

2.2

Entire
Section

@ISAAF and @ISAPP—Checking for Add-Ins

New to 1-2-3 Release 2.2 are two functions that help you check the status of add-in functions and programs. The @ISAAF function checks the status of an add-in function, and also discriminates between add-in and built-in functions. The format for the @ISAAF function is

> @ISAAF(name)

name is the description of the add-in function for which you are testing. You can enter name as a literal string, a string formula, or a reference to a cell that contains a label. Don't include the initial @ sign in the argument. To test for an add-in function such as @D360, use the following formula:

> @ISAAF("D360")

If the formula returns 1, the function is available; if it returns 0, it is not available. @ISAAF also returns 0 if the function is a built-in function.

The @ISAPP function checks whether a particular add-in program has been installed or attached with the Add-in manager. The format of the @ISAPP function is

> @ISAPP(name)

Again, you can enter *name* as a literal string, a string formula, or a reference to a cell that contains a label. To check the status of an add-in program, such as Allways, use the following formula:

> @ISAPP("Allways")

If the name is an AAF or dynamic driver add-in, @ISAPP returns 1 (TRUE); if the name is not an AAF or dynamic driver add-in, @ISAPP returns 0 (FALSE).

Special Functions

The special functions are listed in a separate category because they provide information about cell or range content or worksheet location. Table 6.9 lists 1-2-3's special functions.

Table 6.9
Special Functions

Function	Description
@@(cell address)	Returns the contents of the cell referenced by the cell address in the argument
@CELL(string,range)	Returns the attribute designated by the string for the cell in the upper left corner of the range
@CELLPOINTER(string)	Returns the attribute designated by the string for the current cell
@CHOOSE(offset,list)	Locates the specified entry in a list
@COLS(range)	Computes the number of columns in a range
@ERR	Displays ERR in the cell
@HLOOKUP(key,table, offset)	Locates the specified key in a look-up table and returns a value from that row of the look-up table
@INDEX(range, column-offset, row-offset, worksheet-offset)	Locates an entry in the specified address in a range
@NA	Displays NA in the cell
@ROWS(range)	Computes the number of rows in a range
@VLOOKUP(key,table, offset)	Locates a specified key in a look-up table and returns a value from that column of the look-up table

@@—Referencing Cells Indirectly

The @@ function provides a way of indirectly referencing one cell by way of another cell. The format of the @@ function is as follows:

@@(cell reference)

For example, if cell A1 contains the label 'A2, and cell A2 contains the number 5, the function @@(A1) returns the value 5.

The argument of the @@ function must be a cell reference to the cell that contains the indirect address. Similarly, the cell referenced by the argument of the @@ function must contain a string value that evaluates to a cell reference. This cell can contain a label, a string formula, or a reference to another cell, as long as the resulting string value is a cell reference.

The @@ function is useful primarily in situations where several formulas each have the same argument, and the argument must be changed from time to time during the course of the application. 1-2-3 lets you specify the arguments of each formula through a common indirect address, as shown in the example in figure 6.38.

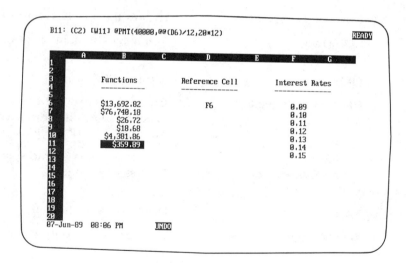

Fig. 6.38. An example of the @@ function in a series of formulas.

In figure 6.38, column B contains a variety of financial functions, all of which use the @@ function to reference 1 of 7 interest rates in column F indirectly through cell D6. When you are ready to change the cell being referenced, you have to change only the label in cell D6 instead of editing all 6 formulas in column B. Figure 6.39 shows the results of the same formulas after the indirect address has been changed from 'F6 to 'F7.

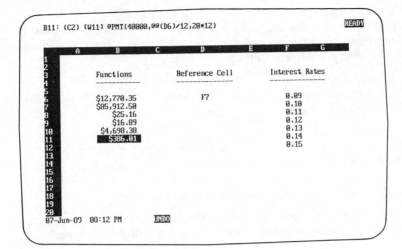

Fig. 6.39.
Formulas using
@@ after
changing an
indirect
reference.

@CELL and @CELLPOINTER—Checking Cell Attributes

The @CELL and @CELLPOINTER functions provide an efficient way to determine the nature of a cell because these functions return up to nine different characteristics of a cell. The @CELL and @CELLPOINTER functions are used primarily in macros and advanced macro command programs (see Chapters 13 and 14).

Cue:
@CELL and
@CELLPOINTER
provide an efficient
way to determine
the nature of a
cell.

The formats of the @CELL and @CELLPOINTER functions are as follows:

@CELL(string,range)

@CELLPOINTER(string)

Both functions have a string argument, which is the *aspect* of a cell you want to examine. The @CELL function, however, also requires the specification of a range; the @CELLPOINTER function works with the current cell.

The following examples illustrate how you can use the @CELL function to examine some cell attributes:

@CELL("address",SALES)
  If the range named SALES is C187..E187, 1-2-3 returns the absolute address $C$187. This is a convenient way of listing the upper left corner of a range's address in the worksheet. To list all the range names and their addresses, use the **/R**ange **N**ame **T**able command.

@CELL("prefix",C195..C195)

If the cell C195 contains the label 'Chicago, 1-2-3 returns ' (indicating left alignment). If, however, cell C195 is blank, 1-2-3 returns nothing; in other words, the current cell appears blank.

@CELL("format",A10)

1-2-3 changes the second argument to range format (A10..A10) and returns the format of cell A10.

@CELL("width",B12..B12)

1-2-3 returns the width of column B as viewed in the current window regardless of whether that width was set using the /Worksheet Column Set-Width command (for the individual column) or the /Worksheet Global Column-Width command (for the default column width).

The other attributes you can examine with either the @CELL or the @CELLPOINTER function include "row", "col", "contents", "type", and "protect".

The difference between @CELL and @CELLPOINTER is important. The @CELL function examines the string attribute of a cell you designate in a range format, such as A1..A1. If you use a single-cell format, such as A1, 1-2-3 changes to the range format (A1..A1) and returns the attribute of the single-cell range. If you define a range larger than a single cell, 1-2-3 evaluates the cell in the upper left corner of the range.

On the other hand, the @CELLPOINTER function operates on the current cell—the cell where the cell pointer was positioned when the worksheet was last recalculated. The result remains the same until you enter a value or press the Calc (F9) key if your worksheet is in Automatic Recalculation mode, or until you press the Calc (F9) key in Manual Recalculation mode.

For example, to determine the address of the current cell, you can enter @**CELLPOINTER**("**address**") in cell B22. If recalculation is set to Automatic, the value displayed in that cell is displayed as the absolute address $B$22. This same address remains displayed until you recalculate the worksheet by making an entry elsewhere in the worksheet or by pressing the Calc (F9) key. The address that appears in cell B22 changes to reflect the position of the cell pointer when the worksheet was recalculated. If recalculation is Manual, you can change the address only by pressing the Calc (F9) key. Figure 6.40 illustrates the use of the @CELLPOINTER function with all the attributes that can be examined by both the @CELLPOINTER and @CELL functions.

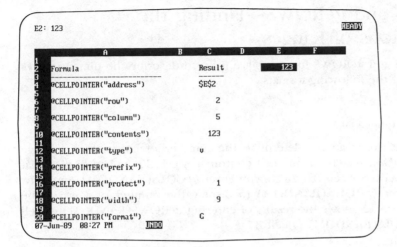

Fig. 6.40.
The
@CELLPOINTER
function used
to examine cell
attributes.

@CHOOSE—Selecting an Item from a List

The @CHOOSE function selects an item from a list based on the item's position in the list. The format of the @CHOOSE function is

   @CHOOSE(offset,list)

The function selects the item in the specified position, or *offset*, in the specified list. Keep in mind that positions are numbered starting with 0. For example, the first position is 0, the second is 1, the third is 2, and so on.

Figure 6.41 shows examples of the @CHOOSE function. The key, or offset, is the specified position. The actual formulas are shown in column B. The lists of items, which can be either values or strings, are shown in columns C through F. And the results of the @CHOOSE function are shown in column H.

Remindor:
@CHOOSE selects
an item from a list.

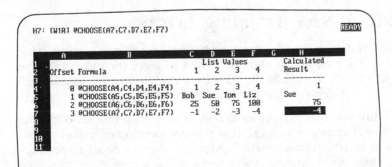

Fig. 6.41.
The @CHOOSE
function used
to select an
item from a
list.

@COLS and @ROWS—Finding the Dimensions of Ranges

The @COLS and @ROWS functions are used to describe the dimensions of ranges, using the following formats:

@COLS(range)

@ROWS(range)

Suppose that you want to determine the number of columns in a range called RANDOM, which has the cell coordinates D4..G9, and to display that value in the current cell. To do so, you enter @**COLS(RANDOM)**. Similarly, you can enter @**ROWS(RANDOM)** to display the number of rows in the range. Figure 6.42 shows the results of entering @ROWS(RANDOM) in cell B5 and @COLS(RANDOM) in cell B7.

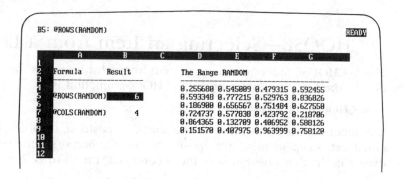

Fig. 6.42.
The @COLS and @ROWS functions used to show range dimensions.

If you specify a single cell (such as C3) as the argument for the @COLS or @ROWS function, 1-2-3 changes the argument to range format (C3..C3) and returns the value 1 for the function.

@ERR and @NA—Trapping Errors

If you find yourself in a situation in which you simply don't know what number to enter for a value, but you don't want to leave the cell blank, you can enter @NA (for "Not Available"). 1-2-3 then displays NA in that cell and in any other cell that depends on that cell.

Another condition you may encounter is that of screening out unacceptable values for cells. For example, suppose that you are developing a checkbook-balancing macro in which checks with values less than or equal to zero are unacceptable. One way to indicate this unacceptability is to use ERR to signal that fact. You might use the following version of the @IF function:

@IF(B9<=0,@ERR,B9)

This statement says: "If the amount in cell B9 is less than or equal to zero, then display ERR on-screen; otherwise, use the amount." Notice that the @ERR function controls the display in almost the same way that @NA does in a previous example.

1-2-3 also uses ERR as a signal for unacceptable numbers—for example, a division by zero or mistakenly deleted cells. ERR often shows up temporarily when you are reorganizing the cells in a worksheet. If the ERR message persists, however, you may have to do some careful analysis to figure out why.

As it does for NA, 1-2-3 displays ERR in any cells that depend on a cell with an ERR value. Sometimes many cells display ERR after you delete rows or columns that contain cells on which other formulas depend. To correct the errors, trace back through the chain of references to find the root of the problem. Use the Undo (Alt-F4) key to return to the worksheet as it was before the change (see Chapter 3).

@HLOOKUP and @VLOOKUP—Looking Up Entries in a Table

The @HLOOKUP and @VLOOKUP functions retrieve a string or value from a table based on a specified key. The operation and format of the two functions are essentially the same except the @HLOOKUP function looks through horizontal tables, and the @VLOOKUP function looks through vertical tables. The functions use the following formats:

@HLOOKUP(key,range row,offset)

@VLOOKUP(key,range column,offset)

Keys are values in labels that the LOOKUP command uses to search through the list. 1-2-3 compares the key specified with the contents of each cell in the first row or column of the table, looking for a cell whose contents match the key.

When you use numeric keys, make sure that the key values ascend in order. If they don't, you may get an ERR. (If the keys are strings, you can list the keys in any order.) With numeric keys, the LOOKUP function is actually searching for the largest value that is less than or equal to the key. Therefore, if it can't find a value that is equal, the function will pick the largest value that is *less than* the key.

The range argument is the area making up the entire look-up table. *Offset* specifies which row or column contains the data you are looking up. The offset argument is always a number, in ascending order, ranging from 1 to the highest number of columns or rows in the look-up table. Number 1 marks the first column to the right of the column that contains key data or the first row below the row that contains key data. When you specify an offset number, it cannot be negative or exceed the correct number of columns or rows.

Cue:
When you use numeric keys, make sure that the key values ascend in order.

Figure 6.43 shows one @HLOOKUP and two @VLOOKUP functions, which together demonstrate 1-2-3's LOOKUP functions.

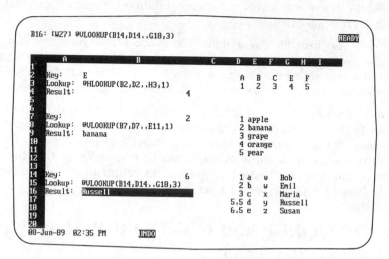

Fig. 6.43.
The
@HLOOKUP
and
@VLOOKUP
functions used
to retrieve
strings and
values from
tables.

The first function, @HLOOKUP, finds the key E in the range defined as D2..H3. If the LOOKUP is successful, the function retrieves the contents of the offset row numbered 1—the value 4. Notice that as with the @CHOOSE function, offset numbering starts at 0. The result of the @HLOOKUP function in cell B3 is shown in cell B4 as 4.

The first @VLOOKUP looks through the vertical table located in the worksheet range D7..E11 for an entry with a numeric key value of 2. The function then returns the string from the number 1 offset column—banana. The key is shown in cell B7, the @VLOOKUP function in cell B8, and the result of the @VLOOKUP function in cell B9.

The second @VLOOKUP function, shown in cell B15, looks through the vertical table located in the worksheet range D14..G18 for an entry with a numeric key value of 6. In figure 6.43, no entries in the table have a key value of 6. In this case, the LOOKUP function picks the table entry with the largest key value that doesn't exceed the argument key.

Watch for three common errors when you construct @HLOOKUP and @VLOOKUP functions. First, when you use a string as the key argument, the LOOKUP function returns ERR if it can't find the string in the LOOKUP table. If a LOOKUP function with a string key returns ERR, first check that you haven't misspelled the string either in the function or in the LOOKUP table.

A second common error is omitting the columns or rows that contain the key and value or string you want returned in the LOOKUP table argument; this situation also generates an ERR condition. The examples in figure 6.43

use cell addresses to specify the table so that the example is easy to understand. However, you will probably want to name your LOOKUP tables, and that can make spotting missing rows or columns tricky.

When you use named ranges for a table argument, make sure that the named range includes both the key column or row and the offset column or row. Accordingly, if you use an @HLOOKUP function with the offset row argument set to 6, your table range should include at least 7 rows. Alternatively, if you use a @VLOOKUP function with the offset column argument set to 3, your table range should include at least 4 columns.

Remember, too, that the key strings or values belong in the first column or row and that column and row numbering starts at 0. Accordingly, the first offset is 0, the second is 1, the third is 2, and so on.

@INDEX—Retrieving Data from Specified Locations

@INDEX, a data management function, is similar to the table-lookup functions. However, @INDEX has some unique features. The format of the @INDEX function is

@INDEX(range,column-offset,row-offset)

Like the table-lookup functions, the @INDEX function works with a table of numbers. But unlike the table-lookup functions, the @INDEX function does not use a test variable and a comparison column (or row). Instead, the @INDEX function requires you to indicate the column-offset and row-offset of the range from which you want to retrieve data. For example, the following function, shown in figure 6.44, returns the value 2625:

@INDEX(L142..S145,3,2)

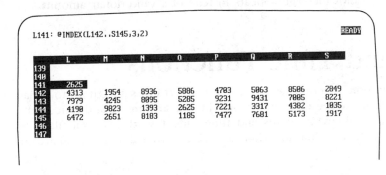

Fig. 6.44.
An example of the @INDEX function.

Notice that the number 0 corresponds to the first column, 1 corresponds to the second column, and so on. The same numbering scheme applies to rows. Using 3 for the column-offset and 2 for the row-offset indicates that you want an item from the fourth column, third row.

With the @INDEX function, you cannot use column or row numbers that fall outside the relevant range. Using either negative numbers or numbers too large for the range causes 1-2-3 to return an ERR message.

The @INDEX function is useful when you know the exact position of a data item in a range of cells and want to locate the item quickly. For instance, the @INDEX function works well for rate quotation systems. Figure 6.45 shows an example of a system for quoting full-page magazine advertising rates.

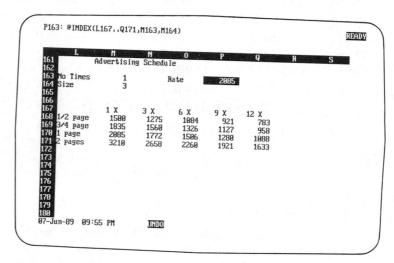

Fig. 6.45.
Use of @INDEX for advertising rate quotations.

In this example, the following function returns a value of 2085:

> @INDEX(L167..Q171,M163,M164)

This value corresponds to the amount in the first column and the third row of the index range. If 6 is entered for the ad frequency (the number of times an ad is run), the ERR message appears instead of a valid dollar amount.

Date and Time Functions

1-2-3's date and time functions allow you to convert dates and times to serial numbers and then use these serial numbers in date arithmetic and time arithmetic—a valuable aid when dates and times affect worksheet calculations and logic. The date and time functions available with 1-2-3 are summarized in table 6.10.

Table 6.10
Date and Time Functions

Function	Description
@DATE(y,m,d)	Calculates the serial number that represents the described date
@DATEVALUE(date string)	Converts a date expressed as a string into a serial number
@DAY(date)	Extracts the day number from a serial number
@HOUR(time)	Extracts the hour number from a serial number
@MINUTE(time)	Extracts the minute number from a serial number
@MONTH(date)	Extracts the month number from a serial number
@NOW	Calculates the serial date and time from the current system date and time
@SECOND(time)	Extracts the second number from a serial number
@TIME(h,m,s)	Calculates the serial number that represents the described time
@TIMEVALUE(time string)	Converts a time expressed as a string into a serial number
@YEAR(date)	Extracts the year number from a serial number

@DATE—Converting Date Values to Serial Numbers

The first step in using dates in arithmetic operations is to convert them to actual numbers, or *serial numbers*, you can then use in arithmetic operations. The most frequently used date function is @DATE, which converts any date into a number you can use in arithmetic operations—and, as importantly, that 1-2-3 can view as a date. The @DATE function uses this format:

@DATE(year,month,day)

You identify a year, month, or day using numbers. For example, you enter the date November 26, 1989 into the @DATE function as the following:

@DATE(89,11,26)

The numbers you enter to represent the year, month, and day need to make up a valid date, or 1-2-3 returns an ERR. For example, you can specify the day argument in February as 29 only during leap years, and never as 30 or 31. When you specify the month as 1 (which represents January), 30 or 31 are valid day arguments because January has 31 days.

As you use the @DATE function, keep a couple of guidelines in mind. First, the internal 1-2-3 calendar starts with the serial number 1—the first date that 1-2-3 recognizes—and that serial number represents January 1, 1900. A single day is represented by the increment 1.

Second, even though 1900 wasn't a leap year, 1-2-3 erroneously assigns the serial number 60 to February 29, 1900. To adjust for this error, subtract 1 from serial numbers that represent dates between January 1, 1900, and March 1, 1900.

Figure 6.46 shows an example of the @DATE function being used to calculate the number of days between the date a loan is originated and the date the loan is paid off. In cases where the lender calculates interest charges using daily compounding, this information is necessary to calculate the final interest charges.

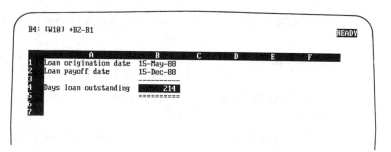

Fig. 6.46.
The @DATE function expressing dates as serial numbers.

Note that the serial dates used in figure 6.46 appear as dates even though they are actually just numbers. Using the **/R**ange **F**ormat **D**ate command sequence, you can format serial numbers that represent dates to appear in one of several ways. When you format the dates, 1-2-3 still works with the dates as serial numbers, but you see the dates in reports and on-screen in formats you recognize. (The **/R**ange **F**ormat commands and the various **D**ate and **T**ime formats available are discussed in detail in Chapter 5.)

@DATEVALUE—Changing Date Strings to Serial Numbers

@DATEVALUE computes the serial number for a string that looks like one of the 1-2-3 date formats you might have set using the **/R**ange **F**ormat command. The @DATEVALUE function uses this format:

@DATEVALUE(date string)

Reminder: *You must construct the date string using one of the five date formats or by referencing a cell that contains one of these formats.*

You need to construct the date string by including one of the five 1-2-3 date formats or by referencing a cell that contains one of the valid date formats. If the string doesn't look like a formatted date, 1-2-3 returns ERR; if it does, 1-2-3 returns the serial number.

Note that if you have reset the default date format for 1-2-3 using the **/W**orksheet **G**lobal **D**efault **O**ther **I**nternational **D**ate command, you need to use the **I**nternational **D**ate format you set as the default as the date string for the @DATEVALUE function. For example, if you reset the default date format to MM/DD/YY, you need to enter the date December 27, 1989, as the following:

@DATEVALUE("12/27/89")

Figure 6.47 shows the @DATEVALUE function converting into serial numbers the date strings that mirror each of the five standard date formats. Column A shows the 1-2-3 date format name; column B shows the date string; column C, the format of the @DATEVALUE function; column D, the unformatted results of the @DATEVALUE function, and column E, the results of the @DATEVALUE function formatted to look like the corresponding date string in column B.

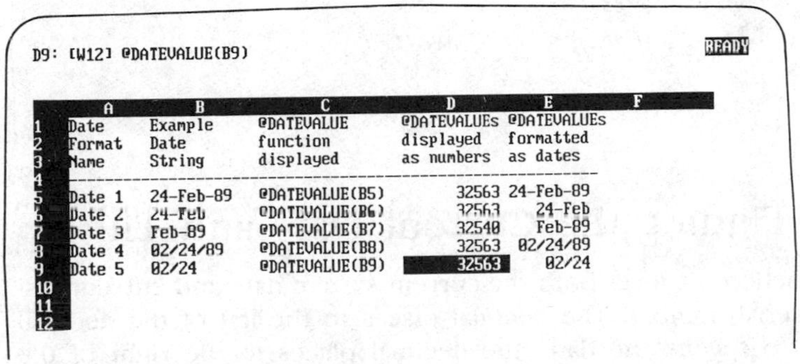

D9: [W12] @DATEVALUE(B9) READY

	A	B	C	D	E	F
1	Date	Example	@DATEVALUE	@DATEVALUEs	@DATEVALUEs	
2	Format	Date	function	displayed	formatted	
3	Name	String	displayed	as numbers	as dates	
4						
5	Date 1	24-Feb-89	@DATEVALUE(B5)	32563	24-Feb-89	
6	Date 2	24-Feb	@DATEVALUE(B6)	32563	24-Feb	
7	Date 3	Feb-89	@DATEVALUE(B7)	32540	Feb-89	
8	Date 4	02/24/89	@DATEVALUE(B8)	32563	02/24/89	
9	Date 5	02/24	@DATEVALUE(B9)	32563	02/24	
10						
11						
12						

Fig. 6.47. *The @DATEVALUE function used to convert date strings to serial numbers.*

Because no year is included in the date string for the second and fifth date formats, 1-2-3 assumes that the year is the same as the system date year—in these cases, 1989. Because no day is included in the date string for the third format, 1-2-3 assumes that the day is the first day of the month. Keep these assumptions in mind for your specific application.

@DAY, @MONTH, and @YEAR—Converting Serial Numbers to Dates

The @DAY, @MONTH, and @YEAR functions convert serial numbers to dates. These functions use the following formats:

@DAY(date)

@MONTH(date)

@YEAR(date)

The @DAY function accepts a valid serial number as its single argument and returns the day of the month—which is a number from 1 to 31. The @MONTH function accepts a valid serial number as its single argument and returns the month of the year—which is a number from 1 to 12. The @YEAR function accepts a valid serial number as its single argument and returns the number of the year—which is a number from 0 (1900) to 199 (2099).

Figure 6.48 illustrates the mechanics of these three date functions. With these functions, you can extract just the component of a date—year, month, or day—you want to manipulate.

Fig. 6.48.
The @YEAR,
@MONTH,
and @DAY
functions used
to extract parts
of a date.

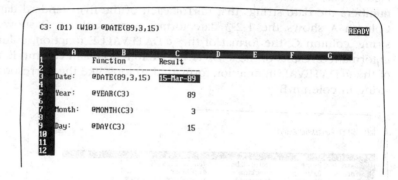

@NOW—Finding the Current Date and Time

The @NOW function retrieves both the current system date and current system time as a serial number. The decimal places to the left of the decimal point are used to specify the date; the decimal places to the right of the decimal point are used to specify the time.

Assuming that you either enter the current date and time when you boot your computer or that you have an internal clock that keeps the date and time for you, this function provides a convenient tool for recording the dates and times worksheets are modified or printed. @NOW does not require an argument.

Figure 6.49 illustrates the result of using @NOW. Column B shows the serial number, which represents the system date and time. Column C shows the serial number formatted as a date. Column D shows the result of the function, formatted to show the current system time.

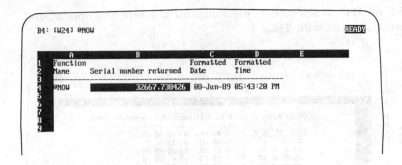

Fig. 6.49.
The @NOW
function used
to insert the
date and time
in a worksheet.

@TIME—Converting Time Values to Serial Numbers

1-2-3 expresses time in fractions of serial numbers between 0 and 1. For example, 0.5 is equal to 12 hours (or 12:00 pm). In addition, 1-2-3 works on military time; 10:00 pm is 22:00 in military time. 1-2-3's timekeeping system may seem a little awkward at first. Use the following general guidelines to help you understand the system:

Reminder:
1-2-3 expresses
time in fractions of
serial numbers
between 0 and 1.

Time Increment	Numeric Equivalent
1 hour	0.0416666667
1 minute	0.0006944444
1 second	0.0000115741

The @TIME function produces a serial number for a specified time of day. The format of the @TIME function is

@TIME(hour number,minute number,second number)

You can use the @TIME function to produce a range of times just as you can use the @DATE function to generate a range of dates. One way to produce a range of times is to use the **/D**ate **F**ill command. For example, to produce a range of times from 8:00 am to 5:00 pm in 15-minute increments, use the following steps:

1. Select **/D**ate **F**ill.

2. Specify the range where you want the times to appear and press Enter.

3. Type **@TIME(8,0,0)** as the Start value and press Enter.

4. Type **@TIME(0,15,0)** as the Step value and press Enter.

5. Type **@TIME(17,0,0)** as the Stop value and press Enter.

6. Use **/R**ange **F**ormat **D**ate **T**ime to display the range in whatever time format you choose, and expand the column widths as necessary.

In figure 6.50, B4..D17 is selected as the range for the times to appear, and the results are formatted with **Time 1**.

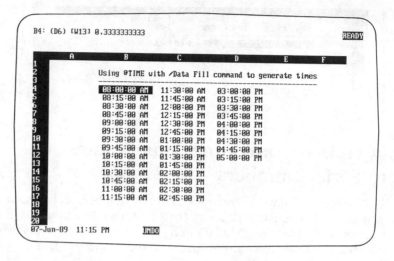

Fig. 6.50.
An example of
the @TIME
function.

```
B4: (D6) [W13] 0.3333333333                                    READY

       A           B             C             D         E         F
1
2              Using @TIME with /Data Fill command to generate times
3      ----------------------------------------------------------------
4      08:00:00 AM   11:30:00 AM   03:00:00 PM
5      08:15:00 AM   11:45:00 AM   03:15:00 PM
6      08:30:00 AM   12:00:00 PM   03:30:00 PM
7      08:45:00 AM   12:15:00 PM   03:45:00 PM
8      09:00:00 AM   12:30:00 PM   04:00:00 PM
9      09:15:00 AM   12:45:00 PM   04:15:00 PM
10     09:30:00 AM   01:00:00 PM   04:30:00 PM
11     09:45:00 AM   01:15:00 PM   04:45:00 PM
12     10:00:00 AM   01:30:00 PM   05:00:00 PM
13     10:15:00 AM   01:45:00 PM
14     10:30:00 AM   02:00:00 PM
15     10:45:00 AM   02:15:00 PM
16     11:00:00 AM   02:30:00 PM
17     11:15:00 AM   02:45:00 PM
18
19
20
07-Jun-89  11:15 PM        UNDO
```

The numeric arguments have certain restrictions. First, the hour number must be between 0 and 23. Second, both the minute number and second number must be between 0 and 59. Finally, although 1-2-3 accepts numeric arguments that contain integers and decimals, only the integer portion is used.

After a time has been interpreted by 1-2-3 as a fraction of a serial number, you can use the **/R**ange Format **D**ate **T**ime command to display the time in a more recognizable way.

@TIMEVALUE—Converting Time Strings to Serial Values

Just like @DATEVALUE and @DATE, @TIMEVALUE is a variation of @TIME. Like @TIME, @TIMEVALUE produces a serial number from the hour, minute, and second information you supply to the function. Unlike @TIME, however, @TIMEVALUE uses string arguments rather than numeric arguments. The format of the @TIMEVALUE function is

@TIMEVALUE(time string)

Reminder:
If the string you
supply doesn't
conform to an
acceptable format,
1-2-3 returns the
ERR value.

The time string must appear in one of the four time formats: **T1**, **T2**, **T3**, or **T4**. If the string conforms to one of the time formats, 1-2-3 displays the appropriate serial number fraction. If you then format the cell, 1-2-3 displays the appropriate time of day. Figure 6.51 shows the results of using the @TIMEVALUE function with the four different acceptable time strings.

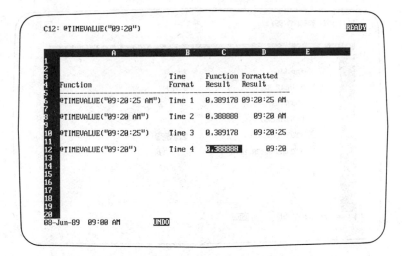

```
C12: @TIMEVALUE("09:20")                                         READY

          A              B      C        D        E
1
2
3                       Time   Function Formatted
4  Function             Format Result   Result
5  ─────────────────────────────────────────────
6  @TIMEVALUE("09:20:25 AM")  Time 1  0.389178 09:20:25 AM
7
8  @TIMEVALUE("09:20 AM")     Time 2  0.388888    09:20 AM
9
10 @TIMEVALUE("09:20:25")     Time 3  0.389178    09:20:25
11
12 @TIMEVALUE("09:20")        Time 4  0.388888       09:20
13
14
15
16
17
18
19
20
08-Jun-89  09:00 AM       UNDO
```

Fig. 6.51.
An example
of the
@TIMEVALUE
function.

The first two time formats, **T1** and **T2**, accept times from 12:00 am to 11:59 am, and from 12:00 pm to 11:59 pm. The last two time formats, which Lotus calls International Time formats, accept military time from 00:00 (12 am) to 23:59 (11:59 pm). The separator character for the international time formats defaults to a colon (:), but you can change this by using the **/W**orksheet **G**lobal **D**efault **O**ther **I**nternational **T**ime command.

@SECOND, @MINUTE, and @HOUR— Converting Serial Numbers to Time Values

The @SECOND, @MINUTE, and @HOUR functions allow you to extract different units of time from a numeric time fraction. These functions use the following formats:

@SECOND(time)

@MINUTE(time)

@HOUR(time)

Figure 6.52 shows that these three functions are the reverse of the @TIME function, just as the @DAY, @MONTH, and @YEAR functions are the reverse of the @DATE function.

Notice that the argument includes both an integer and a decimal portion. Although the integer portion is important for date functions, it is disregarded for time functions, as illustrated by the last example in the figure. You can use these functions for various time-related chores, such as developing a time schedule.

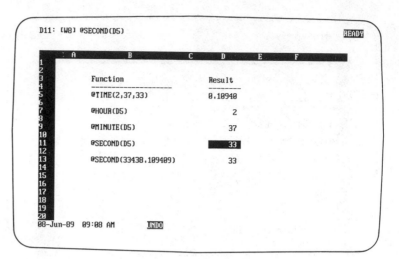

Fig. 6.52.
The @SECOND,
@MINUTE, and
@HOUR
functions used
to extract parts
of a time.

String Functions

1-2-3 has a variety of functions that give you significant power to manipulate strings. *Strings* are labels or portions of labels. More specifically, strings are units of data consisting of connected characters (alphabetic, numeric, blank, and special) that are delimited by quotation marks (" "). The functions specifically designated as string functions are not the only 1-2-3 functions that take advantage of the power and flexibility of strings. For example, logical, error-trapping, and special functions use strings as well as values. The string functions, however, are specifically designed to manipulate strings. Table 6.11 summarizes the string functions available with 1-2-3.

Table 6.11
String Functions

Function	Description
@FIND(search string, overall string, start number)	Locates the start position of one string within another string
@MID(string,start position,length)	Extracts the specified number of characters from a string, beginning with the character start position
@LEFT(string,length)	Extracts the leftmost specified number of characters from the string

Function	Description
@RIGHT(string,length)	Extracts the rightmost specified number of characters from the string
@REPLACE(original string,start number,length, replacement string)	Substitutes the specified number of characters from the original string with the replacement string at the character start number
@LENGTH(string)	Displays the number of characters in the string
@EXACT(string1, string2)	Returns TRUE if string1 and string2 are exact matches; otherwise, returns FALSE
@LOWER(string)	Converts all characters in the string to lowercase
@UPPER(string)	Converts all characters in the string to uppercase
@PROPER(string)	Converts the first character in each word in the string to uppercase, and the remaining characters to lowercase
@REPEAT(string,number)	Copies the string the specified number of times in a cell
@TRIM(string)	Extracts blank spaces from the string
@N(range)	Returns the value contained in the cell in the upper left corner of the range
@S(range)	Returns the string value of the cell in the upper left corner of the range
@STRING(number to convert,decimal places	Converts a value to a string showing the specified number of decimal places

Table 6.11—*continued*

Function	Description
@VALUE(string)	Converts a string to a value
@CLEAN(string)	Removes nonprintable characters from the string
@CHAR(number)	Converts a code number into an ASCII/LICS character
@CODE(string)	Converts the first character in the string into an ASCII/LICS code

Reminder:
You can link strings to other strings using the concatenation operator (&).

You can link strings to other strings by using the *concatenation* operator (&). The discussion of the individual string functions in this section shows several examples of the use of the concatenation operator. Keep in mind that you can't link strings to cells that contain numeric values or that are empty. If you try, 1-2-3 returns an ERR value.

Avoid mixing data types in string functions. For instance, some functions produce strings, whereas others produce numeric results. Be careful not to combine functions from these two different groups unless you have taken all the precautions regarding string functions discussed throughout this section.

The numbering scheme for positioning characters in a label is also something to watch for when using string functions. These positions are numbered beginning with zero and continuing to a number corresponding to the last character in the label. The following example shows the position numbers (0 to 24) for a long label:

```
          111111111122222
0123456789012345678901234
'two chickens in every pot
```

The prefix (') before the label does not have a number because the prefix is not considered part of the label. Nor are negative position numbers allowed. The importance of position numbers is explained further in the next section.

@FIND—Locating One String within Another

@FIND, one of the simplest string functions, is the best function for showing how position numbers are used in strings. The @FIND function locates the starting position of one string within another string. For instance, you could use this function to find at what position the string "every" occurs within the string "two chickens in every pot". The format of the @FIND function is

@FIND(search string,overall string,start number)

The *search string* is the string you want to locate. In this example, the search string is "every". The *overall string* is the target string to be searched. In this example, "two chickens in every pot" is the overall string. Finally, the *start number* is the position number in the overall string where you want to start the search. If you want to start at position 6 and you are using the overall string located in cell A2, you use the following function, as shown in figure 6.53:

@FIND("every",A2,6)

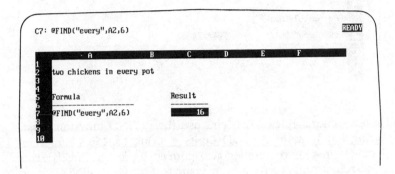

Fig. 6.53.
An example of the @FIND function.

Your result is the number 16—the position of the first (and only) occurrence of "every" in the overall string. If the search string "every" is not found in the overall string, the ERR message is displayed.

In the example, notice that choosing the start number of 6 has no bearing on the outcome of the function. You could just as easily choose 0 (or any other number less than or equal to 16) for the starting position of the search string. If "every" appeared more than once in the overall string, however, the start number could locate its occurrence elsewhere. Suppose that the following overall string appears in cell A2:

'two chickens in every pot, two cars in every garage

Now suppose that you want to locate all the occurrences of "every" in the overall string. The following function returns a value of 16, as before:

@FIND("every",A2,6)

Try changing the start number by adding 1 to the result of the original function. The appropriate function is now

@FIND("every",A2,17)

This new function returns the number 39, the starting location of the second occurrence of "every". Next, add 1 to the second result and use this function:

@FIND("every",A2,40)

The resulting ERR message tells you that you have found all the occurrences of the search string. Figure 6.54 shows the results of using different position numbers.

Fig. 6.54.
Position
numbers used
with the
@FIND
function.

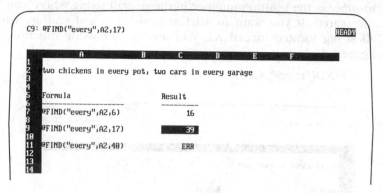

Reminder:
@FIND performs
only exact
searches; upper-
and lowercase are
significant.

Keep in mind a few general rules when you use the @FIND function. First, @FIND (like string functions in general) limits a string to 240 characters. Second, any decimals in a start number are ignored by 1-2-3. Finally, you must enter any search string exactly as you want to find it—@FIND is case sensitive. In the preceding example, if you use a search string of "Every" instead of "every", you get the ERR message instead of a numeric value.

@MID—Extracting One String from Another

Whereas @FIND helps you locate one string within another, the @MID function lets you extract one string from another. This operation is called *substringing*. The format of the @MID function is

@MID(string,start position,length)

The *start* position is a number representing the character position in the string where you want to begin extracting characters. The *length* argument indicates the number of characters to extract. For example, to extract the first name from a label containing the full name "Page Davidson", use this function:

@MID("Page Davidson",0,4)

This function extracts the string starting in position 0 (the first character) and continuing for a length of 4 characters—the string "Page".

Cue:
Use @MID with
@FIND to extract
first and last
names from a list
of full names.

Now suppose that you want to extract the first and last names from a column list of full names and to put those two names in a separate column. To accomplish this, use the @MID and @FIND functions together. Because you know that a blank space will always separate the first and last names, @FIND can locate the position of the blank in each full name. Using this value, you then can set up the functions to extract the first and last names.

If cell A8 contains the full name "Ivan Anderson", as shown in figure 6.55, place the following function in cell B8:

@MID(A8,0,@FIND(" ",A8,0))

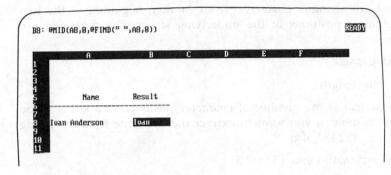

Fig. 6.55.
The @MID function used to extract a substring.

The value of this function appears as "Ivan" because the following returns a value of 4 for the length argument:

@FIND(" ",A8,0)

Next place the following function in cell C8, as shown in figure 6.56:

@MID(A8,@FIND(" ",A8,0)+1,99)

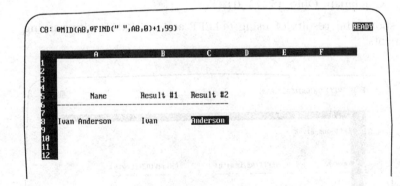

Fig. 6.56.
The @MID and @FIND functions used to locate and extract first and last names.

The @FIND function indicates that the start position is one character beyond the blank space. In addition, the length of the string to be extracted is 99 characters. Although a length of 99 is greater than you need, there is no penalty for this excess. The string that 1-2-3 extracts is "Anderson".

@LEFT and @RIGHT—Extracting Strings from Left and Right

@LEFT and @RIGHT are special variations of the @MID function and are used to extract one string of characters from another, beginning at the left-most and rightmost positions in the underlying string. The functions use these formats:

@LEFT(string,length)

@RIGHT(string,length)

Cue:
Use @RIGHT to
extract the ZIP
code from an
address.

The length argument is the number of character positions in a string to be extracted. For example, if you want to extract the ZIP code from the string "Cincinnati, Ohio 45243", use

@RIGHT("Cincinnati, Ohio 45243",5)

@LEFT works the same way as @RIGHT except that @LEFT extracts from the beginning of a string. For instance, use the following function statement to extract the city in the preceding example:

@LEFT("Cincinnati, Ohio 45243",10)

In most cases, use the following instead of 10 for the length in the function to extract the city from the address:

@FIND(",","Cincinnati, Ohio 45243",0)

Figure 6.57 shows the results of using @LEFT and @RIGHT with varying length arguments.

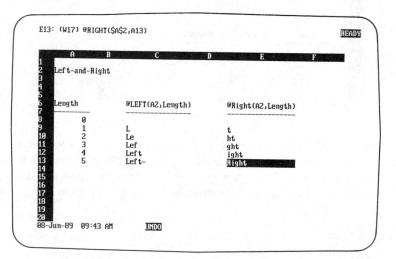

Fig. 6.57.
The length
argument
changed for the
@LEFT and
@RIGHT
functions.

@REPLACE—Replacing a String within a String

The @REPLACE function removes a group of characters from a string and replaces them with another string. The @REPLACE function is valuable for correcting a text entry without having to retype the entire string. @REPLACE numbers the character positions in a string, starting with zero and continuing to the end of the string (up to a maximum of 239). The format of the @REPLACE function is

@REPLACE(original string,start number,length,replacement string)

The *start number* argument indicates the position where 1-2-3 will begin removing characters in the original string. The *length* shows how many characters to remove, and the *replacement string* contains the new characters to replace the removed ones.

Suppose, for example, that the string "This is the original string" appears in cell A2. Figure 6.58 shows several examples of how to use @REPLACE to change words in the string. Notice in the third example in the figure that you can use the @FIND function to locate the string you want to replace instead of starting at 0 and counting the 12 positions to find the start number.

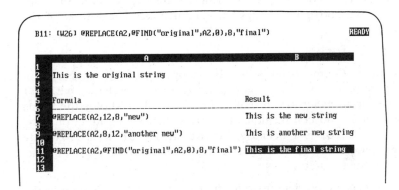

Fig. 6.58.
The @REPLACE function used to alter a string.

@LENGTH—Computing the Length of a String

The @LENGTH function indicates the length of a string. The format of the @LENGTH function is

@LENGTH(string)

Figure 6.59 shows how you can use @LENGTH to find the length of a string. Notice that the function returns the value ERR as the length of numeric values or formulas, empty cells, and null strings.

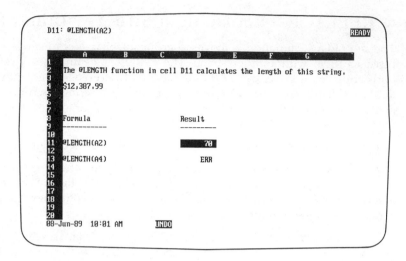

Fig. 6.59.
*The @LENGTH
function used
to find the
length of a
string.*

```
D11: @LENGTH(A2)                                                        READY

          A        B        C        D        E        F        G
 1
 2  The @LENGTH function in cell D11 calculates the length of this string.
 3
 4  $12,387.99
 5
 6
 7
 8  Formula                          Result
 9  ----------                       ----------
10
11  @LENGTH(A2)                          70
12
13  @LENGTH(A4)                         ERR
14
15
16
17
18
19
20
08-Jun-89  10:01 AM        UNDO
```

@EXACT—Comparing Strings

The @EXACT function compares two strings, returning a value of 1 for strings that are alike and 0 for strings that are unalike. The format of the @EXACT function is

   @EXACT(string1,string2)

@EXACT's method of comparison is like the = operator in formulas except that the = operator checks for an approximate match, and the @EXACT function checks for an exact match. For example, if cell A2 holds the string "Marketing Function" and cell B2 holds the string "marketing function", the numeric value of A2=B2 is 1 because the two strings are an approximate match. The numeric value of @EXACT(A2,B2) is 0 because the two functions are not an exact match.

The examples in figure 6.60 demonstrate the use of @EXACT. Notice in the third example that @EXACT cannot compare nonstring arguments. If you try to compare the entry in cell A6 with the blank cell C6, the value of @EXACT(A6,C6) is ERR. In fact, if either argument is a nonstring value, 1-2-3 returns the ERR value. (Note that you can use the @S function, explained later in this chapter, to ensure that the arguments used with @EXACT have string values.)

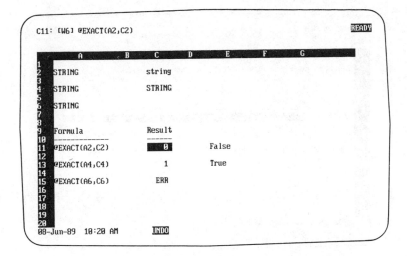

Fig. 6.60.
Strings
compared with
the @EXACT
function.

@LOWER, @UPPER, and @PROPER—
Converting the Case of Strings

1-2-3 offers three functions for converting the case of a string value:

@LOWER(string)   Converts all uppercase letters in a string to
lowercase letters

@UPPER(string)   Converts all the letters in a string to
uppercase letters

@PROPER(string)   Capitalizes the first letter in each word of a
label. (Words are defined as groups of
characters separated by blank spaces.)
@PROPER then converts the remaining letters
in each word to lowercase.

Figure 6.61 gives an example of the use of each function.

None of these three functions works with nonstring values. For instance, if
cell E9 contains a number or a null string (" "), 1-2-3 returns ERR for each of
these functions. (Note that you can use the @S function, explained later in
this chapter, to ensure that the arguments of these functions have string
values.)

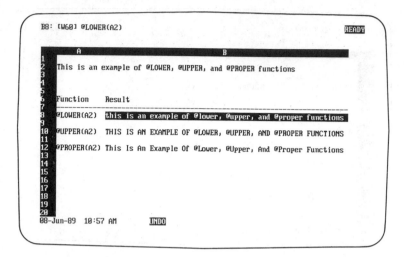

Fig. 6.61.
Functions used to convert the case of alphanumeric strings.

@REPEAT—Repeating Strings within a Cell

The @REPEAT function repeats strings within a cell much as the backslash (\) repeats characters. But @REPEAT has some distinct advantages over the backslash. @REPEAT lets you repeat the character the precise number of times you want—which may be different than the column width in characters. The format of the @REPEAT function is

> @REPEAT(string,number)

Reminder:
@REPEAT copies characters beyond the current column width.

The number argument indicates the number of times you want to repeat a string in a cell. For example, if you want to repeat the string "COGS" three times, you can enter this function:

> @REPEAT("COGS",3)

The resulting string is the following:

> COGSCOGSCOGS

This string follows 1-2-3's rule for long labels. That is, the string will be displayed beyond the right boundary of the column, provided that no entry is in the cell to the right. When you use the backslash to repeat a string, however, 1-2-3 fills the column to the exact column width. If the string doesn't fit within the column width, 1-2-3 truncates it.

The @REPEAT function in figure 6.62 shows you how to generate a dashed line that is one character less than the column width of the current cell. You can enter the formula shown in the figure in one cell and then use the /Copy command to copy it to any other appropriate cell in the worksheet. If you use this technique, do not reference in the @CELL function a cell that contains a formula; otherwise, a circular reference may result.

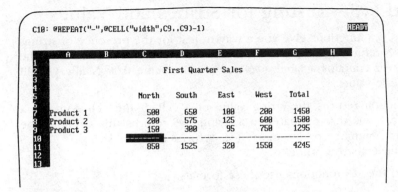

Fig. 6.62.
The @REPEAT function used to generate dashed lines.

@TRIM—Removing Blank Spaces from a String

The @TRIM function deletes blank spaces from the beginning, end, or middle of a string. The format for the @TRIM function is

@TRIM(string)

If more than one space occurs consecutively in the middle of a string, 1-2-3 removes all but one of the blank spaces. For example, the @TRIM function in figure 6.63 removes extra spaces from between the words of a sentence.

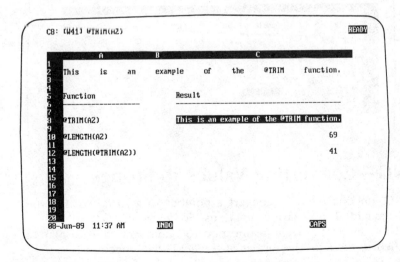

Fig. 6.63.
Unwanted spaces removed with the @TRIM function.

Notice that the value of @LENGTH(A2) is 69, but the value of @LENGTH(@TRIM(A2)) is 41. (To trim characters other than blank spaces, use the @CLEAN function, described later in this chapter.)

@N and @S—Testing for Strings and Values

The @N and @S functions give you a way to test for the presence of strings or values. @N returns the value of a number or formula found in a cell. If the cell is blank or contains a label, @N returns the value 0. @N always will have a numeric value.

The @S function returns the string value of a cell. If the cell contains a string, or a formula that evaluates to a string, @S returns this string. If the cell contains a number or is empty, @S returns the null string (" "). @S always will have a string value.

The @N and the @S functions use these formats:

@N(range)

@S(range)

The argument must be a range or a single-cell reference. If you use a single-cell reference, 1-2-3 adjusts the argument to range format and returns the numeric or string value of the single cell. If the argument is a multicell range, @N and @S return the numeric or string value of the upper left corner of the range. Figure 6.64 shows the results of using the @N and @S functions.

Fig. 6.64.
String functions used for string and numeric values.

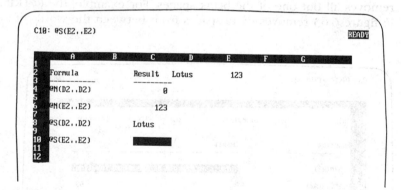

@STRING—Converting Values to Strings

The @STRING function lets you convert a number to a string so that the number can act with 1-2-3's string functions. For example, @STRING can override 1-2-3's automatic right-justification of numbers and display a number justified to the left. The format of the @STRING function is

@STRING(number to convert,decimal places)

1-2-3 uses the fixed-decimal format for the @STRING function. The decimal-places argument represents the number of places to be included in the string. For example, if the *number-to-convert* argument within cell A2 is 22.5, enter @**STRING(A2,2)** in cell C10. The resulting string "22.50" is displayed with left-justification, the default setting (see fig. 6.65).

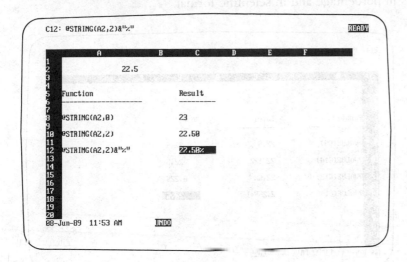

Fig. 6.65.
A number
converted to
a string.

Notice that in the first example in the figure, 1-2-3 rounds the number upward to 23, just as 1-2-3 rounds any number displayed in the fixed-decimal format. The third example shows how to use the @STRING function to display a number as a percentage. The formula @STRING(A2,2)&"%" produces the string "22.50%". Note that to create a string from a number in any format other than fixed decimal, you must add the additional format characters.

Cue:
Use the @STRING
function to display
a number as a
percentage.

@VALUE—Converting Strings to Values

If you have been entering string data but need to use the data as numbers, use the @VALUE function. For example, suppose that you enter model numbers and their quantities as labels. The information on model numbers works fine in the string format; but you want to change the format of the quantity data so that you can add different part quantities together. The format of the @VALUE function, which handles this kind of task, is

@VALUE(string)

Figure 6.66 shows a number of examples of converting labels to numeric values with the @VALUE function. Aside from converting strings in the standard number format (as in the first example in the figure), @VALUE also can convert strings with decimal fractions as well as numbers displayed in scientific format. In the second example, the string "22 1/2" in cell C10 is converted by the function @VALUE(C10) to the number 22.5. Even if cell C10 contained the string "22 3/2", @VALUE would convert the string to the number 23.5. The final two examples in figure 6.66 show how @VALUE converts strings in percentage and in scientific format.

Fig. 6.66.
Labels
converted to
numbers.

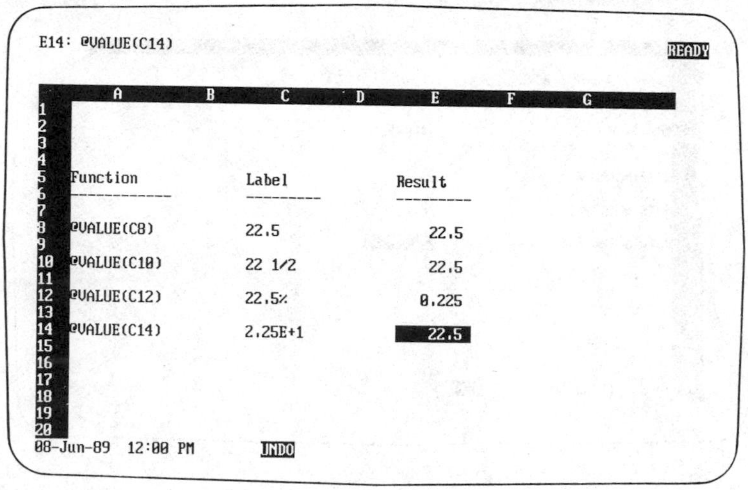

```
E14: @VALUE(C14)                                              READY

         A          B        C        D        E        F        G
 1
 2
 3
 4
 5   Function               Label            Result
 6   _____               _____            _____
 7
 8   @VALUE(C8)             22.5              22.5
 9
10   @VALUE(C10)            22 1/2            22.5
11
12   @VALUE(C12)            22.5%             0.225
13
14   @VALUE(C14)            2.25E+1           22.5
15
16
17
18
19
20
08-Jun-89  12:00 PM          UNDO
```

A few rules are important when you use @VALUE. Although 1-2-3 usually does not object to extra spaces left in a string, the program has trouble with some extra characters, such as trailing percent (%) signs. Currency signs (such as $) that precede the string are acceptable, however. Try experimenting with different extra characters to see how @VALUE reacts. Another point to remember is that a numeric value supplied as an argument for @VALUE simply returns the original numeric value.

@CLEAN—Removing Nonprintable Characters from Strings

Cue:
@CLEAN removes
nonprintable
characters from
data imported into
your worksheet
from other
sources.

Sometimes when you import strings with /File Import (see Chapter 7), particularly by way of a modem, the strings will contain nonprintable characters. The @CLEAN function removes these nonprintable characters from strings (see fig. 6.67). The format of the @CLEAN function is

   @CLEAN(string)

The argument used with @CLEAN must be a string value or a cell reference to a cell containing a string value. 1-2-3 will not accept a cell entry containing @CLEAN with a range argument specified.

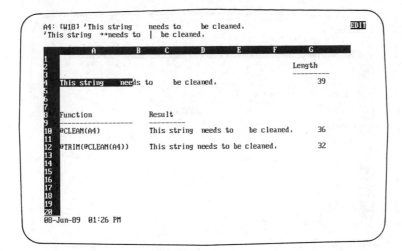

```
A4: [W18] 'This string    needs to    be cleaned.                         EDIT
'This string  ↔needs to  |  be cleaned.
          A          B         C         D         E         F         G
 1
 2                                                                Length
 3                                                                --------
 4  This string      needs to      be cleaned.                      39
 5
 6
 7
 8  Function                    Result
 9  ---------------------       --------
10  @CLEAN(A4)                  This string  needs to    be cleaned.    36
11
12  @TRIM(@CLEAN(A4))           This string needs to be cleaned.        32
13
14
15
16
17
18
19
20
08-Jun-89  01:26 PM
```

Fig. 6.67.
The @CLEAN function used to remove nonprintable characters.

Functions Used with LICS

1-2-3 offers a few special functions for interfacing with the Lotus International Character Set (LICS). (Be aware that the ASCII code number for a given character may not correspond to its LICS code number.) LICS is a character set that allows you to display foreign language characters and mathematical symbols.

The complete set of LICS characters, listed in the Lotus 1-2-3 manual, includes everything from the copyright sign to the lowercase e with the grave accent.

@CHAR—Displaying ASCII/LICS Characters

The @CHAR function displays the ASCII/LICS equivalent of a number between 1 and 255. The format of the @CHAR function is

@CHAR(number)

For example, 1-2-3 represents a ™ sign on-screen with a T. To display the trademark sign on-screen, enter **@CHAR(184)** in a cell. Furthermore, you can use a string formula to concatenate the trademark sign to a product name. For instance, enter the following formula to produce the string "8080T":

+"8080"&@CHAR(184)

When you print the screen display, this string prints as 8080™. Figure 6.68 shows several other examples of the use of the @CHAR function.

Fig. 6.68.
LICS characters
displayed with
the @CHAR
function.

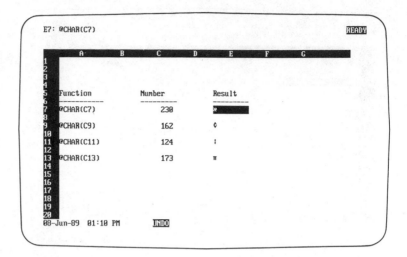

Keep in mind two simple rules when using @CHAR. First, if the numeric argument you are using is not between 1 and 255, 1-2-3 returns an ERR message. Second, 1-2-3 disregards the noninteger portion of the argument.

ASCII/LICS characters also can be displayed by using the Compose (Alt-F1) key together with a compose sequence. See the Lotus 1-2-3 manual for further information and for a list of LICS codes.

@CODE—Computing the ASCII/LICS Code

@CODE examines an ASCII/LICS character and returns a number between 1 and 255. The format of the @CODE function is

@CODE(string)

Reminder:
@CODE returns
the LICS code of
the first character
of the string used
as the argument.

Suppose that you want to find the ASCII/LICS code number for the letter a. You enter @**CODE**("a") in a cell, and 1-2-3 returns the number 97. If you enter @**CODE**("aardvark"), 1-2-3 still returns 97, the code of the first character in the string. Figure 6.69 shows several other examples of the use of the @CODE function.

Remember that if you specify a number as the argument for @CODE (expressed as a number and not as a string), 1-2-3 returns an ERR message.

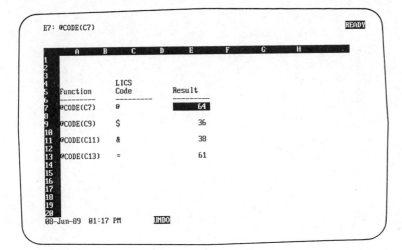

Fig. 6.69.
The @CODE function used to find LICS numbers.

Chapter Summary

This chapter described most of the 92 functions that 1-2-3 provides to make formula and worksheet construction easier and, usually, more error-free. (The 1-2-3 functions that deal specifically with databases are discussed in Chapter 12.)

Managing Files

The commands available when you select /File from 1-2-3's main menu provide a wide range of file management, modification, and protection functions. Some commands are similar to operating system commands. Other commands are related to specific 1-2-3 tasks and applications.

Through the File menu, you can, for example, combine data from several files, extract data from one file to another file, and create a link between two files. You also can give a file "reservation" status so that only one user is permitted to write information to and update the file. This chapter covers the /File commands and the topic of good file management in 1-2-3.

Specifically, this chapter shows you how to do the following:

- Manage a file in memory
- Name files
- Change directories
- Save files to disk
- Retrieve files from disk
- Extract data and combine data
- Use passwords to protect files
- Erase files from disk
- List different types of files
- Transfer files between different programs
- Use 1-2-3 in a multiuser environment

1-2-3's commands for managing worksheet files are accessed from the **/File** option on the menu. From that menu, you can perform operations such as reading files, combining information into the current file, and creating new files. A brief description of these commands follows. The rest of the chapter covers the **/File** commands in more detail.

When you first start 1-2-3, a blank worksheet appears. If you want to build a new worksheet, just use the blank one. If you want to start with an existing file, use the **/File Retrieve** command. **/File Retrieve** replaces the blank worksheet or the current file in memory with a new one.

If you want to combine information into the current file, use the **/File Combine** or the **/File Import** command. With the **/File Combine** command, you can read all or part of a 1-2-3 worksheet file and combine the data into the current file. With the **/File Import** command, you can read a text file and combine the data into the current file.

To create a new file, use the **/File Save** or the **/File Xtract** command. The **/File Save** command saves the file in memory on the disk. The **/File Xtract** command saves part of a file as a new file.

RELEASE

2.2

Usually you work with data files in one directory on your disk. To change the default data directory, use the **/File Directory** command. To see a list of all or some of the files in the current directory, use the **/File List** command. To save a list of files as a table in a worksheet, use the **/File Admin Table** command.

If you want to erase unneeded files on your disk to make room for other files, use the **/File Erase** command.

RELEASE

2.2

If you work with shared files in a network or other multiuser environment, you can use the **/File Admin Reservation** command to control write-access to files. If you have files with formulas that refer to cells in shared files, use the **/File Admin Link-Refresh** command to update these formulas manually.

Managing a File in Memory

In 1-2-3 Releases 2.2 and 2.01, the word *file* refers to a disk-based file that stores information magnetically for the long term. When you build or change a worksheet in memory, the information is lost unless you save it to a disk-based file.

Reading a file from disk produces in the computer's memory an exact copy of the disk file. The file still exists unchanged on disk.

When you save a file, you store on the disk an exact copy of the file that is in the computer's memory. The file still exists unchanged in memory. To manage files on disk, you must first understand how to manage a file in memory.

The computer's memory is your work area. When you use the /Quit 1-2-3 or /Worksheet Erase command, you lose the file in memory. When you use the /File Retrieve command, you replace the current file in memory with another file from the disk. If you save a file before removing it from memory, you can read the file again from disk. If you make changes to a file and do not save it to disk, the changes are lost if you erase the file or replace it in memory.

Naming Files

The exact rules for file names depend on the operating system you use. File names consist of a 1- to 8-character name plus an optional file extension of 1 to 3 characters. The extension usually identifies the type of file. An example of a file name is BUDGET.WK1. In most cases, you choose the file name, and 1-2-3 supplies the extension.

A file name in DOS can contain letters, numbers, and the following characters:

~ ! @ $ % ^ & ( ) - _ { } # '

Spaces are not allowed. All letters convert automatically to uppercase. A file name should include only letters, numbers, the hyphen (-), and the underscore character (_). Other characters may work now but may not work in later versions of DOS or other operating systems. For example, the characters # and ' work with current versions of DOS but not with OS/2. Whether or not you plan to switch to OS/2, a future release of DOS may make these two characters invalid in file names.

The standard extension for 1-2-3 Release 2.2 and Release 2.01 worksheet files is .WK1. When you type a file name, simply type the 1- to 8-character part of the name. 1-2-3 adds the extension for you. 1-2-3 Release 2.2 uses the following extensions:

Cue:
1-2-3 Release 2.2 has two new file extensions, .BAK and .ADN.

.WK1	For worksheet files
.BAK	For backup worksheet files
.PRN	For print-image text files
.PIC	For files in Lotus graph-image format
.ADN	For add-in programs

RELEASE
2.2

RELEASE
2.2

1-2-3 Release 2.01 uses only the .WK1, .PRN, and .PIC extensions.

You can override these standard extensions and type your own. In addition, 1-2-3 can read worksheets that have the following extensions:

.WKS	For 1-2-3 Release 1A worksheet files
.WRK	For Symphony Releases 1 and 1.01 worksheet files
.WR1	For Symphony Releases 1.1, 1.2, and 2 worksheet files

When you execute most file commands, 1-2-3 expects that you want to see the existing files that have .WK* extensions and therefore lists these files in the control panel. The asterisk (*) means "any character"; .WK*, therefore, designates such extensions as .WK1 and .WKS. If you create a file whose extension does not start with .WK, 1-2-3 will not list that file name as a default.

To open a file that has a nonstandard extension, you must type the complete file name and extension. You may want to save a file with a nonstandard extension so that the file does not show up when 1-2-3 lists the worksheet files. For example, you may want to use a nonstandard extension with a file that is part of a macro-controlled system, in which macros retrieve or open the file, so that you do not accidentally retrieve the file outside of the macro. The nonstandard extension "hides" the file from any list of worksheet files. When you want to retrieve the file outside of the macro environment, perhaps to change it, simply type the entire file name and extension.

To change the file list's default extension from .WK* to something else, use the **/F**ile **L**ist **O**ther command and specify the new default extension. To list only Release 2.2 or 2.01 worksheets, use .WK1. To list all versions of 1-2-3 and Symphony worksheet files, use .W*.

Keep in mind that you do not have to accept the default .WK1 extension when you save a file. You can type any extension you want.

Changing Directories

A hard disk is logically separated into a number of directories (also called *subdirectories*). The set of directories leading from the root to the directory containing a file you want is called the *path*, or *directory path*. When you perform file operations in 1-2-3, you usually deal with one directory at a time.

To select the default directory when you start 1-2-3, use the **/W**orksheet **G**lobal **D**efault **D**irectory command. Type the path to the directory that contains the files you use most often and press Enter. In figure 7.1, the sample path name is C:\123\FILES. To save the name of the path permanently, use the **/W**orksheet **G**lobal **D**efault **U**pdate command.

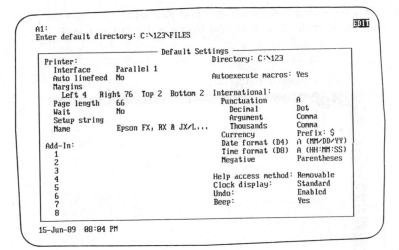

Fig. 7.1.
The sample
default
directory
C:\123\FILES
as displayed in
1-2-3 Release
2.2.

Note how the screen shown in figure 7.1 from 1-2-3 Release 2.2 differs from the screen you see in 1-2-3 Release 2.01 (see fig. 7.2). The prompt in Release 2.01 is Directory at startup:; in Release 2.2 the prompt is Enter default directory. In addition, notice that Release 2.2 displays a settings sheet. A settings sheet lets you see all of the settings rather than just the current setting.

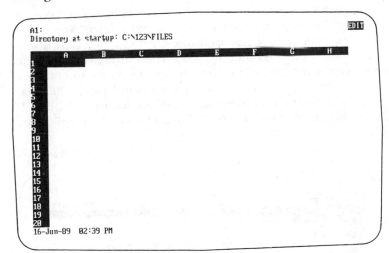

Fig. 7.2.
The sample
default
directory
C:\123\FILES
as displayed in
1-2-3 Release
2.01.

To change the current directory, use the **/F**ile **D**irectory command. 1-2-3 displays the current directory path (see fig. 7.3). You can ignore the current path and type a new one. As soon as you type a character, the previous path clears. Type the directory path you want to use and press Enter. When you perform any other file commands, such as **/File Retrieve**, 1-2-3 assumes that you want to use the current directory and displays the current path.

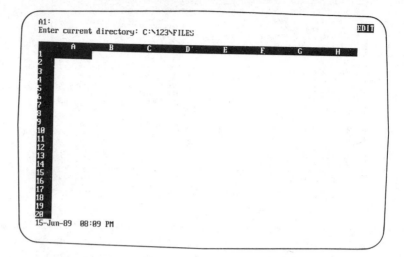

Fig. 7.3.
The current directory.

Saving Files

The **/File Save** command enables you to store on disk a magnetic copy of the file in memory, including all the formats, names, and settings. When you save a file for the first time, the file has no name. 1-2-3 supplies a list of the current worksheet files on the disk (see fig. 7.4). You can either select one of these entries or type a new file name. You should always try to choose a meaningful name for the file. Figure 7.5 shows the control panel after you type the letters **BUD** as the first three characters of the file name BUDGET. After you type the file name, press Enter. 1-2-3 automatically supplies the .WK1 extension.

```
A1: [W14] 'Department 1                                              FILES
Enter name of file to save: C:\123\FILES\*.wk1
CAMBRIDG.WK1   FILE1.WK1     FILE2.WK1      FILE3.WK1    LONDON.WK1
          A          B           C           D          E          F          G
1  Department 1      QTR 1       QTR 2       QTR 3      QTR 4     TOTALS
2                    -----       -----       -----      -----     ------
3  Product 1         4,428       3,170       7,035      9,829     24,462
4  Product 2         4,664       3,340       7,410     10,354     25,768
5  Product 3         9,197       6,328      13,623     17,181     46,329
6  Product 4         7,563       6,651      15,779     21,130     51,123
7  Product 5         7,519       5,896      15,208     20,245     48,868
8  Product 6         5,873       9,558      25,708     18,119     58,458
9                    -----       -----       -----      -----     ------
10                  38,444      34,943      84,763     96,858    255,008
11
```

Fig. 7.4.
A list of file names displayed when you save a file.

```
A1: [W14] 'Department 1                                        EDIT
Enter name of file to save: C:\123\FILES\BUD
        A          B       C        D       E       F      G
1  Department 1   QTR 1   QTR 2    QTR 3   QTR 4   TOTALS
2
3  Product 1      4,428   3,170    7,035   9,829   24,462
4  Product 2      4,664   3,340    7,410  10,354   25,768
5  Product 3      9,197   6,328   13,623  17,181   46,329
6  Product 4      7,563   6,651   15,779  21,130   51,123
7  Product 5      7,519   5,896   15,200  20,245   48,860
8  Product 6      5,073   9,558   25,700  18,119   58,458
9
10                38,444  34,943  84,763  96,858  255,000
11
```

Fig. 7.5.
Typing a new
file name.

When you save a file that has been saved before, the file already has a name.
1-2-3 supplies this name as the default. Figure 7.6 shows the default name for
the BUDGET file (which has been saved before) in the control panel. To
save the file under the same name, press Enter. To save the file under a different name, type the new name and press Enter.

```
A1: [W14] 'Department 1                                        EDIT
Enter name of file to save: C:\123\FILES\BUDGET.wk1
        A          B       C        D       E       F      G
1  Department 1   QTR 1   QTR 2    QTR 3   QTR 4   TOTALS
2
3  Product 1      4,428   3,170    7,035   9,829   24,462
4  Product 2      4,664   3,340    7,410  10,354   25,768
5  Product 3      9,197   6,328   13,623  17,181   46,329
6  Product 4      7,563   6,651   15,779  21,130   51,123
7  Product 5      7,519   5,896   15,200  20,245   48,860
8  Product 6      5,073   9,558   25,700  18,119   58,458
9
10                38,444  34,943  84,763  96,858  255,000
11
```

Fig. 7.6.
The default file
name for a file
you have saved
before.

Suppose that you build a worksheet and are about to save it for the first time.
You type **BUDGET** and press Enter. Later you add to the worksheet and
want to save it again, under the name BUDGET1. You don't want the default
file name BUDGET.WK1; therefore, type **BUDGET1** and press Enter.

Cue:
Save different
versions of your
files under different
names.

Renaming different versions of the same worksheet is a good way to keep
several backup copies accessible while you build a new worksheet. If you
make a catastrophic error and don't discover it until after you have saved the
file, you have earlier versions you can retrieve.

If a file already exists in the same directory under the same file name you
have chosen, 1-2-3 warns you and displays three options: Cancel, Replace,
and Backup as shown in figure 7.7. (Note that 1-2-3 Release 2.01 does not
have the Backup option.) If you do not want to write over the previous file
on disk, choose Cancel to cancel the command. You then can save your file
under a different name.

RELEASE

2.2

```
A1: [W14] 'Department 1                                            MENU
Cancel  Replace  Backup
Cancel command -- Leave existing file on disk intact
           A          B        C         D         E        F        G
1  Department 1      QTR 1    QTR 2     QTR 3     QTR 4    TOTALS
2                   -------  -------   -------   -------  -------
3  Product 1         4,428    3,170     7,035     9,829   24,462
4  Product 2         4,664    3,340     7,410    10,354   25,768
5  Product 3         9,197    6,328    13,623    17,181   46,329
6  Product 4         7,563    6,651    15,779    21,130   51,123
7  Product 5         7,519    5,896    15,208    20,245   48,868
8  Product 6         5,073    9,558    25,708    18,119   58,458
9                   -------  -------   -------   -------  -------
10                  38,444   34,943    84,763    96,858  255,008
11
12
```

Fig. 7.7.
The File Save
menu.

If you want to overwrite the previous file, choose **R**eplace. The previous file with the same name is lost permanently. When you choose **R**eplace, 1-2-3 first deletes the previous file from the disk. If you get a `Disk full` message while saving a file, you must save the file on another disk or erase some existing files to make room to save the file. If you do not save the file successfully, the previous version on disk is lost. You can save the file still in memory on another disk.

RELEASE

2.2

In 1-2-3 Release 2.2, you can save your file under the same name and not lose the previous file on disk by choosing **B**ackup. **B**ackup renames the previous file with a .BAK extension and then saves the new file under the same file name with a .WK1 extension. You then have both files on disk.

Cue:
1-2-3 Release 2.2
users can use the
Backup option to
keep the previous
version of a file as
a backup copy.

You can use the **B**ackup option to save only one file as a backup. If you save the file again and choose **B**ackup, 1-2-3 deletes the current backup file, renames the current .WK1 file with a .BAK extension, and saves the file in memory with a .WK1 extension. If you want to keep the previous file with a .BAK extension, you must copy the file to a different disk or directory, or you must rename the file.

Retrieving Files from Disk

Warning:
The /File Retrieve
command replaces
the current file. If
you made changes
to this file since
the last /File Save
command, the
changes are lost.

The **/F**ile **R**etrieve command enables you to read a file from disk into memory. This command replaces the current file with the new file. If you just started 1-2-3 or if nothing but a blank worksheet is in memory, this command brings a new file into memory. If you have a current file in memory and you changed the file since the last time you saved it, those changes are lost if you use the **/F**ile **R**etrieve command to retrieve another file. 1-2-3 gives no warning that you are about to replace a file you have changed. Therefore, be sure to save your current file before retrieving a new file.

Cue:
Press the Name
(F3) key for a full-
screen list of file
names.

With the **/F**ile **R**etrieve command, 1-2-3 lists, at the prompt requesting you to enter the file name, the files on disk. You can type the file name or point to the file from the list in the control panel. If several files are in the directory, press the Name (F3) key for a full-screen display of file names (see fig. 7.8). Files are listed in alphabetical order, left to right. Point to the file you want to retrieve and press Enter.

```
A1:
Name of file to retrieve: C:\123\FILES\*.wk?                    FILES
          BUDGET.WK1      06/15/89      20:49          2454
BUDGET.WK1      CAMBRIDG.WK1    LONDON.WK1     MONTREAL.WK1   NEWYORK.WK1
SALES1.WK1      SALES2.WK1      SALES3.WK1     SAMPLE.WK1     SIMES.WK1
STATUS.WK1
```

Fig. 7.8.
A list of file names.

Using Wild Cards for File Retrieval

Whenever 1-2-3 prompts you for a file name, you can include the asterisk (*) and the question mark (?) as wild cards in the file name. Wild cards are characters that enable you to make one file name match a number of files. Although you can use wild cards with many of the /File commands, you will probably use these special characters most often with the /File Retrieve command.

The ? matches any one character in the name (or no character if the ? is the last character in the file name's main part or extension). The * matches any number of characters (or no character).

When you use wild cards in response to a file name prompt, 1-2-3 lists only the files whose names match the wild-card pattern. Suppose that you type **SALES?** at the file-name prompt. 1-2-3 lists all file names that start with SALES, followed by any character, such as SALES1, SALES2, and SALES3. If you type **SA***, 1-2-3 lists all file names that start with SA, such as SALES1, SALES2, SALES3, and SAMPLE.

Retrieving Files from Subdirectories

Whenever 1-2-3 prompts you for a file name and gives you a default, the program also lists the complete path, such as C:\123\FILES\BUDGET.WK1. To change the current directory, use the /File Directory command. To retrieve or save a file in another directory without changing the current directory, press Esc twice to clear the path and then type a new path. You also can edit the existing path in the prompt.

When 1-2-3 lists the files in the current directory, the program lists any subdirectories below the current directory, placing a backslash (\) after each directory's name. To read a file in one of the subdirectories, point to the subdirectory name and press Enter. 1-2-3 then lists the files and any sub-

Reminder:
Press Backspace to list a parent directory; select a subdirectory to list the files in that subdirectory.

directories in that subdirectory. To list the files in the parent directory (the directory above the one displayed), press Backspace; 1-2-3 lists the files and subdirectories in that directory. You can move up and down the directory structure this way until you find the file you want.

For those who want to learn more about directories, Que Corporation has many books available. New DOS users should try *MS-DOS QuickStart*. Intermediate users who want to learn more about DOS file and directory management should consult *Using PC DOS*, 3rd Edition, and *MS-DOS User's Guide*, Special Edition, both by Chris DeVoney; and *Managing Your Hard Disk*, 2nd Edition, by Don Berliner.

Retrieving a File Automatically

Usually, when you first start 1-2-3, you have a blank worksheet. If you are in the default directory and save a file under the name AUTO123, however, 1-2-3 retrieves that file automatically when 1-2-3 starts. This capability is useful if you work with macro-driven worksheet files. You can use the AUTO123 file to provide the first menu of a macro-driven system or a menu of other files to retrieve.

Extracting Data and Combining Data

You can take the data from part of a file and use that data to create another, smaller file. For example, you may have a large file that contains budget information from many departments. For each department, you can create an input file that contains only the data for that department.

You also may want to reverse the procedure if you have many departmental input files and want to combine them into one file for company-wide analysis and reporting.

1-2-3 provides the /File Xtract command so that you can save a part of the current file as a new file. 1-2-3 also offers the /File Combine command so that you can combine data from another file into the current file. The following sections discuss these commands.

Extracting Information

The /File Xtract command enables you to save a range in the current file as a separate file. You can use this command to save part of a file before you change it, to break a large file into smaller files so that they can be read in another computer that has less memory, to create a partial file for someone else to work on, or to pass information to another file.

The extracted range can be a single cell or a range of cells. The extracted file contains the contents of the cells in the range, including the cells' formats and protection status; all range names in the file; and all file settings, such as column widths, window options, print ranges, and graph options.

To extract part of a worksheet, choose the **/File Xtract** command and select either **Formulas** or **Values**. When you select **Formulas**, any cells in the extract range that contain formulas are copied into the extracted file as formulas. When you select **Values**, any cells in the extract range in the current file that contain formulas are converted into their current values, and these values are copied into the extracted file. 1-2-3 then acts as if you were saving a file for the first time, prompting you for a file name. Type a file name and press Enter.

Next specify the range to extract and press Enter. For the range, you can type addresses, highlight the range, type a range name, or press the Name (F3) key and point to a range name. If the file name already exists, the **Cancel Replace Backup** menu is displayed.

The extracted range can start anywhere in the current file (see fig. 7.9). The upper left corner of the extracted range becomes cell A1 in the new file (see fig. 7.10). All range names adjust to their new positions.

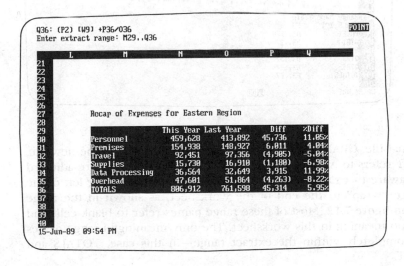

Fig. 7.9.
A highlighted
range to be
extracted.

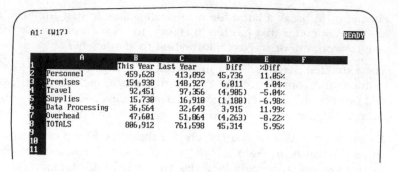

Fig. 7.10.
The extracted
range, which
starts in cell A1
of the new file.

Compare the range name table in the file SALES (see fig. 7.11) with the range name table in the file XVALUES (see fig. 7.12). The XVALUES file was created with the **/File Xtract Values** command from the range F1..F9 in the SALES file. A range name table was added to the extracted file.

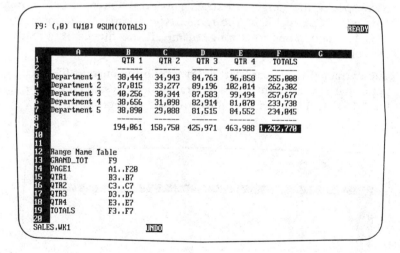

Fig. 7.11.
The SALES file.

In the original file, GRAND_TOT refers to F9 (see fig. 7.11). In the new file, GRAND_TOT refers to A9 (see fig. 7.12). All other range names are adjusted as well. Be aware that range names to the left or above the upper left of the extract range "wrap" to the end of the worksheet, as shown in the range name table in figure 7.12. Most of these range names refer to blank cells and really have no meaning in this worksheet. The only meaningful range names are those completely within the extract range—in this case, TOTALS and GRAND_TOT.

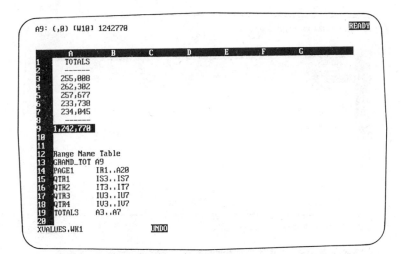

A9: (,0) [W10] 1242770   READY

```
      A        B       C      D      E      F      G
 1   TOTALS
 2   ------
 3   255,000
 4   262,302
 5   257,677
 6   233,738
 7   234,045
 8   ------
 9  1,242,770
10
11
12  Range Name Table
13  GRAND_TOT  A9
14  PAGE1      IR1..A20
15  QTR1       IS3..IS7
16  QTR2       IT3..IT7
17  QTR3       IU3..IU7
18  QTR4       IU3..IU7
19  TOTALS     A3..A7
20
XVALUES.WK1                    UNDO
```

Fig. 7.12.
The extracted
file XVALUES.

The extracted file also has all the other settings of the original file, including print, graph, and data ranges. These settings adjust, as do the range names. For example, the print range in SALES is A1..F20 (see fig. 7.11). In XVALUES, the print range is IR1..A20 (see fig. 7.12). The /Graph x-range (the range that contains the department numbers) is A3..A7 in SALES and IR3..IR7 in XVALUES. As with range names, do not use /Print, /Graph, or /Data settings in an extracted file unless the entire setting range is within the range extracted. In this example, the /Print and /Graph settings are meaningless.

Caution:
Use the /File Xtract command to extract data in cells to a new file, but do not use range names or other settings outside the extracted range.

You should extract formulas only when the formulas in the extract range refer solely to other cells in the extract range. The formulas in figure 7.11 are converted to values in figure 7.12. This fact is important because the formulas in F3..F7 sum a range that was not extracted.

Caution:
Extract formulas only if those formulas refer solely to cells in the extract range.

Figure 7.13 shows the XFORMULA file created with the /File Xtract Formulas command from the range F1..F9 in the SALES file in figure 7.11. This range is the same one extracted with the /File Xtract Values command in figure 7.12. In the SALES file, the formula in F3 is @SUM(E3..B3). In figure 7.13, this formula becomes @SUM(IS3..IV3). Because the cells at the end of the worksheet are blank, all the numbers are zero, and the extracted file is useless. Extracted formulas that refer to cells above or to the left of the extract range are usually incorrect because they "wrap" to the end of the worksheet.

At times you will need to extract formulas. Suppose that you want to extract part of the worksheet from the file SALES, discussed in the preceding section. Figure 7.14 shows the SALES worksheet with a horizontal window used to show the details for Department 1. To extract the range A21..F30 and place it in a separate file, use the /File Xtract Formulas command and specify the range A21..F30. You might name this extract file XSALES1 to remind yourself

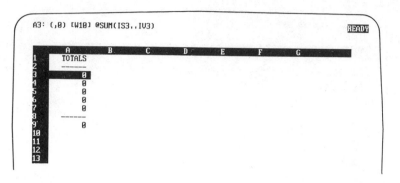

Fig. 7.13.
Meaningless results produced by the /File Xtract Formulas command.

Fig. 7.14.
Two separate parts of the SALES file shown in two windows.

that it is an extract file from SALES for Department 1 (see fig. 7.15). Because all formulas refer to cells in the extracted range, the formulas are still valid. The values in figure 7.15 are identical to those in the range A21..F30 in figure 7.14.

Reminder:
Even absolute cell references adjust with the /File Xtract command.

When you extract formulas, the formulas adjust even if they are absolute. The resulting formulas are still absolute, but they have new addresses. If the formula in F3 in figure 7.11 were @SUM($B$3..$E$3), the formula in A3 in figure 7.13 would be @SUM($IS$3..$IV$3).

Caution:
If the CALC indicator is on, press the Calc (F9) key to calculate the worksheet before you use the /File Xtract Values command.

When you extract values, you get the current value of any formulas in the extract range. If recalculation is set to Manual and the CALC indicator is on, press the Calc (F9) key to calculate the worksheet before you extract a range; otherwise, you may extract outdated values inadvertently.

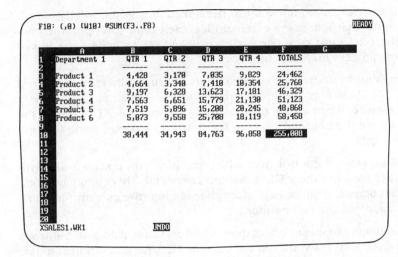

```
F10: (,0) [W10] @SUM(F3..F8)                                    READY

        A          B        C        D        E        F        G
 1 Department 1  QTR 1    QTR 2    QTR 3    QTR 4    TOTALS
 2              ------   ------   ------   ------   ------
 3 Product 1     4,428    3,170    7,035    9,829   24,462
 4 Product 2     4,664    3,340    7,410   10,354   25,768
 5 Product 3     9,197    6,328   13,623   17,181   46,329
 6 Product 4     7,563    6,651   15,779   21,130   51,123
 7 Product 5     7,519    5,896   15,208   20,245   48,868
 8 Product 6     5,073    9,558   25,700   18,119   58,450
 9              ------   ------   ------   ------   ------
10              38,444   34,943   84,763   96,858  255,000
11
12
13
14
15
16
17
18
19
20
XSALES1.WK1              UNDO
```

Fig. 7.15.
*The XSALES1
file, extracted
from SALES.*

Combining Information from Other Files

You can combine information from one or more files into the current file. Depending on your needs and on your version of 1-2-3, you can do this either with formulas (1-2-3 Release 2.2 only) or with the **/File Combine** command (1-2-3 Releases 2.2 and 2.01). A formula can include references to cells in other files, as in figure 7.16. The formula in B3 in the file LSALES refers to the total sales for Department 1 from B10 in the file XSALES1 (see fig. 7.15). Linked worksheets and formulas are described in Chapter 3.

RELEASE
2.2
Cue:
*Linking files is a
new Release 2.2
feature.*

```
B3: (,0) +<<XSALES1.WK1>>B10                                    READY

        A          B        C        D        E        F        G
 1              QTR 1    QTR 2    QTR 3    QTR 4    TOTALS
 2              ------   ------   ------   ------   ------
 3 Department 1  38,444   34,943   84,763   96,858   255,000
 4 Department 2  37,815   33,277   89,196  182,014   262,302
 5 Department 3  40,256   30,344   87,583   99,494   257,677
 6 Department 4  38,656   31,098   82,914   81,070   233,738
 7 Department 5  38,890   29,088   81,515   84,552   234,045
 8              ------   ------   ------   ------   ------
 9             194,061  158,750  425,971  463,988 1,242,770
10
11
12
13
14
15
16
17
18
19
20
LSALES.WK1               UNDO
```

Fig. 7.16.
*A worksheet
with references
to cells in other
files.*

In certain situations, you do not want to use linked files for consolidations. If you use formulas that link many external files, each time you open the consolidation file, 1-2-3 must read parts of each linked file to update the linked formulas. This process may take too long.

You may not want to update the consolidation automatically every time you read in the file. You may want to update the consolidation only once a month, for instance, when all the new detail data is available. The rest of the time, you may use the consolidation file for "what if" analysis, using the previous month's data.

When you want manual control over when and how you update a file with data from other files, use the /File Combine command. This command combines the cell contents of all or part of another file into the current file, starting at the location of the cell pointer.

The /File Combine command offers three options: Copy, Add, and Subtract. Copy enables you to replace data in the current file with data from an external file. With Add, you sum the values of the cells in the external file with the values of the cells in the current file. Subtract enables you to subtract the data in the external file from the data in the current file.

You can use any of the /File Combine options with either an entire file (Entire-File) or a range (Named/Specified-Range). The range can be a single cell or a range of cells. You can specify range addresses, but you should use range names if possible. You easily can make an error if you specify range addresses because when you execute the command, you can't see the external file from which the data is coming.

When you use the /File Combine options, blank cells in the external file are ignored. Cells with data in the external file update the corresponding cells in the current file.

Using the /File Combine Copy Command

In the section "Extracting Information," the /File Xtract command is used with a consolidated file to create separate files for the individual departments. In this section, the process is reversed. The /File Combine Copy command is used to update the consolidated file from the individual departmental files. These examples are typical of how you use the /File Xtract and /File Combine commands. You start with the consolidated file, and each month (or other time period) you extract the departmental files for input and then combine them for consolidated analysis and reporting.

You would use the /File Combine Copy command, for example, if you needed to update the SALES file with new data contained in another file—the file XSALES2, for instance (see fig. 7.17). Making sure that you are in the receiving worksheet, move the cell pointer to the upper left corner of the range to receive the combined data—in this case, C34—and execute the /File Combine Copy command (see fig. 7.18).

After selecting the /File Combine Copy command, you have the choice of combining the whole file or only a range. If you wanted to include, for example, only the values in the range C3..E5 in XSALES2, choose Named/Specified-Range; then specify the range C3..E5 and press Enter. Finally, specify the external file—in this case, XSALES2. Figure 7.19 shows how the data in figure 7.18 has been replaced by the data in figure 7.17.

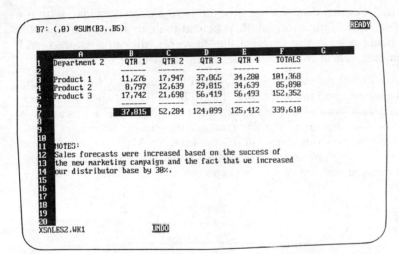

Fig. 7.17.
The XSALES2 file to be combined into SALES.

Fig. 7.18.
The SALES file before the incorporation of new data.

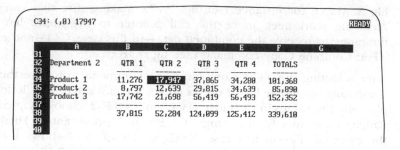

Fig. 7.19.
The SALES file
after the
incorporation
of new data.

C34: (,0) 17947   READY

	A	B	C	D	E	F	G
31							
32	Department 2	QTR 1	QTR 2	QTR 3	QTR 4	TOTALS	
33		-------	-------	-------	-------	-------	
34	Product 1	11,276	17,947	37,865	34,280	101,368	
35	Product 2	8,797	12,639	29,815	34,639	85,890	
36	Product 3	17,742	21,698	56,419	56,493	152,352	
37		-------	-------	-------	-------	-------	
38		37,815	52,284	124,099	125,412	339,610	
39							
40							

In this case, the previous data and the new data had a known format, with no blank cells. Each cell in the external file replaced the data in the current file. If there are blank cells in the external file, however, they are ignored, and the corresponding cell in the current file is left unchanged.

Caution:
If there are blank
cells in the external
file, erase the data
in the target range
before performing
a /File Combine
Copy operation.

Figure 7.20 is a variation of the input file shown in figure 7.17. In figure 7.20, Product 3 is canceled and the sales data erased. If you repeat the /File Combine Copy command to update the file in figure 7.19 with the data shown in figure 7.20 and use the range B3..E5, you get the results shown in figure 7.21. Note that the previous sales figures for Product 3 are not erased and that the totals for the department are wrong. To avoid this error, erase the range in the current file before you incorporate the new data. In this case, erase B34..E36.

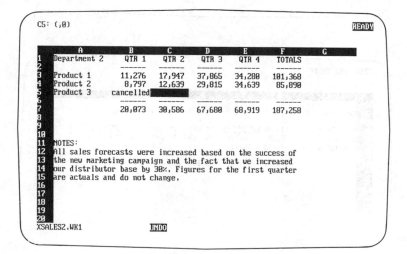

Fig. 7.20.
An input
worksheet with
blank cells to
be incorporated
into the SALES
file.

C5: (,0)   READY

	A	B	C	D	E	F	G
1	Department 2	QTR 1	QTR 2	QTR 3	QTR 4	TOTALS	
2		-------	-------	-------	-------	-------	
3	Product 1	11,276	17,947	37,865	34,280	101,368	
4	Product 2	8,797	12,639	29,815	34,639	85,890	
5	Product 3	cancelled					
6							
7		20,073	30,586	67,680	68,919	187,258	
8							
9							
10							
11	NOTES:						
12	All sales forecasts were increased based on the success of						
13	the new marketing campaign and the fact that we increased						
14	our distributor base by 30%. Figures for the first quarter						
15	are actuals and do not change.						
16							
17							
18							
19							
20							

XSALES2.WK1   UNDO

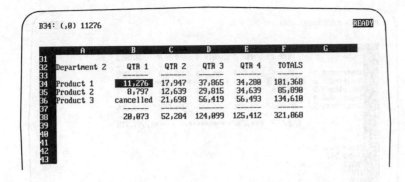

Fig. 7.21.
Incorrect results in the SALES file.

In these examples, only numbers, not formulas, are combined. You can combine formulas if you also combine the data referenced in those formulas. From figures 7.17 and 7.20 you could have incorporated B3..F7 and included the TOTALS formulas in row 7 and column F. Because you also combined the data for these formulas, the formulas would have been correct in figures 7.19 and 7.21.

Be careful when you use the **/**File Combine Copy command with formulas. Formulas—even absolute ones—adjust automatically to their new location after the execution of the **/**File Combine Copy command. In figure 7.17, for example, the formula for the total for QTR 1 in cell B7 is @SUM(B3..B5). If you combined this formula into SALES in figure 7.18, the formula adjusts to @SUM(B34..B36) in cell B38. If the formula in cell B7 of XSALES2 were @SUM($B$3..$B$5), the formula would adjust, after the execution of the **/**File Combine command, to @SUM($B$34..$B$36) in cell B38 of SALES.

If you simply combine the formulas without the data, the formulas are meaningless, and you get incorrect results. Figure 7.22 shows the master consolidation for the SALES file. Because the detail already exists in another worksheet, you could decide to combine only the totals from B7..E7 in figure 7.20 directly into B4..E4. The formula in B7 in figure 7.20 is @SUM(B3..B5). In figure 7.22, the formula adjusts to @SUM(B8192..B2), which is clearly wrong. This formula makes the figures for Department 2 wrong and causes a circular reference. To get what you want in this case, use the **/**File Combine Add command.

Cue:
*Even absolute cell references adjust with the **/**File Combine Copy command.*

Caution:
*Do not use the **/**File Combine Copy command with formulas unless you also incorporate the data referenced by the formulas.*

Using the /File Combine Add and the /File Combine Subtract Commands

The **/**File Combine Add command works somewhat like the **/**File Combine Copy command, but differs in some important ways. The **/**File Combine Subtract command is identical to the **/**File Combine Add command except

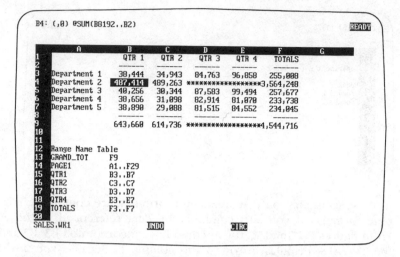

Fig. 7.22.
An erroneous
formula in the
SALES file.

that you subtract instead of add. With that exception, everything that follows about the /**File Combine Add** command applies to the /**File Combine Subtract** command as well.

Instead of replacing the contents of cells in the current file, the /**File Combine Add** command adds the values of the cells in the external file to the values of cells in the current file that contain numbers or are blank. In other words, this command adds a number or a formula result to a number or a blank cell. If the cell in the current file contains a formula, the formula is unchanged by the /**File Combine Add** command.

To update the totals correctly for Department 2 in figure 7.22, move the cell pointer to B4 and use the /**R**ange Erase command to erase B4..E4. Then use the /**File Combine Add Named/Specified-Range** command to add B7..E7 from file XSALES2 in figure 7.20. The result is shown in figure 7.23.

Fig. 7.23.
The SALES file
after being
updated with
the /File
Combine Add
command.

```
B4: (,0) 20073                                                    READY

         A            B        C        D        E        F        G
                    QTR 1    QTR 2    QTR 3    QTR 4    TOTALS
1
2                   ------   ------   ------   ------   ------
3  Department 1     30,444   34,943   84,763   96,858   255,008
4  Department 2     20,073   30,586   67,680   68,919   187,258
5  Department 3     40,256   30,344   87,583   99,494   257,677
6  Department 4     38,656   31,098   82,914   81,070   233,738
7  Department 5     38,890   29,088   81,515   84,552   234,045
8                   ------   ------   ------   ------   ------
9                  176,319  156,059  404,455  430,893 1,167,726
10
11
12 Range Name Table
13 GRAND_TOT     F9
14 PAGE1         A1..F29
15 QTR1          B3..B7
16 QTR2          C3..C7
17 QTR3          D3..D7
18 QTR4          E3..E7
19 TOTALS        F3..F7
20
SALES.WK1                       UNDO
```

The /File Combine Add command adds to the current file the current value of any formulas in the external file. Because you erased the range B4..E4 in SALES in figure 7.22, these blank cells are treated as zeros.

If you had specified a /File Combine Add range of B7..F7 instead of B7..E7, you would have gotten the same result. The total in F7 in figure 7.20 would not be added to the contents of F4 in figure 7.22 because F4 contains the formula @SUM(E4..B4). This formula remains @SUM(E4..B4) after the /File Combine Add because this command has no effect on formulas in the current file.

Be aware that with the /File Combine Add command you can add incorrect formula results. Because the /File Combine Add command converts formulas in the external file to their current values before the command adds them, these values must be current for you to get the correct result.

If XSALES2 in figure 7.20 were set to Manual calculation and the CALC indicator had been on the last time the file was saved, incorrect data could have been added during the execution of the /File Combine command. You can do nothing about this problem when you issue the /File Combine Add command. You must press the Calc (F9) key to calculate the external file before it is saved.

The other way to use the /File Combine Add command is to sum the values from two or more files into one consolidation. If all you wanted was the single row of totals in B9..F9 in figure 7.23, you could add the totals from all the input worksheets directly. First, use the /Range Erase command to erase A3..F7 (you won't be keeping department totals in this example). Make sure that F9 contains @SUM(B9..E9). Then move the cell pointer to B9 and use the /Range Erase command on B9..E9. Finally, use the /File Combine Add command to add the totals from each input file (XSALES1, XSALES2, and so on). This process accumulates the totals from each department.

If you have a separate file for credits or returns, you can use the /File Combine Subtract command to subtract these returns. If the returns are entered as negative numbers, however, you should use the /File Combine Add command to add the negative numbers and thereby correctly decrease the sales totals.

Caution:
Make sure that the CALC indicator is off before you save a file that might be used for a /File Combine Add or Subtract operation.

Protecting Files with Passwords

You can protect worksheet files by using passwords. Once a file is password-protected, no one (including you) can read the file without first issuing the password. This restriction applies to the /File Retrieve, /File Combine, and Translate commands.

You password-protect a file when you specify the file name during a **/File Save** or **/File Xtract** command execution. Type the file name, press the space bar once, press p, and then press Enter (see fig 7.24). 1-2-3 prompts you to type a password of 1 to 15 characters. The password cannot contain spaces. As you type, the cursor moves but nothing appears on-screen.

Fig. 7.24.
Protecting a
file with a
password.

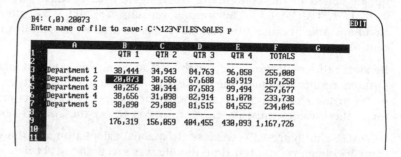

After you type the password, press Enter. You are prompted to type the password again. Type it again and press Enter. Only blank spaces appear where the words have been typed (see fig. 7.25). If both passwords are identical, the file is saved in a special format, and neither you nor anyone else can access the file without first giving the password. If the two passwords do not match, 1-2-3 displays an error message, and you must type the password again.

Fig. 7.25.
The control
panel after you
have typed the
password twice.

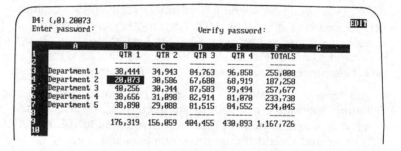

Caution:
If you forget the
password, you
cannot access a
password-protected
file.

Passwords are case-sensitive. When you first assign a password, check the Caps Lock indicator so that you know how you are entering letters.

When you use **Retrieve** or **Combine** with a password-protected file, 1-2-3 prompts you for the password. Only if you type the password correctly will you have access to the file.

When you save a file that has already been saved with a password, 1-2-3 displays the message [PASSWORD PROTECTED] after the file name (see fig. 7.26). To save the file with the same password, just press Enter. To delete the password, press Backspace once to clear the [PASSWORD PROTECTED] message;

then press Enter. To change the password, press Backspace once to clear the [PASSWORD PROTECTED] message, press the space bar once, press p, and press Enter. Finally, assign a new password.

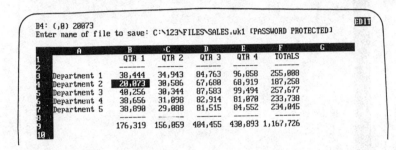

Fig. 7.26.
A password-protected file that is about to be saved again.

Erasing Files

Every time you save a file under a different file name, you use some space on your disk. Eventually you will run out of disk space if you do not occasionally erase old, unneeded files from the disk. Even if you still have disk space left, you will have a harder time finding the files you want to open if the disk contains many obsolete files. Before you erase files, you may want to save them to a diskette in case you ever need them again.

To erase an unneeded file from disk, use the /File Erase command. This command permanently removes the file from disk and frees the disk space for other files. You also can use DOS' ERASE or DEL command to erase files on disk. Within 1-2-3, you can erase only one file at a time.

When you choose the /File Erase command, the menu shown in figure 7.27 appears. Use this menu to select the type of file you want to erase. If you choose Worksheet, 1-2-3 lists all files in the current directory that have .WK* extensions (unless you change the default with the /File List Other command). If you choose Print, 1-2-3 lists all files contained in the current directory that have .PRN extensions. Choosing Graph produces a list of all files contained in the current directory that have .PIC extensions. Choosing Other produces a list in the current directory.

To list some other set of files, choose any of the options in figure 7.27; then type the file specification. To list all worksheet files that start with BUDGET, type **BUDGET*.WK***; to list all backup files, type ***.BAK**; and so on. When the file you want to erase is listed, highlight the file name and press Enter. Choose Yes to confirm that you want to erase the file. 1-2-3 erases the file.

Warning:
Once you erase a file from disk, you cannot recover it without using a special utility program.

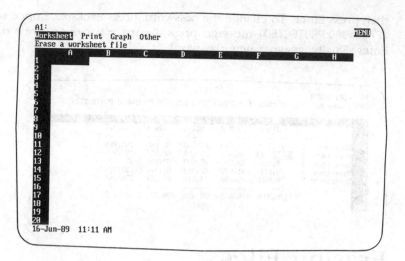

Fig. 7.27.
The File Erase
menu.

Creating Lists and Tables of Files

1-2-3 provides commands to help you keep track of the files you have on disk. You can either list the files or save a table of files in your worksheet. If you work with many files, you may forget the names of certain files or the times they were last updated.

RELEASE
2.2

To see a list of files, use the /File List command. For 1-2-3 Release 2.2, the menu shown in figure 7.28 appears. For 1-2-3 Release 2.01, the first four menu choices appear; Linked does not appear. The Worksheet, Print, Graph, and Other options provide the same lists that they provide with the File Erase menu described earlier. Choose Linked from the File List menu only when there is a worksheet in memory. If there is, 1-2-3 lists all files referenced in formulas to the worksheet.

Fig. 7.28.
The File List or
File Admin
Table menu.

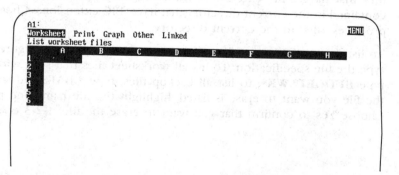

In 1-2-3 Release 2.2, you can save a file list as a table in your worksheet by using the **/File Admin Table** command. You get the same menu as in figure 7.28. If you choose **Worksheet**, you create a table starting at the current position of the cell pointer (see fig. 7.29). You may have to change the column widths to see all the information.

RELEASE

2.2

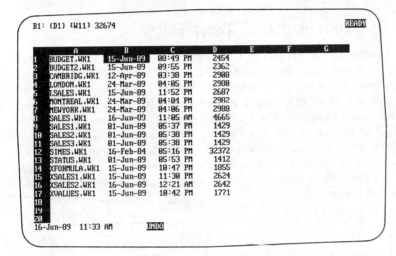

```
B1: (D1) [W11] 32674                                              READY

        A           B            C          D        E      F       G
1   BUDGET.WK1    15-Jun-89   08:49 PM     2454
2   BUDGET2.WK1   15-Jun-89   09:55 PM     2362
3   CAMBRIDG.WK1  12-Apr-89   03:38 PM     2988
4   LONDON.WK1    24-Mar-89   04:05 PM     2980
5   LSALES.WK1    15-Jun-89   11:52 PM     2687
6   MONTREAL.WK1  24-Mar-89   04:04 PM     2982
7   NEWYORK.WK1   24-Mar-89   04:06 PM     2988
8   SALES.WK1     16-Jun-89   11:05 AM     4665
9   SALES1.WK1    01-Jun-89   05:37 PM     1429
10  SALES2.WK1    01-Jun-89   05:38 PM     1429
11  SALES3.WK1    01-Jun-89   05:38 PM     1429
12  SIMES.WK1     16-Feb-84   05:16 PM    32372
13  STATUS.WK1    01-Jun-89   05:53 PM     1412
14  XFORMULA.WK1  15-Jun-89   10:47 PM     1855
15  XSALES1.WK1   15-Jun-89   11:30 PM     2624
16  XSALES2.WK1   16-Jun-89   12:21 AM     2642
17  XVALUES.WK1   15-Jun-89   10:42 PM     1771
18
19
20
16-Jun-89  11:33 AM        UNDO
```

Fig. 7.29.
A list shown in
a worksheet.

The first column lists the file name. The second column lists the date the file was last saved. (You have to format these cells as a date.) The third column lists the time the file was last saved. (You have to format these cells as a time.) The fourth column lists the file size in bytes. These first four columns are included when you choose any of the table options. The list is constructed in a range you specify in the worksheet.

Transferring Files

1-2-3 provides a number of ways to pass data between itself and other programs. The simplest file format is straight text; a straight text file also is called an *ASCII file*. Most programs can create text files. To create a text file in 1-2-3, use the **/Print File** command (see Chapter 8). To read a text file into a worksheet, use the **/File Import** command.

Transferring Files with the /File Import Command

The **/File Import** command is a special type of **/File Combine** command. You combine the information into the current worksheet, starting at the position of the cell pointer. Any existing data in these cells is overwritten. When you execute the /File Import command, 1-2-3 lists the .PRN files contained in the current directory. To list files that have another extension—.TXT, for example—type the appropriate characters (such as *.TXT) and press Enter.

Importing Unstructured Text Files

The typical text file contains lines of data, each line ending with a carriage return. Except for the carriage returns, these text files have no structure. You combine them by using the /File Import Text command. Figure 7.30 shows the result of importing a typical text file into a worksheet. Each line in the text file becomes a long label in a cell. All the data is in column A. If you import a list of names or simply want to see this data, you are finished. In most cases, however, you want to work with this data in separate cells. And you want numbers as numbers and dates as dates, not labels. To make this data usable, use the /Data Parse command. See Chapter 12 for a complete discussion of this command.

Fig. 7.30.
An
unstructured
text file
imported with
the /File
Import Text
command.

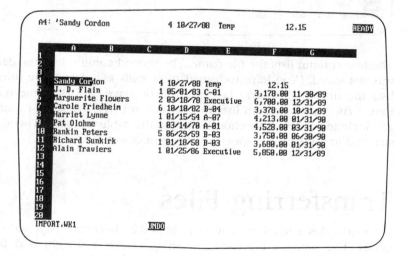

Importing Delimited Files

Some ASCII files are in a special format that enables them to be imported into separate cells without being parsed. This special format is called the *delimited format*. There is a delimiter between each field, and labels are enclosed in quotation marks. A delimiter can be a space, comma, colon, or semicolon. If the labels are not enclosed in quotation marks, they are ignored, and only the numbers are imported.

To import a delimited file, use the /File Import Numbers command. In spite of the name, this command really means "file import delimited." Figure 7.31 is an example of a delimited file. Figure 7.32 shows the results after executing the /File Import Numbers command and adjusting column widths.

```
"Part Name","Part Number","Qty","Cost","Retail"
"Hammer","H0101",12,1.95,3.99
"Wrench","W0998",15,3.25,5.99
"Standard Screw Driver","S0099",30,1.87,1.99
"Phillips Screw Driver","S0101",25,1.27,2.09
"Hack Saw","00201",5,4.22,6.99
"Jig Saw","10020",5,22.94,29.99
```

Fig. 7.31.
A delimited
ASCII file.

```
C2: [W5] 12                                              READY

           A              B          C    D      E      F      G
1   Part Name         Part Number  Qty  Cost   Retail
2   Hammer            H0101         12   1.95   3.99
3   Wrench            W0998         15   3.25   5.99
4   Standard Screw Driver  S0099    30   1.87   1.99
5   Phillips Screw Driver  S0101    25   1.27   2.09
6   Hack Saw          00201          5   4.22   6.99
7   Jig Saw           10020          5   22.94  29.99
8
9
10
11
12
13
14
15
16
17
18
19
20
IMPORTN.WK1              UNDO
```

Fig. 7.32.
The delimited
ASCII file after
executing the
/File Import
Numbers
command and
adjusting
column widths.

Transferring Files with the Translate Utility

Translate is not part of the 1-2-3 worksheet program but is a separate program. Type **trans** from the operating system prompt to execute Translate, or choose Translate from the 1-2-3 Access System menu.

Use Translate to convert files so that they can be read by a different program. You can convert files to 1-2-3 Release 2.2, 2.01, or 2 from the following programs:

- 1-2-3 Release 1A
- Symphony 1.0, 1.1, 1.2, 2.0
- VisiCalc

RELEASE

2.2

- dBASE II, dBASE III, and dBASE III PLUS
- Multiplan
- Products that use the DIF format

RELEASE

2.2

Entire
Section

You can convert files from 1-2-3 Release 2.2, 2.01, or 2 to the following programs:

- 1-2-3 Release 1A
- 1-2-3 Release 3
- Symphony Release 1, 1.01, 1.1, 1.2, and 2
- dBASE II, dBASE III, and dBASE III Plus
- Products that use the DIF format

When you convert 1-2-3 Release 2.2 files to prior releases of 1-2-3 or Symphony, you will lose some information if you use any of the features unique to Release 2.2.

To use Translate, first choose the format or program from which you want to translate; then choose the format or program to which you want to translate (see figs. 7.33 and 7.34). Note that dBASE III Plus is not listed in figure 7.33, but it is available by selecting dBASE III. Finally, choose the file you want to translate. Type the file name of the output file and press Enter.

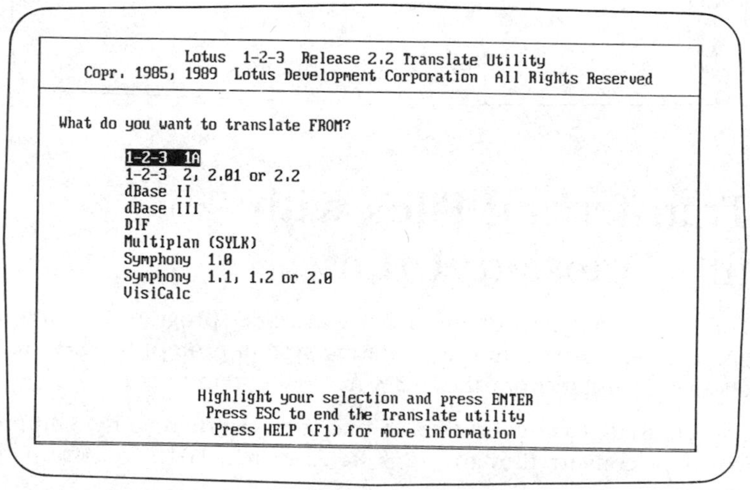

Fig. 7.33.
The menu of choices to translate from other programs to 1-2-3.

```
              Lotus  1-2-3  Release 2.2 Translate Utility
       Copr. 1985, 1989  Lotus Development Corporation  All Rights Reserved

    What do you want to translate FROM?

              1-2-3  1A
              1-2-3  2, 2.01 or 2.2
              dBase II
              dBase III
              DIF
              Multiplan (SYLK)
              Symphony  1.0
              Symphony  1.1, 1.2 or 2.0
              VisiCalc




              Highlight your selection and press ENTER
              Press ESC to end the Translate utility
              Press HELP (F1) for more information
```

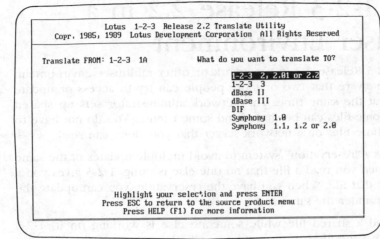

```
            Lotus  1-2-3  Release 2.2 Translate Utility
   Copr, 1985, 1989  Lotus Development Corporation  All Rights Reserved


   Translate FROM: 1-2-3  1A          What do you want to translate TO?

                                      1-2-3  2, 2.01 or 2.2
                                      1-2-3  3
                                      dBase II
                                      dBase III
                                      DIF
                                      Symphony  1.0
                                      Symphony  1.1, 1.2 or 2.0




                   Highlight your selection and press ENTER
                 Press ESC to return to the source product menu
                     Press HELP (F1) for more information
```

Fig. 7.34.
The menu of choices to translate to other programs from 1-2-3.

When you translate to dBASE format, you can translate the entire file or a named range. In most cases, the file contains data in addition to the input range; therefore, make sure that you use the **/Range Name** command to name the database input range. When you translate a file into a dBASE format, the range or entire file must consist only of a database input range.

Using 1-2-3 Release 1A and Symphony Files in Release 2.2, 2.01, or 2

1-2-3 Releases 2.2, 2.01, and 2 can read files created by 1-2-3 Release 1A and all releases of Symphony. Just use the **/File Retrieve** command and specify the complete file name and extension; you do not have to use Translate. The Translate menu seems to give you the option of translating files to 1-2-3 Release 2.2, 2.01, or 2 format from the format for 1-2-3 Release 1A and Symphony (see fig. 7.34). However, if you choose one of these formats, you simply get a message telling you that you do not need to translate the file.

1-2-3 Release 2.2 can write files in 1-2-3 Release 2.01 format without errors if you haven't used any features unique to Release 2.2. Just use the **/File Save** command. Symphony Releases 1.1, 1.2, and 2 also can read these files.

If a file in Release 2.2 format is linked to other worksheets (a unique Release 2.2 feature), for example, ERR will appear in each cell in the worksheet when you execute a **/File Retrieve** command in 1-2-3 Release 2.01 or 2. Formats and settings new with Release 2.2 are lost.

To create a Release 2.2, 2.01, or 2 file that can be read by 1-2-3 Release 1A or Symphony Releases 1 or 1.01, you must use Translate.

RELEASE

2.2

Entire
Section

Using 1-2-3 Release 2.2 in a Multiuser Environment

If you use 1-2-3 Release 2.2 in a network or other multiuser environment, you should be aware that two or more people can try to access or update the same file at the same time. The network administrator sets up shared disks so that some files can be shared and some cannot. You do not have to worry about those files on a network server that you alone can read.

Release 2.2 has a "reservation" system to avoid multiple updates of the same shared file. When you read a file that no one else is using, 1-2-3 gives you a reservation for that file. When you have the reservation, you can update the file and save it under the same name.

When you read a shared file while someone else is working on it, 1-2-3 prompts you that the file is in use and asks whether you want the file without the reservation. If you choose **Yes**, you can access the file in read-only status. The RO status indicator at the bottom of the screen warns you that you cannot save the file under its current name. If you want to save the file, you must give it a different name.

If you have the reservation for a file, you keep the reservation until you remove the file (under the same name) from your worksheet. You can remove the file with the **/Quit**, **/Worksheet Erase**, or **/File Retrieve** command. You also can release the reservation with **/File Save** if you save the file under a different name. You can release the reservation manually with the **/File Admin Reservation Release** command. You still have the file in memory, but you cannot save the file.

When you have a file that contains references to other files, 1-2-3 updates these formulas when you read in the file. If you believe that one or more of these external files were updated since you read your file, use the **/File Admin Link-Refresh** command to update these formulas.

Suppose that you are working on the SALES worksheet, while someone else on the network is editing SALES2. Notice in figure 7.35, the SALES worksheet is linked to cell B8 in the SALES2 worksheet. When a value changes in SALES2 (see fig. 7.36) and the file is saved, your worksheet does not reflect the change. Issue **/File Admin Link-Refresh** to recalculate all links to other files (see fig. 7.37). See Chapter 3 for more information on linking files and using the **/File Admin Link-Refresh** command.

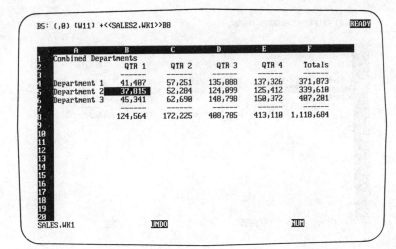

Fig. 7.35.
*The SALES file
linked to the
SALES2 file.*

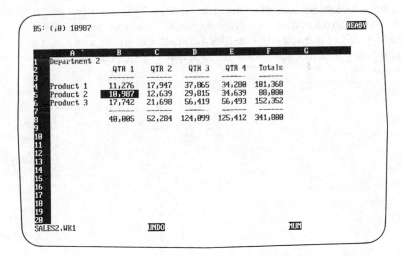

Fig. 7.36.
The SALES2 file.

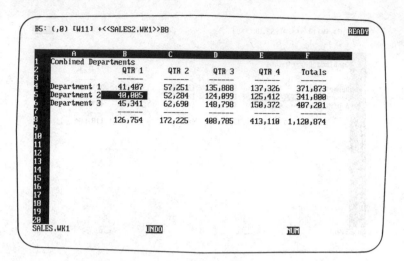

Fig. 7.37.
The updated
SALES file.

Chapter Summary

In this chapter, you learn how to manage files on disk, how to save and read in whole files, and how to extract and combine partial files. You see how to combine text files and translate files in other formats. Creating lists and tables of files to help you keep track of your files on disk and in memory is covered also. Finally, this chapter discusses the special considerations for using 1-2-3 on a network.

Part II

Creating 1-2-3 Reports and Graphs

Includes

Printing Reports

Using Allways: The Spreadsheet Publisher

Creating and Displaying Graphs

Printing Graphs

8

Printing Reports

The 1-2-3 program is a powerful tool for developing information presented in column-and-row format. You can enter and edit your worksheet and database files on-screen as well as store the input on disk. But to make use of your data, you often need it in printed form: as a target production schedule, a summary report to your supervisor, or a detailed reorder list to central stores, for example.

By using 1-2-3's /Print command, you can access many levels of print options to meet your printing needs. You can elect to write directly from 1-2-3 to the printer by using the /Print Printer command. Or use the alternative /Print File command to create a print (.PRN) file. Later, you can produce a printout of the file from within 1-2-3 or from DOS, or you can incorporate the file into a word processing file.

This chapter shows you how to complete the following tasks:

- Choose between /Print Printer and /Print File
- Print using default settings
- Print single or multiple pages
- Exclude segments within a designated print range
- Control paper movement
- Change the default settings
- Test the print format of large print ranges
- Print worksheet contents cell-by-cell
- Prepare output for acceptance by other programs

281

Because you must use the PrintGraph program to print graphs, printing graphs is not covered in this chapter. See Chapter 11 for a complete discussion of the PrintGraph program.

Choosing Between /Print Printer and /Print File

Cue:
Choose /Print File
to create a file to
be incorporated
into a word
processing file.

To start any print operation, you select the **/P**rint command from 1-2-3's main menu. When you select **/P**rint, you next select one of two options (see fig. 8.1). To print to a printer, choose **P**rinter. Choose **F**ile to create a file on disk; later you can print the file from within 1-2-3 or incorporate the file into a word processing file.

Fig. 8.1.
The initial
print decision:
print to the
printer or to a
disk file.

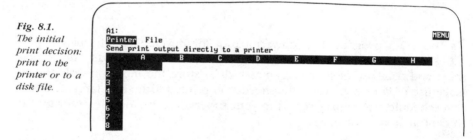

When you choose **F**ile, you are prompted for a file name. Type a name up to eight characters long. You don't need to add a file extension because 1-2-3 automatically assigns the .PRN (print file) extension. You can incorporate the file into a 1-2-3 worksheet again by using the **/F**ile Import command. In this case, the file will not be the same as your original worksheet file; imported .PRN files consist of long labels. (**/F**ile Import is discussed in Chapter 7.) You also can view a .PRN file by using the DOS TYPE command, a word processor's print command, or a special printing routine. See the section "Preparing Output for Other Programs" for more information on printing to a file.

RELEASE

2.2

After you select either **P**rinter or **F**ile, another **P**rint menu is displayed in the control panel. In Release 2.2, the Print Settings sheet is displayed also, showing the current settings (see fig. 8.2).

The **P**rint [**P**,**F**] menu presents the following choices:

Menu Selection	Description
Range	Indicates what section of the worksheet is to be printed
Line	Adjusts the paper line-by-line in the printer

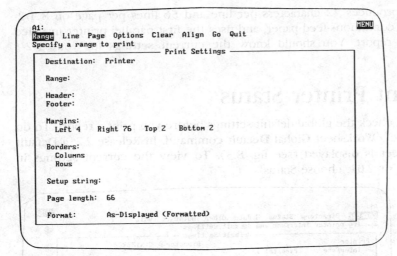

Fig. 8.2.
The main Print menu and the Print Settings sheet.

Menu Selection	Description
Page	Adjusts the paper page-by-page in the printer
Options	Makes available options to change default settings and enhance the appearance of the printout
Clear	Erases settings previously entered
Align	Signals the beginning of each page in the printer
Go	Starts printing
Quit	Exits the Print menu

Regardless of whether you select **Printer** or **File**, you follow the same procedure to print: specify a range to print, select **Go**, and then select **Quit** to return to the worksheet. All other selections are optional. Before you learn about specific selections from the **Print** menu, you need to understand 1-2-3's default print settings.

Understanding the Print Default Settings

To minimize the keystrokes necessary for a print operation, 1-2-3 makes certain assumptions about how you want your copy printed. The usual print operation produces 72 characters per line and 56 lines per page on 8 1/2-by-11-inch continuous-feed paper, and uses the first parallel printer installed to print a report. You should know the current settings for your 1-2-3 program.

Current Printer Status

RELEASE

2.2

Cue:
Use /Worksheet
Global Default to
check current
default print
settings.

You should check the global default settings before you print a report. To do so, issue the **/W**orksheet **G**lobal **D**efault command. In Release 2.2, a Default Settings sheet is displayed (see fig. 8.3). To view the current settings in Release 2.0 or 2.01, choose **S**tatus.

Fig. 8.3.
The Worksheet
Global Default
menu and the
Default Settings
sheet.

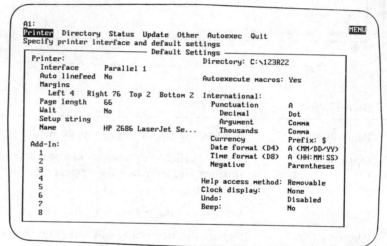

```
A1:                                                                    MENU
Printer Directory Status Update Other Autoexec Quit
Specify printer interface and default settings
                        ┌──────── Default Settings ────────
   Printer:                              Directory: C:\123R22
     Interface      Parallel 1
     Auto linefeed  No                   Autoexecute macros: Yes
     Margins
        Left 4   Right 76  Top 2  Bottom 2   International:
     Page length    66                       Punctuation      A
     Wait           No                          Decimal       Dot
     Setup string                              Argument       Comma
     Name           HP 2686 LaserJet Se...     Thousands      Comma
                                             Currency      Prefix: $
   Add-In:                                   Date format (D4)  A (MM/DD/YY)
     1                                       Time format (D8)  A (HH:MM:SS)
     2                                       Negative          Parentheses
     3
     4                                     Help access method: Removable
     5                                     Clock display:      None
     6                                     Undo:               Disabled
     7                                     Beep:               No
     8
```

The upper left area of the Default Settings sheet indicates the default printer settings. You use **P**rinter to change a setting for the current work session and choose **U**pdate to make the change remain in effect every time you reload 1-2-3.

The settings discussed in this chapter are in the upper left corner of the status screen. The first two settings contain hardware-specific information; the margins and page length sections show page layout. Any setup strings in effect are displayed on-screen. Wait is the setting for manual-feed paper, and Name indicates which specific parallel printer is installed.

Global Default Hardware-Specific Options

If you want to change any of the print settings shown in the default status report, issue the **/W**orksheet **G**lobal **D**efault **P**rinter command. Notice that

the first two options in the menu shown in figure 8.4 correspond to the first
two settings in the default status report: Interface and AutoLF.

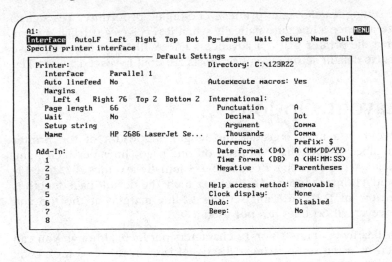

Fig. 8.4
The Worksheet
Global Default
Printer menu.

Use the Interface option to specify one of eight possible connections between your computer and your printer:

1 First parallel port (the default)
2 First serial port
3 Second parallel port
4 Second serial port
5 DOS Device LPT1
6 DOS Device LPT2
7 DOS Device LPT3
8 DOS Device LPT4

Choices 5 through 8 are applicable only if your workstation is part of a local
area network. If you select either serial port option (2 or 4), another menu
appears. From this menu, you must specify one of the following baud rates
(data transmission speed). For example, a 1200 baud rate roughly equals 120
characters per second.

1 110 baud
2 150 baud
3 300 baud
4 600 baud
5 1200 baud
6 2400 baud
7 4800 baud
8 9600 baud
9 19200 baud

Check your printer manual for information about the type of interface and baud rate, if applicable.

Reminder:
Set AutoLF to Yes
for double-spaced
reports.

The AutoLF setting specifies the printer's end-of-line procedure. **Yes** signals the printer to advance a line automatically when it receives a carriage return; **No** means that the printer will not advance a line. With most printers, leave AutoLF in its **No** default setting. If your reports are double-spaced, select **Yes.**

Page Layout Options

For page layout, you must consider the length and width of the printer paper, the number of lines that will print on one page (lines per inch), and the pitch (characters per inch). Because 1-2-3 initially assumes 8 1/2-by-11-inch paper and a printer output of 6 lines per inch, the default page length is 66 lines. Because of 1-2-3's default settings (2-line margins at the top and bottom), however, all 66 lines are not used.

Every line ordinarily contains 10 or 12 characters per inch, although you can vary the pitch by using setup strings (discussed later in this chapter). Look again at figure 8.4. Five options determine default page-layout characteristics:

Option	Message
Left	Default left margin (0..240):4
Right	Default right margin (0..240):76
Top	Default top margin (0..32):2
Bot	Default bottom margin (0..32):2
Pg-Length	Default lines per page (1..100):66

In each message, the number at the end of the message indicates the default value, and the numbers enclosed in parentheses indicate the minimum and maximum values you can select.

To calculate the width of your report, subtract the current left-margin setting (4) from the current right-margin setting (76). Your report will be printed with 72 characters per line.

Reminder:
1-2-3 automatically
reserves 3 lines
each for a header
and footer, even if
you do not enter
any.

To calculate how many lines of your worksheet will actually be printed, you need to subtract not only the lines for top and bottom margins, but also the lines that 1-2-3 automatically reserves for a header and a footer. If you are using all default settings, for example, the actual number of lines (or rows) from your worksheet that will be printed is 56. 1-2-3 assigns 2 lines each for the top and bottom margins, and reserves 3 lines each for a header and a footer. The 6 header and footer lines are reserved even if you do not enter a header or footer. Because the default page length is 66, you subtract 4 lines for top and bottom margins and the 6 lines reserved for a header and footer to get 56 printed lines. (To learn how to enter headers and footers, see the section "Creating Headers and Footers" in this chapter.)

Other Default Options: Wait, Setup, and Name

The final three default printer settings control the way paper is fed to the printer (**Wait**), the size and style of type (**Setup**), and the specific printer you use (**Name**).

If you are using continuous-feed paper or a laser printer or automatic sheet feeder that can feed single sheets, leave the **Wait** option set to **No** (the default). If you are using single sheets of paper, select **Yes** to change the default setting; printing will pause at the end of each page so that you can insert a new sheet of paper. After you insert the page, press Enter to continue printing.

Reminder:
For printing on single sheets of paper, change the **W**ait *option to* **Yes** *to have the printer pause after printing each sheet.*

The default setting for **Setup** is no setup string. This means that no special printer-control codes, such as condensed print, 8 lines per inch instead of 6, or boldface type, are in effect. (For examples of setup strings, see the section "Changing the Print Options" in this chapter.)

The menu that appears after you select **Name** depends on which printers you installed when you installed 1-2-3. For example, you may have installed your 1-2-3 program to print on two different printers: the EPSON printer you have at home and the Toshiba printer at work. In this case, selecting **Name** produces a menu with options **1** (the EPSON) and **2** (the Toshiba).

Remember that if you use the **/W**orksheet **G**lobal **D**efault **P**rinter command to change print settings, the new settings remain in effect for the current work session only. To have the settings remain the default whenever you start 1-2-3, use the **/W**orksheet **G**lobal **D**efault **U**pdate command after you have made the changes you want.

Reminder:
Use **/W**orksheet **G**lobal **D**efault **U**pdate *to make your new default settings "permanent."*

Printing a Draft-Quality Report

1-2-3's **P**rint menu is designed for the simplest to most complex worksheet printing needs. If you want to print a report quickly that neither requires changing any default print settings (such as those for paper size) nor requires special enhancements (such as headers, footers, or different size and style of type), you can print a report with default settings. If you want to dress up your report or have special requirements for paper size, margins, or page length, you need to use the commands available in the **P**rint menu system. To illustrate printing techniques, this chapter uses the large worksheet in figure 8.5, which occupies the range A1..T130.

	A	B	C	D	E	F
	CASH FLOW PROJECTOR			Copyright (C) 1987 Que Corporation		

BALANCES IN WORKING CAPITAL ACCOUNTS

	Dec	Jan	Feb	Mar	Apr	May	Jun	Jul	Aug	Sep	Oct	Nov	Dec	Total
Assets														
Cash	17,355	31,643	34,333	36,657	35,614	29,146	20,000	20,000	20,000	76,623	186,131	337,995	582,796	570,036
Accounts Receivable	493,151	490,780	535,597	577,314	577,314	641,082	641,082	750,544	879,271	989,501	1,097,616	1,370,465	1,218,036	1,218,036
Inventory	163,833	169,209	170,671	189,246	206,788	228,828	269,990	296,527	324,230	345,629	352,687	358,926	358,926	358,926
Liabilities														
Accounts Payable	125,000	130,754	139,851	150,186	163,731	180,350	203,669	225,085	243,320	258,740	267,621	272,747	275,041	275,041
Line of Credit							1,834	8,327	2,035	0	0	0	0	
Net Working Capital	549,339	580,878	604,750	627,003	655,984	692,620	726,289	833,659	978,146	1,153,013	1,368,812	1,594,820	1,884,718	5,388,970

SALES

	Oct	Nov	Dec	Jan	Feb	Mar	Apr	May	Jun	Jul	Aug	Sep	Oct	Nov	Dec	Total
Profit Center 1	27,832	23,864	26,125	31,336	37,954	43,879	51,471	56,953	53,145	54,140	53,614	52,015	48,902	44,091	42,536	570,036
Profit Center 2	13,489	21,444	20,140	22,572	24,888	25,167	32,588	40,140	37,970	34,587	33,463	28,939	24,153	26,701	26,155	358,828
Profit Center 3	126,611	124,382	123,618	131,685	129,044	131,723	139,221	141,539	108,803	147,108	149,803	110,401	112,018	127,956	107,522	1,254,073
Profit Center 4	94,285	92,447	89,010	95,473	98,008	96,986	95,318	103,538	108,146	108,642	104,065	225,000	300,000	325,000	350,000	1,490,000
Profit Center 5										115,000	175,000	225,000	300,000	325,000	350,000	1,490,000
Total Sales	262,417	262,137	258,893	281,066	289,894	297,755	318,598	342,510	349,064	459,477	515,174	569,795	635,063	653,305	677,269	5,388,970

Percent of																
Collections	Cash	10%	10%	10%	10%	10%	10%	10%	10%	10%	10%	10%	10%	10%	10%
	30 Days	20%	20%	20%	20%	20%	20%	20%	20%	20%	20%	20%	20%	20%	20%
	60 Days	50%	50%	50%	50%	50%	50%	50%	50%	50%	50%	50%	50%	50%	50%
	90 Days	20%	20%	20%	20%	20%	20%	20%	20%	20%	20%	20%	20%	20%	20%

	Jan	Feb	Mar	Apr	May	Jun	Jul	Aug	Sep	Oct	Nov	Dec	Total
Cash Collections	263,437	267,077	280,066	292,571	304,827	322,258	350,735	386,447	459,566	526,948	580,275	629,878	4,664,085

PURCHASES

	Oct	Nov	Dec	Jan	Feb	Mar	Apr	May	Jun	Jul	Aug	Sep	Oct	Nov	Dec	Total
Cost of Goods Sold																
Profit Center 1	33%	33%	33%	33%	33%	33%	33%	33%	33%	33%	33%	33%	33%	33%	33%	
	9,185	7,875	8,621	10,341	12,525	14,480	16,985	18,794	17,538	17,866	17,693	17,135	16,138	14,550	14,037	188,112
Profit Center 2	29%	29%	29%	29%	29%	29%	29%	29%	29%	29%	29%	29%	29%	29%	29%	
	3,912	6,219	5,841	6,546	7,218	7,298	9,451	11,641	11,011	10,030	9,704	8,392	7,004	7,743	7,580	103,886
Profit Center 3	50%	50%	50%	50%	50%	50%	50%	50%	50%	50%	50%	50%	50%	50%	50%	
	63,406	62,191	61,809	65,843	64,522	65,862	69,611	70,940	74,902	73,554	73,516	76,720	74,995	72,599	75,255	858,317
Profit Center 4	67%	67%	67%	67%	67%	67%	67%	67%	67%	67%	67%	67%	67%	67%	67%	
	63,171	61,939	59,637	63,967	65,665	64,981	63,663	69,637	72,458	72,790	71,064	75,052	75,011	75,637	72,040	840,229
Profit Center 5	30%	30%	30%	30%	30%	30%	30%	30%	30%	30%	30%	30%	30%	30%	30%	
	0	0	0	0	0	0	0	0	0	34,500	52,500	67,500	90,000	97,500	105,000	447,000
Total Cost of Goods Sold	139,673	138,224	135,908	146,696	149,930	152,621	159,910	170,745	175,908	208,741	224,476	243,746	263,189	267,507	274,075	2,437,543

Inventory	0 Days in Advance	5%	5%	5%	5%	5%	5%	5%	5%	5%	5%	5%	5%	5%	5%	5%
Purchasing	30 Days in Advance	50%	50%	50%	50%	50%	50%	50%	50%	50%	50%	50%	50%	50%	50%	50%
Schedule	60 Days in Advance	30%	30%	30%	30%	30%	30%	30%	30%	30%	30%	30%	30%	30%	30%	30%

Fig. 8.5. *The Cash Flow Projector worksheet.*

		Oct	Nov	Dec	Jan	Feb	Mar	Apr	May	Jun	Jul	Aug	Sep	Oct	Nov	Dec	Total
Inventory Purchases	90 Days in Advance	15%	15%	15%	15%	15%	15%	15%	15%	15%	15%	15%	15%	15%	15%	15%	15%
		$138,873	$141,363	$148,015	$152,072	$157,391	$165,196	$177,452	$192,785	$217,07*	$235,277	$252,180	$265,145	$270,24*	$273,747	$274,075	$2,632,637
Payment	Cash 30%	30%	30%	30%	30%	30%	30%	30%	30%	30%	30%	30%	30%	30%	30%	30%	30%
Schedule	30 Days 40%	40%	40%	40%	40%	40%	40%	40%	40%	40%	40%	40%	40%	40%	40%	40%	40%
	60 Days 30%	30%	30%	30%	30%	30%	30%	30%	30%	30%	30%	30%	30%	30%	30%	30%	30%
Payment for Purchases				$142,612	$147,237	$152,451	$158,137	$166,531	$178,375	$195,47	$215,247	$234,886	$250,999	$262,785	$269,766	$272,795	$2,504,680
OPERATING EXPENSES																	
Profit Center 1		$20,458	$20,760	$20,963	$21,529	$22,329	$22,802	$23,108	$24,099	$24,428	$24,411	$24,42	$25,646	$26,515	$26,639	$26,881	$293,461
Profit Center 2		14,377	15,002	15,587	15,946	16,790	17,355	17,759	18,195	18,610	30,246	19,546	20,348	20,860	21,729	21,785	228,315
Profit Center 3		25,921	26,395	27,339	17,554	28,286	27,464	29,275	29,292	29,578	30,246	30,358	31,041	31,680	32,048	32,525	360,347
Profit Center 4		13,922	14,885	15,801	16,130	16,800	17,651	18,000	18,789	19,70	20,400	20,939	21,589	21,833	22,024	22,154	236,052
Profit Center 5						10,000	1,000	18,000	20,000	22,00	22,470	22,837	22,995	23,344	24,023	24,806	224,495
Corporate Overhead		14,944	15,262	15,801	16,332	16,474	1,933	17,616	18,575	19,278	19,544	18,640	20,225	21,1+2	21,565	22,378	228,702
Total Expenses		$89,622	$92,302	$95,491	$97,491	$110,679	$117,205	$123,777	$128,950	$132,954	$136,237	$138,284	$141,844	$145,394	$148,028	$150,529	$1,571,372
Payment	Cash 70%	70%	70%	70%	70%	70%	70%	70%	70%	70%	70%	70%	70%	70%	70%	70%	70%
Schedule	30 Days 20%	20%	20%	20%	20%	20%	20%	20%	20%	0%	20%	20%	20%	20%	20%	20%	20%
	60 Days 10%	10%	10%	10%	10%	10%	10%	10%	10%	0%	10%	10%	10%	10%	10%	10%	10%
Total Payment for Expenses				$94,266	$96,572	$106,523	$115,928	$121,153	$126,741	$131,256	$134,852	$137,342	$140,571	$143,973	$146,883	$149,515	$1,549,288
CASH FLOW SUMMARY																	
Collection of Receivables					$263,437	$267,077	$280,066	$292,571	$304,82*	$322,2B8	$350,735	$386,447	$459,566	$526,948	$580,275	$629,878	$4,466,085
Other Cash Receipts					0	0	0	0	0	50,000	0	0	0	0	0	50,000	50,000
Cash Disbursements																	
Payment for Purchases on Credit					147,237	152,451	18,137	166,531	178,375	195,471	215,247	234,886	250,999	262,785	269,766	272,795	2,504,680
Operating Expenses					96,572	106,523	3,928	121,153	126,741	131,236	134,852	137,342	140,571	143,973	146,883	149,515	1,549,288
Long-Term Debt Service				13.50%	13.50%	13.50%	13.50%	13.50%	13.50%		13.50%	13.50%	13.50%	13.50%	13.50%	13.50%	137
Interest Payment on Line of Credit					94	21	23	94	32		7,833	7,109	9,315	10,581	11,762	12,767	94,538
Interest Rate					5,340	5,413	5,677	5,930	6,199	6,32	7,109						
Income Tax Payments																	
Other																	
Total Cash Disbursements					249,149	264,387	27,742	293,614	311,265	333,394	357,228	380,154	400,908	417,440	428,611	435,077	4,148,643
Net Cash Generated This Period					$14,288	$2,690	$2,324	($1,043)	($6,448)	($10,280)	($6,493)	$6,293	$58,658	$109,508	$151,864	$244,801	$565,441
ANALYSIS OF CASH REQUIREMENTS																	
Beginning Cash Balance					$17,355	$31,643	34,333	$36,657	$35,614	$29,146	$20,000	$20,000	$20,000	$76,623	$186,131	$337,995	$337,995
Net Cash Generated This Period					14,288	2,690	2,324	(1,043)	(6,448)	(10,980)	6,293	58,658	109,508	151,864	244,801	50,000
Cash Balance before Borrowings					31,643	34,333	36,657	35,614	29,146	18,166	20,000	26,293	78,658	186,131	337,995	582,796	582,796
Minimum Acceptable Cash Balance					20,000	20,000	20,000	20,000	20,000	20,000	20,000	20,000	20,000	20,000	20,000	20,000	20,000
Amount above/(below) Minimum Acceptable Balance	0				11,643	14,333	16,657	15,614	9,146	(1,834)	(6,493)	6,293	58,658	166,131	317,995	562,796	562,796
Current Short-Term Borrowings					0	0	0	0	0	1,834	6,493	(6,293)	(2,035)	0	0	0	0
Total Short-Term Borrowings					0	0	0	0	0	1,834	8,327	2,035	0	0	0	0	0
Ending Cash Balance				$31,643	$31,643	$34,333	$36,657	$35,614	$29,146	$21,000	$20,000	$20,000	$76,623	$186,131	$337,995	$582,796	$582,796

Fig. 8.5. *The Cash Flow Projector worksheet (cont.).*

This section shows you how to print draft-quality reports quickly by using a minimum of commands. Later in the chapter, you learn how to use those commands that enhance reports, change type size and style, and automatically repeat border titles. You also learn how to produce printouts of complete formulas rather than their resulting values.

Printing a Screenful of Data

Before you print any portion of a 1-2-3 worksheet, decide whether the output must be of "report" quality (suitable for official distribution or filing) or whether all you need is a screen print (hard copy of the screen's contents).

Cue:
Pressing PrintScreen (or Shift-PrtSc) prints whatever is on-screen, including the date and time display.

You can, for example, retrieve the Cash Flow Projector file and then press PrintScreen (or Shift-PrtSc) for a screen print (see fig. 8.6). The resultant screen print captures everything on-screen, even such unwanted items as the contents of the highlighted cell A1 and the mode indicator. Such "quick and dirty" printouts may be adequate for interoffice memos and, because they capture the date-time display, for documenting model construction.

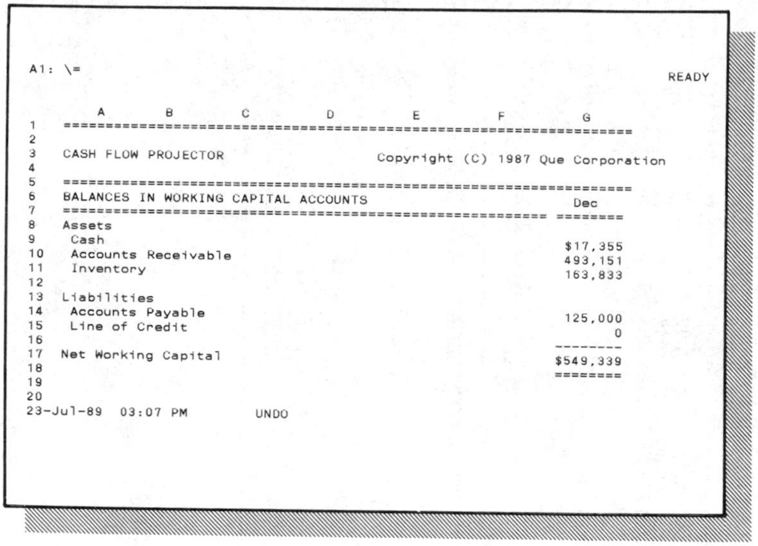

Fig. 8.6.
The result of using the PrintScreen key.

```
A1: \=                                                               READY

         A        B        C        D        E        F        G
   ============================================================================
1
2
3   CASH FLOW PROJECTOR                    Copyright (C) 1987 Que Corporation
4
   ============================================================================
5
6   BALANCES IN WORKING CAPITAL ACCOUNTS                           Dec
7  ============================================================================  ========
8   Assets
9    Cash                                                         $17,355
10   Accounts Receivable                                          493,151
11   Inventory                                                    163,833
12
13  Liabilities
14   Accounts Payable                                             125,000
15   Line of Credit                                                     0
16                                                               --------
17  Net Working Capital                                          $549,339
18                                                               ========
19
20
23-Jul-89   03:07 PM            UNDO
```

Printing Draft-Quality Reports on One Page or Less

If you don't change any of the default print settings, and no other print settings have been entered during the current worksheet session, printing a page or less involves only a few steps. These steps include the following:

1. Choose to print to the printer or file.

2. Highlight the worksheet area you want printed.

3. Choose the command to begin printing.

RELEASE

2.2

Two other steps may be necessary if another person uses your copy of 1-2-3 and has possibly changed either the default print settings or has entered new settings during the current worksheet session. First, you can check the default settings by selecting **/W**orksheet **G**lobal **D**efault. In Release 2.2, the settings sheet is displayed automatically. In Releases 2.0 and 2.01, you have to choose **S**tatus to view the settings. A quick review of the top left section of the status screen indicates whether the printer and page layout settings are the ones you need. Second, you can clear any special settings that may have been entered. To do so, select **/P**rint **P**rinter **C**lear **A**ll to erase any settings.

If you are certain that all default settings are correct and no other settings have been entered, you can print a report of a page or less easily by completing the following sequence of operations. First, check that your printer is on-line and that your paper is positioned where you want the data to print. Next choose **/P**rint **P**rinter. The **P**rint menu appears:

Range   Line   **P**age   **O**ptions   **C**lear   **A**lign   **G**o   Quit

Indicate what part of the worksheet you want to print by selecting **R**ange and highlighting the area. Suppose that you want to print the December data for the working-capital accounts part of the Cash Flow Projector (see fig. 8.5). To print this area, you specify the range A1..G18.

You can use the PgUp, PgDn, and End keys to designate ranges when you print. If you want to designate a range that includes the entire active area of the worksheet, anchor the left corner of the print range, press the End key, and then the Home key.

After you highlight the range you want to print, select **G**o (see fig. 8.7). If you accidentally press Enter after you have already used the **G**o option, the file will print a second time. If this happens, you can stop printing by pressing Ctrl-Break.

Cue:
Use Ctrl-Break to stop printing at any time.

Printing Reports Longer Than One Page

If the area of your worksheet has more rows and columns than can be printed on one page, you can use the basic steps discussed in the preceding section for printing reports on a page or less. Setting the print range, however, so that a new page begins exactly where you want it to begin can sometimes be a bit tricky. Also, if you want to print a section of a large worksheet like the Cash Flow Projector in figure 8.5, you may need to use the

Cue:
If your worksheet is more than one page, use the /Print Printer Options Borders command to repeat the borders on each page.

Fig. 8.7.
The result of
printing one
page with
default settings.

```
=================================================================
CASH FLOW PROJECTOR                  Copyright (C) 1987 Que Corporation
=================================================================
BALANCES IN WORKING CAPITAL ACCOUNTS                        Dec
=================================================================   =========
Assets
  Cash                                                    $17,355
  Accounts Receivable                                     493,151
  Inventory                                               163,833

Liabilities
  Accounts Payable                                        125,000
  Line of Credit                                                0

Net Working Capital                                       --------
                                                         $549,339
                                                          ========
```

/Print Printer Options Borders command so that labels are repeated on each page.

To ensure that information will be printed on the pages as you want, remember that 1-2-3 treats numeric and text data differently when splitting data from one page to the next. Complete numbers will be printed because numbers can span only one cell. On the other hand, text, such as long labels that span several cells, may be split in awkward places from one page to the next.

Suppose that you want to print 6 months of data from the working-capital accounts section in the Cash Flow Projector worksheet in figure 8.5. Suppose also that you want to print your report on 8 1/2-by-11-inch paper, the default paper size. To print the report on this size paper with the default margin settings and a pitch of 10 characters per inch, you need to print on 2 pages.

To print six columns of data from the working-capital accounts section, first check that your printer is on-line and that your paper is positioned where you want the printing to begin. Then choose the /Print Printer command.

Because you want the labels in A6 through A17 in figure 8.5 to print on both pages, you must use the Options Borders command. When you select Options Borders, 1-2-3 asks whether the labels you want repeated are located down a column or across a row. For the sample report, choose Columns. (To print a report on two or more pages and repeat labels that are displayed across a row, you select Rows after choosing Options Borders.)

After you choose Columns, the prompt Enter range for border columns: appears. If your cell pointer is located in the column where the labels appear, press Enter; if not, move your cell pointer to the column and press Enter. To return to the main Print menu, select Quit.

Once you have indicated which column or row of labels you want repeated on each page, you do not need to include those labels in your actual print range. 1-2-3 automatically places those labels in the first column or row on every page. To print the January-through-June data for the working-capital accounts section, highlight the range H6..M18. Notice that this range does not include A6..D18, which is the range that contains the labels.

Next, select **Align**, **Go**, and **Quit**. Choosing **Align** ensures that printing will begin at the top of all succeeding pages after the first. Make sure in particular that you reposition your printer paper and use the **Align** command whenever you have aborted a print job. The printed pages of the working-capital accounts section are shown in figures 8.8 and 8.9. Notice that the column descriptions print on both pages.

Cue:
If you use Ctrl-Break to abort a print job, use /Print Printer Align before you restart printing.

```
BALANCES IN WORKING CAPITAL ACCOUNTS   Jan        Feb        Mar
=====================================  =========  =========  =========
Assets
  Cash                                 $31,643    $34,333    $36,657
  Accounts Receivable                  510,780    533,597    551,287
  Inventory                            169,209    176,671    189,246

Liabilities
  Accounts Payable                     130,754    139,851    150,186
  Line of Credit                             0          0          0
                                       ---------  ---------  ---------
Net Working Capital                    $580,878   $604,750   $627,003
                                       =========  =========  =========
```

Fig. 8.8.
The first page of a report printed on two pages.

```
BALANCES IN WORKING CAPITAL ACCOUNTS   Apr        May        Jun
=====================================  =========  =========  =========
Assets
  Cash                                 $35,614    $29,146    $20,000
  Accounts Receivable                  577,314    611,007    641,802
  Inventory                            206,788    228,828    269,990

Liabilities
  Accounts Payable                     163,731    180,350    203,669
  Line of Credit                             0          0      1,834
                                       ---------  ---------  ---------
Net Working Capital                    $655,984   $692,620   $726,289
                                       =========  =========  =========
```

Fig. 8.9.
The second page of a report printed on two pages.

Hiding Segments within the Designated Print Range

Because the **/Print** commands require you to specify a range to print, you can print only rectangular blocks from the worksheet. Nevertheless, you can suppress the display of cell contents within the range. You can eliminate one or more rows, hide one or more columns, or remove from view a segment that spans only part of a row or column. The results of each of the following illustrations will print on one page, using default settings.

Excluding Rows

To exclude rows from printing, you must mark the rows for omission. Do this by typing a double vertical bar (||) in the blank leftmost cell of the print range of each row you want to omit. Only one of these vertical bars appears on-screen and neither appears on the printout. A row marked in this way will not print, but the suppressed data remains in the worksheet and is used in any applicable calculations.

Suppose that you want to print the cash-flow summary line descriptions from the Cash Flow Projector worksheet. When the **/Print Printer Range** command prompts you for a range to print, specify A94..D112. The printout of the contents of rows 94 through 112 is shown in figure 8.10.

Fig. 8.10.
A printout of
individual
cash-
disbursements
rows.

```
============================================
CASH FLOW SUMMARY
============================================
Collection of Receivables
Other Cash Receipts

Cash Disbursements
 Payment for Purchases on Credit
 Operating Expenses
 Long-Term Debt Service
 Interest Payment on Line of Credit
  Interest Rate
  Payment
 Income Tax Payments
 Other

Total Cash Disbursements

Net Cash Generated This Period
```

Cue:
If necessary, insert a new column A to provide blank cells for the double vertical bars.

Now suppose that you don't want the printout to show the cash-disbursements detail (rows 100 through 109). Do not use a worksheet command to delete the rows. Instead, omit the row from printing by typing a double vertical bar in the leftmost cell of each row to be omitted. Because the leftmost cell is not blank, however, you need to make an adjustment. The simplest method is to insert a new column A and narrow it to a one-column width. Then type || in cell A100 and copy that entry to cells A101..A109.

When you execute the **Print** command, be sure to specify the expanded range A94..E112 (not A94..D112 or B94..E112). Figure 8.11 shows the resulting printout.

Fig. 8.11.
The individual
cash-
disbursements
rows omitted.

```
============================================
CASH FLOW SUMMARY
============================================
Collection of Receivables
Other Cash Receipts

Total Cash Disbursements

Net Cash Generated This Period
```

To restore the worksheet after you have finished printing, delete the vertical bars from the leftmost cells of the marked rows and delete column A.

Excluding Columns

Cue:
Use /Worksheet Column Hide to hide columns you don't want to print.

As you learned from Chapter 4, you can use 1-2-3's **/Worksheet Column Hide** command to mark columns you don't want to display on-screen. If these marked columns are included in a print range, they will not appear on the printout if you use the **/P**rint **P**rinter **O**ptions **O**ther **A**s-Displayed command.

Suppose that you are working with the Cash Flow Projector model and you want to print only the descriptions and the January-through-March sales information contained in the range A21..J40. Issue the **/W**orksheet **C**olumn **H**ide command and specify columns E1..G1 to suppress the October-through-December data. The resulting printout is shown in figure 8.12.

```
==================================================    ==========    =========    =========
SALES                                                       Jan          Feb          Mar
==================================================    ==========    =========    =========
Profit Center 1                                         $31,336      $37,954      $43,879
Profit Center 2                                          22,572       24,888       25,167
Profit Center 3                                         131,685      129,044      131,723
Profit Center 4                                          95,473       98,008       96,986
Profit Center 5
                                                        --------     --------     --------
Total Sales                                            $281,066     $289,894     $297,755
                                                        ========     ========     ========

                          Cash                              10%          10%          10%
Percent of               30 Days                            20%          20%          20%
Collections              60 Days                            50%          50%          50%
                         90 Days                            20%          20%          20%
                                                        --------     --------     --------
Cash Collections                                       $263,437     $267,077     $280,066
                                                        ========     ========     ========
```

Fig. 8.12.
The printout after hiding columns E, F, and G.

To restore the columns, select **/W**orksheet **C**olumn **D**isplay. When the hidden columns (marked with an asterisk) reappear on-screen, you can specify which column or columns to display.

Excluding Ranges

If you want to hide only a partial row, a partial column, or an area that partially spans one or more rows and columns, use the **/R**ange **F**ormat **H**idden command to mark the ranges.

Perhaps your worksheet includes documentation you want to save on disk but omit from the printout. For example, you may want to omit the copyright message in the third row of the Cash Flow Projector worksheet. To omit the message, issue the **/R**ange **F**ormat **H**idden command and specify cell D3. (Although the message spans several cells, it is entered in just D3.) Then print the range A1..G7 (see fig. 8.13).

After you finish printing, select **/R**ange **F**ormat **R**eset and then specify the range D3..D3 to restore the copyright message.

```
=======================================================================
CASH FLOW PROJECTOR
=======================================================================
BALANCES IN WORKING CAPITAL ACCOUNTS                              Dec
=======================================================================  =========
```

Cue:
Use print macros for repeated print operations.

If you find yourself repeating print operations (hiding the same columns, suppressing and then restoring the same documentation messages, and so on), remember that you can save time and minimize frustration by developing and using print macros (see Chapter 14).

Controlling Paper Movement

Unless you specify otherwise, the top of a page is initially marked by the print head's position when you turn on the printer and load 1-2-3. If you print a range containing fewer lines than the default page length, the paper does not advance to the top of the next page; the next print operation begins wherever the preceding operation ended. If you print a range containing more lines than the default page length, 1-2-3 automatically inserts page breaks between pages, but the paper does not advance to the top of the next page after the last page has printed.

If you don't want to accept 1-2-3's automatic paper-movement controls, you can change the controls from the keyboard. You can specify the "top" of a page in any paper position, advance the paper by line or by page, and insert page breaks exactly where you want them.

Using Line, Page, and Align

If you are using continuous-feed paper, position the paper so that the print head is at the top of the page; then turn on the printer. Do not advance the paper manually. Because 1-2-3 coordinates a line counter with the current page-length setting, any lines you advance manually are not counted, and page breaks may crop up in strange places.

If you want to advance the paper one line at a time (to separate several small printed ranges that fit on one page, for example), issue the **/Print Printer Line** command. This command makes the printer skip a line.

If you want to advance to a new page after printing less than a full page, select the **/Print Printer Page** command. Whenever you issue this command, the printer will skip to a new page. (The following section shows how you can embed a page-break symbol in the print range to instruct 1-2-3 to advance automatically.)

In many cases, a faster way to advance the paper is to take the printer off-line, adjust the paper manually, put the printer on-line, and then issue the **/Print Printer Align** command. In fact, whether you adjust the paper off-line in this manner, or on-line with the paper-control commands, you should issue **Align**. Note that **Align** also resets the page counter, which you may not want to do if you are numbering pages in a header or footer (see the section on "Creating Headers and Footers" in this chapter). Whenever you begin a print job at the top of a page, it's a good practice to select **Align** before selecting **Go**.

To print an existing footer on the last page, use the **Page** command at the end of the printing session. If you select the **Quit** command from the **Print** menu without issuing the **Page** command, this final footer will not print. You can reissue the **/Print Printer** command and select **Page** to print the footer.

Reminder:
To print a footer on the last page of the printout, issue the /Print Printer Page command at the end of the print session.

Setting Page Breaks within the Worksheet

Look again at figure 8.5, which shows the entire Cash Flow Projector worksheet. Suppose that you want to print three months of data (October to December) for the sales and purchases sections of the worksheet. To make sure that the purchases section begins printing on a new page, you can insert a page break into the worksheet by using a command or by typing a special symbol.

To enter a page break using 1-2-3's commands, first move the cell pointer to column A and then to one row above the row at which you want the page break to occur. Then select the **/Worksheet Page** command; this command automatically inserts a new blank row containing a page-break symbol (|..).

For example, to insert a page break just above the first separating line in the purchases section, position the cell pointer on A42 and then execute the command. Figure 8.14 shows the inserted row with the double-colon page-break symbol. To remove the inserted row and the page-break symbol after you finish printing, use the **/Worksheet Delete Row** command.

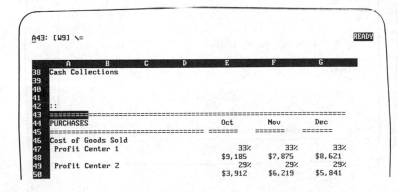

Fig. 8.14.
Inserting a page-break symbol in the worksheet.

As an alternative, insert a blank row into your worksheet where you want a page break, and then type a page-break symbol (|::) into a blank cell in the leftmost column of the print range in that row. The contents of cells in any row marked by the page-break symbol will not print.

Caution:
Inserting a blank row for a page-break symbol may alter formulas or cause other problems.

Be careful when you alter a worksheet. You may alter formula results by inserting rows, or you may accidentally delete the wrong row after you finish printing. You may be able to avoid these problems by typing the page-break symbol into the leftmost column in the print range of a row that is already blank in your worksheet. First check to be sure that the row is blank; use the End and arrow keys to scan across the row.

Changing the Print Options

You can use the /**W**orksheet **G**lobal **D**efault **P**rinter command to change the default print settings. The new default settings remain in effect for all print operations performed in the current work session. If you want the new settings to be in effect whenever you load 1-2-3, select /**W**orksheet **G**lobal **D**efault **U**pdate.

RELEASE

2.2

Reminder:
/Print Printer Options settings override corresponding /Worksheet Global Default Printer settings.

You can change print settings also by using the selections on the **Print Printer Options** menu shown in figure 8.15. As shown in the figure, Release 2.2 displays the current print settings. The **M**argins, **S**etup, and **Pg**-Length options override the /**W**orksheet **G**lobal **D**efault **P**rinter settings for margins, setup strings, and page length. The **H**eader, **F**ooter, and **B**order margins are unique to this menu; they are provided to help you improve the readability of your reports.

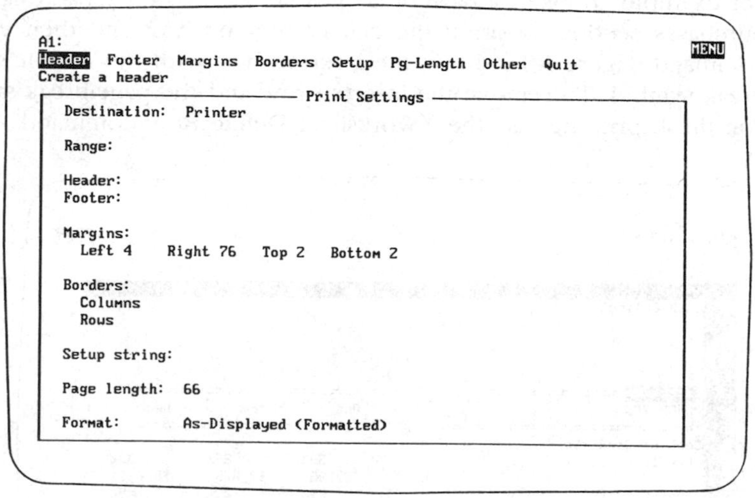

*Fig. 8.15.
The Print Printer [P,F] Options menu and settings sheet.*

```
A1:                                                               MENU
Header Footer  Margins  Borders  Setup  Pg-Length  Other  Quit
Create a header
┌──────────────────── Print Settings ────────────────────┐
│  Destination:  Printer                                   │
│                                                          │
│  Range:                                                  │
│                                                          │
│  Header:                                                 │
│  Footer:                                                 │
│                                                          │
│  Margins:                                                │
│    Left 4      Right 76   Top 2   Bottom 2               │
│                                                          │
│  Borders:                                                │
│    Columns                                               │
│    Rows                                                  │
│                                                          │
│  Setup string:                                           │
│                                                          │
│  Page length:   66                                       │
│                                                          │
│  Format:       As-Displayed (Formatted)                  │
└──────────────────────────────────────────────────────────┘
```

The print settings you use for your worksheet are saved with the file when you execute **/F**ile **S**ave. When you retrieve the file, the settings are still in effect.

Creating Headers and Footers

1-2-3 reserves three lines in a document for a header and an additional three lines for a footer. You can either retain the six lines (regardless of whether you use them) or eliminate all six lines by selecting **O**ther **U**nformatted (illustrated later in this chapter) from the **P**rint **P**rinter **O**ptions menu.

Technically, the **H**eader and **F**ooter options let you specify up to 240 characters of text within one line in each of 3 positions: left, right, and center. But from a practical standpoint, the overall header or footer line cannot exceed the number of characters printed per inch multiplied by the width of the paper in inches minus the right and left margins.

The header text, which is printed on the first line after any blank top margin lines, is followed by two blank header lines (for spacing). The footer text line is printed above the specified bottom-margin blank lines and below two blank footer lines (for spacing).

Although you can enter text manually, 1-2-3 provides special characters for controlling page numbers, entering the current date, and positioning text within a header or footer. These special characters include the following:

Cue:
You can use special characters in your header and footer to enter page numbers, enter the date, and position the text.

Character	Function
#	Automatically prints page numbers, starting with 1.
@	Automatically includes (in the form 29-Jun-87) the date you entered when you started your computer.
|	Automatically separates text: Absence of a | mark left-justifies all text. The first | mark centers text that follows. The second | mark right-justifies remaining text.

To illustrate, reprint the range A1..D17 after adding a header that includes all the preceding special characters. To add the header, select **/P**rint **P**rinter, specify the range A1..G17, and then select **O**ptions **H**eader. At the prompt Enter Header:, type the following:

@|**YOUR FIRM NAME**|#

Next, select **Q**uit from the **P**rint **P**rinter **O**ptions menu; signal the top of the page to the printer, if necessary, by selecting **A**lign; and then select **G**o. The header line shown in figure 8.16 improves the report's appearance.

Fig. 8.16.
The result of
specifying a
header.

```
03-Aug-89                        YOUR FIRM NAME                              1

=====================================================================================

CASH FLOW PROJECTOR

=====================================================================================
BALANCES IN WORKING CAPITAL ACCOUNTS                                   Dec
=======================================================           =========
Assets
   Cash                                                             $17,355
   Accounts Receivable                                              493,151
   Inventory                                                        163,833

Liabilities
   Accounts Payable                                                 125,000
   Line of Credit                                                         0
                                                                  --------
Net Working Capital                                               $549,339
                                                                  ========
```

Whenever the print range exceeds a single-page output, the header is printed on each succeeding page and the page number increases by one. If you have used the special page-number character (#) and want to print your report a second time before you leave the **Print** menu, you can reset the page counter and set the top of the form by selecting **A**lign before you select **G**o.

If you have specified a header line, but the centered or right-justified text doesn't print, make sure that the right-margin setting is appropriate for the current pitch and paper width. To change the header, repeat the sequence to establish the text, press Esc to remove the display of the existing header from the control panel, and press Enter. (You can delete a header or footer without removing other specified options.)

RELEASE

2.2

In Release 2.2, you can include the contents of a worksheet cell in a header or footer. Instead of typing the header or footer text, type \ followed by the address of the cell that contains the label. For example, if a title is in cell A1, you can enter **\A1** as the header.

Reminder:
In Release 2.2,
you can include the
contents of a
worksheet cell in a
header or footer.

Printing Worksheet Borders

A printed report of lines of figures can be difficult, if not impossible, to interpret if you don't know what those figures represent. You can make your report easy to understand by printing specified columns and rows repeatedly on a multipage printout.

If you use the default print settings to print the Cash Flow Projector worksheet, the report contains all necessary information. But without descriptions of what each line of figures represents, some pages may be difficult to interpret.

To improve the report, you need to add certain column or row headings—what 1-2-3 calls *borders*. Selecting **B**orders **C**olumns produces a row that appears as a border to a set of columns; selecting **B**orders **R**ows produces a column that appears as a border to a set of rows. Setting borders in a printout is analogous to freezing titles in the worksheet: **B**orders **C**olumns produces a border like a frozen horizontal title display, and **B**orders **R**ows produces a column like a frozen vertical title display.

Reminder:
*Using **B**orders in printing is analogous to freezing titles on the worksheet.*

To illustrate the process of creating borders, you can modify a small portion of the report—the working-capital accounts information in the range A1..S18. Omit the blank columns (E and F) as well as the initial December column (G); then use the **B**orders **C**olumns command to repeat the account names in columns A through D.

Select **/Print Printer**, specify the range H1..S18, and then select **Options Borders Columns**. When the message Enter range for border columns: appears in the control panel, specify A1..D1. As you can see from the first two pages of the report, the account names are repeated to coincide with the January-through-December dollar amounts (see figs. 8.17 and 8.18).

```
===========================================================================
CASH FLOW PROJECTOR

===========================================================================
BALANCES IN WORKING CAPITAL ACCOUNTS   Jan        Feb        Mar
===========================================================================
Assets
  Cash                               $31,643    $34,333    $36,657
  Accounts Receivable                510,780    533,597    551,287
  Inventory                          169,209    176,671    189,246

Liabilities
  Accounts Payable                   130,754    139,851    150,186
  Line of Credit                           0          0          0
                                    --------   --------   --------
Net Working Capital                 $580,878   $604,750   $627,003
                                    ========   ========   ========
```

Fig. 8.17.
Page 1 of a printed column border.

```
===========================================================================
CASH FLOW PROJECTOR

===========================================================================
BALANCES IN WORKING CAPITAL ACCOUNTS   Apr        May        Jun
===========================================================================
Assets
  Cash                               $35,614    $29,146    $20,000
  Accounts Receivable                577,314    614,997    641,802
  Inventory                          206,788    228,828    269,990

Liabilities
  Accounts Payable                   163,731    180,350    203,669
  Line of Credit                           0          0      1,834
                                    --------   --------   --------
Net Working Capital                 $655,984   $692,620   $726,289
                                    ========   ========   ========
```

Fig. 8.18.
Page 2 of the printed column border.

If the designated border includes part of the print range or the print range includes part of the border, you get the same information printed twice.

If you want to print information with a vertical border on every page, select the **Borders Rows** option. For example, you could use this option if you wanted to print only the liabilities information in rows 13 to 15.

Select the **/Print Printer Options Borders Columns** (or **Rows**) command when you want only borders to be printed. If you select the command accidentally, the cell highlighted by the cell pointer will be entered as either the columns or rows you selected. Should this occur, remove the selection by using the **/Print Printer Clear Borders** command.

Using Setup Strings

Cue:
For special printing effects within a print range, embed setup strings in the worksheet.

Setup strings are optional printer codes you can use to change the size or style of type. To pass setup strings temporarily to the printer, use one of two methods. Either select the **Setup** option and specify the appropriate ASCII code, or embed the code in the worksheet. (Remember that you can establish a "permanent" or default setup string which will be used automatically whenever 1-2-3 is loaded. To do so, use the **/Worksheet Global Default Printer Update** command.)

To illustrate setup strings, you can print portions of the working-capital accounts information in the Cash Flow Projector worksheet. The examples assume that an HP LaserJet printer is being used. (The 1-2-3 Reference Manual contains a "Printer Control Codes" appendix.)

To use the first method, first send a setup string (the decimal code for ASCII must not exceed 39 characters) by executing a 1-2-3 command. Assume that the print range is H1..S18 and that columns A1..D1 are established as a border at the left side of every printed page.

Access the **Print Printer Options** menu, select **Setup**, type **\027(s16.66H** to indicate the line printer font, the smallest type size on an HP LaserJet printer, and then press Enter. At this point, if you were to quit the **Options** menu and issue a **Go** command, the first printed page would contain only January-through-March amounts in small print.

Because you want the January-through-August amounts to fit on the page, you must establish margins that coincide with print pitch. Select **Margins Right** from the **Print Printer Options** menu. Then enter **136** (8 1/2 inches multiplied by 16 characters per inch). Page 1 of the resulting printout is shown in figure 8.19.

To remove the temporary setup string, select **Setup** from the **Print Printer Options** menu, press Esc, and then press Enter. Exit the **Print Printer Options** menu by selecting **Quit** or pressing Esc.

```
==========================================================================================
CASH FLOW PROJECTOR

==========================================================================================
BALANCES IN WORKING CAPITAL ACCOUNTS   Jan       Feb       Mar       Apr       May       Jun       Jul       Aug
==========================================================================================  =========  =========  =========  =========  =========  =========  =========  =========
Assets
  Cash                                $31,643   $34,333   $36,657   $35,614   $29,146   $20,000   $20,000   $20,000
  Accounts Receivable                  510,780   533,597   551,287   577,314   614,997   641,802   750,544   879,271
  Inventory                            169,209   176,671   189,246   206,788   228,828   269,990   296,527   324,230

Liabilities
  Accounts Payable                     130,754   139,851   150,186   163,731   180,350   203,669   225,085   243,320
  Line of Credit                             0         0         0         0         0     1,834     8,327     2,035
                                     ---------  --------- --------- --------- --------- --------- --------- ---------
Net Working Capital                  $580,878  $604,750  $627,003  $655,984  $692,620  $726,289  $833,659  $978,146
                                     ========= ========= ========= ========= ========= ========= ========= =========
```

Fig. 8.19.
Page 1 printed in condensed mode.

You use this method when you want all output from the current print operation to reflect the code condition. In the preceding illustration, for example, the contents in the entire print range, as well as the column borders, are printed in the line printer font.

If you want only a portion within a print range to reflect a special printing characteristic, you can embed a setup string in the worksheet instead of issuing several separate print commands. In blank rows preceding and following the area that requires special treatment, type a double vertical bar (||) and the appropriate ASCII code (or codes) separated by backslashes. (Insert a blank row, if necessary, making sure that it will not disturb any formulas in your worksheet.) The first vertical bar will not appear in the worksheet, and neither the bars nor the print codes will be printed. If you must embed a code in a row that contains data, that data will not be printed.

If you want to print the first few rows of the Cash Flow Projector report in normal type, except for a bold title in row 3, you first select **/Print Printer Clear All** to restore all print settings to default values. Then enter ||\027(s3B in the first cell of the first blank row (A2) to turn on bold on an HP LaserJet printer. Enter ||\027(s0B in the first cell of the next blank row (A4) to turn off bold print. If you specify A1..F8 as the print range, the printed output will be similar to that shown in figure 8.20.

```
=================================================================
CASH FLOW PROJECTOR
=================================================================
BALANCES IN WORKING CAPITAL ACCOUNTS
=================================================================
Assets
```

Fig. 8.20.
The results of embedding a setup string in the worksheet.

You can combine more than 1 print characteristic in a setup string if the combined setup code does not exceed the 39-character limit and your printer supports the combination. Check your printer manual for information about the compatibility of codes. A setup string contains the print-enhancement codes found in the printer manual. Each code consists of a backslash and 3 digits. If the manual says, for example, to use ESC E to turn on emphasized mode, look up the decimal equivalent for ESC (27) and for uppercase E (69). Because each code must contain 3 digits and begin with a backslash, you use \027\069 as the setup string to turn on emphasized mode. (Note: do not include spaces in a setup string.)

Changing the Page Layout

To change the page layout temporarily, use the **Print Printer Options** menu. If you want to change the margins, select the **Margins** option and then select **Left**, **Right**, **Top**, **Bottom**, or **None** from the menu.

Menu Selection	Message
Left	Enter Left Margin (0..240):XX
Right	Enter Right Margin (0..240):XX
Top	Enter Top Margin (0..32):XX
Bottom	Enter Bottom Margin (0..32):XX
None	Release 2.2 only

RELEASE
2.2

The XX at the end of each line denotes the current setting, which you can change. Before making any changes, review the "Understanding the Print Default Settings" section at the beginning of this chapter. Keep in mind general layout considerations such as the number of lines per page, the number of characters per inch, and so on.

Be sure that you set left and right margins that are consistent with the width of your paper and the established pitch (characters per inch). The right margin must be greater than the left margin. And make sure that settings for the top and bottom margins are consistent with the paper's length and the established number of lines per inch.

The specified page length must not be less than the top margin plus the header lines plus one line of data plus the footer lines plus the bottom margin, unless you use the **/Print Printer Options Other Unformatted** command to suppress all formatting. (Information about this command is included in the following section, "Printing a Listing of Cell Contents.") To maximize the output on every printed page of a large worksheet, you can combine the Unformatted option with setup strings that condense print and increase the number of lines per inch.

You can use the **None** margin option, offered in Release 2.2, to eliminate margins when you are printing to a disk file using **/Print File**.

Cue:
Use the None margin option to eliminate margins when you are printing to a disk file.

RELEASE
2.2

Printing a Listing of Cell Contents

You can spend hours developing and debugging a model worksheet and much additional time entering and verifying data. You should safeguard your work not only by making backup copies of your important files but also by printing the cell contents of important worksheets. Be aware, however, that this print job can take a while if you have a large worksheet.

You produce printed documentation of cell contents by selecting Other from the **Print Printer Options** menu and then selecting either **As-Displayed** or **Cell-Formulas**. Choosing **Cell-Formulas** produces a listing that shows the width of the cell (if different from the default), the cell format, cell-protection status, and the contents of cells in the print range, with one cell per line. Selecting **As-Displayed** restores the default instructions to print the range as it appears on-screen.

Cue:
Choose Cell-Formulas to print a listing of formulas in cells.

You can produce a cell-by-cell listing of only the first 7 columns and the first 18 rows of the Cash Flow Projector worksheet, for example, by selecting **/Print Printer**, specifying the range A1..G18, and then selecting **Options Other Cell-Formulas**. Return to the main **Print** menu by choosing **Quit**. Then press **Align** and then **Go**. The resulting one-cell-per-line listing is shown in figure 8.21.

Notice that within the specified print range, the contents of each cell in the first row are listed before the next row is presented. Information enclosed by parentheses indicates a range format established independently of the global format in effect. For example, the (C0) in cell G17 indicates that the cell is formatted (with a **/Range Format** command) as Currency, with zero decimal places.

Information enclosed by square brackets indicates a column width set independently of the global column width in effect. For example, the [W11] in cell G17 indicates that column G is set specifically to be 11 characters wide. Cell content is printed after the column-width and format information. The formula in G17 prints as $549,339 in the printed worksheet.

If you need more extensive documentation and analysis, you may want to purchase an add-in auditing program.

Clearing the Print Options

Selecting **/Print Printer Clear** lets you eliminate all or a portion of the print options you chose earlier. The Clear options include the following:

All   **Range**   **Borders**   **Format**

Fig. 8.21.
A listing
produced by
using the Cell-
Formulas
option.

```
A1:  [W9]  \=
B1:  [W9]  \=
C1:  [W9]  \=
D1:  [W9]  \=
E1:  [W11] \=
F1:  [W11] \=
G1:  [W11] \=
A3:  [W9]  'CASH FLOW PROJECTOR
D3:  (H) [W9]  '          Copyright (C) 1987 Que Corporation
A5:  [W9]  \=
B5:  [W9]  \=
C5:  [W9]  \=
D5:  [W9]  \=
E5:  [W11] \=
F5:  [W11] \=
G5:  [W11] \=
A6:  [W9]  'BALANCES IN WORKING CAPITAL ACCOUNTS
G6:  [W11] ^Dec
A7:  [W9]  \=
B7:  [W9]  \=
C7:  [W9]  \=
D7:  [W9]  \=
E7:  [W11] \=
F7:  [W11] \=
G7:  [W11] ' =========
A8:  [W9]  'Assets
A9:  [W9]  ' Cash
G9:  (C0) [W11] 17355
A10: [W9]  ' Accounts Receivable
G10: (,0) [W11] 493151
A11: [W9]  ' Inventory
G11: (,0) [W11] 163833
A13: [W9]  'Liabilities
A14: [W9]  ' Accounts Payable
G14: (,0) [W11] 125000
A15: [W9]  ' Line of Credit
G15: (,0) [W11] 0
G16: [W11] ' --------
A17: [W9]  'Net Working Capital
G17: (C0) [W11] +G9+G10+G11-G14-G15
G18: [W11] ' ========
```

Cue:
Reset every print
option with /Print
Printer Clear All.

You can clear every print option, including the print range, by selecting **All,** or you can be more specific by using the other choices:

Menu Selection	Description
Range	Removes the previous print-range specification
Borders	Cancels columns and rows specified as borders
Format	Eliminates margins, page-length, and setup string settings

Remember that you can automate many routine print operations by setting up the print macros discussed in Chapter 14. **/Print Printer Clear All** is usually the first instruction in this type of macro.

Preparing Output for Other Programs

Many word processing and other software packages accept ASCII text files. You can maximize your chances of successfully exporting 1-2-3 files to other programs if you use some **Print** commands to eliminate unwanted specifications for page layout and page breaks.

To create a printer file, select **/Print File**. To direct output to a .PRN file instead of to a printer, specify a file name and then specify the range to print. Next, choose **Options Other Unformatted**. Selecting Unformatted removes all headers, footers, and page breaks from a print operation.

To create the .PRN file on disk, quit the **Options** menu, select **Go**, and then choose **Quit** from the **Print File** menu. Follow the instructions in your word processing or other software package to import the specially prepared 1-2-3 disk files.

To restore the default printing of headers, footers, and page breaks, issue the **/Print Printer Options Other Formatted** command. You ordinarily choose Formatted when printing to the printer and Unformatted when printing to a file.

Cue:
In most cases, choose ***Unformatted*** *when printing to a file.*

Chapter Summary

This chapter showed you how to create printed reports from your 1-2-3 worksheets. You learned how to print quickly using the default settings and how to change the defaults. To customize your reports and make them more readable, you can break the worksheet into pages; change the margins and page length; and provide headers, footers, and borders on the printout, as described in this chapter. You also discovered how to take full advantage of your printer's capabilities by passing setup strings to the printer.

Successfully printing large worksheets with a variety of options generally takes practice and some study of your printer manual. Use this chapter as a reference as you continue to experiment. The next chapter shows you how to create more professional looking reports using Allways, a spreadsheet publishing add-in program.

RELEASE

2.2

Entire
Chapter

Using Allways: The Spreadsheet Publisher

Release 2.2 of 1-2-3 is packaged with Allways, a desktop publishing add-in. Release 2.0 or 2.01 users can purchase Allways separately from Lotus Development Corporation. Allways does not claim to be a full-featured desktop publishing program, but this program may be all you need for many desktop publishing tasks involving 1-2-3 reports and graphs.

Allways enables you to produce printed 1-2-3 reports that incorporate a variety of type fonts, lines, shadings, and other formatting features (boldface, underline, and so on). Compare a report printed from 1-2-3 using the 1-2-3 /Print command (see fig. 9.1) with the same report formatted and printed with Allways (see fig. 9.2). As you can see, the difference in presentation quality is dramatic. (All printed figures in this chapter were produced using a Hewlett-Packard LaserJet Series II laser printer.)

In addition to enhanced text formatting, Allways enables you to embed 1-2-3 graphs in your printouts, add enhanced text to your printed graphs, and print 1-2-3 graphs and associated worksheet data from Allways.

This chapter explains all the features you need to use Allways with 1-2-3. In this chapter, you learn to do the following:

- Install, attach, and invoke Allways
- Understand how Allways and 1-2-3 work together
- Format worksheets with special text fonts
- Incorporate 1-2-3 graphs into an Allways document
- Fine-tune the page layout and add titles and borders

309

Fig. 9.1.
A report printed with the 1-2-3 /Print command.

```
                              LaserPro Corporation
                              Balance Sheet
                              October 1, 1989

                               ASSETS
                                             This Year   Last Year Change
Current Assets
Cash                                           247,886     126,473     96%
Accounts receivable                            863,652     524,570     65%
Inventory                                       79,071      53,790     47%
Prepaid expenses                                 9,257      11,718    -21%
Investments                                    108,577      31,934    240%
      Total Current Assets                   1,308,443     748,485     75%

Fixed Assets
Machinery and equipment                        209,906     158,730     32%
Vehicles                                       429,505     243,793     76%
Office furniture                                50,240      36,406     38%
(Accumulated depreciation)                   (101,098)    (64,394)     57%
      Total fixed assets                       588,553     374,535     57%
                                            $1,896,996  $1,123,020     69%

                              LIABILITIES AND SHAREHOLDERS' EQUITY
                                             This Year   Last Year Change
Current Liabilities
Accounts payable trade                         426,041     332,845     28%
Notes payable                                   45,327      23,486     93%
Accrued liabilities                             34,614      26,026     33%
Income taxes payable                            88,645      51,840     71%
      Total Current Liabilities                594,627     434,197     37%

Noncurrent Liabilities
Long-term debt                                 488,822     349,253     40%
Deferred federal tax                           147,844      92,101     61%
      Total Noncurrent Liabilities             636,666     441,354     44%

Shareholders' equity
Common stock                                     1,000       1,000      0%
Opening retained earnings                      246,469      82,531    199%
Profit (loss) for the period                   418,234     163,938    155%
      Total Shareholders' Equity               665,703     247,469    169%
                                            $1,896,996  $1,123,020     69%
```

Fig. 9.2.
A report formatted and printed with Allways.

LaserPro Corporation
Balance Sheet
October 1, 1989

ASSETS	This Year	Last Year	Change
Current Assets			
Cash	247,886	126,473	96%
Accounts receivable	863,652	524,570	65%
Inventory	79,071	53,790	47%
Prepaid expenses	9,257	11,718	-21%
Investments	108,577	31,934	240%
Total Current Assets	1,308,443	748,485	75%
Fixed Assets			
Machinery and equipment	209,906	158,730	32%
Vehicles	429,505	243,793	76%
Office furniture	50,240	36,406	38%
(Accumulated depreciation)	(101,098)	(64,394)	57%
Total fixed assets	588,553	374,535	57%
	$1,896,996	$1,123,020	69%

LIABILITIES AND SHAREHOLDERS' EQUITY	This Year	Last Year	Change
Current Liabilities			
Accounts payable trade	426,041	332,845	28%
Notes payable	45,327	23,486	93%
Accrued liabilities	34,614	26,026	33%
Income taxes payable	88,645	51,840	71%
Total Current Liabilities	594,627	434,197	37%
Noncurrent Liabilities			
Long-term debt	488,822	349,253	40%
Deferred federal tax	147,844	92,101	61%
Total Noncurrent Liabilities	636,666	441,354	44%
Shareholders' equity			
Common stock	1,000	1,000	0%
Opening retained earnings	246,469	82,531	199%
Profit (loss) for the period	418,234	163,938	155%
Total Shareholders' Equity	665,703	247,469	169%
	$1,896,996	$1,123,020	69%

- Print using Allways
- Change the appearance of the screen

Before you use Allways, you must install it and attach it to 1-2-3. Installing Allways is easy with its installation program that copies the necessary files and enables you to set up the program for your computer. You can attach Allways to 1-2-3 only when you need the add-in, or you can set up Allways to attach itself automatically whenever you start 1-2-3. The first sections in this chapter explain how to install Allways and then how to attach it to 1-2-3.

Installing Allways

Allways is installed by running the AWSETUP program on the Allways Setup disk. Before you start the installation, however, make sure that you meet the system requirements listed in the following section.

Understanding System Requirements

To run Allways, you need a copy of 1-2-3 Release 2.0 or above and an IBM PC, XT, AT, PS/2, or compatible with a hard disk. The hard disk should have at least 1.1M of free space.

You can run Allways without a graphics card and adapter although you probably will find Allways easier to use with a graphics monitor (either color or monochrome). When the program runs in Graphics mode, what you see on-screen looks almost exactly like the printout you get—WYSIWYG: "what you see is what you get."

Allways enhances the printed output of almost any type of printer. You get maximum benefit, however, when you use Allways with a laser printer or other printer that provides a similar level of resolution.

Allways takes about 125K of RAM. In some cases, you may need more memory. You cannot use Allways with large 1-2-3 worksheets that leave less than 125K to 150K of free memory. If your computer has expanded memory, you probably will never run into a memory-shortage problem.

A computer with 640K of RAM leaves 362,800 bytes free when 1-2-3 Release 2.2 is loaded and running. With Allways attached to 1-2-3, 300,296 bytes are free to load and build a worksheet. If the 1-2-3 Undo feature and Allways are enabled, however, only 111,912 bytes are available to load and build a worksheet.

Perhaps you have a large worksheet that cannot be loaded when Allways is active, but you want to use Allways to print a portion of the worksheet. To accommodate this need, load the worksheet and use /Files Xtract Values to copy the section of the worksheet you want to print with Allways to a separate, temporary worksheet. Erase the original worksheet using /Worksheet Erase, attach Allways (as described in this chapter), and use /File Retrieve to load the temporary worksheet. Now you can print using Allways.

Using the AWSETUP Program

Use the AWSETUP program on the Allways Setup disk to install Allways. The installation of Allways is a separate task from installing 1-2-3. Insert the Allways Setup disk in drive A, go to drive A (type **A:** on a DOS command line and press Enter), type **AWSETUP**, and press Enter. Follow the instructions on the screen to provide specifications about your printer and monitor. AWSETUP creates a subdirectory called ALLWAYS and copies the appropriate files from the Allways installation disks. When AWSETUP requires another disk, you are prompted to insert that disk.

Release 2.2 includes the /Add-In menu command for accessing add-in programs, but because Releases 2.0 and 2.01 do not have this feature, you must use the Lotus Add-In Manager to access Allways with the older releases. The Lotus Add-In Manager enables you to access the Add-In menu by pressing Alt-F10. This menu is similar to the one that appears when you select /Add-In in 1-2-3 Release 2.2.

The AWSETUP program automatically installs the Add-In Manager in the 123.SET driver set file for 1-2-3 Releases 2.0 and 2.01. If you recall, 123.SET is the file created when you installed 1-2-3. This file contains display and printer information. If you created more than one driver set when you installed 1-2-3, you may want to install the Add-In Manager to those driver sets so that when you start 1-2-3 with a driver set other than 123.SET, you have access to the Add-In Manager.

If you want to use Allways with additional driver sets, you can install the Add-In Manager in those driver sets by following these steps:

1. Working in DOS, set the current drive and directory to the directory that contains the 1-2-3 program (for example, C:\123).

2. Type the following and press Enter (*filename* is the name of the 1-2-3 driver set in which you want to install the Add-In Manager):

    ADD_MGR *filename***.SET**

If you change a 1-2-3 driver set using 1-2-3's installation program, you must install the Add-In Manager in that driver set using these steps before you can use Allways with that driver set. You change driver sets when you update your 1-2-3 program to work with a different display or printer.

Attaching Allways

Before you can use Allways, it must be *attached*, or loaded, into memory. To attach Allways in 1-2-3 Release 2.2, select /Add-In Attach. Choose ALLWAYS.ADN from the list that appears on the screen and press Enter. You then are asked to select the function key you want to use to invoke Allways. Select a number from 7 to 10 to specify the function key. If you select 7, for example, you invoke Allways by pressing Alt-F7. You can choose No-Key if you don't want to invoke Allways using a function key. If you select No-Key, you must invoke Allways by selecting /Add-In Invoke, choosing **ALLWAYS**, and pressing Enter.

If you use Allways frequently, you may want to attach the add-in program automatically when 1-2-3 is loaded. To do this in 1-2-3 Release 2.2, start 1-2-3 and select /Worksheet Global Default Other Add-In Set. The screen shown in figure 9.3 appears. Select a number from **1** to **8** to specify which add-in Allways will be (you can attach as many as eight add-ins to 1-2-3). Select **ALLWAYS.ADN** from the list that appears and press Enter to specify Allways as the desired add-in. Now select the function key you want to use to invoke Allways (No-Key or 7 through **10**).

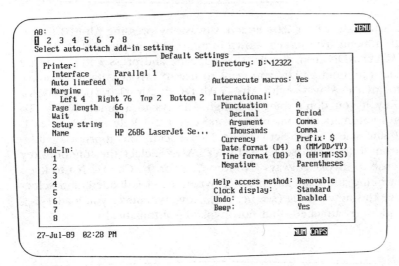

You also have the option of automatically invoking Allways whenever 1-2-3 is started. Because you must give 1-2-3 commands before you can use Allways (to retrieve a file, for example), select No when asked whether you want to invoke Allways automatically when you start 1-2-3. Allways is now attached to 1-2-3 and is available. Additionally, Allways is part of your default system configuration and can be invoked easily, as explained in the following section. Select Quit and choose Update to save this new setting (see fig. 9.4).

Now, whenever you load 1-2-3, the Allways add-in is attached—but not invoked—automatically. To use Allways once it is attached, you must invoke it as described in the following section.

Fig. 9.4.
Updating 1-2-3
Release 2.2 to
attach Allways
automatically.

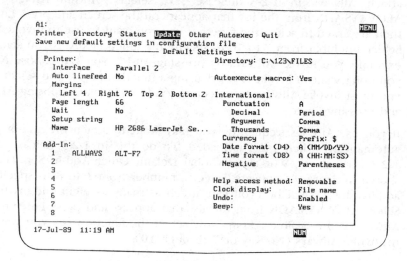

Users of 1-2-3 Release 2.0 or 2.01 attach Allways by pressing Alt-F10 to display the Add-In menu. The screen shown in figure 9.5 appears. Select **Attach**, choose **ALLWAYS.ADN** from the list that appears, and press Enter. You are asked to select the function key you want to use to invoke Allways. Choose **7**, **8**, or **9** to invoke Allways with Alt-F7, Alt-F8, or Alt-F9, respectively, or choose No-Key if you don't want to assign Allways to a function key. To attach Allways automatically whenever you start 1-2-3 Release 2.0 or 2.01, press Alt-F10 and select Setup Set (see fig. 9.6). Specify the appropriate add-in number from **1** to **8** and select **ALLWAYS.ADN**. Select the function key you want to use to invoke Allways (No-Key, **7**, **8**, or **9**). Choose **No** to keep Allways from being automatically invoked when 1-2-3 is loaded, and select Update to save this new setting (see fig. 9.7). Now, whenever you load 1-2-3, the Allways add-in is attached—but not invoked—automatically.

Fig. 9.5.
Pressing Alt-F10
to display the
Add-In menu
in 1-2-3
Release 2.0 or
2.01.

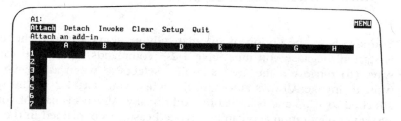

If you want a faster way to attach Allways, create a macro to do this for you. Following are the macros you can use with the various releases of 1-2-3:

Cue:
You can create a macro to attach Allways for you.

\a   /aaALLWAYS˜ 7q   (Release 2.2)
\a   {APP4}aALLWAYS˜ 7q (Release 2.0 or 2.01)

The 7 in these macros specifies Alt-F7 as the invoke key. You can replace this number with *n* (no invoke key), *8* (Alt-F8), *9* (Alt-F9), or, in Release 2.2 only, *10* (Alt-F10).

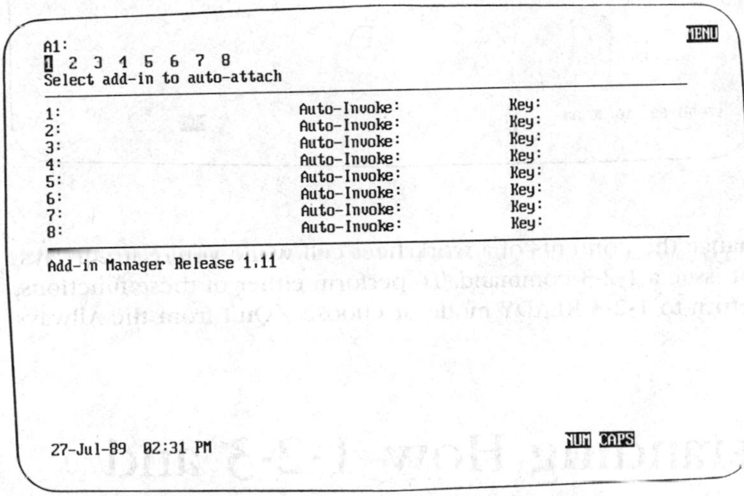

```
A1:                                                    MENU
█ 2  3  4  5  6  7  8
Select add-in to auto-attach

1:                        Auto-Invoke:        Key:
2:                        Auto-Invoke:        Key:
3:                        Auto-Invoke:        Key:
4:                        Auto-Invoke:        Key:
5:                        Auto-Invoke:        Key:
6:                        Auto-Invoke:        Key:
7:                        Auto-Invoke:        Key:
8:                        Auto-Invoke:        Key:

Add-in Manager Release 1.11




27-Jul-89  02:31 PM                        NUM CAPS
```

Fig. 9.6.
Pressing Alt-F10 and selecting Setup Set in 1-2-3 Release 2.0 or 2.01.

Invoking Allways

Once Allways has been attached (loaded into memory), you can invoke the add-in from 1-2-3 at any time. If you specified a function key to use to invoke Allways, press that key (for example, Alt-F7). You also can invoke Allways with the /Add-In command in 1-2-3 Release 2.2 (press Alt-F10 in 1-2-3 Release 2.0 or 2.01), select Invoke, and select **ALLWAYS**.

When you invoke Allways, it displays its own version of the current 1-2-3 worksheet. When Allways is active, pressing the slash (/) key calls the Allways menu instead of the 1-2-3 menu.

Reminder:
When Allways is active, pressing / calls up the Allways menu, not the 1-2-3 menu.

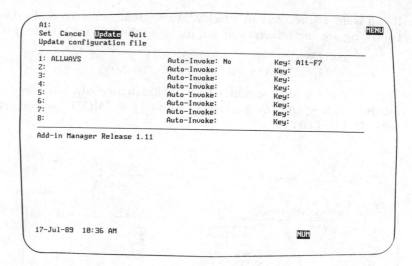

Fig. 9.7.
Updating 1-2-3
Release 2.0 or
2.01 to attach
Allways
automatically.

You cannot change the contents of a worksheet cell while you're in Allways, and you cannot issue a 1-2-3 command. To perform either of these functions, press Esc to return to 1-2-3 READY mode or choose /Quit from the Allways menu.

Understanding How 1-2-3 and Allways Work Together

Allways stores the enhanced formatting information in its own file, separate from the worksheet file. The Allways file has the same first name as your 1-2-3 file, but with the extension ALL. If you save a worksheet file called BUDGET.WK1 with Allways attached, for example, Allways saves an associated BUDGET.ALL file. This file contains all the formatting enhancements selected with Allways. Actions you perform in Allways do not affect the contents of your current 1-2-3 worksheet—except if you use the /Special Justify command (discussed later in this chapter).

Caution:
Don't detach
Allways without
first saving any
changes made in
the current
worksheet.

Allways saves enhanced formatting information only when you use the 1-2-3 /File Save command to save the current 1-2-3 worksheet. If you choose /Add-In Detach or /Add-In Clear (Alt-F10 Detach or Alt-F10 Clear in Release 2.0 or 2.01), Allways is erased immediately from memory and cannot save enhanced formatting. In addition, if you select /**W**orksheet **G**lobal **D**efault **O**ther **A**dd-In **C**ancel to stop Allways from automatically attaching (Alt-F10 **S**etup **C**ancel in Release 2.0 or 2.01.), you also detach the add-in and cannot save enhanced changes.

If Allways is detached by any of these methods before you save the worksheet, your ALL file is not updated and you may loose an extensive amount of formatting work.

Understanding the Allways Screen and Keyboard

Suppose that you load the Balance Sheet file shown in figure 9.8 into 1-2-3. If you invoke Allways (by pressing the appropriate Alt-function key or selecting the add-in from the menu) and press /, the Allways command menu appears (see fig. 9.9). As shown by these figures, the Allways **T**ext mode screen in figure 9.9 is almost identical to the standard 1-2-3 screen. Figure 9.10 shows the Allways screen in Graphics mode. Allways menus work the same way as 1-2-3 menus: press / to display the menu and select a command by typing the first letter of the command or by highlighting it and pressing Enter.

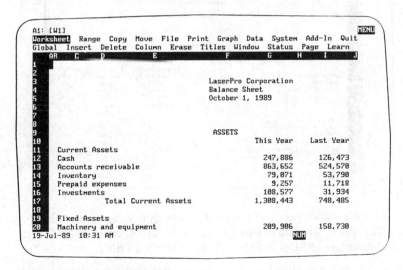

Fig. 9.8.
The worksheet and 1-2-3 menu.

The 1-2-3 and Allways screens are similar in structure. You see the spreadsheet borders (column letters and row numbers) and the clock at the bottom-left corner of the screen. Instead of the 1-2-3 READY indicator, the indicator in the upper right corner of the screen is ALLWAYS. When you are in ALLWAYS mode, you can move the cell pointer or bring up the menu. You

Reminder:
The Allways screen is similar to the 1-2-3 screen; look for the ALLWAYS indicator to determine whether Allways is active.

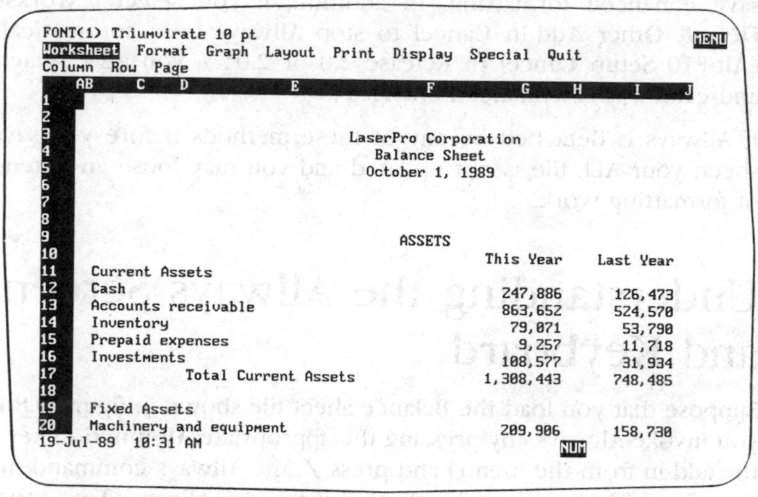

Fig. 9.9.
The worksheet
and Allways
menu in Text
mode.

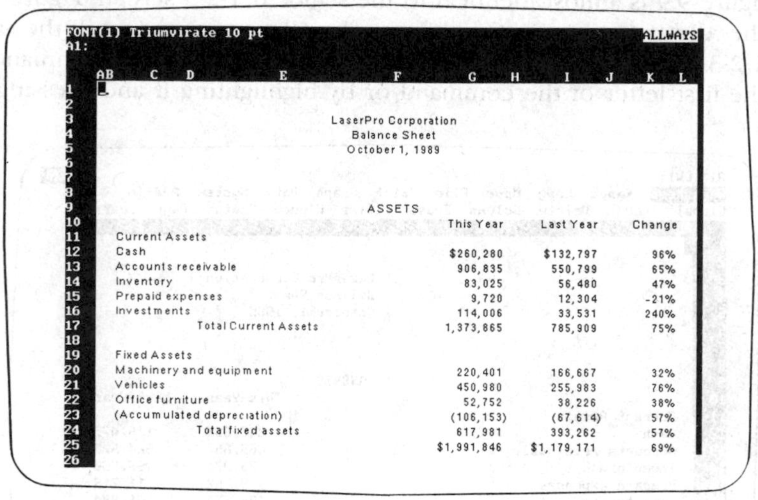

```
FONT(1) Triumvirate 10 pt                                           MENU
Worksheet Format Graph Layout Print Display Special Quit
Column Row Page
    AB  C   D       E              F         G       H    I    J
1
2
3                                    LaserPro Corporation
4                                       Balance Sheet
5                                      October 1, 1989
6
7
8
9                                         ASSETS
10                                             This Year   Last Year
11  Current Assets
12  Cash                                         247,886     126,473
13  Accounts receivable                          863,652     524,570
14  Inventory                                     79,871      53,790
15  Prepaid expenses                               9,257      11,718
16  Investments                                  108,577      31,934
17            Total Current Assets             1,308,443     748,485
18
19  Fixed Assets
20  Machinery and equipment                      209,906     158,730
19-Jul-89  10:31 AM                                          NUM
```

Fig. 9.10.
Allways in
Graphics mode.

```
FONT(1) Triumvirate 10 pt                                        ALLWAYS
A1:
    AB  C   D       E            F        G    H   I   J   K   L
1
2
3                                LaserPro Corporation
4                                   Balance Sheet
5                                  October 1, 1989
6
7
8
9                                      ASSETS
10                                        This Year   Last Year   Change
11  Current Assets
12  Cash                                   $260,280    $132,797      96%
13  Accounts receivable                     906,835     550,799      65%
14  Inventory                               83,025       56,480      47%
15  Prepaid expenses                         9,720       12,304     -21%
16  Investments                            114,006       33,531     240%
17            Total Current Assets        1,373,865     785,909      75%
18
19  Fixed Assets
20  Machinery and equipment                220,401      166,667      32%
21  Vehicles                               450,980      255,983      76%
22  Office furniture                        52,752       38,226      38%
23  (Accumulated depreciation)            (106,153)     (67,614)     57%
24            Total fixed assets           617,981      393,262      57%
25                                       $1,991,846   $1,179,171     69%
26
```

cannot enter or edit data. You must quit Allways and return to 1-2-3 to change data. The mode indicator can display several other messages that 1-2-3 users find familiar: ERROR, HELP, MENU, NAMES, POINT, and WAIT.

As is true in 1-2-3, the top three lines of the screen make up the *control panel*. The first line of the control panel describes the current cell's format (font, bold, underlining, and the like). The second line displays the cell address of the current cell and the contents of that cell (the label, value, or formula). When you are in MENU mode, the second line of the control panel contains the menu options, and the third line displays a description of the highlighted option in the menu.

To move around the Allways screen, use the same cell-pointer movement and GoTo (F5) keys you use in 1-2-3. Note that Allways assigns some function keys the same meanings they have in 1-2-3; these include Help (F1), Name (F3), and GoTo (F5).

Reminder:
Allways assigns to some function keys the same meanings used in 1-2-3.

Other function keys have special meanings in Allways. Shift-F4 enlarges the magnification of the screen display ("zooms in"); F4 decreases the display magnification ("zooms out"). F6 switches between Graphics and Text mode. F10 turns the display of graphs on and off. Table 9.1 lists the Allways function keys.

Table 9.1
Allways Function Keys

Function Key	Use
F1	Help
F3	Name
F4	Zoom out
Shift-F4	Zoom in
F5	GoTo
F6	Graphics/Text mode toggle
F10	Graph display on/off toggle

Allways also uses the Alt versions of a number of keys as "quick keys" or "accelerator keys." These keys are listed in table 9.2. Quick keys enable you to set various cell formats quickly without going through the menus. If a formatting option has two settings (as boldface does), pressing the quick key once turns on the option; pressing the quick key again turns off the option. If the formatting option has more than two settings (as shade does), pressing the quick key cycles through all the options.

Table 9.2
Allways Accelerator Keys for Quick Formatting

Alt Key	Format Applied
Alt-B	Boldface (**S**et, **C**lear)
Alt-G	Show Gridlines (**O**n, **O**ff)
Alt-L	Lines (**O**utline, **A**ll, **N**one)
Alt-S	Shade (**L**ight, **D**ark, **S**olid, **N**one)
Alt-U	Underline (**S**ingle, **D**ouble, **N**one)
Alt-1 to Alt-8	Set font 1 to font 8

In general, changes made to your current 1-2-3 worksheet carry through to Allways. This carry-through principle applies in three areas:

Reminder:
Most changes you make to your 1-2-3 worksheet are carried through to Allways.

- Allways immediately recognizes all changes you make to cells in your 1-2-3 worksheet, whether by direct entry or through a 1-2-3 command.

- Allways reflects in its display and printouts all cell formats assigned in your 1-2-3 worksheet.

- Allways follows the default column widths and label prefixes set in your 1-2-3 worksheet.

Specifying Cell Ranges in Allways

Many Allways commands require you to specify a range. Some commands initially anchor the range for you and some do not. You can tell whether Allways has initially anchored a range by looking for the ANC indicator at the bottom of the screen. In addition to the ANC indicator, a cell range may appear (for example, B2..B5). If the range appears, you know the range is anchored.

To point to a multicell range in POINT mode (when the ANC indicator appears), use any of the cell-pointer movement keys to extend the highlight over the desired range and press Enter. As with 1-2-3, you may choose to type the actual cell address in response to the range prompt rather than point to the range in POINT mode.

If the ANC indicator does not show a range and you want to highlight a range, move the cell pointer to the top left cell of the range and anchor it by pressing period (.). To unanchor a range, press either Esc or Backspace.

Cue:
You can prespecify an Allways range that applies automatically to a series of commands.

To prespecify an Allways range you can invoke when prompted for a range, move the cell pointer to the first cell of the range, press period (.), and extend the range with the arrow keys. Then press / to bring up the Allways command menu. From this menu you can choose any series of commands; the preselected range applies to all commands until you change the range specification (by prespecifying or supplying a new range). Prespecifying a range saves time when you want a series of commands to apply to the same range. If you want to use the following series of commands to format a range of cells, for example, it makes sense to prespecify the range: /Format Shade Light, /Format Lines Outline, and /Format Bold.

Learning To Format with Allways

The heart of Allways' power is its capability to add special text formats to the formats 1-2-3 associates with a cell. The 1-2-3 formats—numeric display and label alignment—carry through automatically to Allways. Allways' formats determine printed typeface, character size, boldface, and other stylistic features such as lines and shading.

Allways' additional formats provide many ways to enhance the appearance of printed text. To assign an Allways format to a cell or range, use the Allways /Format command. To determine the format of a cell, move the cell pointer to the cell. The format displays at the top of the screen, above the current-cell address. If you use Allways in Graphics mode, you actually can see the formatting on the screen.

Understanding Fonts

Most of Allways' formatting effects result from using different text fonts. A *font* consists of a *typeface* (for example, Times Roman), a *point* size, and sometimes an *attribute* (for example, bold or italic). The fonts you have to choose from depend on your printer; Allways can use any font your printer is capable of printing.

Allways comes with three soft fonts: Courier, Times, and Triumvirate. A *soft font* is a file on disk that specifies to a printer how to make a font. Soft fonts are sent to the printer's memory before the document is printed so that the printer can use the information to print the document. If you have a dot-matrix printer, Allways uses your printer's graphics mode to produce these fonts. If you have a laser printer, these three fonts are downloaded automatically to your printer when you use them. Your printer, however, may not have enough memory for larger fonts.

If your printer provides additional fonts, these fonts also are available to Allways. The Hewlett-Packard LaserJet comes with two built-in fonts (Courier and Line Printer), for example, and you can purchase dozens of cartridges to access additional fonts. All of these fonts can be used in Allways.

Reminder:
Allways can use, for worksheet text, any additional laser printer fonts you might have.

Each worksheet can use up to eight different fonts. These eight fonts are stored in a *font set*. The font list displayed in figure 9.11 is the default font set, comprised of Triumvirate and Times fonts. Figure 9.12 displays a worksheet formatted with the default fonts.

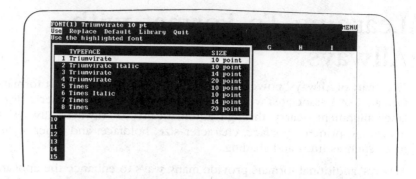

Fig. 9.11.
The default font set offered in Allways.

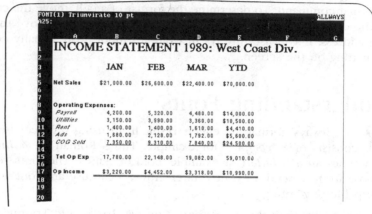

Fig. 9.12.
A worksheet formatted with Times and Triumvirate fonts.

If you want to choose a font from a laser cartridge, use the **/Print Configuration Cartridge** command to select the cartridge you want to use *before* you select the **/Format Font** command. See "Configuring Your Printer" later in this chapter for details.

Using Fonts

With Allways, you can format each cell or range of cells with a different font. You can use up to eight fonts for a single worksheet, but by default, all cells are assigned to font 1.

You assign a font to a cell or range with the Allways **/Format Font** command. Use the cell-pointer movement keys to move to the desired font on the displayed font list. (Alternatively, you can type the number next to the font.) Make sure **Use** is highlighted in the **Format Font** menu and press Enter. Allways then prompts you for a range. When you supply the range and press Enter, the selected font is applied to the specified range. If necessary, Allways adjusts the height of the row to conform to the tallest point size present.

If you change the font size of a paragraph of text, you may find that the text consumes more or fewer columns than it originally did. To respace the text, use the /Special Justify command. This command is similar to 1-2-3's /Range Justify command that word-wraps text within the range you define.

Another way to format with fonts is to use the quick keys. If you have memorized the numbers next to the fonts in the font box, you can press Alt and the desired font number to format a prespecified range.

Replacing Fonts

The list of eight fonts shown in figure 9.5 is the default font set. If the fonts you want are not in the displayed list, you can substitute the desired font for any of the default fonts. Because you are limited to eight fonts per worksheet, you must *replace* one of the existing fonts in the list; you cannot *add* fonts to the list.

To replace one of the fonts in the current set with a font not currently shown, select /Format Font. Highlight the font you want to replace with a new font (choose a font you don't need in the current worksheet). When prompted, you also can type the number next to the font you want to replace. Select Replace from the Format Font menu. A list of all the fonts your printer can produce appears. Highlight the font you want and press Enter. A list of available point sizes for that font displays. Highlight the desired point size and press Enter. The new font is now listed in the font set and can be used immediately or at a later time.

To use the newly added font, select Use from the Format Font menu, highlight the range to which you want to apply the font, and press Enter.

When you replace fonts, any worksheet cells formatted with that particular font number automatically change. Suppose that you used /Format Font Replace to replace Times-20 with Courier Bold-12. All cells in your worksheet previously formatted as Times-20 are automatically reformatted as Courier Bold-12.

Creating Font Libraries

When you use /Format Font Replace to customize the font list for the current worksheet, you may want to save the font set for use with another worksheet file. The font set can be named and saved in a font library to be used over again in any other worksheet. Create font libraries for combinations of fonts you are likely to use in other worksheets. Creating a font library saves you from using the /Format Font Replace command in each worksheet.

To save the current font set in a library, select /Format Font Library Save. Allways prompts you to enter a file name. Type a file name of up to eight characters and press Enter. The file is saved with the extension AFS.

When you want to use a font library, select /Format Font Library Retrieve. Allways displays a list of library files with the AFS extension. Highlight the name of the library you want to use and press Enter. The eight fonts saved in this library display in the font box and you can use any of these fonts on the current worksheet.

If you find that you frequently retrieve the same font library, make it the default font set. To do this, retrieve the font library you want to become the default and select /Format Font Default Update.

Some laser printers have a restricted amount of memory. In general, the larger the point size of a font, the more memory the font takes in the printer's memory. When you download soft fonts to a laser printer, the printer stores the fonts in its memory for use during the printing process. If you get an "out of memory" message on your printer when you print, your printer does not have enough memory to support the font set downloaded to it. Try replacing the large fonts with smaller fonts or using an internal or cartridge font. Internal or cartridge fonts are labeled printer under the column heading KIND when you select /Format Font Replace; soft fonts are labeled soft.

Changing Attributes

Font formats are only one type of format you can apply to a cell or a range. You also can apply boldface, single-underline, and double-underline attributes. If you have a color printer, you can change the color of a range of cells.

The titles in figure 9.13 appear in boldface; the last number in each column is single underlined and the final totals are double underlined.

Fig. 9.13.
A worksheet formatted with boldface, single-underline, and double-underline attributes.

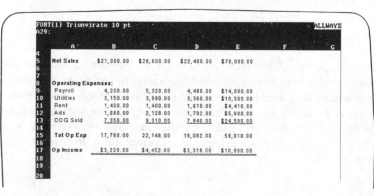

You can use bold formatting to emphasize column headings. To boldface a range, select **/Format Bold Set** and indicate the range to which you want to apply the attribute. If you work in **Graphics** mode, the bold text appears heavier on the screen. Regardless of the mode you use, the first line of the control panel indicates Bold if you have formatted the cell with the **Bold** attribute.

Use the Allways underline formatting option instead of the 1-2-3 repeating label to create underlines. In 1-2-3, you have to enter \- to create a single underline and \= to produce a double underline. This method has several disadvantages. First, you must enter these labels in blank cells, consuming valuable worksheet space. Second, the underlines are not solid and don't look very professional.

Cue:
Use Allways to create professional underlines in your worksheet.

Allways solves these problems by offering true underlining—the same as is available in word processing. You do not use blank rows for the underlines; underlines are solid and appear directly underneath existing cell entries, not in separate cells.

The **Underline** option on the **/Format** menu offers two types of underlining: **Single** and **Double**. The **Underline Single** option can be used at the bottom of a column of numbers, above a total. This option underlines only the characters in the cell—it does not underline the full width of the cell. If the single underline is not long enough, use the **/Format Lines Bottom** command (see "Drawing Lines and Boxes" later in this chapter for details). You probably will use the **Underline Single** option only when the last number in the column is the longest number. The **Underline Double** option is ideal for double underlining grand totals. Unlike single underlining, double underlining *does* span the entire cell width.

Quick keys are available for boldfacing and underlining. To use quick keys, first preselect the range you want to format. To preselect the range, place the cell pointer on the top left cell of the range you want to format, press the period (.) to anchor the highlight, and move the cell pointer to the bottom right cell in the desired range. To boldface, press Alt-B. If the cell is already boldfaced, Alt-B cancels the boldface.

The underline quick key is Alt-U. The first time you press Alt-U, the range is single underlined. The second time, it is double underlined; the third time, underlining is canceled.

You also can cancel boldfacing and underlining using the menu **/Format Bold Clear** and **/Format Underline Clear** commands.

If you have a color printer, such as the Hewlett-Packard PaintJet, you may want to enhance your printouts with different colors. You can print up to eight different colors if your printer has the capability. To change the color of a range, select **/Format Color**. A list of eight colors appears. Choose the color, or type the number of the color you want (from **1** to **8**), and indicate the range you want to affect. Following is a list of the colors and assigned color numbers used by /Format Color:

Color Number	Color
1	Black
2	Red
3	Green
4	Blue
5	Cyan
6	Magenta
7	White
8	Red for negative numbers; black for the rest

Drawing Lines and Boxes

You can make your spreadsheet look more professional by adding horizontal or vertical lines and creating boxes. Figure 9.14 shows how lines and borders can enhance a spreadsheet.

Fig. 9.14.
A box created
with the
/Format Line
command.

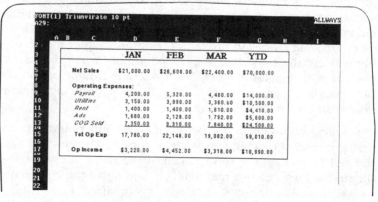

Reminder:
Use /Format Lines
to draw lines
around a range of
cells.

The /Format Lines command enables you to place lines around any part of a cell or range: Outline, Left, Right, Top, Bottom, and All. The Outline option draws lines around the entire range, forming a single box. The spreadsheet in figure 9.14 has an outline border around it. The Left, Right, Top, and Bottom options draw a line along the appropriate side of each selected cell in the range. The All option draws lines around each cell in the range, boxing each cell. The All option is the equivalent of choosing Left, Right, Top, and Bottom for each cell in the range.

The quick key for drawing lines is Alt-L. The first time you press Alt-L, the range is outlined. The second time, the range is boxed; the third time, all lines are cleared. To remove lines using the menu, select /Format Lines Clear.

You can change the weight of the lines in several ways. To change the darkness of lines before you print, use **/Layout Options Line-Weight**. (This command appears as **Line-Weight** in Release 2.2 and as **LineWeight** in earlier releases.) Choose from **N**ormal, **L**ight, and **H**eavy. You may not notice any difference in the line weight on the screen, but the printed copy should reflect the change.

If you need even thicker lines, you can use a different technique that doesn't even use the **/F**ormat **L**ines command. See "Creating Special Effects" later in this chapter for details.

Adding Shades

The **/F**ormat **S**hade command enables you to highlight important areas on the printed worksheet. The column headings in figure 9.15 stand out because of the background shading. You also can create thick horizontal and vertical lines using the **S**olid shade. The thick line under the column headings in figure 9.15, for example, was created by using the **S**olid shade on a narrow row.

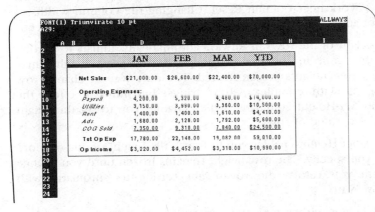

Fig. 9.15.
Headings emphasized with light and solid shades.

Shades can be **L**ight, **D**ark, or **S**olid (black). The **D**ark shade is not as dark as it appears on-screen—you should have no problem reading text in a dark-shaded area on a printed report. Use the **S**olid shade only on blank cells to create thick, solid lines. You cannot see the cell contents if you assign **S**olid to cells containing data. To create a border around a shaded area, use **/F**ormat **L**ines **O**utline.

The quick key for shading is Alt-S. The first time you press Alt-S, the range is lightly shaded. The second time, the range is dark; the third time, it is shaded solid. The fourth time you press Alt-S, all shading is cleared. To remove shading using the menu, choose **/F**ormat **S**hade **C**lear.

Adjusting Column Widths and Row Heights

When you invoke Allways, the width of your 1-2-3 columns carry through to Allways. You can set column width in 1-2-3, but you may want to use Allways' /Worksheet Column Set-Width command for several reasons. First of all, you can adjust a column's width more finely in Allways than in 1-2-3: you can set column widths in one-tenth-inch increments. In addition, once you change fonts, you may discover that you need to change the width of a column. Using Allways to make this change is more convenient than returning to 1-2-3.

Cue:
Use Ctrl-left and Ctrl-right arrows to specify the width of a column as finely as one-tenth inch.

As you can do in 1-2-3, you can adjust the column width visually in Allways, using the left and right arrows to change the width one character at a time. In Allways, however, you can change the width in tenths of a character using Ctrl-left arrow and Ctrl-right arrow. Allways has its own definition for the width of one character: one character width equals the width of a numeric digit in font 1.

To return to the default 1-2-3 column widths after adjusting column widths in Allways, use /Worksheet Column Reset. Changing the column widths in Allways does not affect the column widths in the original 1-2-3 worksheet.

By default, the height of the rows in Allways automatically adjusts to accommodate the largest font in the row. Although Allways row heights may change, the 1-2-3 row heights are unaffected. The only way to change row heights in 1-2-3 is with complex setup strings, but Allways offers the /Worksheet Row Set-Height command, which enables you to set the height of a single row or a range of rows.

/Worksheet Row Set-Height enables you to freeze the height of one or more rows to a value you specify. The row height remains frozen until you change it again or until you return the row-height setting to automatic with /Worksheet Row Auto.

To enter a row height, either type the new point size when prompted or press the up and down arrows to adjust the height of the row one point size at a time. (When specifying the number of points for the row height, remember that one inch has 72 points.) The current row height is displayed when you select /Worksheet Row Set-Height.

When you specify column widths and row heights, remember that column widths are specified in numbers of characters (the width of a character is defined as the width of an Arabic numeral in font 1). Row heights, however, are specified in points. See "Creating Special Effects" later in this chapter for examples of ways to use the /Worksheet Column and /Worksheet Row commands.

Both **/W**orksheet **R**ow Set-Height and **/W**orksheet **C**olumn Set-Width can be used on a multicell prespecified range. Before issuing either command, place the cell pointer on the first row or column to be set, press the period (.) to anchor the highlight, and adjust the highlight to include the desired range of rows or columns.

Cue:
By preselecting a range, you can adjust the height of multiple rows or the width of multiple columns at the same time.

Justifying Text

1-2-3's **/R**ange Justify command word-wraps text within a defined range. If you change the font size of a paragraph of text in Allways, however, you may find that the text consumes more or fewer columns than it did originally. Allways' **/S**pecial Justify command can respace text to fit evenly in the columns.

/Special Justify is the only Allways command that alters the contents of your 1-2-3 worksheet. Make sure that you know the effect this command will have on your worksheet before you use this command. If you have any doubts, save the worksheet before using Allways to respace text.

Reminder:
/Special Justify actually alters the contents of the cells in your 1-2-3 worksheet.

In figure 9.16, text is included at the end of the worksheet report. In 1-2-3, this text stretches across the screen; in Allways, however, you see that the text appears on a narrower line. This occurs because of the font selected in Allways. To make the lines longer, use **/S**pecial Justify to adjust the text. When prompted to enter the range, highlight B59..F62 and press Enter. As happens in 1-2-3, Allways justifies the text (see fig. 9.17).

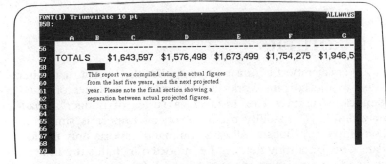

Fig. 9.16.
Text at the bottom of an Allways worksheet appearing on a narrow line.

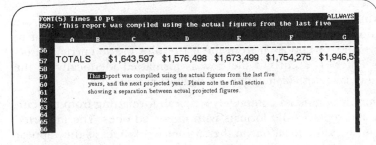

Fig. 9.17.
Using /Special Justify to adjust the text.

Copying and Moving Formats

The /Special Copy command enables you to copy all the formats of a cell or range to another cell or range. The command copies *formats* only, not cell contents (/Special Copy differs from the 1-2-3 /Copy command in this respect). The formatting that can be copied with /Special Copy includes font, boldface, underline, shade, color, and lines. You should find that Allways' /Special Copy command saves you time in formatting.

Cue:
Use /Special Copy to format ranges quickly in your worksheet.

This command is useful when several areas of a worksheet have similar formatting. You can use the /Format commands to format the first area and then use /Special Copy to copy those formats to one or more areas. If you have formatted a range to 14-point Times, in boldface with shading and lines, for example, you save a lot of time by copying the format to another range rather than using four separate /Format commands. When you invoke Allways' /Special Copy command, you are asked to enter the range to copy *from* (the cell or cells containing the formatting) and the range to copy *to* (the target cell or cells).

The /Special Move command also copies formats from the source range to the target range, but at the same time, resets all source-range formats. The source range is set to font 1 and all special formatting (boldface, underline, shades, lines, and colors) is cleared. Like /Special Copy, this command does not affect the cell contents of either the source or target ranges. Because the command resets your source-range formats, use the command with care. In some cases, you may find it safer to use /Special Copy and reset source range formats as necessary with /Format.

Importing Formats

Allways offers a /Special Import command that applies the format of another worksheet on disk to the current worksheet. If you have a series of worksheets with identical structures (for instance, a series of budget spreadsheets), you may find this capability useful. /Special Import is similar to 1-2-3's /File Combine Copy, but the Allways command imports only the formats, not the data. The formatting that can be imported includes the individual cell formats, the font set, layout, print range, and graphs.

To import formats from another file, select /Special Import. You are prompted to enter the name of the file containing the format you want to copy. Type the name, or choose it from the list of files in the current directory, and press Enter. The current file now is formatted identically to the selected file. You can reformat individual ranges if you choose.

The /Special Import command completely strips all formatting from the current worksheet and replaces the formats with imported ones. The imported formats appear in the same locations in the current worksheet as they appear in the imported worksheet. If the two worksheets are not organized identically, formats may appear in unexpected cells. You may be able to fix minor problems using /Special **M**ove to move imported cell formats that do not match up exactly with the current file.

1-2-3 Release 2.2's Undo feature does not work in Allways. If you don't like the results of importing the formats from another file, you cannot undo the formats. The only way to get rid of the new formats is to retrieve the original file (assuming you saved it before importing). Therefore, always save your current worksheet before you execute /Special **I**mport.

Cue:
Because you cannot undo formatting mistakes, save the Allways file before using /Special Import.

Controlling Label Alignment

In 1-2-3, the label contents of a cell can be aligned left, right, or center. Allways does not offer a label-alignment command, although all 1-2-3 label prefixes carry through to Allways.

A centered label always stays centered in the cell. If the label exceeds the width of the cell, the label spills over to adjacent empty cells, both to the left and right. A right-aligned label always stays right aligned; if the label is too long for the cell width, the label spills over to any empty cells to the left. A left-aligned label works the same way: any text too large for the cell spills over to the right. If the cells surrounding the labeled cell are not empty, the long label is truncated to stay within its own cell. Because Allways does not offer the equivalent of 1-2-3's /**R**ange **L**abel command and has no way to edit cells, you must return to 1-2-3 to change a label's alignment.

Creating Special Effects

The various formatting commands that Allways offers can produce special effects that may not be immediately obvious. If you want thicker lines than can be produced with /**F**ormat **L**ines, for example, apply a solid shade to a row or column, and narrow the column width or shorten the row height.

To create a thick vertical line, shade a blank column with /**F**ormat **S**hade **S**olid and narrow the column width with /**W**orksheet **C**olumn **S**et-Width. Set the column width to less than one character (for example, 0.6 character). To create thick horizontal lines, shade a row and shorten the row height. (See "Adding Shades" and "Adjusting Column Widths and Row Heights" earlier in this chapter for details.)

Another unusual effect you can produce is a shadow box (see fig. 9.18). This effect is produced by creating an outline "box" with a short row and narrow column of solid shades. Make sure that you have empty rows and columns around the area to be boxed before you begin. Then use the following steps to create a shadow box:

1. Draw a box around the area with /**Format Lines Outline**. When prompted for the range, include the blank column to the left of the range to be boxed.

2. Narrow the width of the blank left column using /**Worksheet Column Set-Width** (for example, to 0.4 characters).

3. Shade the row under the box using /**Format Shade Solid**. Specify a range starting in the first column of the data/graph area (do not include the first narrow column) and ending one column after the data/graph area.

4. Shorten the height of the shaded row using /**Worksheet Row Set-Height** (for example, to 4 points).

5. Shade the column to the right of the box using /**Format Shade Solid**. Specify a range starting one row down from the top of the data/graph area and ending at the bottom row of the data/graph area.

6. Narrow the width of the shaded column (for example, to 0.4 characters).

Fig. 9.18.
A shadow box.

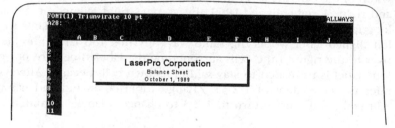

Using 1-2-3 Graphs

Because Allways can print 1-2-3 graphs, you may seldom use the Lotus Print-Graph program. Using Allways to print graphs offers two advantages over PrintGraph: you don't need to exit 1-2-3, and you can print graphs in the middle of a worksheet report. In addition, you can use Allways' formatting features to enhance the graph.

The graphs you use with Allways must reside on a disk in Lotus PIC file format. (Save a graph in PIC format using 1-2-3's /**Graph Save** command.) When you ask Allways to use a 1-2-3 graph, Allways reads the corresponding PIC file from the disk.

Reminder:
Use the 1-2-3 /Graph Save command to save any 1-2-3 graphs you want to use with Allways.

Simply creating and naming a 1-2-3 graph does not save a PIC file and does not give Allways access to the graph. You must use the 1-2-3 /**Graph Save** command to save the current graph in a PIC file. If you make changes to your graph in 1-2-3, you must reexecute /**Graph Save** so that Allways has access to the changes.

To display and print graphs, Allways uses the graph font files (files with the extension FNT) that come with 1-2-3's PrintGraph program. By default, Allways expects these files to be in the same directory as your 1-2-3 program. If the FNT files are in a different directory, copy the files from the PrintGraph disk to the 1-2-3 directory or use the Allways **/G**raph **F**onts-Directory command to point Allways to the disk and directory containing the FNT files.

Reminder:
Allways cannot use 1-2-3 graphs if the font files aren't in the 1-2-3 program directory.

Adding a 1-2-3 Graph

Before you can print a 1-2-3 graph from Allways, you must add the graph to your Allways worksheet with the Allways **/G**raph **A**dd command. You then are prompted for the name of the PIC file containing the graph. Next, specify the range over which you want to paste this graph. The size and shape of the range you specify determines the size and shape of the graph when it is printed.

To print the graph in the middle of a worksheet report, insert blank rows or columns where you want the graph to appear before you add the graph. If you don't, the graph overlays worksheet data. Generally, the graph range should include only blank cells, so be sure that you insert enough rows and columns to make the graph the size you want. Although the graph range is usually blank, you may want to place formatted worksheet text in a graph; see "Enhancing Graphs with /Format" for details on how you can overlay a graph on worksheet text.

Suppose that you want to paste a 1-2-3 bar graph into the middle of a worksheet and then print the worksheet and graph. Also suppose that the graph has been saved in a file called EXP89BAR.PIC. To add this graph, use **/G**raph **A**dd and select EXP89BAR.PIC. Select the range D20..F30 to place the graph in the Allways file. Figure 9.19 shows the Allways screen with the 1-2-3 graph added. Notice that the graph appears as a shaded box when you import the graph; you must turn on the graph display, as explained later in this section, to see the graph.

Once you add a graph, you can change the range in which it resides with the **/G**raph **S**ettings **R**ange command. You may want to change the range to move the graph to another part of the worksheet or to change its size. Another way to adjust the graph range is to change the row heights and column widths of the graph range using the **/W**orksheet **R**ow and **/W**orksheet **C**olumn commands. If you want the graph to be a little larger—but less than a full row or column—increase the column widths or row heights of columns or rows within the graph range with the **/W**orksheet commands.

To erase a graph from the worksheet report, use **/G**raph **R**emove.

When you first add a graph, all you see on-screen is cross-hatching in the specified range, even if you're in **G**raphics mode. Cross-hatching appears

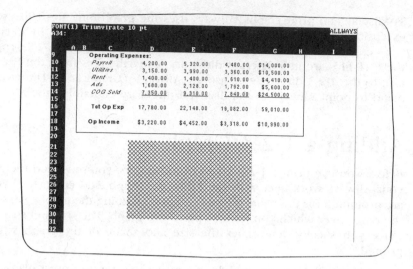

Fig. 9.19.
A graph added
to a worksheet.

Reminder:
When you first add
a graph to an
Allways worksheet,
all you see on-
screen is cross-
hatching in the
range you
specified.

because Allways does not, by default, display graphs. Redrawing the screen slows considerably when a graph is on-screen; Allways therefore does not display the graph, assuming that you don't need to see the graph until you print. The cross-hatching appears to show you where the graph is positioned. (If you're in **T**ext mode, *G* characters fill the graph range instead of cross-hatching.) To display a graph on-screen, execute /**D**isplay **G**raphs **Y**es. When you select **Q**uit, the graph displays on-screen. Alternatively, press F10 to toggle the display of graphs on and off. The graph in figure 9.19 looks like the one in figure 9.20 when the graph display is turned on.

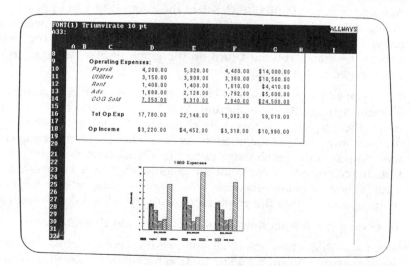

Fig. 9.20.
A graph added
to a worksheet
with graph
display turned
on.

Allways allows as many as 20 graphs per worksheet. To keep track of all these graphs and move to a particular graph, use /Graph GoTo. With this command, you move the pointer to one of the graphs added to the worksheet in the same way you move to specific cells with 1-2-3's GoTo feature. /Graph GoTo is useful when you have many graphs in a large worksheet.

Changing Graph Settings

Allways provides graph settings you can use to add enhancements to a graph. When you execute /Graph Settings, Allways displays a menu and a settings sheet showing all the current settings for the current graph (see fig. 9.21). If your cell pointer was not in a particular graph range, a numbered list of the graphs added to the current worksheet appears after you select /Graph Settings. Use the cursor keys to select one of these graphs, press Enter, and the settings sheet appears.

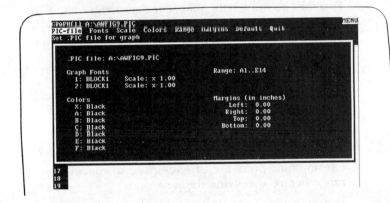

Fig. 9.21
The default graph settings sheet.

Following is a summary of the options available on the **Graph Settings** menu:

Option	Description
PIC-file	Enables you to change the settings for the PIC file associated with a graph you have added. Use this option if you move a PIC file to another disk or directory so that you don't have to redefine specific graph settings. You also may want to use this option if you have renamed a graph file in DOS.
Fonts	Applies to any text placed in the graph with the 1-2-3 /Graph command. The fonts available are the same as those in the Lotus PrintGraph program. You can use two fonts per graph. Font 1 controls the typeface for the top center graph title; font 2 specifies the font for

Option	Description
	all other titles and legends. By default, both fonts are BLOCK1. Change one or both fonts with this command.
Scale	Changes the scale of a graph. The Lotus PrintGraph program does not enable you to change the size of graph fonts. In Allways, however, you can use this command to change the scale (size) of graph text. A scale factor of 1, the default, produces graph text identical in size to PrintGraph. You can specify a scale factor between 0.5 and 3 for either or both of the two available graph fonts. A scale size of 0.5 makes the font half the default size; 3 makes the font three times the default. Increasing the scale size may result in overlapping text.
Colors	Specifies colors for the different data ranges (X, A, B, C, D, E, and F) in a graph in the same way as PrintGraph. Use this setting only if you have a color printer. If you set colors in 1-2-3, you must reset them in Allways.
Range	Changes the size or location of a graph. The current graph range is highlighted on-screen, and you can type the new range or move the cell pointer to highlight a larger or smaller area. If you want to specify a new range entirely different from the existing one, press Esc or Backspace to cancel the old range before specifying the new one.
Margins	Controls the graph's position within the specified range. By default, Allways fills the entire graph range with the graph. If you want more white space around the graph, choose Left, Right, Top, or Bottom. The graph shrinks to fit its new space.
	Left is the amount of space between the left edge of the graph range and the beginning of the graph. Right is the amount of space between the graph and the right side of the graph range. Top refers to the amount of space between the upper edge of the graph range and the top of the graph. Bottom is the amount of space between the graph and the bottom of the graph range. The initial default for all four graph margins is 0. You may enter values between 0 and 9.99 inches.

Option	Description
Default	Sets new default graph settings and returns settings to the default values. /Graph Settings Default Restore returns settings to the default. /Graph Settings Default Update permanently changes the default settings to the current settings. Use this option if you find yourself constantly changing the graph settings to the same values.
Quit	Exits the Graph Settings menu and returns to the Allways main menu.

When you issue /Graph Settings, Allways immediately displays the settings sheet for the current graph if the pointer is in the graph range. If the pointer was not on a graph when the command was issued, you must select the graph you want to work with from a list before the settings sheet for that graph appears. Preselection is an easier and more foolproof way of selecting the correct graph.

Cue:
Before you issue /Graph Settings, preselect a graph by positioning the cell pointer within the range of the graph.

Enhancing Graphs with /Format

When you print *graphs* in Allways, the only font choices you have are Print-Graph fonts. (When you print *worksheet data* in Allways, however, you can choose any eight of the fonts supported by your printer.) You can include other fonts in your graph by typing the text in a worksheet cell and formatting the cell with Allways' /Format command. Because a graph is transparent to any text and formatting in the worksheet behind it, you can add text to the worksheet and have it appear "on" the graph.

A good example of this technique is shown in figure 9.22. **ASSETS** was typed in 1-2-3 in cell AF211; **NOTE**>> was typed in cell AH214. The Allways /Format command was used to format both cells, including formatting AH214 with a double underline. Because the graph is transparent, the formatted text in these two cells shows through and becomes part of the graph.

Another way to use Allways' formatting capabilities with graphs is to use /Format Lines to place an outline border around the graph after it is added. Use /Format Shade to shade the background of the graph.

Setting Up the Page

Before you print from Allways, use the /Layout command to fine-tune the page layout. Figure 9.23 shows the Layout menu and the layout settings for the current worksheet. Notice that many of the options are similar to those

Fig. 9.22.
Using
formatted
worksheet text
to enhance a
graph.

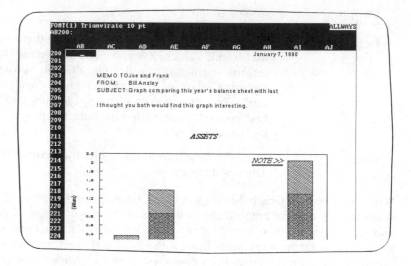

Reminder:
Any headers,
footers, margins,
and borders
specified in 1-2-3
must be respecified
in Allways.

offered in 1-2-3's **Print Printer Options** menu. The headers, footers, margins, and borders you enter in 1-2-3's **Print Printer Options** menu do not transfer into Allways. If you defined headers and footers in 1-2-3, you must use the Allways **/L**ayout command to set them up again. The following sections explain how to use the various options on the Layout menu.

Fig. 9.23.
The Layout
menu.

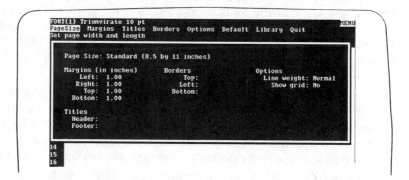

Defining the Page Layout

The default page size is standard letter size (8.5 by 11 inches). Using **/L**ayout **P**ageSize, you can choose **L**egal (8.5 by 14 inches) or **C**ustom. The Custom option lets you define the page width and page length, in inches, to any size you need. Additional page sizes may be listed, depending on your printer.

Allways' /Layout Margins command is similar to 1-2-3's /Print Printer Options Margins command, with several important differences. In 1-2-3, the right and left margins are entered in terms of characters, and the top and bottom margins are entered in terms of lines. In Allways, all margins are entered in inches. In 1-2-3, the right margin is the number of characters that print on the line. In Allways, the right margin is the space between the printed worksheet and the right edge of the page. You can set each of the margins (Left, Right, Top, and Bottom) to a value from 0 to 99.99 inches; 1 is the default.

Although you may think page orientation (landscape and portrait) should be on the Layout menu, it is not. (Landscape orientation prints the page sideways; portrait orientation is the default, with the page up and down.) To specify landscape orientation on a laser printer, use the /Print Configuration Orientation command. See "Configuring Your Printer" later in this chapter for details.

Printing Titles and Borders

Allways' /Layout Titles command is the equivalent of 1-2-3's /Print Printer Options Header and Footer commands. A *header* is a one-line title at the top of every page; a *footer* is a line that prints at the bottom of each page. You do not see these titles on-screen with Allways; they appear only when you print.

As with 1-2-3, you can include special characters in a header or footer. Including the @ symbol prints today's date in that position; including the # symbol prints the page number. Including vertical bar characters (|) separates the text into left-justified, centered, and right-justified sections.

If you type a header as @|**Balance Sheet**|**Page #**, the printed header looks like the following:

8-Aug-89   Balance Sheet   Page 1

Allways reserves three lines on the printout for each header and footer. Remember to figure in these extra lines when you calculate how many lines of text fit on a printed page. Unlike 1-2-3, Allways does not reserve lines for titles if you don't have any titles. Headers and footers are always printed in font 1. To cancel headers or footers, use the /Layout Titles Clear command.

Allways' /Layout Borders command is the same as 1-2-3's /Print Printer Options Borders command. This command specifies a worksheet range (rows or columns) to be printed on every page of a multipage printout. Suppose that the balance sheet shown in figure 9.2 included columns for five years instead of two. You would need two pages to print the report, with the leftmost column as the first column on each page so that you know what each row of data signifies. In Allways, you can specify the rows to print at

Reminder:
Allways reserves three lines at the top and bottom of each page for titles unless you have no titles.

the top or bottom of each page if the worksheet is very long; specify the columns to print at the left side of each page if the sheet is very wide.

To repeat a column or row of text on other pages of the report, follow these steps:

1. Use the Allways **/P**rint **R**ange command to specify a range including the entire report *except* for the border columns and rows.

2. Select **/L**ayout **B**orders **L**eft and highlight any cell in the border column to specify a border column. Select **/L**ayout **B**orders **T**op or **B**ottom and highlight any cell in the border row to specify a border row. If the border has multiple rows or columns, press the period key (.) to anchor the highlight and extend the highlight over the additional rows or columns. Press Enter.

3. Print the report using **/P**rint **G**o.

The border columns and rows should print on each page. Make sure that the **/L**ayout **B**orders range is not included in the **/P**rint **R**ange, or the border range is printed twice on the first page. To cancel borders, use the **/L**ayout **B**orders **C**lear command.

Using Other Layout Options

The **/L**ayout **O**ptions command provides several additional options you can use to affect the way your report looks. The Layout Options menu includes the Line-Weight and Grid commands. This section explains these commands and also describes the **/L**ayout **D**efault and **/L**ayout **L**ibrary commands.

The **/L**ayout **O**ptions Line-Weight command enables you to control the thickness of lines added with the **/F**ormat **L**ines command. After issuing this command, select a line weight of Normal, Light, or Heavy. The weight you select applies to *all* lines in the report. The varied line weight is noticeable only on printers with sufficient resolution (laser printers and high-density dot-matrix printers).

/Layout **O**ptions Line-Weight changes the line weight of *all* lines created with **/F**ormat **L**ines; you cannot change the thickness of individual lines. As mentioned earlier, however, you can vary the thickness of individual lines by using **/F**ormat **S**hade **S**olid, **/W**orksheet **C**olumn **S**et-Width, and **/W**orksheet **R**ow **S**et-Height (see "Creating Special Effects" earlier in this chapter).

The **/L**ayout **O**ptions Grid command produces a printout that looks like ledger paper, with dotted lines following the rows and columns of your text and enclosing every cell on your printout. If you select **/L**ayout **O**ptions Grid Yes, Allways prints grid lines through the entire printout. If you want to enclose only part of your printout in a grid, use /Format Lines All and specify a range. You can use the Alt-G quick key to turn on and off the printing of grids.

The /Layout Default and /Layout Library commands enable you to modify all the layout settings at once. To return all the layout settings to the default values, choose /Layout Default Restore. To change the default settings permanently to those of the current worksheet, use /Layout Default Update. Use /Layout Default Update if you find yourself constantly changing the layout settings to the same values.

Use /Layout Library to create a library of layout settings on disk. If you need certain combinations of layout settings for different types of worksheets, you can save each group of settings and then retrieve it to use later with any worksheet.

To save the current page-layout settings in a library, use /Layout Library Save and specify a file name. The file is given the extension ALS. When you want to use the settings with another worksheet, use /Layout Library Retrieve. If you no longer need a library file, delete it using /Layout Library Erase.

Printing with Allways

The following sections examine each of the options available with the Allways /Print command. You will learn how to configure your printer, specify a print range, set page breaks, specify print settings, and print your document.

Configuring Your Printer

Before you print, select /Print Configuration and check the settings sheet to make sure that Allways is set up to work with your printer. Figure 9.24 displays the configuration for an HP LaserJet II printer. Most of the options on the setting sheet are not changed once you have defined them unless you use more than one printer. The settings are saved automatically when you change them.

If you do not have a laser or high-end dot-matrix printer, you can select only a few configuration options from the Print Configuration menu. When an Epson LQ2550 is the selected printer, for example, only the options Printer and Interface are shown. If the selected printer is a Hewlett-Packard DeskJet or DeskJet Plus, the Cartridge option appears as well. Use Printer to specify the printer you want to use. Select the desired printer from the displayed list. (If you do not see your printer on the list, use the AWSETUP program

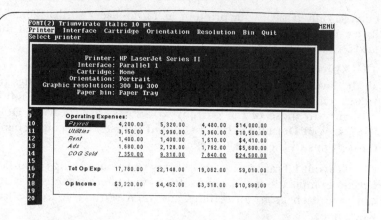

*Fig. 9.24.
/Print
Configuration
used to define
printer options.*

and select the **A**dd a Printer option.) Use the **/P**rint Configuration **I**nterface command to select the printer port to which your printer is attached (Parallel 1, Serial 1, Parallel 2, Serial 2, LPT1:, LPT2:, LPT3:, or LPT4:).

If you have a laser or high-end dot-matrix printer, you can make the following selections from the **P**rint Configuration menu:

Selection	*Description*
Cartridge	Enables you to choose the desired printer cartridge. Some printers have separate cartridges or cards you can purchase to get additional fonts for your printer. The Hewlett-Packard LaserJet, for example, offers a "B" cartridge that includes Helvetica 14-point Bold and Times Roman 8-point and 10-point in bold, medium, or italic. Use this option to select the cartridge you want to use.
Orientation	Sets the orientation of the page to be printed. Choose between **P**ortrait and **L**andscape (sideways) to change the printing orientation. In 1-2-3, you must specify a cumbersome setup string such as **\027E\027&l1O** to print in landscape; in Allways, an easy menu option does the trick.
Resolution	Controls the quality of print in your printer's graphics mode. The HP LaserJet, for example, can print 75, 100, 150, or 300 dots per inch. The higher the resolution, the better the print quality. Your printer, however, may not have enough memory to print a graph at the highest resolution. If you get an "out of memory" message on your printer when you print, or if only part of the range prints, try printing at a lower resolution.

Selection	Description
	Depending on the type of printer you have (laser or dot-matrix), a change in resolution affects different aspects of the printed page. On a dot-matrix printer, both graphs and fonts are printed in the printer's graphics mode and are affected by a change in resolution. On a laser printer, however, the text fonts are downloaded and are unaffected by a resolution change, but the resolution of graphs is affected.
Bin	Sets the feeding method if your printer offers more than one way to feed paper. Your printer may have multiple paper trays and a way to feed paper manually. Depending on the options offered by your printer, this option lists various selections. If you want to feed paper manually, use **/P**rint **C**onfiguration **B**in and select **M**anual Feed. (If you feed paper manually, you also may want to choose **/P**rint **S**ettings **W**ait to pause between pages.)

Specifying a Print Range

Allways' **/P**rint **R**ange **S**et command is the equivalent of 1-2-3's **/P**rint **P**rinter **R**ange command. If you entered a print range in 1-2-3, however, it is not transferred to Allways. You must set the print range in Allways before you print.

Reminder:
Print ranges entered in 1-2-3 are not transferred to Allways.

To specify an Allways print range, select **/P**rint **R**ange **S**et and indicate the range just as you do in 1-2-3: highlight the range with the cell-pointer movement keys, type the range, or use a 1-2-3 range name. If you want to use a 1-2-3 range name, type the range name or press F3 to choose from a list of names when prompted for the print range. After you define your print range, you see a dashed border around the area. If the print area is large, dashed lines appear around each page. To change the page breaks, refer to "Setting Page Breaks" later in this chapter.

If you want to print an Allways graph, you must define its range with **/G**raph **A**dd, as explained earlier in this chapter. Be sure to include the entire graph range in the print range. Remember that when you specify print borders using **/L**ayout **B**orders, do not include the borders range in the print range.

You also can select the range to print before choosing **/P**rint **R**ange. To preselect the range, place the cell pointer in the top left cell in the range, press the period (.), and extend the highlight to the lower right corner of the desired range. When you use **/P**rint **R**ange **S**et, Allways automatically highlights the selected range; press Enter to accept it.

To print the range, assuming that the **P**rint Configuration and **P**rint Settings menus are defined properly, select **/P**rint **G**o. If the selected range exceeds both the width and length of the page, Allways (like 1-2-3) prints the left part of the range from top to bottom and then prints the right parts of the range from top to bottom until the entire range is printed. The dashed lines on the screen let you know where the page breaks occur.

Reminder:
If you choose /Print Go before defining the range, Allways prompts you for the print range.

If you forget to specify the print range before printing a worksheet in 1-2-3, an error message appears, and you then must choose the **/P**rint **P**rinter **R**ange command, define the range, and choose **G**o again. Allways is friendlier when you forget your print range; you are prompted for the print range, and then printing begins. See "Specifying Print Settings" later in this chapter for information on printing only certain pages of the print range.

Setting Page Breaks

After you choose a print range, you see dashed lines around each page in the print range. If you don't like where the page breaks are, use **/W**orksheet **P**age to set new page breaks before you print. You can specify the row or column on which you want Allways to start a new page.

To set a row page break, select **/W**orksheet **P**age **R**ow. Position the pointer on the first row of the new page and press Enter. As shown in figure 9.25, a dashed line appears above the specified row to indicate the new page break.

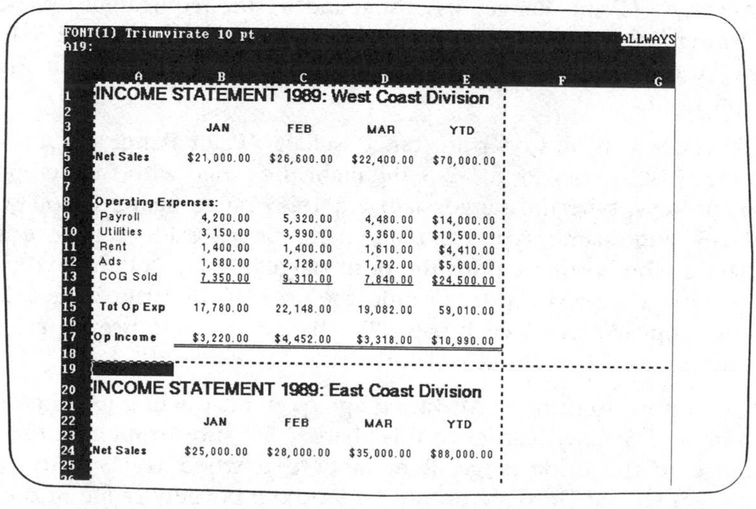

Fig. 9.25.
A worksheet with a page break added.

To tell Allways at which column to start a new page, choose **/W**orksheet **P**age **C**olumn. Position the pointer on the first column of the new page and press Enter. A dashed line appears to the left of the specified column to indicate the new page break. To remove a page break, place the cell pointer on the first row or column of the page and select /**Worksheet Page D**elete.

Specifying Print Settings

Use the /**Print Settings** command to control page numbering, ranges of pages to print, number of copies to print, and print pausing. Figure 9.26 shows the screen that appears when you select this command. The **Print Settings** menu offers the options listed in the following chart.

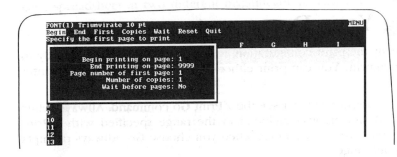

Fig. 9.26.
The Print Settings menu and settings sheet.

Option	Description
Begin and End	Prints the specified page numbers. Normally, Allways prints the entire range specified with /**Print Range Set**. If you want to print only selected pages in the range (for instance, only the ones that changed from a previous printing), set the **Begin** and **End** options accordingly. The **Begin** and **End** values cannot be less than zero or greater than the number of the last page in the document. The **Begin** value must be less than or equal to the **End** value.
First	Specifies the page number for the first page of a document if you include the # symbol in a header or footer. If you are printing your document from several different worksheets, for example, use this option to specify the first page number of each subdocument so that the page numbers are continuous. The default setting is 1.
Copies	Prints the specified number of copies.
Wait	Pauses the printer between pages. The default setting is **No**. If you want to feed individual sheets into the printer, select **Yes** to pause the printer before each new page. Use this option if you selected the **Manual**

The /Display commands *do not* affect the report printout; they simply change how the worksheet looks on-screen. When you select /Display, a menu of options appears:

Option	Description
Mode	Select from **Graphics** and **Text** modes. In **Graphics** mode, formatting displays on-screen close to how it prints. You must have a graphics monitor to use **Graphics** mode. You cannot see formatting on-screen in **Text** mode, although the control panel displays the formatting instructions for the current cell.
Zoom	Choose from **Tiny**, **Small**, **Normal**, **Large**, and **Huge** character display. Figure 9.27 shows **Tiny** magnification; figure 9.28 shows **Large**. The **Zoom** feature does not work in **Text** mode.
Graphs	Choose whether or not to show graphs on-screen. /Display **Graphs Yes** displays the actual graph, instead of cross-hatching, on-screen. When graph display is on, you will notice a delay whenever the screen redraws.
Colors	Select the colors for the screen's **Background**, **Foreground**, and **Highlight** (color monitors only).

You can use the following function keys as quick ways to change some of the display features:

Key	Use
F4	Zoom out (reduce the display)
Shift-F4	Zoom in (enlarge the display)
F6	Toggle between **Graphics** and **Text** modes
F10	Turn on and off the display of graphs

Quitting Allways

You can exit Allways and return to 1-2-3 in two ways: choose /Quit from the Allways main menu or press Esc when you are in ALLWAYS mode. You cannot press Esc to return to 1-2-3 when you are in MENU mode or on the help screens.

Even though you quit Allways, the add-in is still attached and in memory. You can reinvoke Allways in the current work session by pressing Alt and the appropriate function key (for example, Alt-F7) or by selecting /Add-In Invoke and choosing **ALLWAYS.ADN**. (In Release 2.0 or 2.01, press Alt-F10 to display the Add-In menu, and then choose **Invoke**.)

If you don't need to use Allways again during the current work session and want to free the memory Allways consumes, select /Add-In Detach and choose **ALLWAYS.ADN**. Choose /Add-In Clear to remove *all* add-ins from memory. (In Release 2.0 or 2.01, press Alt-F10 to display the Add-In menu, and then choose Detach or Clear.)

Chapter Summary

In this chapter you learned how to use Allways to enhance your 1-2-3 graphs and worksheets when you print them. Allways provides more font capabilities, borders, lines, and shading options than does 1-2-3 and can be used to make an ordinary report something special.

10

Creating and Displaying Graphs

Even if Lotus 1-2-3 provided only spreadsheet capabilities (the *1* in 1-2-3), the program would be extremely powerful. More information can be quickly assembled and tabulated electronically than possibly could be developed manually. Despite the importance of keeping detailed worksheets that show real or projected data, data can be worthless if it cannot be readily understood.

To help decision-makers who are pressed for time or are unable to draw conclusions from countless rows of numeric data—and who may benefit from seeing key figures displayed graphically—Lotus offers graphics capabilities—the *2* in 1-2-3. The program offers five types of basic business graphs as well as limited options for enhancing the appearance of graphs. Although no match for the capabilities of many stand-alone graphics packages, 1-2-3's graphic strength lies in its integration with the worksheet.

This chapter shows you how to do the following:

- Meet minimum requirements for constructing graphs

- Enhance the appearance of a graph

- Preserve the graph on disk

- Edit the current contents of a graph

- Reset some or all graph settings

- Select an appropriate graph type

- Develop all graph types

- Bypass selected 1-2-3 graph limitations

351

Understanding Draft-Quality and Final-Quality Graphs

Selecting **/G**raph from the initial 1-2-3 Release 2.2 menu produces the main **G**raph menu:

RELEASE

2.2

Type **X A B C D E F R**eset **V**iew **S**ave **O**ptions **N**ame **G**roup **Q**uit

Users of 1-2-3 Release 2.01 do not see the **G**roup option on the **G**raph menu. You can create graphs that display nothing more than unlabeled data points in bar (or stack-bar), line (or XY), and pie forms. To do so, select a graph **T**ype; specify a data range or ranges from choices **X**, **A**, **B**, **C**, **D**, **E**, and **F**; and **V**iew the screen output. The result is a draft-quality graph that depicts relationships between numbers or trends across time.

RELEASE

2.2

To improve the appearance of your graphs and produce labeled, final-quality output suitable for business presentations, you can select one or more **O**ptions. Select **S**ave to store a graph for printing. If you plan to recall specifications, use **N**ame to store your graph specifications in the current worksheet. In 1-2-3 Release 2.2, Select **G**roup to perform an operation such as selecting all the data ranges (**X**, **A**, **B**, **C**, **D**, **E**, and **F**) at once.

Suppose that you want to make a quick on-screen comparison of specific data in your current worksheet—quarterly sales information (in range N5..Q5) and the associated gross-profit figures (in range N8..Q8). By issuing the following command sequences, you can produce the minimal graph shown in figure 10.1. (In the **G**raph command sequences in this chapter, keys to be pressed to select menu options and data to be entered are shown in boldface type. Remember that you do not press Enter when you make a menu selection, but you do press Enter after typing data.)

/Graph **T**ype **B**ar
        A N5..Q5 Enter (Sales data range A)
        B N8..Q8 Enter (Gross Profit data range B)
        View

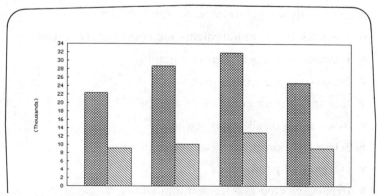

Fig. 10.1.
A minimal, or
draft-quality,
sample graph.

In this graph, the four sets of bars represent quarterly data. The bars are graphed in order from left to right, starting with the first quarter. Within each set, the left bar represents Sales data and the right bar represents the corresponding Gross Profit value. This minimal graph shows the upward movement of sales and gross profit for the first three quarters, followed by a downward trend in the fourth.

Suppose that you want to improve the appearance of this quarterly trend analysis before showing it to your colleagues. To produce the final-quality graph shown in figure 10.2, use the following command sequences:

/Graph Type **Bar**
      A N5..Q5 Enter (Sales data range A)
      B N8..Q8 Enter (Gross Profit data range B)
      X N3..Q3 Enter (Quarterly headings below x-axis)
      Options Titles First **YOUR FIRM NAME** Enter
              Titles Second **MIDWEST REGION** Enter
              Titles X-Axis **1989 OPERATIONS** Enter
              Titles Y-Axis **DOLLARS** Enter
              Legend **A SALES** Enter
              Legend **B GROSS PROFIT** Enter
              Grid Horizontal
              Scale Y-Scale Format Currency **0** Enter

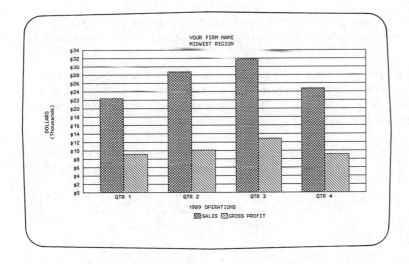

*Fig. 10.2.
A presentation-
quality sample
graph.*

Even those unfamiliar with the data can understand the contents of an enhanced graph.

In this chapter, you learn how to apply all the options to a single line graph. Then you learn how to construct all the other types of 1-2-3 graphs.

Defining the Basic Requirements for a Graph

Before creating your first graph, you must determine whether your hardware supports viewing and printing graphs, whether your 1-2-3 software is correctly installed and loaded, and whether the worksheet on-screen contains data you want to graph. You also should understand which type of graph is best suited for presenting specific numeric data in picture form.

Setting Up Hardware and Software

You use 1-2-3's graphics feature to create and view a graph, store its specifications for later use, and print it. Creating and storing a graph requires only that you have the Lotus system software installed on your equipment and that you correctly select options from the **G**raph menu.

Reminder:
To view a graph on-screen, you need a monitor connected to a graphics-display adapter.

To view a graph on-screen, you need to connect your monitor to a graphics-display adapter. (Without such an adapter, you can construct and save a 1-2-3 graph but you must print the graph to view it.) If you have two monitors installed, one monitor can display the worksheet while the other displays the graph.

To print a graph, you need a graphics printer supported by 1-2-3 and a separate set of PrintGraph instructions. (PrintGraph instructions are explained in Chapter 11.)

To create a graph, first load 1-2-3 and retrieve a worksheet file containing the data you want to graph. Suppose, for example, that you want to graph data from the 1989 CASH FLOW DATA spreadsheet, part of which is displayed in figures 10.3 and 10.4.

Fig. 10.3.
The sample WORKING CAPITAL ACCOUNTS worksheet (January to June).

```
         A         B         C        D         E         F         G         H         I
 1 1989 CASH FLOW DATA
 2
 3 =================================================================================
 4 WORKING CAPITAL ACCOUNTS      Jan       Feb       Mar       Apr       May       Jun
 5 =================================================================================
 6 Current Assets:
 7  Cash                      $31,643   $34,333   $36,657   $35,614   $29,146   $20,000
 8  Accounts Receivable       510,780   533,597   551,287   577,314   614,997   641,802
 9  Inventory                 169,209   176,671   189,246   206,788   228,828   269,990
10                            --------  --------  --------  --------  --------  --------
11    Total Current Assets    711,632   744,601   777,189   819,715   872,970   931,792
12
13 Current Liabilities:
14  Accounts Payable          130,754   139,851   150,186   163,731   180,350   203,669
15  Other Short-term Debt           0         0         0         0         0     1,834
16                            --------  --------  --------  --------  --------  --------
17    Total Current Liabilities 130,754 139,851   150,186   163,731   180,350   205,503
18
19 Net Working Capital       $580,878  $604,750  $627,003  $655,984  $692,620  $726,289
20                           ========   ========  ========  ========  ========  ========
```

```
      A     B     C        J        K        L        M        N        O
 1 1989 CASH FLOW DATA
 2
 3 ======================================================================
 4 WORKING CAPITAL ACCOUNTS    Jul      Aug      Sep      Oct      Nov      Dec
 5 ==============================  ======== ======== ======== ======== ========
 6 Current Assets:
 7   Cash                   $20,000  $20,000  $76,623 $186,131 $337,995 $582,796
 8   Accounts Receivable    750,544  879,271  989,501 1,097,616 1,170,646 1,218,036
 9   Inventory              296,527  324,230  345,629  352,687  358,926  358,926
10                          -------- -------- -------- -------- -------- --------
11     Total Current Assets 1,067,071 1,223,501 1,411,753 1,636,434 1,867,567 2,159,759
12
13 Current Liabilities:
14   Accounts Payable       225,085  243,320  258,740  267,621  272,747  275,041
15   Other Short-term Debt    8,327    2,035        0        0        0        0
16                          -------- -------- -------- -------- -------- --------
17     Total Current Liabilities 233,412 245,355 258,740 267,621 272,747 275,041
18
19 Net Working Capital      $833,659 $978,146 $1,153,013 $1,368,812 $1,594,820 $1,884,718
20                          ======== ======== ======== ======== ======== ========
```

Fig. 10.4.
The sample WORKING CAPITAL ACCOUNTS worksheet (July to December).

To graph information from this spreadsheet's Working Capital Accounts section, you must know which numeric data you can plot and which data (numeric or label) you can use to enhance the graph.

Account names are displayed across columns A, B, and C. Monthly headings and amounts appear in columns D through O. The numeric entries in rows 7, 8, 9, 14, and 15, as well as the formula results in rows 11, 17, and 19, are suitable for graphing as data points.

To develop graphs to view on-screen, select /Graph from the main 1-2-3 menu to display the Graph menu. You always use three options from the main Graph menu: the Type option to indicate the type of graph you want; at least one data series from the choices X, A, B, C, D, E, and F; and the View option to see the graph if you have a graphics-display adapter. (Use the X data series option as a data range only when you create an XY graph, as explained later in this chapter.)

Selecting a Graph Type

Selecting one of the five available graph types is easy. When you select Type from the Graph menu, the following options are displayed:

    Line Bar XY Stack-Bar Pie

By selecting one of these options, you set that graph type and automatically restore the Graph menu to the control panel.

To understand which type of graph best displays specific numeric data, you must know something about plotting points on a graph. The following paragraphs review the two basic terms (*x-axis* and *y-axis*) shown in figure 10.5.

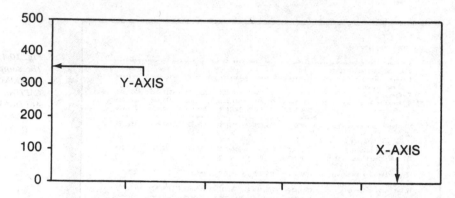

Fig. 10.5.
The graph's x-axis and y-axis.

All graphs (except pie graphs) have two axes: the y-axis (the vertical left edge) and the x-axis (the horizontal bottom edge). 1-2-3 automatically provides tick marks for both axes. 1-2-3 also scales the adjacent numbers on the y-axis, based on the minimum and maximum figures included in the plotted data range(s).

Every point plotted on a graph has a unique location (x,y): *x* represents the time period or the amount measured along the horizontal axis; *y* measures the corresponding amount along the vertical axis. The intersection of the y-axis and the x-axis is called the *origin*. Notice that the origin of the graph shown in figure 10.5 is zero (0). To minimize misinterpretation of graph results and to make graphs easier to compare, use a zero origin in your graphs. Later in this chapter, you learn how to manually change the upper or lower limits of the scale initially set by 1-2-3.

Of the five 1-2-3 graph types, all but the pie graph display both the x-axis and y-axis. Line, bar, and stack-bar graphs display numbers (centered on the tick marks) along the y-axis only. The XY graph displays numbers on both axes. (A general statement about the use of each 1-2-3 graph type precedes the explanation of how to construct that type of graph.)

Specifying a Worksheet Data Range

1-2-3 does not enable you to type data to be plotted on a graph. Do not confuse the process of plotting data points with typing descriptions (such as titles). Entering descriptions is described later in this chapter.

Reminder:
Enter data to be plotted on a graph by highlighting data from the worksheet.

To create a graph, you must specify data from the currently displayed worksheet as a data series in range form. An example of a data series is D7..O7. In 1-2-3, you may plot one data series along the x-axis (the **X** data series) and up to six data series along the y-axis (the **A**, **B**, **C**, **D**, **E**, and **F** data series). To enter a data series from the main **G**raph menu, choose one of the following options:

X A B C D E F

In 1-2-3 Release 2.2, you can select **Group** from the main **Graph** menu to set all x-axis and y-axis data ranges at once. The number of y-axes in the graph is determined by the number of rows or columns specified.

Before you start building a graph, read the following general statements about each graph type:

Graph Type	Comments
Line	Enter as many as six data series after you have accessed separately the **Graph** menu choices **A**, **B**, **C**, **D**, **E**, and **F**. You do not have to start with **A**, nor do you have to select all six data series. The data points in every data series are marked by a unique symbol (see table 10.1 later in this chapter). In 1-2-3 Release 2.2, you can select all data ranges at once with the **/Graph Group** command.
Bar	Enter as many as six data series after you have accessed separately the **Graph** menu choices **A**, **B**, **C**, **D**, **E**, and **F**. You do not have to start with **A**, nor do you have to select all six data series. Multiple data ranges appear on the graph from left to right in alphabetical order. Every data series displayed in black and white has unique shading. Every data series displayed in color is assigned a color. (Shading and screen colors are summarized in table 10.1). In 1-2-3 Release 2.2, you can select all data ranges at once with the **/Graph Group** command.
XY	Enter the data series being plotted as the independent variable by selecting **X** from the main **Graph** menu. Plot at least one dependent variable (you usually select **A**). The unique symbols that mark the data points depend on which A-through-F data series is used with X. The symbols are the same as the Line symbols in table 10.1. In 1-2-3 Release 2.2, you can select all data ranges at once with the **/Graph Group** command.
Stack-Bar	Follow the bar graph instructions. In a stack-bar graph, multiple data ranges appear from bottom to top in alphabetical order.
Pie	Enter only one data series by selecting **A** from the main **Graph** menu. (To shade and "explode" pieces of the pie, also select **B**.)

RELEASE

2.2

Cue:
In 1-2-3 Release 2.2, use /Graph Group to set all data ranges at once.

As you build your graphs, refer to the preceding comments (organized by graph type) and to the summary information (organized by data range) in table 10.1. Table 10.1 (found later in this chapter in the "Using the Legend Option" section) shows each data range with the corresponding default assignments for line symbols, bar shading, and color.

Constructing the Default Line Graph

Reminder:
The minimum steps for creating a graph involve specifying the type of graph, locating on the worksheet the data to plot, and selecting the /Graph View command.

After you have selected the appropriate graph type for the data to be plotted, producing a graph is easy. Using the Net Working Capital values in row 19 of figures 10.3 and 10.4, you can create a line graph of the January-through-June amounts or the January-through December amounts. From 1-2-3's main menu, select **/Graph** to access the **Graph** menu.

Ordinarily, the next step is to select **Type** and choose **Line**. Because this graph is the first you have created after loading 1-2-3, however, and **Line** is the default type, you don't have to make a **Type** selection.

To enter the first data range, choose **A** from the main **Graph** menu. Respond to the Enter first data range: prompt by typing **D19..I19**.

By specifying the type of graph and the spreadsheet location of the data to plot, you have completed the minimum requirements for creating a graph. If you select **View** from the **Graph** menu, you see a graph similar to the graph shown in figure 10.6.

Fig. 10.6.
A default line graph in 1-2-3 Release 2.2.

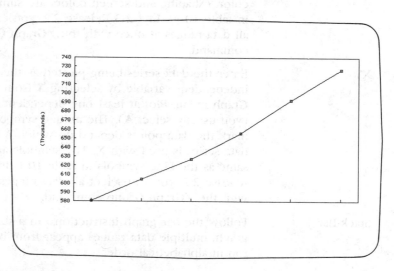

You know what this graph represents, but it does not mean much to anyone else. Although the six data points corresponding to the January-through-June figures have been plotted, none of the points has been labeled to indicate what it represents. In addition, users of 1-2-3 Release 2.01 will notice that the two data points resting on the graph's left and right vertical sides are difficult to see, as shown in figure 10.7.

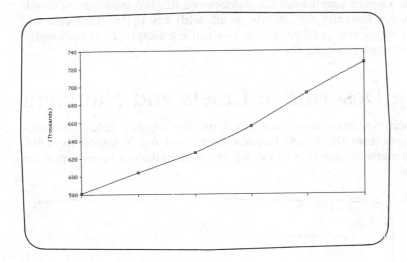

Fig. 10.7.
A default line graph in 1-2-3 Release 2.01.

Because 1-2-3 sets a scale based on minimum and maximum values in the range, 1-2-3 automatically displays the (Thousands) indicator along the y-axis. Also notice that the origin on this initial 1-2-3 line graph is not zero, making the upward trend seem larger than it really is.

Reminder:
1-2-3 automatically enters an indicator of units along the y-axis.

Before delving into the specific characteristics of each graph type, you should be aware of some of the available methods for improving the appearance of your graphs. These methods apply to all graph types, unless stated otherwise.

Enhancing the Appearance of a Basic Graph

As you know, you can create an on-screen graph by selecting from the main **Graph** menu a Type, the appropriate data series (**X**, **A**, **B**, **C**, **D**, **E**, or **F**), and View. If you want to improve the appearance of your graph, select **Options** from the **Graph** menu to access the following submenu:

Legend Format Titles Grid Scale Color B&W Data-Labels Quit

As you add enhancements to your graphs, check the results frequently. If you have only one monitor, select **Quit** to leave the **Graph Options** menu and

Reminder:
As you add enhancements to your graphs, check the results frequently.

return to the main **Graph** menu. Select View from the main **Graph** menu to check the most recent version of the graph. Press any key to exit the graph display and restore the **Graph** menu to the screen.

Cue:
Use Graph (F10) to toggle between displaying the worksheet and displaying the graph.

To view the current graph from the worksheet's READY mode, press Graph (F10). This key instantly redraws the graph with any updated information. Whenever you are not in MENU mode, you can use Graph (F10) to "toggle" between the worksheet and the graph.

Adding Descriptive Labels and Numbers

To add descriptive information to a graph, use the **Legend**, **Titles**, and **Data-Labels** options from the **Graph Options** menu, and the **X** option from the main **Graph** menu. Figure 10.8 shows where these additional items appear on your graph.

Fig. 10.8.
Graph location of descriptive information.

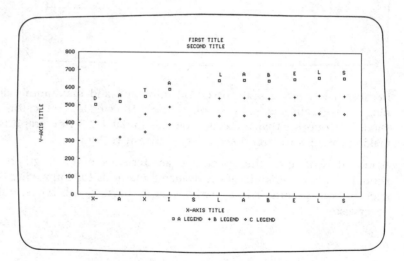

As shown in figure 10.8, data labels appear within the graph. Descriptions entered with the **X** option appear immediately below the x-axis. You can enter as many as four titles: two at the top and one to describe each axis. Legends describing the shading, color, or symbols assigned to data ranges in line or bar graphs appear across the bottom of the graph. The legend line appears in addition to any x-axis title you may have specified.

Using the Titles Option

If you select /**Graph** Options **Titles**, the following options are displayed in the control panel:

First   Second   X-Axis   Y-Axis

You can enter one or two centered titles at the top of your graph. If you enter two titles, both appear the same size on-screen. On the printed graph, however, the title you enter by selecting **First** is twice the size of any other title specified. You can enter titles by typing a new description, specifying a range name, or referencing the cell location of a label or a number already in the worksheet.

Reminder:
The first title you enter with /Graph Options Titles is printed twice the size of other titles.

Suppose that you want to enhance the basic line graph of the Net Working Capital amounts (refer to fig. 10.6). (Figures 10.3 and 10.4 contain the worksheet data for this graph.) In the following paragraphs, you enter four titles; you use cell references for two of the titles and type new descriptions for the others.

Select **Titles First** from the Graph Options menu. When 1-2-3 prompts you for a title, type **ABC Company** and press Enter. The Graph Options menu (*not* the Titles submenu) reappears.

Select **Titles Second** and type **\A19** to make *Net Working Capital* (the contents of cell A19) the second top-centered title.

To reproduce *1989 CASH FLOW DATA* beneath the x-axis, select **Titles X-Axis** and type **\A1**. To enter the fourth title, select **Titles Y-Axis** and type **Actual Dollars**. Now check the graph by selecting **Quit** from the Graph Options menu (restoring the main Graph menu) and then choosing **View**. If you use 1-2-3 Release 2.2, your graph should like the enhanced graph shown in figure 10.9.

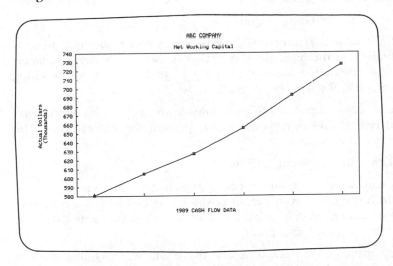

Fig. 10.9.
Titles added to a line graph.

Although all titles appear on-screen in the same print style, when you print the graph you can select one font (such as italic) for the top title and another font for other titles and labels. (For a detailed discussion of this topic, see Chapter 11.)

Cue:
You can change print fonts for the first title.

To edit a title, use the command sequence used to create the title. The existing text, cell reference, or range name appears in the control panel, ready for editing. To change a title made by a cell reference, change the label in the cell or change the cell reference itself. To eliminate a title displayed in the control panel, press Esc and then press Enter.

The x-axis and y-axis titles have no significance when you construct a pie graph. Because a pie graph has no x-axis or y-axis, titles are not used.

Entering Labels within a Graph

After a data series has been graphed, you can enter values or labels to explain each point plotted on the graph. To do so, select **/Graph Options Data-Labels** and then specify the data series to which the data labels are to apply. 1-2-3 Release 2.2 data series include **A**, **B**, **C**, **D**, **E**, **F**, or Group; 1-2-3 Release 2.1 data series include **A**, **B**, **C**, **D**, **E**, or **F**. The **X** data series is used to assign labels to the tick marks on the x-axis. Instead of typing the labels (as you typed the titles), you must specify each data-label range by pointing to an existing range in the worksheet, providing cell coordinates, or specifying a previously determined range name.

Continue to enhance your sample line graph by entering the January-through-June headings from row 4 of the worksheet shown in figure 10.4. First, select **/Graph Options Data-Labels**. The following submenu choices appear on-screen in 1-2-3 Release 2.2:

RELEASE
2.2

   A B C D E F Group Quit

Users of 1-2-3 Release 2.01 do not see the **Group** option. Under this menu is a line explaining that the highlighted **A** option is used to specify data labels for the A range. The only data range currently identified in the Net Working Capital line graph is the A range, defined as D19..I19.

To enter the six abbreviated monthly headings from row 4 in the worksheet, select **A** and type **D4..I4** in response to the prompt for a label range. The following submenu appears:

   Center Left Above Right Below

From this menu, select only one option for each data-label range you are identifying. In other words, you cannot position one cell within a data-label range *above* its associated data point, and another cell in the same data-label range *below* its associated data point.

To continue enhancing your graph, select **Above** and select **Quit**. Return to the main **Graph** menu by selecting **Quit** from the **Graph Options Data-Labels** menu. To check the graph, select **View** from the **Graph** menu. Your graph should resemble the one in shown figure 10.10.

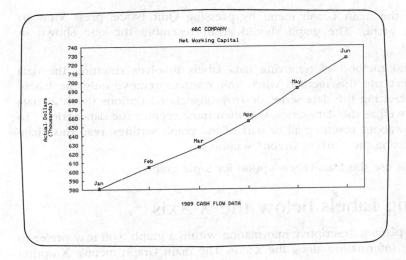

Fig. 10.10.
Data-labels
added within a
line graph.

Cue:
Users of 1-2-3
Release 2.01
should include
blank cells at each
end of the data
range so that
x-axis labels fit
neatly.

Users of 1-2-3 Release 2.01 find that placing labels within a graph often produces less than desirable results. Particularly on line graphs, the first and last labels tend to overlap the graph's edges. To solve this problem, you can expand any data ranges defined for a line graph by including blank cells at each end of the ranges defined.

If you graph more than one data series, attach the data labels to the data series with the largest figures. Then select **Above** to position the data labels above the data points plotted. To enter text or numbers as the plotted points, use the **Center** option and select **/Graph Options Format**. Choose a data series (**A** through **F**, or **Group** in 1-2-3 Release 2.2) and then choose **Neither** so that no lines or symbols appear on the graph. Only the data labels appear.

To edit either the range or position of the data label, use the same command sequence used to create the data label. Edit the current range or specify a different position.

To eliminate a data label, use one of two methods. If you remember both the data series (**A**, **B**, **C**, **D**, **E**, or **F**) and the position (**Center**, **Left**, and so on) specified when you entered the data label, you can follow the original setup sequence, overriding the existing data-label range by substituting any single blank cell in the worksheet. (You cannot eliminate an existing range by pressing Esc as you did to eliminate an unwanted title.)

To remove the January-through-June data labels from the sample Net Working Capital graph, use the following sequence:

Select **/Graph Options Data-Labels A** (data series)
Enter **D1** (blank out the existing range)
Select **Above**

Return to the main **Graph** menu by pressing **Quit** twice; press **View** to check the graph. The graph should again resemble the one shown in figure 10.9.

The second method of removing data labels involves resetting the data series. Don't use this method when you want to remove only the labels. Because resetting the data series destroys associated options (such as data labels) as well as the data series, you then must reenter the data series. (To learn more about resetting all or part of the graph settings, read this chapter's "Resetting the Current Graph" section.)

You cannot use the **Data**-Labels option for a pie graph.

Entering Labels below the X-Axis

Instead of placing descriptive information within a graph, you may prefer to enter label information along the x-axis. The main **Graph** menu's **X** option has two distinct functions: Use it to position labels below the x-axis in line, bar, and stack-bar graphs; or to enter a data series in an XY graph. (XY graphs are discussed later in this chapter.) You also can use the **X** option to identify slices of a pie chart.

Suppose that you want to enter the actual January-through-June Net Working Capital figures as labels below your sample graph's x-axis. Select **X** from the main **Graph** menu and type **D19..I19** when prompted for a range. Then select **View** from the main **Graph** menu. Your graph should look like the one shown in figure 10.11.

Fig. 10.11.
Displaying
values below
the x-axis.

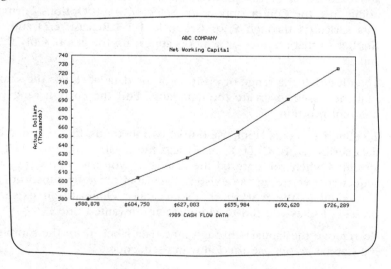

Notice that in the graph shown in figure 10.11, the values used as descriptive labels below the x-axis have the same format shown in the worksheet.

You may remember that entries within the range you specify for descriptions can be either values or labels. To practice entering labels, change the Net Working Capital descriptive amounts to January-through-June headings. To do so, select **X** from the main **Graph** menu and type **D4..I4** when prompted for a range. When you choose **View** from the **Graph** menu to check the graph, your graph should resemble the one shown in figure 10.12.

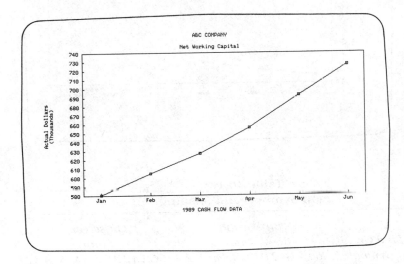

Fig. 10.12.
Displaying labels below the x-axis.

Users of 1-2-3 Release 2.01 find that when x-axis labels or values are longer than 9 or 10 characters, parts of the extreme right or left descriptions may not be displayed. To edit the x-axis labels, select **X** from the main **Graph** menu and override the current range by typing or pointing to a different range. To eliminate the x-axis labels, select **/Graph Reset X**. In 1-2-3 Release 2.2, x-axis labels are staggered to avoid overlap as shown in figure 10.13.

You cannot use the **X** option to enter labels below the x-axis when you construct an XY or pie graph. (The x-axis can be used to place labels *next* to each pie slice in a pie graph, however.)

Using the Legend Option

Whenever a graph contains more than one set of data, you must be able to distinguish between the sets. If you use a color monitor and select Color from the main **Graph** menu, 1-2-3 differentiates data series with color. If the main **Graph** menu's default option **B&W** (black and white) is in effect, data series in line graphs are marked with special symbols; data series in bar-type graphs are marked with unique patterns of crosshatches. Table 10.1 summarizes the assignments of each data range. Notice that crosshatches for 1-2-3 Release 2.01 and 2.2 are different.

RELEASE

2.2

Caution:
In 1-2-3 Release 2.01, parts of x-axis labels longer than 9 or 10 characters may not be displayed. In 1-2-3 Release 2.2, the labels are staggered.

Fig. 10.13.
Staggered
x-axis labels
in 1-2-3
Release 2.2.

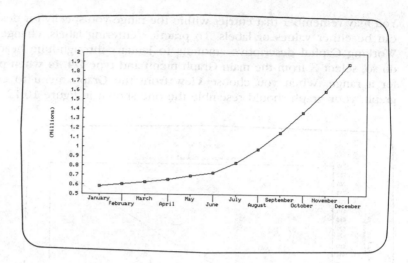

Table 10.1
Graph Symbols and Shading

Data Range	Line Graph Symbol	Bar Graph B&W Shading Release 2.01	Release 2.2	On-screen Color CGA (2.2)	EGA/VGA
A	□			Red	Yellow
B	+			Blue	Violet
C	◇			White	Blue
D	△			Red	Red
E	×			Blue	Cyan
F	▽			White	Green

Reminder:
Choose /Graph
Options B&W
before saving your
graph to make sure
that the data
ranges are shaded
correctly.

If you intend to print the graph on a black-and-white printer, even if you have a color monitor, choose **B&W** before saving the graph. A graph saved under the **Color** option prints on a black-and-white printer as all black.

You may decide to pick one of the data series because you want certain symbols or shadings or, more often, to avoid using certain combinations of symbols or shadings. If you entered only two data items in a line graph and used data ranges **D** and **F**, for example, you would have difficulty distinguishing between the two three-sided assigned symbols—one pointing up and the other pointing down. On the other hand, in 1-2-3 Release 2.01, pairing the E range (widely spaced crosshatches) with the F range (narrowly spaced crosshatches) on a bar graph produces a distinctly different display. To provide explanatory text for data represented by symbols or shadings, use legends below the x-axis.

The most recent version of the sample Net Working Capital line graph displays the square symbol assigned to the data points entered as the A data series (refer to fig. 10.12). Suppose that you want to change the data to reflect two items: Total Current Assets (CA) and Total Current Liabilities (CL), rather than the single item reflecting Net Working Capital.

First, change the second title line to reflect the changed data. Select **/Graph Options Titles Second**, press Esc to remove the current cell reference, and type **Components of Working Capital** as the new second title. Retain the A range but respecify the data range as **Current Assets**. Add a second range, C, and enter the cell range containing **Current Liabilities** as the data range. (Because you don't eliminate the A range, you don't use the **Reset** option.)

To enter the Total Current Assets figures for the first six months of the year, select **/Graph A** and either type **D11..I11** or press Esc once and point to the range. If you remove the anchor from the data series range by pressing Esc, you must reanchor it by pressing the period (.) key. When the main **Graph** menu reappears, select **C** and type **D17..I17** in response to the prompt for a range. Choose **Options Legend A** from the **Graph** menu and, when 1-2-3 prompts you for a legend name, type **TOTAL CA**. Then select **Legend C** and type **TOTAL CL** at the prompt. You may type as many as 19 characters for a legend. Select **Quit** to exit the **Options** menu. When you choose **View**, 1-2-3 displays the modified graph (see fig. 10.14).

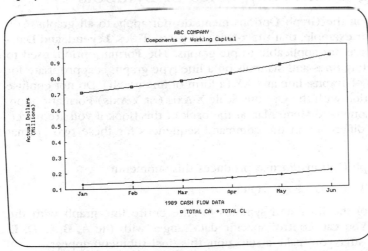

Fig. 10.14.
Adding legends to the line graph.

If you want to edit a legend, use the same command sequence used to create the legend. The existing text, cell reference, or range name appears in the control panel, ready for you to edit. To eliminate a legend that appears in the control panel, press Esc and Enter.

Reminder:
To edit a legend, use the same command sequence you used to create the legend.

Legends are appropriate only for graphs with two or more data series. You cannot use the **Legend** option for pie graphs because pie graphs have only one data series.

Altering the Default Graph Display

All the previously described enhancements involve adding label or number descriptions to the basic minimal graph. 1-2-3 supplies the additional default display items shown in figures 10.12 and 10.14.

In both of these graphs, for example, the numbers, or scale, along the vertical y-axis was set automatically, taking into account the minimum and maximum values in the data ranges plotted. The amounts are displayed in **General** format. 1-2-3 also determines the parenthetical display of (Thousands) shown in figure 10.12 and (Millions) shown in figure 10.14. Within the graphs, 1-2-3 automatically centers the symbols on the data points plotted; black lines are used to connect the symbols, leaving the background clear. All labels included in the x-axis range are displayed below the graphs.

You can change any of these additional default graph display items. To continue enhancing the appearance of a basic graph, change the defaults in the simple line graph. (Additional examples are included in this chapter's explanations of how to develop all graph types.)

Specifying Connecting Lines or Symbols

Reminder:
A few choices on the Graph Options menu do not apply to all graphs.

A few choices on the **Graph Options** menu do not apply to all graphs. You have learned, for example, that the x-axis and y-axis Titles, **Legend**, and Data-Labels options are not applicable to pie graphs. The **Format** option, used to display connecting lines and symbols on a line-type graph, is appropriate for only two types of graphs: line and XY (a form of line graph). Do not confuse this **Format** option with the **Options Scale X-Axis** (or **Y-Axis**) **Format** option. (Refer to the Command-Menu Map at the back of this book if you are uncertain about the difference in the command sequences for these two **Format** options.)

Selecting **/Graph Options Format** produces this submenu:

   Graph A B C D E F Quit

You can control the lines and symbols for the entire line graph with the **Graph** option. You can control specific data ranges with the **A, B, C, D, E,** and **F** options. After you make a selection, this final submenu appears:

   Lines Symbols Both Neither

Use the graph shown in figure 10.12 to learn the mechanics of switching the default setting (**Both**) to **Lines**. (You learn to specify **Neither** or **Symbols** in this chapter's "Line Graphs" section.) Select /**Graph Options Format A Lines Quit**. Then choose **Quit** from the **Options** menu and select **View** to check the graph. As shown in figure 10.15, the square symbols centered on A-range data points are no longer displayed.

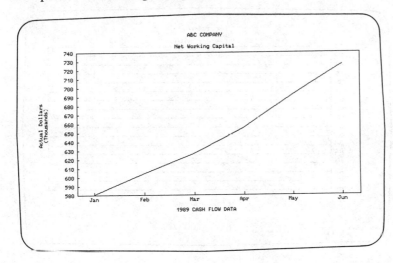

Fig. 10.15.
Suppressing the display of symbols in the line graph.

Experiment with different format displays by repeating the command sequences, first selecting the data ranges you want to change and then selecting a specific format. To restore the default format setting for the sample line graph, select /**Graph Options Format A Both**, return to the main **Graph** menu, and select **View** to restore the graph shown in figure 10.12.

You can use the **Format** option from the **Graph Options** menu for line and XY graphs only.

Reminder:
Use the **Format** option for line and XY graphs only.

Setting a Background Grid

Ordinarily, you use the default (clear) background for graphs. You may encounter situations when you want to impose a grid on a graph so that the data-point amounts are easier to read.

Selecting /**Graph Options Grid** produces this menu:

Horizontal   Vertical   Both   Clear

Horizontal creates a series of horizontal lines across the graph, spaced according to the tick marks on the y-axis. **Vertical** creates a series of vertical lines across the graph, spaced according to the tick marks on the x-axis. **Both** causes both horizontal and vertical lines to appear, and **Clear** clears all grid lines from the graph.

To add horizontal lines to the sample graph, select **/Graph Options Grid Horizontal**. Then select **Quit** from the **Options** menu and press **View**. The graph should look like the one shown in figure 10.16.

Fig. 10.16.
Adding a
horizontal grid
to the line
graph.

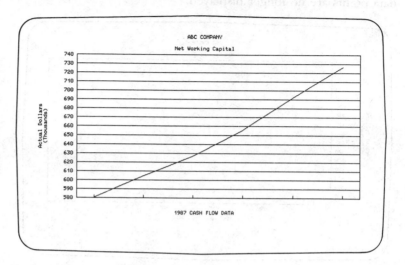

Experiment with different grids, repeating the command sequence and specifying other options. Whenever you want to eliminate a grid display, select **/Graph Options Grid Clear**.

You cannot use the **Grid** option from the **Graph Options** menu for a pie graph.

Changing Axis Scale Settings

You can use the **Scale** option from the **Graph Options** menu to alter three distinct default settings associated with the values displayed along a graph's x-axis and y-axis.

When a line, XY, bar, or stack-bar graph is created, 1-2-3 automatically sets scale values displayed on the y-axis, taking into account the smallest and largest numbers in the data ranges plotted. (For XY graphs only, 1-2-3 also establishes x-axis scale values.)

Reminder:
You can change the upper and lower scale values for the y-axis, but you cannot change the degree of increment between values.

You can change the upper and lower scale values. You cannot, however, determine the size of the increment between the maximum and minimum values (this increment is indicated by tick marks). For example, you cannot change the incremented scale on the y-axis of the graph shown in figure 10.16 from the default of 10,000 to an increment of 25,000 (575, 600, 625, 650, 675, 700, 725, and 750). Furthermore, in 1-2-3 Release 2.01, the increment displayed on the screen may or may not be the increment printed. As you learn in Chapter 11, increments for scale values on printed graphs are the same as, or more closely spaced than, those displayed on-screen.

1-2-3 automatically sets the format of the scale values to **General**—the same default global numeric display you see when you access a blank worksheet. Notice that dollar signs, commas, and decimal points are not displayed along the y-axis shown in figure 10.16. You can change the format to any of the styles available under the **Worksheet Global Format** or **Range Format** menus. Do not confuse the capability of altering the default format of the scale values with bringing in previously formatted worksheet numbers as data labels.

The third automatic scale-related display is the indicator that appears along the y-axis when a line, XY, bar, or stack-bar graph is created. (On an XY graph, an indicator also appears along the x-axis.) This indicator is (Thousands) on the y-axis of the graph shown in figure 10.16.

Although you cannot change the indicator, you can suppress its display. To understand why you might want to suppress display of the indicator, imagine a worksheet containing data with truncated trailing zeros (for example, a sales budget figure of 5,000,000 entered in the worksheet as 5,000). Graphing the truncated figures produces the y-axis indicator (Thousands) when the graph is really showing millions. You can suppress display of the indicator and type a more appropriate indicator as part of the y-axis title.

Select **/Graph Options Scale** to produce this menu:

   Y-Scale   X-Scale   Skip

To initiate changes in the upper or lower scale values, changes in the format of the scale values, or suppression of the scale indicator, select either of the first two options. (The **Scale Skip** command sequence is discussed in the following section.) Selecting either **Y-Scale** or **X-Scale** produces the following submenu:

   Automatic   Manual   Lower   Upper   Format   Indicator   Quit

The **Automatic** and **Manual** options work as a set. To specify maximum (Upper) or minimum (Lower) axis values, select **Manual**; select **Automatic** to restore control to 1-2-3. When you select **Manual**, the entire submenu remains on the screen. After selecting **Manual**, select **Upper** or **Lower**, and respond to the prompt for a new scale value.

If you elect to establish manual limits, remember that you must specify both upper *and* lower settings because selecting **Manual** resets both upper and lower values to zero. Remember also that the upper limit you specify must be larger than the lower limit. You can use negative figures for scale values in line, XY, and bar graphs, but not in stack-bar or pie graphs.

Using the sample graph shown in figure 10.16, practice changing y-axis values by setting a lower value of zero and an upper value of $800,000.

Select **/Graph Options Scale Y**-Scale **Manual Lower** and press **Enter** to accept the 0 displayed in the control panel. Then select **Upper** and enter **800000** (without dollar signs or commas) as the upper limit. Quit the Scale submenu, Quit the Options menu, and press **View**. The graph should resemble the one shown in figure 10.17.

Fig. 10.17.
Changed y-axis
upper and
lower limits.

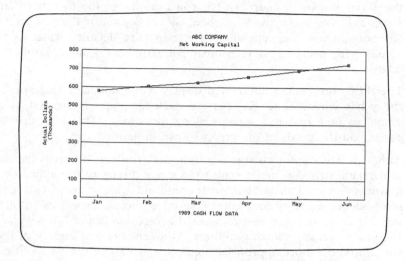

Compare figures 10.16 and 10.17 to see that setting the origin to zero (as is done for most graphs) gives you a different perspective on the magnitude of the increase in working capital. Notice also that 1-2-3 changed the increment between tick marks from $10,000 in figure 10.16, to $100,000 in figure 10.17.

You can change the scale format and suppress the scale indicator with a few keystrokes. Suppose that you want to alter the y-axis title in the graph shown in figure 10.17 to indicate that the y-axis values are in thousands. Also suppose that you want to suppress the automatic scale indicator and change the default **General** format to **Currency** format with zero decimal places.

Select **/Graph Options Titles Y**-Axis and type **(in thousands)** to add this information to the existing Actual Dollars title. Change the display format by selecting **Scale Y**-Scale **Format Currency** and specifying 0 decimal places. To suppress display of the automatic scale indicator, select **Indicator No**. Quit the Scale submenu, Quit the Options menu, and **View** the graph (see fig. 10.18). Compare the graphs shown in figures 10.17 and 10.18.

Now restore the scale indicator by selecting **/Graph Options Scale Y**-Scale (or **X**-Scale) **Indicator Yes**. Change the format and manual limits by repeating the command sequences used to establish the first changes, this time selecting alternative formats or entering alternative upper or lower values. Restore the automatic scale limits by choosing **/Graph Options Scale Y**-Scale (or **X**-Scale) **Automatic**.

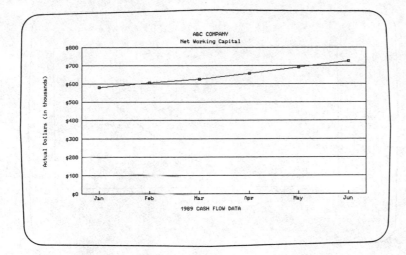

Fig. 10.18.
Changed scale
format and
suppressed
indicator.

Choose /Graph Options Scale X-Scale only when the graph type is XY. Choose Y-Scale for line, XY, bar, and stack-bar graph types. The Format, Indicator, and Manual scale capabilities are not applicable to pie graphs.

Spacing Display of X-Axis Labels

Recall that selecting /Graph Options Scale produces the following options:

    Y-Scale   X-Scale   Skip

The last section explained how to use the first two options. The Skip option determines the spacing of displayed labels—whether all labels or only every *n*th label entered by selecting X from the main Graph menu are to appear below the x-axis. The default setting of 1 causes every label to display. If you set the skip factor to 3, for example, every third label displays.

If the labels are so long that they crowd together or overlap, use the Skip option to improve the display. Technically, you can set a skip factor of 1 to 8,192, but you will seldom need to set the factor higher than 4.

Reminder:
Use /Graph Options
Scale Skip when
you cannot
correctly display
labels for the
x-axis.

Suppose that the monthly headings below the x-axis were spelled out and encompassed the entire year. In 1-2-3 Release 2.01, the labels are overlapped. In 1-2-3 Release 2.2, the labels are staggered and also may still be crowded (refer back to fig. 10.13). To set a skip factor other than the default of 1, select /Graph Options Scale Skip and specify 2. Then return to the main Graph menu and press View. The changed spacing is shown in figure 10.19.

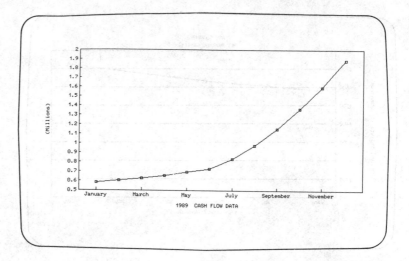

Fig. 10.19.
Skipped labels
on the x-axis.

Only the January, March, May, July, September, and November x-axis labels are displayed in figure 10.19. To restore the default setting and display every label in the range, repeat the command sequence, specifying a skip factor of **1**.

Because using the main menu's **X** option to enter labels below the x-axis applies only to line, bar, and stack-bar graphs, the Scale Skip command sequence does not apply to XY or pie graphs.

Viewing a Graph in Color

The **/Graph Options Color** and **B&W** (black and white) options work as a set to control screen display of color. Setting colors to produce graphs on a color printer or plotter requires command input from the PrintGraph menu (see Chapter 11).

You can select the **B&W** option even if you have a color monitor installed. The initial setting when you load 1-2-3 is **B&W**. The connecting lines in XY or line graphs appear white, amber, or green against a black background; bar or stack-bar data ranges display a unique pattern of crosshatches. Refer to table 10.1 for a summary of the crosshatch patterns assigned to each data range. (Pie graphs have unique capabilities for shading portions of the single data range graphed and are explained in this chapter's "Pie Graphs" section.)

To view graphs on-screen in color, you must use a color monitor. The connecting lines and symbols in XY or line graphs appear in the color assigned to the data range(s) in use; bar or stack-bar segments reflect the color assigned to the data ranges in use. Refer to table 10.1 for a summary of the colors assigned to each data range. (Pie graphs have unique capabilities for coloring the portions of the single data range graphed and are explained in this chapter's "Pie Graphs" section.)

To become familiar with 1-2-3's shading capabilities, convert the line graph shown in figure 10.14 to a bar graph. (Before you convert the line graph, save the settings of the line graph. Save the settings by typing /**Graph Name Create**, typing **Line** for the graph name, and pressing Enter.) To produce the graph shown in figure 10.20, select **T**ype **B**ar. Remember that the shadings used in 1-2-3 Release 2.2 are different from those used in 1-2-3 Release 2.01.

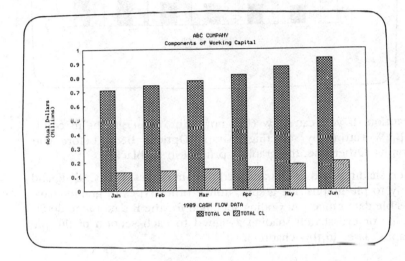

*Fig. 10.20.
Comparative
bar graph in
black and
white.*

Because the left bar in each set represents Total Current Assets in the A data range, the bar is shaded for the A range. The right bar in each set represents Total Current Liabilities, defined as the C data range, and is shaded accordingly. The legends at the bottom of the graph automatically reflect the appropriate black-and-white shading assignments.

If you have a color monitor, you can view this bar graph in color by selecting /**G**raph **O**ptions **C**olor. Quit the **O**ptions menu and press **V**iew. The graph shown in figure 10.21 shows solid shading in the bars, indicating that the **C**olor option is in use.

In the graphs shown in figures 10.20 and 10.21, the left bar in each set represents Total Current Assets in the A data range. On a color monitor, the entire bar is filled with a color (the color depends on the type of graphics adapter you have). The right bar in each set represents Total Current Liabilities in the C data range, and is filled in with a different color. The legends at the bottom of the graph reflect the color assignments.

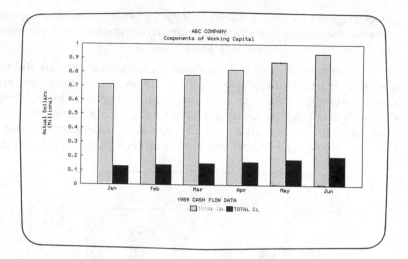

Fig. 10.21.
Comparative
bar graph in
color.

Reminder:
If you print on a
black-and-white
printer, restore the
B&W setting before
you print.

A word of caution: If you can view (but not print) your graphs in color, restore the **B**&W setting by selecting **/G**raph **O**ptions **B**&W before you store your graphs. Otherwise, the graph is printed in all black.

The crosshatch shadings and colors assigned to data ranges A, B, C, D, E, and F do not apply to pie graphs. Pie graphs, unlike other types of graphs, have only one possible data range—A. Coding specified for the B data range determines the color or crosshatch shading assigned to each section of the pie (see "Pie Graphs" later in this chapter).

Preserving the Graph on Disk

You have learned how to create a basic graph and how to use options to enhance display of that graph. All the main **G**raph options (except **R**eset, **S**ave, **N**ame, and **G**roup) have been discussed in detail. This section describes the **S**ave and **N**ame options, which affect preserving the graph for future printing or recall to the screen. (The **R**eset and **G**roup options are discussed just before the explanation of how to develop all graph types.)

Although using 1-2-3 to construct a graph from existing data in a worksheet is easy, having to rebuild the graph whenever you want to print or display it on-screen would be unnecessarily tedious.

Reminder:
*Use /G**raph **S**ave to*
save a graph file
for printing; use
*/G**raph **N**ame to*
view a graph later.
*Always use /**File**
Save to store the*
print-and-display
settings for future
use.

To create a disk file (with the file extension PIC) that can be used only to print the graph, use the **/G**raph **S**ave command. To save with the underlying worksheet the graph specifications that reflect the changes in the worksheet, use **/G**raph **N**ame **C**reate to name the graph; then use **/F**ile **S**ave to save the worksheet.

Saving a PIC File for Printing

Suppose that you have constructed a graph you want to store for subsequent printing with the PrintGraph program or other graphics program. (Print-Graph is discussed in Chapter 11.) After verifying that the graph type chosen is appropriate for your presentation needs, that the graph data ranges have been specified accurately, and that all desired enhancements have been added, choose **/Graph Save** to create a PIC file on disk. 1-2-3 prompts you for a file name and displays (in menu form across the top of the screen) a list of the PIC files in the current directory.

You can use the arrow keys to highlight an existing name, or type a new name as many as eight characters long. (1-2-3 automatically adds the PIC extension.) If a PIC file by the same name already exists in the current directory, you see a **Cancel/Replace** menu similar to the one that appears when you try to save a worksheet file under an existing name. To overwrite the contents of the existing PIC file, select **Replace**. To abort storage of the current graph as a PIC file with that name, select **Cancel**.

If you have set up subdirectories for disk storage, you can store the current graph as a PIC file to other than the current subdirectory without first issuing a **/File Directory** command to change directories. To store the graph, select **/Graph Save**. Press Esc twice to remove the existing current-directory information. Then type the name of the new subdirectory in which you want to store this particular graph.

Remember the following points:

- **/Graph Save** stores only an image of the current graph, locking in all data and enhancements, for the purpose of printing the graph with the PrintGraph program. You also can import the PIC file to another program such as Freelance Plus. At print time, you cannot access the print file to make changes such as adding a label or editing an underlying worksheet figure.

- You cannot recall the graph to screen unless you have named the graph and saved the worksheet, or unless the graph is the last active graph on the current worksheet. Naming graphs is described in the next section.

Creating Graph Specifications for Reuse

If you want to view on-screen a graph created in an earlier graphing session, you must give the graph a name when the graph is originally constructed (and you must save the worksheet, unless the same worksheet is still active). To name a graph, issue the **/Graph Name** command to access the following menu in 1-2-3 Release 2.2:

Use Create Delete Reset Table

RELEASE

2.2

Users of 1-2-3 Release 2.01 do not see the Table option. Only one graph at a time can be the *current* graph. If you want to save a graph you have just completed for subsequent recall to the screen, and you also want to build a new graph, you must first issue a /Graph Name Create command. The only way to store a graph for later screen display is to issue /Graph Name Create, which instructs 1-2-3 to remember the specifications used to define the current graph. If you don't name a graph and then either reset the graph or change the specifications, you cannot restore the original graph without rebuilding it.

When 1-2-3 prompts you for a graph name, provide a name up to 15 characters long. (You can use the same name for the PIC file when you save the graph, and even for the worksheet file when you do a /File Save. Remember, however, that PIC file names and WK1 file names are limited to eight characters each.)

You can use data from a single worksheet to create and name several different graphs. Be sure to save the worksheet before you retrieve a different worksheet file or before you /Quit 1-2-3. Graph specifications are stored with the worksheet file when you issue the /File Save command.

Reminder:
Use /Graph Name
Use when you
want to display
graphs stored in
the current
worksheet.

To recall any named graphs from the active worksheet, select /Graph Name Use. When /Graph Name Use is issued, 1-2-3 displays a list of all the graph names stored in the current worksheet. You also can display the existing graph names by pressing the Name (F3) key. When the names are displayed, you can select the graph you want to redraw by either typing the appropriate name or pointing to the name on the list. By invoking Name Use commands in rapid sequence, you create a "slide show" of 1-2-3 graphics.

To delete a single named graph, use /Graph Name Delete. 1-2-3 lists all the graph names stored in the current worksheet. You can select the graph you want to delete either by typing the appropriate name or by pointing to the name on the list.

Caution:
Use /Graph Name
Reset only when
you want to delete
all graph names.

If you want to delete all the graph names, use /Graph Name Reset. Be careful! /Graph Name Reset does not have a Yes/No confirmation step. Using this command to delete the names of all graphs also deletes the parameters for all the graphs.

Keep in mind that /Graph Name is like /Range Name: the name is available in a future worksheet only if you follow the Name command with /File Save. /Graph Name stores your graph settings in the current worksheet; /File Save then stores the settings with the worksheet. Forgetting to use either /Graph Name or /File Save may result in extra work later.

RELEASE
2.2

Users of 1-2-3 Release 2.2 can use the /Graph Name Table command to list all the named graphs in the worksheet. The resulting table takes up three columns in the worksheet and includes the name, type, and first title line of each graph associated with the worksheet.

When you use **/Graph Name Table**, 1-2-3 prompts you for a range in the worksheet. You need to specify only the first cell of the table's location. To avoid writing over data already in the worksheet, make sure that the area you specify is blank and large enough to hold all the table information. Protected areas of the worksheet cannot be used for a table. After you specify the range, press Enter; 1-2-3 prints a table of graph names with associated data about type and title in the worksheet as shown in figure 10.22.

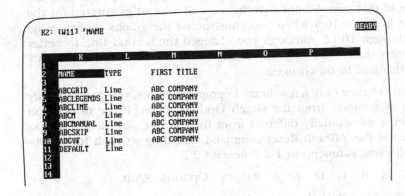

Fig. 10.22.
Using the
/Graph Name
Table
command.

Performing One-Step Graph Operations in 1-2-3 Release 2.2

RELEASE

2.2

Entire
Section

Users of 1-2-3 Release 2.2 have several **Group** commands available when creating graphs. First is the **Group** command in the **Graph** menu. When you select **/Graph Group**, you can set all the data ranges (**X, A, B, C, D, E,** and **F**) at once by typing or pointing to the data range. After you select the range, you must select either **Columnwise** (the first column contains the x-axis labels) or **Rowwise** (the first row contains the x-axis labels). Before using **/Graph Group**, make sure that the data in your worksheet is set up to take advantage of this command. In other words, make sure that no blank rows or columns are in the data and that the data is arranged in the order you want it graphed.

Group commands are also available when you select data labels and legends, or when you reset graph settings (discussed in the next section). To select data labels in a group, use the **/Graph Options Data-Labels Group** command and specify the range containing the data labels. Then select **Columnwise** or **Rowwise**. Finally, choose the placement of the labels from the following options: **Center, Left, Above, Right,** and **Below**. To select legends in one step, use the **/Graph Options Legend Range** command and specify the range.

Because the **Group** commands can save time when creating graphs, it's wise to invest some time in learning to use them.

Caution:
Make sure that data is set up correctly in the worksheet before using 1-2-3's /Graph Group command.

Resetting the Current Graph

You may have noticed that, throughout this chapter, instructions for editing or removing options have been given at the end of each new topic. These instructions are important because 1-2-3 continues to use an enhancement in the next version of the same graph—or in a new graph—unless you take specific actions to remove that enhancement. For example, you can build a series of six different bar graphs by specifying the graph **T**ype for only the first one. Recall that you did not have to respecify the titles entered for the graph shown in figure 10.9 when you constructed the graphs shown in figures 10.10 through 10.12. Although you changed the second title to better explain the new data ranges shown in figure 10.14, that title was the only one of four that had to be changed.

Reminder:
*Use /**G**raph **R**eset when the next graph you want to construct is substantially different from the current one.*

If you want to enhance only a few items in graph contents, you can respecify or eliminate these items from the Graph **O**ptions menu. If the next graph you construct is substantially different from the current one, however, you may want to use the /**G**raph **R**eset command. Selecting /**G**raph **R**eset produces the following submenu in 1-2-3 Release 2.2:

RELEASE 2.2

Graph X A B C D E F Ranges Options Quit

Users of 1-2-3 Release 2.01 do not see **R**anges and **O**ptions on this submenu. Select **G**raph from this submenu only if you do not want to use any of the existing specifications in your new graph. /**G**raph **R**eset **G**raph ensures that no unwanted enhancements from a previous graph carry over into the current one, and usually precedes any graph construction automated by macros. (Chapter 13 describes creating and using macros.)

As an alternative to a total graph reset, you can remove an individual data range (in 1-2-3 Release 2.2, you can specify a group of ranges). All data labels assigned to the reset data range or ranges are eliminated also. By choosing **R**eset **X**, for example, you remove labels displayed below the x-axis, pie-slice labels, or x-axis information for an XY graph. By choosing **R**eset **R**anges, you eliminate all the data ranges (X, A, B, C, D, E, and F) and any data labels associated with the ranges.

If you want to reset only the option settings of the graph, use /**G**raph **R**eset **O**ptions. **R**eset **O**ptions leaves the data ranges intact.

To illustrate the total graph-reset operation as applied to the bar graph shown in figure 10.21, select /**G**raph **R**eset **G**raph. If you then select **V**iew from the main **G**raph menu, you hear a beep and see a blank screen. By removing the graph's data ranges, you have eliminated the essential ingredients for graph production.

The following sections discuss how to construct each type of graph.

Developing Alternative Graph Types

You have learned that you can use 1-2-3 to build five types of graphs: line, bar, XY, stack-bar, and pie.

Because more than one type of graph can accomplish the desired goals, choosing the best graph form may be a matter of personal preference. For example, choosing a line, bar, or pie graph is appropriate if you plan to graph only a single data range. In other situations, only one graph type can do the job. As you work through the remainder of this chapter, take a moment to learn or review the primary uses of each graph type.

Selecting an Appropriate Graph Type

You may want to review the information given earlier in this chapter to refresh your memory about which data ranges are appropriate for each graph type. More information about the use of each graph type is presented in the following chart.

Graph Type	Purpose
Line	To show the trend of numeric data across time. Used, for example, to display monthly working-capital amounts during 1989.
Bar	To show the trend of numeric data across time, often comparing two or more data items. Used, for example, to display total current assets compared to total current liabilities for each month during 1989.
XY	To compare one numeric data series to another numeric data series across time to determine whether one set of values appears to depend on the other. Used, for example, to plot monthly Sales and Advertising Expenses to assess whether a direct relationship exists between the amount of sales and the dollars spent for advertising.
Stack-Bar	To graph two or more data series totaling 100% of a specific numeric category. Used, for example, to graph three monthly data series—Cash, Accounts Receivable, and Inventory (displayed one above the other)—to depict the proportion each comprises of total current assets throughout the year. (Do not use this type of graph if your data contains negative numbers.)

Graph Type	Purpose
Pie	To graph only one data series, the components of which total 100% of a specific numeric category. Used, for example, to graph the January Cash, Accounts Receivable, and Inventory amounts to depict the proportion each comprises of the January current assets. (Do not use this type of graph if your data contains negative numbers.)

Building All Graph Types

Although line graphs were used to show 1-2-3's general graph-enhancement options, most of the options can be used for all graph types. (This chapter has pointed out the options that don't apply to specific types of graphs.)

Next, you focus on each graph type and learn the enhancements that are particularly useful when attached to a specific graph type. To do so, use data in the SALES (by Profit Center) report shown in figures 10.23 and 10.24. The line, bar, and stack-bar types are all appropriate for graphing the monthly sales-by-profit-center information.

Fig. 10.23.
Sample sales data by profit center (January to June).

```
         A          B      C          D          E          F          G          H
 1 ==================================================================================
 2 SALES                   Jan        Feb        Mar        Apr        May        Jun
 3 ==================================================================================
 4 Profit Center 1      $31,336    $37,954    $43,879    $51,471    $56,953    $53,145
 5 Profit Center 2       22,572     24,888     25,167     32,588     40,140     37,970
 6 Profit Center 3      131,685    129,044    131,723    139,221    141,879    149,803
 7 Profit Center 4       95,473     98,008     96,986     95,318    103,538    108,146
 8                      --------   --------   --------   --------   --------   --------
 9 Total Sales         $281,066   $289,894   $297,755   $318,598   $342,510   $349,064
10                      ========   ========   ========   ========   ========   ========
```

Fig. 10.24.
Sample sales data by profit center (July to December).

```
         A          B      I          J          K          L          M          N          O
 1 =============================================================================================
 2 SALES                   Jul        Aug        Sep        Oct        Nov        Dec       Total
 3 =============================================================================================
 4 Profit Center 1      $54,140    $53,614    $52,015    $48,902    $44,091    $42,536   $570,036
 5 Profit Center 2       34,587     33,463     28,939     24,153     27,060     26,701    358,228
 6 Profit Center 3      147,108    147,032    153,440    149,990    145,198    150,510  1,716,633
 7 Profit Center 4      108,642    106,065    110,401    112,018    111,956    107,522  1,254,073
 8                      --------   --------   --------   --------   --------   --------   --------
 9 Total Sales         $344,477   $340,174   $344,795   $335,063   $328,305   $327,269 $3,898,970
10                      ========   ========   ========   ========   ========   ========   ========
```

Line Graphs

In this section, you use the worksheet data in figures 10.23 and 10.24 to create a line graph. Because you are constructing a new graph, reset the previous graph settings to remove any unwanted options carried over from the most recent graph operations. Enter the four data series as the ranges C4..N4, C5..N5, C6..N6, and C7..N7. Although you can choose any four of the menu's six **R**ange options (**A**, **B**, **C**, **D**, **E**, or **F**), enter the data series in order (C4..N4 Profit Center 1 values as the **A** range, C5..N5 Profit Center 2 values as the **B** range, and so on). Entering the data series in order makes the corresponding legend easier to interpret. To produce a graph similar to the one shown in figure 10.25, use the following command sequences:

/**Graph Reset Graph**
      Type Line
      A C4..N4 Enter
      B C5..N5 Enter
      C C6..N6 Enter
      D C7..N7 Enter
      Options Titles First 1989 SALES Enter
           Titles Second SAMPLE COMPANY Enter
           Titles X-Axis SALES BY PROFIT CENTER Enter
           Legend A \A4 Enter
           Legend B \A5 Enter
           Legend C \A6 Enter
           Legend D \A7 Enter
           Quit
     View

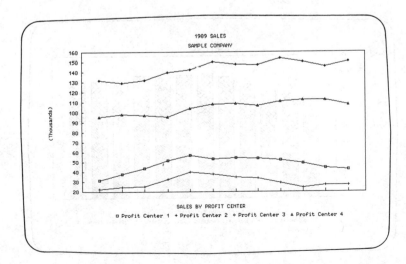

Fig. 10.25.
An enhanced
multiple-line
graph.

Notice that the upper limit of the y-axis is set automatically at $160,000, slightly higher than the highest monthly sales figure ($153,440—the September sales for Profit Center 3).

Recall that 1-2-3 does not automatically set to zero the lower limit of a line graph's y-axis. To make the graph easier to read, select **Options Scale Y**-Scale **Manual Lower** and specify a lower limit of zero. Because 1-2-3 requires that you set both limits if you switch to a manual setting, be sure to specify an upper limit of 160000 after you set the lower limit.

Notice that each of the four legends below the x-axis describes the symbol used for each line in the graph. Always use legends for multiple-line graphs. Without legends, you don't know which line represents which data series (unless you memorize the symbols in table 10.1). If you prefer one symbol to another, pick the data range associated with that symbol when you select a data range or ranges from the main **G**raph menu. (You see how to select data ranges for the set of graphs discussed in the following section.)

Stack-Bar Graphs

You may want to experiment with different graph types when you plot multiple time-series data. If the data-range values combine to produce a meaningful figure (for example, the combined January sales of each profit center equal the total January sales), try using **Stack-Bar** as a graph type. The data ranges in a stack-bar graph appear as bars; these bars are plotted in the order A, B, C, D, E, and F, with the A range closest to the x-axis. After entering the command sequences to create figure 10.25, for example, you can create the stack-bar graph shown in figure 10.26 by selecting **T**ype **Stack-Bar** from the main **G**raph menu and then selecting **V**iew.

Fig. 10.26.
The initial
stack-bar graph
in 1-2-3
Release 2.2.

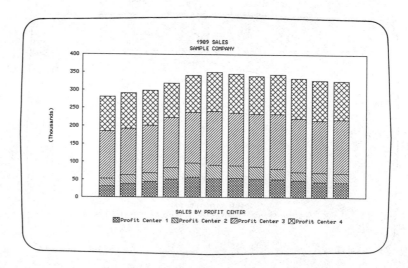

All the options set to produce the line graph shown in figure 10.25 are carried over to the new stack-bar graph. The legends (which showed symbol assignments for the line graph) automatically change to display the crosshatches of a black-and-white bar graph. 1-2-3 also automatically adjusts the upper and lower limits of the y-axis. The new $400,000 upper limit in the current graph exceeds the highest total sales month ($349,064 in June). In a stack-bar graph, the lower limit must always be zero.

Reminder:
In a stack-bar graph, the lower limit of the y-axis must be zero.

Distinguishing between certain patterns of crosshatches can be difficult when those patterns appear together. Although evident in figure 10.26 (produced in 1-2-3 Release 2.2), the problem also exists in figure 10.27 (produced in 1-2-3 Release 2.01). Look at the patterns that represent Profit Centers 3 and 4 in the upper two bars for each month in figure 10.27. To solve this visual problem, keep the profit center information in the same order, but instead of choosing data ranges **A**, **B**, **C**, and **D**, select data ranges **A**, **C**, **E**, and **F**. Reset the **B**, **C**, and **D** ranges and create the new ranges **C**, **E**, and **F**. Finally, enter legends to show that the **C** range is Profit Center 2, the **E** range is Profit Center 3, and the **F** range is Profit Center 4. Assuming that the current graph on your display screen is the same as the one shown in figure 10.26, use the following command sequences to produce the graph shown in figure 10.28:

```
/Graph Reset B
             C
             D
             Quit
        C C5..N5 Enter
        E C6..N6 Enter
        F C7..N7 Enter
        Options Legend C \A5 Enter
                Legend E \A6 Enter
                Legend F \A7 Enter
                Quit
        View
```

Compare figures 10.27 and 10.28 to see that changing the patterns of crosshatches by carefully selecting data ranges makes the information easier to read. If you intend to view the stack-bar graph in color, be sure to assign different or contrasting colors to consecutive bars; otherwise, you cannot differentiate between two distinct data items. (The ranges shown in figure 10.28 are displayed in 1-2-3 Release 2.01 on an EGA or VGA color monitor as yellow [A range], blue [C range], cyan [E range], and green [F range]).

Reminder:
If you want to view a stack-bar graph in color, be sure to assign different colors to consecutive bars.

Fig. 10.27.
The initial
stack-bar
graph in 1-2-3
Release 2.01.

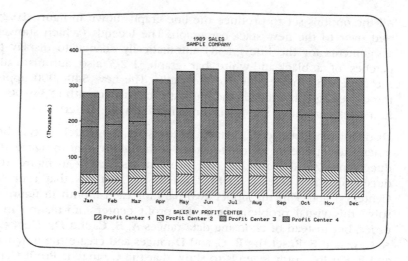

Fig. 10.28.
The stack-bar
graph in 1-2-3
Release 2.01
with revised
patterns of
crosshatches.

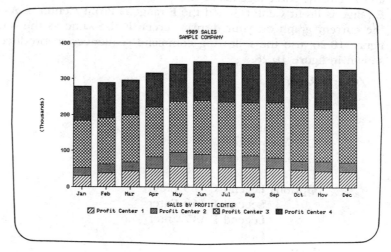

Bar and Comparative Bar Graphs

A bar graph also is appropriate for displaying the worksheet's sales-by-profit-center information (refer to figs. 10.23 and 10.24). By plotting more than one data range, you can produce a comparative bar graph in which the bars are displayed in order of data series entered, with the A range in the leftmost position.

Assuming that the stack-bar graph shown in figure 10.26 (or fig. 10.28 if you use 1-2-3 Release 2.01) is the current graph, add monthly headings below the graph. Experiment with the bar graph by entering the following command sequences:

/Graph Type Bar
            X C2..N2 Enter
            View

Your graph should be similar to the one shown in figure 10.29.

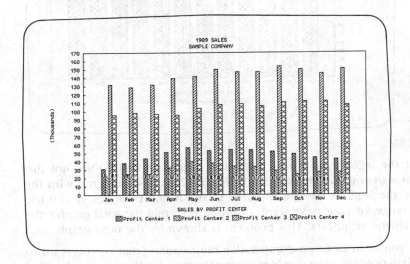

Fig. 10.29.
Four data
ranges in a
comparative
bar graph.

In this graph, each set of four bars clustered together on the x-axis represents sales by profit center. In every set of bars, the left bar represents data range A; the next, data range B; the next, C; and the right bar represents data range D (or A, C, E, and F if you are using 1-2-3 Release 2.01). Monthly headings are centered under each set of bars, and 1-2-3 has automatically revised (to $170,000) the upper scale of the y-axis.

Because the graph display seems crowded when you work with four data ranges, each of which contains 12 numbers, you may prefer to construct additional graphs, each of which compares fewer data series or contains only one data range. To compare only the two top-ranked profit centers according to sales (data ranges C and D), for example, use the following command sequences:

/Graph Reset A
               B
               Quit
               View

Make sure that you reset the A and C ranges if you use 1-2-3 Release 2.01. Compare your results to figure 10.30.

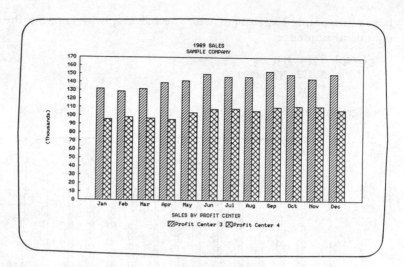

Fig. 10.30. Two data ranges in a comparative bar graph.

Notice that the legends for the deleted data ranges (A and B) are not displayed. Although you may think that the legends have been deleted with the data ranges, the legends are still assigned to the A and B ranges. If you use the A or B range for your next graph (without resetting the total graph), the associated legend reappears. This problem is shown by the next graph.

Ordinarily, you want to graph comparative information (that is, you want to use more than one data series) when the numbers to be plotted are classified by region, division, product line, and the like. By resetting one additional data range in the current example, however, you can produce a simple bar graph of only one profit center.

Suppose that you want to use data in the range O4..O7 to graph each profit center's contribution to total annual sales. To do so, retain the existing bar graph type, x-axis labels, titles, and legends. Before you reestablish data range A as O4..O7, however, reset all the data ranges. Assuming that the graph shown in figure 10.30 is current, use the following command sequences to produce a graph similar to the one shown in figure 10.31:

> /**Graph** **Reset C**
> **D**
> **Quit**
> **A O4..O7** Enter
> **View**

Because you have not changed the four legends used in figure 10.29, these legends are still established (as Profit Center 1, 2, 3, and 4) for data ranges A, B, C, and D, respectively. The legend (Profit Center 1) below the graph shown in figure 10.31 is inappropriate for two reasons: first, it no longer

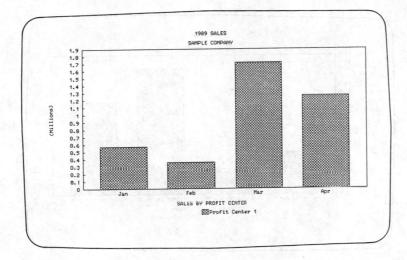

Fig. 10.31.
A bar graph
with an
inappropriate
legend.

applies to the data being graphed; second, a legend is needed only when more than one data series is being graphed. (To remove an unwanted legend, access the existing legend, press Esc, and press Enter.) Furthermore, you need to revise the x-axis labels on this graph.

To correct the appearance of the graph shown in figure 10.31 and add a Currency format to the scale numbers on the y-axis, use the following command sequences:

/Graph **X** A4..A/
        Options Legend **A** Esc Enter
                Scale **Y**-Scale Format Currency **1** Enter
                        Quit
      Quit
    View

The revised bar graph is shown in figure 10.32.

When you graph summary information, especially when the figures are large, you may want to display specific amounts as data-label descriptions within the graph, or as x-axis labels below the graph. The graph shown in figure 10.32, for example, may be easier to understand if each profit center's specific contribution to total annual sales is shown within the graph, above that center's bar. Recall that you can use /Graph Options Data-Labels to enter numbers as well as labels. In this case, raise the upper scale of the y-axis to make room for the data labels and then use the range O4..O7 as a descrip-

Reminder:
Use /Graph Options
Data-Labels to
display specific
amounts as data-
label descriptions
within a graph or
as x-labels below
the graph.

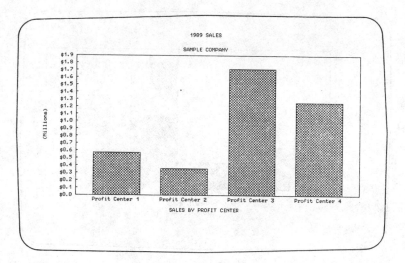

Fig. 10.32.
A corrected bar graph.

tion. Access the main **Graph** menu and apply the following command sequences to the previous settings to produce an improved graph (see fig. 10.33):

/**Graph Options Scale Y**-Scale **Manual**
                 Upper 2000000 Enter
                 Quit
           Data-Labels A O4..O7 Enter
                 Above
                 Quit
         Quit
  View

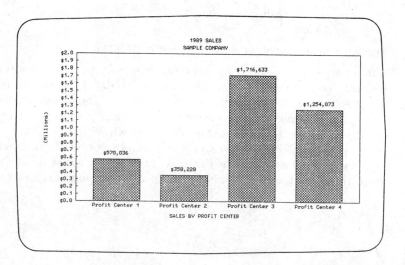

Fig. 10.33.
A bar graph with numeric data labels.

Pie Graphs

Use a pie graph only for plotting a single data series in which all numbers are positive. The main **Graph** menu's **X** and **B** range options, and the **Titles** and **Color** choices from the **Graph Options** menu are the only menu enhancements that apply to a pie graph.

You construct a pie graph by continuing to plot each profit center's contribution to total sales. If you select **/**Graph **T**ype **P**ie **V**iew, carrying over the improved bar graph settings, the graph shown in figure 10.34 displays.

Reminder:
*/Graph **X**, /Graph*
***B**, /Graph **O**ptions*
Titles, and /Graph
*Options **C**olor are*
the only
commands that
affect a pie graph.

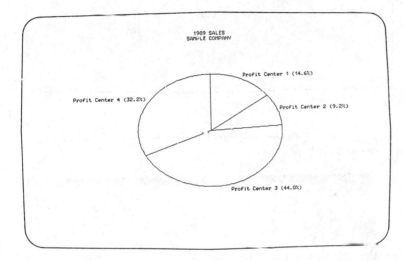

Fig. 10.34.
A basic pie
graph.

1-2-3 automatically calculates and displays in parentheses the percentage of the whole represented by each pie wedge. (You cannot suppress these percentages.) Notice that the profit center labels, entered by using the main **Graph** menu's **X** option, carried over from the previous bar graph.

You can enhance the basic pie graph by adding shading or color. 1-2-3 provides eight different shading patterns for monochrome display, eight different colors for EGA color display, and four colors for CGA color display. Figure 10.35 shows the pie graph shading patterns associated with each of the eight possible code numbers.

Use the **B** data range to specify the shadings or colors for each pie wedge. The B range can be any range that is the same size as the A data range in the worksheet you are plotting as a pie graph. To clarify this process, enter codes **1**, **2**, **4**, and **7** in cells P4, P5, P6, and P7 of the Sales by Profit Center worksheet (see fig. 10.36).

Fig. 10.35.
The crosshatch
shading codes
for pie graphs.

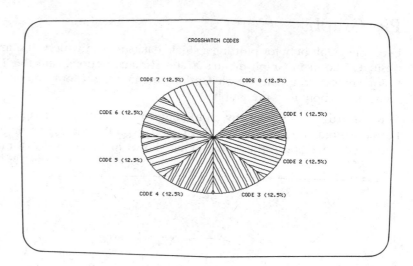

Fig. 10.36.
A worksheet
containing
initial shading
codes.

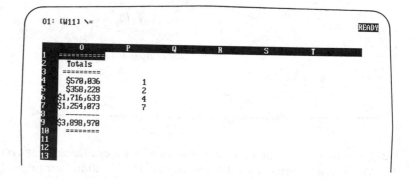

Assuming that all previous pie-graph settings are still in effect, select the **B** data range from the main **Graph** menu and specify **P4..P7** as the B data range. Select **View** to see the enhanced pie graph (see fig 10.37).

Cue:
Create an exploded pie wedge by adding 100 to the wedge's shading code in the B range.

You can "explode" any or all of the wedges by adding *100* to the appropriate numeric shading code in the B range. To illustrate this feature, emphasize Profit Center 3's top performance by adding *100* to the code number in worksheet cell P6 (see fig. 10.38). Press the Graph (F10) key to view the graph. Figure 10.39 shows the Profit Center 3 portion of the pie offset (exploded) from the rest of the graph.

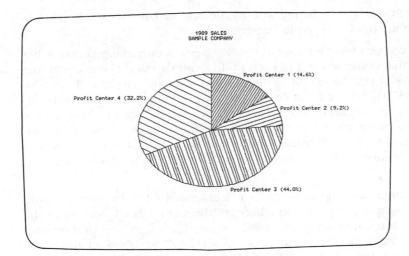

Fig. 10.37.
A shaded pie graph.

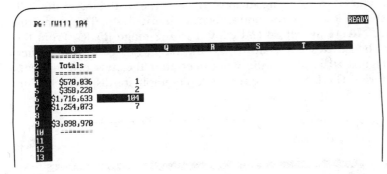

Fig. 10.38.
A worksheet containing code to explode a pie wedge.

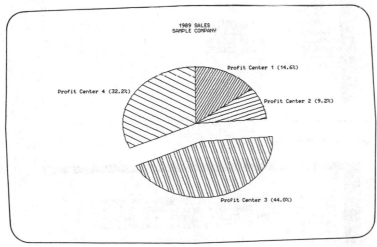

Fig. 10.39.
A pie graph with an exploded wedge.

Marking each segment of the pie with an appropriate label is essential. In this case, you must label each profit center.

The graph can be even more useful if it displays not only the percentage but also the actual dollar amount of each profit center's sales. If you could join the contents of cell A4 (Profit Center 1) with the contents of cell O4 (displayed as $570,036), for example, the graph would display both the percentage of sales and the exact dollar amount of sales for each center. You can use 1-2-3's string functions to join (concatentate) the contents of two such cells. Unfortunately, instead of producing the Currency format (*Profit Center 1 $570,036*), joining cells A4 and O4 produces the label *Profit Center 1 570036.*

You can change the appearance of each extended label by taking a little extra time. Simply retype the numbers as labels (in a blank section of the worksheet) and then string the newly created cells to the profit-center labels. You can type the contents of cells O4..O7 as labels in the range Q4..Q7, for example, or use **/R**ange Value to copy the range O4..O7 to Q4..Q7. Edit each cell by inserting an apostrophe at the beginning of the cell. Your screen should look like the one shown in figure 10.40. Then type the formula **+A4&": "&Q4** in cell R4 and copy it to the range R5..R7. From the **Graph** menu, choose **Reset X Quit.** Assign the range R4..R7 to **X** and then select View. Figure 10.41 shows the worksheet after the new cell contents have been entered. The labels in the resulting pie graph are displayed in **Cur**rency format (see fig. 10.42).

Fig. 10.40.
New cell contents (in text format) for string labels.

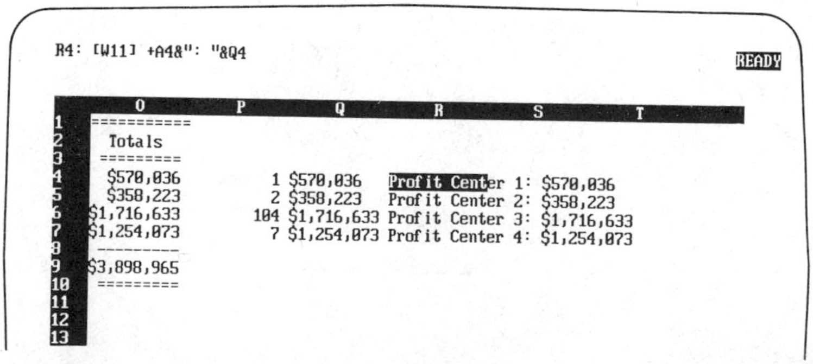

Fig. 10.41.
A worksheet display of new cell contents.

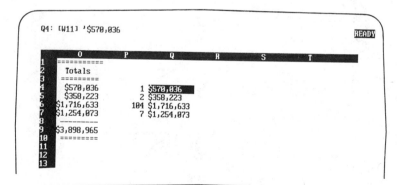

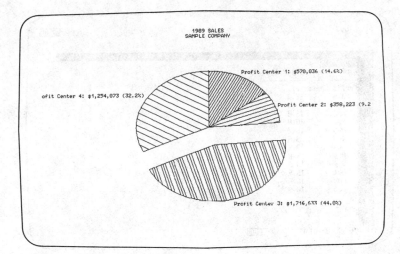

Fig. 10.42. A pie graph with string labels.

XY Graphs

The XY graph, often called a *scatter plot*, is a unique variation of a line graph. In this type of 1-2-3 graph, two or more different data items from the same data range can share the same x-axis value. Instead of showing time-series data, XY graphs show the relationships between different attributes of data items—age and income, for example, or educational achievements and salary. Think of one data item as the independent variable and consider the other item to be dependent on the first. Use the main Graph menu's X data range to enter the independent variable; use one of the A, B, C, D, E, or F options to enter the other item. If the relationship between the two items is strong, the symbols that represent each item tend to cluster in a straight-line pattern.

Suppose that you want to create a graph showing a correlation between the amount a profit center spends on advertising and the sales generated by that profit center. Imagine that, somewhere in the spreadsheet, information has been tabulated to record each profit center's share of advertising dollars spent. To create an XY graph for Profit Center 1, use the sample % of Advertising Budget data for Profit Center 1 (see fig. 10.43) and the monthly Sales data for Profit Center 1 from the worksheet shown in figures 10.23 and 10.24.

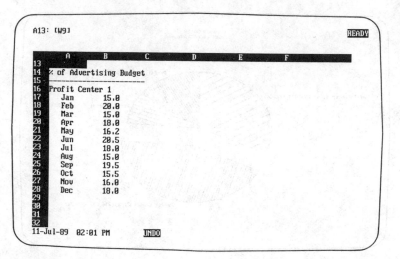

Fig. 10.43.
A sales spreadsheet containing advertising data.

Using the amount of advertising dollars expended as the independent variable, with sales as the dependent variable, construct an XY graph that includes titles and labels. To do so, issue the following command sequences:

/Graph Reset Graph
Type XY
A C4..N4 Enter
X B17.B28 Enter
Options Titles First SALES vs SHARE OF ADVERTISING Enter
     Titles Second PROFIT CENTER 1 Enter
     Titles X-Axis % of Advertising Budget Enter
     Quit
View

The initial XY graph should look like the one shown in figure 10.44.

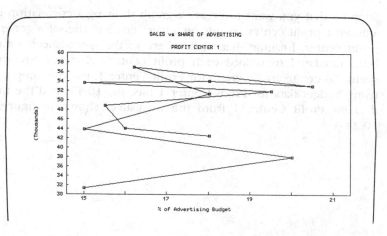

Fig. 10.44.
An initial XY graph with connecting lines.

Because the graph shown in figure 10.44 displays the default lines and symbols typical of line graphs, using the XY graph to determine whether a relationship exists between the two data series plotted is difficult, at best. But by using a setting frequently applied to XY graphs, you can suppress display of the lines and make the graph easier to read. Assuming that the XY graph shown in figure 10.44 is the current graph, issue the following command sequences:

Cue:
To create a scatter plot, use an XY graph without lines connecting the data points.

/Graph Options Format Graph Symbols
                        Quit
            Quit
    View

The revised graph should resemble the one shown in figure 10.45.

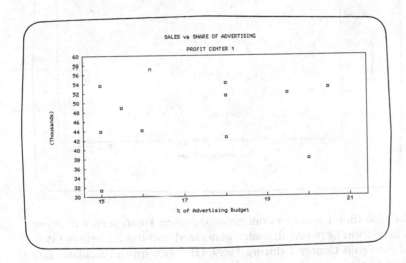

Fig. 10.45.
An XY graph
that displays
symbols only.

An XY graph without lines connecting the data points is called a scatter plot. If the symbols in a scatter plot seem to cluster along a single, imaginary, straight line fitted among the data points, a strong relationship exists.

At first glance, the widely scattered data points shown in figure 10.46 seem to indicate no strong dependency of sales dollars on advertising dollars spent. Before you draw conclusions, however, manually reset the lower scale limits of the y-axis to zero. If you use 1-2-3 Release 2.01, set the x-axis to 0; if you use 1-2-3 Release 2.2, set the x-axis to 1. To avoid distortion in the graph caused by scale differences, use the following command sequences and compare the results with figure 10.46:

/Graph Options Scale Y-Scale Manual
      Upper **60000** Enter
      Lower **0** Enter
      Quit
    Scale X-Scale Manual
      Upper **22** Enter
      Lower **1** (**0** in Release 2.01) Enter
      Quit
    Quit
  View

Fig. 10.46.
An XY graph
with the origin
set at zero.

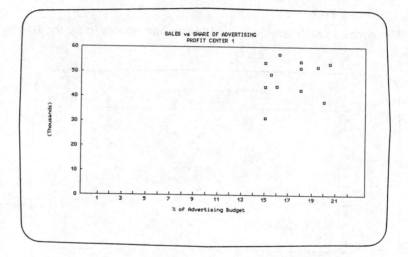

Aren't you glad you didn't jump to conclusions? Figure 10.46 seems to show a significant correlation between the sales generated and the advertising dollars expended for Profit Center 1 during 1989. (If you want to calculate data for a regression line to plot through the scattered symbols, use the **/D**ata **R**egression command.)

Bypassing Selected 1-2-3 Limitations

Now that you have learned when to use and how to construct the five 1-2-3 graph types, and how to use options to enhance them, you should be able to create most of your graphs by accepting the program's graphics defaults and selecting other menu options.

A few common problem areas exist, however. You may find, for example, that the worksheet data you want to graph is not in a continuous range. You may not like the size of a single-range bar graph or the way 1-2-3 positions data points on a line graph's axes in 1-2-3 Release 2.01. Perhaps you like the moveable title capability found in many stand-alone graphics software programs, which is not an option with 1-2-3. With a little experimentation, you may be able to overcome these apparent limitations.

Graphing Noncontinuous Ranges

Although 1-2-3 requires that a graph's data ranges be continuous, you can get around this limitation by creating continuous ranges in a blank area of the worksheet. Suppose that the Sales by Profit Center spreadsheet included not only monthly data but also quarterly summary information (see figs. 10.47 and 10.48).

Cue:
To graph noncontinuous ranges, use blank areas of the worksheet.

Fig. 10.47.
The Sales spreadsheet with quarterly summary data (January to June).

	A B	C	D	E	F	G	H	I	J
1	============	=========	=========	=========	=========	=========	=========	=========	=========
2	SALES	Jan	Feb	Mar	Qtr1	Apr	May	Jun	Qtr2
3	====================	=========	=========	=========	=========	=========	=========	=========	=========
4	Profit Center 1	$31,336	$37,954	$43,879	$113,169	$51,471	$56,953	$53,145	$161,569
5	Profit Center 2	22,572	24,888	25,167	72,627	32,588	40,140	37,970	110,698
6	Profit Center 3	131,685	129,044	131,723	392,452	139,221	141,879	149,803	430,903
7	Profit Center 4	95,473	98,008	96,986	290,467	95,318	103,538	108,146	307,002
8		--------	--------	--------	--------	--------	--------	--------	--------
9	Total Sales	$281,066	$289,894	$297,755	$868,715	$318,598	$342,510	$349,064	$1,010,172
10		========	========	========	========	========	========	========	========

Fig. 10.48.
The Sales spreadsheet with quarterly summary data (July to December).

	A B	K	L	M	N	O	P	Q	R
1	============	=========	=========	=========	=========	=========	=========	=========	=========
2	SALES	Jul	Aug	Sep	Qtr3	Oct	Nov	Dec	Qtr4
3	====================	=========	=========	=========	=========	=========	=========	=========	=========
4	Profit Center 1	$54,140	$53,614	$52,015	$159,769	$48,902	$44,091	$42,536	$135,529
5	Profit Center 2	34,587	33,463	28,939	96,989	24,153	27,060	26,701	77,914
6	Profit Center 3	147,108	147,032	153,440	447,580	149,990	145,198	150,510	445,698
7	Profit Center 4	108,642	106,065	110,401	325,108	112,018	111,956	107,522	331,496
8		--------	--------	--------	--------	--------	--------	--------	--------
9	Total Sales	$344,477	$340,174	$344,795	$1,029,446	$335,063	$328,305	$327,269	$990,637
10		========	========	========	========	========	========	========	========

If you wanted to graph only the monthly sales information for profit center 1, you might be tempted to hide columns F, J, N, and R, and then specify the range C4..R4. Try it! Because the cell entries in hidden columns are graphed, the result is a line, bar, or pie graph with 16 data points plotted, not the 12 data points you need.

You can create separate continuous ranges by pointing to data in noncontinuous ranges. To clarify this procedure, enter the cell contents in the range A12..F16 by typing +A4 in cell A13 and copying cell A13 to A14..A16, repeating the process as shown in figure 10.49.

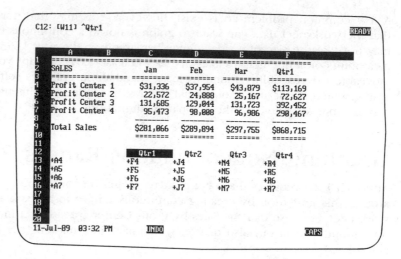

Fig. 10.49.
Cell contents
(in Text
format) for
continuous
ranges.

To verify that your screen display reflects the quarterly summary figures created in continuous ranges, compare your screen and figure 10.50.

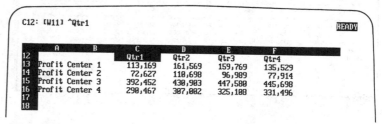

Fig. 10.50.
A cell display
after creating
continuous
ranges.

If you want to create a comparative bar graph of the quarterly sales information, use the following command sequences (refer to fig. 10.51):

/Graph Reset Graph
        Type Bar
        A C13..F13 Enter
        B C14..F14 Enter
        C C15..F15 Enter
        D C16..F16 Enter
        X C12..F12 Enter
        Options Titles First 1989 SALES Enter
                Titles Second SAMPLE COMPANY Enter
                Titles X-Axis SALES BY PROFIT CENTER Enter
                Legend A \A13 Enter
                Legend B \A14 Enter
                Legend C \A15 Enter
                Legend D \A16 Enter
                Quit
        View

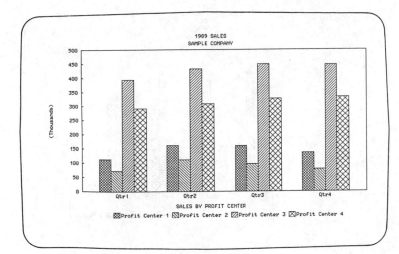

Fig. 10.51.
A bar graph
that uses newly
created
continuous
ranges.

Using Blank Cells To Alter Spacing

You can use blank cells or ranges to improve the default appearance of many
1-2-3 graphs. Notice that, in figure 10.51, the leftmost and rightmost bars
rest close to the left and right sides of the graph. In 1-2-3 Release 2.01, the
bars rest against the sides of the graph. A line graph in 1-2-3 Release 2.01 has
the first and last data points in each range plotted on the graph's right and
left sides. Graphs can be easier to read when each data range is preceded and
followed by a blank cell.

To illustrate the concept, use the quarterly summary data from figure 10.49.
First, move the range C12..F16 one column to the right (to D12..G16).
Expand each data range to include six cells (a blank, four quarterly figures,
and another blank). Then apply the following command sequences to the
current graph:

    /Graph **A C13..H13** Enter
             B C14..H14 Enter
             C C15..H15 Enter
             D C16..H16 Enter
             X C12..H12 Enter
             View

The graph displayed on your screen should look like the slightly revised
comparative bar graph shown in figure 10.52.

You also can change the display by using totally blank ranges. If you used
data from figure 10.50 to graph quarterly data only for Profit Center 1
(adjusting the options accordingly), for example, the resulting graph resembles the one shown in figure 10.53.

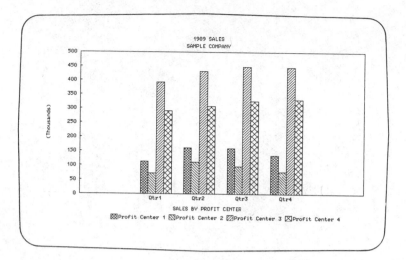

Fig. 10.52.
*Using blank
cells to alter
bar graph
display.*

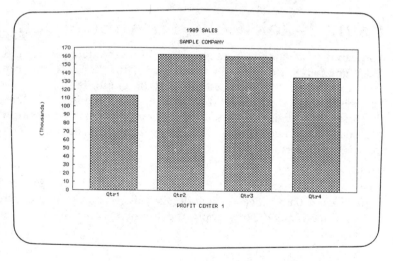

Fig. 10.53.
*A bar graph
created by
referencing
noncontinuous
data.*

Cue:
*To narrow the bars
of a bar graph,
add blank data
ranges.*

To improve the appearance of the graph, you can narrow the bars by adding additional blank data ranges. If you add a single range of blank cells as the B range (a single blank cell, such as C17 in the current example, will do), the results are less than satisfactory (see fig. 10.54).

Although the bars shown in figure 10.54 are narrower than the original bars, the bars are not centered in the frame of the graph. The location of the bars suggests that data that ought to be graphed is missing. To keep the bars centered, add an equal number of blank ranges on both sides of each data range. For example, use the worksheet, shown in figure 10.50 and subsequently changed, to graph the data range D13..G13 as the B range, enter a blank A

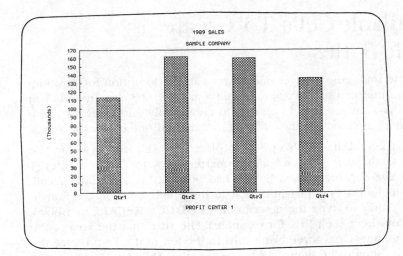

Fig. 10.54.
A graph displaying the wrong way to change bar width.

range (any blank cell such as C17), and enter a blank C range (any blank cell such as C17). Figure 10.55 reflects the addition of an even number of blank ranges.

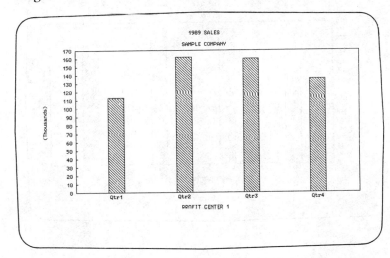

Fig. 10.55.
A graph displaying bars positioned correctly in the frame of the graph.

Now compare the default display (shown in fig. 10.52) to the revised display shown in figure 10.55. Both are "correct." Deciding which to use is a matter of individual preference. You should avoid creating bar graphs such as the one shown in figure 10.54, however, because the bars are not centered in the frame of the graph. Inadvertently creating a blank range is easy when you position the cell pointer on a blank cell, access **A**, **B**, **C**, **D**, **E**, or **F** from the main **Graph** menu, and press Enter instead of Esc to leave the submenu without specifying a range.

Using Blank Cells To Create Movable Titles

Although some software packages offer a moveable title option for positioning descriptive information anywhere within a graph, 1-2-3 does not. As you have learned, you can use 1-2-3's options to create only four titles: two centered above the graph, one to the left of the y-axis, and one below the x-axis.

Cue:
*For more freedom in placing titles, use blank spaces with the **D**ata-Labels option.*

You can use 1-2-3's **D**ata-Labels option to place text selectively within the graph. Suppose that the reduced fourth-quarter sales for Profit Center 1 (refer to fig. 10.54) were caused by the bad publicity of a product recall. You want to include this explanatory text in the graph, close to the fourth-quarter data. To do so, type the description **PRODUCT RECALL** in a blank area of the worksheet (cell F18, for example). (Be sure that the area of the worksheet you choose has three blank cells to the left of it.) To produce the moveable title shown in figure 10.56, enter the **D**ata-Labels command sequences that set the B range to position the range C18..F18 above the bars.

Fig. 10.56.
Setting a moveable title within the graph.

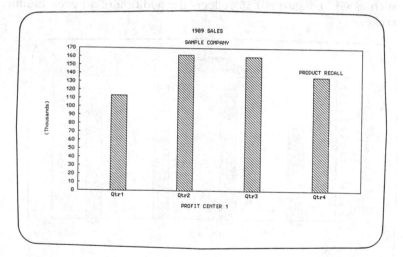

Chapter Summary

You have learned a great deal about 1-2-3 graphs from this chapter: how to create and enhance all five graph types, how to store graphs for printing as well as for subsequent recall to the screen, and how to use your imagination to produce alternative graph displays. The next chapter explains how to print graphs.

11

Printing Graphs

Chapter 10 showed you how to use 1-2-3 to create and display graphs. Because the main 1-2-3 program cannot print graphics, you must use the PrintGraph program to print the graphs you saved in graph (.PIC) files. If you are using Release 2.2, you can use Allways to print graphs rather than use the PrintGraph program. Allways provides many options not available in PrintGraph. With Allways, you can use available options to customize and improve the quality of your printed graphs, and you can print worksheet data and graphs together. See Chapter 9 for a complete description of Allways.

You can use the PrintGraph program for quick printouts of graphs; you also can choose from a variety of optional print settings for enhancing the appearance of graphs. This chapter shows you how to perform the following tasks:

- Access the PrintGraph program
- Use the status screen
- Print a graph using PrintGraph default settings
- Select or alter hardware-related settings
- Change graph size, font, and color settings
- Control paper movement from the keyboard
- Establish temporary PrintGraph settings

Accessing the PrintGraph Program

To access PrintGraph directly from the operating system, type **pgraph** at the operating system prompt. (The PrintGraph program should reside in the current directory for a hard disk system; for a floppy disk system, the disk that contains the PrintGraph program should be in the active drive.) If you use a driver set other than the default 1-2-3 set, you also must type the name of that driver set (**pgraph hp**, for example) to reach the main PrintGraph menu.

Rather than starting from the operating system, you are more likely to use PrintGraph immediately after you have created a graph. If you originally accessed 1-2-3 by typing **lotus**, select **/Quit Yes** to return to the Access menu. Then select **PrintGraph**. If you are using 1-2-3 on a floppy disk system, you are prompted to remove the 1-2-3 System disk and insert the PrintGraph disk, unless you use a member of the IBM PS/2 family. For the PS/2 and other systems with 3 1/2-inch disk drives, the PrintGraph program resides on the System disk.

Caution:
Save your
worksheet before
you use the 1-2-3
/System command.

Alternatively, if you have sufficient RAM, you can use the **/System** command to access the operating system and then PrintGraph. Instead of having to reload 1-2-3 after you leave PrintGraph, you can return directly to 1-2-3 by typing **exit** at the system prompt. Be careful!. Before you use this technique, save your worksheet. Also, use the **/Worksheet Status** command to check remaining internal memory (RAM) before you attempt to use **/System**—you must have at least 256K of remaining RAM to run PrintGraph and 1-2-3 simultaneously without overwriting your worksheet.

Producing Basic Printed Graphs

When you select **PrintGraph** from the 1-2-3 Access menu or type **pgraph** at the operating system prompt, the following menu appears:

Image-Select Settings Go Align Page Exit

Reminder:
Printing a graph
can be as easy as
selecting the image
to be printed and
then choosing Go.

Printing a graph can be a simple procedure if you accept PrintGraph's default print settings. If the correct hardware configuration has been specified, you can produce a half-size, block-font, black-and-white graph on 8 1/2-by-11-inch continuous-feed paper simply by marking a graph for printing and then printing it. You choose **Image-Select** to mark a graph for printing and **Go** to print the graph.

Suppose that you want to print the line graph saved in the WCLINE.PIC file. Make sure that the current printer and interface specifications accurately reflect your hardware, that you're using continuous-feed paper, and that the printer is on-line and positioned at the top of a page. Then you can print the default graph by issuing the following command sequences:

Image-Select **WCLINE**
Go

Figure 11.1 shows the printout of the graph. This graph is centered upright (zero degrees rotation) on the paper and fills about half of an 8 1/2-by-11-inch page. The titles are printed in the default BLOCK1 font.

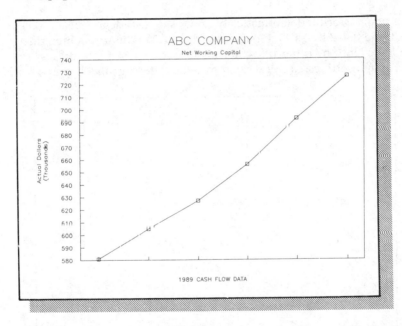

Fig. 11.1.
A sample graph
printed with
default settings.

If you want to enhance this default graph, you can do so by using any or all of PrintGraph's many special features. These special capabilities (which are not available in the main 1-2-3 program) include the production of high-resolution output on special printers and plotters; enlargement, reduction, and rotation of graph printouts; and the use of several additional colors and font types. If you're using Release 2.2, you can use Allways to enhance your graph with additional formatting options.

RELEASE

2.2

To illustrate PrintGraph's size and font options, issue the following command sequences:

> **Image-Select WCLINE**
> **Settings Image Size Full**
> > **Quit**
> > **Font 1 ITALIC1**
> > **Font 2 ROMAN1**
> > **Quit**
> > **Quit**
> **Align**
> **Go**

The resulting graph is printed automatically on its side (90 degrees rotation) and almost fills an 8 1/2-by-11-inch page (see fig. 11.2). The top center title is printed in italic font; the other titles, in roman font. (These font options, as well as other graph settings, are described in detail later in this chapter.)

Fig. 11.2.
A sample graph printed with font and size changes.

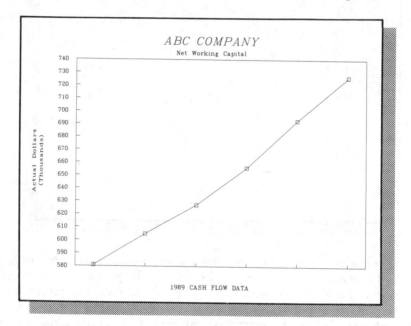

Comparing On-Screen Graphs to Printed Graphs

Reminder:
The printed graph will not be exactly the same as the screen display you see with /Graph View.

As you create and prepare to print graphs, note that a printed graph looks different from its on-screen display. For example, if you compare figure 11.3 (which captures the on-screen display of a stacked-bar graph) with figure 11.4 (which shows the same graph printed), one difference is immediately apparent.

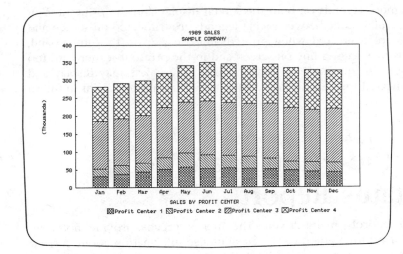

Fig. 11.3.
The screen display of a sample stacked-bar graph.

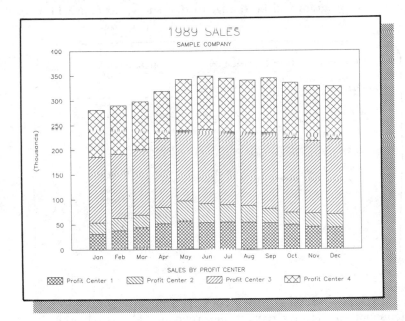

Fig. 11.4.
The printed sample stacked-bar graph.

You can see at a glance that the two top center titles in the on-screen version appear to be the same size but that, in the printed graph, the first title has been changed to a larger pitch.

You also may find other differences depending on whether you are using 1-2-3 Release 2.2 or Release 2.01. For example, if you're using Release 2.01 and create a line, bar, or stack-bar graph that contains more legends than can fit in one line across the bottom of your screen, 1-2-3 may cut off part or

RELEASE

2.2

all of one or more legends on both the screen display and the printout. You also may find a difference between what legends are truncated on-screen and what legends are truncated when printed. Release 2.2, on the other hand, wraps legends to a second line on-screen and in the printout if there are too many legends to fit on one line. Text labels on pie charts may display and print in a truncated form in Release 2.01, but will display and print in full in Release 2.2.

Using the PrintGraph Menu and Status Report

PrintGraph is entirely menu-driven. The menu screens provide not only instructions for printing graph (.PIC) files but also information about current print conditions. If you are using a hard disk, the screen displayed when you enter the PrintGraph program will be similar to that shown in figure 11.5.

Fig. 11.5.
The default
status screen.

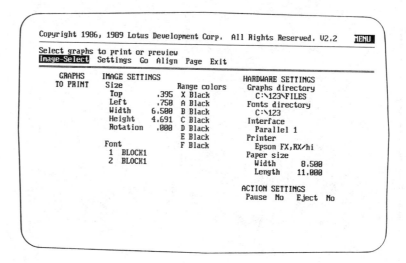

```
Copyright 1986, 1989 Lotus Development Corp.  All Rights Reserved.  V2.2   MENU

Select graphs to print or preview
Image-Select  Settings  Go  Align  Page  Exit

     GRAPHS      IMAGE SETTINGS                    HARDWARE SETTINGS
    TO PRINT     Size            Range colors      Graphs directory
                   Top     .395   X Black            C:\123\FILES
                   Left    .750   A Black          Fonts directory
                   Width  6.500   B Black            C:\123
                   Height 4.691   C Black          Interface
                   Rotation .000  D Black            Parallel 1
                                  E Black          Printer
                 Font             F Black            Epson FX,RX/hi
                 1  BLOCK1                         Paper size
                 2  BLOCK1                           Width    8.500
                                                     Length  11.000

                                                  ACTION SETTINGS
                                                  Pause No   Eject No
```

The first three text lines, which display a copyright message and two levels of current menu options, always remain on-screen. In the area below the double solid line, option selections are updated continually. (The status report disappears temporarily when you select a printer, graphs to print, and a font style.)

Cue:
Check the
PrintGraph status
report before
printing any
graphs.

Before you select the **Go** command to begin printing a graph, get in the habit of checking the status report. As you can see from figure 11.5, the settings displayed in the status report are organized in four areas in Release 2.2: GRAPHS TO PRINT, IMAGE SETTINGS, HARDWARE SETTINGS, and ACTION SETTINGS.

The areas are named GRAPH IMAGES SELECTED, IMAGE OPTIONS, HARDWARE SETUP, and ACTION OPTIONS (in Release 2.01). Each of these areas is directly related to either the **Image-Select** or **Settings** option on the **PrintGraph** menu.

For example, a list of graphs you can select for printing appears under GRAPHS TO PRINT (GRAPH IMAGES SELECTED in Release 2.01), on the left side of the status report. (In fig. 11.5, no graphs have been selected for printing.) To make changes to the other three status-report areas, you first select **Settings** from the main **PrintGraph** menu. When you select **Settings**, the following menu appears:

    Image   Hardware   Action   Save   Reset   Quit

If you choose **Image**, you can change the size, font, and color of the graph; the updated revisions are displayed in the status report's IMAGE SETTINGS area (IMAGE OPTIONS in Release 2.01). The settings shown in figure 11.5 will produce a black-and-white, half-size graph in which all titles, labels, and legends are printed in block style.

To alter the paper size, printer, or disk-drive specifications displayed in the HARDWARE SETTINGS area (HARDWARE SETUP in Release 2.01), you select **Hardware**. The instructions in figure 11.5 tell PrintGraph to look for .PIC files in the C:\123\FILES subdirectory, to look for font program files in the C:\123 directory, to print on standard-size paper, and to use an EPSON printer.

To control when a new page starts, select **Action** from the **Settings** menu. Then update the ACTION SETTINGS section (ACTION OPTIONS in Release 2.01) of the status report by changing both the **Pause** and **Eject** options from **No** to **Yes**.

The following sections discuss how to make changes to each of these settings.

Cue:
*To give you a chance to change PrintGraph settings between graphs, change the **Pause** and **Eject** options to **Yes**.*

Establishing the Physical Print Environment

The physical print environment includes the following: disk drives that contain your graph files, printer type and name, paper size, and printer actions to control print delay and paper movement.

In figure 11.5, current physical-environment settings are displayed under HARDWARE SETTINGS and ACTION SETTINGS (HARDWARE SETUP and ACTION OPTIONS in Release 2.01). For example, the HARDWARE SETTINGS information shows that the files to be graphed are located in the subdirectory C:\123\FILES; the ACTION SETTINGS show that the printer will not pause between printing two or more selected graph images.

Before you select any graphs for printing and before you select options that will affect the printed image, you should understand each Hardware and Action option.

When you select Settings Hardware, you see the following menu:

Graphs-Directory Fonts-Directory Interface Printer Size-Paper Quit

The Graphs-Directory and Fonts-Directory options pertain to disk-drive specifications; Interface and Printer determine the current printer name and type; and Size-Paper permits you to specify paper length and width in inches.

Changing the Graphs Directory

Reminder:
The graphs you want to print must be located in the current graphs directory.

In figure 11.5, the current graphs directory is C:\123\FILES. This means that you store your .PIC files in a directory named FILES that is a subdirectory of a directory named 123. You can change this directory, for example, if you want to print .PIC files from a floppy disk. To do so, insert the floppy disk in drive A and select Settings Hardware Graphs-Directory from the main PrintGraph menu. Type a: at the following prompt (Release 2.2)

Enter directory containing graph (.PIC) files

or this prompt in Release 2.01:

Enter directory containing picture files

Then type the new drive or directory. You don't have to erase the previous setting by pressing Esc or the Backspace key. The setting is updated in the upper right corner of the status report as you type (see fig. 11.6).

Fig. 11.6.
A status report showing a revised graphs directory.

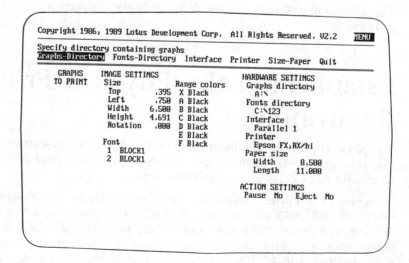

To restore C:\123\FILES as the current graphs directory, select Settings Hardware Graphs-Directory again and type **C:\123\FILES**.

Changing the Fonts Directory

Whenever you print a graph, you use PrintGraph's font files, which contain program instructions for font styles. These files are located on the same disk that holds the PrintGraph program. (Available font styles are discussed in this chapter's "Selecting Fonts" section.) As you can see from figure 11.5, the location of the fonts directory is C:\123.

If you need to change this directory, use the Settings Hardware Fonts-Directory command. For example, Lotus delivers the PrintGraph program with drive A as the default drive for the fonts directory. To change to C:\123, select **Settings Hardware Fonts-Directory** and type **C:\123**. You also might change the directory if you moved the files to another directory or renamed the directory.

Reminder:
PrintGraph's font files must be located in the current fonts directory.

Setting the Type and Name of the Current Printer

In addition to setting the graphs and fonts directories, you must specify the printer or plotter you'll use to print the selected graph images. To do so, you use two Settings Hardware menu options: Interface and Printer. Interface sets the type of connection to a graphics printer; Printer establishes a specific type of printer.

You can direct the graph output to one of two parallel printers, one of two serial printers, or one of four DOS devices (usually set up as part of a local area network). If you need to determine whether a printer is parallel or serial, consult your printer manual.

Selecting **Settings Hardware Interface** produces eight menu choices, labeled 1 through 8, which represent the physical connections between your computer and your printer:

1   Parallel 1
2   Serial 1
3   Parallel 2
4   Serial 2
5   DOS Device LPT1
6   DOS Device LPT2
7   DOS Device LPT3
8   DOS Device LPT4

In figure 11.7, option 3 (Parallel 2) is highlighted in the menu. (The default setting is Parallel 1.)

Fig. 11.7.
The Settings
Hardware
Interface menu.

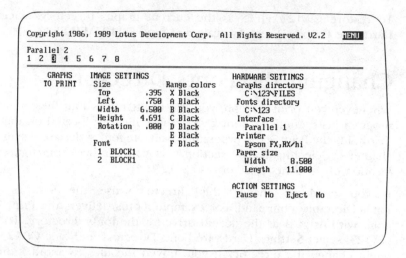

```
Copyright 1986, 1989 Lotus Development Corp. All Rights Reserved. V2.2   MENU

Parallel 2
1 2 3 4 5 6 7 8

     GRAPHS    IMAGE SETTINGS                    HARDWARE SETTINGS
     TO PRINT  Size              Range colors      Graphs directory
                 Top      .395    X Black             C:\123\FILES
                 Left     .750    A Black           Fonts directory
                 Width   6.500    B Black             C:\123
                 Height  4.691    C Black           Interface
                 Rotation .000    D Black             Parallel 1
                                  E Black           Printer
               Font               F Black             Epson FX,RX/hi
               1  BLOCK1                            Paper size
               2  BLOCK1                              Width     8.500
                                                      Length   11.000

                                                  ACTION SETTINGS
                                                  Pause  No  Eject  No
```

If you specify a serial interface, you also must select a baud rate. Baud rates determine the speed at which data is transferred. Because each printer has specific requirements, consult your printer manual for the appropriate rate. Many serial printers accept more than one baud rate. A general guideline is to choose the fastest rate your printer will accept without corrupting the data. A baud rate of 1200 is normally a safe choice.

After you have specified the appropriate interface, PrintGraph again displays the **H**ardware menu so that you can name the printer attached to the designated interface.

To select a printer, you must have installed one or more printers when you installed 1-2-3. If you installed three printers (an Epson FX-80, an IBM Graphics, and a Toshiba, for example) to run with 1-2-3, a list of these printers is displayed when you select **P**rinter from the **S**ettings **H**ardware menu (see fig. 11.8).

Fig. 11.8.
The Settings
Hardware
Printer display.

```
Copyright 1986, 1989 Lotus Development Corp. All Rights Reserved. V2.2   POINT

Select graphics printer or plotter


   Printer or Plotter name and Resolution
--------------------------------------------------  Space bar marks or unmarks selection
# Epson-FX and RX series-Low density                ENTER selects marked device
  Epson-FX and RX series-High density               ESC exits, ignoring changes
  IBM-Graphics Printer-Low density                  HOME moves to beginning of list
  IBM-Graphics Printer-High density                 END moves to end of list
  Toshiba-P1350 series·                             ↑ and ↓ move highlight
                                                    List will scroll if highlight
                                                    moved beyond top or bottom
```

Notice that the list includes not three, but five options. You can print at either high or low density (dark or light print). If you use a high-density option, the printed graph will be of high quality, but printing will take more time.

Instructions for selecting an option appear on-screen, and a number sign (#) marks the current printer. To mark or unmark a selection, press the space bar. The highlighted line, # Epson-FX and RX series-Low density, tells you that the current printer is an Epson FX or RX and that you have chosen to print at low density. If you want to select another printer, press the space bar to remove the # mark from the Epson FX and RX series; then reposition the highlighted bar and mark the new device by pressing Enter.

Cue:
Use a low-density option for faster, draft-quality printing.

Changing the Paper Size

Along with selecting your printer, you should set your paper size. The default paper size is 8 1/2 by 11 inches, but you can print your graph on different sized paper by selecting Settings Hardware Size-Paper. When you select Size-Paper, the following options are displayed:

    Length   Width   Quit

Select **Length** or **Width** and specify the appropriate number of inches. To adjust the paper size to the 14-inch paper used in wide-carriage printers, for example, select Settings Hardware Size-Paper **Width** and then type **14**. Remember that this command changes the size of the paper, not the size of the graph. (Changing the size of a graph is discussed in "Adjusting Size and Orientation" in this chapter.) Be sure to select a paper size that can accommodate the specified graph size.

Reminder:
The Size-Paper option tells PrintGraph to print on a different paper size, but does not change the size of the graph.

Making the Printer Pause between Graphs

If you have selected more than one .PIC file for a single print operation, you can make the printer pause between printing the specified graphs. If you are using a manual sheet-feed printer, for example, you can pause to change the paper. Or you may want to stop printing temporarily so that you can change the hardware settings, directing the output to a different printer. (You cannot change the font, color, and size options during the pause.)

If you want the printing operation to pause, select Settings Action **Pause Yes** before you select **Go** from the main PrintGraph menu. After each graph has been printed, the printer pauses and beeps. To resume printing, press the space bar. To restore the default setting so that all currently specified graphs will print nonstop, choose Settings Action **Pause No**.

Ejecting the Paper To Start a New Page

Another Action option that applies to "batching" several graphs in one print operation is Eject. When you select Settings Action Eject Yes, continuous-feed paper advances to the top of a new page before the next graph is printed. Use the alternative default setting, Eject No, to print two (or more) half-size (or smaller) graphs on a single page.

Do not confuse the Settings Action Eject Yes command with the PrintGraph menu's Page command. (The Page option is described in "Completing the Print Cycle" in this chapter.) Both commands advance the paper to the top of a new page. Settings Action Eject Yes is appropriate when you use a single Go command to print more than one selected graph; the paper advances automatically after each graph has been printed. You select PrintGraph Page, on the other hand, whenever you want to advance the paper one page at a time before or after a printing session.

Controlling the Appearance of Printed Graphs

You've learned about the physical print environment needed to produce a graph: the printer type and name, the disk-drive location of required files, and the paper size and movement. Now that you're familiar with the mechanics of producing a graph, you learn about options that affect the printed graph's appearance. These options are displayed in the status screen, under IMAGE SETTINGS in Release 2.2 or IMAGE OPTIONS in Release 2.01.

If you select Settings Image from the PrintGraph menu, you see the following menu:

  Size   Font   Range-Colors   Quit

Use these options to change the size of a graph, to specify one or two print styles in a single graph, and to select colors. (As you know, you use the 1-2-3 /Graph commands to enter graph enhancements such as titles, legends, and labels.)

Adjusting Size and Orientation

The Size option lets you adjust the size of graphs and decide where, and at what angle, the graphs are printed on a page. You determine the size of the graph by specifying the desired width and height; you set the graph's position on the page by specifying the top and left margins. You also can rotate the graph a specified number of degrees on the page.

When you select **Settings Image Size**, you see the menu shown in figure 11.9. The default **H**alf option automatically produces a graph that fills half of a standard-size 8 1/2-by-11-inch page. Figure 11.9 shows the following default assignments:

Top	.395 (inches)
Left	.750 (inches)
Width	6.500 (inches)
Height	4.691 (inches)
Rotation	.000 (degrees)

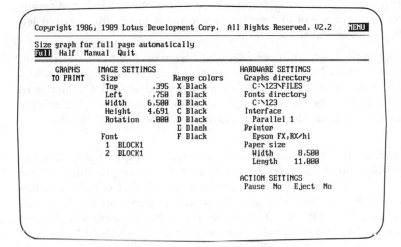

Fig. 11.9.
The Settings
Image Size
menu.

Because these settings are the default, you don't have to use the **S**ize option if you want to print a graph with these dimensions centered upright on a standard-size page.

Width refers to the horizontal graph dimension produced on a page. The width of the half-size graph shown in figure 11.1 is the x-axis. In a zero-rotation graph, the ratio of x-axis size (width) to y-axis size is 1.386 to 1.

The **F**ull option automatically determines a combination of the width, height, top, left, and rotation settings to produce a graph that fills an 8 1/2-by-11-inch page. The top of this horizontal graph (90 degrees rotation) lies along the left edge of the paper. The automatic assignments for a full-size graph include the following:

Top	.250 (inches)
Left	.500 (inches)
Width	6.852 (inches)
Height	9.445 (inches)
Rotation	90.000 (degrees)

The width of the full-size graph shown in figure 11.2 is the y-axis, which has been changed automatically to 6.852 inches. In a graph rotated 90 degrees, the ratio of x-axis size (height) to y-axis size is 1.378 to 1.

If you want to change any or all of the size settings, select Manual from the Settings Image Size menu. Then select one or more of the following options:

> Top Left Width Height Rotation Quit

To position a printed graph at a location other than the automatic distances from the edges of the paper, change the margin settings. If you want to center a half-size graph at the top of 11-by-14-inch paper, for example, specify a different left margin by selecting Settings Image Size Manual Left and typing **3.5** as the revised number of inches. When you press Enter, the updated left margin is displayed in the status report.

Determine the appropriate number of inches by working from the default values. You know that a half-size graph is centered automatically on an 8 1/2-inch page and that changing to paper 14 inches wide adds 5 1/2 inches to the width. Add half of the increase (2.75 inches) to the default left margin (.75 inches) to calculate the total number of inches (3.5) for the new margin.

Cue:
The x- to y-axis ratio should remain at 1.38 to 1 for every combination of width and height setting.

When you change the Width and Height settings, be sure to maintain the basic x- to y-axis ratio of approximately 1.38 to 1. For example, suppose that you want to produce an upright (zero rotation) graph that is only 3 inches high. You know that the x-axis dimension should exceed the y-axis dimension and that, at zero rotation, the x-axis is the width. Multiply the desired height of 3 inches by 1.38 to calculate the proportionate width (4.14 inches) of the graph.

Be sure that the combined dimensions (margin, width, and height) do not exceed the size of the paper. If a graph exceeds the physical bounds of the paper, 1-2-3 will print as much of the graph as possible and then truncate the rest.

Although you can set rotation anywhere between 0 and 360 degrees, you will use 3 settings (0, 90, or 270) for most graphs. To print an upright graph, use 0; to position the graph's center titles along the left edge of the paper, use 90; use 270 to position the graph's center titles along the right edge of the paper.

Selecting Fonts

Cue:
Select Font 1 to print the top title in one typeface; then select Font 2 for the remaining text.

You can use different character types, or fonts, in a printed graph. For example, you can print a graph's top title in one character type (Font 1) and then select a different font (Font 2) for the remaining titles, data labels, x-labels, and legends. If you want to use only one print style, your Font 1 choice is used for all descriptions.

When you select **Settings Image Font 1**, you see the options shown in figure 11.10. BLOCK1 is the default font. The number after the font name—for example, BLOCK1 and BLOCK2—indicates the darkness (density) of the printed characters. Notice that four of the fonts permit alternative print-density specifications. If you choose BLOCK2, for example, the printed characters will be darker than those produced by choosing BLOCK1. Figure 11.11 shows a sample of each font style.

```
Copyright 1986, 1989 Lotus Development Corp.  All Rights Reserved.  V2.2    POINT

Select font 1

        FONT         SIZE
        -----------------          Space bar marks or unmarks selection
     ⊞ BLOCK1        5732          ENTER selects marked font
       BLOCK2        9273          ESC exits, ignoring changes
       BOLD          8684          HOME moves to beginning of list
       FORUM         9767          END moves to end of list
       ITALIC1       8974          ↑ and ↓ move highlight
       ITALIC2       11865            List will scroll if highlight
       LOTUS         8686            moved beyond top or bottom
       ROMAN1        6843
       ROMAN2        11615
       SCRIPT1       8064
       SCRIPT2       18367
```

Fig. 11.10.
The Settings
Image Font 1
options.

This is BLOCK1 type
This is BLOCK2 type
This is BOLD type
This is FORUM type
This is ITALIC1 type
This is ITALIC2 type
This is LOTUS type
This is ROMAN1 type
This is ROMAN2 type
This is SCRIPT1 type
This is SCRIPT2 type

Fig. 11.11.
Samples of
fonts available
in PrintGraph.

Two of these fonts (italic and script) may be difficult to read, especially on half-size graphs produced on a nonletter-quality printer. Before you print a final-quality draft in darker density, print the graph at the lower density so that you can determine whether the font and size settings are correct.

Cue:
Print the graph at the faster, low-density setting to check font appearance before you print the final version at the high-density setting.

Choosing Colors

If you have a color printing device, you can use the PrintGraph program to assign colors to all parts of a graph. Select **S**ettings **I**mage **R**ange-Colors to display the following menu:

X A B C D E F Quit

For all graph types except pie, use the **X** option to assign a single color to the edges of the graph, any background grid, and all displayed options other than legends and data labels. Use **A**, **B**, **C**, **D**, **E**, and **F** to assign a different color to every data range used. The color set for an individual data range is used also for any data label or legend assigned to that data range.

You use a different method to determine the print colors for a pie graph. Because you create a pie graph by using only data in the A range, and because each wedge of the pie is assigned a B-range shading code, you must use the appropriate shading codes to determine which colors will print. First, associate each code with the following **I**mage **R**ange-Colors menu options:

Range-Colors Option	*B-Range Shading Option*
X	Shading code ending in 1 (101 or 1)
A	Shading code ending in 2
B	Shading code ending in 3
C	Shading code ending in 4
D	Shading code ending in 5
E	Shading code ending in 6
F	Shading code ending in 7

When you select an option from the **S**ettings **I**mage **R**ange-Colors menu, a menu of colors is displayed. The number of colors displayed depends on the capabilities of the current printer (named in the HARDWARE SETTINGS area of the PrintGraph status report). If your printer does not support color printing, only the **B**lack option appears. To choose a color for each range, highlight that color and press Enter. In figure 11.12, the assigned colors are listed in the IMAGE SETTINGS (or IMAGE OPTIONS in Release 2.01) section of the Print-Graph status report.

If you know that you will print a specific graph in color, select **/G**raph **O**ptions **C**olor before you store that graph as a .PIC file. If you store the graph in black and white and then print it in color, the crosshatch markings and the colors assigned to the ranges both will print.

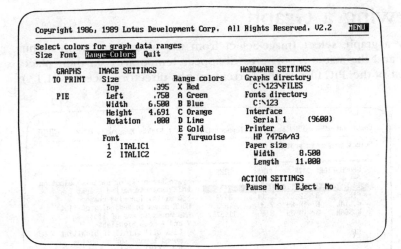

Fig. 11.12.
A sample status report after selecting colors.

The figure shows a screen with the following text:

```
Copyright 1986, 1989 Lotus Development Corp. All Rights Reserved. V2.2    MENU

Select colors for graph data ranges
Size  Font  Range-Colors  Quit

GRAPHS        IMAGE SETTINGS              HARDWARE SETTINGS
TO PRINT      Size            Range colors  Graphs directory
              Top      .395   X Red           C:\123\FILES
PIE           Left     .750   A Green       Fonts directory
              Width   6.500   B Blue          C:\123
              Height  4.691   C Orange      Interface
              Rotation .000   D Line          Serial 1      (9600)
                              E Gold        Printer
              Font            F Turquoise     HP 7475A/A3
               1  ITALIC1                   Paper size
               2  ITALIC2                     Width      8.500
                                              Length    11.000

                                            ACTION SETTINGS
                                            Pause  No  Eject  No
```

Saving and Resetting PrintGraph Settings

After you have established current **Hardware**, **Action**, and **Image** settings and completed the current printing operation, you select one of two options from the **Settings** menu: **Save** or **Reset**. Both of these options apply to the entire group of current settings.

If you choose **Save**, the current options are stored in a file named PGRAPH.CNF; this file will be read whenever PrintGraph is loaded. Select **Reset** to restore all **Hardware**, **Action**, and **Image** settings to PrintGraph's default settings or to the options saved during the current session—whichever occurred most recently. Image-Selected graphs are not reset.

Completing the Print Cycle

After you have accepted the default options or selected other **Hardware**, **Action**, and **Image** options, you access the main **PrintGraph** menu to complete the printing operation. From this menu, you select the graph(s) to be printed, adjust the paper alignment, and select **Go**.

Previewing a Graph

To preview a graph, select **Image-Select** from the main **PrintGraph** menu. The menus and the status report area disappear temporarily; in their place, you see a list of the .PIC files in the current graphs directory (see fig. 11.13).

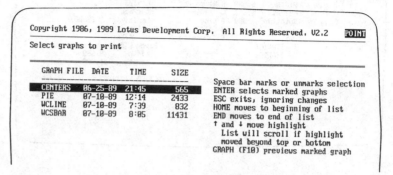

```
Copyright 1986, 1989 Lotus Development Corp. All Rights Reserved. V2.2    POINT

Select graphs to print


    GRAPH FILE  DATE      TIME    SIZE
    ----------------------------------
    CENTERS    06-25-89  21:45     565    Space bar marks or unmarks selection
    PIE        07-10-89  12:14    2433    ENTER selects marked graphs
    WCLINE     07-10-89   7:39     832    ESC exits, ignoring changes
    WCSBAR     07-10-89   8:05   11431    HOME moves to beginning of list
                                          END moves to end of list
                                          ↑ and ↓ move highlight
                                            List will scroll if highlight
                                            moved beyond top or bottom
                                          GRAPH (F10) previews marked graph
```

Instructions for selecting graphs are displayed on-screen. The last item on the list of instructions indicates that pressing the Graph (F10) key displays the highlighted graph on-screen. (If you are using Release 2.01, some of the text differs on your screen.) To verify that the graph shown is the one you want to print, use the Graph key to preview it. Size and font options are not displayed in this preview, and you can't see rotation or half-size results. But the preview does give a good idea of what the printed graph will look like—in some instances, a better idea than /Graph View. For example, legend titles that are too wide to print appear complete when viewed on-screen with /Graph View, but not with the Graph (F10) key.

Selecting a Graph

Selecting graphs you want to print is easy. Simply select **Image-Select** and then mark the file you want to print. To mark the files for printing, use the cursor-movement keys to position the highlighted bar on the graph you want to select. Then press the space bar to mark the file with a # symbol. The space bar acts as a toggle key; use the same action to remove any unwanted marks. If necessary, continue to mark additional graphs. (In fig. 11.14, two graphs have been marked for printing.) After you press Enter to accept the currently marked graphs for printing, the updated status report is displayed again.

```
Copyright 1986, 1989 Lotus Development Corp. All Rights Reserved. V2.2   POINT

Select graphs to print
_____

   GRAPH FILE  DATE     TIME    SIZE
   ----------------------------------   Space bar marks or unmarks selection
 # CENTERS     06-25-89 21:45    565    ENTER selects marked graphs
   PIE         07-18-89 12:14   2433    ESC exits, ignoring changes
   WCLINE      07-18-89  7:39    832    HOME moves to beginning of list
 # WCSBAR      07-18-89  8:05  11431    END moves to end of list
                                        ↑ and ↓ move highlight
                                          List will scroll if highlight
                                          moved beyond top or bottom
                                        GRAPH (F10) previews marked graph
```

Fig. 11.14.
.PIC files
marked for
printing.

Controlling Paper Movement

The main **PrintGraph** menu's **Align** option sets the program's built-in, top-of-page marker. When you choose Align, PrintGraph assumes that the paper in the printer is aligned correctly at the top of the page. Using the page-length information you provided when you installed the graphics device, Print-Graph then inserts a form feed at the end of every page. Regularly selecting Align before selecting **Go** is a good practice.

Reminder:
To ensure that the graph lines up properly on the printed page, select Align before selecting Go.

The **Page** option advances the paper one page at a time. At the end of a printing session, this option advances continuous-feed paper to help you remove the printed output. While you are using the PrintGraph program, control the movement of paper from the keyboard, not from the printer. Although many printers have controls that allow you to scroll the paper one line at a time, PrintGraph does not recognize these controls. For example, if you scroll the paper three lines but do not realign it, PrintGraph will be three spaces off when you issue the next form-feed command.

Printing the Graph

To print a graph, you must select **Go** from the main **PrintGraph** menu. After you select Go, you see in the screen's menu area messages indicating that picture and font files are loading. Then the graphs are printed. Printing a graph takes much longer than printing a similar-sized worksheet range, especially if you are printing in high-density mode.

If you want to interrupt the process of printing a graph or series of graphs, use the Ctrl-Break key combination. Then press Esc to access the **PrintGraph** menu.

Cue:
To stop PrintGraph while printing is in progress, press Ctrl-Break.

Exiting the PrintGraph Program

To leave the PrintGraph program, choose **Exit** from the main **PrintGraph** menu. The next screen to appear depends on the method you used to access PrintGraph. If you entered PrintGraph from the 1-2-3 Access System, the Access menu reappears. Select **Exit** to restore the operating system prompt, or select another Access menu option. If you entered PrintGraph by typing **pgraph** from the operating system prompt, the operating system prompt is restored.

If you want to enter 1-2-3 after you have exited PrintGraph and restored the operating system prompt, remember how you originally accessed the operating system prompt (before you typed **pgraph**). If you were using 1-2-3 and selected **/**System to reach the operating system prompt, type **exit** and press Enter to return to the 1-2-3 worksheet. If you were not using 1-2-3 before the PrintGraph session, type **123**, or type **lotus** and then select **123** from the Access menu.

Chapter Summary

The mechanics of printing a graph are simple. The PrintGraph utility program provides a menu-driven approach to mark graphs for printing and to specify settings involving the physical print environment. You also must create and store the graphs within the 1-2-3 program, correctly install hardware, and use PrintGraph to print the results.

With the conclusion of this chapter, you have learned all the fundamentals of 1-2-3. Part III, which begins with Chapter 12, introduces you to advanced 1-2-3 topics: using 1-2-3's database management features, creating keyboard macros, and using 1-2-3's advanced macro commands. Many users do not approach the advanced topics until they have used 1-2-3 for a while. If that is your preference, keep this book handy as a reference as you continue to use 1-2-3; then return to Part III when you are ready.

Part III

Customizing 1-2-3

Includes

Managing Data

Using Macros To Customize Your Worksheet

Introducing the Advanced Macro Commands

12

Managing Data

In addition to the electronic worksheet and business graphics, 1-2-3 has a third element: data management. Because the entire 1-2-3 database resides in the worksheet within main memory (RAM), 1-2-3's database feature is fast, easy to access, and easy to use.

1-2-3's database is quick because the program reduces the time required to transfer data to and from disks. By doing all the work inside the worksheet, 1-2-3 saves the time required for input and output to disk.

The 1-2-3 database is easily accessed because Lotus Development Corporation has made the entire database visible within the worksheet. You can view the contents of the whole database by using worksheet windows and cursor-movement keys to scroll through the database.

The ease of use is a result of integrating data management with the program's worksheet and graphics functions. The commands for adding, modifying, and deleting items in a database are the same ones you have already seen for manipulating cells or groups of cells within a worksheet. And creating graphs from ranges in a database is as easy as creating them in a worksheet.

This chapter shows you how to complete the following:

- Create a 1-2-3 database
- Enter, modify, and maintain data records
- Carry out Sort and Query operations
- Load data from ASCII files and other programs
- Apply data with other /Data commands
- Use database statistical functions

427

Defining a Database

A database is a collection of data organized so that you can list, sort, or search its contents. The list of data might contain any kind of information, from addresses to tax-deductible expenditures.

In 1-2-3, the word *database* means a range of cells that spans at least one column and more than one row. This definition, however, does not distinguish between a database and any other range of cells. Because a database is actually a list, its manner of organization sets it apart from ordinary cells. Just as a list must be organized to be useful, a database must be organized to permit access to the information it contains.

Remember nonetheless that in 1-2-3 a database is similar to any other group of cells. This knowledge will help you as you learn about the different **/Data** commands covered in this chapter. You can use these database commands in what you might consider "nondatabase" applications in many instances.

The smallest unit in a database is a *field*, or single data item. For example, if you were to develop an information base of present or potential corporate contributors for a not-for-profit organization, you might include the following fields of information:

Company Name
Company Address
Contact Person
Phone Number
Last Contact Date
Contact Representative
Last Contribution Date

A database *record* is a collection of associated fields. For example, the accumulation of all contributor data about one company forms one record. In 1-2-3, a *record* is a row of cells within a database, and a *field* is a single cell.

You must set up a database so that you can access the information it contains. Retrieval of information usually involves key fields. A database *key field* is any field on which you base a list, sort, or search operation. For example, you could use ZIPCODE as a key field to sort the data in the contributor database and assign contact representatives to specific geographic areas. And you could prepare a follow-up contact list by searching the database for the key field LAST CONTACT DATE in which the date is less than one year ago.

Reminder:
The 1-2-3 database resides in the worksheet's row-and-column format.

The 1-2-3 database resides in the worksheet's row-and-column format. Figure 12.1 shows the general organization of a 1-2-3 database.

Labels (*field names*) describing the data items appear as column headings. Information about each specific data item (*field*) is entered in a cell in the appropriate column. In figure 12.1, the highlighted cell (D6) represents data for the second field name in the database's fourth record.

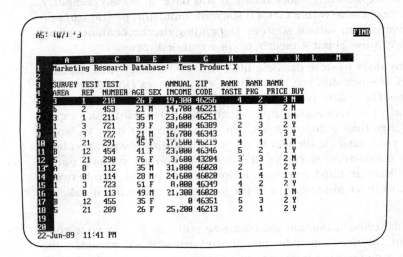

```
D6: [W12] 'FIELD R4F2                                        READY

        A      B      C        D        E        F        G
1                  FIELD    FIELD    FIELD    FIELD    FIELD
2                  NAME 1   NAME 2   NAME 3   NAME 4   NAME 5
3    RECORD#  1             FIELD R1F2
4    RECORD#  2             FIELD R2F2
5    RECORD#  3             FIELD R3F2
6    RECORD#  4 FIELD R4F1  FIELD R4F2 FIELD R4F3 FIELD R4F4 FIELD R4F5
7    RECORD#  5             FIELD R5F2
8    RECORD#  6             FIELD R6F2
9    RECORD#  7             FIELD R7F2
10   RECORD#  8             FIELD R8F2
11   RECORD#  9             FIELD R9F2
12   RECORD# 10             FIELD R10F2
13
14
```

Fig. 12.1.
The general organization of the 1-2-3 database.

In the marketing research database shown in figure 12.2, the highlighted row (row 5) contains all fields of information concerning the first record.

```
A5: [W7] '3                                                  FIND

      A     B      C     D  E     F      G     H    I    J    K   L  M
1   Marketing Research Database:   Test Product X
2
3   SURVEY TEST  TEST          ANNUAL ZIP   RANK RANK RANK
4   AREA   REP   NUMBER AGE SEX INCOME CODE  TASTE PKG  PRICE BUY
5    3     1     210    26  F   19,300 46256   4    2    3 N
6    b     2     453    21  M   14,700 46221   1    3    2 N
7    3     1     211    35  M   23,600 46251   1    1    1 N
8    1     3     721    39  F   38,000 46389   2    3    2 Y
9    1     3     722    21  M   16,700 46343   1    3    3 Y
10   5     21    291    45  F   17,500 46219   4    1    1 N
11   B     12    454    41  F   23,000 46346   5    2    1 Y
12   5     21    290    76  F    3,600 43204   3    3    2 N
13*  A     8     112    35  M   31,000 46820   2    1    2 Y
14   A     8     114    28  M   24,600 46820   1    4    1 Y
15   1     3     723    51  F    8,000 46349   4    2    2 Y
16   a     8     113    49  M   21,300 46828   3    1    1 N
17   B     12    455    35  F        0 46351   5    3    2 Y
18   5     21    289    26  F   25,200 46213   2    1    2 Y
19
20
22-Jun-89  11:41 PM
```

Fig. 12.2.
The highlighted record.

Understanding Database Limits

The major disadvantage of 1-2-3's database capabilities is the limitation the program imposes on the size of the database. With some popular database programs, you can load only portions of your database at once; with 1-2-3, the entire database must be in memory before you can perform any data-management operations.

Theoretically, the maximum number of records you can have in a 1-2-3 database corresponds to the maximum number of rows in the worksheet (8,192 rows minus 1 row for the field names). Realistically, however, the

Reminder:
You must load the entire 1-2-3 database into memory before you can perform any data-management operations.

number of records in a specific database is limited by the amount of available memory: conventional memory (RAM), expanded memory, and disk storage. You also must consider the room needed within the database to hold data extracted by Query commands.

A typical computer system with 640K of conventional memory can store in a single 1-2-3 Release 2.2 database only about 2,000 records of the type shown in figure 12.2. For large databases, you need to add expanded memory to your computer.

When you add expanded memory to your computer, it operates as though more than the conventional 640K of memory—up to 8 megabytes—is available. Because adding this memory is really a hardware trick to fool the operating system (DOS), restrictions are imposed on this memory. Expanded memory is designed to work with the Lotus/Intel/Microsoft Expanded Memory Specification (LIM EMS), currently at version 4.0. To add expanded memory to a computer with an 8088, 8086, or 80286 microprocessor, you usually install an expanded memory board. If you have an 80386 computer, your computer may come with a LIM 4.0 software emulator, or you can purchase this software from various sources. Depending on the contents of the database, 1-2-3 can use about 4 megabytes of expanded memory.

Reminder:
The size of a worksheet in memory is usually different from the amount of space it takes up on a disk.

If you use floppy disks to store database files, you are limited by the capacity of the disk. A 5 1/4-inch disk can hold either 360 kilobytes (low density) or 1.2 million bytes (high density). A 3 1/2-inch disk can hold either 720 kilobytes (low density) or 1.44 million bytes (high density). A hard disk's capacity is much higher than a floppy disk's. The only time you have to worry about whether your database file will fit on your hard disk is when you have so much other information stored on the disk that you are running out of available space. Keep in mind that there is not a direct relationship between the size of a worksheet in memory and the amount of space it will take up on your disk.

When you estimate the maximum database size you can use on your computer equipment, be sure to include enough blank rows to accommodate the maximum output you expect from extract operations.

If you can deal with 1-2-3's memory constraints and the somewhat time-consuming method of using menu options to manipulate data, you'll have a powerful data-management tool.

Creating a Database

When you select **Data** from the 1-2-3 main menu, the following options are displayed in the control panel:

Fill Table Sort Query Distribution Matrix Regression Parse

The **Sort** and **Query** (search) options are true data-management operations. Both are described in detail in this chapter. The other options (**Fill**, **Table**, **Distribution**, **Matrix**, **Regression**, and **Parse**) are considered, more appropriately, data-creation operations. They too are described in this chapter. First, let's discuss creating a database.

You can create a database as a new database file or as part of an existing worksheet. If you decide to build a database as part of an existing worksheet, choose a worksheet area you will not need for anything else. This area should be large enough to accommodate the number of records you plan to enter. If you add the database to the side of the worksheet, be careful about inserting or deleting worksheet rows that might also affect the database. If you add a database below an existing worksheet, be careful not to disturb predetermined column widths in the worksheet portion when you adjust the column widths of the database fields.

After you decide which area of the worksheet to use, you create a database by specifying field names across a row and entering data in cells as you would for any other 1-2-3 application. The mechanics of entering database contents are simple; the most critical step in creating a useful database is choosing your fields accurately.

Caution:
Place your database where it won't be affected by inserting or deleting columns or rows or by changing column widths in other applications.

Determining the Required Output

1-2-3's data-retrieval techniques rely on locating data by field names. Before you begin typing the kinds of data items you think you may need, write down the output you expect from the database. You also need to consider any source documents already in use that provide input to the file. For example, you might use the following information from a sample database:

Company Name
Company Address
Contact Person
Phone Number
Last Contact Date
Contact Representative
Last Contribution Date

When you are ready to set up these items in your database, you must specify for each information item a field name, the column width, and the type of entry.

You might make a common error in setting up your database if you choose a field name (and enter data) without thinking about the output you want from that key field. Suppose that you establish GIFTDATE as a field name to describe the last date a contribution was made. Then you enter record dates as labels in the general form XX/XX/XX. Although you can search for a GIFT-

DATE that matches a specific date, you won't be able to perform a math-based search for all GIFTDATEs within a specified period of time or before a certain date. To get maximum flexibility from 1-2-3's **/D**ata commands, enter dates in the following form (see Chapter 6 for more information on functions):

@DATE(year number,month number,day number)

Reminder:
The format of your data (date, labels, numbers) affects how you can sort and search the data.

After you decide on the output, you then need to choose the level of detail needed for each item of information, select the appropriate column width, and determine whether you will enter data as a number or as a label. For example, if you want to be able to sort by area code all records containing telephone numbers, you should enter telephone numbers as two separate fields: area code (XXX) and the base number XXX-XXXX. Because you will not want to perform math functions on telephone numbers, enter them as labels.

To save memory and increase data-entry speed and accuracy, code as much information as possible. For example, if you need to query only about work-loads, plan to use the first, middle, and last initials of each contact representative in the database instead of printing a list of their full names.

If you enter database content from a standard source document, such as a marketing research survey form, you can increase the speed of data entry by setting up the field names in the same order as the corresponding data items on the form.

Be sure to plan your database carefully before you establish field names, set column widths and range formats, and enter data.

Entering Data

After you plan your database, you can build it. To help you understand how the process works, let's create a sample marketing research database as a new database in a blank worksheet. After you select the appropriate area of the worksheet for the database, you enter the field names across a single row (see fig. 12.3).

The highlighted bar rests on row 4, the field-name row. The field names must be labels, even if they are the numeric labels '1, '2, and so on. Although you can use more than one row for the field names, 1-2-3 processes only the values that appear in the bottom row. For example, the first field name in the marketing research database (rows 3 and 4 of column A) is SURVEY AREA, but only AREA (the portion in row 4) is referenced as a key field in sort or query operations.

Reminder:
Keep all field names unique; any repetition of field names confuses 1-2-3

Keep in mind that all field names should be unique; any repetition of names confuses 1-2-3 when you search or sort the database. The field names in figure 12.3 are acceptable because, although the words in row 3 are repeated (two TESTs and three RANKs), each key-field name in row 4 is unique.

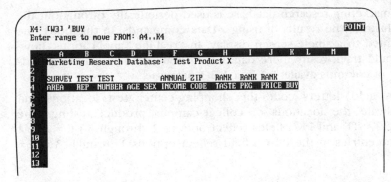

Fig. 12.3.
Creating field
names in a
database.

To control the manner in which cells are displayed on-screen, use 1-2-3's Format and Column Set-Width options. In figure 12.2, notice that the range format in column F is the comma format with zero decimal places, and that column widths on the worksheet vary from 4 to 7 characters.

Note also that whenever a right-justified column of numeric data is adjacent to a left-justified column of label information (AGE..SEX or INCOME..CODE, for example), the data looks crowded. You can insert blank columns to change the spacing between fields, but if you plan to search values in the database, do not leave any blank rows.

Cue:
Insert blank
columns between
fields to prevent
crowding data.

After you alter the column widths, enter the title and field names, and add columns, you can add records to the database. To enter the first record, move the cursor to the row directly below the field-name row and then enter the data across the row in the normal manner.

In the sample marketing research database, the contents of the AREA, REP, NUMBER, SEX, CODE, and BUY fields are entered as labels; the contents of the AGE, INCOME, TASTE, PKG, and PRICE fields are entered as numbers. Figure 12.4 shows the initial data and the column spacing for this database.

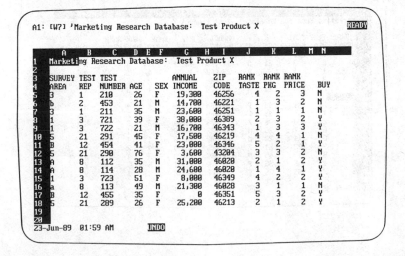

Fig. 12.4.
The marketing
research
database.

This sample marketing research database is used periodically throughout the chapter to illustrate the results of using /Data commands. In this book, the fields are limited to a single screen display. In "real-life" applications, however, you would track many more data items. You can maintain 256 fields (the number of columns available) in a 1-2-3 database.

In the AREA field, letters code the shopping-center test locations and numbers indicate the locations of college-campus product testing. The entries in the TASTE and PKG fields reflect options 1 through 5 (1 = most favorable); the entries in the PRICE field reflect options 1 through 3 (1 = too high).

Modifying a Database

After you collect the data for your database and decide which field types, widths, and formats to use, creating and maintaining the accuracy of a database is easy.

To add and delete records in a database, use the same 1-2-3 commands for inserting and deleting rows you use for any other application. Because records correspond to rows, you begin inserting a record with the /Worksheet Insert Row command. You then fill in the various fields with the appropriate data. Figure 12.5 shows an example of inserting a record in the middle of a database. Instead of inserting a record in the middle of a database, however, you probably will enter the record at the end of the database and then use 1-2-3's sorting capabilities, illustrated in the next section, to rearrange the order of database records.

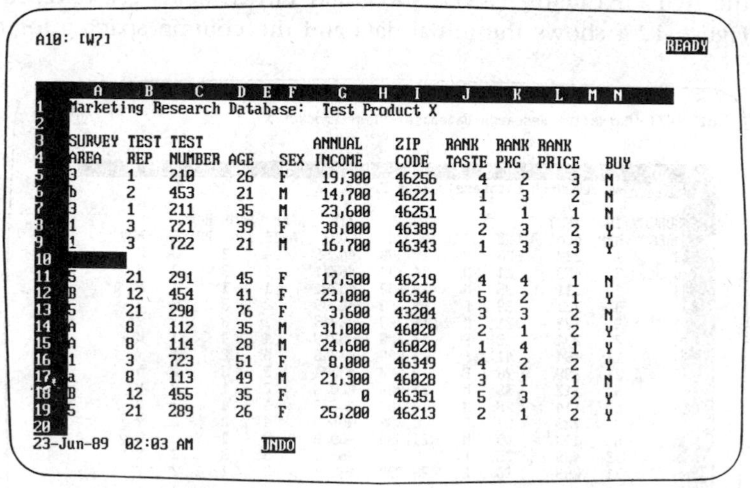

Fig. 12.5.
Inserting a
record row in
the database.

```
A10: [W7]                                                    READY

      A      B     C    D E F    G       H I    J     K    L  M  N
 1 Marketing Research Database:  Test Product X
 2
 3 SURVEY TEST  TEST                 ANNUAL   ZIP   RANK RANK RANK
 4 AREA   REP   NUMBER AGE  SEX INCOME    CODE  TASTE PKG  PRICE  BUY
 5 3      1     210    26   F   19,300    46256   4    2    3    N
 6 b      2     453    21   M   14,700    46221   1    3    2    N
 7 3      1     211    35   M   23,600    46251   1    1    1    N
 8 1      3     721    39   F   38,000    46389   2    3    2    Y
 9 1      3     722    21   M   16,700    46343   1    3    3    Y
10
11 5      21    291    45   F   17,500    46219   4    4    1    N
12 B      12    454    41   F   23,000    46346   5    2    1    Y
13 5      21    290    76   F   3,600     43204   3    3    2    N
14 A      8     112    35   M   31,000    46020   2    1    2    Y
15 A      8     114    28   M   24,600    46020   1    4    1    Y
16 1      3     723    51   F   8,000     46349   4    2    2    Y
17 a      8     113    49   M   21,300    46028   3    1    1    N
18 B      12    455    35   F   0         46351   5    3    2    Y
19 5      21    289    26   F   25,200    46213   2    1    2    Y
20
23-Jun-89  02:03 AM            UNDO
```

To delete records, move your cell pointer to the row or rows you want to delete and use the **/W**orksheet **D**elete **R**ow command. Because you do not have an opportunity to verify the range before you issue the command, be extremely careful when you specify the records to be deleted. If you are using Release 2.2 and accidentally delete a row you want to keep in your database, use Undo (Alt-F4) immediately to restore the original row. If you want to remove only inactive records, consider first using the **E**xtract command to store the extracted inactive records in a separate file before you delete the records.

The process of modifying fields in a database is the same as that for modifying the contents of cells in any other application. As you learned in Chapter 3, you change the cell contents either by retyping the cell entry or by using the Edit (F2) key and editing the entry. If you need to change one or more cells, each containing the exact same data, with an exact replacement, use the **/R**ange **S**earch command. (See Chapter 4 for a discussion of this command.) Using **/R**ange **S**earch, for example, is the easiest way to update a database containing a company name that has changed.

To add a new field to a database, position the cell pointer anywhere in the column that will be to the right of the newly inserted column. Issue the **/W**orksheet **I**nsert **C**olumn command and then fill the field with values for each record. For example, to insert a DATE field between the NUMBER and AGE fields in the marketing research database, position the cell pointer on any cell in the AGE column, issue the **/W**orksheet **I**nsert **C**olumn command, and then type the new field name in D3 and D4 (see fig. 12.6).

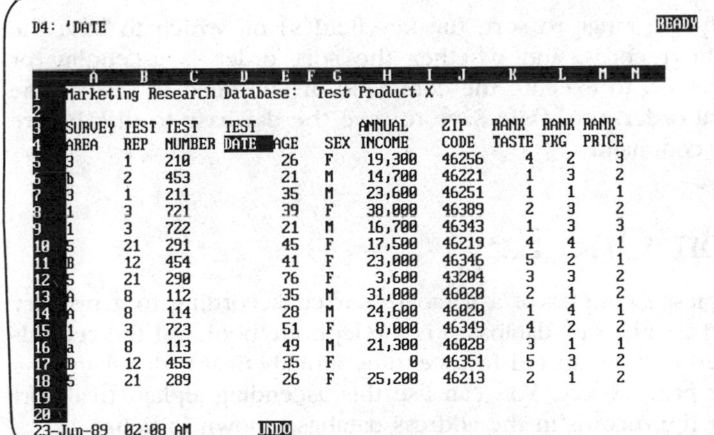

```
D4: 'DATE                                                              READY

       A     B     C     D  E F G   H       I      J     K    L    M   N
 1  Marketing Research Database:   Test Product X
 2
 3  SURVEY TEST  TEST  TEST              ANNUAL  ZIP    RANK RANK RANK
 4  AREA   REP   NUMBER DATE AGE  SEX INCOME  CODE   TASTE PKG  PRICE
 5   3      1    210         26   F    19,300  46256    4    2    3
 6   b      2    453         21   M    14,700  46221    1    3    2
 7   3      1    211         35   M    23,600  46251    1    1    1
 8   1      3    721         39   F    38,000  46389    2    3    2
 9   1      3    722         21   M    16,700  46343    1    3    3
10   5     21    291         45   F    17,500  46219    4    4    1
11   B     12    454         41   F    23,000  46346    5    2    1
12   5     21    290         76   F     3,600  43204    3    3    2
13   A      8    112         35   M    31,000  46020    2    1    2
14   A      8    114         28   M    24,600  46020    1    4    1
15   1      3    723         51   F     8,000  46349    4    2    2
16   a      8    113         49   M    21,300  46028    3    1    1
17   B     12    455         35   F        0   46351    5    3    2
18   5     21    289         26   F    25,200  46213    2    1    2
19
20
23-Jun-89  02:08 AM        UNDO
```

*Fig. 12.6.
Inserting a column for a new field.*

To delete a field, position the cell pointer anywhere in the column you want to remove and then use the **/W**orksheet **D**elete **C**olumn command. If you use Release 2.2 and accidentally delete a column, you can use the Undo (Alt-F4) key to restore the column.

All other commands, such as those for moving cells, formatting cells, displaying the contents of worksheets, and so on, are the same for both database and other worksheet applications.

Sorting Database Records

1-2-3's data-management capability lets you change the order of records by sorting them according to the contents of the fields. Selecting /Data Sort produces the following menu:

Data-Range Primary-Key Secondary-Key Reset Go Quit

Reminder:
Do not include the field-name row when you are designating a data range for sorting your database.

To sort the database, start by designating a data range. This range must be long enough to include all of the records to be sorted and wide enough to include all of the fields in each record. Remember not to include the field-name row in this range. (If you are unfamiliar with how to designate ranges or how to name them, see Chapter 4.)

The data range does not necessarily have to include the entire database. If part of the database already has the organization you want or if you don't want to sort all the records, you can sort only a portion of the database.

After choosing the data range, you must specify the keys for the sort. *Keys* are the fields to which you attach the highest precedence when the database is sorted. The field with the highest precedence is the Primary-Key, and the field with the next highest precedence is the Secondary-Key. You must set a primary key, but the secondary key is optional.

Caution:
Use /File Save before sorting your database, in case you need to restore the original order.

After you specify the range to sort, the key field(s) on which to base the reordering of the records, and whether the sort order is ascending or descending, select Go to execute the command. If you need to restore the file to its original order, use /File Save to save the database to disk before you issue a Sort command.

Sorting on One Key

One of the simplest examples of a database sorted according to a primary key (often called a single-key database) is a telephone book. All the records in the telephone book are sorted in ascending alphabetical order using the last name as the primary key. You can use this ascending alphabetical sort order to reorder the records in the address database shown in figure 12.7.

To sort the records alphabetically on the LAST name field, select /Data Sort Data-Range. At the prompt for a range to sort, enter A2..F19. After you specify the range, the Data Sort menu is displayed again so that you don't have to enter /Data Sort at the beginning of each command. If you are using Release

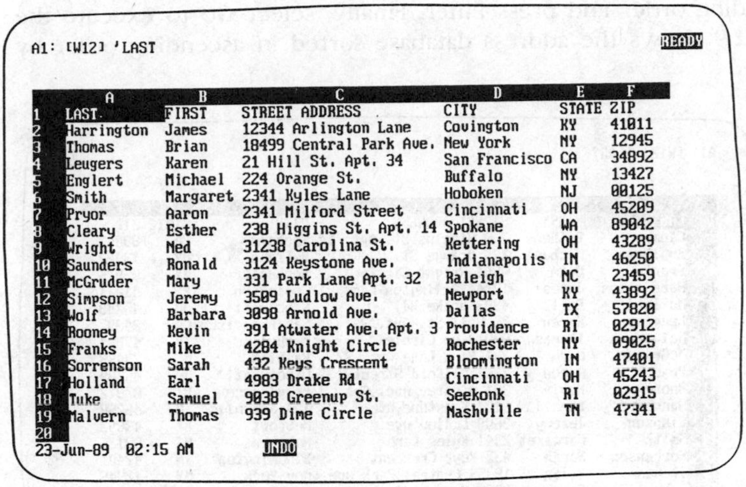

```
A1: [W12] 'LAST                                              READY

       A          B          C                   D              E     F
1  LAST.       FIRST      STREET ADDRESS .        CITY           STATE ZIP
2  Harrington  James      12344 Arlington Lane    Covington      KY    41811
3  Thomas      Brian      18499 Central Park Ave. New York       NY    12945
4  Leugers     Karen      21 Hill St. Apt. 34     San Francisco  CA    34892
5  Englert     Michael    224 Orange St.          Buffalo        NY    13427
6  Smith       Margaret   2341 Kyles Lane         Hoboken        NJ    00125
7  Pryor       Aaron      2341 Milford Street      Cincinnati     OH    45209
8  Cleary      Esther     238 Higgins St. Apt. 14 Spokane        WA    89042
9  Wright      Ned        31238 Carolina St.      Kettering      OH    43289
10 Saunders    Ronald     3124 Keystone Ave.      Indianapolis   IN    46250
11 McGruder    Mary       331 Park Lane Apt. 32   Raleigh        NC    23459
12 Simpson     Jeremy     3589 Ludlow Ave.        Newport        KY    43892
13 Wolf        Barbara    3898 Arnold Ave.        Dallas         TX    57820
14 Rooney      Kevin      391 Atwater Ave. Apt. 3 Providence     RI    02912
15 Franks      Mike       4284 Knight Circle      Rochester      NY    09025
16 Sorrenson   Sarah      432 Keys Crescent       Bloomington    IN    47401
17 Holland     Earl       4983 Drake Rd.          Cincinnati     OH    45243
18 Tuke        Samuel     9038 Greenup St.        Seekonk        RI    02915
19 Malvern     Thomas     939 Dime Circle         Nashville      TN    47341
20
23-Jun-89  02:15 AM           UNDO
```

Fig. 12.7.
The unsorted address database.

2.2, notice that a settings sheet is displayed when you select **/D**ata **S**ort. This sheet indicates any data range and primary and secondary key settings you may have entered (see fig. 12.8).

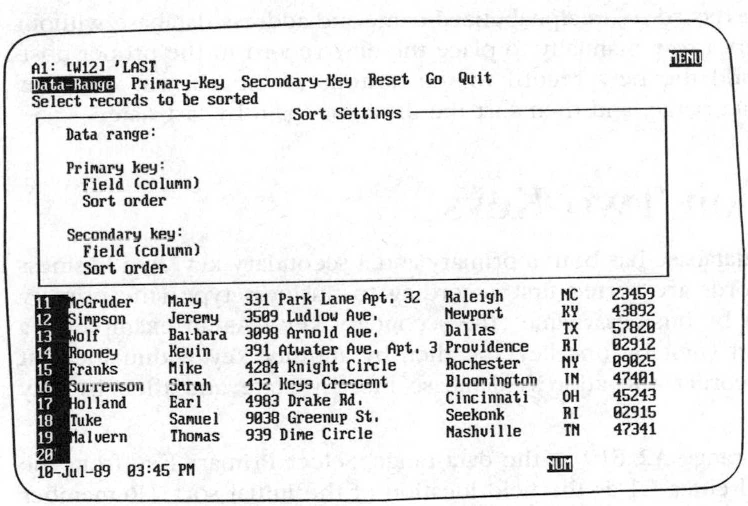

RELEASE
2.2

```
A1: [W12] 'LAST                                              MENU
Data-Range  Primary-Key  Secondary-Key  Reset  Go  Quit
Select records to be sorted
                           ─── Sort Settings ───
    Data range:

    Primary key:
       Field (column)
       Sort order

    Secondary key:
       Field (column)
       Sort order

11 McGruder    Mary      331 Park Lane Apt. 32   Raleigh      NC  23459
12 Simpson     Jeremy    3589 Ludlow Ave.        Newport      KY  43892
13 Wolf        Barbara   3898 Arnold Ave.        Dallas       TX  57820
14 Rooney      Kevin     391 Atwater Ave. Apt. 3 Providence   RI  02912
15 Franks      Mike      4284 Knight Circle      Rochester    NY  09025
16 Sorrenson   Sarah     432 Keys Crescent       Bloomington  IN  47401
17 Holland     Earl      4983 Drake Rd.          Cincinnati   OH  45243
18 Tuke        Samuel    9038 Greenup St.        Seekonk      RI  02915
19 Malvern     Thomas    939 Dime Circle         Nashville    TN  47341
20
10-Jul-89  03:45 PM           NUM
```

Fig. 12.8.
The settings sheet displayed when you select /Data Sort in Release 2.2.

After choosing the data range, select **P**rimary-**K**ey and then enter or point to the address of any entry (including blank or field-name cells) in the column that contains the primary-key field. For example, enter **A1** as the **P**rimary-**K**ey in the address database. 1-2-3 then asks you to enter a sort order (A or D). A stands for Ascending and D for Descending. For this example, choose **A**scending order and press Enter. Finally, select **G**o to execute the sort. Figure 12.9 shows the address database sorted in ascending order by last name.

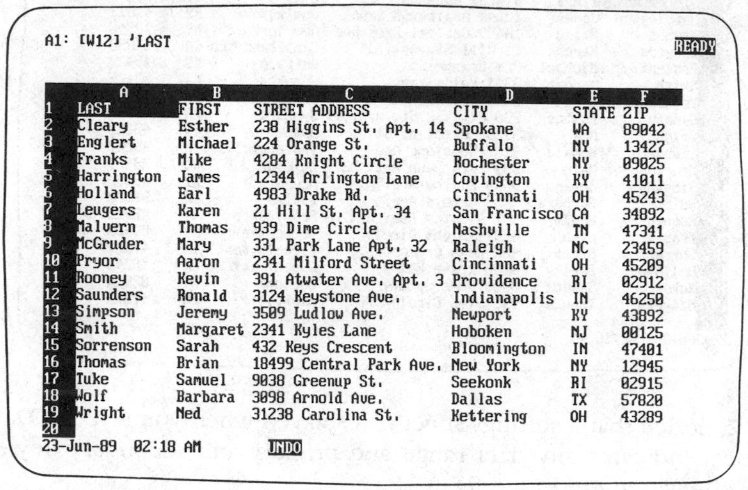

Fig. 12.9.
The address
database sorted
by LAST name.

```
A1: [W12] 'LAST                                                    READY

      A           B         C                    D            E     F
 1  LAST        FIRST     STREET ADDRESS         CITY        STATE ZIP
 2  Cleary      Esther    238 Higgins St. Apt. 14 Spokane    WA    89042
 3  Englert     Michael   224 Orange St.         Buffalo      NY    13427
 4  Franks      Mike      4204 Knight Circle     Rochester    NY    09025
 5  Harrington  James     12344 Arlington Lane   Covington    KY    41011
 6  Holland     Earl      4983 Drake Rd.         Cincinnati   OH    45243
 7  Leugers     Karen     21 Hill St. Apt. 34    San Francisco CA   34892
 8  Malvern     Thomas    939 Dime Circle        Nashville    TN    47341
 9  McGruder    Mary      331 Park Lane Apt. 32  Raleigh      NC    23459
10  Pryor       Aaron     2341 Milford Street    Cincinnati   OH    45209
11  Rooney      Kevin     391 Atwater Ave. Apt. 3 Providence  RI    02912
12  Saunders    Ronald    3124 Keystone Ave.     Indianapolis IN    46250
13  Simpson     Jeremy    3509 Ludlow Ave.       Newport      KY    43892
14  Smith       Margaret  2341 Kyles Lane        Hoboken      NJ    00125
15  Sorrenson   Sarah     432 Keys Crescent      Bloomington  IN    47401
16  Thomas      Brian     18499 Central Park Ave. New York    NY    12945
17  Tuke        Samuel    9838 Greenup St.       Seekonk      RI    02915
18  Wolf        Barbara   3098 Arnold Ave.       Dallas       TX    57820
19  Wright      Ned       31238 Carolina St.     Kettering    OH    43289
20

23-Jun-89  02:18 AM          UNDO
```

Cue:
Add a new record
to a sorted
database by
entering the record
at the bottom of
your database and
then resorting the
database.

You can add a record to an alphabetized name-and-address database without having to insert a row manually to place the new record in the proper position. Simply add the new record to the bottom of the current database, expand the data range, and then sort the database again by last name.

Sorting on Two Keys

A double-key database has both a primary and a secondary key. In a business directory, records are sorted first according to business type (the primary key) and then by business name (the secondary key). As an example of a double-key sort (first by one key and then by another key within the first sort order), reorder the address database first by state and then by city within state.

Designate the range A2..F19 as the data range. Select **P**rimary-Key from the **S**ort menu and enter **E1** as the field location of the initial sort. (Remember that you can specify any cell in column E.) Press **A** for ascending order for the sort by STATE. Select **S**econdary-Key, enter **D1**, and choose **A** for ascending sort order by CITY. Finally, issue the **G**o command. Figure 12.10 shows the results of the two-key sort.

As you can see, records are now grouped first by state in alphabetical order (California, Indiana, Kentucky, and so on) and then by city within state (Bloomington, Indiana before Indianapolis, Indiana). When you determine

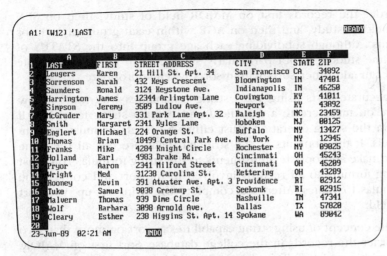

Fig. 12.10.
The address database sorted by CITY within STATE.

```
A1: [W12] 'LAST                                              READY

       A          B           C                  D          E      F
1    LAST       FIRST       STREET ADDRESS       CITY       STATE ZIP
2    Leugers    Karen       21 Hill St. Apt. 34  San Francisco CA  34892
3    Sorrenson  Sarah       432 Keys Crescent    Bloomington   IN  47401
4    Saunders   Ronald      3124 Keystone Ave.   Indianapolis  IN  46258
5    Harrington James       12344 Arlington Lane Covington     KY  41011
6    Simpson    Jeremy      3589 Ludlow Ave.     Newport       KY  43892
7    McGruder   Mary        331 Park Lane Apt. 32 Raleigh      NC  23459
8    Smith      Margaret    2341 Myles Lane      Hoboken       NJ  00125
9    Englert    Michael     224 Orange St.       Buffalo       NY  13427
10   Thomas     Brian       10499 Central Park Ave. New York   NY  12945
11   Franks     Mike        4284 Knight Circle   Rochester     NY  09025
12   Holland    Earl        4983 Drake Rd.       Cincinnati    OH  45243
13   Pryor      Aaron       2341 Milford Street  Cincinnati    OH  45289
14   Wright     Ned         31238 Carolina St.   Kettering     OH  43289
15   Rooney     Kevin       391 Atwater Ave. Apt. 3 Providence RI  02912
16   Tuke       Samuel      9038 Greenup St.     Seekonk       RI  02915
17   Malvern    Thomas      939 Dine Circle      Nashville     TN  47341
18   Wolf       Barbara     3098 Arnold Ave.     Dallas        TX  57820
19   Cleary     Esther      238 Higgins St. Apt. 14 Spokane    WA  89042
20

23-Jun-89  02:21 AM        UNDO
```

whether to use a primary or secondary key, be sure to request a reasonable sort. For example, do not try to sort first on city and then on state within city. Also, whenever possible, you may want to place the key fields at the leftmost column in your database. With this placement, you won't have to hunt for the results of the sort.

Sorting on More Than Two Keys

Although 1-2-3 seems to limit you to sorting on only two keys, you can bypass this apparent limitation by using the program's *string* capabilities. Suppose that you want to reorder the four fields of student information in the college database shown in figure 12.11.

```
A1: [W7] 'STATUS                                             READY

       A        B            C     D    E    F    G    H
1    STATUS   MAJOR         SEX  AGE
2    Full     Accounting    M    22
3    Part     Finance       F    19
4    Full     Accounting    F    27
5    Full     Marketing     F    33
6    Full     Administration M   20
7    Part     Finance       M    19
8    Part     Accounting    F    26
9    Full     Accounting    F    35
10   Full     Marketing     F    19
11   Full     Accounting    F    20
12   Full     Finance       M    19
13   Full     Finance       M    31
14   Full     Finance       M    26
15   Part     Accounting    F    29
16   Full     Accounting    F    42
17   Part     Accounting    M    27
18   Part     Finance       F    48
19   Part     Marketing     F    33
20   Part     Administration M   19
23-Jun-89  02:24 AM        UNDO
```

Fig. 12.11.
The unsorted college database.

You can reorder the records first on MAJOR field of study, then on SEX within each field of study, and then on AGE within each group of male or female students. Although subdividing each age group into the STATUS of full- or part-time student is not particularly significant in this small sample database, you can add other sorts within sorts when appropriate.

To generate accurate sorts using 1-2-3 string capabilities, you must follow certain rules. You must create a new field and enter a string formula. All fields joined in the string operation must either be labels or must be converted to labels. If the contents of the stringed fields are not all the same size, you must make appropriate adjustments to the string formula. You must copy the string formula to all records involved in the sort and convert the resultant formulas to values. After you complete the string set-up, you sort on the new field.

To illustrate the concept of using string capabilities to sort on more than two keys, let's reorder the records in the college database. Sort first on MAJOR, then on SEX within major, followed by AGE within sex, and then STATUS within age.

As the first step in the sort process, you create a new field and enter a string formula (see fig. 12.12). To create the new field name, enter **SORT-KEY** in cell E1. Then enter the formula **+B2&" "&C2&" "&@STRING(D2,0)&" "&A2** in cell E2. Notice that the formula appears in the control panel and that the results of the formula display the label fields concatenated (strung together) in the highlighted cell.

Fig. 12.12.
Entering a string formula for a multiple-key sort.

```
E2: +B2&" "&C2&" "&@STRING(D2,0)&" "&A2                        READY

      A        B               C     D    E          F       G       H
1  STATUS  MAJOR             SEX   AGE  SORT-KEY
2  Full    Accounting        M      22  Accounting M 22 Full
3  Part    Finance           F      19
4  Full    Accounting        F      27
5  Full    Marketing         F      33
6  Full    Administration    M      20
7  Part    Finance           M      19
8  Part    Accounting        F      26
9  Full    Accounting        F      35
10 Full    Marketing         F      19
11 Full    Accounting        F      20
12 Full    Finance           M      19
13 Full    Finance           M      31
14 Full    Finance           M      26
15 Part    Accounting        F      29
16 Full    Accounting        F      42
17 Part    Accounting        M      27
18 Part    Finance           F      48
19 Part    Marketing         F      33
20 Part    Administration    M      19
23-Jun-89  02:29 AM          UNDO
```

The following listing breaks down the formula in cell E2 so that you can better understand it:

Formula piece	Description
+B2	Indicates the initial sort on MAJOR
&	String concatenation symbol
" "	Places a space after the contents of B2
&C2&" "	Indicates the secondary sort on SEX
&@STRING	Begins to add a third sort dimension on AGE. @STRING converts a numeric field to a label field. All stringed fields must be labels; otherwise, the formula returns an ERR message.
(D2,0)&" "	Encloses the numeric field D2 in parentheses, followed by a comma and specifies decimal places (in this case, zero)
&A2	Adds a fourth sort dimension on STATUS

As the next step in setting up a sort that uses string capabilities, you need to copy the new formula to all the other fields in column E that fall within the specified data range. Figure 12.13 shows the results of copying the formula in E2 to the range E3..E20. (The cell pointer has been moved to E4 to show that the cell contents are currently in formula form.)

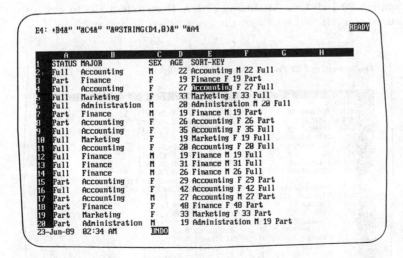

Fig. 12.13.
The results of
copying the
string formula.

For the string sort to work properly, you must convert the new formulas in column E to values. Use **/R**ange **V**alue and specify E2..E20 as both the range to copy FROM and the range to copy TO. This step converts all the formulas to values. As you can see from figure 12.14, the column E display does not change. But if you compare figures 12.13 and 12.14, notice that the control panel in the figure 12.13 displays cell E4's formula content, whereas the control panel in figure 12.14 displays the contents of cell E4 as nonformula data.

Fig. 12.14.
Changing the string formulas to values.

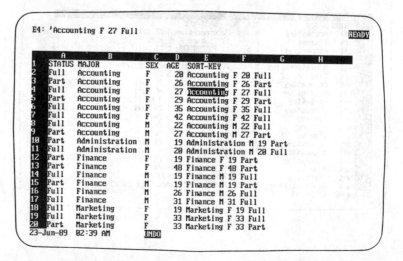

To begin the sort operation, select **/D**ata **S**ort **D**ata-Range and specify A2..E20 as the range to sort. Select **P**rimary-Key, enter any cell in column E (E1, for example), and choose **A**scending order. Then select **G**o to execute this sort. Your screen should look like the one shown in figure 12.15.

Fig. 12.15.
The results of executing a multiple-key sort.

Notice that major fields of study are grouped alphabetically, that study fields are subdivided into female and male categories, and that each of these subgroups is further sorted by age. For example, the 6 female accounting majors rank in age from 20 to 42 years. Splitting a duplicate age (Finance M 19 or Marketing F 33, for example) into a fourth subdivision (by status) does not produce meaningful data.

You can bypass 1-2-3's limited menu selections by stringing together any three (or more) meaningful sort keys. For example, try a different string sort on the college database. This time, use full- or part-time STATUS as the primary key, followed by SEX within STATUS, and then by MAJOR within SEX. The control panel in figure 12.16 displays the string formula required to set up this sort.

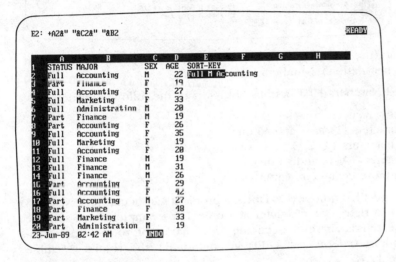

Fig. 12.16.
Entering an alternative sort-string formula.

If you copy the formula down column E, change the formulas to values, and execute the sort, the results of this alternative sort appear as shown in figure 12.17.

Determining the Collating Sequence

The order in which the records appear after the sort depends on the ASCII numbers of the contents of the primary and secondary keys. For this reason, you should not include blank rows past the end of the database when you designate the data range. Because blanks have precedence over all the characters in a sort, these blank rows appear at the top of your sorted database.

By using the Install program, you can determine the order of precedence that 1-2-3 uses for sorting text strings by specifying one of these choices:

Caution:
Do not include blank rows past the end of the database when you designate the data range for a sort.

Reminder:
You can use the Install program to change the order of precedence that 1-2-3 uses for sorting.

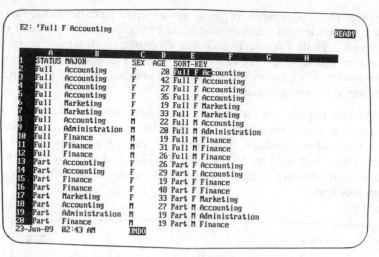

Fig. 12.17.
The results of the alternative string sort.

Numbers First (the default sort order if you do not specify another sort order during installation), Numbers Last, or ASCII.

The ASCII and Numbers First options both sort in the following order:

Blank spaces
Special characters (!, #, $, and so on)
Numeric characters (1, 2, 3, 4, and so on)
Alpha characters (A, b, and so on)
Special compose characters (international characters)

When you've specified numbers as labels, a problem can occur because 1-2-3 sorts from left to right, one character at a time. For example, if you sort the marketing research database in ascending order according to the representative who administered the test (REP, in column B), the results resemble those in figure 12.18.

Fig. 12.18.
An erroneous ascending sort.

```
B4: [W5] 'REP                                                    READY

     A    B     C    D E F   G       H    I     J    K    L M N
 1  Marketing Research Database:    Test Product X
 2
 3  SURVEY TEST TEST            ANNUAL   ZIP  RANK RANK RANK
 4  AREA   REP  NUMBER AGE  SEX INCOME   CODE TASTE PKG PRICE  BUY
 5  3      1    211    35   M   23,600   46251  1    1    1    N
 6  3      1    210    26   F   19,300   46256  4    2    3    N
 7  B      12   455    35   F        0   46351  5    3    2    Y
 8  B      12   454    41   F   23,000   46346  5    2    1    Y
 9  b      2    453    21   M   14,700   46221  1    3    2    N
10  5      21   290    76   F    3,600   43204  3    3    2    N
11  5      21   291    45   F   17,500   46219  4    4    1    N
12  5      21   289    26   F   25,200   46213  2    1    2    Y
13  1      3    723    51   F    8,000   46349  4    2    2    Y
14  1      3    721    39   F   38,000   46389  2    3    2    Y
15  1      3    722    21   M   16,700   46343  1    3    3    Y
16  a      8    113    49   M   21,300   46028  3    1    1    N
17  A      8    114    28   M   24,600   46020  1    4    1    Y
18  A      8    112    35   M   31,000   46020  2    1    2    Y
19
20
23-Jun-89  02:47 AM          UNDO
```

Although you would expect the records to be sorted in ascending order on the REP field, notice that the 12 in rows 7 and 8 appears before the 2 in row 9, and that 21 appears before 3. This problem occurs because 1-2-3 sorts the numbers 1 character at a time when sorting labels. To bypass the problem, enter a zero (0) before each single-character REP field. Figure 12.19 shows the corrected sort.

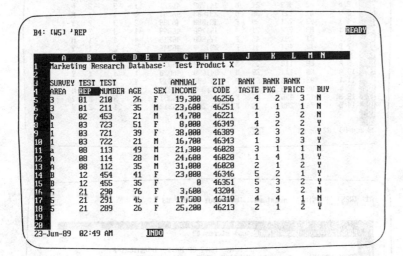

Fig. 12.19.
The corrected
ascending sort.

Restoring the Presort Order

If you sort the original contents of the database on any field, such as the REP field, you cannot restore the records to their original order. If you add a "counter" column to the database before any sort, however, you can reorder the records on any field and then restore the original order by resorting on the counter field.

Figure 12.20 shows the counter field NUM, which has been added in column A. After you sort the database on a particular column, you can sort again on the NUM field to restore the records to their original order.

Cue:
Add a "counter"
field to your
database in case
you want to restore
records to their
original order.

Searching for Records

You have learned how to use the Sort option to reorganize information from the database by sorting records according to key fields. In this section, you learn how to use Query, the Data menu's other data-retrieval command, to search for records and then edit, extract, or delete the records you find.

You can use the tools inventory database shown in figure 12.21 to learn the basic concepts of 1-2-3's search (also called *query*) operations.

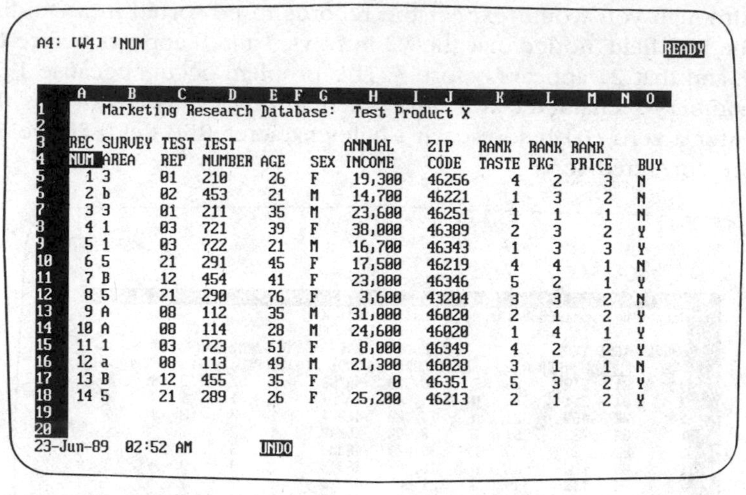

Fig. 12.20.
Inserting a counter field in an original database.

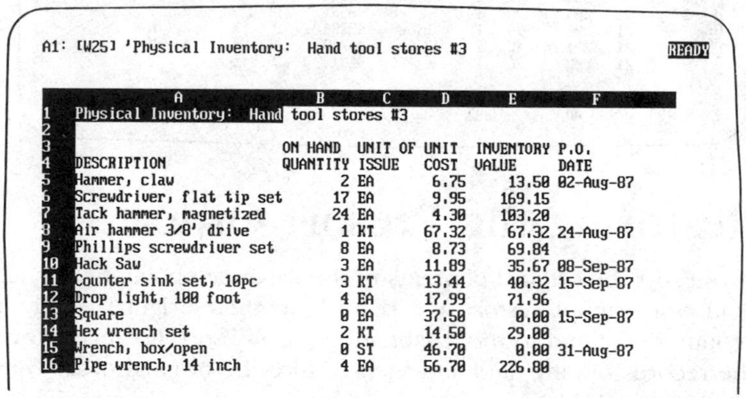

```
A4: [W4] 'NUM                                                    READY

       A    B      C     D     EFG      H        I    J    K     L    M   N   O
1           Marketing Research Database:   Test Product X
2
3     REC SURVEY TEST  TEST               ANNUAL   ZIP    RANK  RANK RANK
4     NUM AREA   REP   NUMBER AGE   SEX   INCOME   CODE   TASTE PKG  PRICE  BUY
5      1 3       01    210    26    F     19,300   46256   4    2    3      N
6      2 b       02    453    21    M     14,700   46221   1    3    2      N
7      3 3       01    211    35    M     23,600   46251   1    1    1      N
8      4 1       03    721    39    F     38,000   46389   2    3    2      Y
9      5 1       03    722    21    M     16,700   46343   1    3    3      Y
10     6 5       21    291    45    F     17,500   46219   4    4    1      N
11     7 B       12    454    41    F     23,000   46346   5    2    1      Y
12     8 5       21    290    76    F     3,600    43204   3    3    2      N
13     9 A       00    112    35    M     31,000   46020   2    1    2      Y
14    10 A       00    114    28    M     24,600   46020   1    4    1      Y
15    11 1       03    723    51    F     8,000    46349   4    2    2      Y
16    12 a       00    113    49    M     21,300   46028   3    1    1      N
17    13 B       12    455    35    F     0        46351   5    3    2      Y
18    14 5       21    289    26    F     25,200   46213   2    1    2      Y
19
20
23-Jun-89  02:52 AM              UNDO
```

Fig. 12.21.
The initial tools inventory database.

```
A1: [W25] 'Physical Inventory:  Hand tool stores #3              READY

                A               B       C     D        E       F
1     Physical Inventory: Hand tool stores #3
2
3                            ON HAND UNIT OF UNIT  INVENTORY P.O.
4     DESCRIPTION            QUANTITY ISSUE  COST  VALUE     DATE
5     Hammer, claw              2     EA     6.75    13.50 02-Aug-87
6     Screwdriver, flat tip set 17    EA     9.95   169.15
7     Tack hammer, magnetized   24    EA     4.30   103.20
8     Air hammer 3/8' drive     1     KT    67.32    67.32 24-Aug-87
9     Phillips screwdriver set  8     EA     8.73    69.84
10    Hack Saw                  3     EA    11.89    35.67 08-Sep-87
11    Counter sink set, 10pc    3     KT    13.44    40.32 15-Sep-87
12    Drop light, 100 foot      4     EA    17.99    71.96
13    Square                    0     EA    37.50     0.00 15-Sep-87
14    Hex wrench set            2     KT    14.50    29.00
15    Wrench, box/open          0     ST    46.70     0.00 31-Aug-87
16    Pipe wrench, 14 inch      4     EA    56.70   226.80
```

Looking for records that meet certain conditions is the simplest form of searching a 1-2-3 database. To determine when to reorder items, for example, you can use a search operation to find any records with an on-hand quantity of less than four units.

Once you have located the information you want, you can extract the found records from the database to another section of the worksheet separate from the database. For example, you can extract all records with a specified purchase order (P.O.) date and print the extracted area as a record of pending purchases.

With 1-2-3's search operations, you also have the option of looking for only the first occurrence of a specified field value. Using this feature, you can develop a unique list of field entries. For example, you can search the ISSUE field to extract a list of the different units of issue. Finally, you can delete all inventory records for which quantity on-hand equals zero (if you don't want to reorder these items).

Understanding the Minimum Search Requirements

To initiate any search operation, you need to select the operation from the **Data Query** menu:

Input Criteria Output Find Extract Unique Delete Reset Quit

If you are using Release 2.2, notice that a settings sheet is displayed when you select /**Data Query**. This setting sheet indicates any input, criteria, or output ranges that may have been entered for the current worksheet (see fig. 12.22).

```
A1: [W25] 'Physical Inventory:  Hand tool stores #3              MENU
Input  Criteria Output Find  Extract Unique Delete  Reset Quit
Specify range that contains records to search
                    ───── Query Settings ─────
     Input range:

     Criteria range:

     Output range:

 7  Tack hammer, magnetized       24 EA      4.30    103.20
 8  Air hammer 3/8' drive          1 KT     67.32     67.32 24-Aug-87
 9  Phillips screwdriver set       8 EA      8.73     69.84
10  Hack Saw                       3 EA     11.89     35.67 08-Sep-87
11  Counter sink set, 10pc         3 KT     13.44     40.32 15-Sep-87
12  Drop light, 100 foot           4 EA     17.99     71.96
13  Square                         0 EA     37.50      0.00 15-Sep-87
14  Hex wrench set                 2 KT     14.50     29.00
15  Wrench, box/open               0 ST     46.70      0.00 31-Aug-87
16  Pipe wrench, 14 inch           4 EA     56.70    226.80
```

Fig. 12.22.
The settings sheet displayed when you select /*Data Query in Release 2.2.*

You can use the first three options to specify ranges applicable to the search operations. You must specify **Input** and **Criteria**, which give the locations of the search area and the search conditions, respectively, in all **Query** operations. (If you are using Release 2.01, Criterion appears rather than Criteria within the **Data Query** menu and when used in prompts that are displayed in the control panel.) You must establish an output range only when you select a **Query** command that copies records or parts of records to an area outside the database.

The last two options signal the end of the current search operation. **Reset** removes all previous search-related ranges so that you can specify a different search location and conditions. **Quit** restores the main **Data** menu.

The four options in the middle of the **Query** menu perform the following search functions:

Option	Description
Find	Moves down through a database and positions the cursor on records that match given criteria. You can enter or change data in the records.
Extract	Creates copies, in a specified area of the worksheet, of all or some of the fields in certain records that match the given criteria.
Unique	Similar to **Extract**, but recognizes that some of the field contents in the database may be duplicates of other cell entries in the same fields. Eliminates duplicates as entries are copied to the output range.
Delete	Deletes from a database all the records that match given criteria and shifts the remaining records to fill in the gaps that remain.

To perform a **Query** operation, you must specify both an input range and a criteria range and select one of the four search options. (Before issuing a **Unique** or **Extract** command, you must also specify an output range.)

Determining the Input Range

The input range for the **/Data Query** command is the range of records you want to search. The specified area does not have to include the entire database. In the tools inventory database, specifying an input range of A4..F16 defines the area of search as the entire database. Entering A4..B16 as the input range limits the search area to the fields for tool descriptions and on-hand quantities.

Reminder:
You must include the field name in the input range whether you search all or only part of a database.

Whether you search all or only part of a database, you must include the field-name row in the input range. If the field names occupy space on more than one row, specify only the bottom row to start the input range. In the tools inventory database, for example, even though rows 3 and 4 both contain portions of the field names, you enter A4..F16 instead of A3..F16 for the input range.

Next, select **/Data Query Input** and specify the range by typing or pointing to a range or by using an assigned range name. You do not have to specify the range again unless the search area changes.

Determining the Criteria Range

When you want 1-2-3 to search for records that meet certain criteria, you must be able to talk to 1-2-3 in terms the program will understand. Suppose that you want to identify all records in the address database that contain OH in the STATE field. When the database is on-screen and 1-2-3 is in READY mode, type **STATE** in cell H2 and **OH** in cell H3 (see fig. 12.23). Type **Criteria Range** in cell H1 only if you want the documentation it provides; cell H1 is not directly involved in the search command.

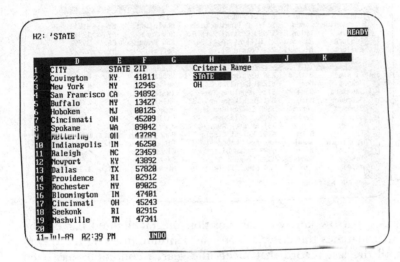

Fig. 12.23.
Establishing a
single search
condition.

Select **/D**ata **Q**uery and specify A1..F19 as the input range. The **Q**uery menu is displayed in the control panel as soon as you enter the input range. Select **C**riteria and then type, point to, or name the range H2..H3 as the location of your search condition. The **Q**uery menu is displayed again.

You can use numbers, labels, or formulas as criteria. A criteria range can be up to 32 columns wide and 2 or more rows long. The first row must contain the field names of the search criteria, such as STATE in row 2. The rows below the unique field names contain the actual criteria, such as OH in row 3. The field names in the input range and the criteria range must match.

By entering the input and criteria ranges, you have completed the minimum requirements for executing a **F**ind or **D**elete command. Be sure to enter the specific field names above the conditions in the worksheet (in READY mode) before you use the **/D**ata **Q**uery **C**riteria command sequence.

Caution:
The criteria range
must include the
field name(s) in the
first row and
criteria in the
second row.

Issuing the Find Command

When you select **F**ind from the **Q**uery menu, a highlighted bar rests on the first record (in the input range) that meets the conditions specified in the criteria range. In figure 12.24, the highlighted bar rests on the first record that includes OH in the STATE field.

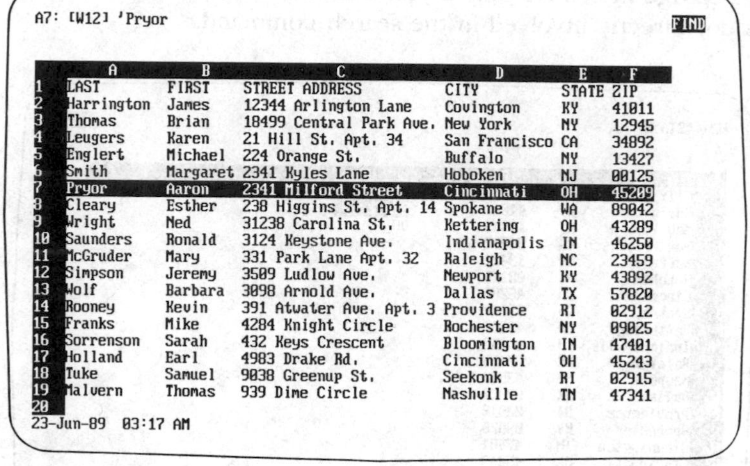

Fig. 12.24.
The first record highlighted in a find operation.

```
A7: [W12] 'Pryor                                                    FIND

     A          B         C                     D           E     F
1  LAST       FIRST     STREET ADDRESS         CITY        STATE ZIP
2  Harrington James     12344 Arlington Lane   Covington   KY    41011
3  Thomas     Brian     10499 Central Park Ave. New York   NY    12945
4  Leugers    Karen     21 Hill St. Apt. 34    San Francisco CA  34892
5  Englert    Michael   224 Orange St.         Buffalo     NY    13427
6  Smith      Margaret  2341 Kyles Lane        Hoboken     NJ    00125
7  Pryor      Aaron     2341 Milford Street    Cincinnati  OH    45209
8  Cleary     Esther    238 Higgins St. Apt. 14 Spokane    WA    89042
9  Wright     Ned       31238 Carolina St.     Kettering   OH    43289
10 Saunders   Ronald    3124 Keystone Ave.     Indianapolis IN   46250
11 McGruder   Mary      331 Park Lane Apt. 32  Raleigh     NC    23459
12 Simpson    Jeremy    3509 Ludlow Ave.       Newport     KY    43892
13 Wolf       Barbara   3098 Arnold Ave.       Dallas      TX    57820
14 Rooney     Kevin     391 Atwater Ave. Apt. 3 Providence RI    02912
15 Franks     Mike      4284 Knight Circle     Rochester   NY    09025
16 Sorrenson  Sarah     432 Keys Crescent      Bloomington IN    47401
17 Holland    Earl      4983 Drake Rd.         Cincinnati  OH    45243
18 Tuke       Samuel    9038 Greenup St.       Seekonk     RI    02915
19 Malvern    Thomas    939 Dime Circle        Nashville   TN    47341
20
23-Jun-89  03:17 AM
```

Reminder:
The up- and down-arrow keys let you highlight the previous and next records that match the search criteria.

By using the down-arrow key, you can position the highlighted bar on the next record that matches the criteria. You can continue pressing the down-arrow key until the last record that meets the search conditions has been highlighted (see fig. 12.25). Notice that the mode indicator changes from READY to FIND during the search.

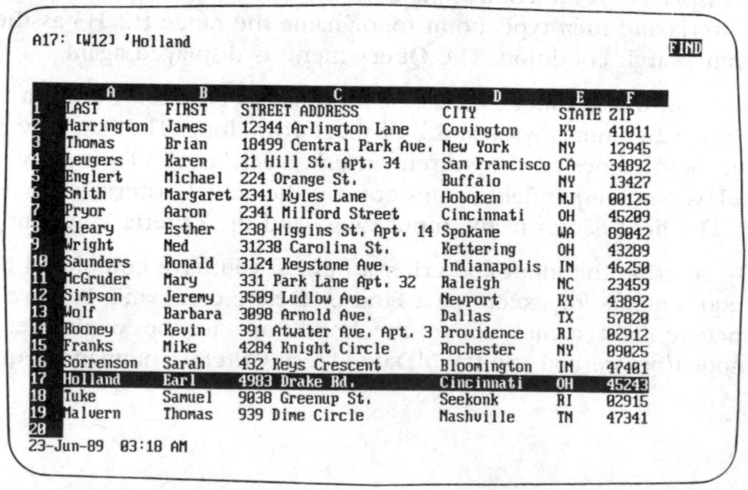

Fig. 12.25.
The last record highlighted in a find operation.

```
A17: [W12] 'Holland                                                 FIND

     A          B         C                     D           E     F
1  LAST       FIRST     STREET ADDRESS         CITY        STATE ZIP
2  Harrington James     12344 Arlington Lane   Covington   KY    41011
3  Thomas     Brian     10499 Central Park Ave. New York   NY    12945
4  Leugers    Karen     21 Hill St. Apt. 34    San Francisco CA  34892
5  Englert    Michael   224 Orange St.         Buffalo     NY    13427
6  Smith      Margaret  2341 Kyles Lane        Hoboken     NJ    00125
7  Pryor      Aaron     2341 Milford Street    Cincinnati  OH    45209
8  Cleary     Esther    238 Higgins St. Apt. 14 Spokane    WA    89042
9  Wright     Ned       31238 Carolina St.     Kettering   OH    43289
10 Saunders   Ronald    3124 Keystone Ave.     Indianapolis IN   46250
11 McGruder   Mary      331 Park Lane Apt. 32  Raleigh     NC    23459
12 Simpson    Jeremy    3509 Ludlow Ave.       Newport     KY    43892
13 Wolf       Barbara   3098 Arnold Ave.       Dallas      TX    57820
14 Rooney     Kevin     391 Atwater Ave. Apt. 3 Providence RI    02912
15 Franks     Mike      4284 Knight Circle     Rochester   NY    09025
16 Sorrenson  Sarah     432 Keys Crescent      Bloomington IN    47401
17 Holland    Earl      4983 Drake Rd.         Cincinnati  OH    45243
18 Tuke       Samuel    9038 Greenup St.       Seekonk     RI    02915
19 Malvern    Thomas    939 Dime Circle        Nashville   TN    47341
20
23-Jun-89  03:18 AM
```

The down- and up-arrow keys let you position the cursor to the next and previous records that match the search criteria set in the criteria range. Use the Home and End keys to position the cursor on the first and last records in the database, even if those records do not fit the search criteria. In FIND mode, you can use the left- and right-arrow keys to move the cursor to different fields in the current highlighted record. Then enter new values or use the Edit (F2) key to update the values in the field. One caution: If you change the record so that it no longer satisfies the criteria and then move away from that record, you cannot use the down- or up-arrow key to return to the record during the find operation.

To end the find operation and return to the **Data Query** menu, press Enter or Esc. To return directly to READY mode, press Ctrl-Break.

Listing All Specified Records

The Find command has limited use, especially in a large database, because the command must scroll through the entire file if you want to view each record that meets the specified criteria. As an alternative to the Find command, you can use the **Extract** command to copy to a blank area of the worksheet only those records that meet the conditions. (Before you issue the command, you must define the blank area of the worksheet as an output range.) You can view a list of all the extracted records, print the range of the newly extracted records, or use the **/File Xtract** command to copy the extracted records to a new file on disk.

Cue:
Copy extracted records to a new file by using /File Xtract.

Defining the Output Range

Choose a blank area in the worksheet as the output range to receive records copied in an extract operation. Designate the range to the right or below the database. In figure 12.26, for example, both the criteria range and the output range have been placed below the records in the address database.

In the first row of the output range, copy the names of only those fields whose contents you want to extract. You do not have to copy these names in the same order as they appear in the database. (In figure 12.26, the output-range entry in cell A27 is for documentation purposes only, and all field names in row 28 have been reproduced in the existing order of the database.)

The field names in both the criteria and output ranges must match the corresponding field names in the input range. To avoid mismatch errors, use the **/Copy** command to copy the database field names in the criteria and output ranges.

Reminder:
Field names in the criteria and output ranges must match the corresponding field names in the input range.

Select **/Data Query Output**; then type, point to, or name the range location of the output area. You can create an open-ended extract area by entering

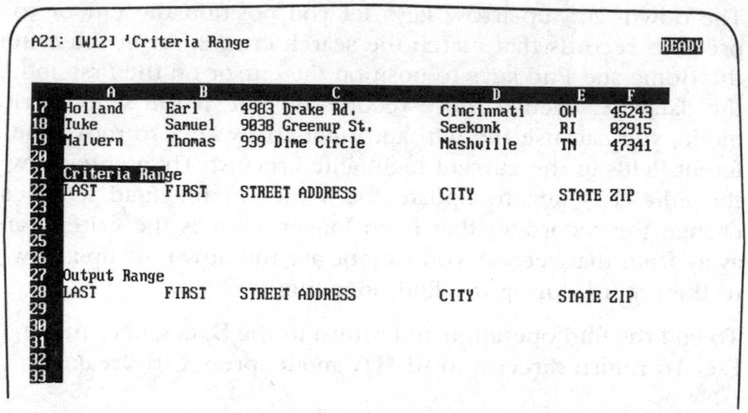

Fig. 12.26.
The criteria
range and
output range.

```
A21: [W12] 'Criteria Range                                              READY

         A          B          C                    D          E    F
   17 Holland     Earl       4983 Drake Rd.        Cincinnati  OH   45243
   18 Tuke        Samuel     9838 Greenup St.      Seekonk     RI   02915
   19 Malvern     Thomas     939 Dime Circle       Nashville   TN   47341
   20
   21 Criteria Range
   22 LAST        FIRST      STREET ADDRESS        CITY        STATE ZIP
   23
   24
   25
   26
   27 Output Range
   28 LAST        FIRST      STREET ADDRESS        CITY        STATE ZIP
   29
   30
   31
   32
   33
```

only the field-name row as the range, or you can set the exact size of the extract area.

Caution:
If you do not allow sufficient room in the output range for extracted records, the extract operation aborts.

To limit the size of the extract area, enter the upper left to lower right cell coordinates of the entire output range. The first row in the specified range must contain the field names; the remaining rows must accommodate the maximum number of records you expect to receive from the extract operation. Use this method when you want to retain additional data that is located below the extract area. For example, as you can see in figure 12.26, naming A28..F36 as the output range limits incoming records to eight (one row for field names and one row for each record). If you do not allow sufficient room in the fixed-length output area, the extract operation aborts, and the message too many records for output range is displayed on-screen.

To create an open-ended extract area that does not limit the number of incoming records, specify as the output range only the row that contains the output field names. For example, by naming A28..F28 as the output range in figure 12.26, you define the output area without limiting the number of records.

Caution:
The extract operation overwrites all existing data in the output range.

An extract operation first removes all existing data from the output range. If you use only the field-name row to specify the output area, all data below that row is destroyed to make room for the unknown number of incoming extracted records.

Executing the Extract Command

To execute an **Extract** command, you must type the search conditions in the worksheet; type the output field names in the worksheet; and set the input, criteria, and output ranges from the **Data Query** menu.

To accelerate what seems to be a time-consuming setup process, establish standard input, criteria, and output areas and then store the range names for these locations. Keeping in mind the limit of 32 criteria fields, you might establish a single criteria range (such as the range A22..F23 in figure 12.26) that encompasses all the key fields on which you might search. By establishing such a range, you save the time needed to respecify a criteria range for each extract on different field names; but if the criteria range contains many unused field names, you lose some speed of execution.

To illustrate the extract process applied to the address database, you can create a list of all records with OH in the STATE field. Assuming that rows 22 and 28 contain the field names, enter **OH** in cell E23. Select **/D**ata Query and specify the input (A1..F19), criteria (A22..F23), and output ranges (A28..F28). Then choose **E**xtract from the **Q**uery menu. The output range in figure 12.27 contains three extracted records, each of which meets the condition of STATE = OH.

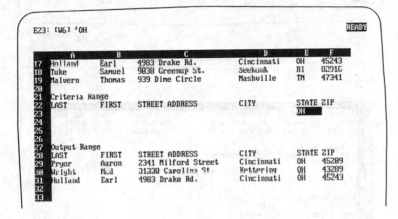

Fig. 12.27.
*A full-record
extract on an
"exact match"
label condition.*

You do not have to extract entire records or maintain the order of field names within the extracted records. For example, you can combine the first- and last-name fields in a new field (NAME) and then extract only the NAME and CITY information from records that have OH in the STATE field. To do this, type **NAME** in cell G1 and then type the string formula **+B2&" "&A2** in cell G2 (see fig. 12.28).

After you copy the contents of cell G2 to the range G3..G19, use the **/R**ange Value command to convert the formulas in G2..G19 to values. Next, use **/R**ange Erase to erase the field names in row 28. Type the new field **NAME** in cell A28, skip column B (for spacing purposes), and enter the second output field **CITY** in cell C28. Then respecify the output range as A28..C28. Expand both the input and criteria ranges to include the new column G. This operation extracts the name and city information for all records of individuals living in Ohio (see fig. 12.29).

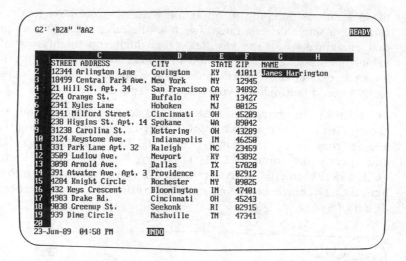

Fig. 12.28.
Creating the NAME field in the address database.

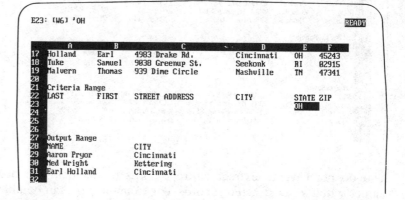

Fig. 12.29.
A partial-record extract on a single label condition.

Creating More Complex Criteria Ranges

In addition to an "exact match" search on a single label field, 1-2-3 permits a wide variety of record searches: on exact matches to numeric fields; on partial matches of field contents; on fields that meet formula conditions; on fields that meet all of several conditions; and on fields that meet either one condition or another. Let's look first at variations of queries on single fields.

Using Wild Cards in Criteria Ranges

You can use 1-2-3's wild cards for matching labels in database operations. The characters ?, *, and ~ have special meaning when used in the criteria range. The ? character instructs 1-2-3 to accept any character in that specific position and can be used only to locate fields of the same length. You can use the * character, which tells 1-2-3 to accept any and all characters that follow, on field contents of unequal length. By placing a tilde (~) symbol at the beginning of a label, you tell 1-2-3 to accept all values except those that follow. Table 12.1 illustrates how you can use wild cards in search operations.

Reminder:
You can use wild cards for matching labels in database operations.

**Table 12.1
Using Wild Cards in Search Operations**

Enter	To find
N?	NC, NJ, NY, and so on
BO?L?	BOWLE but not BOWL
BO?L*	BOWLE, BOWL, BOLLESON, BOELING, and so on
SAN*	SANTA BARBARA, SAN FRANCISCO
SAN *	SAN FRANCISCO
~N*	Strings in specified fields that do not begin with the letter N

Use the ? and * wild-card characters when you are unsure of the spelling used in field contents. Be sure that the results of any extract operation that uses a wild card are what you need. And be extremely careful when you use wild cards in a Delete command. If you are not careful, you may remove more records than you intend.

Entering Formulas in Criteria Ranges

To set up formulas that query numeric fields in the database, you can use the following relational operators:

>	Greater than
>=	Greater than or equal to
<	Less than
<=	Less than or equal to
=	Equal to
<>	Not equal to

Create a formula that references the first field entry in the numeric column you want to search. 1-2-3 tests the formula on each cell down the column until the program reaches the end of the specified input range.

You can place the formula anywhere below the criteria range's field-name row (unlike text criteria, which must appear directly below the associated field name). For example, you can use a formula based on information already in the marketing research database to extract the records of test participants who are at least 45 years old. First, type the formula **+D5>=45** in cell D22 (see fig. 12.30).

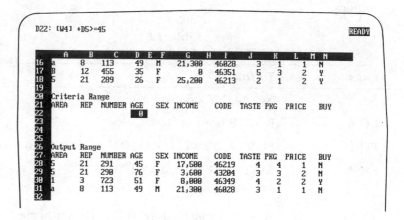

Fig. 12.30.
Extracting
records with a
relative
formula
condition.

Notice that the formula is displayed in the control panel and that a zero (0) is displayed in cell D22. The formula checked whether the contents of cell D5 (AGE = 26) were greater than or equal to 45 and returned zero (0) to indicate a false condition. (To better understand the search condition, you could use the **/R**ange **F**ormat **T**ext command to change the display from O to the formula. But the AGE column in this example is so narrow that the full formula cannot be displayed.)

After you specify the input, criteria, and output ranges correctly, executing an extract operation produces four records for which AGE equals or exceeds 45 years. A criterion of +D5>45 would extract only three records; the formula +D5=45 would extract only one record.

To reference cells outside the database, use formulas that include absolute cell addressing. (For addressing information, refer to Chapter 4.) Suppose that immediately after you issue the preceding command (to extract records based on AGE), you want to extract the records of those marketing research database respondents whose income exceeds the average income of all respondents. To do this, you must return to READY mode. Then determine the average income by entering **@AVG(G5..G18)** in a blank cell (G24) away from all database ranges (see fig. 12.31).

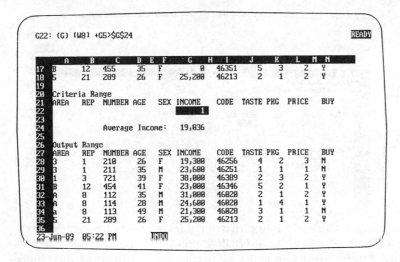

Fig. 12.31.
Extracting
records with a
mixed formula
condition.

Next, type the formula **+G5>$G$24** as the criterion under INCOME in cell G22. The +G5 tells 1-2-3 to test (starting in cell G5) income contents against the average income in cell G24 and to continue down column G to the end of the input range (row 18), testing each subsequent income cell against the average income in cell G24.

With the program still in READY mode, press the Query (F7) key to repeat the most recent query operation. Use the shortcut method only when you do not want to change the locations of the input, criteria, and output ranges. As you can see from figure 12.31, the extracted records indicate that eight of the marketing research database participants have incomes greater than the average income of all respondents.

Specifying AND Conditions

Now that you have seen how to base a find or extract operation on only one criterion, you learn how to use multiple criteria for your queries. You can set up multiple criteria as AND conditions (in which all the criteria must be met) or as OR conditions (in which any one criterion must be met). For example, searching a music department's library for sheet music requiring drums AND trumpets is likely to produce fewer selections than searching for music appropriate for drums OR trumpets.

Indicate two or more criteria, all of which must be met, by specifying the conditions on the criteria row immediately below the field names. The multi-

Reminder:
You can set up
multiple criteria for
your queries with
AND or OR
conditions.

ple criteria in row 24 of the college database requests those records for which MAJOR equals Accounting and SEX equals Male (see fig. 12.32). If you then issue an **E**xtract command, 1-2-3 extracts two records that meet both conditions.

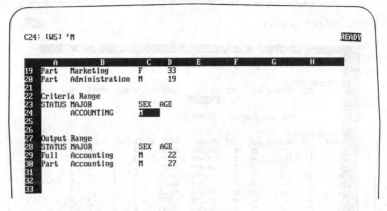

Fig. 12.32.
An initial two-field logical AND search.

When you maintain a criteria range that includes many fields, you quickly can extract records based on an alternative condition. For example, access READY mode, change M to F in cell C24 (under SEX), and press the Query (F7) key. 1-2-3 immediately copies the records of female accounting majors to the extract range (see fig. 12.33).

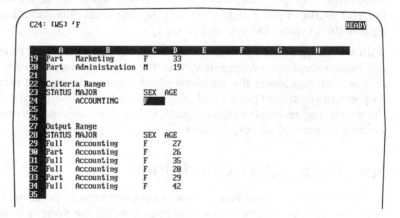

Fig. 12.33.
A revised two-field logical AND search.

You can continue to add conditions that must be met. Enter the additional criteria in the row immediately below the field-name row. For example, the extracted records in figure 12.34 are limited to female accounting majors under 30 years old.

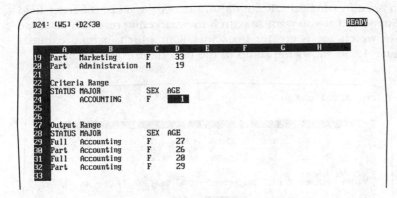

D24: [W5] +D2<30   READY

	A	B	C	D	E	F	G	H
19	Part	Marketing		33				
20	Part	Administration	M	19				
21								
22	Criteria Range							
23	STATUS MAJOR		SEX	AGE				
24		ACCOUNTING	F	1				
25								
26								
27	Output Range							
28	STATUS MAJOR		SEX	AGE				
29	Full	Accounting	F	27				
30	Part	Accounting	F	26				
31	Full	Accounting	F	20				
32	Part	Accounting	F	29				
33								

Fig. 12.34.
A three-field logical AND search.

Specifying OR Conditions

Criteria placed on the *same* row have the effect of a logical AND; they tell 1-2-3 to find or extract on this field condition AND this field condition AND this field condition and so on. Criteria placed on *different* rows have the effect of a logical OR; that is, find or extract on this field condition OR that field condition and so on. You can set up a logical OR search on one or more fields.

Searching a single field for more than one condition is the simplest use of an OR condition. To illustrate the concept, extract from the tools inventory database those records whose unit of issue is either KT (kit) or ST (set).

Under the ISSUE criteria field, type one condition immediately below the other (see fig. 12.35). Be sure to expand the criteria range to include the additional row. As you can see from the output range in figure 12.35, four records in the tools database have either KT or ST for a unit of issue.

Caution:
Make sure that your criteria range includes all rows that contain the multiple criteria.

C21: [W8] 'ST   READY

	A	B	C	D	E	F
12	Drop light, 100 foot		4	EA	17.99	71.96
13	Square		0	EA	37.50	0.00 15-Sep-87
14	Hex wrench set		2	KT	14.50	29.00
15	Wrench, box/open		0	ST	46.70	0.00 31-Aug-87
16	Pipe wrench, 14 inch		4	EA	56.70	226.80
17						
18	Criteria Range					
19	DESCRIPTION	QUANTITY	ISSUE	COST	VALUE	DATE
20			KT			
21			ST			
22						
23	Output Range					
24	DESCRIPTION	QUANTITY	ISSUE	COST	VALUE	DATE
25	Air hammer 3/8' drive		1	KT	67.32	67.32 24-Aug-87
26	Counter sink set, 10pc		3	KT	13.44	40.32 15-Sep-87
27	Hex wrench set		2	KT	14.50	29.00
28	Wrench, box/open		0	ST	46.70	0.00 31-Aug-87

Fig. 12.35.
A logical OR search within a single field.

You also can specify a logical OR condition on two or more different field conditions. Suppose that you want to search the marketing research database for records in which age is greater than 50 OR in which income exceeds $25,000. Figure 12.36 shows the setup of the criteria in rows 22 and 23.

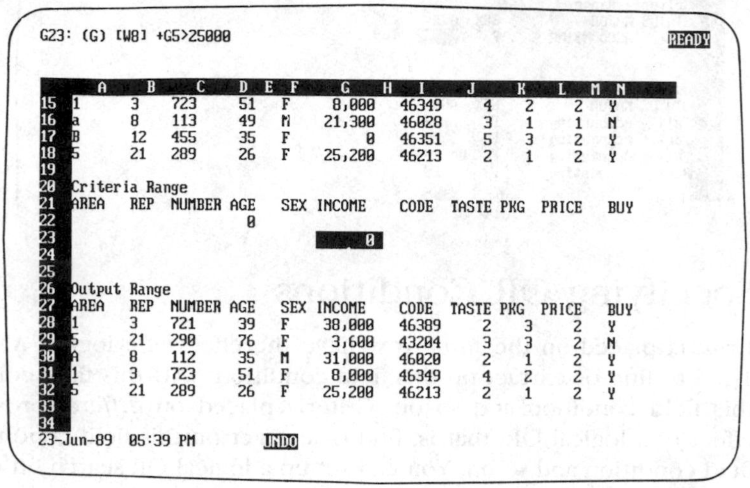

Fig. 12.36.
A logical OR search on two fields.

```
G23: (G) [W8] +G5>25000                                              READY

         A      B      C    D E F      G      H    I     J       K   L M N
15  1      3    723    51  F      8,000   46349   4     2       2   Y
16  a      8    113    49  M     21,300   46028   3     1       1   N
17  B     12    455    35  F          0   46351   5     3       2   Y
18  5     21    289    26  F     25,200   46213   2     1       2   Y
19
20  Criteria Range
21  AREA  REP  NUMBER AGE    SEX INCOME    CODE TASTE PKG  PRICE    BUY
22                     0
23                             0
24
25
26  Output Range
27  AREA  REP  NUMBER AGE    SEX INCOME    CODE TASTE PKG  PRICE    BUY
28  1      3    721    39  F     38,000   46389   2     3       2   Y
29  5     21    290    76  F      3,600   43204   3     3       2   N
30  A      8    112    35  M     31,000   46020   2     1       2   Y
31  1      3    723    51  F      8,000   46349   4     2       2   Y
32  5     21    289    26  F     25,200   46213   2     1       2   Y
33
34
23-Jun-89  05:39 PM          UNDO
```

Type **+D5>50** in cell D22. In the next row, enter **+G5>25000** in cell G23. (Remember that you can type formulas under any field name; you could have entered the two formulas in cells A22 and A23, for example.) Adjust the criteria range to include the OR condition by expanding the criteria range down a row.

When you issue the **E**xtract command, 5 records are copied to the output range (see fig. 12.36). Although rows 29 and 31 in figure 12.36 do not reflect INCOME contents exceeding $25,000, they do contain AGE contents over 50. Only one condition OR the other had to be met before the copy was made.

To add other OR criteria, move to a new row, enter each new condition, and expand the criteria range. If you reduce the number of rows involved in an OR logical search, be sure to contract the criteria range.

Although no technical reason prevents you from mixing AND and OR logical searches, the results of such a mixed query operation may not be of much use. Follow the format of placing each AND condition in the row immediately below the criteria field-name row, and each OR condition in a separate row below. For example, if you want to search the marketing research database for records in which BUY equals Y (Yes) and INCOME is either less than $10,000 or greater than $30,000, erase the AGE search condition in cell D22 and then enter the AND/OR conditions in the following cells:

G	H	I	J	K	L	M	N
22 +G5<10000							Y
23 +G5>30000							Y

By specifying these conditions, you tell 1-2-3 to search for records in which INCOME is less than $10,000 and the BUY response is "Yes" (row 22) OR for records in which INCOME is greater than $30,000 and the BUY response is "Yes" (row 23). The criteria range (A21..N23) remains unchanged. Repeating the Y in cell N23 is critical (even though you have entered Y in cell N22) because if 1-2-3 finds a blank cell within a criteria range, the program selects all records for the field name above that blank cell.

You should test the logic of your search conditions on a small sample database in which you can verify search results easily by scrolling through all records and noting which of them should be extracted. For example, if the marketing research database contained hundreds of responses, you could test the preceding AND/OR search conditions on the small group of 14 records. (Issuing an **Extract** command should copy to the output area only the records in rows 8, 13, 15, and 17.)

Entering String Searches

If you want to search on the partial contents of a field, you can use functions in a formula. Suppose that you can remember only the street name "Keystone" for a record you want to extract from the address database. If you safely can assume that all street addresses start with a number and have a space before the street name (XXX Streetname), you can use the formula shown in the control panel of figure 12.37 as the search criteria.

Cue:
Use string functions to search on the partial contents of a field.

```
C23: [W24] @MID(C2,@FIND(" ",C2,0)+1,8)="keystone"                    READY

        A         B          C                    D          E     F
10  Saunders   Ronald    3124 Keystone Ave.    Indianapolis  IN   46250
11  McGruder   Mary      331 Park Lane Apt. 32 Raleigh       NC   23459
12  Simpson    Jeremy    3589 Ludlow Ave.      Newport       KY   43892
13  Wolf       Barbara   3098 Arnold Ave.      Dallas        TX   57820
14  Rooney     Kevin     391 Atwater Ave. Apt. 3 Providence  RI   02912
15  Franks     Mike      4284 Knight Circle    Rochester     NY   09025
16  Sorrenson  Sarah     432 Keys Crescent     Bloomington   IN   47401
17  Holland    Earl      4983 Drake Rd.        Cincinnati    OH   45243
18  Tuke       Samuel    9038 Greenup St.      Seekonk       RI   02915
19  Malvern    Thomas    939 Dime Circle       Nashville     TN   47341
20
21  Criterion Range
22  LAST       FIRST     STREET ADDRESS        CITY          STATE ZIP
23                                        0
24
25
26
27  Output Range
28  LAST       FIRST     STREET ADDRESS        CITY          STATE ZIP
29  Saunders   Ronald    3124 Keystone Ave.    Indianapolis  IN   46250
23-Jun-89  05:44 PM         UNDO
```

Fig. 12.37.
Using a function condition to search a string.

The double quotation marks (" ") in the formula instruct 1-2-3 to start the search after a blank space is encountered (between the street number and street name). The 1,8 portion of the formula instructs the program to search on the first through the eighth character positions matching "Keystone," thereby eliminating any need to know whether "Street," "Ave.," "Avenue," and so on, is part of the field. Issuing the **E**xtract command produces one record in the output range (row 29). You also could use compound criteria and search on both CITY and part of the STREET ADDRESS field. (See Chapter 6 for an in-depth description of functions.)

Using Special Operators

To combine search conditions within a single field, use the special operators #AND# and #OR#. Use the special operator #NOT# to negate a search condition.

Use #AND# or #OR# to search on two or more conditions within the same field. Suppose that you want to extract from the tools inventory database all records with an August 1987 purchase-order date (DATE). Establish the criteria by requesting an extract of all dates later than July 31, 1987 AND earlier than September 1, 1987. In figure 12.38, the formula condition has been entered in cell A20. (Keep in mind that you do not have to type a formula under the associated field name—DATE, in this example.) The extracted records are displayed in rows 25 through 27.

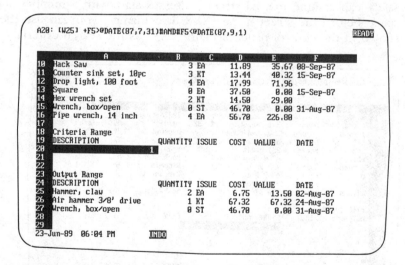

Fig. 12.38.
*Extracting
records with
the special
#AND#
operator.*

You use the #AND#, #OR#, and #NOT# operators to enter (in one field) conditions that could be entered some other way (usually in at least two fields). For example, you could enter **+C5="KT"#OR#C5="ST"** in a single cell in row 20 (any cell in the criteria range A19..F20) as an alternative criteria entry to select all units of issue as KT or ST in the tools inventory database.

Use #NOT# at the beginning of a condition to negate that condition. For example, if the tools inventory database had only three units of issue—KT, ST, and EA—you could select all KT or ST units of issue by specifying the criterion **#NOT#"EA"** in cell C20 of the criteria range A19..F20.

Performing Other Types of Searches

In addition to the Query and Find commands, you can use the Data menu's Unique and Delete commands for searches. By issuing the Unique command, you can produce (in the output range) a copy of only the first occurrence of a record that meets a specified criteria. And you can update the contents of your 1-2-3 database by deleting all records that meet a specified criterion with the Delete command. After entering the conditions, you need to specify only the input and criteria ranges before you issue the Delete command.

Reminder:
Use the /Data Unique command to copy only the first occurrence of a record in the output range.

Searching for Unique Records

Ordinarily, the Unique command is used to copy into the output area only a small portion of each record that meets the criteria. For example, if you want a list of issues used in the tools inventory database, set up an output range that includes only the unit of ISSUE (see fig. 12.39). To search all records, leave blank the row below the field-name row in the criteria range A19..F20. Then, with the input range defined as A4..F16 and the output range set at A24, select Unique to produce (in rows 25 through 27) a list of the three units of issue.

A24: [W25] 'ISSUE					READY
	A	B	C	D	E	F
9	Phillips screwdriver set	8 EA	8.73	69.84	
10	Hack Saw	3 EA	11.89	35.67	08-Sep-87
11	Counter sink set, 10pc	3 KT	13.44	40.32	15-Sep-87
12	Drop light, 100 foot	4 EA	17.99	71.96	
13	Square	0 EA	37.50	0.00	15-Sep-87
14	Hex wrench set	2 KT	14.50	29.00	
15	Wrench, box/open	0 ST	46.70	0.00	31-Aug-87
16	Pipe wrench, 14 inch	4 EA	56.70	226.80	
17					
18	Criteria Range				
19	DESCRIPTION	QUANTITY ISSUE	COST VALUE		DATE
20					
21					
22					
23	Output Range				
24	ISSUE				
25	EA				
26	KT				
27	ST				
28					
23-Jun-89 06:10 PM	UNDO				

Fig. 12.39.
The results of issuing a Unique command.

As another example, you can produce (from the college database) a list of the majors selected by current students. To do so, you specify in the output area only the field name MAJOR, leave blank the row under field names in the criteria range, and execute the Unique command.

Deleting Specified Records

As you know, you can use the /Worksheet Delete Row command to remove records from a worksheet. If you want a fast alternative to this "one-by-one" approach, use the Delete command to remove unwanted records from your database files. Before you select Delete from the Query menu, simply specify the range of records to be searched (input range) and the conditions for the deletion (criteria).

Suppose that you want to remove from the address database all records with a STATE field beginning with the letter N. To do so, specify an input range of A1..F19, a criteria range of A22..F23, and use the criterion N* in cell E23 (see fig. 12.40). Then issue the Delete command. The remaining records pack together in rows 2 through 14, and the input range automatically adjusts to A1..F14.

Fig. 12.40.
The results of issuing a Delete command.

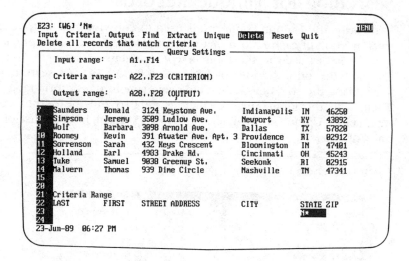

Be extremely careful when you issue the Delete command. To give you the opportunity to verify that you want to select the Delete command, 1-2-3 displays the following menu:

Cancel   Delete

Choose Cancel to abort the delete operation. Select Delete to verify that you want to execute the delete operation.

You can guard against deleting the wrong records by doing one (or both) of two things. Before you issue a **Query Delete** command, you can use **/File Save** to save the database using a name such as TEMP. Then, if the logic of the delete conditions proves faulty, you can retrieve this copy. Or you can perform an extract on the delete conditions, view the records to verify that they should be removed, and then perform the delete operation.

Loading Data from Other Programs

Lotus provides several means of importing data from other applications. The Translate utility (see Chapter 7) has options for converting data directly to 1-2-3 worksheets from VisiCalc, DIF, dBASE II, dBASE III, and dBASE III Plus files. You then can access the data by using the **/File Retrieve** or **/File Combine** commands from the current worksheet.

Use the **/File Import** command to read into a current worksheet the data stored on disk as a text file. Depending on the format, these files may be read directly to a range of cells or a column of cells. Specially formatted "numeric" data can be read directly to a range of worksheet cells. ASCII text can be stored as long labels in a single column with one line of the report per cell. You then must disassemble these labels into the appropriate data values or fields by using functions or the **/Data Parse** command.

Finally, you can use certain advanced macro commands to read and write an ASCII sequential file directly from within 1-2-3 advanced macro command programs (see Chapter 14).

Using the /Data Parse Command

The **/Data Parse** command is a flexible and easy method of extracting numeric, string, and date data from long labels and placing it in separate columns. Suppose that you typed inventory data in a report composed with the WordPerfect word processing program, and you want to load the print-image file in 1-2-3. After you load the file by using the **/File Import** command, you must reformat the data by using the **/Data Parse** command.

The **/File Import** command loads the inventory data into the range A1..A16 (see fig. 12.41). Visually, the data is formatted in a typical worksheet range such as A1..G16, but the display is misleading. The current cell-pointer location is A5; the entire contents of the row exist only in that cell.

Reminder:
Use /Data Parse to split long labels imported from text files into separate text, number, or date fields.

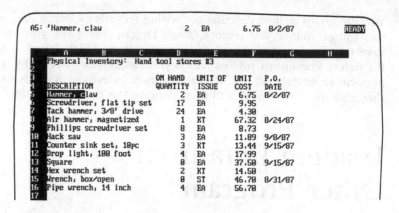

Fig. 12.41.
The results of
issuing a /File
Import
command.

To break down the long label to columns, move the cursor to the first cell to be parsed and select **/D**ata **P**arse. The following menu appears:

    Format-Line   Input-Column   Output-Range   Reset   Go   Quit

Use **F**ormat-Line to create or edit a newly inserted line in the data to be parsed. The Format-Line command specifies the pattern or patterns for splitting the long labels into numbers, labels, and dates.

Use **I**nput-Column for specifying the range of cells to be parsed. The output range denotes the upper left corner cell of a block of cells that will hold the parsed data.

Reset clears the previously set input-column range and output range. **G**o performs the parse, based on the specified input-column, format-line, and output ranges.

To parse the data in figure 12.41, follow these steps:

1. Move the cursor to A3, the first cell that contains the data you want to break into columns. (You do not have to parse the title in cell A1.)

2. Parse the column headings in cells A3..A4, using one format line; and then parse the data in A5..A16, using another format line.

Different format lines are necessary because the data is a mixture of label, numeric, and date data, and because all the headings are labels. Select **F**ormat-Line **C**reate. A suggested format line is inserted in the data at A3, and the remaining worksheet content moves down one line.

After creating a format line, you can edit it by selecting **F**ormat-Line again and choosing **E**dit. Use the format line to mark the column positions and the type of data in those positions. **P**arse uses the format line to break down the data and move it to its respective columns in the output range.

Combinations of certain letters and special characters comprise format lines. The letters denote the beginning position and the type of data; special symbols define the length of a field and the spacing.

Symbol	Purpose
D	Marks the beginning of a date field
L	Marks the beginning of a label field
S	Marks the beginning of a skip position
T	Marks the beginning of a time field
V	Marks the beginning of a value field
>	Defines the continuation of a field. Use one > for each position in the field (excluding the first position).
*	Defines blank spaces (in the data below the format line) that may be part of the block of data in the following cell

Add as many format lines as you need in your data. In the inventory example, you need to enter another format line at cell A6 and specify the format criteria for the data records that follow. A suggested format line is shown in figure 12.42. To restore the **P**arse menu, press Enter after you finish editing. (Note that the **P**arse Settings sheet shown in figure 12.42 is included only in Release 2.2, not in Release 2.01.)

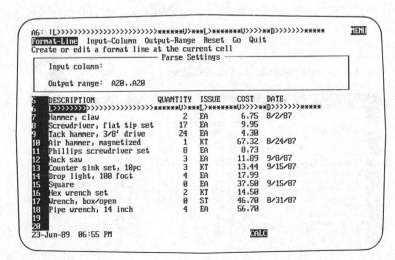

Fig. 12.42.
Editing a
format line in
a parse
operation.

After setting up two format lines in the inventory example, select **Input-Column** from the **Parse** menu. Point to or type the range A3..A18; this range includes format lines, column headings, and data. Continue by selecting **Output-Range** from the **Parse** menu and by specifying A20 as the upper left corner of a blank range to accept the parsed data. Complete the operation by selecting the **G**o option (see fig. 12.43).

Fig. 12.43.
The results
from a parse
operation.

```
A22: 'Hammer, claw                                                    READY

         A        B        C        D      E       F        G       H
15 Square                            0      EA     37.50   9/15/87
16 Hex wrench set                    2      KT     14.50
17 Wrench, box/open                  0      ST     46.70   8/31/87
18 Pipe wrench, 14 inch              4      EA     56.70
19
20            ON HAND  UNIT OF  UNIT        P.O.
21 DESCRIPTIQUANTITY  ISSUE    COST        DATE
22 Hammer, c     2     EA        6.75      31991
23 Screwdriv    17     EA        9.95
24 Tack hamm    24     EA        4.3
25 Air hamme     1     KT       67.32      32013
26 Phillips      8     EA        8.73
27 Hack saw      3     EA       11.89      32028
28 Counter s     3     KT       13.44      32035
29 Drop ligh     4     EA       17.99
30 Square        0     EA       37.5       32035
31 Hex wrenc     2     KT       14.5
32 Wrench, b     0     ST       46.7       32020
33 Pipe wren     4     EA       56.7
34
23-Jun-89  07:00 PM              UNDO
```

The data displayed in individual cells may not be exactly what you want. You can make a few changes in the format and column width, and you also can add or delete information to make the newly parsed data more usable. These enhancements are not part of the **Parse** command, but they usually are necessary after importing and parsing data.

To produce the final inventory database shown in figure 12.44, follow these steps:

Fig. 12.44.
Improving the
appearance of
parsed data.

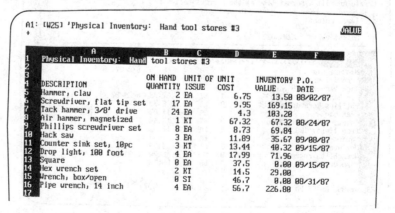

```
A1: [W25] 'Physical Inventory: Hand tool stores #3                    VALUE
+
         A              B      C        D        E         F
1 Physical Inventory:  Hand tool stores #3
2
3
4 DESCRIPTION          ON HAND  UNIT OF  UNIT    INVENTORY P.O.
                       QUANTITY ISSUE    COST    VALUE     DATE
5 Hammer, claw              2   EA        6.75     13.50   08/02/87
6 Screwdriver, flat tip set 17  EA        9.95    169.15
7 Tack hammer, 3/8' drive   24  EA        4.3     103.20
8 Air hammer, magnetized     1  KT       67.32     67.32   08/24/87
9 Phillips screwdriver set   8  EA        8.73     69.84
10 Hack saw                  3  EA       11.89     35.67   09/08/87
11 Counter sink set, 10pc    3  KT       13.44     40.32   09/15/87
12 Drop light, 100 foot      4  EA       17.99     71.96
13 Square                    0  EA       37.5       0.00   09/15/87
14 Hex wrench set            2  KT       14.5      29.00
15 Wrench, box/open          0  ST       46.7       0.00   08/31/87
16 Pipe wrench, 14 inch      4  EA       56.7     226.80
17
```

1. Delete rows A3..A19 to remove the unparsed data and to move the parsed data up under the title.

2. Expand column A to make it 25 characters wide and contract column C to make it 8 characters wide.

3. Reformat the P.O. DATE range in column E to the Date 4 format.

4. Insert at column E a column for the inventory value.

5. Widen the new column E to 10 characters (the P.O. DATE should be column F).

6. Add the INVENTORY and VALUE headings in cells E3 and E4, respectively.

7. Enter in cell E5 the formula that computes the inventory value (**+B5*D5**).

8. Copy the formula in cell E5 to cells E6..E16.

9. Use **/R**ange **F**ormat to format D5..E16 to the comma (2 decimal places) format.

Noting Cautions about Using /Data Parse

If you are parsing a value that continues past the end of the field, the data is parsed until a blank is encountered or until the value runs into the next field in the format line. This means that if you parse labels, you need to make sure that the field widths in the format line are wide enough so that you can avoid losing data because of blanks. If you parse values, the field widths are less critical.

Caution:
Make sure that the column widths are wide enough to accept the complete value or label you want in the field.

Experiment on small amounts of data until you are comfortable using the **/D**ata **P**arse command. After you understand how this command works, you will find many more applications for it. Every time you develop a new application, you should consider whether existing data created on another software program can be imported and then changed to 1-2-3 format by using the **/D**ata **P**arse command.

Using Database Statistical Functions

1-2-3's database statistical functions are similar to the worksheet statistical functions, but they have been modified to manipulate database fields. Like the standard statistical functions, the database statistical functions perform in one simple statement, calculations that would otherwise require several statements. This efficiency and ease of application make these excellent tools. 1-2-3's database functions are listed in table 12.2.

Table 12.2
Database Functions

Function	Description
@DCOUNT	Gives the number of items in a list
@DSUM	Sums the values of all the items in a list
@DMIN	Gives the minimum of all the items in a list
@DMAX	Gives the maximum of all the items in a list
@DSTD	Gives the standard deviation of all the items in a list
@DVAR	Gives the variance of all the items in a list
@DAVG	Gives the arithmetic mean of all the items in a list

The general form of these functions is

@DFUNCTION(input range, offset, criteria range)

The input and criteria ranges are the same as those used by the /Data Query command. The input range specifies the database or part of a database to be scanned, and the criteria range specifies which records are to be selected. The offset indicates which field to select from the database records; the off-set value must be either zero or a positive integer. A value of zero indicates the first column, a one indicates the second column, and so on.

The following example uses the database statistical functions. The example involves computing the mean, variance, and standard deviation of the average interest rates offered by money market funds for a given week. If you are unfamiliar with the concepts of mean, variance, and standard deviation, you can read more about them in Chapter 6.

Figure 12.45 shows the money market returns database and the results of the various database functions. The functions and their ranges include the following:

Count	@DCOUNT(A3..B20,1,D13..D14)
Mean	@DAVG(A3..B20,1,D13..D14)
Variance	@DVAR(A3..B20,1,D13..D14)
Std. Dev.	@DSTD(A3..B20,1,D13..D14)

Maximum @DMAX(A3..B20,1,D13..D14)

Minimum @DMIN(A3..B20,1,D13..D14)

```
D13: [W12] 'WEEK 1                                              READY

              A              B      C      D          E
 1 Money Market Database (7 day average yield)   Database Statistics
 2                                              ─────────────────
 3 NAME                     WEEK 1              Count       17
 4 Alliance Group Capital Reserves   7.7        Mean       7.7
 5 Bull & Bear Dollar Reserves       7.7        Variance  0.057
 6 Carnegie Cash Securities          7.4        Std Dev   0.238
 7 Colonial Money Market             7.9        Maximum    8.2
 8 Equitable Money Market Account    7.8        Minimum    7.3
 9 Fidelity Group Cash Reserves      8.0
10 Kemper Money Market               7.7
11 Lexington Money Market            8.1
12 Money Market Management           7.8        Criteria Range
13 Paine Webber Cash                 7.9        WEEK 1
14 Prudential Bache                  7.4        +WEEK 1>?
15 Saint Paul Money Market, Inc.     7.6
16 Shearson T-Fund                   8.2
17 Short Term Income Fund            7.9
18 Standby Reserves                  7.6
19 Summit Cash Reserves              7.3
20 Value Line Cash Fund              7.7
25-Jun-89  05:05 PM        UNDO
```

Fig. 12.45.
Statistical functions used with a money market database.

Figure 12.45 shows that the week's mean return for 17 different money market funds works out to an annual percentage rate of 7.7 (cell E4) with a variance of .057 (cell E5). This result means that about 68 percent of the money market funds return between 7.46 and 7.94 percent annually.

One Std. Dev. below mean 7.7 - .238   7.46

One Std. Dev. above mean 7.7 + .238 + 7.94

The result of the @DMIN function (cell E8) shows that Summit Cash Reserves returns the lowest rate at 7.3 percent. This value is almost 2 standard deviations below the mean. That figure (2 standard deviations below the mean) is computed as follows:

Two Std. Devs. below mean 7.7 - (2 * .238) = 7.22

Because approximately 95 percent of the population falls within plus or minus 2 standard deviations of the mean, Summit Cash Reserves is close to being in the lowest 2.5 percent of the population of money market funds for that week; 5 percent is divided by 2 because the population is assumed to be normal. (See Chapter 6 for a further discussion of how to interpret the statistical functions.)

Conversely, the Shearson T-Fund returns 8.2 percent, the highest rate. The @DMAX function has determined the highest rate to be just over 2 standard deviations above the mean, the highest 2.5 percent of the population.

By setting up the proper criteria, you can analyze any portion of the database you want. How do the statistics change if funds returning less than 7.5 percent are excluded from the statistics? Figure 12.46 gives the answer.

Fig. 12.46.
A money fund
analysis with
funds earning
less than 7.5
percent
excluded.

```
D14: (T) [W12] +WEEK 1>7.5                                        READY

              A                    B   C      D        E
 1  Money Market Database (7 day average yield)   Database Statistics
 2  ─────────────────────────────────────────── ─────────────────────
 3  NAME                         WEEK 1           Count      14
 4  Alliance Group Capital Reserves   7.7         Mean       7.8
 5  Bull & Bear Dollar Reserves       7.7         Variance   0.031
 6  Carnegie Cash Securities          7.4         Std Dev    0.175
 7  Colonial Money Market             7.9         Maximum    8.2
 8  Equitable Money Market Account    7.8         Minimum    7.6
 9  Fidelity Group Cash Reserves      8.0
10  Kemper Money Market               7.7
11  Lexington Money Market            8.1
12  Money Market Management           7.8         Criteria Range
13  Paine Webber Cash                 7.9         WEEK 1
14  Prudential Bache                  7.4         +WEEK 1>7.5
15  Saint Paul Money Market, Inc.     7.6
16  Shearson T-Fund                   8.2
17  Short Term Income Fund            7.9
18  Standby Reserves                  7.6
19  Summit Cash Reserves              7.3
20  Value Line Cash Fund              7.7
25-Jun-89  05:11 PM         UNDO
```

The database statistical functions can tell you a great deal about the database as a whole and about how to interpret the values contained in it. If you add several more weeks' data to the database, as shown in figure 12.47, you can use the database statistical functions to analyze all or part of the larger database.

Fig. 12.47.
Additional
money fund
data.

```
J3: [W9] @DCOUNT(A3..G20,3,I13..I14)                             READY

       D       E       F       G     H      I          J
 1                                          Database Statistics
 2                                          ────────────────────
 3   WEEK 3  Week 4  Week 5  WEEK 6         Count        17
 4    7.9     7.9     8.0     8.0           Mean         7.9
 5    7.8     7.8     7.8     7.9           Variance    0.058
 6    7.5     7.5     7.6     7.6           Std Dev     0.240
 7    7.9     8.0     8.0     8.0           Maximum      8.3
 8    7.9     8.0     8.0     8.1           Minimum      7.4
 9    8.1     8.2     8.2     8.3
10    7.8     7.8     7.8     7.9
11    8.2     8.3     8.3     8.3
12    7.9     8.0     8.0     8.0           Criteria Range
13    8.0     8.0     8.1     8.1           WEEK 3
14    7.5     7.6     7.7     7.7           +WEEK 3>7
15    7.7     7.7     7.8     7.8
16    8.3     8.3     8.4     8.4
17    8.1     8.2     8.2     8.2
18    7.8     7.8     7.9     7.9
19    7.4     7.4     7.5     7.6
20    7.7     7.7     7.8     7.9
25-Jun-89  05:32 PM         UNDO
```

You can use all the methods you have seen so far to interpret the statistics in figure 12.47. The input, offset, and criteria ranges used for the data from the third week of the example are as follows:

Input range	A3..G20
Offset	3 (for the fourth column)
Criteria range	I13..I14

From this information, you can determine how the formulas have been set up for each week. The criteria range displayed in figure 12.47 (I13..I14) shows the criteria used to select the values for the third week.

Building Tables

Reminder:
Table building
automates the
"what if" process.

Table building is an extended version of the "what if" process. In fact, you could duplicate the functions performed by the table-building feature by performing repeated "what if" analyses. Doing so would take a prohibitive amount of time, however. Table building automates the "what if" process so that you can make a thorough analysis with a minimal amount of effort. The /Data Table command is the host command for the table-building function.

Table building automates the "what if" process through iteration: 1-2-3 takes sets of values and substitutes them one at a time for existing values in the worksheet. You provide the values for substitution and tell 1-2-3 where to substitute them. The program automatically records the results.

Although the /Data Table command may take some time to learn, you will find it to be one of the most powerful commands in 1-2-3. In fact, the strength of this command rivals similar commands in more sophisticated mainframe decision-support systems. When you consider the command's strength with its ease of implementation, you'll find the /Data Table a useful feature of 1-2-3.

The purpose of the /Data Table command is to structure the "what if" analysis. The command lets you build a table of input values that the program substitutes one at a time into your model. 1-2-3 then records the results in the table next to the input values.

To demonstrate a simple example, you can build a table of interest rates and show their effect on the monthly payments of a 30-year mortgage, as shown in figure 12.48.

By using the /Data Table 1 command, you can have 1-2-3 substitute in appropriate input cells the interest rates you have entered in a column. After calculating the results, 1-2-3 lists the monthly payments in the column next to the interest rates.

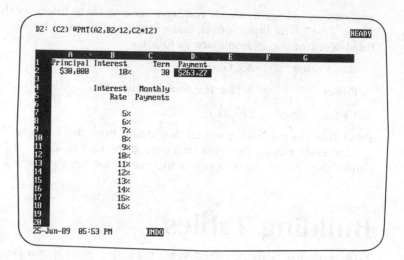

Fig. 12.48.
A worksheet for
monthly
payment
analysis.

Before entering the **/D**ata Table **1** command, you enter the interest-rate values in a column. (To enter those values, use the **/D**ata Fill command, covered in the next section.) Cells B7..B18 hold the interest rates. For the next step, you need to enter either the appropriate formula for calculating the results or the cell address from which to draw those results. This entry goes next to the column of interest rates and one row above the first entry.

Because the **/R**ange Format Text command was issued for cell C6, causing the formula rather than the value to be displayed, enter **+D2** in cell C6, as shown in figure 12.49. You also could enter in C6 the formula for computing the value, @PMT(A2,B2/12,C2*12).

Fig. 12.49.
The worksheet
before /Data
Table 1 is
issued.

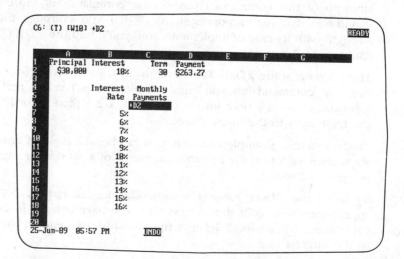

Next, issue the /Data Table **1** command; 1-2-3 prompts for a table range, a range of cells that includes the column of interest rates, and the column where the results are to appear. In this example, enter B6..C18. Notice that this range specification includes the formula row (see fig. 12.49). Then the program prompts for an input cell. This is the cell to which all the values in the column of interest rates correspond. Enter B2.

While 1-2-3 calculates the results, the WAIT mode indicator flashes in the upper right corner of the screen. When the calculation is finished, the sign changes to READY. Now the table contains all the payment values (see fig. 12.50).

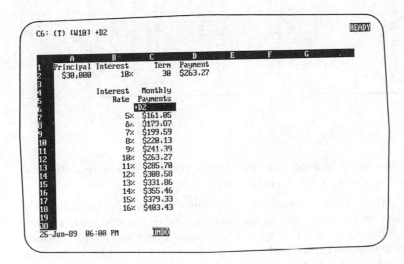

Fig. 12.50.
The worksheet
after issuing
/Data Table 1.

If you would like to try some other input values, you can change the values and then press the Table (F8) key to recalculate the table automatically. When the table is recalculated, 1-2-3 uses the command parameters you specified in the previous /Data Table command.

A more complicated example, shown in figure 12.51, uses the /Data Table **2** command. This command requires two input variables instead of one. Using more variables increases the breadth of the sensitivity analyses you can perform. This example is designed to show the effects of changes in order quantity and order point on total cost. You want the combination of order point and order quantity that minimizes cumulative costs-to-date at the end of a 12-month period.

The lower left portion of figure 12.51 shows the result of using the /Data Table **1** command to calculate the effect of different order quantities on cost. The /Data Table **2** command creates a much more extensive table, as shown in the lower right portion of the figure. This table shows the effect on cost of

Fig. 12.51.
Inventory
analysis with
the /Data
Table
command.

	A	B Jan	C Feb	D Mar	E Apr	F May	G Jun	H Jul	I Aug	J Sep	K Oct	L Nov	M Dec
1	Month												
2		Jan	Feb	Mar	Apr	May	Jun	Jul	Aug	Sep	Oct	Nov	Dec
3	Beginning Inventory	43	15	39	28	10	38	18	45	21	11	39	20
4	Past Demand for Month	28	16	11	18	12	20	13	24	10	12	19	22
5	Ending Inventory	15	-1	28	10	-2	18	5	21	11	-1	20	-2
6	Quantity Ordered	0	40	0	0	40	0	40	0	0	40	0	40
7	Setup Costs ($10 per order)	$0.00	$10.00	$0.00	$0.00	$10.00	$0.00	$10.00	$0.00	$0.00	$10.00	$0.00	$10.00
8	Inventory Costs ($.2/unit)	$3.00	$0.00	$5.60	$2.00	$0.00	$3.60	$1.00	$4.20	$2.20	$0.00	$4.00	$0.00
9	Shortage Costs ($1/unit)	$0.00	$1.00	$0.00	$0.00	$2.00	$0.00	$0.00	$0.00	$0.00	$2.00	$0.00	$2.00
10	Total Costs for Month	$3.00	$11.00	$5.60	$2.00	$12.00	$3.60	$11.00	$4.20	$2.20	$11.00	$4.00	$12.00
11	Cum Cost From Last Month	$0.00	$3.00	$14.00	$19.60	$21.60	$33.60	$37.20	$48.20	$52.40	$54.60	$65.60	$69.60
12	Cumulative Costs to Date	$3.00	$14.00	$19.60	$21.60	$33.60	$37.20	$48.20	$52.40	$54.60	$65.60	$69.60	$81.60
15	Order Quantity Input Cell	40											
16	Order Point Input Cell	8											

DATA TABLE 1 -->

	Order Quant	Cumulative Cost
21	+M12	+M12
22	25	$104.00
23	26	$109.60
24	27	$106.40
25	28	$98.00
26	29	$99.60
27	30	$102.40
28	31	$95.20
29	32	$91.60
30	33	$94.60
31	34	$95.60
32	35	$86.60
33	36	$88.80
34	37	$84.60
35	38	$93.20
36	39	$93.60
37	40	$81.60
38	41	$81.60
39	42	$85.20
40	43	$87.00
41	44	$90.00
42	45	$88.60
43	46	$86.80
44	47	$86.40
45	48	$88.40
46	49	$90.40
47	50	$98.00

(vertical label between the two tables: "Order Point")

DATA TABLE 2 --> Order Quantity

	38	39	40	41	42	43	Average
1	$91.20	$103.80	$96.40	$96.00	$93.20	$91.60	$95.37
2	$91.20	$103.80	$96.40	$93.80	$93.20	$91.60	$95.00
3	$91.20	$86.40	$96.40	$93.80	$93.20	$91.60	$92.10
4	$91.20	$86.40	$96.40	$93.80	$93.20	$91.60	$92.10
5	$90.40	$86.40	$81.60	$93.80	$84.80	$91.60	$88.10
6	$90.40	$86.40	$81.60	$93.80	$94.80	$91.60	$89.77
7	$90.40	$86.40	$81.60	$81.60	$94.80	$91.60	$89.77
8	$93.20	$89.40	$81.60	$81.60	$94.80	$87.00	$87.93
9	$93.20	$93.60	$81.60	$81.60	$85.20	$87.00	$87.03
10	$93.20	$93.60	$87.20	$81.60	$85.20	$97.00	$89.63
11	$93.20	$93.60	$94.00	$88.60	$85.20	$90.00	$90.77
12	$88.80	$93.60	$94.00	$88.60	$93.60	$90.00	$91.43
13	$88.80	$93.60	$94.00	$88.60	$93.60	$98.60	$92.87
14	$96.40	$93.60	$94.00	$96.40	$93.60	$98.60	$95.50
15	$110.40	$100.20	$100.80	$103.80	$100.80	$106.00	$103.67
16	$110.40	$108.60	$100.80	$103.80	$100.80	$106.00	$105.07
17	$110.40	$108.60	$103.80	$109.20	$106.00	$106.00	$106.47
18	$110.40	$116.40	$108.80	$103.80	$109.20	$106.00	$109.10
19	$110.40	$116.40	$108.60	$109.20	$109.20	$106.00	$109.10
20	$110.40	$116.40	$114.40	$112.00	$109.20	$114.60	$112.83
21	$110.40	$116.40	$122.40	$112.00	$109.20	$114.60	$114.17
22	$110.40	$116.40	$122.40	$122.00	$117.60	$114.60	$115.57
23	$110.40	$116.40	$122.40	$122.00	$117.60	$114.60	$115.57
24	$110.40	$116.40	$122.40	$128.40	$117.60	$123.20	$119.73
25	$110.40	$116.40	$122.40	$128.40	$117.60	$123.20	$119.73
26	$118.00	$116.40	$122.40	$128.40	$117.60	$123.20	$121.00

order point and order quantity. The result is a more complete analysis, the advantage of the **/D**ata Table **2** command.

To use the **/D**ata Table **2** command, you enter the values for variable 2 (order quantity, in this example) in the row just above the first entry of variable 1 (order point). In this example, these values begin in cell F21. Notice also that you enter **+N13**, the address of the formula for cost-to-date, in the row directly above the first entry of variable 1, cell E21 in the example. Again, the Text format is used so that the cell displays +N13.

When you issue the **/D**ata Table **2** command, 1-2-3 calls for a table range and input cells for variables 1 and 2. You enter the following information for these parameters:

Table Range	E21..K47
Input Cell Variable 1	B16
Input Cell Variable 2	B15

After you enter this information, 1-2-3 begins building the table of results. You may have to wait for the **/D**ata Table **2** command to work.

Note that you find no *one* correct answer concerning the effect of changes in order quantity and order point on total cost. This limited analysis, however, shows that on average an order point of about 9 and an order quantity of about 41 are best.

The advantage of the /Data Table command is that it allows you to perform extensive sensitivity analyses and display the results in a tabular format. You can perform analyses that you might not otherwise perform, given the time required. The power you gain from combining this command with macros and special database statistical functions can be great.

Filling Ranges with Numbers

To fill ranges, you use the /Data Fill command. This command is useful when combined with the other database commands mentioned earlier in this chapter, especially /Data Table and /Data Sort.

/Data Fill fills a range of cells with series of numbers that increase or decrease by a specified increment or decrement. For an example of the use of /Data Fill, look at the year numbers used as titles in the sales forecast shown in figure 12.52.

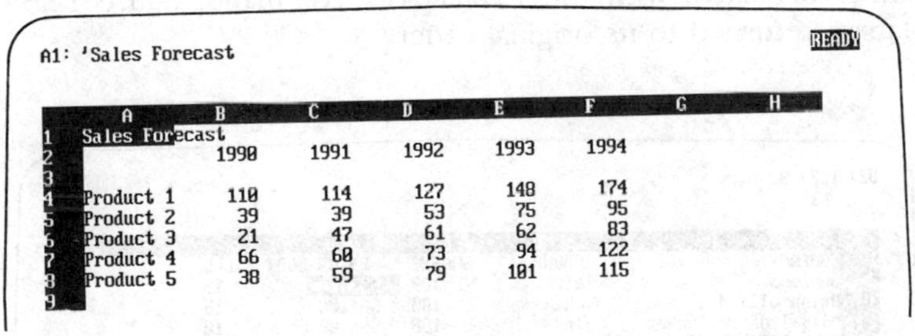

Cue:
Use the /Data Fill command to automate the process of entering a series of numbers or dates that increment at the same value.

```
A1: 'Sales Forecast                                          READY

      A          B       C       D       E       F       G       H
1  Sales Forecast
2               1990    1991    1992    1993    1994
3
4  Product 1    110     114     127     148     174
5  Product 2     39      39      53      75      95
6  Product 3     21      47      61      62      83
7  Product 4     66      60      73      94     122
8  Product 5     38      59      79     101     115
9
```

Fig. 12.52.
Entering year numbers with /Data Fill.

When you issue the /Data Fill command, 1-2-3 first prompts you for the starting number of the series. The program then asks for the step (or incremental) value to be added to the previous value. Finally, 1-2-3 prompts you for the ending value.

To enter a sequence of year numbers for a five-year forecast beginning in 1990, you need to start by specifying the range of cells to be filled. For this example, chose B2..F2 and then enter the beginning value, **1990**. The incremental or step value in this example is **1**. The ending value is **1994** for a five-year forecast.

One disadvantage of the /Data Fill command for year numbers is that you can't center or left-justify the numbers after you create them. As numbers, they will always be right-justified. If you want your year numbers centered or left-justified, you should type them as labels instead.

You can use the /Data Fill command to build a list of interest rates, as shown in figure 12.49. In that figure, specify B7..B18 for the range of cells to be filled, **.05** for the starting value, and **.01** for the step value. For the ending value, let 1-2-3 default to 8,192, which is far beyond the ending value actually needed. The /Data Fill command, however, fills only the specified range and doesn't fill cells beyond the end of the range.

The /Data Fill command is useful with /Data Sort. Suppose that you're going to sort a database, and you want to be able to restore the records to their original order if you make a mistake in sorting them. You need only add a field to the database and use /Data Fill to fill the field with consecutive numbers. Then you can sort your database. If you find that the sort results are unacceptable, you simply sort the database on the new field to return the database to its original order. Figure 12.53 shows a stocks database after it is sorted by number of shares with the /Data Sort command; figure 12.54 shows the database returned to its original order.

Fig. 12.53.
A stocks database sorted by number of shares.

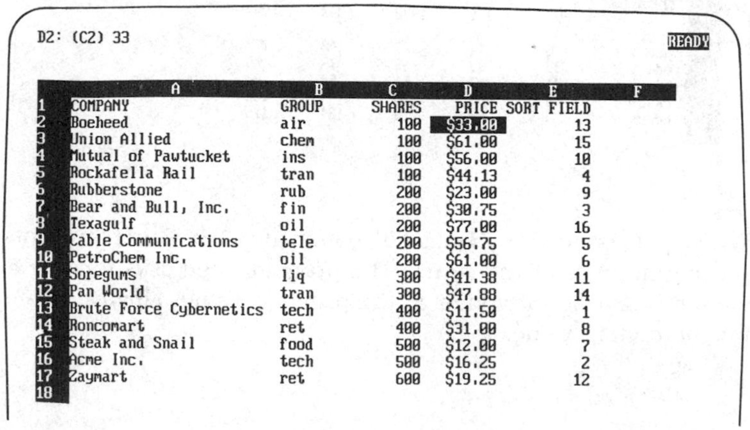

```
D2: (C2) 33                                    READY

          A                B       C      D       E      F
 1 COMPANY              GROUP   SHARES  PRICE SORT FIELD
 2 Boeheed              air       100  $33.00        13
 3 Union Allied         chem      100  $61.00        15
 4 Mutual of Pautucket  ins       100  $56.00        10
 5 Rockafella Rail      tran      100  $44.13         4
 6 Rubberstone          rub       200  $23.00         9
 7 Bear and Bull, Inc.  fin       200  $30.75         3
 8 Texagulf             oil       200  $77.00        16
 9 Cable Communications tele      200  $56.75         5
10 PetroChem Inc.       oil       200  $61.00         6
11 Soregums             liq       300  $41.38        11
12 Pan World            tran      300  $47.88        14
13 Brute Force Cybernetics tech   400  $11.50         1
14 Roncomart            ret       400  $31.00         8
15 Steak and Snail      food      500  $12.00         7
16 Acme Inc.            tech      500  $16.25         2
17 Zaymart              ret       600  $19.25        12
18
```

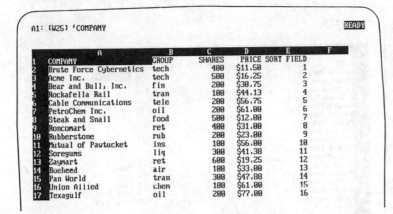

Fig. 12.54.
*A stocks
database
returned to the
original order.*

In these examples, regular numbers for the beginning, incremental, and ending values are used, but you also can use formulas and functions. If you want to fill a range of cells with incrementing dates, after you set the range, you can use the @DATE function to set the start value—for example, @DATE(89,6,1). You can use also a cell formula, such as +E4, for the incremental value. In this case, E4 may contain the increment 7 so that there can be increments of one week at a time. You can enter the stop value @DATE(89,10,1), for example. Or if the stop date is in a cell, you can give that cell address as the stop value. 1-2-3 allows many different combinations of commands.

Reminder:
*You can use
formulas and
functions in
beginning, step,
and end values
with /Data Fill.*

Figuring Frequency Distributions

The command for creating frequency distributions in 1-2-3 is the **/D**ata **Di**stribution command. A *frequency distribution* describes the relationship between a set of classes and the frequency of occurrence of members of each class. A list of consumers with their product preferences illustrates using the **/D**ata **D**istribution command to produce a frequency distribution (see fig. 12.55).

To use the **/D**ata **D**istribution command, you first specify a values range, which corresponds to the range of taste preference numbers in this example. After specifying B3..B18 for the values range, you set up the range of intervals at D3..D7, in what 1-2-3 calls the bin range. If you have evenly spaced intervals, you can use the **/D**ata **F**ill command to enter the values for the bin range.

Fig. 12.55.
Using /Data
Distribution to
analyze taste
preference data.

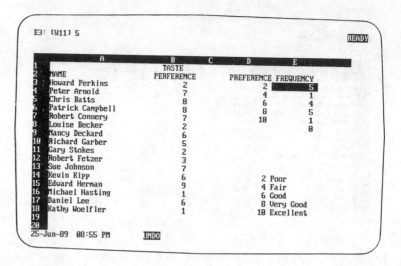

When you specify these ranges and enter the **/Data Distribution** command, 1-2-3 creates the results column (E3..E8) to the right of the bin range (D3..D7). The results column, which shows the frequency distribution, is always in the column to the right of the bin range and extends one row farther down.

The values in the results column represent the frequency of distribution of the numbers in the values range for each interval. The first interval in the bin range is for values greater than zero and less than or equal to two; the second, for values greater than two and less than or equal to four, and so on. The last value in the results column, in cell E8, shows the frequency of left-over numbers (that is, the frequency of numbers that don't fit into an interval classification).

The **/Data Distribution** command can help you create understandable results from a series of numbers. The results are easily graphed, as shown in figure 12.56.

A manufacturer looking at this graph would probably start looking for another product or start trying to improve the taste of the current product.

Using the /Data Regression Command

The **/Data Regression** command gives you a free multiple-regression analysis package within 1-2-3. Most people will probably never use this advanced feature. But if you need to use it, 1-2-3 saves you the cost and inconvenience of buying a stand-alone statistical package for performing a regression analysis.

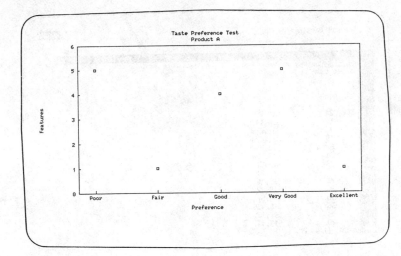

Fig. 12.56. The graph of results from the /Data Distribution command.

Use /Data Regression when you want to determine the relationship between one set of values (the dependent variable) and one or more other sets of values (the independent variables). Regression analysis has a number of uses in a business setting, including relating sales to price, promotions, and other market factors; relating stock prices to earnings and interest rates; and relating production costs to production levels.

Think of linear regression as a way of determining the "best" line through a series of data points. Multiple regression does this for several variables simultaneously, determining the "best" line relating the dependent variable to the set of independent variables. As an example, consider a data sample showing annual earnings versus age. Figure 12.57 shows the data; figure 12.58 shows the data plotted as an XY graph.

The /Data Regression command can simultaneously determine how to draw a line through these data points and how well the line fits the data. When you invoke the command, the following menu appears:

X-Range   **Y**-Range   **O**utput-Range   **I**ntercept   **R**eset   **G**o   **Q**uit

Use the **X**-Range option to select one or more independent variables for the regression. The /Data Regression command can use as many as 16 independent variables. The variables in the regression are columns of values, which means that you must convert any data in rows to columns with /**R**ange **T**ranspose before you issue the /Data Regression command. In this example, the x-range is A7..A20.

The **Y**-Range option specifies the dependent variable. The y-range must be a single column; therefore, select C7..C20.

Fig. 12.57.
Annual earnings versus age data.

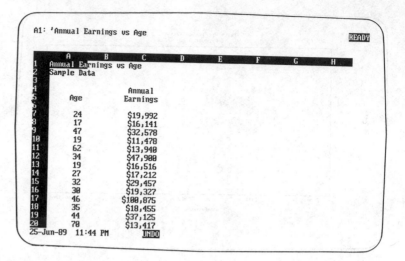

Fig. 12.58.
The XY graph of annual earnings versus age.

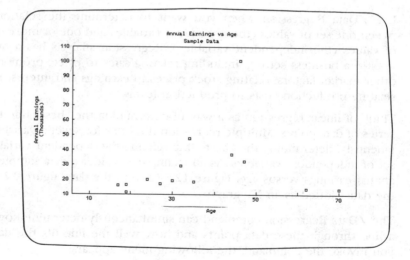

The **Output-Range** option specifies the upper left corner of the results range. This should be an unused section of the worksheet—the output is written over any existing cell contents.

The **Intercept** option lets you specify whether you want the regression to calculate a constant value. Calculating the constant is the default, but you may need to exclude a constant in some applications.

Figure 12.59 shows the results of using the **/Data Regression** command in the annual earnings versus age example. The results include the value of the constant and the coefficient of the single independent variable you specified with the **X**-Range option. The results also include a number of regression statistics that describe how well the regression line fits the data. In this case, the r-squared value and the standard errors of the constant and the regression coefficient all indicate that the regression line does not explain much of the variation in the dependent variable.

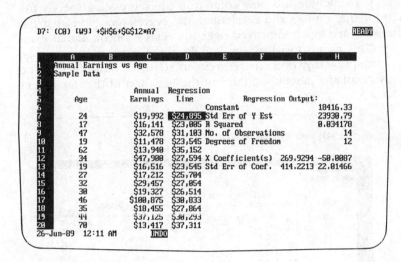

Fig. 12.59.
The results of
/Data
Regression on
annual
earnings versus
age.

The new data in column D is the computed regression line. These values consist of the constant plus the coefficient of the independent variable times its value in each row of the data. This line can be plotted against the original data, as shown in figure 12.60.

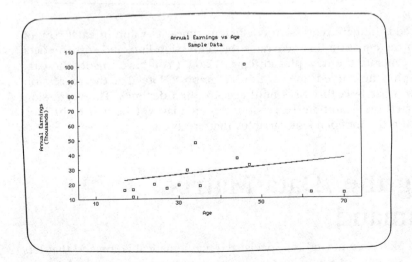

Fig. 12.60.
The plot of
annual
earnings versus
age data, with
regression line.

Looking at the annual earnings versus age plot, you notice that income appears to rise with age until about age 50; then income begins to decline. You can use the /Data Regression command to fit a line that describes such a relationship between annual earnings and age. In figure 12.61, the database is sorted by age. Column B has been added and contains the square of the age in column A. To include this new column in the regression, specify the range A7..B20 for the x-range and recalculate the regression. Note that the regression statistics are much improved over the regression of annual earnings versus age. This means that the new line fits the data more closely than the previous example. (However, the regression statistics indicate that the regression only "explains" about one-third of the variation of the dependent variable.)

Fig. 12.61.
Annual
earnings versus
age and the
square of age.

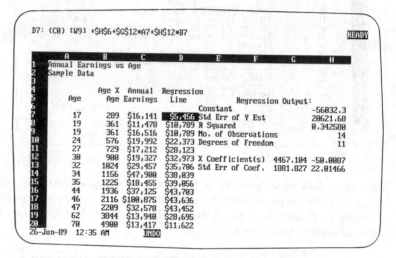

You must add the new regression coefficient times its value in each row of the data to the equation that generates the regression line, and sort the data by age, to generate the new plot in figure 12.62. (You have to sort the data by age to plot the curved line on the XY graph.) Note that the regression line is now a parabola that rises until age 45, then declines. The regression line generated by a multiple regression may or may not be a straight line, depending on the independent variables that are used.

Using the /Data Matrix Command

The /Data Matrix command is a specialized mathematical command that lets you solve systems of simultaneous linear equations and manipulate the

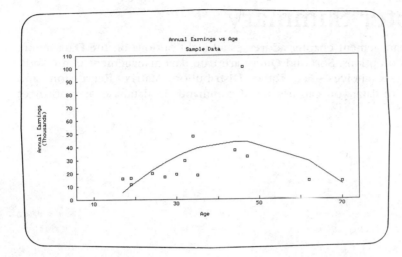

*Fig. 12.62.
The plot of
annual
earnings versus
age, with
revised
regression line.*

resulting solutions. This command is powerful but has limited application in a business setting. If you are using 1-2-3 for certain types of economic analysis or for scientific or engineering calculations, you may find this command valuable.

The **/D**ata Matrix command has a menu with two options: Invert and Multiply. The **I**nvert option lets you invert a nonsingular square matrix of up to 90 rows and columns. Just select the Invert option and highlight the range you want to invert. Then select an output range to hold the inverted solution matrix. You can place the output range anywhere in the worksheet, including on top of the matrix you are inverting.

The time required to invert a matrix is proportional to the cube of the number of rows and columns. A 10-by-10 matrix takes about 6 seconds, and a 90-by-90 matrix takes almost 1 hour on an IBM PC with no math coprocessor. If you are going to use 1-2-3 to invert matrices, you may want to invest in an 8087, 80287, or 80387 math coprocessor for your computer.

The **M**ultiply option allows you to multiply two rectangular matrices together in accordance with the rules of matrix algebra. The number of columns in the first matrix must equal the number of rows in the second matrix. The result matrix has the same number of rows as the first matrix and the same number of columns as the second.

When you select **/D**ata Matrix Multiply, 1-2-3 prompts you for three ranges: the first matrix, the second matrix, and the output range. Multiply is fast compared to Invert, but may still take some time if you multiply large matrices.

Chapter Summary

The data-management chapter addresses all eight options on the **Data** menu. The first two options, **S**ort and **Q**uery are true data-management commands. The other six choices—**F**ill, **T**able, **D**istribution, **M**atrix, **R**egression, and **P**arse—create data; you can use these commands in database or worksheet applications.

13

Using Macros To Customize Your Worksheet

In addition to all the capabilities available from the commands in 1-2-3's main menu, two other features considerably enhance the powers of 1-2-3: macros and advanced macro commands. Using 1-2-3's macros and the advanced macro commands of 1-2-3 Release 2.2 (or the Command Language commands of 1-2-3 Release 2.01), you can automate and customize 1-2-3 for your particular applications. First, you can reduce multiple keystrokes to as few as a two-keystroke operation with 1-2-3 macros. Press two keys, such as Alt-Z, and 1-2-3 does the rest, whether you're formatting a range, creating a graph, or printing a worksheet. Second, you can control and customize worksheet applications with 1-2-3's powerful advanced macro commands.

Think of macros as the building blocks for advanced macro command programs. When you begin to add advanced macro commands to simple keystroke macros, you can control and automate many of the actions required to build, modify, and update 1-2-3 models. At the most sophisticated level, 1-2-3's advanced macro commands can be used as a full-fledged programming language for developing custom business applications.

This chapter introduces the concept of macros; explains how to create, use, and debug macros; and provides numerous examples that you can copy for your own applications. The next chapter introduces you to the advanced macro commands, helps you learn their functions and applications, and shows you how to create programs with them.

Defining a Macro

Before releasing 1-2-3 to the public in 1983, Lotus decided to describe macros as *typing alternatives*. This name was later deemphasized in favor of the term *macros*. In its most basic form, a macro is simply a collection of keystrokes. Keystrokes can be commands or simple text and numeric entries. Macros provide an alternative to typing data and commands from the keyboard—hence the name "typing alternative."

By creating a simple macro, for example, you can automate the sequence of seven keystrokes necessary to format a cell in Currency format. You can execute the seven keystrokes by pressing as few as two keys.

The Elements of Macros

A macro is nothing more than a specially named *text cell*. Macros are created by entering keystrokes (or representatives of those strokes) into a worksheet cell. Suppose, for example, that you want to create a simple macro to format the current cell to appear in Currency format with no decimal places. The macro would look like this:

    '/rfc0˜˜

You enter this macro into the worksheet in exactly the same way you enter any other label: by typing a label prefix followed by the characters in the label. The label prefix informs 1-2-3 that what follows should be treated as a label. If this prefix is not used, 1-2-3 automatically interprets the next character, /, as a command to be executed immediately instead of stored in the cell. Any of the four 1-2-3 label prefixes (', ", |, or ^) work equally well. (The ' symbol is used frequently because labels are usually aligned at the left edge of the cells.) If you use the | prefix at the beginning of a macro line, the prefixed line does not print if the print range begins in the column with the | symbol.

All macros that begin with certain nontext characters (/, \, +, −, (, $, #, @, ., or any number—1-2-3 interprets all other characters as text characters) must be started with a label prefix. Otherwise, 1-2-3 interprets the characters that follow as numbers or commands.

The next four characters in the sample macro represent the command used to create the desired format. After all, /rfc is simply shorthand for **/R**ange **F**ormat **C**urrency. The number 0 informs 1-2-3 that no digits are to be displayed to the right of the decimal. If you were entering this command from the keyboard, you would type the 0 in response to a prompt. In the macro, the 0 is simply assumed by 1-2-3.

At the end of the macro are two characters called *tildes*. When used in a macro, the tilde (˜) represents the Enter key. In this case, the two tildes signal that the Enter key should be pressed twice. Think about this for a moment. If you were entering this command from the keyboard, you would have to press Enter twice: once after supplying the 0 for the number of decimals, and again to signal that the format should be applied to the current cell.

Users of 1-2-3 Release 2.2 have the option of creating macros with the Learn feature. To create a macro this way, you select the **/Worksheet Learn Range** command and choose a range of blank cells down a single column large enough to store all the keystrokes you want to include in the macro. Because each cell holds no more than 40 characters, make sure you specify a range large enough for your macro when storing keystrokes in LEARN mode. Press Learn (Alt-F5) to turn on the Learn feature. Then type the keystrokes of the macro; in this case, type **/rfc0** and press Enter twice. When you are finished typing the keystrokes of the macro, press Learn (Alt-F5) again. The final step is to name the macro. The Learn feature and naming macros are described in detail later in this chapter.

RELEASE

2.2

1-2-3 also uses symbols other than the ˜ to stand for keystrokes. Look at the following macro:

'/rfc0˜.{END}{RIGHT}˜

This macro is similar to the one you just looked at, except that this macro causes the cell pointer to move. This macro can be used to format an entire row instead of just one cell.

Once again, notice the ' at the beginning of the macro and the ˜ symbol at the end. Notice also the phrase {END}{RIGHT} in the macro. The {END} in this phrase stands for the End key on the keyboard. The {RIGHT} represents the right-arrow key. This phrase has the same effect in the macro as these two keys have when they are typed in sequence from the keyboard. The cell pointer moves to the next boundary between blank and nonblank cells in the row.

Symbols and words within braces are used to represent all the special keys on the IBM PC keyboard. In every case, the name of the key (that is, RIGHT for the right arrow, or CALC for function key F9) is enclosed in braces. For example, {UP} represents the up-arrow key, {END} stands for the End key, and {GRAPH} represents the Graph (F10) key. Braces also are used to enclose advanced macro commands (also referred to as the Command Language in versions of 1-2-3 before Release 2.2). These commands are discussed in the next chapter. If you enclose in braces a phrase that is not a key name or an advanced macro command, 1-2-3 returns the error message Unrecognized key Range name {...}(A1), where {...} represents the invalid key name and (A1) indicates that the error occurred in cell A1.

RELEASE

2.2

In 1-2-3 Release 2.2, abbreviated key names can be used for arrow-key names. The symbols {U}, {D}, {L}, and {R} can be used in place of {UP}, {DOWN}, {LEFT}, and {RIGHT}.

Table 13.1 shows the complete list of special key representations.

Table 13.1
Special Key Representations in Macros

Keys	Action
Function Keys	

RELEASE

2.2

Keys	Action
{HELP}	Accesses 1-2-3's on-line help facility (same as F1); also enables you to capture this keystroke in a {GET} advanced macro command so that you can access customized help screens for a particular macro.
{EDIT}	Edits contents of current cell (same as F2).
{NAME}	Displays list of range names in the current worksheet (same as F3).
{ABS}	Converts relative reference to absolute (same as F4).
{GOTO}	Jumps cell pointer to cell coordinates (same as F5).
{WINDOW}	Moves cell pointer to other side of split screen (same as F6). In 1-2-3 Release 2.2, turns the display of settings sheets on or off when applicable.
{QUERY}	Repeats most recent query operation (same as F7).
{TABLE}	Repeats most recent table operation (same as F8).
{CALC}	Recalculates worksheet (same as F9).
{GRAPH}	Redraws current graph (same as F10).
Cell Pointer-Movement Keys	
{UP}	Moves cell pointer up one row.
{U}	Can be used instead of {UP} in Release 2.2.
{DOWN}	Moves cell pointer down one row.

RELEASE

2.2

Keys	Action
{D}	Can be used instead of {DOWN} in Release 2.2.
{LEFT}	Moves cell pointer left one column.
{L}	Can be used instead of {LEFT} in Release 2.2.
{RIGHT}	Moves cell pointer right one column.
{R}	Can be used instead of {RIGHT} in Release 2.2.
{BIGLEFT}	Moves cell pointer left one screen.
{BIGRIGHT}	Moves cell pointer right one screen.
{PGUP}	Moves cell pointer up 20 rows.
{PGDN}	Moves cell pointer down 20 rows.
{HOME}	Moves cell pointer to cell A1.
{END}	Used with {UP}, {DOWN}, {LEFT}, or {RIGHT} to move cell pointer to next boundary between blank and nonblank cells in the indicated direction. Used with {HOME} to move cell pointer to lower right corner of the defined worksheet.

Editing Keys

Keys	Action
{DELETE} or {DEL}	Used with {EDIT} to delete a single character from a cell definition.
{INSERT}	Toggles the editor between INSERT and OVERTYPE modes.
{ESCAPE} or {ESC}	Indicates the Esc key.
{BACKSPACE} or {BS}	Indicates the Backspace key.

Special Keys

Keys	Action
{BREAK}	Indicates the Ctrl-Break key. (Note: {Ctrl-Break} does not stop a macro.)
~	Indicates the Enter key.
{~}	Causes tilde to appear as ~.
{{} and {}}	Causes braces to appear as { and }.

RELEASE 2.2

RELEASE 2.2

RELEASE 2.2

RELEASE 2.2

In addition to these key representations, simple keystroke macros can use the ? symbol in braces ({}). {?} is used to make a macro pause so that the user can enter something manually—a range of cells, text, values, and the like. (See Chapter 14 for a detailed explanation of {?}.)

Function Key Grammar

Cue:
You can include a repetition factor within cell pointer-movement key representations.

To specify more than one use of a special key, you can include repetition factors inside the braces of a special-key phrase. You can use the following statements, for example:

{PGUP 3}	Press the PgUp key three times in a row.
{RIGHT JUMP}	Press the right-arrow key the number of times indicated by the value in the cell called JUMP.

Creating, Using, and Debugging Macros

The best macros are simple macros. Most users create macros to automate simple, repetitive tasks. When you start to use macros in your worksheets, keep several considerations in mind. Developing a macro involves some planning. You begin by defining the actions you want that macro to perform; then you determine the sequence of keystrokes necessary to accomplish those actions. After planning your macro, you face the problem of where to put it; you want your macros out of the way, but easily accessible from your main work area. You should document your macro when you enter it so that you can understand what it does if, after three months, you decide to change it. After entering a macro, you need to name it so that you can execute it. Sometimes, your macro may not work right the first time and needs "debugging." The following sections of this chapter deal with these considerations.

Planning Your Macro

Cue:
Step through the series of actions you want a macro to perform before you start creating the macro.

As already mentioned, a macro can be thought of as a substitute for keyboard commands. Because a macro is a substitute for keystrokes, the best way to plan a macro is to use the keyboard to step through the series of instructions you intend to include, one keystroke at a time. Do this before you start creating the macro. Take notes about each step as you go; then translate the keystrokes you have written down into a macro that conforms to the syntax rules. Users of 1-2-3 Release 2.2 can use the Learn feature, described later in this chapter, to create macros.

Macro syntax rules are summarized in the following list:

- Macro lines beginning with a command sequence (for example, /rfc) or certain nontext characters must be preceded by a label prefix.

- Commands are represented in macros with the first letters of the commands alone.

- The tilde (˜) is used to represent the action of pressing the Enter key in a macro.

The keystroke approach usually works well for simple macros. Stepping through an operation with the keyboard is an easy way to build simple macros.

For more complex macros, the best approach is to break a large macro into smaller macros that execute in series. Each small macro performs one simple operation; the series of simple operations together perform the desired application, such as printing a report, creating a graph or amortization table, or sorting a database.

This approach starts with an application's results. What is the application supposed to do or to produce? What form must the results take? If you start with the desired results and work backward, you lower the risk of producing the wrong results with your application.

Next, consider input. What data is needed? What data is available, and in what form? How much work is involved in moving from the data to the results?

Finally, look at the process. How do you analyze available data? How do you produce the desired results using 1-2-3? How can necessary calculations be divided into a series of tasks, each of which a simple macro can perform?

This "divide and conquer" method of breaking a complex task into simpler pieces is the key to successful development of complex worksheets, whether or not they include macros. Although this method entails initial work as you analyze and plan your macros, less work is required by the time your application functions properly.

Placing Your Macro

Many users create macros in the same worksheet containing the models with which the macros are used. You can, however, have a worksheet file containing nothing but macros (see "Creating a Macro Library in 1-2-3 Release 2.01" later in this chapter).

If you place macros in the same worksheet as your model, place the macros outside the area occupied by your main model. Organizing in this way helps keep you from accidentally overwriting or erasing part of a macro as you create your model (see fig. 13.1).

Caution:
Locate your macros in a worksheet area outside your main model.

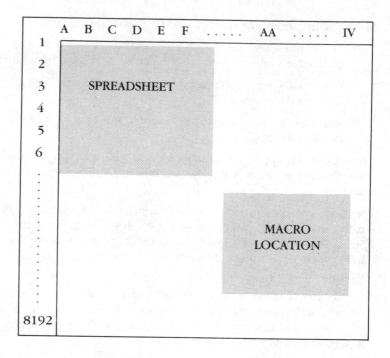

Fig. 13.1.
Positioning
macros outside
the worksheet
area.

Depending on how much space you want to leave on your worksheet for spreadsheet or database applications, you can reserve for your macros either the topmost rows of the worksheet or a few columns to the right of the area where you build most applications.

Macros are frequently put in column AA in this book (the macro name is in column AA; the macro text begins in AB). This column was selected for several reasons. Because the models in this book rarely require more than 26 columns, you don't have to worry about overwriting the macro area with the model. Also, because column AA is close enough to the origin, the macro area can be easily reached with the Tab key.

No rule says that you must place your macros in the same place in every model. In models that you use frequently, place the macros wherever it is most convenient. In small models, you may want to put your macros in column I. Column I lies just off the home screen when all the columns have a width of 9.

The range name MACROS is typically applied to the area of the sheet containing the macros. This allows quick access to macros with the GOTO command and the range name MACROS.

Experienced 1-2-3 users should note that, because Lotus has reworked the way 1-2-3 uses memory, placing macros outside the basic rectangle containing your model no longer consumes large amounts of memory. Placing macros outside the rectangle, however, causes the End-Home key sequence to place the cell pointer at the lower right corner of the overall worksheet, including the macro area, instead of at the lower right corner of the model. Placing macros outside the rectangle makes the End-Home key sequence less useful.

Documenting Your Macros

Professional programmers usually write programs that are *self-documented*, or *internally documented*. This means that the program contains comments that help explain each step. In the BASIC programming language, these comments are in REM (for REMark) statements. In the following program, for example, the REM statements explain the action taken by the other statements.

```
10  REM This program adds two numbers
20  REM Enter first number
30  INPUT A
40  REM Enter second number
50  INPUT B
60  REM Add numbers together
70  C = A+B
80  REM Display Result
90  Print C
```

You also should document your 1-2-3 macros. The best way to do this is to place the comments next to the macro steps in the column to the right of the macro. In the simple macro shown in figure 13.2, the macro name is in column AA, the macro itself is in column AB, and the comments are in column AC.

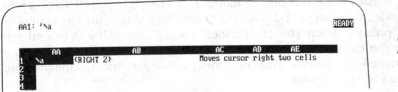

Fig. 13.2.
A suggested macro layout.

Including comments in your macros makes them far easier to use. Comments are especially useful when you have created complex macros important to the overall design of the worksheet. Suppose that you have created a complex macro but have not looked at it for a month. Then you decide to modify the macro. Without built-in comments, you may have a difficult time remembering what each step of the macro does.

Cue:
Documenting your macros makes debugging and modifying them easier.

RELEASE

2.2

Entire
Section

Creating Macros with the Learn Feature

1-2-3 Release 2.2 offers users a simplified way to create macros. This simplified approach to macros is called the Learn feature. To create a macro with the Learn feature, use the **/W**orksheet **L**earn **R**ange command. At the prompt Enter learn range:, enter the range where you want to locate the macro either by typing it or pointing to it. The range you enter should be either a single cell or a single-column range. If you enter a range such as AB1..AD20, 1-2-3 changes it to AB1..AB20. Once you enter the range location, begin to create the macro by pressing Learn (Alt-F5). When you press the Learn key, the LEARN indicator appears at the bottom of the screen as shown in figure 13.3.

Cue:
1-2-3 Release 2.2 users can use the Learn (Alt-F5) key to create macros.

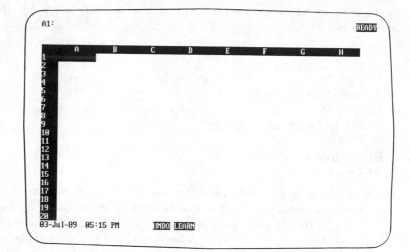

Fig. 13.3.
The LEARN indicator displayed after pressing Alt-F5 in 1-2-3 Release 2.2.

To enter a macro like the one in figure 13.2, simply type **{RIGHT 2}** in LEARN mode. As you type, 1-2-3 functions normally, displaying the results of your key presses. When you are finished, press Learn (Alt-F5) to end the macro. As you can see in figure 13.4, you get the same result as you would if you had typed the macro. The only thing missing is the documentation, which you can still provide.

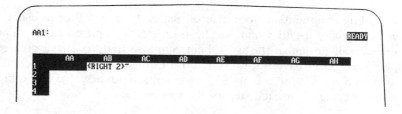

Fig. 13.4.
A macro created with the Learn feature.

If the macro you enter is too large for the specified range, you get the error message Learn range is full. If this happens, make the range larger using the /Worksheet Learn Range command. When you get the error message, notice that 1-2-3 includes as much of the macro as the range permits. Press Esc to return to READY mode, select /Worksheet Learn Range, and specify a new range directly under the previous range. Next, activate Learn and continue creating your macro from the point at which the error message appeared. If you want to cancel the current learn range, use the /Worksheet Learn Cancel command.

One thing to keep in mind about the Learn feature is that all keystrokes are recorded, even ones made in error. If in Learn mode you type /W instead of /R, for example, and you then press Esc to correct the error, the macro still contains this error. To correct an error in a short macro, start the process again. To start again, press Alt-F5 to exit the Learn feature; use the /Worksheet Learn Erase command to erase the macro you started to create. Now begin your macro again from scratch. If you make an error after entering a long macro, you may find it easier to edit the macro rather than creating it over again. You edit a macro created with the Learn feature the same way you edit a normal macro: press Edit (F2) from the cell containing the error.

Caution:
The Learn feature records all keystrokes, even those made in error.

To include an existing macro within the one you are recording, enter in braces the range name of the macro you want to include (for example, {MONTHS}).

1-2-3 does not record some keystrokes when you use the Learn feature. 1-2-3 does not record any /Worksheet Learn commands and does not record the following keystrokes: Compose (Alt-F1), Learn (Alt-F5), Run (Alt-F3), Undo (Alt-F4), Shift, Num Lock, and Scroll Lock.

Naming Macros

A macro entered in the worksheet must be given a name. The name must be located in the cell immediately to the left of the cell where the macro begins. The name you assign to a macro can be invoked directly from the keyboard and must meet certain special conditions. If you're using 1-2-3 Release 2.01, the macro name must be only one character, it must be an alphabetic character (or the number 0), and it must be preceded by a backslash (\ ). If you're using 1-2-3 Release 2.2, you have two macro-naming options: you can name a macro using the method used for 1-2-3 Release 2.01 (a backslash and a letter) or assign to the macro a range name of up to 15 characters.

RELEASE

2.2

1-2-3 Release 2.01 provides one way to invoke a macro—by pressing the Alt key and the letter in the macro name following the backslash. 1-2-3 Release 2.2 provides two methods for invoking macros. If you named a macro with a backslash and letter, invoke it by pressing Alt and the letter, or display a list of all macro names by pressing Run (Alt-F3). If you named a macro in 1-2-3 Release 2.2 with a range name of up to 15 characters, you must invoke the macro by pressing Run (Alt-F3). If you want to run a macro by pressing Alt and a letter key, you must name the macro with the backslash and a single alphabetic character.

Suppose that you have just built the macro shown in figure 13.5. Now you need to name this macro so that you can invoke it from the keyboard. Although you can give the macro any one-letter name, it is always a good idea to choose a name that in some way describes the macro. Obviously, creating descriptive one-letter names is difficult. In this case, for example, you could choose the name \d (for *dollar*) or \f (for *format*). Probably the best name for this macro is \$, but because the symbol $ is not a letter, \$ is not a legal macro name.

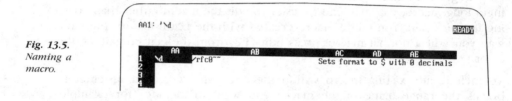

Fig. 13.5.
Naming a macro.

Suppose that you decide to name the macro \d. To assign the name, issue the command **/R**ange Name Create. Next, type the name you selected —**\d**—and press Enter. 1-2-3 then prompts you for the range to name. If the cell pointer is currently on cell AB1, you can press Enter to assign the specified name to the current cell. Otherwise, move the cell pointer to the desired cell or type the cell coordinates from the keyboard.

Some macros require more than one row of space. Look at the simple two-row macro in figure 13.6. To name this macro, you need to assign a name to only the first cell in the range that contains the macro. In this case, you could assign the name \c to cell AB1. You can, however, assign a name to the entire range AB1..AB2. Because you must leave at least one blank cell between macros, 1-2-3 "knows" that it has come to the end of a macro when it encounters a blank cell.

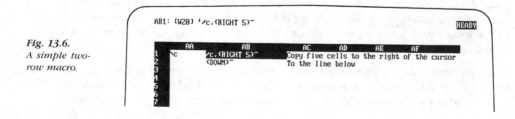

Fig. 13.6.
A simple two-row macro.

A variation on the **/R**ange Name Labels command can be very useful when you want to name a macro. The **R**ight option in the **R**ange Name Labels menu enables you to name a range using the contents of the cell immediately to the left of the range. Suppose that you have created the macro shown in figure 13.7.

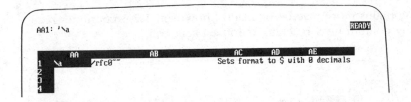

Fig. 13.7.
Naming a
macro with
/Range Name
Labels.

With your cell pointer on cell AA1, name the macro using the **/R**ange Name Labels **R**ight command. Using this command, you assign the name \a to the range AB1.

If you import macros from an external library file, you can use the **/R**ange Name Labels command to create names for the imported macros. In fact, one of the macros described in this chapter automatically imports a worksheet file and names all the macros in the file.

Executing Macros

In 1-2-3 Release 2.01, all macros except those named \0 are executed, or invoked, by pressing the Alt key, followed by the letter name of the macro. (Macros named \0 are executed automatically when the file in which they are included is retrieved.) If the macro you want to use is named \a, for example, you invoke it by pressing Alt-A. The \ symbol in the name represents the Alt key.

As soon as the command is issued, the macro starts to run. If no bugs or special instructions are built into the macro, it continues to run until it is finished. You will be amazed at the speed of macros; commands are issued faster than you can see them.

In 1-2-3 Release 2.2, not only can you invoke a macro by pressing the Alt key and the letter of the macro name, you also can invoke a macro by pressing the Run (Alt-F3) key. When you press Run (Alt-F3), a display such as the one shown in figure 13.8 appears. Range names, including all macro names, are displayed. If you want to see more than a single line of range names, press Name (F3) to produce a full-screen display (see fig. 13.9). To invoke one of the macros listed, point to it and press Enter.

RELEASE

2.2

Many macro keystrokes or commands can be stored in a single cell. Macros that are especially long or include special commands must be split into two or more cells, as in the example shown in figure 13.6. Splitting a macro into several cells is no problem. When executing a macro, 1-2-3 starts in the first cell until all the keystrokes stored there are used. 1-2-3 then moves down one cell to continue execution. If the cell below is blank, the program stops.

If that cell contains more macro commands, however, 1-2-3 continues reading down the column until reaching the first blank cell.

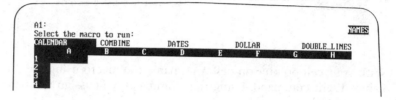

Fig. 13.8.
Results of
pressing Run
(Alt-F3) in
1-2-3 Release
2.2.

Fig. 13.9.
Results of
pressing Name
(F3) after
pressing Run
(Alt-F3) in
1-2-3 Release
2.2.

Cue:
Use /Range Justify
to edit a macro
text cell to make
the lines shorter.

If you use Learn to create macros, 1-2-3 stores approximately 40 characters in one cell. (The number of characters per cell varies because 1-2-3 does not break any element within curly braces.) All the characters are displayed if no entries appear in the cells immediately to the right or if the macro is 40 or more characters wide. If you want to split a long line into shorter lines, you must edit each line. A quick way to edit a cell to make the lines shorter is to insert a space where you want the line to break and then use **/R**ange Justify.

Using Automatic Macros

Reminder:
A macro named
\0 is executed
automatically when
its file is retrieved.

1-2-3 offers an exciting macro feature called *automatic macro execution.* This technique allows the user to create a special macro that executes automatically when the sheet is loaded. Use this type of macro, for example, whenever you want to retrieve a worksheet file and position the cell pointer in a special section of the worksheet as soon as the file is opened. The automatic macro is created just like any other macro. The only difference is in its name. The macro that you want to execute automatically must have the name \0 (backslash zero); therefore you can have only one automatic macro per worksheet.

An even more powerful feature of 1-2-3 is its capability to load a worksheet file automatically. When 1-2-3 loads, it automatically searches the current disk drive for a special worksheet file named AUTO123.WK1. If this file is on the disk, 1-2-3 automatically loads it. If the file contains a macro named \0, the macro is automatically executed.

You can use these features of 1-2-3 to create completely automated programs. First, as soon as you access the 1-2-3 program, the AUTO123.WK1 file is automatically loaded. Second, the /0 macro begins to run automatically without your pressing Alt-0 to invoke it. When combined with menus and macro commands, the automatic execution feature makes macros a remarkably user-friendly tool.

Note: The automatic macro cannot be executed using the Alt-0 key combination. If you need to execute the macro from the keyboard, press Run (Alt-F3), highlight the macro name, and press Enter.

Cue:
To invoke a \0 macro from the keyboard, press Run (Alt-F3), highlight the macro name, and press Enter.

You can have only one automatic macro in each worksheet. This macro can be as large as you want, however, and can include as many steps as you wish. The automatic macro also can access other macros in the sheet.

Avoiding Common Errors

Like all computer programs, macros are literal creatures and cannot discern an error in the code. You recognize immediately, for example, that {GOTI} is a misspelling of {GOTO}. A macro cannot make this distinction. The macro tries to interpret the misspelled word; because the macro is unable to do so, the result is an error message.

Because macros cannot second-guess what you mean, you must be extremely careful when you build your macros so that they have no errors. Misplaced spaces and tildes can cause difficulty for 1-2-3. No matter how careful you are, however, some errors are going to slip through.

The greatest problem most beginners have with macros is forgetting to represent all the required Enter keystrokes in the macros. This oversight can lead to some dismaying results. The missing ~ after {RIGHT 5} in the macro in figure 13.10, for example, causes the {DOWN} command to be included in the definition of the FROM range of the /Copy command, instead of defining the TO range. The result of running this macro is shown in figure 13.11. As you can see, the /Copy command in the macro stopped in the middle of its execution because of the missing keystroke (the tilde).

Caution:
Misplaced tildes (~) and spaces will cause problems when running your macro.

Fig. 13.10.
A macro with a
missing ˜

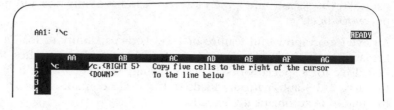

Fig. 13.11.
The result of
running the
macro with the
missing ˜

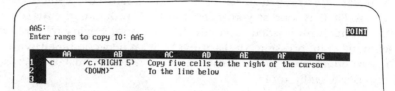

Another problem beginners have with 1-2-3 macros is remembering that the cell references included in macros are always absolute. Cell references do not change when cells are moved about or deleted from the sheet. The following simple macro, for example, erases the contents of cell A6:

'/re˜ A6˜

Suppose that you move the contents of cell A6 so that they now lie one cell to the right. To do this, select /Move, press Enter, press the right-arrow key, and press Enter again. Because you still want to erase the same cell contents from the sheet, you may expect the macro to read as follows:

'/re˜ B6˜

If you try this example, however, you see that the macro does *not* change.

If you think about it for a second, the static nature of macros makes perfect sense. A macro is nothing but a label. You wouldn't expect other labels to change when the sheet is changed. If you created the label 'A15A15A15A15, for example, you wouldn't expect it to change to 'C15C15C15C15 if you inserted two columns in the sheet to the left of column A. Macros are no different.

The absolute nature of cell references within macros is a strong argument in favor of using range names. Because a range name remains associated with the same range even when the range is moved, range names within macros (and other formulas) follow the cells to which they apply, eliminating the problem described.

Debugging a Macro

Almost no program works perfectly the first time. In nearly every case, errors exist that cause the program to malfunction. Programmers call these problems *bugs*, and the process of eliminating the errors *debugging the program*.

Like programs written in other programming languages, 1-2-3 macros may need to be debugged before they can be used. 1-2-3 has an extremely useful tool that helps make debugging fairly simple: the Step function. When 1-2-3 is in STEP mode, all macros are executed one step at a time. 1-2-3 pauses between each keystroke stored in the macro, enabling the user to follow along step by step with the macro as it executes.

Reminder:
1-2-3's STEP mode (accessed by pressing Alt-F2) enables you to run a macro one step at a time.

Step through the "buggy" macro shown in figure 13.10. This macro was supposed to copy the contents of five cells to the next line. If you ran this macro, you would see the screen shown in figure 13.11. Figure 13.11 gives no indication that the line below has been included in the FROM range. All you know is that the macro ends with 1-2-3 waiting for you to specify the TO range.

Once an error is discovered, you must first get out of the macro and into READY mode by pressing Esc once or more times. When the mode indicator reads READY, you can start debugging the macro.

Assume that you don't know what the problem is with the macro. You should enter STEP mode and rerun the macro. To invoke the single-step mode, press Alt-F2. When you do this, the STEP status indicator appears. This indicator changes as soon as you start the macro to be debugged. If you are using 1-2-3 Release 2.2, the STEP indicator disappears and two pieces of information appear in the lower left corner of the screen: the macro's cell address and the contents of that cell. The current macro instruction appears in reverse video. If you are using 1-2-3 Release 2.01, the STEP indicator changes to SST when you start the macro to be debugged. When you start the macro to be debugged after you press Alt-F2, the macro moves forward one step at a time. After each step, the macro pauses and waits for you to press a key before continuing. Although any key can be used, the space bar is recommended to step through a macro.

RELEASE

2.2

As you step through the macro, which was executed with the cell pointer in cell AA5, each command appears in the control panel. In the example, just before the error occurs, the control panel looks like that in figure 13.12.

Thanks to STEP mode, when the error occurs, you easily can pinpoint the location of the error in the macro. Once the error is identified, exit STEP mode by pressing Alt-F2 again. Then abort the macro by pressing Esc one or more times until the READY indicator appears.

Fig. 13.12.
The macro just
before the error
occurs in STEP
mode.

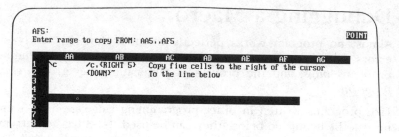

Editing the Macro

Cue:
To correct a
macro, don't
rewrite it; just edit
the cell with the
erroneous
instruction.

You now are ready to repair the error in the macro. Fixing an error in a macro is as simple as editing the cell that contains the erroneous code. You don't need to rewrite the cell; you need only to change the element in error. In the example, first move the cell pointer to cell AB1 and press Edit (F2) to enter EDIT mode. Because the error is a missing ˜, fixing the macro is easy. Just type ˜   (the editor inserts the typed character at the end of the existing cell contents) and press Enter to exit EDIT mode.

Although editing complex macros can be tougher than editing simple ones like this one, the concept is the same. Use 1-2-3's cell editor (accessed by pressing Edit [F2]) to correct the cell that contains the error.

Creating Simple Macros

Now that you have been introduced to the elements of macros and to some of the considerations in using macros, it's time for you to create some simple but useful macros of your own. The following examples provide simple typing-alternative macros. In the next chapter, you learn how to use advanced macro commands to go beyond simple typing-alternative macros. The macros discussed here are useful in various situations and can significantly enhance your productivity as a 1-2-3 user.

Reviewing Some Examples of Macros

The 1-2-3 beginner may try to avoid macros until he or she is fairly comfortable with 1-2-3 in general. You don't need to know everything about 1-2-3 before you begin to use macros. This section contains a number of macros that you can use right away.

A Macro To Format a Range

Macros can be *open-ended* or *close-ended*. Close-ended macros complete the command operation; open-ended macros stop before the command operation is complete to let the user finish the command manually.

One of the macros already created in this chapter makes an excellent open-ended macro. The close-ended macro used to change a cell to the **Currency** format ('/rfc0˜˜) can be converted to an open-ended macro through the removal of the second tilde from the end of the macro:

'/rfc0˜

This macro works precisely like its close-ended brother, except that here the macro does not complete the formatting command. Instead, it ends, leaving the command open and waiting for a range to be provided. When you use this macro, you enter the range from the keyboard and then press Enter.

This macro can be very useful. Sometimes you may have only one cell to format; at other times, you may want to format a whole row. This macro can be used in both situations. If you want to format only one cell, for example, place the cell pointer on the cell to be formatted and execute the macro. When the macro is finished, press Enter to complete the command. This applies the format to only the current cell. If you want to format an entire row, execute the macro and use the arrow keys to point to the range to be formatted.

Open-ended macros frequently specify every part of the command except the range to which the command applies. The range is provided from the keyboard. Such an open-ended macro enables you to apply a format or a command to any range in the sheet. You can simplify many **/R**ange commands by condensing them into open-ended macros.

A Macro To Erase a Range

For an example of how to simplify a **/R**ange command with an open-ended macro, consider the following macro:

'/re

This macro starts the **/R**ange **E**rase command but stops before assigning the range to be erased. The range is supplied from the keyboard. This macro is a quick way to erase any portion of the worksheet.

A Simple Pointing Macro

One of the most useful types of macros is a pointing macro. The following macro inserts in the current cell a formula to add the value of the cell three cells to the right to the value of the cell two cells down:

    '+{RIGHT 3}+{DOWN 2}

If the current cell is C17, the formula is as follows:

    +F17+C19

Notice that this macro includes nothing but mathematical symbols and cell pointer-movement key representations.

Macros To Enter Text

Although you normally enter macros from 1-2-3's READY mode, you also can invoke a macro from MENU mode or while you are entering a label or formula into the sheet. These alternatives enable you to create macros that enter commonly used phrases into the worksheet. Suppose that the word *expense* occurs a number of times in a given sheet. The word occurs by itself and in combination with other words, as in *sales expense* and *office expense*.

You can create a macro that enters the word *expense* in the current cell. The macro would look like this:

    ' expense

Notice that a space appears at the beginning of the macro. This space separates the word *expense* from any other word in the cell when the macro is invoked. Also notice that this is an open-ended macro (no final ~ appears). Other words can be appended in the cell after *expense*.

Suppose that you want to enter the label *expense--miscellaneous* in cell A55. First, invoke the macro to enter *expense* into the cell. Next, complete the phrase from the keyboard. The completed cell looks like this:

    ' expense--miscellaneous

Press Enter to close the cell. To enter the label *Telephone expense (Local)*, type **Telephone**, execute the macro, and type **(Local)** before pressing Enter.

This kind of macro can save time when you set up a large worksheet. Create a number of "common word" macros to use when you want to enter labels throughout the sheet.

A Macro To Create Headers

The simple macro in figure 13.13 can be used to create a row of column headers in the worksheet. Each cell contains the abbreviation of the name of a month.

Essentially, this macro scrolls across a row, inserting the name of one month in each cell before moving on. Notice the use of {RIGHT} to stand for the right-arrow key (→).

A Macro To Date the Worksheet

Thanks to 1-2-3's built-in date functions, you can date your worksheets with the @NOW function. The obvious way to date a sheet is to enter the @NOW function in an appropriate cell. But you encounter a problem with dating a worksheet this way. When the sheet is reloaded into memory after being saved, the program automatically recalculates the date, changing it before you view the sheet and defeating the purpose of dating the sheet in the first place.

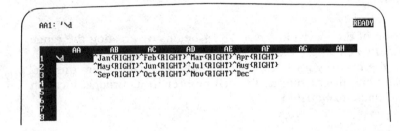

Fig. 13.13.
A macro for entering abbreviated months as centered column heads.

A macro solution to this problem exists. The simple macro in figure 13.14 automatically dates the sheet and ensures that the current date remains in the sheet.

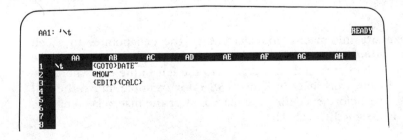

Fig. 13.14.
A macro that enters the system date in a cell with the range name DATE.

This macro assumes that the range name DATE has been assigned to a single cell somewhere in the sheet. The macro goes to the range with the name DATE and inserts the value of @NOW there. The cell DATE can be formatted in any way you choose for the best display of the date.

The third line of the macro is your old friend, the formula-to-value conversion. This line converts the contents of the DATE cell from the @NOW function to the actual numeric value of the @NOW function. This conversion keeps the date from being updated automatically the next time the sheet is loaded.

Cue:
Use /rncHERE to mark and return to the cell you started with.

The one problem with this macro is that it doesn't automatically return you to the point from which you started. Instead, the macro leaves the cell pointer on the DATE cell. This can be remedied, however, with the use of /rncHERE. If you modify the macro in figure 13.14 as follows, the cell pointer returns to its original location:

```
/rncHERE
{GOTO}DATE~
@NOW~
{EDIT}{CALC}
{GOTO}HERE~
/rndHERE~
```

This modification of the macro in figure 13.14 begins by creating the range name HERE for the cell where the cell pointer is located when the macro is invoked. Next, the macro goes to the cell named DATE and enters the current date. Finally, the macro returns the cell pointer to its original location and deletes the range name HERE.

A Macro To Name Macros

Although the **/R**ange Name Labels command is a convenient way to name macros, you can speed the process by creating a macro that automatically names another macro. This macro condenses the **/R**ange Name command into two keystrokes:

```
'/rnlr~
```

Before you execute this macro, you must move the cell pointer to a cell containing the *name* of the macro you want to name. Remember that the macro name must be in the cell immediately to the left of the cell where the macro begins. In the worksheet in figure 13.15, for example, move the cell pointer to cell AA1 before executing the macro. After the macro is complete, the name \w is assigned to cell AB1.

Creating a standard macro area in your worksheet makes the naming macro even simpler to use. Suppose that you decide to store your macros in column AB. This means that the names for the macros lie in column AA. You can then modify the range-naming macro to look like figure 13.16.

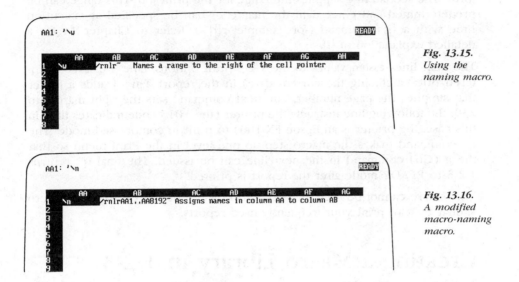

Fig. 13.15.
*Using the
naming macro.*

Fig. 13.16.
*A modified
macro-naming
macro.*

This macro names every cell in column AB with the cell references in column AA. If you use this macro, however, make sure that no "garbage" is in column AA, but only true macro names. Otherwise, the wrong names are assigned to the macros in column AB.

A Macro To Print the Worksheet

Macros can be used to automate complex tasks repeated frequently. Printing a large worksheet is such a task. Several steps are involved in readying the worksheet for printing: specifying the print range; aligning the paper in the printer; and specifying such options as borders, headers, footers, and margins. Although the design of a printing macro may vary from application to application, the sample model in figure 13.17 demonstrates many of the ways a macro can help with this task.

Cue:
Save time by
automating
worksheet printing
with a macro.

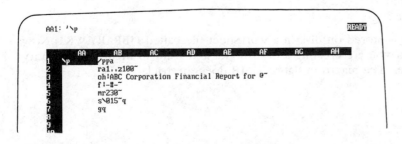

Fig. 13.17.
*A basic print
macro.*

This macro looks complex but is really very simple. The first line invokes the 1-2-3 /**P**rint **P**rinter **A**lign command, used to set the location of the top of form. The second line supplies the range for the print job. This range can be predetermined and entered in the macro or can be specified at execution time with a {?} command (for example, r{?}˜). Refer to Chapter 14 for a detailed explanation of {?}.

The next lines assign values to the 1-2-3 print options. Line 3 inserts a centered title (including the current date) in the report. Line 4 adds a footer that supplies the page number. The next command sets the right margin to 230; the following line instructs the printer (the \015 code indicates that, in this case, the printer is an Epson FX-100) to print in compressed mode. The q˜ command makes the macro step up one level in the **P**rint menu so that the g (**G**o) command in the next line can be issued. The final q˜ returns 1-2-3 to READY mode after the report is printed.

This macro cannot be used for every worksheet, but you can create a macro similar to it to print your frequently used reports.

Creating a Macro Library in 1-2-3 Release 2.01

Once you have become comfortable with macros and have developed a few that you find yourself using repeatedly, you may want to develop a *macro library* in 1-2-3 Release 2.01. A macro library is a worksheet containing several macros. A library typically also includes the name labels associated with each macro and any internal documentation you have written.

If you decide to create a macro library, you need the simple macro shown in figure 13.18. This macro loads into memory a set of macros that you have on disk and names each macro in the set. To create a macro library, you enter macros into a worksheet file that contains nothing but macros. Then assign the file a special name such as LIBRARY. The macro in figure 13.18 must be included in any other worksheet with which you want to use the macros in your macro library. Suppose that you have a macro library that contains the following macros:

\a   /rfc0˜˜
\b   /re.

This library is stored on disk in a worksheet file called LIBRARY.WK1. Now suppose that you are creating a new model and want to include this library in the model. The macro in figure 13.18 does the trick.

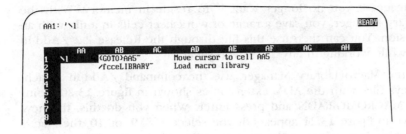

Fig. 13.18.
*A macro for
loading a
macro library.*

This macro performs two operations. It first moves the cell pointer to cell AA5 and then loads the file LIBRARY.WK1. The two macros in LIBRARY.WK1 are loaded into cells AA5 and AA7.

You can combine this macro with the one in figure 13.16 to create the macro shown in figure 13.19.

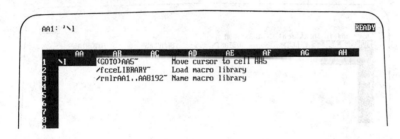

Fig. 13.19.
*A macro for
loading and
naming a
macro library.*

This macro loads and names the macro library. (Although columns AA and AB are used here, you can use any range you want to store your macros.)

Using the Macro Library Manager Add-In of 1-2-3 Release 2.2

RELEASE

2.2

Entire
Section

Users of 1-2-3 Release 2.2 can create a macro library worksheet as described in "Creating a Macro Library in 1-2-3 Release 2.01" or can use the Macro Library Manager add-in. You can use either method to develop a macro library, but if you use the Macro Library Manager add-in, you can put those macros to work more easily.

Attaching and Detaching the Macro Library Manager

Like any add-in product, you must "attach" the Macro Library Manager to 1-2-3 Release 2.2 before you can use it. You also must "detach" the Macro

Library Manager if you no longer want it to reside in memory. With the Macro Library Manager, you save a range of worksheet cells in a file with an MLB extension. You can then use this file through the Release 2.2 **/Add-In** command while working in any 1-2-3 worksheet.

To attach the Macro Library Manager, use the command **/Add-In Attach.** 1-2-3 displays files with the ADN extension as shown in figure 13.20. Point to the file MACROMGR.ADN and press Enter. When you do this, the new menu shown in figure 13.21 appears. If you select **7**, **8**, **9**, or **10**, the Macro Library Manager is attached to the corresponding Alt-function key combination. If you choose **7** from the menu in figure 13.21, for example, the Macro Library Manager is attached to Alt-F7. This means that you can invoke the Macro Library Manager by pressing Alt-F7. If you choose **No-Key** from the menu, you can invoke the program only from the command menu using **/Add-In Invoke.**

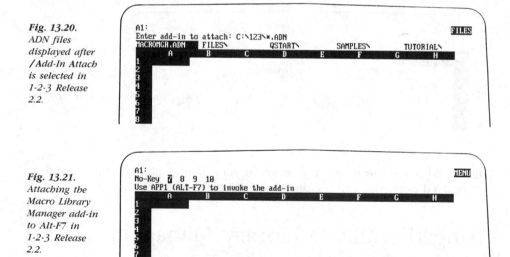

Fig. 13.20.
ADN files
displayed after
/Add-In Attach
is selected in
1-2-3 Release
2.2.

Fig. 13.21.
Attaching the
Macro Library
Manager add-in
to Alt-F7 in
1-2-3 Release
2.2.

To detach the Macro Library Manager, use **/Add-In Detach.** 1-2-3 lists the add-in programs currently in memory as shown in figure 13.22 (in this case, only one program is in memory). Point to MACROMGR and press Enter.

Invoking and Using the Macro Library Manager

If you attach the Macro Library Manager to an Alt-function key combination, you invoke it by pressing those keys (for example, Alt-F7). If you choose **No-Key**, you must use the **/Add-In Invoke** command. Names of add-in pro-

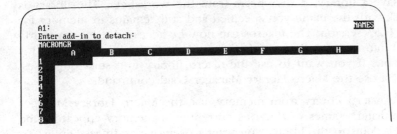

Fig. 13.22.
A list of resident add-in programs displayed with /Add-In Detach in 1-2-3 Release 2.2.

grams currently in memory appear in the control panel when you issue this command. You invoke the add-in program by pointing to it and pressing Enter.

Once you invoke the Macro Library Manager, the menu shown in figure 13.23 appears. Before you can use this menu, you must create a macro library. Press Esc to return to READY mode if you do not have a macro library. If you have a macro library like the one described in the preceding section, save it with the Macro Library Manager **S**ave command. The prompt Enter name of macro library to save: appears as shown in figure 13.24 when you select **S**ave. After you enter a macro library name, you are prompted for a range. After you enter the range of cells containing the macros that you want to include in the macro library, a password menu appears. Select **Y**es or **N**o for a password. (A password protects a macro library from being edited or viewed in STEP mode but does not prevent someone from loading and using the library.) 1-2-3 saves libraries with the MLB extension.

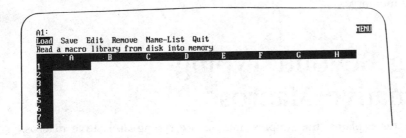

Fig. 13.23.
1-2-3 Release 2.2's Macro Library Manager menu.

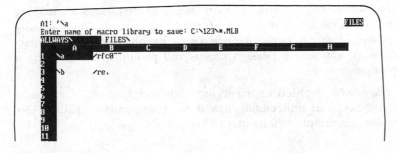

Fig. 13.24.
Saving a macro library with the Macro Library Manager in 1-2-3 Release 2.2.

When you save a library, it disappears from the worksheet. The library is saved on disk with the name you specified and still remains in memory for the current 1-2-3 session. The macros can now be accessed from any worksheet loaded into memory because the library is in the "background" and is always available. If you want to use the macro library in a subsequent session, you must use the Macro Library Manager Load command.

To remove a macro library from memory, use the Macro Library Manager **R**emove command. Names of libraries currently in memory appear in the control panel. Point to the library you want to remove and press Enter. To load a macro library, use the Macro Library Manager Load command. Load brings up library names in the control panel; point to the one you want to load.

Caution:
Choose a blank range to edit data with the Macro Library Manager.

To edit a macro library, use the Macro Library Manager **E**dit command. This command copies the macro library from memory into the current worksheet. Edit individual cells in the usual way—by pressing Edit (F2). You must be careful to choose a blank, unprotected range for the data to be edited because the Macro Library Manager writes over existing data when it copies a library into a worksheet.

The Macro Library Manager **N**ame-List command creates a list of range names in the worksheet. When you choose this command, macro library names appear in the control panel. Select a library by pointing to it and pressing Enter. The Macro Library Manager **Q**uit command, like other 1-2-3 **Q**uit commands, affects only the menu and not the macro library.

Remember that the Macro Library Manager enables the current library to remain in memory even after a worksheet is erased or a new worksheet is loaded into memory.

Going Beyond Typing-Alternative Macros

As this chapter explains, the simplest macros are typing-alternative macros. After you master creating and using this type of macro, you can move beyond simple keystroke macros to more sophisticated ones containing advanced macro commands. The advanced macro commands tremendously expand the power of simple keystroke macros by enabling you to link macros, call macros as subroutines, design menus and prompts, and perform a wide variety of other tasks.

Chapter 14 provides a detailed explanation of advanced macro commands, but to help you begin to understand how these commands enhance 1-2-3 macros, consider the sample macro that follows.

Suppose that you have created in column A a column of row heads similar to those shown in figure 13.25. Later you decide to indent each label one character. Indenting a single label is not difficult. You simply edit the cell by pressing Edit (F2), move the cursor to the far left of the cell by pressing the Home key, position the cursor one character to the right by pressing →, and then type a space. Finally, you press Enter to end the edit. Repeating this process 20 times, however, can be tedious.

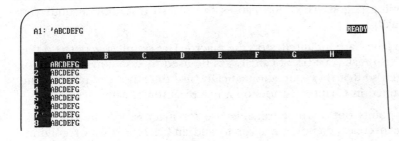

Fig. 13.25.
A column of row heads.

To automate this process, you can create a macro that contains a sequence of keystrokes for indenting and also uses one of 1-2-3's advanced macro commands (see fig. 13.26). The first two lines of the macro are simply keystroke selections; the third line includes the BRANCH command. This command causes the macro to loop so that the sequence of keystrokes repeats nonstop. When you run the macro, it automatically indents the entire column of heads (see fig. 13.27). To stop the macro after it has changed all of the heads, press Ctrl-Break and then Esc.

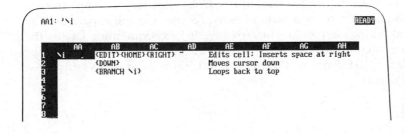

Fig. 13.26.
A macro for inserting a space in a column of row heads.

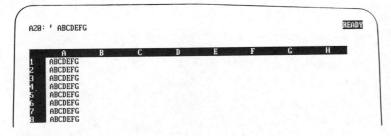

Fig. 13.27.
Row heads after running the macro.

Following is a more specific description of what each element in the macro does. Before invoking the macro, position the cell pointer in the cell containing the first head. After you press Alt-I, the macro begins by invoking EDIT mode and moving the cursor to the first space in the current cell. Line 2 of the macro moves the cell pointer down one row.

The statement in line 3 tells the macro to continue processing at the cell named \i. If you remember that this macro is named \i, you will realize that line 3 tells the macro to start over again. This kind of device is called a *loop* in programming jargon. This loop causes the macro to continue until you stop it manually.

Once all the labels are indented, stop the macro. The simplest way to do this is to press Ctrl-Break. Ctrl-Break can always be used to stop a macro. Macros can be written so that they stop automatically; use the advanced macro commands explained in Chapter 14 to stop a macro automatically.

This macro points out another valuable use for macros: *editing* the worksheet. You can create complex macros to add and delete rows or columns throughout the worksheet. Editing-type macros are most useful when the editing task must be performed repeatedly. When you have a repetitive editing task, try to create a macro to perform the job automatically.

Chapter Summary

By establishing the habit of creating macros for your most frequent 1-2-3 tasks, you save time and increase efficiency. Think of the operations you perform most often, jot down the series of keystrokes needed to complete each operation, and begin your own macro library. As you become experienced in creating and using keystroke macros, begin experimenting with the advanced macro commands of 1-2-3 Release 2.2 or the Command Language of 1-2-3 Release 2.01. Turn to Chapter 14 and learn about 1-2-3's advanced macro commands.

14

Introducing the
Advanced Macro
Commands

In addition to 1-2-3's keyboard macro capabilities, the program contains a powerful set of commands offering many features of a full-featured programming language. 1-2-3 Release 2.2 includes 50 commands called the advanced macro commands. 1-2-3 Release 2.01 provides 41 such commands (referred to as the Command Language in Que's *Using 1-2-3*, Special Edition). Throughout this chapter, these commands are referred to as the advanced macro commands. Both versions of 1-2-3 also include the original /x commands of 1-2-3 Release 1A. With the advanced macro commands, you can customize and automate 1-2-3 for your worksheet applications.

In the preceding chapter, you learned how to use macros to automate keystrokes to save time and streamline your work. This chapter explains the various advanced macro commands you can use to perform a variety of programming tasks.

This chapter is not designed to teach programming theory and concepts, but rather to introduce you to the capabilities of programming with the advanced macro commands. If you want to try your hand at programming, if you want to become your company's 1-2-3 expert, or if you are interested in developing template models to distribute on the open market, you should begin by reading this chapter.

Why Use the Advanced Macro Commands?

Programs created with the advanced macro commands give you added control and flexibility in the use of your 1-2-3 worksheets. With the advanced macro commands, you control such tasks as accepting input from the keyboard during a program, performing conditional tests, repeatedly performing a sequence of commands, and creating user-defined command menus.

You can use the advanced macro commands as a full-featured programming language to develop custom worksheets for specific business applications. For example, by developing advanced macro command programs that guide users to enter and change data on a worksheet, you can ensure that data is entered correctly. Even novice users who aren't familiar with all of 1-2-3's commands and operations can use this type of program application.

After learning the concepts and parts of the advanced macro commands discussed in this chapter, you'll be ready to develop programs that perform the following tasks:

- Create menu-driven spreadsheet/database models
- Accept and control input from a user
- Manipulate data within and among files
- Execute tasks a predetermined number of times
- Control program flow
- Set up and print multiple reports
- Make intelligent decisions based on user input
- Execute multiple programs based on decisions made within programs

As you become more experienced with the advanced macro commands, you'll be able to take full advantage of their power in order to do the following:

- Disengage or redefine the function keys
- Develop a complete business system—from order entry to inventory control to accounting
- Operate 1-2-3 as a disk-based database system—limiting the size and speed of the file operation only to those of the hard disk

If you want to take 1-2-3 to its practical limits, the set of advanced macro commands is the proper vehicle, and your creativity can be the necessary fuel.

What Are the Advanced Macro Commands?

The 1-2-3 Release 2.2 advanced macro commands are a set of 50 "invisible" commands (41 in 1-2-3 Release 2.01). These commands are called invisible because, unlike the command instructions invoked through the 1-2-3 menu and function keys, the advanced macro commands cannot be invoked from the keyboard. You can use these commands only within macro and advanced macro command programs.

The program in figure 14.1 illustrates how you can use the advanced macro commands. With commands such as MENUBRANCH and BRANCH, you can create custom menus to assist and prompt the user. The program in figure 14.1 begins by creating a range name wherever the user has positioned the cell pointer before invoking the program. The second line continues by displaying a custom help screen. The third line uses the MENUBRANCH command to display a menu with three options: to select the next help screen, to select the previous help screen, or to return to the original cell-pointer position in the worksheet. The BRANCH command in the last line of the first two options causes the program to redisplay the menu after the user has selected either the next or the previous help screen.

Reminder:
You can invoke advanced macro commands only from within macro and advanced macro command programs—not from the keyboard.

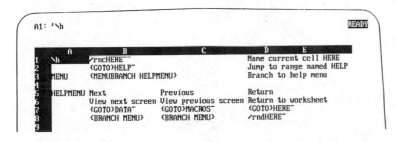

Fig. 14.1. Advanced macro command program using MENUBRANCH and BRANCH.

Notice that the program branches to range names and not to cell addresses. You will probably want to use this convention. Not only does this practice make the program easier to read, but as you move cells, insert and delete rows and columns, and rearrange your worksheet, 1-2-3 updates the range name address. Your program, then, continues to operate on the correct cells and ranges.

Cue:
Design your program so that it branches to range names, not to cell addresses.

As you read this chapter, you will learn about the commands for accepting input, controlling programs, making decisions, manipulating data, enhancing programs, and manipulating files. You will find tables that list and describe these commands throughout the text.

1-2-3's /x Commands

In addition to the 50 advanced macro commands of 1-2-3 Release 2.2 (41 commands in 1-2-3 Release 2.01), 1-2-3 includes a set of 8 /x commands. These commands were included in the original 1-2-3 Release 1A to provide a "limited" programming capability that went beyond simple keystroke macros. All 8 /x commands have advanced macro command counterparts. The 8 /x commands and their advanced macro command counterparts consist of the following:

/x Command	Description	Advanced Macro Command Alternative
/xi	Sets up an If-then-else condition	IF
/xq	Quits execution	QUIT
/xg	Instructs a program to continue at a new location	BRANCH
/xc	Runs a subroutine	{name}
/xr	Returns to the next line of the macro calling this routine	RETURN
/xm	Creates a menu	MENUBRANCH
/xn	Accepts input of only numeric entries	GETNUMBER

/xl	Accepts input of only labels	GETLABEL

Six of these commands work exactly like their advanced macro command counterparts: /xi, /xq, /xg, /xc, /xr, and /xm. For example, /xq performs exactly like the advanced macro command QUIT. When inserted into a program, both commands produce the same result.

The remaining /x commands—/xn and /xl—work a little differently than their comparable advanced macro commands. You use these commands to prompt the user for text and numeric data and then place the data in the current cell. Before GETLABEL and GETNUMBER (the advanced macro command counterparts) can do the same tasks, some programming is required. /xn, unlike GETNUMBER, does not allow users to enter alphabetical characters (except range names and cell addresses). /xn also does not let the user simply press Enter in response to the prompt.

Except in the special instances in which /xn and /xl perform differently from their advanced macro command counterparts, you should not use the /x commands in new programs developed in Release 2.01 or 2.2. /x commands are beneficial, however, because they enable you to run and modify in Release 2.01 or 2.2 those programs originally developed in Release 1A.

The Elements of Advanced Macro Command Programs

In the examples that follow, you will see how you can incorporate macros with the advanced macro commands to produce complete, efficient programs that take 1-2-3's macro capability far beyond simply automating keystrokes. Advanced macro command programs contain the advanced macro commands and all the elements that can be included in macros. Programs can include the following:

1. Keystrokes used for selecting 1-2-3 commands (for example, /rfc0)

2. Range names and cell addresses

3. Keywords for moving the cell pointer (see Chapter 13 for a list of keywords)

4. Keywords for function keys (see Chapter 13)

5. Keywords for editing (see Chapter 13)

6. Key representation for Enter:

7. Advanced macro commands

Advanced Macro Command Syntax

Like the keywords used in macros (discussed in Chapter 13), all commands in the advanced macro commands are enclosed in braces. Just as you must represent the right-arrow key in a macro as {RIGHT}, you must enclose a command such as QUIT in braces:

{QUIT}

Some commands amount to just a single command enclosed in braces. For example, to quit a macro during its execution, you use the command {QUIT}; no arguments are given. Many other commands, however, require additional arguments within the boundaries of the braces. The arguments that follow commands have a grammar similar to the grammar used in 1-2-3 functions. The general syntax of commands that require arguments is

{COMMAND argument1,argument2,...,argumentN}

When you use the BRANCH command to transfer program control to a specific location in the program, for example, you must follow the word BRANCH with the cell address or range name indicating where the program should branch. In the command {BRANCH rangename}, rangename is the argument.

An argument can consist of numbers, strings, cell addresses, range names, formulas, or functions. The command and the first argument are separated by a space, and for most commands, arguments are separated by commas (with no spaces). As you study the syntax for the specific commands described in this chapter, keep in mind the importance of following the conventions for spacing and punctuation.

Creating, Using, and Debugging Advanced Macro Command Programs

With advanced macro command programs, as with macros, you must keep several considerations in mind to ensure that your programs are efficient and error-free. You begin by defining which actions you want the program to perform and determining the sequence of those actions. Then you develop the program, test it, debug it, and cross-check its results for all possible operations.

If you have created keyboard macros, you have a head start on creating advanced macro command programs. These programs share many of the conventions used in the keyboard macros presented in Chapter 13. If you haven't experimented with 1-2-3 macros, you should take some time to review Chapter 13's simple keystroke macros before you try to develop advanced macro command programs. You also should review Chapter 13's discussions of creating, using, and debugging macros—many of the concepts are related to advanced macro command programs. For users who have created macros and read Chapter 13, the following text gives a brief overview.

Like keyboard macros, advanced macro command programs should be carefully planned and positioned in the worksheet. If you have macros you use with many different worksheets, you may want to group those macros in a separate file. When the time comes to use them, users of 1-2-3 Release 2.2 can use the Macro Library Manager to load the file into memory; users of 1-2-3 Release 2.01 can use the procedures explained in Chapter 13 on creating a macro library. If, however, you have a macro that is specific to one file, you should store the macro either in the topmost rows of your worksheet or in a few columns to the right of the area in which you enter most applications.

You enter advanced macro command programs just as you enter macros—as text cells. You must use a label prefix to start any line that begins with a nontext character (such as / or <) so that 1-2-3 does not interpret the characters that follow as numbers or commands.

After you decide where to locate your program and begin entering program lines, keep several considerations in mind. Remember to document your advanced macro command programs as you would document macros—to the right of each program line. Because advanced macro command programs are usually more complex than macros, documenting each line is essential. A documented program is easier to debug and change than an undocumented one.

Reminder:
Document each line of your advanced macro command program.

As described in Chapter 13, the way you name and invoke macro programs depends on which version of 1-2-3 you are using—Release 2.01 or 2.2.

You can name both 1-2-3 Release 2.01 and 2.2 macros or advanced macro command programs by using the backslash key and a letter character. To invoke macros and macro programs named with the backslash and letter, simply press and hold down the Alt key while pressing the appropriate letter key.

Reminder:
You can name advanced macro command programs with the backslash key and a letter character.

Alternatively, if you are using Release 2.2, you can name macros and macro programs with descriptive range names consisting of up to 15 characters. You invoke macros and macro programs with range names by using the Run (Alt-F3) key.

In 1-2-3 Release 2.01, macros or advanced macro command programs you named by using the backslash key and 0 are automatically executed when a worksheet is loaded. The same holds true for 1-2-3 Release 2.2 as long as the /Worksheet Global Default Autoexec setting is Yes (the default).

After you develop and start to run your program, you may need to debug it. Like macros, advanced macro command programs are subject to such problems as missing tildes (~) and misspelled keywords and range names. Another problem is the use of cell addresses that remain absolute in the program but have changed in a worksheet application. You can solve the cell-address problem by using range names in place of cell addresses wherever possible.

To debug advanced macro command programs, you use 1-2-3's STEP mode as you would for simple keyboard macros. Before you execute the program, press Record (Alt-F2) to invoke STEP mode. Then execute your advanced macro command program. Press any key or the space bar to activate each operation in the program. When you discover the error, press Record (Alt-F2) to turn off STEP mode; then press Esc and edit your program.

The Advanced Macro Commands

Using the power of the advanced macro commands, you can make 1-2-3 applications easier to use; you can enhance the features of 1-2-3's regular commands; and you can customize 1-2-3 for special worksheet applications. In the following sections, the advanced macro commands are grouped into six categories: accepting input, controlling programs, making decisions, manipulating data, enhancing programs, and manipulating files.

Commands for Accepting Input

The ?, GET, GETLABEL, GETNUMBER, and LOOK commands provide for all possible types of input into a 1-2-3 file (see table 14.1). You can use these commands to provide the operator with a more user-friendly interface than that of 1-2-3's standard commands and operations. For example, you can use these commands to create prompts that help the user enter data more easily. These commands also make easier the process of performing simple edit checks on the input before storing it in the worksheet.

Table 14.1
Commands for Accepting Input

Command	Description
{?}	Accepts any type of input
{GET}	Accepts a single character into the location specified
{GETLABEL}	Accepts a label into the location specified
{GETNUMBER}	Accepts a number into the location specified
{LOOK}	Places the first character from the type-ahead buffer into the location specified

The ? Command

The ? command causes the program to pause while you enter any type of information. During the pause, no prompt is displayed in the control panel; you can move the cell pointer to direct the location of the input. The program continues executing after you press the Enter key. The format for the ? command is as follows:

{?}   Accepts any type of input

For example, the following one-line program combines macro commands and an advanced macro command to create a file-retrieve program:

/fr{NAME}{?}~

This program displays all files in the current drive and directory and then pauses to accept input from the user. In this instance, you can either type the file name or simply move the cell pointer to a file name and press Enter.

Even if you press Enter after you type a {?} entry, you still must include a tilde (~) at the end of the menu sequence.

The GET Command

The GET command places a single keystroke into a target cell. The program can analyze or test the keystroke in a number of ways and then use the test results to change the flow of the program. The format for the GET command is as follows:

{GET location}   Accepts single keystroke into range defined
                          by location

Reminder:
Be sure to include a tilde (~) at the end of the menu sequence, even if you press Enter after typing a {?} entry.

The following example illustrates how you can use GET:

```
{GET CAPTURE}
{IF CAPTURE = "Y"}/fs~ r~
{GOTO}SALES~
```

The GET statement traps individual keystrokes in a cell named CAPTURE. The second line evaluates CAPTURE. If the keystroke in CAPTURE is the letter Y, the file is saved automatically. If CAPTURE contains any other keystroke, /fs~ r~ is ignored. In either case, control is passed to the third line of the program, which places the cell pointer at the beginning of the range SALES.

The GETLABEL Command

The GETLABEL command accepts any type of entry from the keyboard. The prompt, which must be a string enclosed in quotation marks, is then displayed in the control panel. With this command, the entry is placed in the location cell as a label when the user presses the Enter key. The format for the GETLABEL command is as follows:

```
{GETLABEL prompt,location}       Accepts label into location
```

The following example illustrates how you can use GETLABEL in a macro program:

```
{GETLABEL "Enter order date (MM/DD/YY): ",ENTRY}~
{GOTO}ORDER~ @DATEVALUE(ENTRY)~ /rfd1~
```

The GETLABEL statement displays a prompt and accepts a label date into the cell named ENTRY. The second line places in the cell named ORDER a formula that converts the label date to a numerical date and then formats the cell to appear as a date.

Figure 14.2 shows how to use GETLABEL with the IF, BRANCH, and BEEP commands (discussed later in this chapter) to prompt the user for a description of a part. If the user makes an incorrect entry, the second GETLABEL command displays an error message, and the program pauses until the user presses any key. Remember that whatever is entered in response to the prompt is stored in DESC.

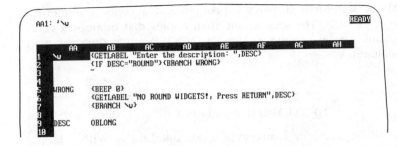

Fig. 14.2.
Using the GETLABEL command with other commands for more complex string input.

GETLABEL versus /xl

GETLABEL and /xl are identical except for one /xl command feature. Suppose, for example, that you write the /xl command as follows:

    /xlprompt˜˜

The label entered in response to the prompt is placed at the cell pointer's current location. You cannot write this kind of instruction with the GETLABEL command; 1-2-3 displays an error message if you don't specify a location for the argument. Using the /xl command is much more convenient than using the GETLABEL command, for example, in a subroutine in which the location of the destination cell changes with each subroutine call. By using /xl in such a situation, you don't have to specify the location at which the label will be placed.

The GETNUMBER Command

The GETNUMBER command accepts only numerical entries. If you enter a label, ERR is displayed in the cell. The prompt, which must be a string enclosed in quotation marks, is displayed in the control panel, and the entry is placed in the cell when you press Enter. The format for the GETNUMBER command is as follows:

    {GETNUMBER prompt,location}˜   Accepts the number into location

Consider the following example:

    {GETNUMBER "Enter classification code: ",CLASS}
    {HOME}{DOWN @COUNT(A2,A5000)}{DOWN}/cCLASS˜˜

The GETNUMBER statement displays a prompt and accepts a numerical entry into the cell CLASS. The second line then copies that numerical entry into the next blank row in column A. The @COUNT function finds the next open row in column A.

GETNUMBER versus /xn

The GETNUMBER and /xn commands work differently. With GET-NUMBER, a blank entry or a text entry causes ERR to be displayed in the cell location. With /xn, however, if the entry is a blank or a text entry, Invalid number input is displayed. After pressing the Esc key, the user is again prompted for a number. This difference can be useful in some applications. If, for example, you accidentally press Q (a letter) instead of the 1 key, the /xn command returns an error message. You also can use the /xn command in the following form:

/xnprompt˜

This command reads a numeric value into the current cell instead of into a specified location. (See the discussion at the end of the GETLABEL section.)

The LOOK Command

The LOOK command checks 1-2-3's type-ahead buffer. If any keys are pressed after the program starts executing, the first keystroke is placed in the target cell location. The LOOK command frequently is used to interrupt processing until you press a key. The general form of the command is as follows:

{LOOK location}   Places first character from type-ahead buffer into location

When the LOOK command is executed, the keyboard type-ahead buffer is checked, and the first character is copied into the indicated location. This means that you can type a character at any time, and the program will find it when the LOOK command is executed. An IF statement can then check the contents of location. Because the character is not removed from the type-ahead buffer, you must use the character or dispose of it before the program needs keyboard input or ends.

Commands for Controlling Programs

The commands shown in table 14.2 (BRANCH, MENUBRANCH, MENUCALL, RETURN, QUIT, ONERROR, BREAKON, BREAKOFF, WAIT, DISPATCH, DEFINE, and RESTART in both 1-2-3 Release 2.01 and 2.2 and SYSTEM in Release 2.2) allow varying degrees of control in 1-2-3 programs. These commands, used alone or in combination with decision-making commands, afford the programmer precise control of program flow.

Table 14.2
Commands for Controlling Programs

Command	Description
{BRANCH}	Continues program execution at the location specified
{MENUBRANCH}	Prompts user with menu found at the location specified
{MENUCALL}	Like MENUBRANCH, except that control returns to the statement after the MENUCALL
{RETURN}	Returns from a program subroutine
{QUIT}	Ends program execution
{ONERROR}	Traps errors, passing control to the branch specified
{BREAKON}	Enables the {BREAK} key
{BREAKOFF}	Disables the {BREAK} key
{WAIT}	Waits until the specified time
{DISPATCH}	Branches indirectly via the location specified
{DEFINE}	Specifies cells for subroutine arguments
{RESTART}	Cancels a subroutine
{SYSTEM}	Executes the specified operating-system command

RELEASE
2.2

The BRANCH Command

The BRANCH command causes program control to pass unconditionally to the cell address indicated in the BRANCH statement. The program begins reading commands and statements at the cell location indicated in the location argument. Program control does not return to the line from which it was passed unless directed to do so by another BRANCH statement. The general format of the BRANCH command is as follows:

{BRANCH location}   Continue program execution in cell specified
                      by location

The following example shows you how BRANCH can be used:

{GOTO}ENTRY˜ @COUNT(RANGE)˜
{BRANCH START}

The first line places the cell pointer in the cell named ENTRY and then enters an @COUNT function. The second line passes program control to the cell named START, regardless of any commands that may follow the BRANCH command (in either the same cell location or the cell below). Program commands are read beginning in the cell named START.

BRANCH is an unconditional command unless it is preceded by an IF conditional statement, as in the following example:

{IF C22 = "alpha"}{BRANCH G24}{GOTO}S101˜

The IF statement must be in the same cell to act as a conditional testing statement. For more information, see the discussion of the IF command.

The MENUBRANCH Command

The MENUBRANCH command defines and displays in the control panel a menu-selection structure from which you can initiate as many as eight individual programs. You select the desired menu item as you would make a selection from a 1-2-3 command menu. The format of the MENUBRANCH command is as follows:

{MENUBRANCH location}   Executes menu structure at location

The menu invoked by the MENUBRANCH command consists of one to eight consecutive columns in the worksheet. Each column corresponds to one item in the menu. The upper left corner of the range named in a MENU-BRANCH statement must refer to the first menu item; otherwise, you receive the following error message:

```
Invalid use of Menu macro command
```

Each menu item consists of three or more rows in the same column. The first row is the menu option name. Try to keep the option name items short so that they all will fit on the top line of the control panel. If the length of the option name exceeds 80 characters, 1-2-3 displays the following error message:

```
Invalid use of Menu macro command
```

Be careful to choose option names that begin with different letters. If two or more options begin with the same letter and you try to use the first-letter technique to access an option, 1-2-3 selects the first option it finds with the letter you specified.

The second row in the menu range contains descriptions of the menu items. The description is displayed in the bottom row of the control panel when the cell pointer highlights the name of the corresponding menu option. Each description can contain up to 80 characters of text. The description row must be present, even if it is blank.

The third row begins the actual program command sequence. Once the individual programs have been executed, program control must be directed by statements at the end of each individual program. No empty columns can exist between menu items; the column immediately to the right of the last menu item must be empty. You can supplement the 1-2-3 menu structure by creating a full-screen menu (for enhancement purposes only).

In figure 14.3, the MENUBRANCH statement produces a menu structure that begins in cell AB4. The individual programs begin in row 6 in each column. Each of these programs must contain a statement in order for the program to continue after the main task has been completed.

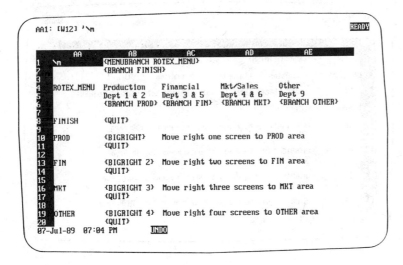

Fig. 14.3.
A program using the MENUBRANCH command.

Suppose, for example, that you are using the corporate personnel database and that you have entered the program shown in figure 14.3. When the MENUBRANCH statement is executed, 1-2-3 displays in the control panel the menu beginning at the cell ROTEX_MENU. (Note: The **/R**ange **N**ame **L**abel **R**ight command is used to assign the name ROTEX_MENU to the cell in which the label Production resides. Production is the first menu item.)

You can select the desired menu item either by moving the cell pointer with the arrow keys or by pressing the first letter of the menu item. You can also back out of a menu by pressing Esc, as you can when using the 1-2-3 command menus. The bottom line of the control panel contains a description of the menu item currently highlighted by the user. For instance, when you move the cell pointer to Financial, the third-line description is Dept 3 & 5.

The MENUCALL Command

The MENUCALL command is identical to the MENUBRANCH command except that 1-2-3 executes the menu program as a subroutine. After the individual menu programs have been executed, program control returns to the cell immediately below the cell that contains the MENUCALL statement. The format of the MENUCALL command is as follows:

{MENUCALL location}   Like MENUBRANCH except MENUCALL acts as a subroutine

Suppose that you replace the MENUBRANCH command in figure 14.3 with MENUCALL. The results are shown in figure 14.4.

Fig. 14.4.
Using the
MENUCALL
command in
place of
MENUBRANCH.

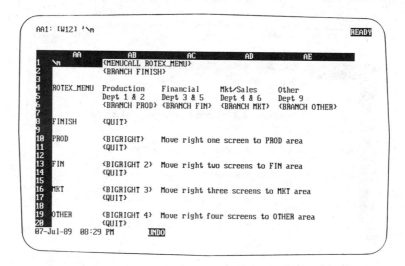

When you use MENUCALL, 1-2-3 returns to the statement immediately following the MENUCALL whenever the program reads a blank cell or a {RETURN}. Suppose, for example, that you select the Financial menu option, which causes 1-2-3 to branch to FIN. The first statement in FIN moves the cell pointer right two screens. When 1-2-3 encounters the {RETURN} statement, however, the flow of execution shifts back to the statement following the MENUCALL: the {BRANCH FINISH} statement.

533 : Introducing the Advanced Macro Commands **533**

Keep in mind that pressing Esc has the same effect with MENUCALL as it does with MENUBRANCH. Execution shifts to the statement following the MENUCALL statement.

The advantage of MENUCALL is that you can call the same menu from several different places in a program and continue execution from the calling point after the MENUCALL is finished.

Subroutines {name}

A subroutine is an independent program that can be run from within the main program. Calling a subroutine is as easy as enclosing the name of a routine in braces—for example, {SUB}. When 1-2-3 encounters a name in braces, the program passes control to the named routine. Then, when the routine is finished (when 1-2-3 encounters a blank cell or a {RETURN}), program control passes back to the command in the cell below the cell that called the subroutine.

Using subroutines can decrease creation time. For example, rather than include the same program lines to display a help screen in each advanced macro command program you create, type the program lines once to create the help screen and call those lines as a subroutine from each program.

You can isolate a problem much more easily if you use subroutines. If you suspect that a subroutine is creating a problem, you can replace the call to the subroutine with a {BEEP}. Then run the program. If the program runs correctly, beeping when the subroutine should be called, you know that the problem is in the subroutine.

Subroutines are easy to enhance. If you decide to add new commands, you can modify your subroutine once. All programs that call that subroutine will reflect the new commands.

The greatest benefit of a subroutine, however, is that any program can use it. Simply create the subroutine once and then call it at any time from any program. When the subroutine is finished, program execution returns to the originating program.

The RETURN Command

The RETURN command indicates the end of subroutine execution and returns program control to the cell immediately below the cell that called the subroutine. When 1-2-3 reads the RETURN, control returns to the main program (or other subroutine) at the location after the subroutine call. Do not confuse RETURN with QUIT, which ends the program completely. You can use RETURN with the IF statement to return conditionally from a subroutine. The form of this command is as follows:

{RETURN}   Returns control from a subroutine

In figure 14.5, line one places the cell pointer in AA101 and then calls the subroutine {SUB}. After {SUB} is executed, the RETURN command passes control to the next command after the subroutine call, placing the cell pointer in the HOME position and then copying the range of cells entered by the subroutine into the range identified by the HOME position as its upper left corner.

Fig. 14.5.
Using the
RETURN
command.

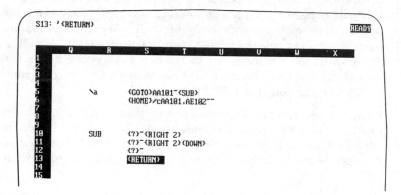

1-2-3 also ends a subroutine and returns to the calling routine when the program encounters, while executing the subroutine, a cell that either is blank or contains a numeric value. Although this method of returning from a subroutine works, the RETURN command is preferred because it delimits a particular set of macro keywords and advanced macro command instructions as a subroutine.

The QUIT Command

The QUIT command forces the program to terminate unconditionally. Even without a QUIT command, the program will terminate if it encounters (within the program sequence) a cell that is empty or contains an entry other than a string. A good practice, however, is always to include a QUIT statement at the end of your programs to indicate that you intend execution to stop. (Conversely, do not put a QUIT command at the end of a program that you intend to call as a subroutine.) The form of the QUIT command is as follows:

{QUIT}   Halts program execution

In the following example, the QUIT command forces the program sequence to terminate unconditionally:

{HOME}/fs˜ r{QUIT}

The program does not terminate unconditionally when QUIT is preceded by an IF conditional testing statement, as shown in the following example:

{IF SAMPLE<>0}{QUIT}
{BRANCH STAT}

In this example, QUIT terminates the program only if the value in the cell named SAMPLE is not equal to 0. Otherwise the program branches to the cell named STAT.

The ONERROR Command

The processing of advanced macro command programs is usually interrupted if a system error (such as Disk drive not ready) occurs during execution. By sidestepping system errors that normally would cause program termination, the ONERROR command allows programs to proceed. The general format of the command is as follows:

{ONERROR branch,message}   Traps errors; program control passes
                                      to branch

The ONERROR command passes program control to the cell indicated by the first argument. Any errors can be recorded in the message cell (the optional second argument).

As a general rule, you should always make sure that your ONERROR statement is executed by the program before an error takes place. Therefore, you may want to include an ONERROR statement near the start of your programs. Because you can have only one ONERROR statement in effect at a time, you should take special precautions to write your programs so that the corect ONERROR is active when its specific error is most probable.

In figure 14.6, the ONERROR statement acts as a safeguard against leaving drive A empty or not closing the drive door. If an error occurs, program control passes to S10, and the error message in V10 is displayed. Because S10 is the file-save sequence, this program will not continue until drive A contains a disk and the drive door has been closed.

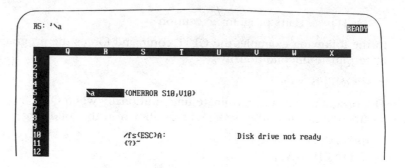

Fig. 14.6.
Using the
ONERROR
command to
prompt users to
close the drive
door.

The BREAKOFF Command

The easiest way to stop a program is to issue a Ctrl-Break command. However, 1-2-3 can eliminate the effect of a Ctrl-Break while a program is executing. By including a BREAKOFF command in your program, you can prevent the user from stopping the program before it completes. Note that before you use a BREAKOFF statement, you must be certain that the program has been fully debugged. Often, while debugging an advanced macro command program, you may need to issue a Ctrl-Break command to halt the program and make a "repair."

The BREAKOFF command disables the Ctrl-Break command during program execution. The format of the BREAKOFF command is as follows:

> {BREAKOFF}   Disables Ctrl-Break sequence

When a 1-2-3 menu structure is displayed in the control panel, you can halt program execution by pressing Esc, regardless of the presence of a BREAK-OFF command.

Cue:
To halt program
execution when a
menu structure is
displayed in the
control panel,
press Esc.

BREAKOFF is used primarily to prevent the user from interrupting a process and destroying the integrity of data in the worksheet. You will not need to use BREAKOFF unless you are developing extremely sophisticated programs; in such applications, however, BREAKOFF can be an important safeguard against problems.

The BREAKON Command

To restore the effect of Ctrl-Break, use the BREAKON command. The format of this command is as follows:

> {BREAKON}   Enables Ctrl-Break sequence

You will probably want a simple one-line program that issues a BREAKON, just in case something happens to your original program during execution. You also may want to make sure that the last statement in your program before QUIT is BREAKON. Including BREAKON allows you to use Ctrl-Break to stop program execution or stop command executions.

Because any Ctrl-Break commands in the keyboard buffer are executed as soon as the BREAKON command is executed, be sure that you place BREAKON where the program can stop safely. Figure 14.7 demonstrates how you can use the BREAKOFF and BREAKON commands.

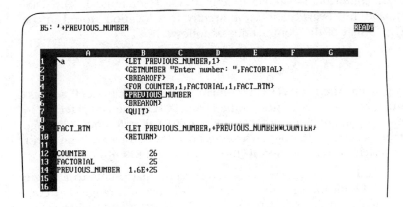

Fig. 14.7.
Using the
BREAKON and
BREAKOFF
commands.

The WAIT Command

The WAIT command causes the program to pause until an appointed time. The general form of the WAIT command is as follows:

{WAIT argument}   Waits until time or elapsed time specified by argument

The WAIT statement in the following example makes the message display for five seconds:

```
{GOTO}PRINTMAC~
MAKE SURE THE PRINTER IS ON-LINE, AND PRESS ENTER
{WAIT @NOW+@TIME(0,0,5)}
/ppr
PRINT_RANGE~
gpq
```

The serial time-number must contain a date plus a time. If you want the program to wait until 6 p.m. today to continue, you can use the following expression:

{WAIT @INT(@NOW)+@TIME(18,0,0)}

To make the program pause for 50 seconds, use this expression:

{WAIT @NOW+@TIME(0,0,50)}

The DISPATCH Command

The DISPATCH command is similar to the BRANCH command. The DISPATCH command, however, branches indirectly to a location stored in the argument. The format of the command is as follows:

{DISPATCH location}   Branches indirectly to the address stored in location

The location given as the DISPATCH argument should contain a cell address or range name that is the destination of the DISPATCH. If the cell referred to by the location argument does not contain a valid cell reference or range name, an error occurs, and program execution either stops with an error message or transfers to the location in the current ONERROR command.

The location must be a cell reference or range name that points to a single cell reference. If the location is either a multicell range or a range that contains a single cell, the DISPATCH acts like a BRANCH statement and transfers execution directly to location.

In figure 14.8, the DISPATCH statement selects the subroutine to be executed, based on the input in the cell number generated by the GETLABEL statement. The string formula in the DISPATCH command concatenates the word SUB and the menu selection number entered by the user. Because the name of every subroutine begins with the word SUB, the DISPATCH command passes program control to the subroutine specified by the user.

Fig. 14.8.
An example of
the DISPATCH
command.

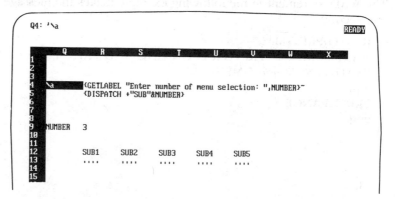

The DEFINE Command

An important subroutine feature of 1-2-3 is the capability of passing arguments by using only the keyword version of the subroutine call. A subroutine called with arguments must begin with a DEFINE statement that associates each argument with a specific cell location. The format of the subroutine call is as follows:

{DEFINE loc1:Type1,...}   Specifies cells for subroutine arguments where loc1, loc2, and so on are names or cell references for the cells in which to place the arguments passed from the main program

You can use one or more arguments, separated by commas. The type is either STRING or VALUE and is optional; the default is STRING. If an argument is STRING, the text of the corresponding argument in the subroutine call is placed in the indicated cell as a string value (label).

If an argument is VALUE, the corresponding argument in the subroutine call is treated as a formula, and its numeric or string value is placed in the argument cell. An error occurs if the corresponding argument in the subroutine call is not a valid number, string, or formula. You do not, however, have to put a string in quotation marks or have a leading plus sign (+) in a formula that uses cell references.

Passing arguments to and from subroutines is important if you want to get the most out of 1-2-3's subroutine capabilities. Subroutines with arguments simplify program coding and make the resulting macros easier to trace. Subroutine arguments are almost essential when you are developing a subroutine to perform a common function that you will use again and again.

The RESTART Command

Just as you can call subroutines from the main program, you also can call one subroutine from another. In fact, as 1-2-3 moves from one subroutine to the next, the program saves the addresses of where it has been. This technique is called *stacking*, or saving addresses on a stack. By saving the addresses on a stack, 1-2-3 can trace its way back through the subroutine calls to the main program.

If you decide that you don't want 1-2-3 to return by the path it came, you can use the RESTART command to eliminate the stack. In other words, the RESTART command allows a subroutine to be canceled at any time during execution. You will not need to use this command until you are an expert at writing advanced macro command programs. Once you reach this point, however, this command is helpful. You normally use the RESTART command with an IF statement under a conditional testing evaluation. The format for this command is as follows:

{RESTART}   Cancels a subroutine

Figure 14.9 illustrates how you can use RESTART to prevent a user from omitting data in a database. This example combines the GETLABEL, GET-NUMBER, and BRANCH commands to produce a simple database application for entering product information. GETLABEL and GETNUMBER are used to prompt the user for product data. If the product item number and price are omitted, RESTART prevents the user from continuing to enter new data. In the last line, BRANCH loops to repeat the process for entering a new record.

Fig. 14.9.
Using RESTART
in a database
application.

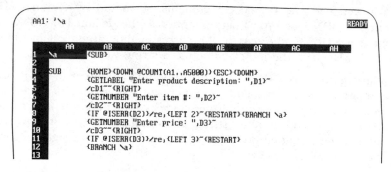

```
AA1: '\a                                                              READY

          AA        AB        AC        AD        AE        AF        AG        AH
1    \a        {SUB}
2
3    SUB       {HOME}{DOWN @COUNT(A1..A5000)}{ESC}{DOWN}
4              {GETLABEL "Enter product description: ",D1}~
5              /cD1~~{RIGHT}
6              {GETNUMBER "Enter item #: ",D2}~
7              /cD2~~{RIGHT}
8              {IF @ISERR(D2)}/re,{LEFT 2}~{RESTART}{BRANCH \a}
9              {GETNUMBER "Enter price: ",D3}~
10             /cD3~~{RIGHT}
11             {IF @ISERR(D3)}/re,{LEFT 3}~{RESTART}
12             {BRANCH \a}
13
```

The SYSTEM Command

Using the following format, Release 2.2's SYSTEM command executes any operating-system or batch command:

{SYSTEM command}   Executes the named command

The following shows how SYSTEM executes the batch file PARK:

{SYSTEM "PARK"}

The operating-system command you execute with SYSTEM can be any operating-system or batch command, and you have up to 125 characters with which to specify it.

Reminder:
Be sure to save
your files before
testing a macro
that uses SYSTEM.

Keep in mind some warnings when you use SYSTEM. First, if you attempt to load a memory-resident program, you may not be able to resume 1-2-3. Second, some batch commands may not let you resume 1-2-3. For these two reasons, you will want to be particularly careful to save your files before you begin testing a macro that uses SYSTEM. Also remember that if all you want to do is access the operating system during a 1-2-3 session, the /System menu command provides a convenient way to do this.

Commands for Making Decisions

The advanced macro commands for decision-making, shown in table 14.3, give you the capabilities of true programming languages such as BASIC. With the three commands (IF, FOR, and FORBREAK) presented in the following sections, you can test for numeric and string values. The IF command provides the kind of conditional logic available in many high-level languages. FOR and FORBREAK offer a conditional looping capability, allowing you to control how many times a group of commands is activated.

Table 14.3
Commands for Making Decisions

Command	Description
{IF}	Conditionally executes statements after IF
{FOR}	Activates a loop a specified number of times
{FORBREAK}	Terminates a FOR loop

The IF Command

The IF statement uses IF-THEN-ELSE logic to evaluate the existence of certain numeric and string values. The advanced macro command IF, commonly used to control program flow and enable the program to perform based on criteria provided by the user, is the functional equivalent of the IF command in BASIC. The form of the IF command is as follows:

{IF condition}{true} or {false} Executes true or false statements based on result of a condition; if the logical expression is true, the remaining commands on the same line are executed

These commands ordinarily include a BRANCH command to skip the {false} statements. If the expression is false, execution skips the commands (after the IF command) on the current line and continues on the next line.

As the following examples illustrate, IF statements can check for a variety of conditions, including the position of the cell pointer, a specific numeric value, or a specific string value. The following illustrates how IF can check the position of the cell pointer:

```
{IF @CELLPOINTER("row")=200}{BRANCH TEST}
{DOWN}{?}
{BRANCH SAMPLE}
{QUIT}
```

In this example the IF statement checks to see whether the current location of the cell pointer is row 200. If the cell pointer is on row 200, program control passes to the cell named TEST, where a QUIT command is executed. If the cell pointer is not on row 200, the cell pointer moves down a row, accepts input, and then branches back to the first line of the example, where the IF statement again checks to see whether the cell pointer is located on row 200.

The next example illustrates how you can use the IF command to evaluate a cell's value:

```
{IF LISTPR<19.95}{LET LISTPR,19.95}~ {QUIT}
{LET LISTPR,LISTPR*1.10}~
```

The IF statement evaluates the value in the cell named LISTPR. If value is less than 19.95, the program converts that value to 19.95, and program execution is halted. If the value in cell LISTPR is 19.95 or greater, the second line of the program replaces the value in cell LISTPR with the value represented by the equation (LISTPR*1.10).

The IF command also can evaluate a string value. You can, for example, develop IF statements that complete certain operations depending on whether the user enters Y (Yes) or N (No). Suppose, for example, that you want to test the value in a single-cell range called NEW_RECORD. If the value in NEW_RECORD is Y (for Yes), you want to add a new record to a database. Otherwise, you want to modify an existing record in the database. Your program can include the following statements:

```
{IF NEW_RECORD="Y"}{BRANCH NEW_ROUTINE}
{BRANCH MOD_ROUTINE}
```

The IF statement adds significant strength to 1-2-3's advanced macro commands. The IF statement's one disadvantage, however, is that if you want to execute more than one command after the logical test, the THEN clause must contain a branching statement or a subroutine call. What's more, if the code in the THEN clause does not branch or execute a QUIT command, the program continues its execution right through the ELSE clause.

The FOR and FORBREAK Commands

The FOR command is used to control the looping process in a program by calling a subroutine to be executed a certain number of times. FOR enables you to define the exact number of times the subroutine will be executed. The format of the FOR command is as follows:

{FOR counter,start,stop,step,routine}   Activates a loop a specific number of times

The FOR statement contains five arguments. The first argument is a cell that acts as the counter mechanism for the loop structure. The second argument is the starting number for the counter mechanism; the third is the completion number for the counter mechanism. The fourth argument is the incremental value for the counter mechanism, and the fifth is the name of the subroutine. Arguments 2, 3, and 4 can be values, cell addresses, or formulas. Arguments 1 and 5, however, must be range names or cell addresses. Because multiple loops are permitted, you need to be careful of the logical flow of multiple looping structures.

Notice how FOR is used in the simple example in figure 14.10. The FOR statement, in the first line of the program, controls how many times the program loops to format a column of values. The FOR statement begins by using the range named COUNT, located at B5, as a counter to keep track of how many times the program should loop. The second argument, 1, is the start number for the counter; the next argument, 5, is the stop number. The program keeps track of the looping process by comparing the counter against the stop number, and stops executing if the counter value is larger than the stop number.

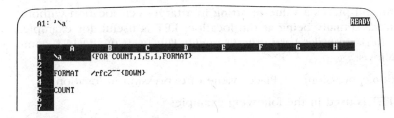

Fig. 14.10. Using FOR to control the number of loops in a formatting program.

The FOR statement's next argument, 1, is the step number—the value by which the counter is to be incremented after each loop. The last argument, FORMAT, is the name of the routine to be executed.

If you want to end the processing of a FOR command based on something other than the number of iterations, such as a conditional test, you can use the FORBREAK command. When you use this command, 1-2-3 interrupts the processing of the FOR command and continues execution with the command that follows the FOR statement.

Commands for Manipulating Data

The LET, PUT, CONTENTS, and BLANK commands allow precise placement of data within worksheet files. These commands, described in table 14.4, function similarly to menu commands such as /Copy, /Move, and Erase but provide capabilities that go beyond these simple operations.

Table 14.4
Commands for Manipulating Data

Command	Description
{LET}	Places value of expression in the location specified
{PUT}	Places value into cell within range
{CONTENTS}	Stores contents of the specified source into the specified destination
{BLANK}	Erases the cell or range

The LET Command

The LET command places a value or string in a target cell location without the cell pointer's actually being at the location. LET is useful, for example, for placing criteria in a database criteria range. The form of the LET command is as follows:

{LET location,expression}   Places value of expression in location

Notice how LET is used in the following example:

{IF PRICE> = 250000}{LET COM,"High"}~
{LET PAY,@ROUND(@PMT(PRIN,INT/12,TERM),0)}~

The LET statement in the first line is executed only if the condition in the IF statement is true. Regardless of the outcome of the first line, the LET statement in the second line is executed. The first line places a label in a cell; the second line places a value representing the formula (in the program) in a cell.

You can use a string value with the LET command. In fact, you even can use a string formula. Suppose, for example, that the cell named FIRST contains the string "Robert" and that LAST holds the string "Hamer". The following statement stores "Robert Hamer" in NAME:

{LET NAME,FIRST&" "&LAST}

Like the DEFINE command, the LET command allows you to specify :STRING and :VALUE suffixes after the argument. The :STRING suffix stores the text of the argument in the location, whereas the :VALUE suffix evaluates the argument as a string or numeric formula and places the result in the location. When a suffix is not specified, LET stores the argument's numeric or string value if it is a valid formula; otherwise, the text of the argument is stored. For example, the following statement stores "Robert Hamer" in NAME:

{LET NAME,FIRST&" "&LAST:VALUE}

The next statement, however, stores the string FIRST&" "&LAST in NAME:

{LET NAME,FIRST&" "&LAST:STRING}

Instead of using the LET command, you could move the cell pointer to the desired location with {GOTO} and enter the desired value into the cell. The LET command, however, has the advantage of not disturbing the current location of the cell pointer.

You also can use the **/D**ata Fill command to enter numbers, but not to enter string values. Overall, the LET command is a convenient and useful means for setting the value of a cell from within a program.

The PUT Command

The PUT command places a value in a target cell location determined by the intersection of a row and a column in a defined range. The form of the PUT command is as follows:

{PUT range,col,row,value}   Places value into cell within range

The PUT statement contains four arguments. The first argument defines the range into which the value will be placed. The second argument defines the column offset within the range; the third, the row offset within the range. The fourth indicates the value to be placed in the cell location. The first argument can be a range name or cell address. The second, third, and fourth arguments can be values, cell references, or formulas. Consider, for example, the following PUT statement:

{PUT TABLE,S1,S2,ARG4}

This statement places the contents of the cell named ARG4 into the range named TABLE at the intersection defined by the values in cells S1 and S2. The following examples show the results of different variations of this command. Keep in mind that the row and column offset numbers follow the same conventions followed by functions (the first column is number 0, the second is number 1, and so on).

{PUT A10..H40,0,1,21}   Places the number 21 in A11

{PUT A10..H40,4,6, Jack}   Places the label "Jack" in E16

{PUT A10..H40,7,30,4^2}   Places the number 16 in H40

The CONTENTS Command

The CONTENTS command stores the contents of the source cell in the destination cell, optionally assigning an individual cell width and/or cell format. If either width or format is not specified, the CONTENTS command uses the column width or format of the source location to format the string. The format of the CONTENTS command is as follows:

{CONTENTS   destination,source,width,format}   Stores contents of source to destination

Consider, for example, the following CONTENTS statement:

{CONTENTS THERE,HERE,11,121}

This statement places the contents of the cell named HERE in the cell named THERE, gives the individual cell a width of 11, and formats the entry as a full international date. Suppose, for example, that you want to copy the number 123.456, which resides in cell A21, to cell B25 and change the number to a string while you copy. The statement for this step is as follows:

{CONTENTS B25,A21}

The contents of cell B25 are displayed as the string '123.456 with a left-aligned label-prefix character.

Next, suppose that you want to change the width of the string when you copy it. Rather than display the string as 123.456, you want to display it as 123.4. You get the desired result by changing the statement to the following:

{CONTENTS B25,A21,6}

This second statement uses a width of 6 to display the string. The least significant digits of the number are truncated to create the string. If the number cannot be displayed in the specified width through the specified format, a string of asterisks (*) is displayed instead of the number. This statement works just like 1-2-3's normal worksheet formatting commands. For example, if you use /Range Format on a cell so that the contents are longer than what can be displayed in the cell, the cell shows a string of asterisks rather than the value.

Finally, suppose that you want to change the display format of the string while you copy it and change its width. The following string changes the display format to **Currency 0**:

{CONTENTS B25,A21,5,32}

The number used for the format number in this statement is listed among the CONTENTS command format numbers that appear in table 14.5. The result of the statement is the number $123.

Table 14.5
Numeric Format Codes for CONTENTS Command

Code	Destination String's Format
0	Fixed, 0 decimal places
1–15	Fixed, 1 to 15 decimal places
16–31	Sci (Scientific), 0 to 15 decimal places
32–47	Currency, 0 to 15 decimal places
48–63	Percent, 0 to 15 decimal places
64–79	Comma, 0 to 15 decimal places
112	+/− Bar Graph
113	General
114	**D1** (DD-MMM-YY)
115	**D2** (DD-MM)
116	**D3** (MMM-YY)
121	**D4** (Long International)
122	**D5** (Short International)
119	**D6** (HH:MM:SS AM/PM time format)
120	**D7** (HH:MM AM/PM time format)
123	**D8** (Long International time format)
124	**D9** (Short International time format)
117	Text format
118	Hidden format
127	Current window's default display format

In the following examples of the CONTENTS command with 123.456 as the number in cell A21, the width of column A is 9, and the display format for cell A21 is Fixed **2**.

Command	What is displayed
{CONTENTS B25,A21}	123.46 in Fixed **2** format
{CONTENTS B25,A21,4}	**** in a column 4 characters wide
{CONTENTS B25,A21,5,0}	123 with 0 decimal places in Fixed **2** format

The CONTENTS command is somewhat specialized but is useful in situations that require converting numeric values to formatted strings. Using the Text format, CONTENTS can convert long numeric formulas to strings. This application is particularly useful for debugging purposes.

The BLANK Command

The BLANK command erases a range of cells in the worksheet. Although this command works similarly to the /**R**ange **E**rase command, using BLANK has a few advantages over using /**R**ange **E**rase in your advanced macro command programs. Because BLANK works outside the menu structure, it is faster than /**R**ange **E**rase.

The format of the BLANK command is as follows:

{BLANK location}   Erases the range defined by location

In the following example, the BLANK statement erases RANGE1:

{BLANK RANGE1}
{IF S23<0}{BLANK RANGE2}

The second line executes the {BLANK RANGE2} statement only if the conditional IF statement tests true.

Commands for Enhancing Programs

The commands shown in table 14.6 (BEEP, PANELOFF, PANELON, WINDOWSOFF, WINDOWSON, FRAMEOFF, FRAMEON, BORDERSOFF, BORDERSON, GRAPHON, GRAPHOFF, INDICATE, RECALC, and RECALC-COL) can "dress up" your program or recalculate a portion of your worksheet. With skillful placement, these commands can add the polish that a solid program structure needs to become a smooth, easy-to-use application. This catch-all group of maintenance-oriented commands includes commands to sound your computer's speaker, control the screen display, and selectively recalculate portions of the worksheet. Two commands in this group—WIN-DOWSOFF and PANELOFF—can increase the execution speed of large advanced macro command programs significantly.

Table 14.6
Commands for Enhancing Programs

Command	Description
{BEEP}	Sounds one of the computer's four beeps
{PANELOFF}	Suppresses display in the control panel
{PANELON}	Reactivates the display in the control panel
{WINDOWSOFF}	Suppresses redisplay of the current window; in Release 2.2 also used to turns off the display of settings sheets
{WINDOWSON}	Enables redisplay of the current window; in Release 2.2 also used to turn on the display of settings sheets
{FRAMEOFF}	Suppresses the display of the worksheet frame (column border letters and row border numbers)
{FRAMEON}	Displays the worksheet frame (column border letters and row border numbers)
{BORDERSOFF}	Functions the same as FRAMEOFF
{BORDERSON}	Functions the same as FRAMEON
{GRAPHON}	Displays the current graph and/or sets the named graph
{GRAPHOFF}	Removes the graph displayed by GRAPHON
{INDICATE}	Resets the control panel indicator to the string specified (up to five characters in 1-2-3 Release 2.01; up to 240 characters in 1-2-3 Release 2.2)
{RECALC}	Recalculates a specified portion of the worksheet row-by-row
{RECALCCOL}	Recalculates a specified portion of the worksheet column-by-column

RELEASE

2.2

Entire
Section

The BEEP Command

The BEEP command activates the computer's speaker system to produce one of four tones. Each argument (1–4) produces a different tone. The BEEP command is commonly used to alert the user to a specific condition in the program or to draw the user's attention. The format of the BEEP command is as follows:

{BEEP number} or {BEEP}   Sounds one of the computer's four beeps

Consider the following BEEP statement:

{IF A35>50}{BEEP 2}

This statement produces a sound if the condition in the IF statement is true. If the condition is not true, program control passes to the next cell below the IF statement.

The PANELOFF Command

The PANELOFF command freezes the control panel, prohibiting the display of program commands in the control panel during program execution. Be aware, however, that the advanced macro commands such as MENU-BRANCH, MENUCALL, GETLABEL, GETNUMBER, and INDICATE override the PANELOFF command.

You can use this command to reposition or delete messages from the control panel, regardless of the cell pointer's current location. The format of the PANELOFF command is as follows:

{PANELOFF}   Suppresses display of control panel

RELEASE

2.2

If you are using Release 2.2, then in addition to using PANELOFF without an argument, you can use PANELOFF with the argument [clear]:

{PANELOFF[clear]}

This form of PANELOFF erases cell pointer information, the mode indicator, and the contents of the status line.

In the following example, the PANELOFF command suppresses display in the control panel of the /Copy command in the second line:

{PANELOFF}
/cC27..E39~ AB21~

The PANELON Command

The PANELON command unfreezes the control panel. This command is commonly used immediately before a GETLABEL or GETNUMBER command. The format of the PANELON command is as follows:

{PANELON}   Reactivates the display in the control panel

The following example shows how you can use PANELON:

{PANELOFF}
/cC27..E39˜ AB21˜
{PANELON}
{GETLABEL "Enter location code: ", AB20}˜

In this example the PANELON command reactivates the control panel so that the prompt for the GETLABEL statement is displayed.

The WINDOWSOFF Command

By using the WINDOWSOFF command, you can freeze the lower part of the screen and have just the control panel show the changes that occur as a result of the commands activated in your program. The WINDOWSOFF command freezes the current screen display, regardless of whether the program is executing.

WINDOWSOFF is particularly useful when you are creating applications for beginning 1-2-3 users. WINDOWSOFF enables you to display only those screen changes that the user must see, freezing other changes that might confuse beginners. The command has an additional function in Release 2.2: you can use the command to turn off the display of settings sheets—the windows that are displayed and that show special settings when you select certain commands, such as /Worksheet Global Default, /Worksheet /Global Status, /Graph Type, and /Data Sort. The format of the WINDOWSOFF command is as follows:

RELEASE

2.2

{WINDOWSOFF}   Suppresses screen display; also can turn off the
                  display of settings sheets in Release 2.2

Consider the following example:

{WINDOWSOFF} /cS24˜ Z12˜ {CALC}

In this example, the WINDOWSOFF command prevents the automatic screen-rebuilding associated with the /Copy command or the Calc (F9) key. Using the WINDOWSOFF and PANELOFF commands can have a significant effect on program execution time. In one complex application, the use of the WINDOWSOFF and PANELOFF commands to freeze the screen reduced execution time by 50 percent, from 5 minutes to 2 1/2 minutes. Speed reduction depends, of course, on the particular application.

You can use WINDOWSOFF with PANELOFF to create a graph "slide show" for business meetings. These commands allow you to display a sequence of graphs uninterrupted by intervening worksheet screens. The program in figure 14.11 demonstrates how to use the WINDOWSOFF and PANELOFF commands to eliminate screen shifting and to reduce execution time for such a presentation.

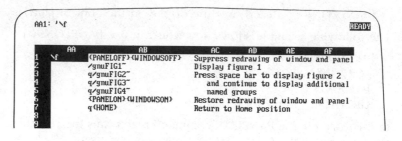

Fig. 14.11.
Using
WINDOWSOFF
and PANELOFF
for a graphics
slide show.

The PANELOFF and WINDOWSOFF commands in AB1 suppress redrawing of the window and panel. The commands in AB2 through AB5 display four different graphs. In AB6, the PANELON and WINDOWSON commands restore redrawing of the window and panel (see this chapter's section on the WINDOWSON command). The program ends in AB7 by returning the worksheet display with the cell pointer located at the HOME position.

Be aware that if something goes wrong with your program while the WINDOWSOFF command is in effect, you won't get a normal updating of your worksheet window. Unless you have a simple one-line program already preset for issuing the WINDOWSON command (see the following section on WINDOWSON), you may have to reboot 1-2-3 and start your application over to recover the use of the screen. Therefore, the wise practice is to develop and test your programs without the WINDOWSOFF and WINDOWSON commands; then add these commands to the debugged and tested program.

The WINDOWSON Command

RELEASE

2.2

The WINDOWSON command unfreezes the screen, allowing the display of executing program operations. This command is commonly used to allow the display of the 1-2-3 menu structures. The command has an additional function in Release 2.2: you can use WINDOWSON to turn on the display of settings sheets (which by default do not display while a macro is running).

Keep in mind that if a WINDOWSOFF command is in effect, two consecutive WINDOWSON commands are needed to turn on the display of settings sheets. The format of the WINDOWSON command is as follows:

{WINDOWSON}   Enables redisplay of the current window; also can turn on the display of settings sheets in Release 2.2

In figure 14.11, the WINDOWSON command in AB6 activates the display of the worksheet screen after all graphs have been shown.

The FRAMEOFF and BORDERSOFF Commands

RELEASE

2.2

Entire
Section

The FRAMEOFF and BORDERSOFF commands, new with Release 2.2, are identical in function. These commands remove from the screen display the column border letters and row border numbers, using the following formats:

{FRAMEOFF}   Supresses display of the worksheet frame or border

{BORDERSOFF} Supresses display of the worksheet borders or
              frame

After you execute a FRAMEOFF or BORDERSOFF command within an advanced macro command program, the worksheet frame display continues to be suppressed until either the command program encounters a FRAMEON or BORDERSON command, or the command program completes execution. FRAMEOFF and BORDERSOFF are effective when you want to change the screen interface temporarily or during the active time a macro is running. With FRAMEOFF and BORDERSOFF, for example, you can display a help screen, customized menus, or custom applications such as a database form without having to display these in the worksheet column-row border.

The FRAMEON and BORDERSON Commands

RELEASE

2.2

Entire
Section

The FRAMEON and BORDERSON commands, which are new with Release 2.2 and identical in function, redisplay the worksheet frame (column border letters and row border numbers) originally suppressed by a FRAMEOFF or BORDERSOFF command. The formats for the FRAMEON and BORDERSON commands are as follows:

{FRAMEON}   Redisplays the worksheet frame or border

{BORDERSON}   Redisplays the worksheet border or frame

The following example shows a simple program using FRAMEOFF and FRAMEON:

{FRAMEOFF}{?}
{FRAMEON}{?}
{FRAMEOFF}{?}

The program initially suppresses the display of the worksheet frame until you press a key, then redisplays the worksheet frame until you press a key, and then again suppresses the worksheet frame until you press a key.

If you construct this macro yourself, note that even though the last FRAME-OFF command doesn't have a matching FRAMEON command, the worksheet frame still is redisplayed when the command program ends. This program functions the same way if BORDERSOFF and BORDERSON are substituted for FRAMEOFF and FRAMEON.

The GRAPHON Command

The GRAPHON command, new with Release 2.2, can set the currently named graph, display the currently named graph, or first set and then display the currently named graph. The format for the GRAPHON command is as follows:

{GRAPHON named-graph,no-display}   Displays the current graph or another named graph, or sets the current graph without displaying it

To display a full-screen view of the currently named graph, simply use the command alone, as in the following:

{GRAPHON}

To display a graph other than the one currently named, reset the currently named graph and then display it. For example, if you have a graph setting named FIGURE1, you use the following structure:

{GRAPHON FIGURE1}

In either of the preceding two cases, 1-2-3 continues to display a full-sized version of the graph until the command program completes execution or until the command program encounters a GRAPHOFF command, another GRAPHON command, or a command that displays a prompt or menu (such as GETLABEL or MENUCALL).

To change the named graph but not display it, you use the no-display argument. For example, suppose that want a graph setting named FIGURE1 to be the current graph setting, but you don't want the graph displayed. You use the following structure:

{GRAPHON FIGURE1,no-display}

The following example shows these alternative command formats:

```
{GRAPHON FIG1}
{WAIT @NOW + @TIME(0,0,3)}
{GRAPHON FIG2, no-display}
{GRAPHON}
{WAIT @NOW + @TIME(0,0,3)}
{GRAPHOFF}
```

The first line of the program sets the current graph as FIG1 and displays it for three seconds, as indicated by the WAIT command in line 2. The third line sets the current graph setting as FIG2 but does not display it. The fourth line displays the current graph—just set as FIG2—for three seconds. The last line of the program redisplays the worksheet by executing the GRAPHOFF command.

The GRAPHOFF Command

The GRAPHOFF command, new with Release 2.2, removes the named graph from the display and redisplays the worksheet. The format for using the GRAPHOFF command, illustrated in the example presented in the GRAPHON section, is as follows:

{GRAPHOFF}

For more information about the GRAPHOFF command, refer to the preceding section on GRAPHON.

The INDICATE Command

The INDICATE command alters the mode indicator in the upper right corner of the 1-2-3 screen. This command is commonly used to provide custom indicators. In Release 2.01, INDICATE accepts a string argument of up to five characters. In Release 2.2, the string argument can be the width of your screen (up to 240 characters) When you use the INDICATE command in Release 2.01, you have to enter a string; you cannot use a cell address or range name. In Release 2.2, you can reference a cell that contains either the string or a formula that evaluates to a string. The format of the INDICATE command is as follows:

RELEASE

2.2

{INDICATE string}   Resets mode indicator to string (Release 2.01 or 2.2)

or

{INDICATE cell}   Resets mode indicator to string in referenced cell (Release 2.2)

Suppose, for example, that you want to display the message START in the upper right corner of the screen. You can use the following INDICATE command:

{INDICATE START}

Unless you clear your indicator, using {INDICATE} displays the START message until you exit from 1-2-3.

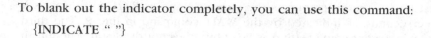

To blank out the indicator completely, you can use this command:

{INDICATE " "}

The RECALC and RECALCCOL Commands

Two macro commands, RECALC and RECALCCOL, allow you to recalculate a portion of the worksheet. This feature can be useful in large spreadsheets in which the recalculation time is long and in which you need to recalculate certain values before you proceed to the next processing step in your macro. The commands for partial recalculation use the following formats:

{RECALC location,condition,iteration-number}

and

{RECALCCOL location,condition,iteration-number}

In these commands, location is a range or range name that specifies the cells whose formulas are to be recalculated. The condition and iteration-number arguments are optional.

If the condition argument is included, the range is recalculated repeatedly until the condition has a logical value of TRUE (1). Remember that the condition must be either a logical expression or a reference to a cell within the recalculation range that contains a logical expression. If the condition is a reference to a cell outside the recalculation range, the value of the condition—either TRUE (1) or FALSE (0)—does not change, and the condition does not control the partial recalculation.

If the iteration-number argument is included, the condition argument must also be specified (the value 1 makes the condition always TRUE). The iteration-number specifies the number of times that formulas in the location range are to be recalculated.

The RECALC and RECALCCOL commands differ in the order in which cells in the specified range are recalculated. The RECALC command performs the calculations by row of all the cells in the first row of the range, then all the cells in the second row, and so on. The RECALCCOL command performs the calculations by column of all the cells in the first column of the range, followed by all the cells in the second column, and so on. If you use both commands, only cells within the specified range are recalculated.

Use RECALC to recalculate the range when the formulas in the range refer only to other formulas in rows above or to the left of themselves in the same row in that range. Use RECALCCOL to recalculate the range when the formulas in the range refer only to other formulas in columns to the left or to cells above themselves in the same column.

You may have to use CALC if formulas in the range refer to other formulas located below and to their right, or if formulas refer both to cells in rows above and to the right and to cells in columns below and to the left.

You need to include in the range only those cells you want to recalculate. The formulas in the recalculation range can refer to values in cells outside the range; however, those values are not updated by the RECALC or RECALCCOL. When either the RECALC or RECALCCOL command is executed, the partial recalculation occurs immediately. However, the results do not appear on-screen until the screen is redrawn. Program execution may continue for some time before a command that updates the screen is executed. In the interim, the recalculated numbers, although not visible on-screen, are available for use in calculations and conditional tests. If the program ends and you want to be sure that the recalculated numbers are on-screen, use the PgUp and PgDn keys to move the window away from and back to the recalculated range. The current values are displayed in the recalculated range.

Within a program, you may need to use CALC, RECALC, or RECALCCOL after commands such as LET, GETNUMBER, and ?, or after 1-2-3 commands such as /Range Input. You do not need to recalculate after invoking 1-2-3 commands such as /Copy and /Move; 1-2-3 automatically recalculates the affected ranges after such commands, even during program execution.

Recalculating a portion of the worksheet can cause some formulas (those outside a recalculated range that reference formulas within the range) to fail to reflect current data. If this problem should occur in your application, be sure to perform a general recalculation at some point before the end of your program.

Caution:
Some formulas may fail to reflect current data if you recalculate only a portion of the worksheet.

Commands for Manipulating Files

Nine commands give 1-2-3 the capability of opening, reading, writing, and closing a sequential data file containing ASCII text data: OPEN, CLOSE, READ, READLN, WRITE, WRITELN, SETPOS, GETPOS, and FILESIZE. This capability allows 1-2-3 applications to read and write files used by other business applications. Although the /File Import and /Print File commands provide a limited capability to manipulate foreign files, the file manipulation commands shown in table 14.7 provide a capability equal to the sequential file commands in BASIC or other programming languages.

Warning: The file manipulation commands are programming commands. To read from and write to foreign files successfully, you must understand exactly how these commands work and how the sequential files you are manipulating are organized. If you write to a file containing another application, be sure to back up the file before trying to write to it from within 1-2-3.

Reminder:
Before writing to a "foreign" file from within 1-2-3, be sure to back up that file.

Table 14.7
Commands for Manipulating Files

Command	Description
{OPEN}	Opens a file for reading, writing, or both
{CLOSE}	Closes a file opened with {OPEN}
{READ}	Copies specified characters from the open file to the specified location
{READLN}	Copies the next line from a file to the specified location
{WRITE}	Copies a string to the open file
{WRITELN}	Copies a string plus a carriage-return line-feed sequence to the open file
{SETPOS}	Sets a new position for a file pointer
{GETPOS}	Records a file pointer position in the specified location
{FILESIZE}	Records the size of the open file in the specified location

Used with caution, this group of commands can open up the world of outside files to your 1-2-3 applications. If you need to process external data files, these commands make the task possible with 1-2-3.

The OPEN Command

The OPEN command opens a disk file, providing access so that you can write to or read from that file. You can specify in the command's second argument whether you want to read only, write only, or both read from and write to the file.

Note that 1-2-3 allows only one file to be open at a time. If you want to work with more than one file in your application, you have to open each file before using it and then close it again before opening and using the next file.

The format of the OPEN command is as follows:

{OPEN filename,access-mode}   Opens file for reading, writing, or both

The filename argument can be a string, an expression with a string value, or a single-cell reference to a cell that contains a string or a string expression. The string must be a valid operating-system file name or path name. You can specify a file in the current directory by its name and extension. A file in another directory may require a drive identification, a subdirectory path, or a complete operating-system path in addition to the file name and extension.

The access-mode argument is a single character string that specifies whether you want to read only ("R"), write only ("W"), or both read from and write to the file ("M" or "A"):

"R"　　　Read access opens an existing file and allows access with the READ and READLN commands. You cannot write to a file opened with Read access.

"W"　　　Write access opens a new file with the specified name and allows access with the WRITE and WRITELN commands. Any existing file with the specified name is erased and replaced by the new file.

"A"　　　In Release 2.2, Append access opens an existing file and allows both read (READ and READLN) and write (WRITE and WRITELN) commands. Append access is like Modify access except that Append access places the byte pointer at the end of the file. (Modify places the byte pointer at the beginning of the file.)

RELEASE

2.2

"M"　　　Modify access opens an existing file with the specified name and allows both read (READ and READLN) and write (WRITE and WRITELN) commands. Note that the "M" (Modify) argument cannot create a new file.

The OPEN command succeeds if it is able to open the file with the access you requested. If the OPEN command succeeds, program execution continues with the cell below the OPEN command. Any commands after OPEN in the current cell are ignored.

The OPEN command fails with an error if the disk drive is not ready. You should use an ONERROR command to handle this possibility.

If the access mode is READ or MODIFY but the file does not exist on the indicated directory, the OPEN command fails, and program execution continues with the commands after the OPEN command in the current cell. To handle the failure, you can place in the same cell as the OPEN command one or more commands after OPEN. The most common practice is to place a BRANCH or a subroutine call after the OPEN command to transfer the operation to a macro that deals with the failure.

The following examples (with explanations) illustrate the use of the OPEN command:

　　　{OPEN "PASTDUE",R}{BRANCH FIXIT}

　　　　Opens the existing file named PASTDUE in the current directory for reading. If the file cannot be opened, branches to the routine FIXIT.

{OPEN "C:\DATA\CLIENTS.DAT",W}

Opens the new file named CLIENTS.DAT in drive C, subdirectory DATA, for writing.

{OPEN file,A}{BRANCH RETRY}

Opens the file whose name is in the cell FILE for Append access (Release 2.2). If the file cannot be opened, branches to the routine RETRY.

{OPEN file,M}{BRANCH RETRY}

Opens the file whose name is in cell FILE for Modify access. If the file cannot be opened, branches to the routine RETRY.

Figure 14.12 shows an example of using all the file commands except READ and WRITE (which are similar to READLN and WRITELN). The program named \o uses the OPEN command to open a user-specified file. This program illustrates how to deal with Disk drive not ready and File not found errors. After prompting you for the file name, an ONERROR command sets the error jump to the routine that handles such problems as the drive's not being ready. Next, the OPEN command is used with the BRANCH that follows it. This BRANCH handles such problems as a File not found error.

Fig. 14.12.
A program that
uses the file
commands.

```
       A     A        B            C              D        E    F        G
       1     \o {GETLABEL "Enter Filename: ",FILE}            \w {GETLABEL "Enter text to write: ", BUFFER}
       2        {GETLABEL "R, W, A, or M access mode: ",a)       {WRITELN BUFFER}{WRITERR}
       3        {ONERROR NOTREADY,MESSAGE}                     ~
       4        {IF @UPPER(a)="R"}{OPEN FILE,R}{BRANCH OPENERR}
       5        {IF @UPPER(a)="W"}{OPEN FILE,W}{BRANCH OPENERR} \s {GETNUMBER "Enter file postion: ",FILEPOINTER}
       6        {IF @UPPER(a)="A"}{OPEN FILE,A}{BRANCH OPENERR}    {SETPOS FILEPOINTER}{NOTOPEN}
       7        {IF @UPPER(a)="M"}{OPEN FILE,M}{BRANCH OPENERR} ~
       8        ~
       9                                                       \g {GETPOS FILEPOINTER}{NOTOPEN}
      10     \r {READLN BUFFER}{READERR}                       ~
      11        ~
      12                                                       \f {FILESIZE SIZE}{NOTOPEN}
      13     \c {CLOSE}{NOTOPEN}                               ~
      14        ~
      15
      16        A        M
      17        MESSAGE
      18        FILE       TEST.TXT
      19        BUFFER
      20        CHAR
      21        FILEPOINTER              242
      22        SIZE                     242
      23
      24        OPENERR   {GETLABEL "Could not open file.",char}
      25
      26        NOTREADY  {GETLABEL "DISK DRIVE NOT READY.",char}
      27
      28        READERR   {GETLABEL "READ FAILED. No file open, end of file, or (W)rite access",char}
      29
      30        WRITERR   {GETLABEL "WRITE FAILED. No file open or (R)ead access",char}
      31
      32        NOTOPEN   {GETLABEL "No file open",char}
```

The CLOSE Command

The CLOSE command closes a currently open file. If no file is open, CLOSE has no effect. CLOSE does not take an argument. The CLOSE command is particularly important for files you are writing or modifying; if you don't close a file, you can lose the last data written to the file. The format of the CLOSE command is as follows:

{CLOSE}   Closes a file opened with {OPEN}

Although under most circumstances 1-2-3 automatically closes a file that you do not close, you should make it a practice to use CLOSE when you are finished using any file opened with OPEN. The use of the CLOSE command is illustrated in the program labeled \c in figure 14.12.

The READ Command

The READ command reads a specified number of characters from the currently open file, beginning at the present file pointer location. The characters read from the file are placed in the worksheet at the cell location indicated. The format of the READ command is as follows:

{READ bytecount,location}   Copies the specified number of characters from a file to the location specified

The bytecount argument specifies the number of bytes to read, starting at the current position of the file pointer, and location is the cell to read into. READ places the specified number of characters from the file into the location cell as a label. Bytecount can be any number between 1 and 240 (the maximum number of characters in a 1-2-3 label). If bytecount is greater than the number of characters remaining in the file, 1-2-3 reads the remaining characters into the specified location. After the READ command is executed, the file pointer is positioned at the character following the last character read.

Consider, for example, the following statement:

{READ NUM,INFO}

This statement transfers information from the open file into the cell location named INFO. The amount of information transferred is determined by the contents of the cell named NUM, which can contain either a value or a formula.

The READ command is useful primarily when you want to read a specific number of characters into the buffer. A data file that contains fixed-length records, for example, can be read conveniently by the READ command with the bytecount argument specified as the record length.

You should not use READ with ASCII text files from a word processor or text editor. Such files generally have variable-length lines terminated with a carriage-return and line-feed sequence. Instead, use the READLN command, which is described next. READ is used much like the READLN command in the \r program in figure 14.12.

The READLN Command

The READLN command reads one line of information from the currently open file, beginning at the file pointer's current position. The characters read are placed in the cell location in the current worksheet. The READLN command format is as follows:

{READLN location}   Copies the next line from the file to the location

Consider, for example, the following statement:

{READLN HERE}

This statement copies a line from an open file into the cell named HERE. The line is determined by the SETPOS command. (SETPOS is discussed later in the chapter.)

Use READLN to read a line of text from a file whose lines are delimited by a carriage-return and line-feed combination. For instance, use READLN to read the next line from an ASCII text file. ASCII text files are created with 1-2-3's **/P**rint File command. Also referred to as print files, these files are assigned the .PRN file extension by 1-2-3. READLN is best suited to reading files that are print images. The program labeled \r in figure 14.12 illustrates the use of READLN.

Using READ and READLN

If you attempt to read past the end of the file, if no file is open, or if the file was opened with Write access, the READ or READLN command is ignored, and program execution continues in the same cell. Otherwise, after the READ or READLN command is completed, program execution continues on the next line. You can place a BRANCH or subroutine call after the READ or READLN command to handle the problem of an unexecuted READ or READLN statement.

The WRITE Command

The WRITE command writes a string of text to the currently open file. The WRITE command has the following format:

{WRITE string}   Copies a string to the open file

The string argument can be a literal string, a range name or cell reference to a single cell that contains a string, or a string expression. Because WRITE does not place a carriage-return and line-feed sequence at the end of the string, multiple WRITE statements can be made to concatenate text on a single line. WRITE is suited to creating or updating a file that contains fixed-length database records. The WRITE command is used in much the same way as the WRITELN command is used in the \w program in figure 14.12.

If the file pointer is not at the end of the file, 1-2-3 overwrites the existing characters in the file. If the file pointer is at the end of the file, 1-2-3 extends the file by the number of characters written. And if the file pointer is past the end of the file (see the discussion of the SETPOS command later in this section), 1-2-3 extends the file by the amount indicated before writing the characters.

The WRITELN Command

The WRITELN command is identical to the WRITE command except that WRITELN places a carriage-return and line-feed sequence after the last character written from the string. The WRITELN command format is as follows:

{WRITELN string}   Copies a string plus a carriage-return line-feed
                        sequence to the open file

WRITELN is useful when the file being written or updated uses the carriage-return and line-feed sequence to mark the end of its lines or records. In many applications, several WRITE statements are used to write a line to the file; then a WRITELN is used to mark the end of the line. The WRITELN command is illustrated in the \w program in figure 14.12.

The SETPOS Command

The SETPOS command sets the position of the file pointer to a specified value. The format of the command is as follows:

{SETPOS file-position}   Sets a new position for a file pointer

File-position is a number, or an expression resulting in a number, that specifies the character at which you want to position the pointer. The first character in the file is at position 0, the second at position 1, and so on. Suppose, for example, that you have a database file with 100 records that are each 20 bytes long. To access the first record, you can use the following commands:

{SETPOS 0} {READ 20,buffer}

To read the 15th record, you can use the following commands:

{SETPOS (15-1)*20} {READ 20,buffer}

Nothing prevents you from setting the file pointer past the end of the file. If the file pointer is set at or past the end and you execute a READ or READLN command, the command does nothing, and program execution continues with the next command on the same line (error branch). If the file pointer is set at or past the end and you execute a WRITE or WRITELN command, 1-2-3 first extends the file to the length specified by the file pointer and then, starting at the file pointer, writes the characters.

If you inadvertently set the file pointer to a large number with SETPOS and write to the file, 1-2-3 attempts to expand the file and writes the text at the end. If the file will not fit on the disk, the WRITE command does nothing, and program execution continues with the next command on the same line (error branch). If the file will fit on the disk, 1-2-3 extends the file and writes the text at the end.

If a file is not currently open, SETPOS does nothing, and execution continues with the next command on the same line as the SETPOS command. Otherwise, when the SETPOS command is completed, execution continues on the next line of the program. You can place a BRANCH command or a subroutine call after the SETPOS command to handle the problem of an unexecuted statement. SETPOS is illustrated in the \s program in figure 14.12.

The GETPOS Command

The GETPOS command allows you to record the file pointer's current position. The form of this command is as follows:

{GETPOS location}   Records a file pointer position in the specified position

The current position of the file pointer is placed in the cell indicated by location, where location is either a cell reference or a range name. If location points to a multicell range, the value of the file pointer is placed in the upper left corner of the range.

The GETPOS command is useful if you record in the file the location of something you want to find again. You can use GETPOS to mark your current place in the file before you use SETPOS to move the file pointer to another position. You can use GETPOS to record the locations of important items in a quick-reference index. GETPOS is illustrated in the \g program in figure 14.12.

The FILESIZE Command

Another file-related command, FILESIZE, returns the length of the file in bytes. The form of the command is as follows:

{FILESIZE location}   Records the size of the open file in the
                       specified location

The FILESIZE command determines the current length of the file and places this value in the cell referred to by location. Location can be a cell reference or range name. If location refers to a multicell range, the file size is placed in the cell in the upper left corner of the range. FILESIZE is illustrated in the \f program in figure 14.12.

Chapter Summary

As you work with the 1-2-3 advanced macro commands, you soon discover that your powerful spreadsheet program has an extremely powerful programming language. Although 1-2-3's advanced macro commands make many things possible, be aware of some practical limitations. For example, because 1-2-3 is RAM-based, you must limit the size of your files. In addition, 1-2-3 may not always execute programming commands with lightning speed. You almost always have a tradeoff of capabilities; the most difficult applications may take a good deal of time to execute.

If you are an adventurer who wants to develop efficient, automated, customized models, and if you can live with the programming limitations, the advanced macro commands are for you. This chapter has provided the groundwork for developing such models. As you become more experienced with the advanced macro commands, turn to other Que titles for help in becoming an expert advanced macro command programmer.

Part IV

Quick Reference
Guide to 1-2-3

Includes

Troubleshooting

1-2-3 Command Reference

Troubleshooting

This section addresses many of the problems you may encounter while using 1-2-3 and offers a variety of creative solutions. First-time users of 1-2-3 find that this section can help them untie knots that seem hopelessly snarled but are really only minor inconveniences when understood correctly.

Experienced users undoubtedly derive even greater benefit from the problems and solutions presented here. As your use of the program becomes increasingly complex and sophisticated, so do the problems and errors you encounter. Although first-time users face problems that momentarily seem insurmountable, the most perplexing problems in using 1-2-3 are those faced by power users who push the program to its limits.

You can use this section in two different ways:

1. Read this entire section after you read the rest of the book and begin to use 1-2-3. You also can read the rest of this book and this section segment by segment. Most people learn 1-2-3 in segments—learning how to build a simple worksheet before they learn to incorporate complex formulas and functions, for example. Users later learn to print reports, and then to create graphs. Much later, perhaps, users learn to create and use macros or to use the program's database-management capabilities. You can use this section the same way: after you learn the basics of one area of the program, read through the applicable portion of the troubleshooting section. Reading this section before you encounter problems can help you avoid those problems.

2. Refer to this section as you encounter problems. The section is arranged to provide easy reference. The titles in the upper right corner of the right-hand pages contain the name of the general area of problems covered on that page (for example, *Worksheet Problems*). As each problem is introduced, a more specific designation (for example, *Data-Entry Problem #1*) appears in the left margin, followed by a brief description of the problem. A quick scan of the heads and the margins takes you to the area that describes your problem. Using this section as a reference can be even easier if you have already read the section, as recommended in the first method.

The topics in this troubleshooting section are arranged as they appear in the book, in the following order:

1. *Installation*: This section should be read before you install 1-2-3. Some potentially disastrous installation problems cannot be remedied—they can only be avoided. Some installation problems, however, can be remedied after they occur. This section covers problems with drivers and with hard-disk installation.

2. *Worksheet*: Covers problems in the basic worksheet environment—the environment in which you probably will encounter your first problems.

3. *Commands*: Covers the use of 1-2-3 commands in the worksheet.

4. *Functions*: Solves a variety of basic and highly complex problems associated with functions.

5. *File operations*: Addresses problems encountered while transferring and combining data from different files, using different directories, and saving and retrieving files.

6. *Printing*: Answers many printing problems and provides many creative and useful tips. Printing is a troublesome area for most people who struggle to "get their reports to look exactly like they're supposed to look."

7. *Graphing*: Helps you through the maze of graphing options that make this area as difficult as printing.

8. *Data Management*: Provides guidance through possibly the most troublesome feature of 1-2-3. Many of the highly sophisticated database management systems (DBMS) on the market are much more powerful than 1-2-3's database. Nevertheless, 1-2-3's capabilities are considerable, complex, and unfamiliar to many users who enter this area reluctantly. Once you start to use 1-2-3's database capabilities, you quickly and frequently may encounter problems. Overcoming these problems with the help of this section can open doors to a much more extensive and rewarding use of 1-2-3.

9. *Macros*: Helps you with many of the problems associated with macros. Macros and the advanced macro commands are among 1-2-3's most powerful features. Many users have fun with macros because they can learn a little at a time, building their skills slowly. As the skills build, so do the problems. This section provides invaluable assistance.

This Troubleshooting reference section cannot be, and is not meant to be, a comprehensive listing of all the problems you may encounter with 1-2-3.

This section sometimes echoes and reinforces explanations given elsewhere in this book. More often, this section extends your knowledge and your skills beyond the explanations given elsewhere. The ultimate problem solver must be the individual user, but this section can help by solving specific problems and by showing a pattern of creative thinking for solving problems as they occur.

Other books extend the assistance given here. Especially recommended are *1-2-3 Tips, Tricks, and Traps*, 2nd Edition; *1-2-3 for Business*, 2nd Edition; *1-2-3 Macro Library*, 2nd Edition; and *1-2-3 Command Language*—all published by Que.

Troubleshooting Installation

Problems with Drivers

DRIVER PROBLEM #1:

You cannot print and you cannot display graphs on a color monitor.

Explanation: The program requires a file, called a *driver set*, that describes the equipment used in your system. This file must have the extension SET. When you use 1-2-3, the program looks for a file (called 123.SET) containing the driver set. The System disk contains an initial driver set called 123.SET. This driver set uses a Universal Text Display driver that works with almost any display but cannot display graphs. The initial driver set also has no support for printers.

Solution: Run the Install program and follow the prompts to describe your computer system. If you don't give the driver set a special name, the Install program names it 123.SET.

Note: If you use different displays on your computer system or if your display has more than one mode for displaying text, you may need several driver sets. You can use Install to set up different driver sets and give them individual names. To tell the program to use a driver set other than 123.SET, specify the name of the driver SET file when you execute the program. If you run Install and name a driver set COLOR.SET, you must specify this name whenever you run a 1-2-3 program. Instead of typing **123** (or **lotus** or **pgraph**) at the DOS prompt, type **123 color** (or **lotus color** or **pgraph color**).

If you always use the same display with your system, let Install name your driver set 123.SET. Then you can forget about it when you execute 1-2-3.

DRIVER PROBLEM #2:

The system hangs at the copyright screen, forcing you to reboot; or you get an error message about the driver set and are returned to DOS.

Explanation: The default Universal Text Display driver works with almost any display. If you have a color monitor and try to start the program with a driver set for a monochrome monitor, or vice versa, however, you confuse the system.

Solution: If the driver set is not called 123.SET, make sure that you specified the proper driver set when you executed 1-2-3. Suppose that 123.SET is set up for a monochrome monitor and the color-monitor driver is in a file called COLOR.SET. Be sure to specify COLOR when you use a color monitor.

If you are using 123.SET, rerun Install and check the type of display installed in the driver set.

If the driver set seems to be correct, test to see whether the original driver set on the System disk runs correctly. If you execute the program from the hard disk, put the System or Backup disk in drive A and, at the C> prompt, type the following:

123 A:123

If the original driver set runs correctly, you can be certain that you specified an incorrect driver set and must rerun Install. If the computer still hangs, the problem involves the switch setting for the math coprocessor.

Alternative Explanation #1: Lotus looks at the PATH statement in your AUTOEXEC.BAT file and finds and uses the wrong 123.SET file. This situation is most likely to occur on a local area network.

Alternative Solution #1: One possible solution is to delete the other 123.SET file or files if they are not needed. If you want to keep the other files, edit the AUTOEXEC.BAT file so that the PATH statement searches the subdirectories in the appropriate order.

Alternative Explanation #2: Two sets of switches located within an IBM Personal Computer tell the computer what kind of monitor you have, how much memory and how many floppy disk drives you have, and so on. The XT contains one set of switches. Although the AT has no switch settings, its SETUP program serves the same purpose.

One of the switch settings on the PC or XT tells the computer whether you have a math coprocessor chip installed. This special chip can perform math functions many times faster than the regular microprocessor in your computer. In most cases, a computer with a math coprocessor executes mathematical computations faster than the same computer without one. (A math coprocessor does not make the computer run faster for other tasks.) The amount of time saved in a worksheet recalculation depends on the kinds of calculations in the worksheet. In a PC or XT, the math coprocessor is an 8087 chip; in an AT, it is an 80287 chip.

Beginning with Release 2.0, 1-2-3 uses the math coprocessor if one is installed. If you do not have a math coprocessor but the switch settings indicate that you do, the system hangs as soon as you try to run the program.

You may have owned a PC for years and not been aware that this switch setting was not set properly. Your computer operates properly as long as you do not run programs that try to use the math coprocessor. Some editions of the *IBM Guide to Operations* show the switch settings reversed.

Alternative Solution #2: The PC switch is in position 2 of switch bank 1 (SW1). The XT has only 1 switch bank. If you do not have a math coprocessor, set the position 2 switch ON. If you have a math coprocessor, set the switch OFF.

If you have an AT, run its SETUP program, making sure that you have not indicated that you have a math coprocessor if none is installed. If you have a Personal System/2, this error should not occur because SETUP determines whether you have a math coprocessor installed.

DRIVER PROBLEM #3:

You have access to several printers and plotters you use occasionally for printing worksheets and graphs, but keeping track of all the driver sets for these different configurations is difficult.

Explanation: 1-2-3 lets you use only the printers and plotters in your driver set. If you put all your output devices in different driver sets, you must remember which driver set to use whenever you execute the program.

Solution: Do not set up different driver sets for each printer or plotter. Put them all in one set.

You must use more than one driver set only when you change either the physical display or the mode in which 1-2-3 displays information. (1-2-3 Display Information is an option with some display systems. With an Enhanced Graphics Adapter [EGA] monitor, for example, you can display text in either 25 rows × 80 columns or 25 columns × 43 rows.)

If you switch equipment and use different printers and plotters, you can install them all in one driver set. Whenever you specify a text printer, Install asks whether you have another printer. If you sometimes attach another printer to your system, answer **Yes** and then select the other printer. You can complete this step for as many as four different text printers you may attach to your computer. Repeat the step for any printers or plotters you may attach to your computer for printing graphs.

You can have as many as 17 graphics printers or plotters installed in a driver set. Because the program does not expect more than one printer or plotter to be used at a time, you can install more than one, even when only one is attached. Then, when working in 1-2-3, use the **/W**orksheet **G**lobal **D**efault **P**rinter **N**ame command to select the printer currently attached to your computer. If the printer you select as the default printer is to remain the default, you must select **Update** from the **W**orksheet **G**lobal **D**efault menu. This command saves the defaults to disk; whenever you start 1-2-3, the same defaults are in effect.

If you attach printers to different ports on your computer, you must use the **/W**orksheet **G**lobal **D**efault **P**rinter **I**nterface command to tell 1-2-3 which printer interface to use. Parallel printers usually use the Parallel 1 port. If you have more than one parallel-printer port, you must specify the one to which the printer is connected. If you use a serial printer, you must specify which serial port (interface) you use (usually Serial 1). If you use a local area network and printed output is redirected to another computer, you may have to specify DOS device LPT1:, LPT2:, LPT3:, or LPT4:.

In the PrintGraph program, use **Settings Hardware Printer** to specify the printer or plotter. 1-2-3 then lists all the graphic printers and plotters included in your driver set (see fig. T.1). Use **Settings Hardware Interface** to specify the correct LPT or COM port. After you make the changes, use **Settings Save** to make the new settings the default.

If you print using the Allways add-in available in Release 2.2, use **/Print Configuration Printer** to indicate the printer or plotter to use; use **/Print Configuration Interface** to specify the printer port.

RELEASE

2.2

```
Copyright 1986, 1989 Lotus Development Corp.  All Rights Reserved. V2.2   POINT

Select graphics printer or plotter


   Printer or Plotter name and Resolution
----------------------------------------- Space bar marks or unmarks selection
 Epson·FX and RX series·Low density        ENTER selects marked device
 Epson·FX and RX series·High density        ESC exits, ignoring changes
 HP·LaserJet+ or LaserJet II·Med den.      HOME moves to beginning of list
 HP·LaserJet+ or LaserJet II·High den.     END moves to end of list
                                           ↑ and ↓ move highlight
                                              List will scroll if highlight
                                              moved beyond top or bottom
```

Fig. T.1.
A list of all graph output devices in the driver set.

Problems with Hard Disk Installation

Versions of 1-2-3 *before* Release 2.2 were copy protected. Users of Release 2.2 will not encounter the copy protection problems discussed in this section.

WARNING:

Problems with copy protection on a hard disk can cost you the use of the System disk. Problems with copy protection can happen if the hard disk fails completely, if you restore the entire hard disk, or, possibly, if you use a utility program to reorganize your hard disk.

You must troubleshoot a hard disk problem before it happens. If you run COPYHARD or use Install to move the copy protection to a hard disk, you must be careful not to lose the protection information permanently. Do not restore 1-2-3 over a good copy of the program and do not use a reorganize program if you want to avoid copy protection problems.

HARD DISK PROBLEM #1:

You used the DOS BACKUP and RESTORE commands to restore your hard disk, and now you can't execute 1-2-3.

Explanation: The copy protection files written to the hard disk by COPY-HARD or Install are hidden, read-only files. Because they are DOS files, these hidden files are backed up if you back up the entire hard disk. If you restore the hard disk from a floppy disk and, in the process, restore the hidden files, the copy protection information appears invalid to 1-2-3. You must use your Backup System disk and contact either your dealer or Lotus for a replacement disk.

Solution: If you have backed up your entire disk, you must use the /P parameter when you use the DOS RESTORE command. (This parameter indicates that you want DOS to prompt you before it restores any files that have been changed or that are marked read-only.) Then you can answer **No** to the Restore any read-only files? prompt.

Alternative Solution: A safer solution is to use Install's Advanced Options to remove the copy protection from the hard disk before you start a full disk backup. After you install the program again on a hard disk, back up only your data directories.

Notes:

1. If your hard disk fails, you may not be able to recover the copy protection. Before a hard disk fails completely, you usually receive warnings that something is wrong. If you start receiving data errors, seek errors, or other disk errors, immediately remove the copy protection. Use the System disk to start 1-2-3 until you have either replaced your hard disk or made sure that it is not failing.

2. Hard disks are most vulnerable to failure when they are new. Do not use COPYHARD or Install to install the copy protection on a hard disk unless you have used the disk for at least two weeks with no disk-related errors.

3. Because you cannot restore the copy protection information from a backup floppy disk to a hard disk, you cannot restore copy protection information to another hard disk. If you must move the 1-2-3 program to a different hard disk, you must remove the copy protection information from the first disk and reinstall it on the other disk.

4. Many of the hard-disk utilities available on the market can optimize disk performance, recover lost files, and rearrange files and directories. Some of these utilities may also destroy the 1-2-3 copy protection information.

Before you use one of these hard-disk utilities, ask your vendor whether the utility has been tested on 1-2-3 Release 2.0 or later. If you have any doubt, remove the copy protection information before you use the utility to reorganize your hard disk.

Troubleshooting the 1-2-3 Worksheet

Problems with Data Entry

DATA-ENTRY PROBLEM #1:

After you type a label that starts with a number, the program beeps and puts you in EDIT mode.

Explanation: When you begin typing information in a cell, 1-2-3 changes the READY mode indicator in the screen's upper right corner to either LABEL or VALUE. If the first character you type is a number or a symbol used in a formula, the program assumes that you are typing a value. If you then type any character that is invalid for a value entry, 1-2-3 beeps, moves the cursor to the first character it rejected, and switches to EDIT mode.

Solution: To type a label such as **353 Sacramento Street**, you must first type a label prefix, such as an apostrophe ('), so that 1-2-3 knows you are entering a label. If you forget to enter the prefix and 1-2-3 beeps, press Home and insert the apostrophe.

If the label is a valid numeric entry, you get a numeric calculation that you don't want instead of an error. If you type **(317)-573-2500** as a telephone number, for example, 1-2-3 evaluates the entry as a formula and displays –2756. Edit the field to change it from a number to a label by inserting a label prefix.

DATA-ENTRY PROBLEM #2:

When you finish writing a complex formula, 1-2-3 automatically switches to EDIT mode if the formula is invalid. If you cannot find the error immediately, you have to press Esc. You lose the entire formula and have to start again.

Explanation: When you type an invalid formula, 1-2-3 refuses to accept the entry and switches to EDIT mode. You must provide a valid entry before you can continue.

Solution: Make the formula a valid entry by converting it to a label: press the Home key, type an apostrophe, and press Enter. Then you can work on the problem until you find and correct the error. You may choose to work on another part of the worksheet and return to the formula later.

You may have used a range name in the formula without having created the range name. If you forgot to create a range name, convert the formula to a label, create the range name, and then edit the formula to remove the label prefix.

Note: Here is a method for debugging complex formulas. Suppose that you enter the following formula in a cell:

@IF(@ISERR(A1/A2),@IF(A2=0),0,@ERR),A1/A2)

When you press Enter, 1-2-3 beeps and switches to EDIT mode. If the error isn't obvious, you are stuck. You cannot exit EDIT mode unless you either fix the error or press Esc, erasing the contents of the cell. Because the program accepts anything as a label, you can insert a label prefix at the beginning of the entry and then press Enter. Then copy the formula to another cell and work on it until you find the error.

In this case, begin by eliminating the compound @IF from the formula. To do so, copy the formula to a blank cell (a work area) and then erase the middle @IF statement, replacing it with a zero:

@IF(@ISERR(A1/A2),0,A1/A2)

Because this formula works, the problem must be in the @IF statement you erased. Again, copy the original formula to the work area. Now delete everything except the middle @IF:

@IF(A2=0),0,@ERR)

You can see that you should erase the right parenthesis that follows A2=0. Make the change and test it:

@IF(A2=0,0,@ERR)

When this segment works, erase the work cell and correct the original formula:

@IF(@ISERR(A1/A2),@IF(A2=0,0,@ERR),A1/A2)

You may write formulas longer and more complex than this example. To debug them, simply convert them to labels and test them, one part at a time.

Problems with Circular References

CIRCULAR REFERENCE PROBLEM #1:

The CIRC indicator suddenly appears after you enter a formula.

Explanation: Whenever the worksheet is recalculated and a CIRC indicator appears at the lower right corner of the screen, 1-2-3 is warning you about a *circular reference*. Circular references are formulas that refer to themselves, either directly or indirectly. Because they usually are errors, you should correct circular references as soon as they occur.

An example of the most common direct circular reference is shown in figure T.2. In this example, the @SUM function includes itself in the range to be summed. Whenever the worksheet recalculates, this sum increases. In the example in figure T.2, the cell was calculated four times after it was entered.

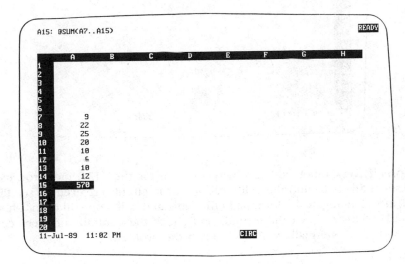

Fig. T.2.
A direct
circular
reference.

Solution: Change the @SUM formula to include the cells through A14, excluding A15; the CIRC indicator disappears.

CIRCULAR REFERENCE PROBLEM #2:

The CIRC indicator appears after you enter a formula, but the formula does not refer to itself.

Explanation: 1-2-3 is warning you about an indirect circular reference, which is tricky to find and fix. None of the formulas refers to itself, but two or more formulas refer to each other. Each formula in figure T.3 seems reasonable, for example, but A1 refers to A3, A2 refers to A1, and A3 refers to A2. You have no way of evaluating these formulas. The numbers increase whenever the worksheet recalculates.

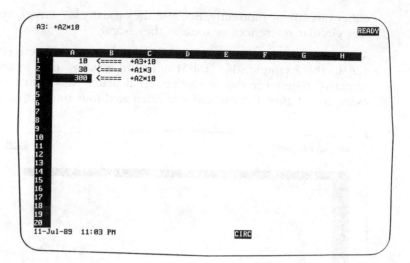

Fig. T.3.
An indirect
circular
reference.

Solution: If you cannot find an obvious reason for the CIRC indicator, use /Worksheet Status to find the cell location of the circular reference (see fig. T.4). If, after looking at the formula in the indicated cell, you still cannot find the problem, write down the formula and check the contents of every cell referenced. You eventually will track down the problem.

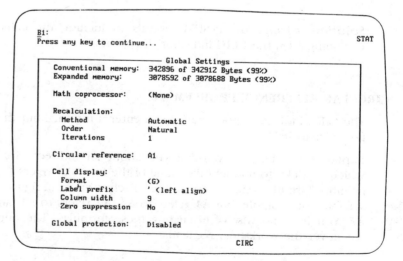

Fig. T.4.
/Worksheet
Status shows a
circular
reference.

Alternative Explanation: @CELL("width") can cause an annoying circular reference if you use the cell address containing this function to determine the width of the column that contains the formula. If cell C9 contains the following formula, for example, a circular reference occurs:

@CELL("width",C9..C9)

Alternative Solution: Because all the cells in the column must be the same width, change the formula to refer to another cell in the same column:

@CELL("width",C8..C8)

CIRCULAR REFERENCE PROBLEM #3:

You have a formula that is supposed to be a circular reference and you don't know how many times to recalculate to get the correct answer.

Explanation: Even deliberate circular references can be a problem. Figure T.5 shows a profit calculation in which total profit depends on the amount of the executive bonus. The bonus, however, is based on profits—a legitimate circular reference. Every time 1-2-3 recalculates, the profit figure comes closer to the right answer. The problem lies in knowing how many recalculations you need. In general, recalculate until the change in the results is insignificant.

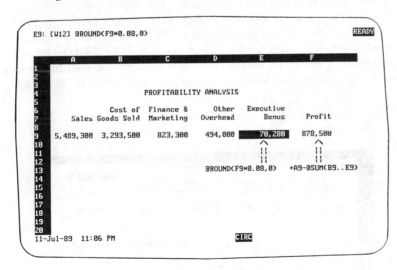

Fig. T.5.
A deliberate circular reference.

Solution: You can recalculate manually if this is a one-time calculation and the worksheet is small. Use @ROUND to set the required precision. In figure T.5, the bonus is rounded to whole dollars. Press Calc (F9) to calculate the worksheet; continue pressing Calc (F9) until the profit number does not change. In the example shown in figure T.5, you must calculate the worksheet four times before the profit figure stops changing.

Alternative Solution: If the circular reference is part of a large worksheet, recalculation may take an inordinate amount of time. Use the macro in figure T.6 to recalculate only part of the worksheet until you get the correct answer.

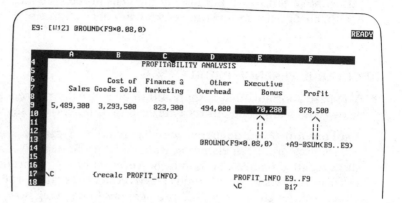

Fig. T.6.
A macro with a {RECALC} that resolves a circular reference.

If the numbers change often and you want to recalculate automatically, use the macro in figure T.7 to recalculate the profit information until PROFIT is equal to OLD PROFIT in cell F5. Figure T.7 shows the result of executing the macro. In most cases, cell F5 would be hidden. This macro works because {RECALC} proceeds row by row and F5 is above PROFIT. If OLD PROFIT were below PROFIT, this macro would not work because the two numbers would always be the same and the macro would stop at the first {RECALC}.

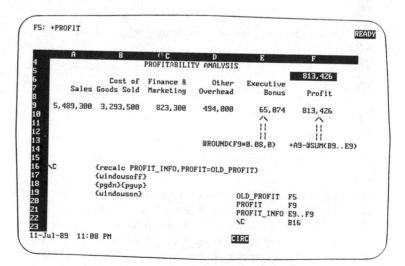

Fig. T.7.
A macro that automatically solves a circular reference.

CIRCULAR REFERENCE PROBLEM #4:

An ERR is created in one of the cells in an intentional circular reference. This causes all the cells in the circular reference to return ERR also. You remove the source of the ERR, but the remaining cells continue to show an ERR.

Explanation: Cells depending on a cell that returns an ERR also return an ERR. If two or more cells with ERR refer to each other, the result is always ERR. Once the cells in the circular reference have been contaminated, you may not be able to eliminate all the ERRs no matter how many times you recalculate after you correct the original error.

Solution: First break the circular reference; then correct the error and recalculate. The fastest way to break the circular reference is to copy to a work area the cells that evaluate to ERR and then erase the original ERR cells. Calculate the worksheet. This should cause the ERR indicators to disappear. Finally, copy the formulas back to the original cells and erase the work area.

Problems Resulting in ERR

ERR PROBLEM #1:

A formula that had been working correctly suddenly changes to ERR.

Explanation: A valid formula can be destroyed by certain subsequent entries. When 1-2-3 cannot evaluate part of a formula, it changes that part of the formula to ERR. The total result is ERR.

Moves, deletes, erases, and certain entries can destroy a formula or make it invalid. If you move a cell or a range to a cell referenced in a formula, the program replaces the reference with ERR (see fig. T.8).

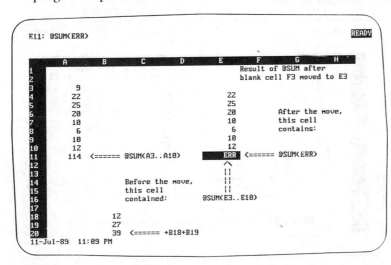

Fig. T.8.
Moving turns a formula to ERR.

Solution: If you want to move a value into a cell after you refer to that cell in a formula, you cannot use the /Move command. Instead, use /Copy and then erase the original cell.

If you want to move a formula to a cell after you have referred to the cell in a formula, do not use the /Move command. Instead, use the /Copy command, following these four steps:

1. Edit the formula to convert it to a label.

2. Copy the label to the cell.

3. Edit the label to convert it back to a formula.

4. Erase the original cell.

You convert the formula to a label to prevent relative cell references from changing when you copy the formula. If you want the cell references to change when you copy the formula to its new location, copy the cell as a formula; do not convert it to a label.

ERR PROBLEM #2:

Formulas change to ERR after you delete a row or a column somewhere else in the worksheet.

Explanation: Although you seldom deliberately delete a row or column containing information used in formulas, deleting such information accidentally is not unusual. The /Worksheet Delete Row or Column command deletes the entire row or column without giving you a chance to inspect the row or column; you can see only the usual screen of information. Information contained in the row or column may be somewhere off-screen. Figure T.9 shows the effect of deleting row 18. As in the example in figure T.8, the referenced cell changes to ERR.

Fig. T.9.
Deleting turns
a formula to
ERR.

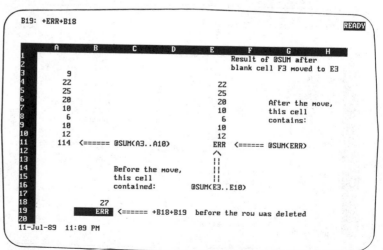

Solution: Avoid this problem by checking the worksheet carefully before you delete rows or columns. To check a row, move the cell pointer to the row and press End-left arrow and End-right arrow. If the cell pointer moves from column A to column IV, the row is empty. Use End-up arrow and End-down arrow to see whether a column is empty from row 1 to row 8192.

Even this method is not foolproof. A formula can legitimately refer to a blank cell. Perhaps the cell is to contain data that has not yet been entered. If you delete the row or column containing the referenced cell, the formula that refers to the cell changes to ERR.

The most foolproof way to avoid this error is to do the following:

1. Save the worksheet.

2. In a blank cell, put an @SUM formula that sums the entire active area (from A1 to End-Home—the key sequence to move to the end of the active area).

3. Delete the desired row or column. If recalculation is set to manual, press Calc (F9) to recalculate the worksheet.

If your @SUM formula changes to ERR, you know that somewhere a cell changed to ERR when you deleted the row or column. Search the worksheet until you find the ERR. If the formula is in error, correct it. If the deleted row or column is needed, retrieve the worksheet you saved before the deletion.

ERR PROBLEM #3:

String formulas change to ERR after you erase a cell or a range.

Explanation: With numeric formulas, cells can usually contain a number, a string, or be blank. Blank cells and cells containing strings are treated as zeros in numeric calculations. (In Release 2.0, however, blank and string cells are not always treated as zeros. One of the reasons Lotus upgraded Release 2.0 to Release 2.01 is that in Release 2.0, numeric formulas often resulted in ERR when any referenced cell contained a string formula.)

Even in Release 2.01 and 2.2, however, string formulas are not as forgiving as numeric formulas. A string formula results in ERR if any referenced cell is blank or contains numeric values. If you erase a cell used in a string formula, the string formula changes to ERR. This may be an acceptable change if you plan to enter new data in the cell. Figure T.10 shows some examples of numeric and string formulas.

Fig. T.10.
Blank cells and
numbers cause
ERR in string
functions.

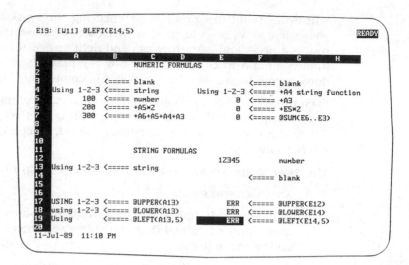

Solution: If you are sure that you will complete the blank cells before you print the worksheet, nothing needs to be done. In fact, you can leave the ERR to remind you that data is missing.

If the data is optional, you must trap the possible error in the formula. You can test for a null string in the cell before referencing the cell in the formula. A blank cell is treated as though it contains a null string (""). The following formula, for example, concatenates the strings in A1 and B1 if both contain strings:

+A1&B1

If A1 always contains a string and B1 may be blank, change the formula to the following:

+A1&@IF(B1="","",B1)

If A1 is either blank or a number, the result is ERR, and the program warns you that something is wrong. If B1 is blank, no error occurs, and the formula equates to the contents of A1.

Here's another formula that behaves in a similar manner:

+A1&@S(B1..B1)

The @S function avoids errors, filtering out anything that is not a string—even filtering out a value. This formula works if B1 contains a label, number, or is blank.

Problems with Memory Management

MEMORY PROBLEM #1:

While working on a large worksheet, you run out of memory.

Explanation: Running out of memory is one of the most common problems in 1-2-3. Because the program was the first spreadsheet to allow full use of 640K of memory, most users assumed that they would never run out of memory. Users kept building bigger worksheets, eventually ran out of memory, and then had to redesign their entire worksheets.

Solution: You have several ways to avoid running out of memory. Because none of these methods is foolproof, use /Worksheet Status frequently to check available memory when you build large worksheets.

Proper worksheet design is the best way to avoid memory problems. Don't try to put an entire accounting system into one worksheet. Don't try to use one worksheet for all your product-line forecasts, even if the worksheets for all the products lines are identical. Instead, build separate worksheets based on a single template. Not only do properly designed worksheets save memory, they also speed recalculation. (The larger the worksheet, the longer you wait when you recalculate.)

Sophisticated analysis models can require a dozen or more separate worksheets. Each of these worksheets can either print a detailed report or (for a smaller, consolidated report) extract data to be combined into a summary report. If you use 1-2-3 Release 2.2, remember that you can use file-linking formulas to "pull" information from a file stored on disk instead of extracting and combining data.

RELEASE

2.2

Alternative Solution #1: Another way to avoid memory problems is to make sure that your computer has the maximum amount of memory. If you want to build large worksheets, you need at least 640K, the maximum amount of memory that normal programs can use. Memory has become so inexpensive that most of the new computers on the market, including the IBM Personal System/2, include at least 640K of standard memory. If your computer has 256K, you can add 384K for as little as $100 to $150.

Because 1-2-3 users wanted to build increasingly larger worksheets, Lotus (working with Intel and Microsoft) developed the LIM expanded memory specification (EMS). This hardware and software specification lets a program use memory that exceeds the 640K limit. To use expanded memory, a program must know about EMS. Although you cannot use EMS with older programs, you can use as many as 8 megabytes of expanded memory with 1-2-3 Release 2.0 and later. Because a normal memory board doesn't work with more than 640K, however, you must buy a special memory expansion board designed to be an EMS board.

Expanded memory works in both the PC, PC XT (and compatibles), and the PC AT (and compatibles). AST Research, Inc. has devised an extended EMS (EEMS). Since AST Research enhanced EMS, Lotus/Intel/Microsoft also enhanced EMS, calling it EMS 4.0. EMS, EMS 4.0, and EEMS boards provide the same expansion capabilities for 1-2-3 worksheets.

Using expanded memory does not solve all memory problems. Although certain parts of worksheets—labels, formulas, decimal numbers, and integers larger than 32,767—can use expanded memory, everything else must be in regular memory (up to 640K). Additionally, 4 bytes must be in regular memory for every cell stored in expanded memory. You can have a maximum of approximately 100,000 individual cell entries before you run out of regular memory, which means that you can run out of memory and still have megabytes of expanded memory that you have not used (and cannot use).

RELEASE
2.2

Alternative Solution #2: The two add-in programs that come with Release 2.2 (Macro Library Manager and Allways)—and any other add-in programs you may have purchased—consume extra memory when attached to 1-2-3. If you don't need the add-in when working with a large worksheet, detach it to free up some memory for the worksheet. In Release 2.2, use the /Add-In Detach command.

RELEASE
2.2

Alternative Solution #3: The Undo feature in Release 2.2 consumes about 190K of RAM when it is enabled—about half of the RAM available when Undo is disabled. Although the Undo feature is invaluable when you want to "take back" the last command you gave, you may not be able to afford the RAM space the feature consumes. To disable Undo, use /Worksheet Global Default Other Undo Disable.

Alternative Solution #4: Because formulas take up more space than numbers, you can use formulas to build a worksheet. Using the /Range Value command, you can convert the formulas to numbers. Use this method with any numbers that do not change when you update the worksheet. (Be sure to save the original template with the unconverted formulas in case you later discover that you need the formulas.)

Because the results of the /Data Table command are numbers, not formulas, you can save memory by converting large tables of formulas to data tables. Repeat the /Data Table command to recalculate the tables if the values in the input cells change. Do not use this technique in a large worksheet if you frequently recalculate the data table—recalculation could take several minutes or even hours.

Alternative Solution #5: The shape of the active area also can affect the total amount of memory used by the worksheet. The active area is defined as a rectangle starting in cell A1 and ending in the last row and last column that contains data or a range format, or is unprotected. A worksheet with a value in G3 and a format in A12, for example, has an active area from A1 to G12. A worksheet with cell AF4 unprotected and a label in B300 has an active area from A1 to AF300.

Although Lotus states that the memory-management scheme uses no memory for empty cells, this statement does not appear to be true. Putting the number 1 in cells A1, A2, B1, and B2 of an otherwise empty sheet, for example, uses 32 bytes of memory. Putting the number 1 in cells A1, A8192, IV1, and IV8192 of an otherwise empty sheet uses 65,506 bytes of memory. (In fact, simply formatting or unprotecting the four cells uses 65,506 bytes—even though you enter no data at all in the worksheet.)

If memory is a problem, keep the shape of the active area in your worksheet as small as possible. To move the cell pointer to the lower right corner of the active area of any worksheet, press End-Home. You may be surprised to discover that a stray entry is costing you quite a bit of memory.

Alternative Solution #6: If you frequently move, insert, and delete rows and columns when you build large worksheets, you may run out of memory. When you move data or delete rows and columns, not all the memory is recovered. You usually can recover the memory by saving the worksheet and retrieving it again.

Troubleshooting 1-2-3 Commands

Problems with Range Names

RANGE NAME PROBLEM #1:

A range name that was valid suddenly results in an ERR.

Explanation: Moving and deleting cells and ranges can change formulas to ERR (see the "Problems Resulting in ERR" section of this Troubleshooting guide). Moving and deleting cells and ranges also cause the loss of range names. Both ranges and range names are identified by the upper left corner cell and the lower right corner cell. If you move a cell or a range of cells to one of these corner cells, the range name is lost. Suppose that you are working with the range-name table shown in figure T.11. After a few move and delete operations, issue the /**R**ange **N**ame **T**able command and notice the range-name table changes (see fig. T.12). As you can see, you have lost the range names whose upper left or lower right corners were affected. Because the TOTALS range was not affected, its range remains the same.

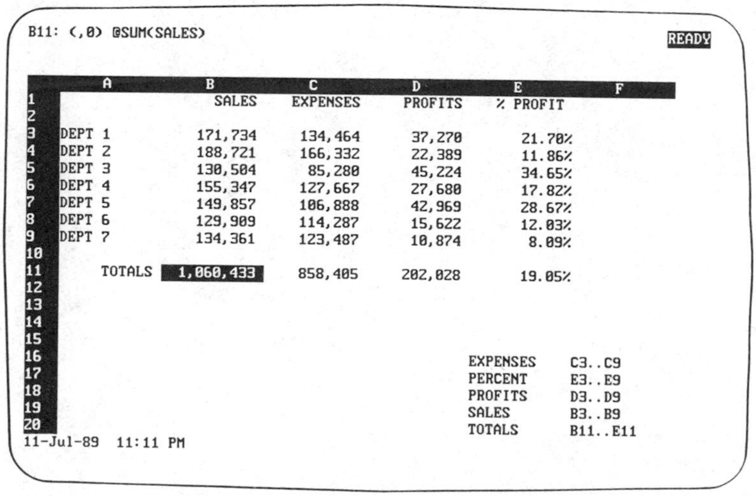

Fig. T.11.
A range-name
table.

```
B11: (,0) @SUM(SALES)                                              READY

        A          B          C          D          E          F
1                 SALES    EXPENSES    PROFITS    % PROFIT
2
3   DEPT 1      171,734    134,464     37,270      21.70%
4   DEPT 2      188,721    166,332     22,389      11.86%
5   DEPT 3      130,504     85,280     45,224      34.65%
6   DEPT 4      155,347    127,667     27,680      17.82%
7   DEPT 5      149,857    106,888     42,969      28.67%
8   DEPT 6      129,909    114,287     15,622      12.03%
9   DEPT 7      134,361    123,487     10,874       8.09%
10
11         TOTALS  1,060,433    858,405    202,028      19.05%
12
13
14
15
16                                      EXPENSES    C3..C9
17                                      PERCENT     E3..E9
18                                      PROFITS     D3..D9
19                                      SALES       B3..B9
20                                      TOTALS      B11..E11
11-Jul-89  11:11 PM
```

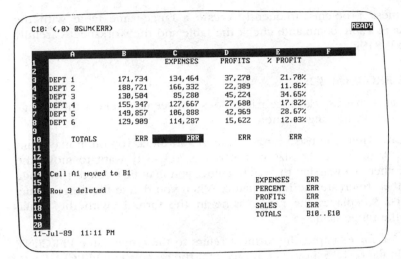

```
C10: (,0) @SUM(ERR)                                              READY

         A           B         C         D         E          F
1                            EXPENSES  PROFITS  % PROFIT
2
3   DEPT 1         171,734   134,464    37,270     21.70%
4   DEPT 2         188,721   166,332    22,389     11.86%
5   DEPT 3         130,504    85,280    45,224     34.65%
6   DEPT 4         155,347   127,667    27,680     17.82%
7   DEPT 5         149,857   106,888    42,969     28.67%
8   DEPT 6         129,909   114,287    15,622     12.03%
9
10     TOTALS         ERR      ERR       ERR        ERR
11
12
13
14  Cell A1 moved to B1
15                                     EXPENSES   ERR
16  Row 9 deleted                      PERCENT    ERR
17                                     PROFITS    ERR
18                                     SALES      ERR
19                                     TOTALS     B10..E10
20
11-Jul-89  11:11 PM
```

Fig. T.12.
A range-name table after moving and deleting.

Solution: Although both ranges and range names are lost in the same manner, using range names provides an easy way to audit these errors. Keep a current range-name table in all your worksheets. After you make any changes, re-create the range-name table and look for ERR.

Caution: If you lose a range name and then save and later retrieve the file, something strange may happen—the lost range names may no longer be lost. The cell that was erased or had data moved into it, however, is changed to cell IV8192. As an example, figure T.13 shows the same worksheet as figure T.12 after the file has been saved and retrieved. The effect on macros that use these range names can be disastrous.

```
C10: (,0) @SUM(ERR)                                              READY

         A           B         C         D         E          F
1                            EXPENSES  PROFITS  % PROFIT
2
3   DEPT 1         171,734   134,464    37,270     21.70%
4   DEPT 2         188,721   166,332    22,389     11.86%
5   DEPT 3         130,504    85,280    45,224     34.65%
6   DEPT 4         155,347   127,667    27,680     17.82%
7   DEPT 5         149,857   106,888    42,969     28.67%
8   DEPT 6         129,909   114,287    15,622     12.03%
9
10     TOTALS         ERR      ERR       ERR        ERR
11
12
13
14  Cell A1 moved to B1
15                                     EXPENSES   C3..IV8192
16  Row 9 deleted                      PERCENT    E3..IV8192
17                                     PROFITS    D3..IV8192
18                                     SALES      B3..IV8192
19                                     TOTALS     B10..E10
20
11-Jul-89  11:12 PM
```

Fig. T.13.
A range-name table after the file is saved and retrieved.

To avoid these problems, frequently create a range-name table with the /Range Name Table command; check the table and the worksheet carefully for ERR or IV8192.

RANGE NAME PROBLEM #2:

A valid formula that uses a range name does not seem to reflect the change in the location of the range name.

Explanation: When you use a range name in a formula, you often may want to increase or decrease the size of the range. You may want to move the range altogether. To reassign the range name, you may first delete the range name and then re-create the range name. When you delete the range name, however, 1-2-3 replaces the range name in the formula with the actual address of the range name.

In figure T.14, for example, the formula refers to the range name PERCENT in cell B1. In figure T.15, however, notice that the range name PERCENT was moved to cell B2, but the formula uses the old address of PERCENT before it was deleted and re-created.

Fig. T.14.
A formula using the range name PERCENT.

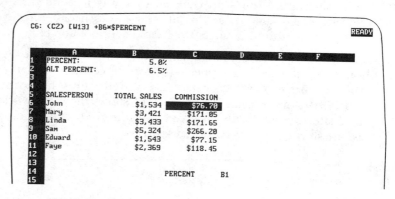

Fig. T.15.
A formula referencing a cell with the range name PERCENT.

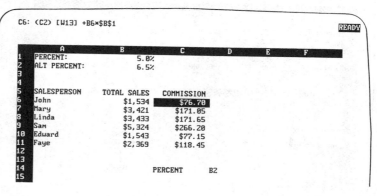

Solution: Rather than deleting a range name, reassign it. Issue the /**R**ange Name **C**reate command, choose the proper range name, and when prompted with Enter range:, either type the new range or point to the new range. Pointing to the new range requires that you know whether the range name is assigned to a single cell or a group of cells.

If the range name is assigned to a single cell, the cell reference may be, for example, B2. Move the cell pointer to the new location of the range name and press Enter. If the range name is assigned to a group of cells, however, press the Esc key before moving the cell pointer. The reference, B2..B5, for example, becomes B2. Now, move the cell pointer to the upper left corner of the new range, press period, and highlight the entire range for the range name. Press Enter to assign the range name to the new address; the formula reflects the appropriate cells.

RANGE NAME PROBLEM #3:

A range name looks correct in the range-name table, but the macros and formulas that refer to the named range do not work properly.

Explanation: This problem occurs when you use a range name that is also a cell address. If you set up a complex report and give individual pages the range names P1, P2, and P3, for example, the printed report contains only the cells P1, P2, and P3. If you give a macro the range name GO2 and then {BRANCH GO2}, the macro branches to cell GO2 and, probably, stops at a blank cell instead of reinvoking the macro.

Solution: Never name a range with a combination of one or two letters and a number. Don't even use a range name such as TO4; a range name that is not a valid cell address in the current version of 1-2-3 may be a valid cell address in a future release.

Problems with Relative and Absolute Addressing

ADDRESSING PROBLEM #1:

After you copy a formula to other cells, the copied formulas are incorrect — the addresses are wrong.

Explanation: One of 1-2-3's handiest built-in features is the automatic formula adjustment for relative cell addressing when a formula is copied. Relative addressing is so natural and automatic that you no longer think about it.

Consider the following formula in cell A4:

+A1+A2−A3

When the cell pointer is positioned in A4, the program displays this formula on the top line of the control panel. You think of the formula as "add the contents of A1 and A2 and subtract the contents of A3." If you copy the formula from A4 to B4, it becomes the following:

+ B1 + B2 − B3

This result, which is exactly what you would expect after you have gained some experience in using 1-2-3, depends on *relative addressing*. Each formula is stored with addresses relative to the cell that contains the formula. Internally, 1-2-3 interprets the formula as "add the contents of the cell three rows up and the cell two rows up and subtract the contents of the cell one row up." This is the same formula originally in A4 and copied into B4.

You frequently do not want the cell references to change when you copy a formula. If you copy the cell references as relative addresses, you get the wrong formula. In figure T.16, for example, the formula for percent of total was written in C2 and copied to C3..C13. The relative addressing adjustment changes the formula in C3 from + B2/B14 to + B3/B15.

Fig. T.16.
Relative and
absolute
addressing.

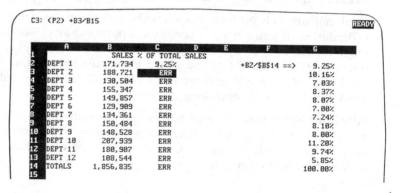

Solution: Specify an address as absolute when you *write* the formula, not when you copy it. To make an address absolute, precede the column and the row of the cell address with a dollar sign ($). If you use the pointing method to specify a range or a cell address, make the address absolute by pressing the Abs (F4) key when you point to the cell. If you type a cell address manually, make the address absolute by pressing Abs after you type the address.

The formula in C2 should be + B2/$B$14. When you copy this formula, the relative address (B2) changes, but the absolute address ($B$14) does not change.

Problems with Recalculation

RECALCULATION PROBLEM #1:

As your worksheets become larger, recalculation becomes annoyingly slow.

Explanation: Whenever you add or change a cell, 1-2-3 recalculates the entire worksheet. At first, this recalculation is almost instantaneous, and you can ignore the delay. As you add formulas and include more complex formulas and string functions, the delay increases noticeably and becomes annoying. Your work can slow down dramatically if you add data to many cells in a large worksheet.

Solution: Upgrade to Release 2.2. This version of the program offers "minimal recalculation" to speed worksheet recalculation. Only cells affected by a change in the worksheet are recalculated.

RELEASE 2.2

Alternative Solution: If you don't have Release 2.2 or you still notice a delay in recalculation, change recalculation to Manual using /Worksheet Global Recalculation Manual. You experience no delay the next time you make an entry because no recalculation occurs. To warn you that the information in some of the cells may be incorrect, the CALC indicator appears at the bottom of the screen. Press Calc (F9) when you want the program to recalculate the worksheet. The CALC indicator disappears until you make another entry.

RECALCULATION PROBLEM #2:

When you print reports after you have updated the worksheet, some of the data is incorrect. You may have a similar problem when you use the /File Xtract Values and /Range Value commands. In all cases, the resulting values are not current.

Explanation: When recalculation is manual, the current values of any formula in the worksheet may be incorrect if you change the information in cells that the formula uses. Generally, you cannot expect 1-2-3 commands to recalculate the worksheet (even when getting the correct answer requires a recalculation).

Solution: If you use a macro to print reports, to extract data as values, or to convert formulas to values with /Range Value, add {CALC} to the macro before it executes the commands. If you don't use a macro, press Calc (F9) to recalculate manually.

RECALCULATION PROBLEM #3:

When you use the /File Combine Add or Subtract command or 1-2-3 Release 2.2's file-linking capability to transfer information from another worksheet, the transferred data is not current.

RELEASE 2.2

RECALCULATION PROBLEM #4:

You want to see only a few values on a large worksheet that takes a long time to recalculate, but you spend an inordinate amount of time recalculating.

Explanation: On large, complex models that can take several minutes to recalculate, you almost always use manual recalculation. If you build or change the model or enter data in one section, however, you often want to see the current values in only that area. Continually pressing Calc (F9) causes you to lose time while you wait for the program to recalculate the entire worksheet.

Solution: You can recalculate only part of a worksheet in one of several ways.

To recalculate a single cell, simply edit the cell. Press Edit (F2) and then press Enter.

To recalculate a range of cells, copy the range to itself. Figure T.17 shows a range that is part of a large worksheet. To recalculate the cells in only the range BC65..BH75, copy the range BC65..BH75 to BC65. All the cells in the range recalculate when 1-2-3 copies them to themselves.

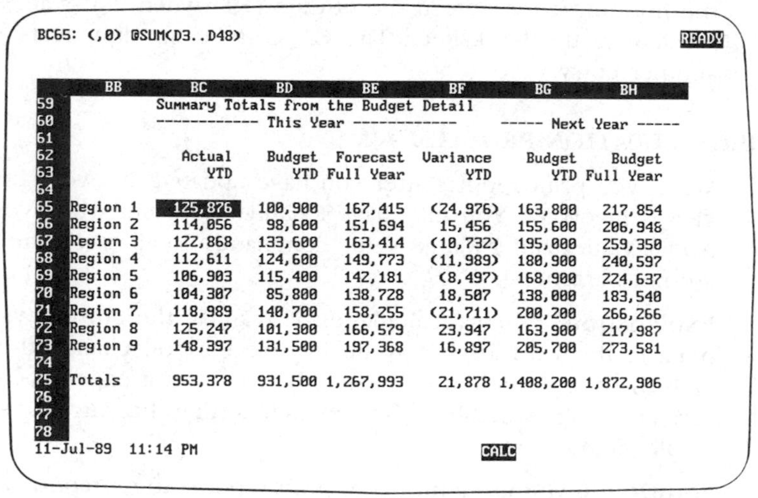

Fig. T.17.
A range that is part of a large worksheet.

```
BC65: (,0) @SUM(D3..D48)                                              READY

         BB        BC        BD        BE        BF        BG        BH
59                Summary Totals from the Budget Detail
60                ------------ This Year ------------    ----- Next Year -----
61
62                Actual    Budget  Forecast  Variance    Budget    Budget
63                YTD       YTD     Full Year YTD         YTD     Full Year
64
65    Region 1   125,876   100,900  167,415  (24,976)   163,800   217,854
66    Region 2   114,056    98,600  151,694   15,456    155,600   206,948
67    Region 3   122,868   133,600  163,414  (10,732)   195,000   259,350
68    Region 4   112,611   124,600  149,773  (11,989)   180,900   240,597
69    Region 5   106,903   115,400  142,181   (8,497)   168,900   224,637
70    Region 6   104,307    85,800  138,728   18,507    138,000   183,540
71    Region 7   118,989   140,700  158,255  (21,711)   200,200   266,266
72    Region 8   125,247   101,300  166,579   23,947    163,900   217,987
73    Region 9   148,397   131,500  197,368   16,897    205,700   273,581
74
75    Totals     953,378   931,500 1,267,993  21,878  1,408,200 1,872,906
76
77
78
11-Jul-89  11:14 PM                              CALC
```

To recalculate part of a worksheet using a macro, use the macro commands {RECALC} and {RECALCCOL}.

RECALCULATION PROBLEM #5:

Because your worksheet is large, you keep recalculation on Manual and use the partial-recalculation methods described in the preceding solution. But the partial recalculation sometimes produces incorrect results.

Explanation: When you recalculate the entire worksheet, 1-2-3 uses natural-order calculation as the default. In other words, unless you change the recalculation order to **R**owwise or **C**olumnwise using **/W**orksheet **G**lobal **R**ecalculation, 1-2-3 always calculates a cell after calculating the results of all the cells to which that cell refers. This step avoids problems that occurred in older spreadsheet programs that calculated only across rows or down columns. With natural-order calculation, formulas can be anywhere in the worksheet; with other calculation methods, formulas are correct after one recalculation only when they refer to cells above or to the left of the cell being recalculated. Formulas that refer to a cell address below and to the right of the cell being recalculated are known as *forward references*.

The worksheet shown in figure T.18 contains forward references. When you press Calc (F9), the program calculates the correct answer. Figures T.19, T.20, and T.21 show the results of different methods of partial recalculation. Certain combinations produce correct results, but others are incorrect.

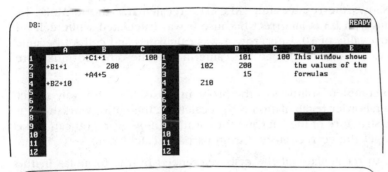

Fig T.18.
A worksheet with forward references.

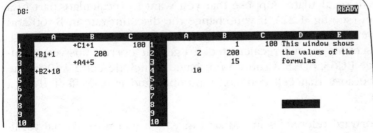

Fig. T.19.
A worksheet with forward references before recalculation.

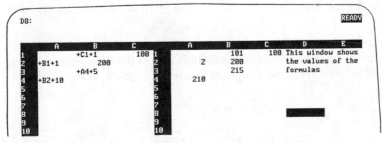

Fig. T.20.
Forward references after recalculation by column.

Fig. T.21.
Forward
references after
recalculation
by row.

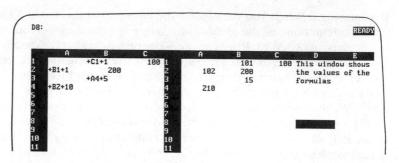

Figure T.19 shows the same formulas as figure T.18 before any calculation. Figure T.20 shows the results after /Copy or {RECALCCOL} recalculates the formulas by column. The formula in A2 is incorrect because it was calculated while cell B1 still contained a value of 1. Later, column B was calculated and cell B1 became 101, but it was too late to change the value in A2. The other formulas are correct.

Figure T.21 shows the results after {RECALC} recalculates the formulas by row. The formula in B3 is incorrect because it was calculated while cell A4 still contained a value of 10. Later, row 4 was calculated and cell A4 became 210, but it was too late to change the value in B3. The other formulas are correct.

Solution: No complete solution to the problem exists. The only way to get complete natural-order recalculation is to recalculate the entire worksheet. If you know the structure of the data and the formulas, however, you can make sure that you get the correct answer from partial recalculation.

First, be sure to recalculate all the cells referenced by the formulas in the area you want to recalculate. Suppose that you want to recalculate part of a large worksheet (see fig. T.22). If you change the discount rate in BA60 and then recalculate the range BD65..BD75, you get an incorrect answer because the average discounts are not recalculated. To get the correct answer, recalculate the range BC65..BD75. (You do not have to include cell BA60 in the recalculation because that cell contains a number and is not affected by a recalculation.)

Try to avoid forward references in the area in which you want partial recalculation. If no forward references are present, partial recalculations can work.

If you cannot avoid forward references, you still can get the correct answer if you pay attention to how partial recalculation proceeds. When you copy a range or use {RECALCCOL}, the program recalculates each cell, starting at the upper left corner of the range and continuing down each column. When it reaches the bottom of each column, 1-2-3 starts recalculating at the top of the next column in the range.

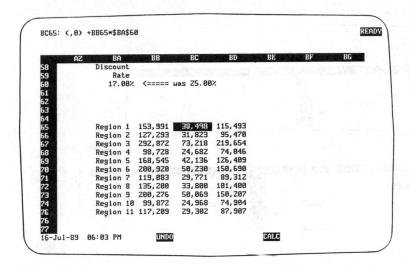

Fig. T.22.
A range that is a part of a large worksheet.

If you use {RECALC}, 1-2-3 recalculates each cell, starting at the upper left corner of the range and continuing across each row. When it reaches the rightmost cell of each row, 1-2-3 starts recalculating at the leftmost cell in the next row.

The following rules apply to partial recalculation:

1. If you use /Copy or {RECALCCOL} for a partial recalculation, the results may be incorrect for a formula that refers to another formula in a column to its right or below it in the same column.

2. If you use {RECALC} for a partial recalculation, the results may be incorrect for a formula that refers to another formula in a row below it or to its right in the same row.

3. Formulas that refer to cells containing values are correct using any recalculation method.

If you must use partial recalculation on a range with forward references, the only solution involves more than one recalculation. You must {RECALC} or {RECALCCOL} once for every *nested forward reference* in the range. A nested forward reference is a formula that refers forward to a formula that refers forward (and so on) to a cell. Figure T.23 shows a series of forward references. Each {RECALC} resolves one additional forward reference.

After you have determined how many nested forward references you need to recalculate, add that number of {RECALC} or {RECALCCOL} statements to your macro.

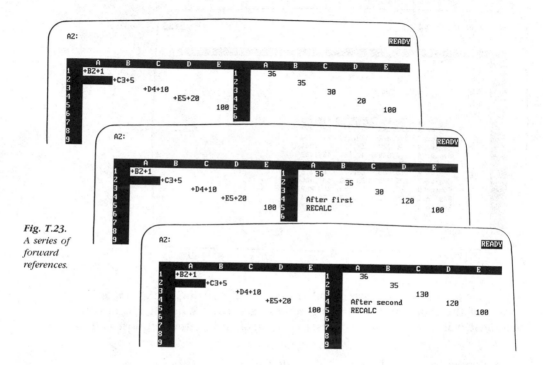

Fig. T.23.
A series of
forward
references.

Miscellaneous Problems

SPLIT SCREEN PROBLEM #1:

When you split the screen into two windows to look at two parts of the worksheet simultaneously, the second window moves with the first one, and you cannot control the second window.

Explanation: You split the 1-2-3 screen for one of two reasons: to keep part of a large table in sight at all times, or to look at two completely different parts of a worksheet at the same time. The first of these reasons is the more common of the two. Figure T.24 shows an example of this kind of split screen. The totals are always displayed in the bottom window. When you scroll the top window, the bottom window scrolls with it, ensuring that the columns in both windows always match (see fig. T.25). This synchronized scrolling is the default (the **S**ync option on the **W**orksheet **W**indow menu) when you split the screen (horizontally or vertically) into two windows. In a vertical split, the same rows are displayed in the left and right windows.

E7: (,0) 150222 READY

	A	B	C	D	E	F	G
1		BUDGET SUMMARIES					
2							
3							
4							
5		January	February	March	April	May	June
6		-------	-------	-------	-------	-------	-------
7	Region 1	129,767	136,256	143,069	150,222	157,733	165,620
8	Region 2	125,297	131,562	138,140	145,047	152,300	159,915
9	Region 3	114,807	120,547	126,575	132,903	139,548	146,526
10	Region 4	121,220	127,281	133,645	140,327	147,343	154,710
11	Region 5	135,937	142,734	149,871	157,364	165,233	173,494
12	Region 6	113,055	118,708	124,643	130,875	137,419	144,290
13	Region 7	130,880	137,424	144,295	151,510	159,085	167,039
14	Region 8	100,316	105,362	110,630	116,162	121,970	128,068
15	Region 9	106,299	111,614	117,194	123,064	129,207	135,667
16	Region 10	125,816	132,106	138,712	145,647	152,930	160,576
17	Region 11	135,100	141,855	148,948	156,395	164,215	172,426
18	Region 12	105,713	110,999	116,549	122,377	128,495	134,920
	A	B	C	D	E	F	G
49	TOTALS	4,989,312	5,238,778	5,500,717	5,775,753	6,064,540	6,367,768

11-Jul-89 11:20 PM

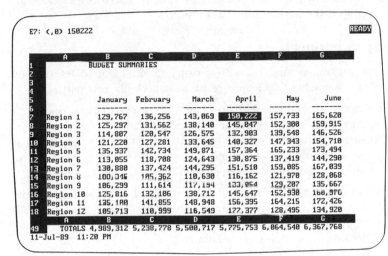

Fig. T.24. The display split into two windows.

N7: (,0) @SUM(B7..M7) READY

	H	I	J	K	L	M	N
1							
2							
3							
4							
5	July	August	September	October	November	December	Totals
6	-------	-------	-------	-------	-------	-------	-------
7	173,901	182,596	191,726	201,312	211,378	221,946	2,065,526
8	167,910	176,306	185,121	194,377	204,096	214,301	1,994,374
9	153,852	161,345	169,622	178,103	187,088	196,359	1,827,275
10	162,446	178,568	179,097	188,051	197,454	207,327	1,937,469
11	182,169	191,277	200,841	210,883	221,428	232,499	2,163,730
12	114,807	120,547	126,575	132,903	139,548	146,526	1,548,896
13	121,220	127,281	133,645	140,327	147,343	154,710	1,714,759
14	135,937	142,734	149,871	157,364	165,233	173,494	1,607,170
15	113,055	117,708	124,643	130,875	137,419	144,290	1,491,025
16	130,880	137,424	144,295	151,510	159,085	167,039	1,746,020
17	126,575	132,903	139,548	146,526	153,852	161,345	1,779,688
18	133,645	140,327	147,343	154,710	162,446	178,568	1,636,092
	H	I	J	K	L	M	N
49	6,686,156	7,020,464	7,371,487	7,740,061	8,127,064	8,533,417	79,415,518

11-Jul-89 11:21 PM

Fig. T.25. The windows scroll in sync.

When you split the screen to look at two completely different parts of a worksheet (data and macros, for example), you probably do not want to use synchronized scrolling. You want to move the cell pointer around the data area in one window while the other window remains fixed on a specific macro.

Solution: To eliminate synchronized scrolling, specify /Worksheet Window Unsync after you split the screen into two windows.

DATA DESTRUCTION PROBLEM #1:

Occasionally, by making a mistake with /Copy, /Move, or /Delete, you destroy part of the worksheet and then must painstakingly reconstruct it.

Explanation: Unlike modeling languages and statistical-analysis packages, spreadsheets such as 1-2-3 do not separate the model from the data. (The *model* is composed of formulas and macros that do not change. The *data* is the information you continually enter and change.) When you use 1-2-3 to enter data, you risk accidentally changing the model as well.

RELEASE
2.2

Solution: In Release 2.2, if the Undo feature is enabled, you can undo some mistakes with Undo (Alt-F4). You can enable the Undo feature with /Worksheet Global Default Other Undo Enable. Use /Worksheet Global Default Update to save this setting permanently.

Alternative Solution: Always keep a backup copy of all worksheets. (Keep two or three backup copies of critical worksheets.) If you destroy a worksheet, you can recover it from the backup file.

You can use /Worksheet Global Protection Enable to prevent the worksheet from being destroyed. Protected cells cannot be changed. If you try to change a protected cell, the program beeps and displays the warning message Protected cell and does not change the contents of the cell.

Use /Range Unprot (/Range Unprotect in 1-2-3 Release 2.01) to unprotect the cells you want to change. After you have completed the worksheet and are ready to use it, turn on the protection feature by issuing /Worksheet Global Protection Enable before you enter data.

TEMPLATE PROBLEM #1:

At the beginning of every month, you must carefully erase all the data from the past month to prepare for the new month. If you leave old data, the information for the new month is incorrect.

Explanation: This problem is related to the preceding one. Because 1-2-3 does not distinguish between the model and the data, the program cannot present a blank model for the next month's data.

Solution: Although 1-2-3 cannot distinguish between the model and the data, you can. Build a model, or *template*: a worksheet that contains all necessary formulas, formats, and macros but no data. Save this worksheet and make a backup copy. Use the model every month to start the new month. After you add data to the file, always be sure to save it under a different name from that of the template. You may name a budget template BUDGET, for example. Retrieve BUDGET every month, saving it as BUD0889 in August 1989; BUD0989 in September 1989; and so on.

SEARCH AND REPLACE PROBLEM #1:

RELEASE
2.2

You used Release 2.2's **/R**ange **S**earch command with the **A**ll option to search for and replace text, and it replaced text in the middle of words, leaving you with many replacements you didn't intend. For example, you replaced *her* with *him*, and 1-2-3 replaced *here* with *hime* and *other* with *othim*, and so on.

Explanation: 1-2-3 searches for the text you specified and finds it whether it is a whole word or part of a word. To rephrase, 1-2-3 looks for a string of characters and doesn't care where these characters appear. If you use the **A**ll option, all replacements are made automatically, and you cannot confirm each one.

Unless you are 100 percent sure that you want to replace all occurrences of a string, use the **R**eplace and **N**ext options instead of **A**ll. **R**eplace replaces the current word and moves on to the next occurrence. **N**ext finds the subsequent occurrence without replacing the current one. Using these options is a safer way to search for and replace text.

Solution: If the Undo feature was enabled before you performed **/R**ange **S**earch, press Undo (Alt-F4) to cancel the replace. If Undo was not active, you can use the search and replace command to reverse the search and replace. The word you searched for would be the word you replace and the word you replaced would be the word you search for. If you first replaced all occurrences of *her* with *him*, reverse the command by replacing *him* with *her*. However, do not use the **A**ll option or you may end up with more *her*s than you started with!

ADD-IN PROBLEM #1:

RELEASE
2.2

You detached an add-in application (such as Allways or the Macro Library Manager) with the **/A**dd-In **D**etach command (Release 2.2 only), but the application still attaches each time you load 1-2-3.

Explanation: The /**A**dd-In **D**etach and /**A**dd-In **C**lear commands remove the application or applications from memory during the *current* work session only. If the add-in attaches each time you load 1-2-3, you must have attached the application with the /**W**orksheet **G**lobal **D**efault **O**ther **A**dd-In **S**et command. This command attaches (and also can invoke, if you specify) an add-in application automatically for every work session.

Solution: Use the /**W**orksheet **G**lobal **D**efault **O**ther **A**dd-In **C**ancel command so that the add-in does not automatically attach. Be sure to use /**W**orksheet **G**lobal **D**efault **U**pdate to save this setting.

Troubleshooting Functions

FUNCTION PROBLEM #1:

You get apparent rounding errors even when you have not rounded off.

Explanation: When you use formats such as Fixed, comma (,), and Currency with a fixed number of decimal places, 1-2-3 keeps the number to 15 decimal places but rounds off the display. Examples of apparent rounding errors are shown in figure T.26.

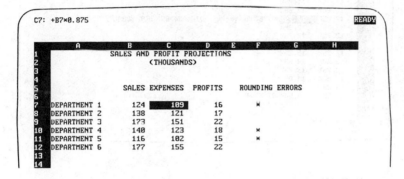

Fig. T.26.
A worksheet with rounding errors.

Solution: To avoid such rounding errors, use the @ROUND function to round off numbers to the same precision shown in the display (see fig. T.27).

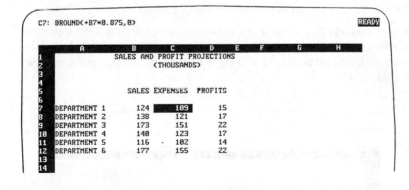

Fig. T.27.
Rounding errors eliminated by @ROUND.

FUNCTION PROBLEM #2:

Two numbers that should be equal sometimes test as unequal.

Explanation: This can be a sneaky problem. Figure T.28 shows what should be two identical columns of numbers. Column A was created using **/Data Fill**; column B, using a formula. The @IF formula in column C indicates that some of the numbers are not equal. This problem can occur with fractions because computers process numbers in binary and then convert the numbers to decimal to display them. The problem does not occur with integers.

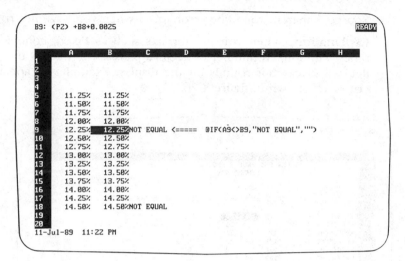

Fig. T.28.
Numbers that should be equal may not test as equal.

Solution: Use @ROUND when you compare two fractions.

FUNCTION PROBLEM #3:

You get ERR when you try to combine numbers and strings.

Explanation: Although 1-2-3 has a full complement of string functions, you cannot mix strings and numbers in the same function. Figure T.29 shows the effect of trying to build an address by using words from strings and a number for the ZIP code.

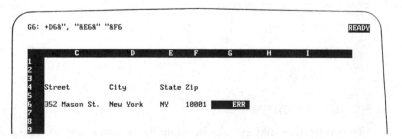

Fig. T.29.
An error when numbers mix with strings.

Solution: Use the @STRING function to convert a number to its equivalent string (see fig. T.30). Then use the converted number in a string function.

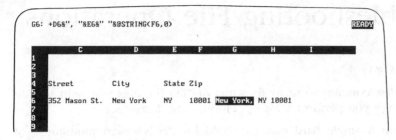

Fig. T.30.
*A function that
converts a
number to a
string.*

FUNCTION PROBLEM #4:

You want to use string functions on a field, but you are not sure whether a number or a string will be entered in the field.

Explanation: Functions work on either strings or numbers, but not on both. If you don't know what a cell contains and you guess incorrectly, you risk getting ERR or an incorrect result.

Solution: You can test a cell to see whether it contains a number or a string and then, depending on the contents of the cell, use the appropriate functions. Suppose that you want to concatenate the contents of A1 and B1 using the following formula:

+A1&B1

The ampersand (&), which is a string concatenation operator, causes an error if either A1 or B1 is blank or contains a number. Assume that you know A1 contains a string but you don't know whether B1 contains a string, a number, or is blank. To concatenate B1 to A1 only if B1 contains a string, use the following formula:

+A1&@S(B1)

The @S function is a filter and does nothing if the cell contains a string. If the cell does not contain a string, however, it returns a null string. The formula therefore results in either A1 (if B1 does not contain a string) or in A1&B1 (if B1 contains a string).

To concatenate the contents of B1 regardless of whether B1 contains a number or a string, you need a more complex formula (see fig. T.31).

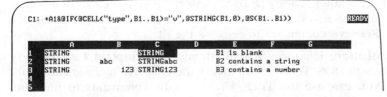

Fig. T.31.
*A formula that
handles
numbers,
strings, or
blank cells.*

In the formula in figure T.31, if the type is "v" (for *value*), the contents of the cell are converted to a string. If the cell is blank, the @S function filters it out, and the cell is ignored. If the cell contains a string, the @S function does nothing, and the two strings are concatenated.

Troubleshooting File Operations

FILE PROBLEM #1:

Your hard disk contains so many files that finding the files you want is difficult; whenever you perform a file operation, long delays occur.

Explanation: A single hard disk can hold hundreds—even thousands—of files. If that many files were placed in one subdirectory, however, keeping track of them could be impossible. In addition, DOS slows significantly if you have more than approximately 112 or 224 files (depending on which version of DOS you use) in one subdirectory.

If you try to put all the files in the root directory, DOS reaches an absolute limit and doesn't let you save additional files.

Solution: Set up separate subdirectories for different applications and users.

The default directory should contain the subdirectory of files you use most often. To specify the name of this subdirectory, use /**W**orksheet **G**lobal **D**efault **D**irectory.

To reach files in other subdirectories, use /**F**ile **D**irectory. This command changes the directory until you either use /**F**ile **D**irectory again or return to the default directory by quitting and reentering 1-2-3.

FILE PROBLEM #2:

You want to retrieve a file not in the default directory, but you don't remember which directory contains the file.

Explanation: You can see only the files in the current directory. The file you want is in another subdirectory, but 1-2-3 does not list all of the disk's subdirectories.

Solution: Select /**F**ile **L**ist and choose **W**orksheet, **P**rint, **G**raph, or **O**ther, depending on the type of file for which you're looking. 1-2-3 displays a list of all files of that type and all subdirectories on the current directory. To search forward through a chain of directories, move the pointer to the directory you want and press Enter. To search backwards through the chain of directories, use the Backspace key. When you locate the file, use the /**F**ile **D**irectory and **F**ile **R**etrieve commands to retrieve the file.

Alternative Solution: Use the /**S**ystem command to suspend 1-2-3 temporarily and return to DOS. This method makes the DOS TREE command available to you. You can use the TREE, CD, and DIR commands to find the subdirectory and file you want.

After you have located the file, return to 1-2-3 by typing **exit** at the DOS prompt. Then you can use the **/File D**irectory and **/File R**etrieve commands to read the file.

FILE PROBLEM #3:

While building a large worksheet, you fear making a mistake that may destroy part of the worksheet and cost you hours of work.

Explanation: Sooner or later, everyone destroys part or all of an important worksheet. The greater your proficiency in 1-2-3, the larger and more complex the worksheets you can build—and the more disastrous the errors you can make.

Solution: In Release 2.2, if the Undo feature is enabled, you can undo a mistake by pressing the Undo (Alt-F4) key. Enable the Undo feature with **/W**orksheet **G**lobal **D**efault **O**ther **U**ndo **E**nable. Use **/W**orksheet **G**lobal **D**efault **U**pdate to save this setting permanently.

RELEASE

2.2

Alternative Solution: You may have no recourse once you destroy a worksheet; you may not be able to restore it. The only solution may be to avoid the problem by preparing for it.

You can best prepare for this problem by saving your worksheet frequently when you make many changes or write macros. Be sure to save the worksheet under a different name. (If you use the same file name, you may save the file two or three times after making a disastrous error before discovering that you made an error.)

If you are developing a worksheet, for example, save it under a name that includes a sequence number (such as BUDGET1, BUDGET2, BUDGET3, and so on). When you reach BUDGET10 and have done some testing, you can consider erasing BUDGET1. At least once during each development session, save the worksheet to a floppy disk. This backup copy is an additional safeguard.

If you enter data in a worksheet daily, save the worksheet under a name that includes the date (BUD0809 or BUD0810, for example).

Remember that time spent storing data is minimal compared to the time you may have to spend reentering lost data and rebuilding lost macro-driven worksheets.

FILE PROBLEM #4:

Some formulas brought in by **/F**ile **C**ombine **C**opy are meaningless.

Explanation: Using **/F**ile **C**ombine **C**opy is similar to using **/C**opy within a worksheet. The same rules about relative addressing apply in both instances. If you combine (pull in) part of another worksheet containing formulas that refer to cells in the combined area, the formulas stay the same in relation to the cells to which they refer. If you combine formulas that refer to cells outside the combined area, however, these formulas become references to cells somewhere else in the current worksheet. These formulas may become meaningless, leading to incorrect results.

Figure T.32 shows the result of combining the data in J10..K15. Because the formula in K10 refers to cell G10, which is a blank cell in this worksheet, the result in K10 is zero. In the original worksheet, the corresponding cell contained a price and the formula gave a correct result.

Fig. T.32.
Formulas may
be meaningless
after using
/File Combine.

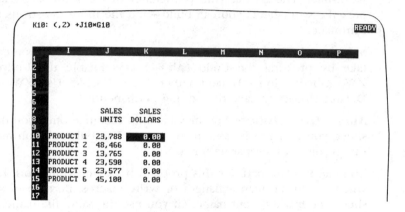

Solution: You can use /File Combine Add to combine into the current worksheet the values from another worksheet. The formulas in the other worksheet are converted to numbers. If you don't want any of the formulas from the other worksheet, use /File Combine Add for the entire range. If you want some of the formulas from the other worksheet, first use /File Combine Copy to get the formulas. Then, to get the numbers, use /File Combine Add on a different range.

Note: /File Combine Add has pitfalls of its own. As 1-2-3 executes the /File Combine Add command, 1-2-3 checks each cell in the current worksheet. If a cell is blank or contains a number, the corresponding value from the file being combined is added to that cell. If the cell in the current worksheet contains a formula, 1-2-3 skips that cell, regardless of what the corresponding cell in the file being combined may contain. /File Combine Add also combines only numeric values—not strings.

FILE PROBLEM #5:

You used /File Combine Add and got old values.

Explanation: When combining cells that contain formulas, /File Combine Add combines the values produced by the formulas rather than the formulas themselves. If the file is set for Manual recalculation and was saved without a recalculation, some of the formulas may not reflect current values.

Solution: If you intend to use a worksheet later for **/File Combine Add** or **Subtract**, always calculate the worksheet before saving it.

FILE PROBLEM #6:

After you use **/File Import Numbers** to read an ASCII file, some of the information is lost and some of it looks scrambled.

Explanation: **/File Import Numbers** works only when the data in the ASCII file is in a precise format. Each field must be separated by commas or spaces, and each string must be enclosed in double quotation marks. 1-2-3 ignores data not in this format but imports whatever data it finds and recognizes as numbers. Ordinarily, the result is a useless mess. Following is an example of correct and incorrect ASCII file formats for use with 1-2-3:

Correct:"John","Doe",26,45000,"Manager"
Incorrect: John,Doe,26,45000,Manager

Solution: Using **/File Import Text**, read in the ASCII data as a series of long labels. Then use **/Data Parse** to separate the data into individual cells that can be used by 1-2-3.

FILE PROBLEM #7:

You used **/File Import Text** and **/Data Parse** to import a text file, but the dates are not in a format that 1-2-3 recognizes.

Explanation: When you use **/Data Parse**, 1-2-3 recognizes only numbers and dates with certain formats. If dates are not in a format that the program recognizes, 1-2-3 converts the dates to a string.

Solution: In many cases, no solution is necessary. You can leave the dates as labels unless you plan to use date arithmetic on them. If you must convert the labels to dates, however, you can do so using string functions and @DATEVALUE.

Figure T.33 shows a directory listing redirected to a text file, imported into 1-2-3, and parsed. The dates in column L are labels because, with the dashes (−) between the date fields, 1-2-3 did not recognize them as dates.

The string function in the control panel in figure T.33 converts the string to a valid 1-2-3 date format. @DATEVALUE then converts to a date the string that looks like a date. After this conversion, you use the **/Range Format Date** command to format the cell so that it looks like a date.

Fig. T.33.
String functions
and
@DATEVALUE
to convert a
date.

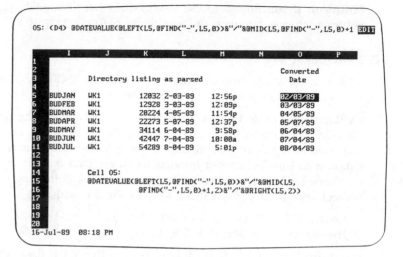

```
O5: (D4) @DATEVALUE(@LEFT(L5,@FIND("-",L5,0))&"/"&@MID(L5,@FIND("-",L5,0)+1  EDIT

         I        J       K        L        M        N        O        P
  1
  2                                                              Converted
  3               Directory listing as parsed                     Date
  4
  5   BUDJAN   WK1       12032  2-03-89    12:56p              02/03/89
  6   BUDFEB   WK1       12928  3-03-89    12:09p              03/03/89
  7   BUDMAR   WK1       20224  4-05-89    11:54p              04/05/89
  8   BUDAPR   WK1       22273  5-07-89    12:37p              05/07/89
  9   BUDMAY   WK1       34114  6-04-89     9:58p              06/04/89
 10   BUDJUN   WK1       42447  7-04-89    10:00a              07/04/89
 11   BUDJUL   WK1       54289  8-04-89     5:01p              08/04/89
 12
 13
 14               Cell O5:
 15               @DATEVALUE(@LEFT(L5,@FIND("-",L5,0))&"/"&@MID(L5,
 16                  @FIND("-",L5,0)+1,2)&"/"&@RIGHT(L5,2))
 17
 18
 19
 20
 16-Jul-89   08:18 PM
```

FILE PROBLEM #8:

To save a backup copy, you use **/F**ile **D**irectory to change the directory to
A:\ and then use **/F**ile **S**ave to save the file. Later, you notice that the file
was not saved on drive A.

Explanation: When you save a file, 1-2-3 remembers the entire path last
used to save the file or, if you haven't saved the file, to retrieve it. 1-2-3 does
not consider the current directory. By changing the directory and executing
/File **S**ave, you saved the file in the original directory.

Suppose that the file BUD0810 was read from the default directory
C:\DATA\123. You change the directory to A:\ and use **/F**ile **S**ave. 1-2-3
ignores the fact that the current directory is A:\ and displays the default path
in the prompt Enter save file name: C:\DATA\123\BUD0810.

Solution: Clear the previous path explicitly by pressing Esc three times.
Then retype the file name. Because you gain nothing by changing the current directory, leave it alone and include drive A in the file name. In this
example, after pressing Esc once, you see the following:

    Enter save file name: C:\DATA\123*.WK1

Pressing Esc again displays the following:

    Enter save file name: C:\DATA\123\

When you press Esc a third time, you see this:

    Enter save file name:

At this prompt, type **A:\BUD0810** and press Enter. The file is saved on drive A.

Caution: The next time you save this file, it is saved on drive A unless you specifically erase the existing path and type the drive C path.

FILE PROBLEM #9:

You used the **/File Save Backup** option when you saved a file in Release 2.2. Now you want to use the backup file, but it doesn't appear on the file retrieve list.

Explanation: Backup files are saved with the extension .BAK. The **/File Retrieve** command only lists files with the extension .WK*.

Solution: To retrieve a backup file, type the complete file name, including the .BAK extension. You also can select the file from a list of backup files by selecting **/File Retrieve**, typing ***.BAK**, and pressing Enter.

RELEASE

2.2

Troubleshooting Printing

PRINTING PROBLEM #1:

You have a multiple-page report that spans different sections of the worksheet. Specifying all the different print ranges is a laborious task.

Explanation: The program remembers only the last print range specified. If a report has multiple print ranges, you must specify each one whenever you print the report.

Solution: Create a macro. If you are not familiar with macros, read Chapters 13 and 14 to learn how to write a simple macro for printing a report and for general information about how to write macros and use advanced macro commands.

Give each page or print range a descriptive name (PAGE1, PAGE2, and so on) and then instruct your macro to print each page (see fig. T.34). Although you may make a few errors the first time you write the macro, the finished macro always prints an error-free report.

Fig. T.34.
A simple print
macro.

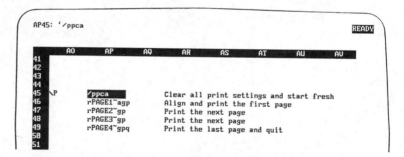

PRINTING PROBLEM #2:

Your print macro usually works as you want it to, but after you change the print options to print a different report, the standard reports print incorrectly.

Explanation: 1-2-3 remembers the print settings from the last report you printed. If you print a special report on wider paper, or with different margins, headers, footers, and setup strings, for example, these settings affect the next report you print with the macro.

Solution: At the beginning of your print macro, use the **/Print Printer Clear All** command to reset all printer options to their defaults and to clear everything else (see fig. T.34). The macro should then specify the printer options you want. In this way, you can include in one worksheet several print macros that don't interfere with one another.

PRINTING PROBLEM #3:

After you have made changes to the worksheet, your reports sometimes print data that is not current.

Explanation: In Manual recalculation mode, 1-2-3 prints the worksheet as of the last recalculation.

Solution: If you specify the printing options manually, press Calc (F9) before you start the /Print command. If you use a macro to print, begin the macro with {CALC}.

PRINTING PROBLEM #4:

Although you calculated correctly the number of lines per page when you set up your print ranges, the report runs off the end of the page and then skips a page.

Explanation: You must tell the program the exact length (in print lines) of a page. The default for 6 lines per inch on 11-inch paper is 66 lines. Because 1-2-3 automatically reserves 3 lines at the top and 3 lines at the bottom of each page, however, the maximum print range on a page is only 60 lines (These extra lines provide 1 line for a header or a footer—even if none is specified—and 2 lines between the print range and the header or footer.) If you specify top and bottom margins, you must subtract them from 60 (not 66) to determine the maximum number of lines in a one-page print range.

Solution: If you are not trying to pack the maximum number of lines onto each page, you can adjust your print ranges to fit the number of available lines.

If you don't use headers, footers, or borders, you can recover the use of the six lines by using /Print Printer Options Other Unformatted. This print setting eliminates automatic page breaks, headers, footers, and borders.

To skip to the next page, specify page breaks manually with /Print Printer Page. You also can specify page breaks manually by inserting page-break codes into the worksheet with /Worksheet Page. Neither of these Page commands is affected when you print with /Print Printer Options Other Unformatted.

PRINTING PROBLEM #5:

When you set up your print ranges, you considered margins and the six lines mentioned in the preceding problem. But 1-2-3 occasionally skips a page between pages.

Explanation: You can use one of two methods to skip to the next page when you print reports: you can specify a long report and let 1-2-3 skip automatically to a new page whenever it prints a full page or encounters a page-break code, or you can specify individual print ranges for each page and use the /Worksheet Page command to tell the program to skip to the next page. Under certain conditions, the two methods conflict and both send a page break to the printer, resulting in a blank page.

With top and bottom margins of 0, you can have a one-page print range of as many as 60 lines. If 1-2-3 encounters a print range of exactly 60 lines, the program automatically tells the printer to skip to the next page. If your macro also sends a page break, you get a blank page.

Solution: Either restrict your print ranges to 59 lines (minus the number of lines for top and bottom borders) or do not issue a **P**age command after a 60-line page. Count the number of lines you want on a page before printing the page.

PRINTING PROBLEM #6:

You do not want to print certain information in the middle of a print range.

Explanation: You have documented assumptions, shown intermediate results that clarify a calculation, and added comments to make your worksheets easier to understand. You may not want to include this information in your final printed reports.

Solution: This problem has several solutions. Pick those that best meet your needs.

Two solutions skip only rows:

- Specify multiple print ranges that skip any rows you do not want printed. (This method is practical only if you use a macro to print and if you do not add comments after completing the worksheet.)

- Use a special label prefix, the vertical bar (|), to tell 1-2-3 not to print a row. (The | symbol is located on the backslash key.) Whenever 1-2-3 sees this label prefix in the leftmost cell of a row in a print range, the program does not print that row. Except for printing, the | label prefix and the left-aligned label prefix (') act the same way. The contents of the cell are displayed normally.

To skip one or more columns in the middle of a print range, use the /Worksheet Column Hide command to hide the column before you print it. After you have printed the range, "unhide" the column by using the /Worksheet Column Display command.

To skip a few cells in a range of other cells you are printing, use /Range Format Hidden to hide the values of specific cells. Use /Range Format Reset to display the values of the cells again.

PRINTING PROBLEM #7:

You want to print a report twice, but the second copy, instead of starting at page 1, begins with the next page number of the first copy.

Explanation: With 1-2-3, you can build a report from many separate sections of a worksheet. If you use page numbers in headers or footers, every page starts with the next page number because the program assumes that you are producing one report.

Solution: Issue the /**Print Printer Align** command after /**Print Printer P**age to instruct 1-2-3 to start again at page 1. Because Align also tells the program that you have adjusted the paper to the top of the page, always issue the **Page** command before the **Align** command to prevent your pages from being misaligned.

PRINTING PROBLEM #8:

You don't want to bother specifying individual print ranges for a long report.

Explanation: If your report is more than five pages long, setting up the range names and writing the macro to print the report can be tedious. If the report grows longer as time passes (if it contains year-to-date details, for example), you want to avoid adding range names and changing the macro constantly.

Solution: Let 1-2-3 automatically break your report. 1-2-3 forces a page break after every full page and automatically inserts any headers or footers you specify. If you specify borders using /**Print Printer O**ther **B**orders **R**ows, 1-2-3 prints titles at the top of the range on every page, you simply specify one print range (see fig. T.35).

```
B1: [W15] 'EMPLOYEE LIST                                        READY

        A          B        C      D         E       F      G
                                                          /Print
 1           EMPLOYEE LIST                                Printer
 2                                                        Options
 3    Name        Name                             ←──    Borders Row
 4    First       Last     Age   SS No.    Dept.         A1..E5
 5    ─────────   ────────  ───  ────────  ──────
 6  Tim          Black      24   545-94-7146   Prod.  ←──
 7  Mary         Stanley    35   768-55-4765   Prod.
 8  John         Malone     58   479-78-1921   Sales
 9  Albert       Smith      25   658-45-1685   Mktg.
10  Joan         Jones      35   295-55-1701   Prod.     /Print
11  William      Aikel      32   122-11-1878   Sales     Printer
12  Linda        Manning    41   362-61-1589   Admin.    Range
13  Andrea       Oleo       42   393-21-9663   Prod.     A6..E110
14  Julie        Fredricks  23   291-25-1123   Sales
15  Bill         Albert     55   159-75-1752   Prod.
16  Jake         Wilone     20   141-40-3454   Sales
17  Fred         Cradle     58   192-78-1155   Prod.
18  Steve        Cray       63   893-83-1465   Mktg.
19  Leo          Apple      54   327-27-1613   Prod.
20  Andy         Jenkins    34   644-90-7025   Sales  ←──

16-Jul-89  09:14 PM      UNDO                          CAPS
```

Fig. T.35.
Specifying one print range to print titles at the top of every page.

1-2-3 also splits vertically a report too wide to print on a single page. The program prints as much material as possible on one page and then prints the "right side" of the report on a separate page. If you have titles at the left of the print range that you want to print on the right-side page, set these titles with **/P**rint **P**rinter **O**ther **B**orders **C**olumns. Do not include the cells defined as borders in the print range. If you do, the titles will print twice—once as borders and once as part of the print range.

PRINTING PROBLEM #9:

You let 1-2-3 handle page breaks automatically, but the program separates information that you want kept on one page.

Explanation: When you specify a long report and let the program separate it automatically into pages, every page has the same number of print lines. The resulting report may split information you do not want separated: paragraphs of explanation or multiple-line descriptions of accounts, for example.

Solution: Leave the report as one print range and insert page-break characters manually wherever you want a page to end. To insert a page-break character, move the cell pointer to the cell in the leftmost column of the row that you want to start on a new page. Then use **/W**orksheet **P**age to instruct 1-2-3 to insert a row above the cell pointer and put a page-break character (|::) in the cell.

PRINTING PROBLEM #10:

When you used **/W**orksheet **P**age to specify a page break, the command inserted a row through a macro or a database in the same row as the print range.

Explanation: 1-2-3 inserts a page break by inserting a row across the entire worksheet. The blank row is inserted through anything spanning that row.

Solution: Instead of using **/W**orksheet **P**age to insert a page break, you can indicate where you want the new page by typing the page-break character as a label.

In the leftmost column of the row that you want to start on the new page, type the page-break character—a vertical-bar label prefix followed by two colons (|::). 1-2-3 treats this label as a page-break character, except that no blank row is inserted in the worksheet. Remember that you must type the page-break character in a blank line (or a line you do not want to print anyway) in your print range because the row with the page-break character does not print.

Alternative Solution: If you store your macros in the Macro Library Manager (included with Release 2.2), you do not have to worry about the /Worksheet Page or /Worksheet Insert Row commands affecting your macros because macros are not included in the worksheet at all when the Macro Library Manager is used.

PRINTING PROBLEM #11:

You used /Print Printer Other Setup to specify the setup string to tell the printer to print compressed print, but the report wraps to a new line after 72 characters, even though additional space remains on the line.

Explanation: Because 1-2-3 cannot interpret a setup string, it does not recognize either the size of the characters you print or the width of the paper you use. The print settings indicate to the program the amount of material that can fit across a line and down a page.

Solution: Whenever you change the print pitch, change the right margin. With a default left margin of 4 and a default right margin of 76, the 72-character print line matches the standard 72 data characters that 1-2-3 displays on-screen.

If you change the line spacing to something other than six lines per inch, you also must change the Pg-Length to match the new setting.

Troubleshooting Graphing

GRAPHING PROBLEM #1:

Because your worksheet uses many different graphs, selecting the graph ranges and other specifications is a slow, tedious process.

Explanation: 1-2-3 has one current active graph. To use many different graphs in one worksheet, you must specify each one separately.

Solution: Although 1-2-3 has only one current active graph, you can save a library of graphs within the worksheet. After you have specified a graph completely, use the /Graph Name Create command to save the specification under a name you choose.

Repeat the process for each graph, giving each a different name. To recall any graph, issue the /Graph Name Use command and either type the name of the appropriate graph or point to its name in the list of graph names.

When you save the worksheet, the graph names and settings are saved also. Be sure you save the worksheet; if you forget to save, the names and settings are lost.

RELEASE
2.2

Alternative Explanation: Before Release 2.2, each data range (X, A, B, C, D, E, and F), legend, and data label had to be specified separately. Release 2.2 offers commands for specifying graph ranges as a group.

Alternative Solution: Use the /Graph Group command in Release 2.2 to specify the X and A through F ranges at the same time. Use /Graph Options Legend-Range to specify all legends and /Graph Options Data-Labels Group to indicate all data-label ranges.

GRAPHING PROBLEM #2:

You don't like the patterns used by some of the graph ranges.

Explanation: 1-2-3 has a fixed set of patterns for each graph range (A through F). If a graph displays certain ranges next to one another, looking at the two patterns may strain your eyes. Figure T.36 shows the B and C ranges next to each other.

Solution: If you have fewer than six ranges to graph, skip the ranges whose patterns you don't want to use. You do not have to specify ranges in order. Figure T.37 shows the preceding graph with ranges A and D specified.

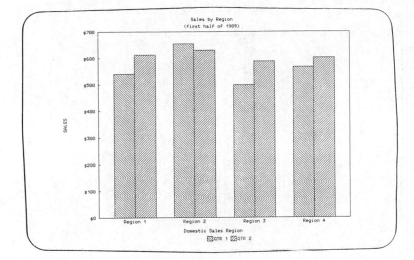

Fig. T.36.
The B and C
ranges can be
hard on your
eyes.

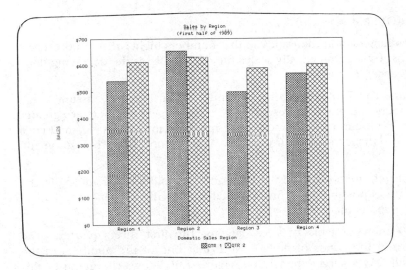

Fig. T.37.
Using the A
and D ranges.

GRAPHING PROBLEM #3:

You want to separate the bars in your graphs, but the program automatically puts them side by side.

Explanation: In a bar graph with multiple ranges, each graph range touches the one next to it even if there is ample room to separate them.

Solution: You can specify a range of blank cells (or zeros) as a dummy graph range. 1-2-3 displays the dummy range as a bar with zero height—the same as a space between the bars. The bar graph in figure T.38 shows that the A and C ranges, which contain data, are separated by B and D ranges of blank cells.

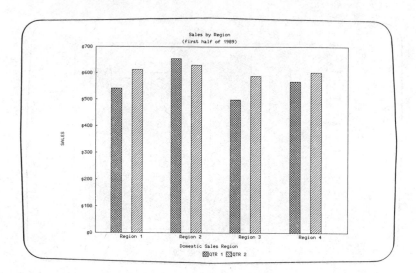

Fig. T.38.
Blank B and D
ranges add
spacing to the
graph.

GRAPHING PROBLEM #4:

You are graphing data in thousands so that numbers higher than 1,000 represent millions. 1-2-3 automatically scales the data and adds the deceiving notation (Thousands) to the y-axis.

Explanation: This problem can be extremely confusing. 1-2-3 assumes that all the numbers you graph represent units. If the largest numbers are greater than 1,000, 1-2-3 automatically scales the numbers into thousands and adds the notation (Thousands) to the y-axis. You cannot stop this automatic scaling.

If you graph information already in thousands (or millions, or more) in the worksheet (as is possible for a financial statement), the (Thousands) indicator on the graph is incorrect.

Figure T.39 shows a table of sales data for the first three quarters. The numbers are in thousands of dollars. Note that one of the numbers in the table (in cell D5) is larger than 1,000. Figure T.40 shows the graph of this data with the incorrect y-axis label.

Fig. T.39.
Data with
numbers in
thousands.

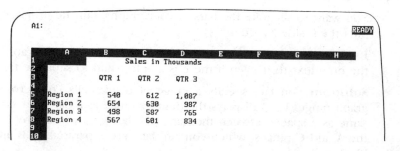

A	B	C	D	E	F	G	H
			Sales in Thousands				
	QTR 1	QTR 2	QTR 3				
Region 1	540	612	1,087				
Region 2	654	630	987				
Region 3	498	587	765				
Region 4	567	601	834				

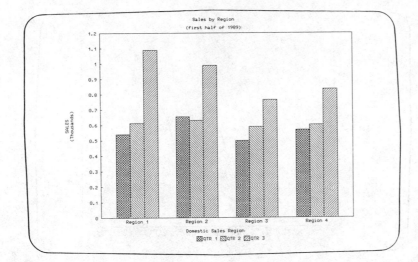

*Fig. T.40.
An incorrect
scaling
notation.*

Solution: Although you cannot stop the automatic scaling, you can turn off the indicator. To do so, use the /Graph Options Scale Y-Scale Indicator command. When prompted, select No. Then use either /Graph Options Titles Second (or Y-Axis) to insert the correct scaling indicator on the axis (see fig. T.41).

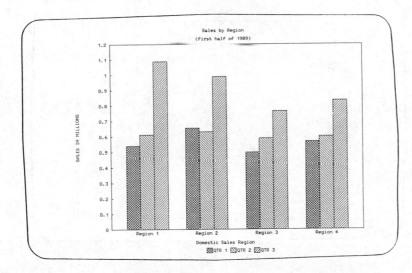

*Fig. T.41.
A graph with
the scaling
indicator
turned off.*

GRAPHING PROBLEM #5:

Your graph's x-axis ranges overlap or are crowded together.

Explanation: You can fit only a limited number of x-axis labels or numbers on a graph before they start to overlap or are split into two rows (see fig. T.42).

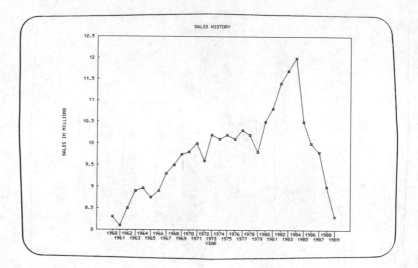

Fig. T.42.
Overcrowded
x-axis labels.

Solution: Use the **/Graph Options Scale Skip** command to skip a specific number of x-axis entries between the entries displayed on the graph. Figure T.43 shows the preceding graph after **Skip 3** was specified.

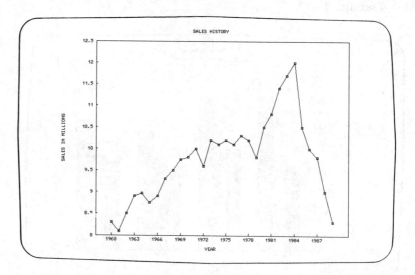

Fig. T.43.
A graph in
which every
third x-axis
label is
skipped.

GRAPHING PROBLEM #6:

After waiting 30 minutes for a graph to print, you discover an error and must print the graph again.

Explanation: This is a common problem. The graph display does not show exactly what the printed graph looks like. The display, for example, doesn't show the different type fonts specified for the text portion of your graph. Missing legends and incorrect data can be overlooked easily on the display.

Solution: Speed up the process of printing a graph by specifying the lowest possible density for your printer. Select **PrintGraph Settings Hardware Printer** to see a list of all the printers and densities included in your driver set (see fig. T.44). Most printers have at least two densities; some have three or four. Depending on the density, the difference in print time for a full-page graph can range from a few minutes to an hour or more. Although the lowest density may not be acceptable for printing material that you show to someone else, you can use it for a quick test print.

```
Copyright 1986, 1989 Lotus Development Corp.  All Rights Reserved. v2.2   PRINT

Select graphics printer or plotter

 Printer or Plotter name and Resolution
 ----------------------------------------------  Space bar marks or unmarks selection
 # Epson FX and RX series High density           ENTER selects marked device
   Epson FX and RX series High density           ESC exits, ignoring changes
   HP LaserJet+ or LaserJet II Med den.          HOME moves to beginning of list
   HP LaserJet+ or LaserJet II High den.         END moves to end of list
                                                 ↑ and ↓ move highlight
                                                 List will scroll if highlight
                                                 moved beyond top or bottom
```

Fig. T.44. Choose a low-density graph to speed printing.

You also can get a quick test print by specifying an unusually small size. To do so, choose **PrintGraph Settings Image Size Manual** and specify a small **Width** and **Height** for the test print. To produce a graph that covers one-quarter of a page, for example, specify a **Width** of 2.345 inches and a **Height** of 3.5 inches. These numbers are half the size you would specify for a half-page graph.

When you are confident that the graph is correct, print it full-size in the print density you want.

Troubleshooting Data Management

DATA MANAGEMENT PROBLEM #1:

You set up a criteria range, but all the records are selected.

Explanation: When you choose **/D**ata **Q**uery **F**ind, **E**xtract, **U**nique, or **D**elete, 1-2-3 uses the criteria range as a filter to select records from the database. If the criteria range is not exact, the **Q**uery commands do not work correctly.

Solution: Reissue the **/D**ata **Q**uery **C**riteria command. When 1-2-3 high-lights the old range, check it carefully, looking for the following errors:

1. *Does the first row of the criteria range contain field names?* If not, the criteria range does nothing.

2. *Do the field names match exactly the field names in the database?* If any field names in the criteria range do not match the names in the database, the label and number matches in those fields are ignored. Don't take chances with incorrect field names when you build your criteria range. Copy the field names from the database to ensure that the names are identical.

3. *Does the criteria range contain any blank rows?* Blank rows are the most common error in criteria ranges that select all records. Each row is a separate selection test; if a record in the database passes any one test, that record is selected. Because a blank row has no tests, all records are selected.

4. *Do any compound tests use #NOT# or <> (not equal)?* Compound tests can be extremely tricky and can produce results just the opposite of the results you are trying to produce. Here is an example of an erroneous compound test:

    +B5<>100#OR#B5<>200

    The purpose of this test is to select all records except those in which the value in column B is either 100 or 200. This written statement makes sense, but the effect of the formula is to select all records in which the value in column B is anything *but* 100 *or* 200. The test selects all records because if the value is 100, it passes the test because it is not 200; if the value is 200, it passes the test because it is not 100. The correct way to write the test is as follows:

    +B5<>100#AND#B5<>200

DATA MANAGEMENT PROBLEM #2:

You set up a criteria range, but none of the records is selected.

Explanation: Each field in a row in a criteria range can be a separate test. To be selected, a record must pass all the tests in the same row. If you write the selection tests incorrectly, it may be impossible for a record to pass all of them. This problem is most common when you use the #AND#, #OR#, and #NOT# operators in your selection tests.

Solution: Carefully check the selection tests in your criteria range for tests such as the following:

+B5>100#AND#B5<0

This test tells 1-2-3 to select records only when the value in column B is both greater than 100 and less than zero. Because this result is impossible, no records are selected.

Also make sure that the test's format matches the data in the field you are testing. If you use label matches or string functions on numeric data, or if you use number matches on strings, nothing is selected.

Alternative Explanation: A common problem occurs when you erase a cell in the criteria range by pressing the space bar. When you do the query, 1-2-3 tries to find a record with a value equal to a space, and is unable to do so.

Alternative Solution: Place the cell pointer underneath each field name in the criteria range. The cell may appear to be blank, but look at the control panel for an apostrophe—this indicates a space is in the cell. Use /Range Erase to erase the space from the cell.

DATA MANAGEMENT PROBLEM #3:

You set up a criteria range, but only the first record is selected or all the records after the first one are selected.

Explanation: The addresses used in formula matches are treated as relative addresses, based on the first record in the database. Any cell addresses in formula matches use the first record in the database. If your criteria range includes the following test, row 4 contains the field names for this database and row 5 is the first record in the database:

+B5>100

When the criteria range is used to select records, 1-2-3 first tests the first record. If the value in B5 is greater than 100, the record is selected; if not, the record is not selected.

Then 1-2-3 adjusts the formula and moves down one row to the next record. At the second record, the test is as follows:

+B6>100

The cell addresses change for each record in the database, as though you had copied the formula down one row before making the test. The program does this automatically.

Suppose that you want to compare a field in the database (B5) to a field outside the database (AG67). The test might be as follows:

+B5>AG67

1-2-3 handles the test on the first record in the manner described in the preceding example, selecting the record if the test is true. When 1-2-3 moves to the second record, the test is changed to the following:

+B6>AG68

AG68 may either be blank or contain data that does not pertain to the values in column B in your database.

Solution: If you make the cell references that address cells outside the database absolute, they don't adjust as 1-2-3 moves down the data records. If you change the test in the preceding example, for example, 1-2-3 compares all the values in column B to the contents of AG67:

+B5>$AG$67

DATA MANAGEMENT PROBLEM #4:

A **/Data Query Find** command works correctly, but **/Data Query Extract** (or Unique) does not.

Explanation: You can use the same settings for Find, Extract, or Unique. Because Find ignores the output range, you can test whether the problem lies in the criteria range or in the output range. If Find works but Extract or Unique does not, something is wrong with the output range.

Solution: The field names in the output range must match the field names in the database. If the names do not match, 1-2-3 selects the correct records but does not copy any fields to the output range. To ensure that the field names match, copy them from the database.

DATA MANAGEMENT PROBLEM #5:

As your database grows, the output from Extract commands grows also. You keep filling the output range and getting an error message.

Explanation: When you define an output range, you can define the number of rows that you want 1-2-3 to use. If the output of the Extract (or Unique) commands contains more records than you have specified, the Query stops and you see the error message Too many records for Output range.

You must enlarge the size of the output range and then rerun the Extract.

Solution: Specify as the output range only the row containing the field names. 1-2-3 uses this specification to enable the use of as many rows as necessary for **Extract** or **Unique**.

If you use this solution, however, be sure not to put anything below the output range. If you do, you lose valuable data because the next time you issue an **Extract** or **Unique** command, 1-2-3 erases everything below the field names before copying the selected records. (1-2-3 erases data from one row below the output-range field names to the bottom of the worksheet.)

Troubleshooting Macros

MACRO PROBLEM #1:

You write a macro, but when you press the Alt key and the letter of the name of the macro, nothing happens.

Explanation: You must use a precise name format for macros executed from the keyboard with the Alt key. The range name must be exactly two characters: the first is always a backslash; the second is a letter from A to Z or the number 0 (for macros executed automatically). If you name your macro anything else and try to execute it by pressing the Alt key, 1-2-3 does not recognize it as a macro.

In Release 2.2, a second type of macro name is available: a name up to 15 characters long. Macros with these kinds of names are not executed with the Alt key. They are invoked by pressing Run (Alt-F3).

Solution: Use /Range Name Create to check the macro's range name. 1-2-3 lists, in alphabetical order, all the range names in the worksheet. Range names that start with a backslash are at the end of the list. If you don't see the desired range name listed, you haven't named your macro. Even experienced programmers make this seemingly trivial mistake, which is the most common reason a macro doesn't work.

If the range name is in the list, make sure that you have included the backslash. Although the letter A is a valid range name, for example, it is not a valid name for a macro used with the Alt key.

Another common error is to use a slash (/) instead of a backslash (\) when you name a macro. If the range name is on the list, check carefully to make sure that it starts with a backslash.

If the macro name is listed and looks valid, highlight it and press Enter. 1-2-3 highlights the range with that name. The range should contain only one cell—the first cell of the macro. The contents of the macro must be a label or a string-valued function. If the cell is blank or contains a numeric value, the macro does not work.

MACRO PROBLEM #2:

After you write a few macros, you move some data. The macros now refer to the wrong addresses.

Explanation: Macros are not like formulas; addresses in macros do not change automatically when you move data used by the macro. In fact, a macro is nothing more than a label. 1-2-3 does not adjust the contents of labels when you move data because the program does not know that labels contain addresses.

Solution: *Never* use cell addresses in macros. Always give range names to all the cells and ranges you use in macros and use these range names in the macros. Then, if you move the ranges or insert and delete rows and columns, the range names adjust automatically, and the macro continues to refer to the correct cells and ranges.

MACRO PROBLEM #3:

Your macro seems to work correctly, but after you execute the macro, the display is wrong.

Explanation: 1-2-3 does not update the display or recalculate the worksheet during certain macro commands. Figure T.45 shows a macro (\a) that has just been executed. Although the contents of cell A1 should be 100, the cell is blank. And although the worksheet is set for **A**utomatic recalculation, the CALC indicator is on.

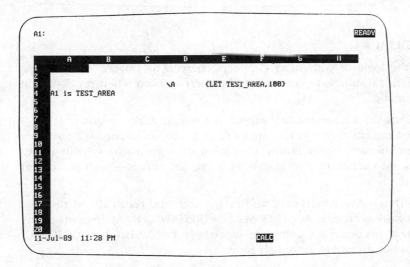

Fig. T.45.
The macro does not update the display.

Solution: To display the update, add a tilde (˜) to the end of the macro. If you add a tilde to the macro in figure T.45, 1-2-3 displays 100 as the contents of A1, and the CALC indicator vanishes (see fig. T.46). Some macro commands such as {RECALC} and {RECALCCOL} require other commands that force 1-2-3 to update the display. The PgDn-PgUp key combination (in a macro, use {PgDn} and {PgUp}) is the easiest way to update the display.

Fig. T.46.
A ˜ at the end
of the macro
updates the
display.

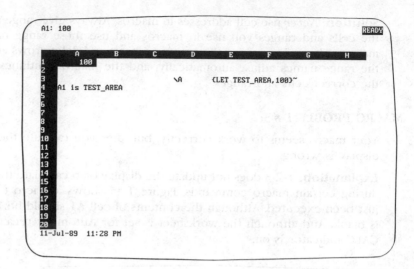

MACRO PROBLEM #4:

Although the logic of your macro appears correct, the macro never works properly. Critical values do not seem to be current, even when recalculation is on **Automatic**.

Explanation: On a large worksheet, macros would execute slowly if 1-2-3 recalculated the entire worksheet after every macro command. 1-2-3 seldom recalculates the worksheet during execution of a macro. If critical values change during execution, the macro uses the old values—not the current ones.

Solution: Determine which cells and ranges must be recalculated to make the macro work correctly. Add {RECALC} or {RECALCCOL} statements to the macro where necessary. A complete worksheet recalculation with {CALC} works also, but usually is extremely slow.

The macro shown in figure T.47 tests incorrectly for a valid entry. In this macro, {GETNUMBER} finds the old value because the test in IP_TEST (cell C12) is not updated after {GETNUMBER}. To correct the problem, add a {RECALC} to the macro (see fig. T.48). In this case, a tilde works if the worksheet is set for **Automatic** recalculation. A {RECALC} or {RECALCCOL} is required in **Manual** recalculation mode.

In figure T.48, the macro branches to PROCESS if the test in C12 is 1 (true) and branches to ERROR_ROUTINE if the test is not 1 (false). These routines perform whatever processing you need in your worksheet.

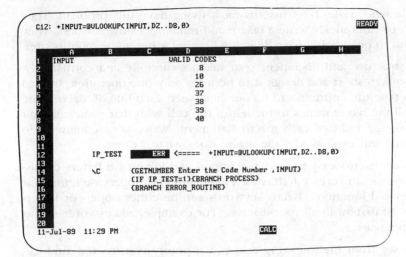

Fig. T.47.
A macro that
requires
recalculation to
work correctly.

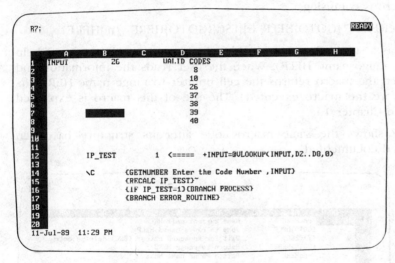

Fig. T.48.
A macro with
{RECALC}.

MACRO PROBLEM #5:

You need to change a macro you wrote earlier, but you can't remember how it works.

Explanation: This common problem surprises users when they first start to work with macros. After having painstakingly written, tested, and debugged a macro, you use it successfully in your worksheet. Because you wrote the macro, you know exactly what it does and how it operates. When you have to change it, you are amazed that you can't remember how it works.

Even people who write 1-2-3 macros for a living have this problem. They think that they can quickly write a macro and remember how it works. They write the macro quickly but have difficulty figuring it out a few months later.

Solution: Structure and document your macros carefully and consistently. Keep each macro short and design it to perform only one operation. Instead of trying to type the entire macro on one line, keep each line of macro code short. Put all the range names to the left of the cell with that name, and put comments to the right of each macro statement. Write your comments in plain language and explain why the macro does what it does.

To make your macros easy to read, use upper- and lowercase letters consistently. Always use lowercase letters for commands and uppercase letters for range names and functions. Macro keywords can be either upper- or lowercase, but be consistent in all your macros. (For example, all keywords in this book are uppercase.)

As you can see from the following example, a poorly constructed, undocumented macro is confusing:

\h   /rncHERE˜˜{GOTO}HELP˜{?}{ESC}{GOTO}HERE˜/rndHERE˜

This macro is a subroutine that provides the operator with a page of help text (at the range name HELP). When the user reads the information and presses Enter, the macro returns the cell pointer to range name HERE (its position before the macro executed). The use of this macro is explained more fully in Chapter 14.

Figure T.49 shows the same macro code after its structure has been improved and documented.

Fig. T.49.
A well-constructed macro.

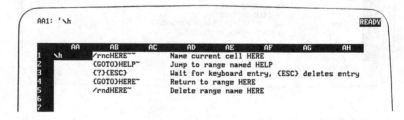

RELEASE

2.2

If you are recording a macro with Release 2.2's Learn feature, make sure that you type the first letters of the menu commands rather than highlighting the menu options. If you highlight menu options, the keys you press to move the pointer are recorded. If you use the right-arrow key to highlight the /Copy menu option, for example, the /Copy command records as /{R}{R}˜ instead of /c. This type of macro is very difficult to decipher later on.

MACRO PROBLEM #6:

Although your macro seems correct, it starts to beep in the middle of some commands and puts some commands in a label.

Explanation: The macro may look correct, but 1-2-3 does not interpret the macro in the way you anticipated. Either something is missing, or the macro contains extraneous keystrokes.

Solution: This problem commonly occurs if you forget to include tildes (to indicate Enter) in a macro. You can use one of two methods to find errors:

1. Press Step (Alt-F2) to put macro execution in STEP mode. When you execute the macro, 1-2-3 executes a single keystroke and waits for you to press a key (which key doesn't matter). When you press a key, you signal the program to execute the next macro keystroke. As you watch the macro execute in slow motion, you usually can see where the error lies. In Release 2.2, watch the bottom left corner of the screen. The macro keystrokes are highlighted one at a time as they are executed. This display helps you see exactly what step you are on in the macro. (With some macros, the single step approach can be painfully slow, however.)

   RELEASE

   2.2

2. Play "computer" and execute the macro manually. First, print the macro; then replay it from the keyboard, doing exactly as the macro indicates, keystroke by keystroke. Unless the problem is one of recalculation that happens only during macro execution, you can find the error if you follow the script faithfully. If the macro works when you execute it manually, change recalculation to **Manual** and try again.

MACRO PROBLEM #7:

You have written a series of handy macros for your worksheet, but you cannot remember all their names. You may even run out of letters for macro names.

Explanation: You can name only 26 macros (A to Z) per worksheet for use with the Alt key. Release 2.2 enables an unlimited number of macros because macro names can follow the same rules as range names (up to 15 characters). Remembering even 20 macros in several worksheets boggles the mind.

RELEASE

2.2

Solution: Use menus to execute macros. Menus are easier to learn than many of the macro keywords. You can have a large macro-driven worksheet with hundreds of macros, only one of which (\m) is executed from the keyboard. This one macro is used to bring up the main menu. A series of hierarchical menus can contain any number of macros, each of which can have any valid range name. (Only macros executed from the keyboard require special names that start with a backslash.)

If you use more than five macros, put them in a menu so that you don't have to remember their names. Refer to Chapter 14 for information about creating a menu of macros.

RELEASE

2.2

Alternative Solution: Release 2.2 enables macro names of up to 15 characters (the same as any range name). Take advantage of this capability and use long, descriptive macro names. Macros with names longer than one character, however, cannot be executed with the Alt key; you must use Run (Alt-F3) and press Name (F3) to display a list of macro names from which you can choose.

MACRO PROBLEM #8:

You wrote a macro containing an error. It destroyed your worksheet.

Explanation: A macro can do anything that you can do from the keyboard. A macro can erase all or part of the worksheet, quit 1-2-3, and erase a file on the disk. If you don't prepare for possible catastrophic errors, you can lose hours—even days—of work.

Solution: Always save your worksheet before you test a macro. Then, if the macro destroys something, you still have the data on disk. If part of the macro saves the file, make sure that you first save the file with a different name. Saving the file is futile if the macro erases most of the worksheet and then saves the destroyed file with the name of the original file.

In fact, using a macro to save a file automatically is so dangerous that you should save your files manually until you are completely familiar with macro programming and the advanced macro commands. Some people believe that saving files with a macro is always too dangerous to attempt.

RELEASE

2.2

MACRO PROBLEM #9:

You are recording a macro with Release 2.2's Learn feature, and you get the message Learn Range Full. Macro recording stops.

Explanation: When defining the learn range with /Worksheet Learn Range, you did not specify enough cells to hold all your recorded keystrokes. When you record, each complete command is stored in a single cell. /wir~, for example, is considered a complete command; only those five keystrokes are stored in a cell. You must therefore specify a range of cells, down a single column, when defining a learn range. Specify a long learn range so that macro recording is not interrupted with the Learn Range Full message.

Solution: When you get this error message, press Esc to clear the error. Redefine a longer learn range with the /Worksheet Learn Range command. To continue recording where you left off, press Learn (Alt-F5) to turn on the Learn feature. After you are done recording, you may need to edit the keystrokes in the learn range to customize or fine-tune the macro.

1-2-3 Command Reference

Worksheet Commands   /W

The /Worksheet commands control the display formats, screen organization, protection, and start-up settings for the entire worksheet. If you want to change these settings for only a *portion* of the worksheet, use the /Range commands. To change settings that affect the *entire* worksheet, however, use the /Worksheet commands shown in the following menu map. Commands new with Release 2.2 are highlighted.

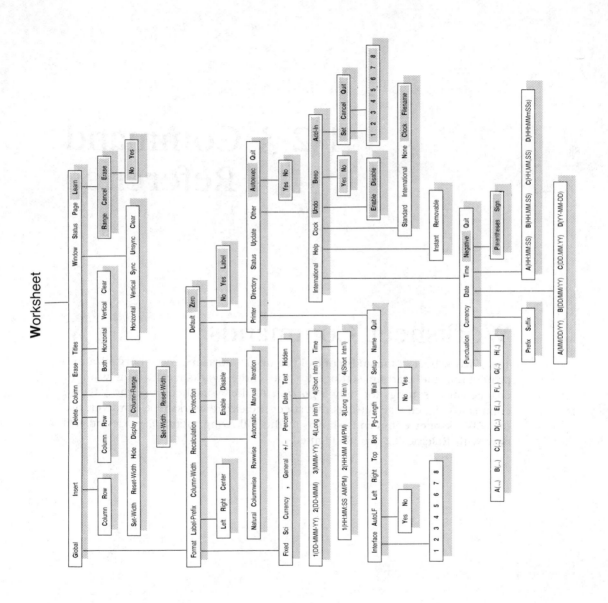

Worksheet Global Format *   /WGF*

Purpose

Selects how most numeric values and formula results should appear.

The **/W**orksheet **G**lobal **F**ormat command formats the *entire* worksheet, but the appearance of previously entered values and formulas does not change.

Reminders

- Before you use /wgf, decide on a format for numeric data.

- If you want to format only a portion of the worksheet, use **/R**ange **F**ormat instead of /wgf.

- Use the **D**ate format option of the /wgf command when most values on your spreadsheet are dates; otherwise, use **/R**ange **F**ormat **D**ate.

Procedures

1. Type **/wgf**

2. Use the right- and left-arrow keys to select a **F**ormat menu choice. The second menu line displays an example of how the highlighted format appears.

3. Select one of the following formats:

Menu Item	Description
Fixed	Fixes the number of decimal places displayed. If the setting is 3 decimal places, the number 1.2345, for example, appears as 1.235.
Sci (Scientific in Release 2.01)	Displays in scientific notation large or small numbers. In a 2-decimal format, the number 950000, for example, appears as $9.50E+05$.
Currency	Displays the default currency symbol (for example, $ or £) and commas. Currency is often used for the first row and the bottom line of financial statements. In a 2-decimal format, 24500.254, for example, appears as $24,500.25.
	Marks thousands and multiples of thousands. In a 2-decimal format, 24500.254 appears as 24,500.25.
General	Suppresses zeros after the decimal point, uses scientific notation for large or small

	numbers, and serves as the default decimal display
+/−	Creates horizontal bar graphs or time-duration graphs on computers that do not have graphics. A positive number displays as + symbols; a negative number, as − symbols. The number of symbols equals the integer value of the cell contents. For example, 6.23 appears as + + + + + +.
Percent	Displays a decimal number as a percentage followed by a percent sign (%). In a 2-decimal format, .346 appears as 34.60%.
Date	Displays serial date and time numbers (those entered through the use of @DATE, @DATEVALUE, @TIME, @NOW, and @TIMEVALUE functions) in one of five customary formats. One selection under **Date** formats the **Time** display.

1 DD–MMM–YY	12–Jan–51
2 DD–MMM	12–Jan
3 MMM–YY	Jan–51
4 Long Intn'l	01/12/51
5 Short Intn'l	01/12

Time:

1 HH:MM:SS AM/PM	1:04:34 PM
2 HH:MM AM/PM	1:04 PM
3 Long Intn'l	13:04:34
4 Short Intn'l	13:04

Text	Evaluates formulas as numbers but displays formulas as text. Numbers in cells appear in **General** format.
Hidden	Hides cell contents from display and printing but evaluates contents. Use this command to hide confidential notes or variables.

4. After you select **Fixed**, **Sci** (**Scientific** in Release 2.01), **Currency**, comma (,), or **Percent**, type the number of decimal places. 1-2-3 normally truncates trailing zeros, but these appear for the number of decimal places you set.

5. Press Enter.

Important Cues

- Use **/R**ange **F**ormat to format only a portion of the worksheet.

- Use **T**ext format to display formulas used in data tables and to document formulas and their locations.

- If you enter a number too large for the formatted cell, the cell fills with asterisks. To remove them, move the pointer to the cell, select **/W**orksheet **C**olumn **S**et-Width, press the right-arrow key until the column is wide enough to display the entire number, and press Enter.

- /wgf commands round only the display of numbers. Stored numbers are retained to 15-decimal precision; the stored numbers, not the displayed numbers, are used in calculations.

- To display non-USA formats or determine the display of negative numbers in comma or **C**urrency format, use **/W**orksheet **G**lobal **D**efault **O**ther **I**nternational. Type **/wgdoi** and select one of the following formats:

Menu Item	Description
Punctuation	Changes numeric punctuation
Currency	Specifies currency symbol and positions the symbol before (**P**refix) or after (**S**uffix) the value
Date	Changes international date formats
Time	Changes international time formats
Negative	Displays negative numbers enclosed in parentheses (select **P**arentheses) or preceded by a minus sign (select **S**ign)
Quit	Restores the **/W**orksheet **G**lobal **D**efault options

Cautions

- /wgf rounds displayed numbers to the specified decimal setting, but calculations are performed to 15-decimal precision. To keep apparently wrong values from being displayed, use @ROUND to round formula results so that calculated results match displayed values.

- Other operators may enter percentage values incorrectly if you use the **P**ercent format. You should thus include a screen prompt to remind operators to place a percent sign (%) after percentages. 1-2-3 automatically divides the entry by 100.

For more information, see /Range Format, /Worksheet Global Default, and Chapter 5.

RELEASE
2.2

Worksheet Global Label-Prefix /WGL

Purpose

Selects how you want text labels aligned throughout the worksheet.

Labels narrower than the cell width can be aligned to the left, right, or center. Labels longer than the cell width are left-aligned. Previously entered labels do not change.

Reminders

- Before you begin building the worksheet, decide how to align the labels. Use /Worksheet Global Label-Prefix to select left alignment (the default setting), right alignment, or center alignment.

- If you use /wgl after you begin to build the worksheet, existing labels are not affected. Any alignment previously set with /Range Label is not altered by /wgl.

- To change the alignment of labels in a single cell or a range of cells, use /Range Label.

Procedures

1. Type **/wgl**

2. Select one of the following:

Menu Item	Description
Left	Aligns label with cell's left edge
Right	Aligns label with cell's right edge
Center	Centers label in a cell

3. Type the labels as you want them to appear on the worksheet.

Important Cues

- To override the global label alignment as you enter data in a single cell, enter one of the following prefixes before you type the label:

Label Prefix	Function
' (apostrophe)	Aligns label to the left (default)
" (quotation mark)	Aligns label to the right
^ (caret)	Centers label in the cell
\ (backslash)	Repeats character to fill the cell

Note: The backslash (\ ) label prefix cannot be selected with /wgl.

- The label prefix appears as the first character in the control panel when the cell pointer is positioned on a cell that contains a label. Use /Worksheet Status or /Worksheet Global (Release 2.2 only) to show the global label prefix.

- You must enter a label prefix in front of labels that begin with a number or formula symbol. You must supply a prefix for an address or part number, for example, as in the following:

Correct	Incorrect
'2207 Cheyenne Dr.	2207 Cheyenne Dr.
"34-567FB	34-567FB

- To turn a number into a label, position the cell pointer on the number you want to change and press Edit (F2). Then press Home to move the cursor to the beginning of the number; type the label prefix and press Enter.

- Because every line of macro code must be entered as a string, a label prefix must precede text used as macro code. For example, if your macro line begins with the command sequence /ppooc, you must precede the entry with a label prefix, as in '/ppooc; otherwise, the keystrokes in the macro select the command instead of typing macro code.

- Preserve a formula that has an unidentified error by adding a label prefix before the formula. Consider the following formula:

  +B5*@PMT(B16B12/12,B14*12)

If you enter this formula, 1-2-3 signals an error and enters EDIT mode. (The problem is a missing comma after B16.) If you can't find the error, press Home to move to the beginning of the formula. Type an apostrophe and press Enter. The formula will then be accepted as a text label. You can return to the formula later to look for the error and make the correction. Delete the apostrophe and press Enter after you make the correction.

- Document formulas by temporarily adding a label prefix and then copying the label to another part of the worksheet. To do this procedure, move the cell pointer to the formula and press Edit (F2). Next, press Home to move the cell pointer to the front of the formula; type an apostrophe and press Enter. The formula is changed to text, and you can copy the text formula to a documentation area of your spreadsheet. Use the Edit, Home, and Del keys to remove the apostrophe from the original formula so that the formula can operate normally.

- To turn a numeric label into a number, use EDIT mode and delete the label prefix.

Caution

Numbers or formulas preceded by a label prefix have the value of zero when evaluated by a numeric formula. In a database query, you must use text searches to search for numbers that have a label prefix.

For more information, see Chapters 4 and 13.

Worksheet Global Column-Width   /WGC

Purpose

Sets the column width for the entire worksheet.

Reminder

Before you use /wgc, decide the column widths you need for the worksheet, and position the cell pointer so that an average column width is displayed.

Procedures

1. Type **/wgc**

2. Enter a number for the column width used most frequently; or press the right- or left-arrow key to increase or decrease the column width, respectively.

3. Press Enter.

Important Cues

- Use **/W**orksheet **C**olumn **S**et-Width to set individual columns so that numbers and labels display correctly. When the column width is too narrow for the value entered, asterisks are displayed in the cell.

- Any global column width can be set to a new width with **/W**orksheet **C**olumn **S**et-Width or **/W**orksheet **C**olumn **C**olumn-Range **S**et-Width (Release 2.2 only). Column widths previously set with these two commands will override the global column width.

- The default column width for all columns is 9 characters. Column width settings can range from 1 to 240 characters.

- You can see the current setting for the global column width by selecting **/W**orksheet **S**tatus. In Release 2.2, the **/W**orksheet **G**lobal command displays a screen of your current global settings.

Caution

If you use a split worksheet and change the column width in one or both windows, settings used in the bottom or right windows are lost when the windows are cleared. 1-2-3 keeps the column widths used in the top window of a horizontal split or the left window of a vertical split.

For more information, see Chapter 4.

Worksheet Global Recalculation   */WGR*

Purpose

Sets **Automatic** or **Manual** recalculation modes for the entire worksheet.

Reminders

- Recalculation can be set to **Automatic** or **Manual**. Manual recalculation should be used to increase data-entry speed in large worksheets or databases. By selecting either the **Columnwise** or **Rowwise** option, you can have 1-2-3 calculate formulas in a particular order. You also can use /wgr to calculate a formula many times to ensure correct results.

- If you change recalculation to **Columnwise** or **Rowwise**, enter formulas in a specific order so that they will be calculated correctly. 1-2-3's default settings are **Natural** and **Automatic** recalculation.

- Release 2.2 offers "minimal recalculation" when recalculation is set to **Natural**. This setting causes 1-2-3 to recalculate only the cells affected by a worksheet change.

RELEASE

2.2

Procedures

1. Type **/wgr**

2. Select one of the following:

Menu Item	Description
Natural	Calculates formulas in the order the results are needed (the normal worksheet setting for the order of recalculation)
Columnwise	Starts at the top of column A and recalculates downward; then moves to column B
Rowwise	Starts at the beginning of row 1 and recalculates to the end; then continues through the following rows
Automatic	Recalculates whenever cell contents change (the normal worksheet setting for when recalculation occurs)

Menu Item	Description
Manual	Recalculates only when you press Calc (F9) or when {CALC} is encountered in a macro. The CALC indicator appears at the bottom of the screen when recalculation is advised.
Iteration	Recalculates the worksheet a specified number of times

3. If you selected **Iteration**, enter a number from 1 to 50. The default setting is 1. **Iteration** works with **Columnwise** and **Rowwise** recalculations or with **Natural** recalculation when the worksheet contains a circular reference.

4. If you selected **Columnwise** or **Rowwise** recalculation, you may need to repeat Step 1 and select **Iteration** in Step 2. In Step 3, enter the number of recalculations necessary for correct results. Columnwise and **Rowwise** recalculations often require multiple calculations in order for all worksheet results to be correct.

Important Cues

RELEASE
2.2

- Display the current recalculation setting by selecting **/Worksheet Status** or **/Worksheet Global** (Release 2.2 only).

- Columnwise or **Rowwise** recalculation often requires multiple recalculations. Set the number of automatic recalculations by selecting **/wgr** and choosing **Iteration**.

Caution

When you use **Manual** recalculation, the screen display is not valid when the CALC indicator appears at the bottom of the screen. This indicator means that changes have been made on the worksheet, and you need to press Calc (F9) so that 1-2-3 will recalculate the worksheet to reflect the changes.

For more information, see Chapter 4.

Worksheet Global Protection   /WGP

Purpose

Protects the entire worksheet from being changed, except for cells unprotected by a range command (**/Range Unprot**).

Reminder

Before you enable worksheet protection, save time by making sure that your worksheet is complete. After the worksheet is protected, you must disable protection or unprotect a range before you can modify the worksheet.

Procedures

1. Type **/wgp**

2. Select one of the following options:

Menu Item	Description
Enable	Protects the worksheet. Only cells specified with **/R**ange Unprot (Unprotect in 2.01) can be changed.
Disable	Unprotects the worksheet. Any cell can be changed.

Important Cues

- Before or after you protect the entire worksheet, you can use **/R**ange Unprot (Unprotect in Release 2.01) to specify cells that can be changed.

- While **/W**orksheet **G**lobal **P**rotection is enabled, use **/R**ange Unprot to indicate the cells that can be changed.

- Protected cells display a PR on the first line of the control panel. Unprotected cells display a U on the first line of the control panel.

- **/W**orksheet **G**lobal **P**rotection works with the **/R**ange Unprot and **/R**ange Input commands to restrict the cell pointer to unprotected cells. This arrangement keeps inexperienced users from entering data in cells that already store information.

- Use **/W**orksheet **G**lobal **P**rotection **D**isable on a data table before you execute **/D**ata **T**able. Otherwise, the data table can be disabled.

Cautions

- Macros that change cell content can change only unprotected cells. When you program macros, include code necessary to enable or disable protection.

- **/W**orksheet **E**rase is one of the few commands that can be used while **/W**orksheet **G**lobal **P**rotection is enabled.

*For more information, see **/Worksheet Erase** and Chapter 4.*

Worksheet Global Default   /WGD

Purpose

Specifies display formats and start-up settings for hardware.

With this command, you can control how 1-2-3 works with the printer; which disk and directory are accessed automatically; which international displays are used; and which type of clock is displayed. The settings can be saved so that each time you start 1-2-3, the specifications go into effect. For temporary changes, see the **File** or **Print** menu options.

Reminder

Before you set the interface for serial printers, find out the baud rate of your printer. The printer should be set to standard operating-system serial printer settings of 8 bits, no parity, and 1 stop bit (2 stop bits at 110 baud). These printer settings can be set with microswitches (DIP switches in your printer) and are normally preconfigured at the factory.

Procedures

1. Type **/wgd**

2. Select the setting you want to change:

Menu Item	Description
Printer	Specifies printer settings and connections. Choose from the following options:
	Interface
	Selects parallel or serial port from 8 settings, **1** through **8**. The menu displays each of the 8 ports. The initial setting is **1** (Parallel 1).
	AutoLF
	Tells 1-2-3 whether your printer inserts its own line feed or whether 1-2-3 should insert a line feed. If the printer is printing double-spaces or overlapped printing, choose the opposite setting.
	Left
	Sets left margin. Default: 4, 0-240
	Right
	Sets right margin. Default: 76, 0-240
	Top
	Sets top margin. Default: 2, 0-32
	Bot
	Sets bottom margin. Default: 2, 0-32
	Pg-Length
	Sets page length. Default: 66, 1-100

Menu Item	Description
	Wait
	Pauses for paper insert at the end of each page. Select **No** or **Yes**.
	Setup
	Creates initial printer-control code
	Name
	Selects from multiple printers
	Quit
	Returns you to the default **Printer** menu
Directory	Specifies directory for read or write operations. Press Esc to clear. Type the new directory and press Enter.
Status	Displays settings for **/Worksheet Global Default**
Update	Saves to disk the current global defaults for use during the next start-up
Other	Provides the following options:
	International
	Specifies display settings for **Punctuation, Currency, Date, Time,** and **Negative** (Release 2.2 only) formats
	Help
	Enables you to choose whether the Help file is immediately accessible from disk (**Instant**) or whether the Help file is on a removable disk (**Removable**)
	Clock
	Enables you to choose between **Standard** and **International** date and time formats or to have **None** displayed on the screen. **Clock** (Release 2.2 only) displays the date and time set by other commands, and **Filename** (Release 2.2 only) displays the file name instead of the date and time.

RELEASE
2.2

Menu Item	Description

Undo

Offers two options: **E**nable, which enables the Undo feature; and **D**isable, which disables the Undo feature (Release 2.2 only). If Undo is enabled, you can cancel an operation after you have executed it. If you erase a range accidentally, for example, you can press Undo (Alt-F4) to "unerase."

Beep

Offers two options: **Y**es, which turns the computer's sound on; and **N**o, which turns it off (Release 2.2 only). If you choose **N**o, you won't hear a beep when you make an error.

Add-in

Enables you to specify an add-in application to be attached automatically each time you load 1-2-3 (Release 2.2 only). You also designate the key combination (Alt-F7, Alt-F8, Alt-F9, or Alt-F10) that invokes the add-in.

Offers three options: **S**et, which attaches one of up to eight add-ins you establish; **C**ancel, which detaches previously set add-ins; and **Q**uit, which restores the **W**orksheet **G**lobal **D**efault menu

Autoexec   Provides two options: **Y**es, which automatically executes autoexecute macros (\0); and **N**o, which stops autoexecute macros from executing (Release 2.2 only)

Quit   Returns you to the worksheet

Important Cues

- Changes made with /**W**orksheet **G**lobal **D**efault are good only while 1-2-3 is running. To save the settings so that they load automatically at start-up, select /**W**orksheet **G**lobal **D**efault **U**pdate. On a disk-based system, make certain that the 1-2-3 System disk is in the current drive. Use the DIR command to verify that the 123.CNF file has been updated.

RELEASE
2.2

- If Release 2.2's Undo feature is enabled, you can reverse the last command issued. You can undo such commands as **/R**ange **E**rase, **/W**orksheet **E**rase, **/F**ile **R**etrieve, and **/D**ata **S**ort.

For more information, see Chapter 5.

Worksheet Global Zero   */WGZ*

Purpose

Suppresses zeros in displays and printed reports so that only nonzero numbers appear; displays a text string instead of a zero (Release 2.2 only).

When **/W**orksheet **G**lobal **Z**ero is in effect, zeros from formulas and typed entries are hidden or displayed with a specified label.

Reminder

Protect hidden zeros in the worksheet by using the **/W**orksheet **G**lobal **P**rotection and **/R**ange **U**nprot (**U**nprotect in Release 2.01) commands. Doing so prevents users new to 1-2-3 from typing over or erasing necessary hidden zero values or formulas.

Procedures

1. Type **/wgz**

2. Choose one of the following options:

Menu Item	Description
No	Displays as zeros those cells containing a zero or a result of zero
Yes	Displays as blank those cells containing a zero or a result of zero
Label	Displays a custom label that replaces those cells containing a zero or zero result

RELEASE
2.2

3. If you chose Label, enter the label you want displayed. All zeros will be replaced with this label. Precede the label with an apostrophe (') for left alignment or with a caret (^) for center alignment. The default label alignment is right alignment.

Important Cues

- The worksheet's default setting is No so that zeros are displayed in normal operation.

- Suppressed zeros in formulas and typed entries are still evaluated as zeros by other formulas.

- The **/W**orksheet **G**lobal **Z**ero command is a temporary setting; it needs to be reset every time the file is retrieved.

Caution

If zeros are suppressed, you can easily erase or write over portions of the worksheet that appear blank but contain suppressed zeros. To prevent accidental erasures and typeovers, use **/**Worksheet **G**lobal **P**rotection **E**nable and **/R**ange **U**nprot.

For more information, see **/Worksheet Global Protection, /Range Prot, /Range Unprot**, *and Chapter 4.*

Worksheet Insert [Column, Row]   /WIC or /WIR

Purpose

Inserts one or more blank columns or rows in the worksheet. Use this command to add space for formulas, data, or text.

Reminder

Before you use /wi, do one of the following:

- Place the cell pointer in the column that you want to move to the right when one or more columns are inserted.

- Place the cell pointer in the row that you want to move down when one or more rows are inserted.

Procedures

1. Type **/wi**

2. Select one of the following:

Menu Item	Description
Column	Inserts column(s) at the cell pointer; moves the current column right
Row	Inserts row(s) at the cell pointer; moves the current row down

3. Insert more than one column by moving the cell pointer right to highlight one cell for each additional column. Insert more than one row by moving the cell pointer down to highlight one cell for each additional row.

4. Check to make sure that the number of highlighted cells equals the number of columns or rows you want inserted.

5. Press Enter.

Important Cues

- Addresses and ranges adjust automatically to the new addresses created when columns or rows are inserted.
- Check all worksheet areas for composition, lines, and layout that may have changed. Use /Move to reposition labels, data, and formulas.

Cautions

- Cell addresses in macros do not adjust automatically. Adjust cell addresses in macros to reflect the inserted column(s) or row(s). Range names in macros will remain correct.
- Make certain that inserted columns and rows do not pass through databases, print ranges, or a column of macro code. Macros will stop executing if they reach a blank cell. Database and data-entry macros may stop or work incorrectly if they encounter unexpected blank columns or rows in the database or data-entry areas.
- Inserting rows and columns uses up conventional memory. Keep this fact in mind when designing large worksheets.

For more information, see Chapters 4 and 13.

Worksheet Delete [Column, Row]   /WDC or /WDR

Purpose

Deletes one or more columns or rows from the worksheet.

When you use /wd, the entire column or row and the information and formatting it contains are deleted and cannot be recovered. (Release 2.2 users can recover a deleted column(s) or row(s) if the Undo feature was enabled before the deletion took place.)

RELEASE **2.2**

Reminders

- Before you delete a column or row, use the End and arrow keys to make sure that distant cells in that column or row do not contain needed data or formulas.
- Before you invoke /wd, place the cell pointer on the first column or row to be deleted.

Procedures

1. Type **/wd**

2. Select one of the following:

Menu Item	Description
Column	Deletes column(s) at the cell pointer. Remaining columns to the right move left.
Row	Deletes row(s) at the cell pointer. Remaining rows below move up.

3. Delete more than one column by moving the cell pointer right to highlight one cell for each column being deleted. Delete more than one row by moving the cell pointer down to highlight one cell for each row being deleted.

4. Make certain that the number of highlighted cells equals the number of columns or rows you want deleted.

5. Press Enter.

Important Cues

- /Worksheet Delete deletes all the data and formulas in the column or row. To erase a small portion of a worksheet, use /Range Erase.

- Whenever you highlight a series of rows or columns, you can return to a single highlighted row or column by pressing Esc.

- Formulas, named ranges, and ranges in command prompts are adjusted automatically to the new cell addresses after you delete a column or row.

- Use /Move when you need to reposition a portion of the worksheet and cannot delete a column or row.

RELEASE
2.2

- If the Undo feature is enabled in Release 2.2, you can use the Undo (Alt-F4) key combination to reverse accidental deletions of rows or columns.

Cautions

- Formulas that refer to deleted cells have the value ERR.

- Deleting a row that passes through an area containing macros can create errors in the macros. Deleting code in the middle of the macro causes problems, and deleting a blank cell between two macros merges their code.

- Deleting a column or row that defines a corner of a command range or range name causes formulas depending on that range to produce ERR. Also, deleting the beginning or ending row in a database or @SUM column causes problems. If you must delete the row or column, delete the corresponding range name, delete the row or column, re-create the range name, and correct the formulas.

For more information, see Chapter 4.

Worksheet Column [Set-Width, Reset-Width]

/WCS or /WCR

Purpose

Adjusts the column width of an individual column.

Columns wider than 9 characters are needed to display large numbers, to display dates, and to prevent text from being covered by adjacent cell entries. Narrow column widths are useful for short entries, such as (Y/N), and for organizing the display layout.

Reminders

- Make certain that changing the width of a column does not destroy the appearance of displays in another portion of the worksheet.
- Move the cell pointer to the widest entry in the column before you use /wcs.

Procedures

To set a new column width, do the following:

1. Type **/wc**
2. Select **Set**-Width.
3. Enter the new column width by typing the number of characters or by pressing the left- or right-arrow key to shrink or expand the column.
4. Press Enter.

To change the column width to the default width specified under /Worksheet Global Column-Width, do the following:

1. Type **/wc**
2. Select **Reset**-Width.
3. Press Enter.

Important Cues

- Asterisks appear in a cell whose column is too narrow to display numeric or date information.
- Text entries wider than the cell may be partially covered by text or numeric entries in the cell to the right.
- Use **/Worksheet Global Column-Width** to set the column width for columns that were not set individually with **/Worksheet Column**.
- If you are using Release 2.2, choose **/Worksheet Column Column-Range** to adjust the width of a range of columns.

RELEASE
2.2

Caution

Changing a column's width throughout the entire worksheet can alter the appearance of display screens you already have created.

For more information, see Chapter 4.

Worksheet Column Column-Range /WCCS or /WCCR [Set-Width, Reset-Width]

Purpose

Adjusts the column width of a range of columns.

When you have several adjacent columns that require the same column width setting, you can adjust them all at once by specifying a range of columns. This command saves you from having to use /Worksheet Column Set-Width on each individual column.

Reminders

- Make certain that changing the width of a column does not destroy the appearance of displays in another portion of the worksheet.

- Before you use /wcs, move the cell pointer to the first column you want to set.

Procedures

To set a new column width of a range of columns, do the following:

1. Type **/wcc**

2. Select **Set-Width**.

3. Move the cell pointer to highlight the columns (one cell in each column is sufficient). Press Enter.

4. Enter the new column width by typing the number of characters or by pressing the left- or right-arrow key to shrink or expand the column.

5. Press Enter.

To change the width of a range of columns to the default width specified under /Worksheet Global Column-Width, do the following:

1. Type **/wcc**

2. Select **Reset-Width**.

3. Move the cell pointer to highlight the columns (one cell in each column is sufficient). Press Enter.

Important Cues

- Asterisks appear in a cell whose column is too narrow to display numeric or date information.

- Text entries wider than the cell may be partially covered by text or numeric entries in the cell to the right.

- Use /Worksheet Global Column-Width to set the column width for columns that were not set individually with /Worksheet Column Column-Range or /Worksheet Column Set-Width.

Caution

Changing a column's width can alter the appearance of display screens you have already created.

For more information, see Chapter 4.

Worksheet Column [Hide, Display]   /WCH or /WCD

Purpose

The /wch command hides individual columns or a range of columns. Use /wch to hide columns of information when you prepare confidential financial reports or want to display only the results of calculations.

/wcd redisplays a hidden column or a range of hidden columns.

Reminders

- Make certain that hiding the display of a column does not destroy the appearance of displays in another portion of the worksheet.

- Move the cell pointer to the column you want to hide. If you plan to hide a range of columns, position the cell pointer at one corner of the range.

- Move the cell pointer to the column or range of columns you want to redisplay. When displaying a range of previously hidden columns, position the cell pointer at one corner of the range.

Procedures

To hide a column, do the following:

1. Type **/wc**

2. Select **Hide**.

3. Specify the column to be hidden by pressing the left- or right-arrow key and then pressing Enter. To hide a range of adjacent columns, specify the range by typing the range address, by entering a range name, or by pressing the period (.) key to anchor the range and moving the pointer to the opposite corner of the range.

4. To hide nonadjacent columns, repeat Steps 1 through 3.

To display a column previously hidden, do the following:

1. Type **/wc**

2. Select **D**isplay. Hidden columns are marked with an asterisk (*) beside the column letter.

3. Move the cell pointer to the column you want to redisplay and press Enter. If you want to redisplay a range of columns, specify the range by typing the range address, by entering a range name, or by pressing the period (**.**) key to anchor the range and moving the pointer to the opposite corner of the range. After you press Enter, the specified columns are displayed.

Important Cues

- Use /wch to suppress the printing of unnecessary columns.

- You can use /wch to suppress columns in the current window without affecting the display in other windows. When the windows are cleared, the settings used in the top window of a horizontal split or the left window of a vertical split are kept; the settings used in the bottom or right windows are lost.

- When preparing reports, use /wch to hide the display of unnecessary data and reduce the number of printed columns.

Cautions

- Be sure that other operators who use your worksheet are aware of the hidden columns. Although the values and formulas of hidden columns work properly, the display may be confusing if data appears to be missing.

- When cells are hidden on an unprotected worksheet, ranges copied or moved to the hidden area overwrite existing data.

For more information, see Chapter 4.

Worksheet Erase /WE

Purpose

Erases the entire worksheet and resets all cell formats, label prefixes, and command settings to their original values.

Use this command to erase the worksheet so that you will have a fresh work area.

Reminder

To use the current worksheet again, be sure to save the worksheet before you use /Worksheet Erase.

Procedures

1. Type **/we**

2. Select one of the following:

Menu Item	Description
No	Cancels the command. Use this option if you realize that you don't want to erase the whole worksheet.
Yes	Erases the entire worksheet

3. In Release 2.2, if you haven't saved your latest changes, 1-2-3 warns you and displays another Yes/No menu. Choose **Yes** to erase without saving. Choose **No** to cancel the command.

RELEASE **2.2**

Important Cues

● You don't have to erase a worksheet before you load a new one. The /File Retrieve command automatically erases the current worksheet when the new worksheet is loaded.

● If you accidentally erase without saving, use the Undo command to bring back the worksheet. Undo must be enabled, however, before you execute the erase.

RELEASE **2.2**

Caution

Make certain that you want to erase the entire worksheet. If portions of it can be used in the following worksheet, you may want to use /Range Erase to erase only the unusable portions.

For more information, see **/File Save** *and Chapter 4.*

Worksheet Titles   /WT

Purpose

Retains the display of column and row headings that would otherwise scroll off the screen.

Reminders

● You can "freeze" cell contents horizontally (in rows), vertically (in columns), or both ways.

- Move the cell pointer so that the column headings you want frozen on the screen occupy the top row of the worksheet. Also move the cell pointer so that the column containing the leftmost row heading will be frozen at the left edge of the screen.

- Move the cell pointer one row below the lowest row to be used as a title, and one column to the right of the columns that contain row headings.

Procedures

1. Type **/wt**

2. Select one of the following:

Menu Item	Description
Both	Creates titles from the rows above the cell pointer and from the columns to the left of the cell pointer
Horizontal	Creates titles from the rows above the cell pointer
Vertical	Creates titles from the columns to the left of the cell pointer
Clear	Removes all frozen title areas so that all worksheet areas scroll

Important Cues

- To return the worksheet to normal, select the **/W**orksheet **T**itles **C**lear command.

- If you have split the worksheet into two windows with **/W**orksheet **W**indow, each window can have its own titles.

- Press Home to move the cell pointer to the top left corner of the unfrozen area.

- Press GoTo (F5) to move the cell pointer inside the title area. This action creates duplicates of the frozen rows and columns. The double appearance can be confusing.

- The cell pointer can enter title areas when you are entering cell addresses in POINT mode.

- **/W**orksheet **T**itles can be useful for displaying protected screen areas when **/R**ange **I**nput is active. Position titles so that they display labels and instructions adjacent to the unprotected input range.

- /Worksheet **Titles** is especially useful for freezing column headings over a database or an accounting spreadsheet. You also can freeze rows of text that describe figures in adjacent cells.

For more information, see Chapter 4.

Worksheet Window /WW

Purpose

Displays two parts of the worksheet at the same time. You can choose to split the worksheet horizontally or vertically. The two parts of the worksheet can scroll separately or together, following the same cell pointer movements.

Reminders

Before you use /ww, do the following:

- Decide whether you want the worksheet split horizontally or vertically.

- If you want two horizontal windows, move the cell pointer to the top row of what will become the lower window.

- For two vertical windows, move the cell pointer to the column that will become the left edge of the right window.

Procedures

1. Type **/ww**

2. Of the following options, select **H**orizontal or **V**ertical to set a window:

Menu Item	*Description*
Horizontal	Splits the worksheet into two horizontal windows at the cell pointer
Vertical	Splits the worksheet into two vertical windows at the cell pointer
Sync	Synchronizes rows or columns within windows so that they move together. Windows are in Sync when they are first opened.
Unsync	Unsynchronizes two windows so that they can move independently of each other. You can then simultaneously view different rows and columns in the worksheet. A window will move only when it contains the cell pointer.
Clear	Removes the inactive window (the one that does not contain the cell pointer)

3. Repeat Steps 1 and 2 and select Unsync if you want the windows to move independently of each other. You can then simultaneously view different rows and columns in the worksheet.

4. Press the Window (F6) key to move the cell pointer into the opposite window. Move the cell pointer to position the second window as needed.

Important Cues

- Each window can have different column widths. When /Worksheet Window Clear is selected, the settings used in the top or left window determine the column width for the remaining worksheet.

- Horizontal windows are useful when you work with databases. The criteria range and database column labels can appear in the upper window while the data or extracted data appears in the lower window.

- You can use /Worksheet Window to display messages, instructions, warnings, help text, and so on, without having to leave the worksheet.

Caution

Always clear windows and reposition the screen before you invoke windows in a macro. Macros that split windows may become "confused" if the window configuration differs from what the macros "expect."

For more information, see Chapter 4.

Worksheet Status   /WS

Purpose

Displays the current global settings that help you operate the worksheet.

You also can use /ws to check available memory.

Reminder

The screen displays the status of the following information:

Available memory (Conventional, Expanded)
Math coprocessor
Recalculation (Method, Order, Iterations)
Circular reference
Cell Display (Format, Label prefix, Column width, Zero suppression)
Global Protection

You can check the worksheet's status whenever a worksheet is displayed.

Procedures

1. Type /**ws**

2. Press any key (such as the space bar) to return to the worksheet.

Important Cues

- The disk-file size of the saved worksheet cannot be calculated from the amount of memory used.

- You can reduce the size of a worksheet by deleting unnecessary formulas, labels, and values. Use /**R**ange Format **R**eset to reset the numeric format for unused areas; then save the revised worksheet to a file and retrieve a smaller version.

- The Circular Reference status displays a single cell within a ring of formulas that depend on each other. The Circular Reference status shows (in this ring) only one cell address at a time.

- In Release 2.2, the /**W**orksheet **G**lobal command also can be used to display a list of current global settings.

For more information, see Chapter 4.

RELEASE
2.2

Worksheet Page   /WP

Purpose

Manually inserts page breaks in printed worksheets. 1-2-3 automatically inserts page breaks when the printing reaches the bottom margin. For some reports, however, you may want page breaks to occur at designated rows. The /**W**orksheet **P**age command indicates to the printer where manually selected page breaks should occur.

Reminders

- If you will need to reuse the worksheet in a form without page breaks, save the worksheet before you insert the page breaks.

- Before you use /wp, move the cell pointer into column A and to one row below where you want the page break to occur.

Procedures

1. Type /**wp**

2. Press Enter.

3. A row is inserted where the page will break, and a double colon (::) appears in the left column.

Important Cues

- Use **/R**ange **E**rase to remove the page break.

- **/W**orksheet **P**age overrides the **/P**rint **F**ile **O**ptions **O**ther **U**nformatted command, which normally suppresses page breaks. If you need to print to disk without using page breaks, make sure that you use **/R**ange **E**rase to remove the page-break markers.

Caution

Do not make entries in the row that contains the page-break marker (::). Entries in this row do not print.

For more information, see Chapter 4.

RELEASE
2.2

Worksheet Learn   /WL

Purpose

Specifies a worksheet range where keystrokes will be recorded when you turn on the Learn feature.

By recording your keystrokes, you can make macros quickly and efficiently. **/W**orksheet **L**earn saves you from having to write down or memorize the keystrokes for your macros and then from having to enter the macro code in the worksheet.

Reminders

- Decide where you want to store your macros. Ideally, macros should be stored to the right and below your active worksheet area so that when you make insertions or deletions in your worksheet, you don't affect your macros.

- Place the cell pointer at the top of the column where you want keystrokes to be stored.

Procedures

To specify a range for recording keystrokes, do the following:

1. Type **/wlr**

2. Highlight cells within a single column and press Enter.

3. When you are ready to begin recording keystrokes, press the Learn (Alt-F5) key combination. Enter all keystrokes to be recorded and press Learn (Alt-F5) to turn off the recording.

4. Press Calc (F9) to transfer the captured keystrokes to the learn range.

5. Go to the learn range and edit the macro keystrokes, if necessary.

6. Name the macro with **/R**ange Name Create.

To clear or cancel a learn range, do the following:

1. Type **/wl**

2. Select one of the following:

Menu Item	Description
Cancel	Cancels an existing learn range. This command does not erase any keystrokes in the learn range.
Erase	Clears all the keystrokes presently recorded in the learn range

3. If you choose **Erase**, a No/Yes menu appears. Choose **Yes** to erase the learn range; choose **No** to cancel the command.

Important Cues

- Specify a long learn range to allow plenty of room for the keystrokes to be stored. Each full command will be recorded in a single cell. For example, /wir~ would be considered one complete command and would be the only keystrokes stored in a cell.

- If you don't specify a long enough learn range, you will get the message **Learn Range Full**, and the Learn feature will be turned off automatically. If you get this error message, press Esc to clear the error message, define a longer learn range, and turn on the Learn feature again (by pressing Learn [Alt-F5]) to continue recording where you left off.

- When recording keystrokes, type the first letter of the commands in the menus so that your macros will be easier to read. If you highlight menu options, the pointer movement keystrokes will record. (If you choose the **/C**opy command by highlighting the option Copy instead of pressing C, for example, /{R}{R}~ will record instead of /C.)

- Each time you turn on the Learn feature, keystrokes will be recorded in the currently specified learn range. If you already had keystrokes in the learn range, the most recent keystrokes will be appended to the keystrokes you have already recorded.

- If you make a mistake while recording keystrokes, you may want to start over again. Simply turn off recording by pressing Learn (Alt-F5), and use **/W**orksheet Learn Erase to clear what has been recorded. You can then turn on the Learn feature again.

Range Commands /R

/Range commands control the display formats, protection, and manipulation of portions of the worksheet. (If you want to affect the entire worksheet, as by inserting an entire column, look at the /Worksheet command menu.) /Range commands new with Release 2.2 are highlighted in the following menu map.

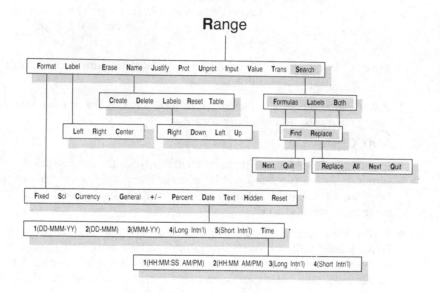

Range Format */RF*

Purpose

Prepares cells so that they display with a specific format for both values (numbers) and formula results.

/Range Format formats a cell or range of cells so that numbers appear in a specific format: with fixed decimal places, as currency, with commas only, in scientific notation, or as dates. These formats affect both the screen display and printing.

Reminders

- Use /Worksheet Global Format to format the majority of the worksheet's cells that will contain numeric data. Use /Range Format to reset formats for areas that differ.

- Use /Worksheet Global Format to format new numbers entered throughout the worksheet. Numbers entered in ranges formatted with /Range Format will not be affected.

- Move the cell pointer to the upper left corner of the range you want to format.

Procedures

1. Type /rf

2. Select a format from the following menu items:

Menu Item	Description
Fixed	Fixes the number of decimal places displayed
Sci (Scientific in Release 2.01)	Displays large or small numbers, using scientific notation
Currency	Displays currency symbols (such as $ or £) and commas
, (comma)	Inserts commas to mark thousands and multiples of thousands
General	Displays values with up to 10 decimals or in scientific notation
+/−	Creates horizontal bar graphs or time-duration graphs on computers that do not have graphics. Each symbol equals one whole number. Positive numbers display as plus (+) symbols; negative numbers, as minus (−) symbols.
Percent	Displays a decimal number as a whole number followed by a percent (%) sign
Date	Displays serial date numbers in the following five formats; provides the Time option, which offers four time formats

1 DD–MMM–YY	12–Jan–51
2 DD–MMM	12–Jan
3 MMM–YY	Jan–51
4 Long Intn'l	01/12/51
5 Short Intn'l	01/12

Time:

1 HH:MM:SS AM/PM	1:04:34 PM
2 HH:MM AM/PM	1:04 PM
3 Long Intn'l	13:04:34
4 Short Intn'l	13:04

Text	Continues to evaluate formulas as numbers, but displays formulas as text on-screen
Hidden	Hides contents from the display and printing but still evaluates contents
Reset	Returns the format to current /Worksheet Global format

3. If 1-2-3 prompts, enter the number of decimal places to be displayed. The full value of a cell—not the value displayed—is used for calculation. (See the first caution.)

4. If you select **D**ate or **T**ime, also select a format number to indicate how you want the date or time to appear.

5. Specify the range by entering the range address, highlighting the range, or using an assigned range name.

6. Verify that the specified range is correct.

7. Press Enter.

Important Cues

- /**R**ange **F**ormat **H**idden is the only format that affects labels. All other /**R**ange **F**ormat commands work on values and numeric formulas.

- Dates and times are generated from serial date and time numbers created with @DATE, @DATEVALUE, @TIME, @NOW, and @TIMEVALUE.

- If you use a format other than **G**eneral, asterisks fill the cell when a value is too large to fit the cell's current column width. (In the **G**eneral format, values that are too large are displayed in scientific notation.)

- Use /**W**orksheet **G**lobal **D**efault **O**ther **I**nternational to display non-USA formats or determine the display of negative numbers in comma or **C**urrency format. Select one of these international format options: **P**unctuation, **C**urrency, **D**ate, or **T**ime. Or select **N**egative and choose **P**arentheses or **S**ign to enclose negative numbers in parentheses or to precede negative numbers with a minus sign, respectively.

- Range formats take precedence over /**W**orksheet **G**lobal formats.

Cautions

- /**R**ange Format rounds only the appearance of the displayed number. The command does not round the number used for calculation. This difference can cause displayed or printed numbers to appear to be incorrect. In some worksheets, such as mortgage tables, results may be significantly different than expected. Enclose numbers, formulas, or cell references in the @ROUND function to ensure that the values in calculations are truly rounded.

- Use the **F**ixed decimal format to enter percentage data. Use the **P**ercent format to display or print results. The **P**ercent format displays a decimal numeral in percentage form; a decimal numeral such as .23 is displayed as 23%. If the **P**ercent format is used for data entry, most users will see numerals in percentage form (such as 23%) and attempt to enter similar percentages (.24 as 24, for example), producing grossly incorrect entries (such as 2,400%). If the **P**ercent format is used, numeric entries should be followed by a percent sign, as in 24%. The trailing percent sign causes 1-2-3 to divide the value by 100.

For more information, see /**Worksheet Global Format**, /**Worksheet Global Default**, *and Chapters 5 and 6.*

Range Label   /RL

Purpose

Selects how you want to align text labels in their cells.

Labels narrower than the cell width can be aligned to the left, right, or center. To change how numbers appear on-screen, use either /**R**ange Format or /**W**orksheet **G**lobal Format.

Reminders

- Move the cell pointer to the upper left corner of the range containing the cells you want to align.

- Use /**W**orksheet **G**lobal **L**abel-Prefix to align the majority of labels on the worksheet. After building the worksheet "skeleton" of text, align labels and set column widths by using /**R**ange **L**abel and /**W**orksheet **C**olumn **S**et-Width.

Procedures

1. Type **/rl**

2. Select one of these menu items:

Menu Item	Description
Left	Aligns labels with cell's left edge
Right	Aligns labels with cell's right edge
Center	Centers labels in cell

3. Specify the range by entering the range address, highlighting the range, or using an assigned range name. Figure R.1 shows a highlighted range ready to be aligned to the right.

Fig. R.1.
The highlighted range A5..A12 about to be aligned to the right.

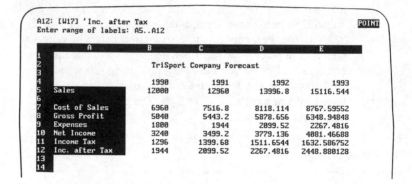

4. Press Enter.

Important Cues

• The label prefix appears on the first line of the control panel.

• Alignment works only for text smaller than the cell width. Text larger than the cell width is left-aligned. The text that exceeds the cell width "squeezes" out the cell's right edge.

• To align labels in a cell manually, enter one of these label prefixes before typing the label:

Label Prefix	Function
' (apostrophe)	Aligns label to the left
" (quotation mark)	Aligns label to the right
^ (caret)	Centers label in the cell
\ (backslash)	Repeats character to fill a cell*

Note that this prefix can't be selected from the menu.

- The worksheet starts with labels left-aligned. Use /Worksheet Global Label-Prefix to set the label prefix used by text entries in areas not specified with /Range Label.

- /Range Label does not affect values (numeric cell entries). Values are always right-aligned.

- Labels beginning with numbers or formula symbols require label prefixes. Enter the label prefix before entering the numbers or symbols. This process is necessary for such items as addresses, part numbers, Social Security numbers, and phone numbers, as in the following examples:

Correct	Incorrect
'2207 Cheyenne Dr.	2207 Cheyenne Dr.
"34-567FB	34-567FB

- Use a label prefix to preserve formulas that have errors you have not yet identified. For example, if you have a problem with the formula +B5*@PMT(B16B12/12,B14*12), and you don't have time to look for the error (a comma is missing after B16), use an apostrophe label prefix to turn the formula into text. Later, when you have more time, use EDIT mode to remove the apostrophe to change the text back to a formula. Then correct the formula error.

- Document formulas by inserting a label prefix before each formula and copying the formula as a label to your worksheet documentation area. Later, remove the label prefix from the original formula to restore it to its original, operable form.

Cautions

- /Range Label Center does not center labels on the screen or page. You must center the text manually by moving the cell pointer with the text and following these steps:

  1. Enter the text if you have not done so already.

  2. Determine how many leading spaces are necessary to center the text on-screen.

  3. Press Edit (F2); then press Home. The cursor moves to the label prefix at the beginning of the text.

  4. Move the cell pointer right one character and insert spaces in front of the first character to center it.

  5. Press Enter.

- Macro code text must be in the form of labels. If you don't place a label prefix before the macro commands, such as /wglr, your keystrokes select menu items.

• Numbers or formulas preceded by label prefixes have a value of zero when evaluated by a numeric formula. (In Release 2.0, however, a formula [but not a function] that references a label returns an ERR; Release 2.01 eliminates this bug.) In a database query, you must use text searches to search for these numbers that have label prefixes.

For more information, see /Worksheet Global Label-Prefix, /Range Format, and Chapter 5.

Range Erase   /RE

Purpose

Erases the contents of a single cell or range of cells.

Reminders

• Use /Worksheet Erase if you want to erase the entire worksheet.

• If you have any doubts about erasing a range of cells, use /File Save to save the worksheet to a file before erasing the range. Erased cells cannot be recovered. (Release 2.2 users can restore erased cells if the Undo feature was enabled before the erasure took place.)

• Move the cell pointer to the upper left corner of the range to be erased.

Procedures

1. Type /re

2. Specify the range to be erased: enter the range address, highlight the range, or use an assigned range name. Figure R.2 shows a highlighted range to be erased.

Fig. R.2.
The highlighted range about to be deleted.

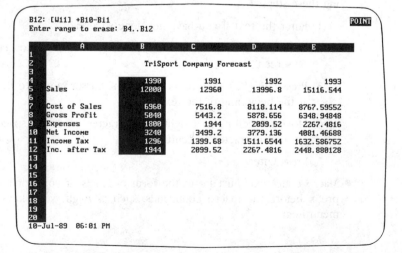

3. Press Enter.

Important Cues

- To erase protected cells, you must first remove worksheet protection by using /Worksheet Global Protection Disable.

- Erasing data or formulas may produce an ERR display in formulas that depend on the erased data or formulas.

- Erasing a range does not change the format, label prefix, or protection status assigned to the cells.

- If the Undo feature is enabled in Release 2.2, you can press Undo (Alt-F4) if you accidentally erase the wrong range.

RELEASE
2.2

Cautions

- /Worksheet Delete can be dangerous if you use it to remove a record from a database. You can unintentionally delete a row that looks blank on-screen but contains cells with important data off-screen. Use instead /Range Erase and sort down empty records.

- Be careful not to erase formulas or values hidden with /Worksheet Global Format Hidden or /Range Format Hidden.

For more information, see **/Worksheet Delete**, **/Worksheet Erase**, *and Chapter 4.*

Range Name   /RN

Purpose

Assigns an alphabetical or alphanumeric name to a cell or a range of cells. (See the caution about alphanumeric range names.)

Instead of column-and-row cell addresses, use range names to make formulas and macros easy to read and understand.

Reminder

Consider all the possible ways to use range names in your specific 1-2-3 application. Consider, for example, how range names can be used in formulas and macros or used for setting print ranges, moving the cell pointer to different areas of the worksheet, and setting data ranges for graphs.

Procedures

To create a range name that describes a single cell or range of cells, follow these steps:

1. Move the cell pointer to the cell or upper left corner of the range of cells to be named.

2. Type **/rn**

3. Select **Create.**

4. When prompted to enter the range name, press Name (F3) to see a full-screen display of names already in use. If the name you want to use is listed, delete it before you create another range by that name. Press Esc to exit from the list.

5. Type a range name of as many as 15 characters. Avoid using symbols other than the underline.

6. Press Enter.

7. To specify the range to be named, enter the range address or highlight the range.

8. Press Enter.

To create range names from labels, follow these steps:

1. Move the cell pointer to the upper left corner of the column or row of labels.

2. Type **/rn**

3. Select **Labels.**

4. Select one of these menu items:

Menu Item	Description
Right	Uses the labels to name the cell to the right of each label
Down	Uses the labels to name the cell below each label
Left	Uses the labels to name the cell to the left of each label
Up	Uses the labels to name the cell above each label

5. By entering the range address or highlighting the range, specify the range of labels to be used as names. Verify that the range encloses only labels.

6. Press Enter.

To delete a range name, follow these steps:

1. Type **/rn**

2. Select **Delete** to delete a single range name. Select **Reset** to delete all range names.

3. If you select **D**elete, highlight the range name and press Enter. The addresses in formulas of the deleted range names revert to normal cell addresses.

To display the names and addresses of existing range names, follow these steps:

1. Move the cell pointer to a clear area of the worksheet. (The area should be two columns wide and contain sufficient rows to hold all range names.)

2. Type **/rn**

3. Select **T**able.

4. Press Enter to create a table of range names and their associated addresses.

Important Cues

- Use a range name when you enter a function. Instead of entering a function as @SUM(P53..P65), for example, type it as @SUM(EXPENSES).

- Similarly, use a range name when you respond to a prompt. For example, when the program requests a print range, provide a range name, as in the following:

      Enter print range: **JULREPORT**

- Undefined range names remain in formulas, although the formulas result in ERR. Use the **/R**ange **N**ame **C**reate or **L**abels command to redefine the name.

- To move the cell pointer rapidly to the upper left corner of any range, press GoTo (F5) and then enter the range name, or press Name (F3) to display a list of range names. After you have entered the range name or selected a name from the list, press Enter.

- In Release 2.2, you can press Name (F3) while you are building a formula. A list of range names displays, and you can select the name to use in the formula.

RELEASE 2.2

- To print a list of range names, use **/R**ange **N**ame **T**able and press Shift-PrtSc after the list appears.

- **/M**ove moves range names with cells if the entire range is included in the block to be moved.

- Macro names are range names; therefore, macros must be named through the use of /rnc or /rnl.

Cautions

- A range name can be alphanumeric (as in SALES87), but avoid creating a range name that looks like a cell reference (for example, AD19). Such a range name does not function correctly in formulas.

- Always delete existing range names before re-creating them in a new location. If you don't delete an original range name, formulas that used the original name may be wrong.

- Do not delete columns or rows that form the corner of a named range. Doing so produces an ERR in formulas.

- Moving the upper left or lower right corner of a named range shifts the cell addresses that the range name defines.

- When two named ranges have the same upper left corner, moving one of the corners moves the address location for both range names. To move a corner of overlapping named ranges, first delete one range name, move the range, and then re-create the deleted range name in its original location.

- /**R**ange **N**ame **T**able does not update itself automatically. If you move, copy, or change range names, you must re-create the range name table.

For more information, see Chapter 4.

Range Justify   */RJ*

Purpose

Fits text within a desired range by wrapping words to form complete paragraphs.

Use /**R**ange **J**ustify to join and "wordwrap" automatically any lines of text in adjacent vertical cells to form a paragraph. /**R**ange **J**ustify redistributes words so that sentences are approximately the same length.

Reminders

- Delete any blank cells or values between vertically adjacent cells you want to join. Blank cells or values stop text from justifying.

- Move the cell pointer to the top of the column of text you want justified. Make sure that the cell pointer is in the first cell containing the text. In the first line of the control panel, you should see the first words of the text from the first row of the column.

- Remember that unless you specify a range for /rj, other cells are moved to reflect the justification.

Procedures

1. Type /**rj**

2. Highlight the range in which you want the text to be justified. If you choose not to specify a range for the justification, highlight only the first row of the text column.

3. Press Enter, and the text will be justified. If you specified a range, worksheet cells within the highlighted range are justified; cells outside the highlighted range are not moved.

Important Cues

- /Range Justify justifies all contiguous text in a column until justification is stopped by nonlabel cell contents (a blank cell, a formula, or a value).

- If you are uncertain about the results of /Range Justify, save your worksheet with /File Save before using /Range Justify. In Release 2.2, you can use Undo (Alt-F4) to restore the worksheet to its status before the command if you get unexpected results.

- Enter long lists of single-word labels as a single text line and justify the line down a column. Enter the words with a single space between them, and make certain that the column width is only wide enough to contain the longest word.

- Use /File Import to import text from word processors (ASCII text files only). Once in 1-2-3, the text can be justified with /Range Justify to fit the worksheet.

Cautions

- If the specified range is not large enough to hold the justified text, 1-2-3 displays an error message. To solve this problem, enlarge the range or move the text to a new location. If you enlarge the range, you may need to move other cell contents.

- Using /Range Justify on protected cells results in an error. Remove protection with /Worksheet Global Protection Disable.

For more information, see /Move, /File Import, /Worksheet Page, and Chapter 5.

RELEASE
2.2

Range Prot and Range Unprot   /RP and /RU

Purpose

/Range Prot (Protect in Release 2.01) enables you to restore the identification of worksheet cells from unprotected to protected. /Range Unprot (Unprotect in Release 2.01) enables you to make changes to cells in a protected worksheet.

Use /Range Unprot and /Worksheet Global Protection to protect worksheets from accidental changes. /Range Unprot identifies which cells' contents can be changed when /Worksheet Global Protection is enabled. Cells not identified with /Range Unprot cannot be changed when /Worksheet Global Protection is enabled.

Reminder

Move the cell pointer to the upper left corner of the range you want to identify as unprotected. /Worksheet Global Protection may be enabled or disabled.

4. Make data entries, using normal methods. Press Esc or Enter to exit from /Range Input and return to normal cell pointer movement.

Important Cues

- /Range Input restricts your key selections to Esc; Enter; Edit; Help; Home; End; and the left-, right-, up-, and down-arrow keys. Use standard alphanumeric keys for data entry and editing.

- /Range Input is most valuable when used within macros. Within macros, the command can be used to restrict data entry to one worksheet range for one part of the macro and to another worksheet range for another part of the macro.

For more information, see /Range Name, /Range Unprot, and Chapter 4.

Range Value   /RV

Purpose

Converts formulas in a range to their values so that you can copy only the values to a new location. This command rapidly converts formula results to unchanging values for database storage.

Reminders

- Check to see that the destination area is large enough to hold the copied values, which will replace existing cell contents.

- Move the cell pointer to the upper left corner of the range containing the formulas.

Procedures

1. Type /rv

2. Specify the source range by typing the range address, highlighting the range, or using a range name.

3. Press Enter.

4. Specify the upper left corner cell of the destination range by typing a cell address or range name, or by moving the cell pointer to this location.

5. Press Enter. The values appear in the destination range and preserve the numeric formats used in the original formulas.

Important Cues

- /Range Value copies labels and string formulas and converts string (text) formulas to labels.

- Use /Copy to copy formulas without changing them into values.

Cautions

- **/R**ange Value overwrites data in the destination (TO) range. Be sure that the destination range is large enough to receive the data without overwriting adjacent cell contents you don't want to alter.

- If you make the destination range the same as the source range, formulas in the range are converted to their values. These values, however, overwrite the formulas they came from. The formulas are replaced permanently.

For more information, see **/Copy** *and Chapter 4.*

Range Trans   /RT

Purpose

Reorders columns of data into rows of data, or rows of data into columns of data.

/Range Trans (**Transpose** in Release 2.01) is useful when you want to change data from spreadsheet format (headings on left, data in rows) to database format (headings on top, data in columns), or vice versa.

Reminders

- In Release 2.01, make sure that the range to be transposed does not contain formulas. If the range contains formulas, use **/R**ange Value to change the formulas into constant values. Release 2.2 changes formulas to values.

- Transpose the new data to a clear worksheet area. The transposed data overwrites any existing data.

- Move the cell pointer to the upper left corner of the range of cells you want to transpose.

RELEASE
2.2

Procedures

1. Type **/rt**

2. Specify the range to be transposed: type the range address, highlight the range, or use an assigned range name.

3. Press Enter.

4. When 1-2-3 displays the TO prompt, move the cell pointer to the upper left corner of the destination cells where the transposed data will be copied.

5. Press Enter.

Figure R.4 shows data in A6..B10 transposed to D6..H7.

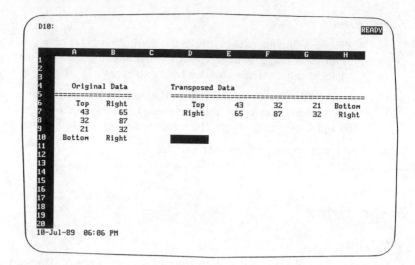

Fig. R.4.
Data in A6..B10
transposed to
D6..H7.

Important Cue

Transposed formulas will usually be incorrect. If the range to be transposed contains formulas, use **/R**ange Value to change the formulas to values; then transpose the range.

Caution

Do not use the same upper left corner for the source (FROM) and the destination (TO) ranges. Not all the data will transpose correctly.

For more information, see **/Range Value** *and Chapter 4.*

RELEASE
2.2

Range Search   */RS*

Purpose

Finds or replaces text within a label or formula. The search and replace can be limited to a range.

Use this command to search databases quickly or to find locations on a worksheet. The command also is useful for finding and replacing cell references, functions, and range names in formulas.

Reminder

Place the cell pointer at one corner of the range to search.

Procedures

To find a text string in labels or formulas, do the following:

1. Type **/rs**

2. Type the cell addresses or highlight or type a range name to specify the range you want searched. Press Enter.

3. Enter the text string you want to find. You may use either upper- or lower-case text; the **/R**ange **S**earch command is not case-sensitive. Press Enter.

4. Choose one of the following:

Menu Item	Description
Formulas	Searches through formulas
Labels	Searches through labels
Both	Searches through both formulas and labels

5. Select **F**ind. The cell containing the first occurrence of the string is highlighted.

6. Select one of the following:

Menu Item	Description
Next	Finds the next occurrence
Quit	Stops the search

7. When no more occurrences are found, press Esc or Enter to return to READY mode.

To replace one string with another, do the following:

1. Type **/rs**

2. Type the cell addresses or highlight or type a range name to specify the range you want searched. Press Enter.

3. Enter the text string you want to find. You may use either upper- or lower-case text; the **/R**ange **S**earch command is not case-sensitive. Press Enter.

4. Choose one of the following:

Menu Item	Description
Formulas	Searches through formulas
Labels	Searches through labels
Both	Searches through both formulas and labels

5. Select **R**eplace.

6. Type the replacement string. Press Enter. The cell containing the first occurrence is highlighted.

7. Select one of the following:

Menu Item	Description
Replace	Replaces the found text with the replacement text, then finds the next occurrence
All	Replaces all occurrences of found text
Next	Finds the next occurrence without replacing the current text
Quit	Stops the search

8. When no more occurrences are found, press Esc or Enter to return to READY mode.

Important Cues

- Use the **R**eplace command to substitute one range name for another in formulas, or one constant for another.

- Type the replacement text in the desired combination of upper- and lower-case letters.

- You cannot search for values that appear in cells by themselves. You can search for numbers only if they appear in a label or in a formula.

- You can search and replace any part of a formula: a number, an @function, an operator, a range name, or a range.

Caution

Beware of replacing with **A**ll. 1-2-3 searches for the text string and finds it whether it is a whole word or part of another word. You can easily replace text or formulas you did not want to replace. Use the **R**eplace and **N**ext options to be on the safe side.

For more information, see Chapter 4.

Copy and Move Commands

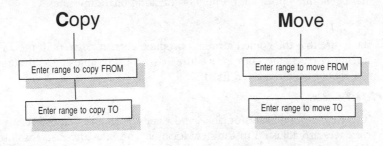

Copy

Enter range to copy FROM

Enter range to copy TO

Move

Enter range to move FROM

Enter range to move TO

Copy   /C

Purpose

Copies formulas, values, and labels to new locations. The cell addresses in copied formulas either change to reflect the new location or stay fixed, depending on whether you use relative or absolute cell references.

Reminders

- Make sure that the worksheet contains enough blank space to receive the cell or range of cells being copied. Copies replace the original contents of cells.

- If the receiving cell address is not close to the cell or range of cells being copied, note the address before entering /Copy, so that you can type the TO address. Pointing across a long distance to the TO address can be tedious.

- Before you issue the /Copy command, move the cell pointer to the upper left corner of the range you want copied. If you are copying one cell, put the cell pointer on that cell.

Procedures

1. Type /c

2. The FROM prompt requests the range of the cells to be copied. Enter the range to be copied by typing the range name or range address or by highlighting the range.

3. Press Enter.

4. At the TO prompt, specify the upper left corner of the worksheet section where you want the duplicate to appear. Move the cell pointer to the upper left corner position, and press the period (.) key to anchor the first corner. If you want multiple adjacent duplicates, you can highlight additional cells that define the upper left corners of the additional duplicates.

5. Press Enter.

6. Make sure that the copied formulas produce correct answers. If the answers are not correct, the copy procedure has probably adjusted cell addresses that should have remained fixed.

Important Cues

- /Copy creates duplicates of labels and values. Formulas that use relative cell references are adjusted to the new location; formulas that use absolute cell references remain fixed.

- You can make single or multiple copies, depending on the range you enter at the TO prompt. Enter the ranges as follows:

Original Range FROM	Desired Copies	Duplicate Range TO
One cell	Fill an area	Row, column, or range
Rectangular area	One duplicate	Upper left cell of duplicate, outside original range
Single column	Multiple column	Adjacent cells across a row, formed from the top cell of each duplicate column
Single row	Multiple rows	Adjacent cells down a column, formed from the left cell in each duplicate row

Cautions

- Overlapping FROM and TO ranges (original and duplicate) can cause formulas to yield incorrect results. To avoid producing incorrect results, move the cell pointer off the original cell before anchoring the TO range with a period. With Release 2.2, if you get unexpected results, you can restore the precopy worksheet by using the Undo (Alt-F4) key.

- If the worksheet area to be copied to does not have enough room to receive the copied range, the contents of the existing cells will be covered by the copied data. To fix this problem, use /Move to move existing data, or use /Worksheet Insert to insert blank columns or rows before you execute the /Copy command.

For more information, see /Worksheet Insert Column, /Worksheet Insert Row, /Range Value, /Range Name, and Chapter 4.

Move   /M

Purpose

Reorganizes your worksheet by moving blocks of labels, values, or formulas to different locations.

Cell references and range names used in formulas stay the same, which means that formula results do not change.

Reminders

- Make sure that you have enough blank space in the receiving area of the worksheet to receive the cell or range of cells being moved. The moved data replaces the original contents of cells.

- Before you issue the /Move command, position the cell pointer on the top left corner of the range to be moved. If you want to move one cell, place the cell pointer on that cell.

Procedures

1. Type /**m**

2. The FROM prompt requests the range of the cells to be moved. Highlight a range, or enter the original range by typing the range name or range address.

3. Press Enter.

4. At the TO prompt, enter the address of the single upper left corner of the range to which the cells will be moved. Do so by typing the cell address, typing a range name, or highlighting the cell with the cell pointer.

5. Press Enter.

Important Cues

- /Move does not change cell addresses. The range names and cell references in the formula remain the same.

- Use /Copy when you want to create at a new location a duplicate range of cells while keeping the original range intact.

- Range names move with the moved cells if the named area is completely enclosed.

Cautions

- If the worksheet does not have enough room to receive the range of cells being moved, the existing cells will be replaced by the moved data. You can use **/Move** to move cell contents to make room, or you can add rows and columns by using **/Worksheet Insert**.

- Moving the anchor cell and/or the diagonally opposite cell of a named range moves the corner(s) of the named range to the new location as well. If you have doubts about what is being moved, save the worksheet, delete the old range name, make the move, and then re-create the range name. With Release 2.2, if you get unexpected results, you can restore the premove worksheet by using the Undo (Alt-F4) key combination.

- Be careful when moving a named range that has the same upper left corner as another range. Moving one range changes the upper left corner for both named ranges.

For more information, see **/Worksheet Insert**, **/Copy**, **/Range Name**, *and Chapter 4.*

File Commands

File commands are used to save and retrieve worksheets, extract a small worksheet from a larger worksheet, combine two worksheets, import ASCII data, and select the drive and directory for storage. The following menu map shows the /File commands. Commands new with Release 2.2 are highlighted.

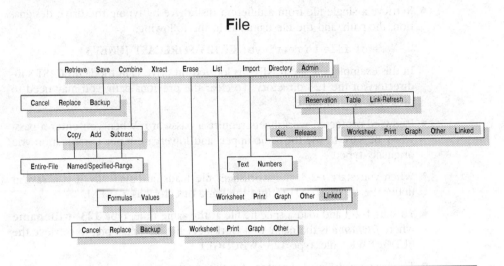

File Retrieve   /FR

Purpose

Loads the requested worksheet file from disk.

Reminder

Before you begin working on a new worksheet, use /File Save to save the current worksheet. When a new worksheet is loaded, it replaces the worksheet currently displayed.

Procedures

1. Type /fr

2. Select the name of the file you want to retrieve, either by typing the name or by using the right- or left-arrow key to point to your selection.

3. Press Enter.

Important Cues

- You can display a list of file names by pressing Name (F3) in response to the prompt

  `Name of file to retrieve:`

  Use the arrow keys to move to the file name you want and then press Enter. To return to the menu without making a selection, press Esc.

- Retrieve a single file from a different disk drive by typing the drive designation, the path, and the file name, as in the following:

  `Name of file to retrieve:` **C:\123\FORECAST\JUNEV3**

  In this example, the file JUNEV3 is located on drive C in the FORECAST subdirectory of the 123 directory. To clear the previous path, you may need to press Esc several times.

- Password-protected worksheets require a password. When you enter a password, be sure to use the same upper- and lowercase letter combination you originally typed.

- When you start 1-2-3, the worksheet file loads automatically if you save it under the name AUTO123 into the same directory as 123.EXE.

RELEASE 2.2

- To start 1-2-3 and load a specific file at the same time, type **123 -wfilename** where *filename* is the name of a worksheet file. For example, to retrieve the BUDGET.WK1 file, type **123 -WBUDGET**.

- To change a drive or directory for the current work session, use the **/File Directory** command.

- Use **/Worksheet Global Default Directory** to change the directory that 1-2-3 uses on start-up. Use **/Worksheet Global Default Update** to save the settings to the System disk.

RELEASE 2.2

- To retrieve a Release 2.2 backup file, type the complete file name, including the .BAK extension. Alternatively, you can select the file from a list of backup files by typing ***.BAK** and pressing Enter.

RELEASE 2.2

- If you are using Release 2.2 on a network, and another user has the rights to save the file you are retrieving, you will see a Yes/No menu. Choose **Yes** to retrieve the file, knowing that you will not be able to save any changes. Choose **No** to cancel the retrieve command.

Caution

The retrieved file replaces the worksheet in memory. Before retrieving a new worksheet, use **/File Save** to store your current worksheet.

*For more information, see **/File Save**, **/File Combine**, **/Worksheet Global Default Directory**, **/File Directory**, and Chapter 7.*

File Save /FS

Purpose

Saves the current worksheet and settings to disk so that they can be retrieved later.

Reminders

- Remember to save frequently to guard against data loss in case of power failure or human error.

- Name files so that they are easy to remember and group together. If you give related files similar names (such as TRENDV1, TRENDV2, and TRENDV3), you can use the DOS wild cards * and ? to copy and erase files.

Procedures

1. Type **/fs**

2. You can enter the file name for the worksheet by using the default name displayed; by highlighting an existing name; by typing a new name; or by entering a new drive designation, path name, and file name.

3. Press Enter.

4. If a file already exists under the name you have selected, choose one of the following:

Menu Item	Description
Cancel	Cancels the save operation
Replace	Replaces an existing file with the current file
Backup	Creates a backup file (available in Release 2.2 only). The previous saved version will have the extension .BAK, and the current file will have the extension .WK1.

Important Cues

- Write file names of up to eight characters by using the letters A through Z, the numbers 0 through 9, and the underline character (_) or hyphen (-). Spaces cannot be used. In Release 2.2, file names can be as long as the operating system allows. DOS allows up to eight characters in a file name.

- Password protection prevents unauthorized access to 1-2-3 worksheets. If you save worksheets with a password, the password must be entered before the file can be retrieved. To save a file with a password, follow these steps:

  1. Type **/fs**

  2. Type the file name, press the space bar, and press P.

  3. Press Enter.

RELEASE
2.2

4. Type a password of up to 15 characters (no spaces). A blank appears in place of each letter. Be sure to remember the upper- and lowercase letter combination. When you retrieve the file, you must enter the password exactly as it was created.

5. Press Enter.

6. After the Verify prompt appears, type the password again, exactly as you typed it the first time, and press Enter.

- To change a protected file's password, use the Backspace key to erase the Password Protected message displayed when you use /File Save. Then repeat Steps 2 through 6.

- From the list of existing files on disk, you can select a file name to save to. When prompted for a name, press Esc to remove the default file name. Press Name (F3), use the arrow keys to move to the file name you want to replace, and press Enter.

- Use /File List to display the size and the date of the existing files.

- Use /File Xtract to save a range of cells from the current worksheet to a file on disk.

Cautions

- Saving a worksheet under an existing file name replaces the previous file. This means that you can accidentally write over files you want to keep. A safer practice is to save each copy under a different name and delete outdated versions later, using /File Erase or the operating system's ERASE or DEL command. In Release 2.2, use the Backup option when you save.

RELEASE
2.2

- The Backup feature in Release 2.2 creates only one backup per file. If you choose Backup, and a backup already exists for that file, the previous backup will be deleted.

- After executing /File Save, do not remove your data disk until the light on your disk drive goes off. Pay no attention to the READY indicator. Wait several seconds after the READY indicator has disappeared before you remove the disk. If you remove the disk prematurely, information can be lost.

*For more information, see /**File Directory**, /**File Erase**, /**File Xtract**, and Chapter 7.*

File Combine   /FC

Purpose

Combines values or formulas from one worksheet with data in another worksheet. Any part of a saved file can be combined with the current file.

Reminders

- Remember that /File Combine can be used three different ways: to copy the contents from the file worksheet to the current worksheet; to add values from the file worksheet to the current worksheet; and to subtract incoming values from the numeric values in the current worksheet.

- Use /File Import and /Data Parse to bring ASCII files into the current worksheet and organize them. To send your file to an ASCII text file, use /Print File to print the file to disk.

- Before you issue /File Combine, move the cell pointer to the upper left corner of the range in which the data will be combined.

Procedures

1. Type **/fc**

2. Select one of the following choices:

Menu Item	Description
Copy	Copies incoming cell contents over the cells in the current worksheet. Cells in the current worksheet that correspond to blank incoming cells do not change. Labels and formulas in the current worksheet are replaced.
Add	Adds values from cells in the file worksheet to cells containing blanks or values in the current worksheet. Labels and formulas in the current worksheet are not changed.
Subtract	Subtracts values from cells in the file worksheet from the corresponding blanks or values in the current worksheet. Labels and formulas in the current worksheet are not changed.

3. Select how much of the saved worksheet file you want to use:

Menu Item	Description
Entire-File	Combines the entire file worksheet with the current worksheet. Use when the file worksheet has been created with /File Xtract and contains only raw data.
Named/ Specified-Range	Combines information from a named range or address on the file worksheet into the current worksheet. Use when the file worksheet is a full worksheet that contains information other than the information being combined.

4. If you select Entire-File, choose a file name from the menu by pressing the right- or left-arrow key, by typing the file name, or by pressing Name (F3) to display a list of file names and then using the arrow keys to select the file. Press Enter. If you select Named/Specified-Range, you are asked to enter the range name (or the coordinates of the range address) and the file name.

Important Cues

RELEASE
2.2

- If you will frequently combine a small portion from a file, first give that portion a range name. Use **/Range Name** to name the portion of the file and save the file back to disk.

- In Release 2.2, you can consolidate data by creating a formula that refers to other worksheet files. You may want to use this linking technique rather than /fc because the former doesn't require you to incorporate the data each time the data changes in one of the worksheets.

- /fcc combines values, labels, and formulas. All cell references, relative and absolute, are adjusted to reflect their new locations on the worksheet. Cell references are adjusted according to the upper left corner of the combined data range (the cell-pointer location). Combined formulas adjust for the difference between the cell pointer and cell A1 on the current worksheet.

- When creating worksheets, you can save time by using **/File Xtract** and **/File Combine** to merge parts of existing worksheets to form the new one.

- Use /fcc to copy sections of a macro file to your worksheet so that you don't have to type the macros on every new worksheet. Keep your favorite macros in one worksheet; be sure to give each macro a range name and an address that includes all the macro's code and documentation. You can use /fcc to copy the macro into the new worksheet, but you need to use **/Range Name Create** or **/Range Name Label** to rename the macro on the new worksheet.

- When you use **/File Combine Add**, cells in the incoming file that contain labels or string formulas are not added.

- Use **/File Combine Subtract** to subtract the values in the incoming worksheet from the values in the current worksheet. When an existing cell is empty, the incoming value is subtracted from zero.

- Create a macro with **/File Combine** to consolidate worksheets.

Cautions

- Data copied into the current worksheet replaces existing data. Blank cells in the incoming worksheet do not overwrite the contents of the cells in the current worksheet.

- Range names are not brought to the new worksheet when a file is combined. This arrangement prevents possible conflicts with range names in the current worksheet. After combining files, you must re-create range names with **/R**ange Name Create or **/R**ange Name Label.

For more information, see **/Range Name Create**, **/Range Name Label**, **/File Xtract**, *and Chapter 7.*

File Xtract /FX

Purpose

Saves to disk a portion of the current worksheet as a separate worksheet.

You can save the portion as it appears on the worksheet (with formulas) or save only the results of the formulas (values).

Reminder

Position the cursor at the upper left corner of the range you want to extract before you start the **/F**ile Extract command.

Procedures

1. Type **/fx**

2. Choose one of the following:

Menu Item	Description
Formulas	Saves as a new worksheet both the formulas and cell contents from the current worksheet
Values	Saves as a new worksheet labels and the results from formulas

3. Specify a file name other than that of the current worksheet. If you want to overwrite the data in a particular file, select that file name from the menu.

4. Highlight the range of the worksheet to be extracted as a separate file. Enter the range by typing the range address (such as B23..D46), by typing the range name, or by moving the cell pointer to the opposite corner of the range.

5. Press Enter.

6. If the name selected in Step 3 already exists, choose one of the following:

Menu Item	Description
Cancel	Cancels the extract operation
Replace	Replaces the existing file with the extract range you specified

RELEASE
2.2

Backup   Saves the extracted range under the name specified in Step 3; renames the existing file with the extension .BAK

Important Cues

- If you used /fxf to save a portion of a worksheet, the extracted file can function as a normal worksheet.

- To freeze a worksheet so that formulas and results don't change, extract a file with **/F**ile **X**tract **V**alues. When you retrieve the file, the formulas are replaced with values. Use this option when you extract "actual" data.

- Use **/F**ile **X**tract to save memory when a worksheet becomes too large. Separate the worksheet into smaller worksheets that require less memory.

- Increase worksheet execution speed and save memory by breaking large worksheets into smaller ones with **/F**ile **X**tract **F**ormulas.

Caution

Make sure that the extracted worksheet does not use values or formulas outside the extract range.

*For more information, see **/F**ile **C**ombine and Chapter 7.*

File Erase   /FE

Purpose

Erases 1-2-3 files from disk.

Use /fe to erase unnecessary files from disk so that you have more available disk space.

Reminders

- Use the operating system's ERASE or DEL command to remove a large number of files. From within 1-2-3, select the **/S**ystem command, use ERASE or DEL at the system prompt, and return to 1-2-3 by typing **EXIT** and pressing Enter.

- Before you use /fe, use **/F**ile **D**irectory to specify the drive designation and the directory that contains the file(s) you want to erase.

- Deleted files cannot be recovered (undeleted) using 1-2-3 or DOS.

Procedures

1. Type **/fe**

2. Select the type of file you want to erase:

Menu Item	Description
Worksheet	Displays worksheet files with .WK? extensions
Print	Displays ASCII text files created with **/P**rint or another program. The file extension must be .PRN.
Graph	Displays files created with **/G**raph, which end with the extension .PIC
Other	Displays all files in the current drive and directory

3. Type the path and the name of the file, or use the arrow keys to highlight the file you want to erase.

4. Press Enter.

5. By selecting **Yes** or **No** from the menu, verify that you do or do not want to erase the file.

Important Cues

- You can erase files from different drives or directories either by specifying the drive designation, path, and file name or by changing the settings with **/F**ile **D**irectory.

- If you are using Release 2.2 on a network, you cannot erase a file reserved by a user. Also, you cannot erase files assigned the read-only attribute by DOS.

For more information, see **/File Directory**, **/File List**, *and Chapter 7.*

RELEASE
2.2

File List   /FL

Purpose

Displays all file names of a specific type that are stored on the current drive and directory.

Lists the files that are referenced in (linked to) formulas in the current file (Release 2.2 only).

/fl displays the size of the file (in bytes) and the date and time the file was created.

RELEASE
2.2

Reminder

Use **/F**ile **L**ist to select different directories and display the current files.

Procedures

1. Type **/fl**

2. Select the type of file you want to display:

Menu Item	Description
Worksheet	Displays worksheet files with .WK? extensions
Print	Displays ASCII text files created with /**P**rint or another program. The file extension must be .PRN.
Graph	Displays files created with /**G**raph, which end with the extension .PIC
Other	Displays all files in the current drive and directory
Linked	Displays all worksheet files linked to the current file by formulas

3. Use the arrow keys to highlight individual file names. If the list of file names extends off the screen, use the arrow keys, PgDn, or PgUp to display the file names.

4. Display files from a different directory by moving the cursor to a directory name (such as \BUDGET) and pressing Enter.

5. Press Enter to return to the worksheet.

Important Cues

- Before you use /**F**ile **E**rase, use /fl to check your file listing.

- 1-2-3 displays the date and time each file was created or last updated so that you can find the most recent version of a file. (Date and time values are accurate only if you supply the correct entries at start-up. The computer's date and time values can be reset at the system prompt through the DATE and TIME commands.)

- To create a permanent list of files directly in your worksheet, use /**F**ile **A**dmin **T**able (Release 2.2 only).

*For more information, see /**File Erase**, /**File Directory**, /**File Admin Table**, and Chapter 7.*

File Import   */FI*

Purpose

Brings ASCII text files from other programs into 1-2-3 worksheets.

Many software programs use ASCII files to exchange data with other programs. Most databases, word processors, and spreadsheets have a method of printing ASCII files to disk.

Reminders

- Remember that you can use /File Import two different ways to transfer data into a 1-2-3 worksheet. The first method reads each row of ASCII characters as left-aligned labels in a column; the second method reads into separate cells text enclosed in quotation marks, or numbers surrounded by spaces or separated by commas.

- Be sure that you have enough room on the worksheet to receive the imported data; incoming characters replace the current cell contents. One row in an ASCII file is equal to one row in the worksheet. The number of columns depends on whether the incoming ASCII data is pure text (a single column) or delimited text (multiple columns).

- Before you issue /fi, move the cursor to the upper left corner of the range in which you want to import data.

Procedures

1. Type **/fi**

2. Choose how to import the ASCII file:

Menu Item	Description
Text	Makes each row of characters in the ASCII file a left-aligned label in the worksheet. Labels will be in a single column from the cell pointer down.
Numbers	Enters each row of characters in the ASCII file into a row in the worksheet. Text enclosed in quotation marks is assigned to a cell as a label. Numbers surrounded by a space or separated by commas are assigned to a cell as values. Other characters are ignored. Only numbers are imported if the input file is nondelimited.

3. Select or type the name of the ASCII print file. Do not type the .PRN extension.

4. Press Enter.

Important Cues

- By default, only files that have a .PRN extension are listed. You can list other files, however, by typing *. with the desired extension and pressing Enter. You also can type the complete file name, including the extension.

- 1-2-3 cannot import ASCII files that have more than 8,192 rows or more than 240 characters per row. If necessary, you can use a word processor to read, modify, and divide the ASCII files into smaller files before saving them to disk as ASCII files.

- Display ASCII files by using the operating system's TYPE command.

- You can print the ASCII file by pressing Ctrl-P before issuing the operating system's TYPE command or by using the following command:

   TYPE   *<filename.ext>*   **PRN**

   To disconnect the printer, press Ctrl-P again when printing is complete.

- You can separate ASCII text files that are not delimited by quotation marks or commas. Use **/File I**mport **T**ext to bring the file into the worksheet. Use **/D**ata **P**arse to separate the resulting long label into separate cells of data.

Cautions

- Incoming data replaces existing cell contents. If you are unsure of the size of the file you are importing, use the operating system's TYPE command to review the ASCII file.

- Word processing files contain special control codes that 1-2-3 cannot handle. Be sure to save your word processing document as an ASCII file before you try to import it into 1-2-3.

For more information, see **/Data Parse** *and Chapter 7.*

File Directory   /FD

Purpose

Changes the current disk drive or directory for the current work session.

Reminder

Sketching how your directories and subdirectories are arranged on your hard disk makes /fd easier to use. Include the types of files stored in different directories. The DOS TREE command or other utility programs are useful for managing your hard disk layout.

Procedures

1. Type **/fd**

2. If the displayed drive and directory are correct, press Enter. If you want to change the settings, type a new drive letter and directory name; then press Enter.

Important Cues

- Access another drive and directory temporarily by selecting /fr or /fs and pressing Esc twice to clear the current drive and directory from the command line. (If you want to access another directory on the same drive, press the Backspace key as many times as necessary to clear the current directory from the command line.) Then type the drive designator and directory name, including a final backslash (\ ). Then either type a file name or press Enter to see a list of file names on that drive or directory; move the cursor and press Enter to select a name from the list.

- Display current file names and directories by selecting /File List, choosing Other, and pressing Name (F3). Press Backspace to go to the parent directory.

- You can change 1-2-3's start-up drive and directory by using /Worksheet Global Default Directory to enter a new drive or directory. Save this new setting to the System disk by using /wgdu.

Caution

When specifying drive letters and path names, be sure to enter the correct symbols. The most common mistakes include using a semicolon (;) instead of a colon (:) after the drive designator, using a slash (/) instead of a backslash (\ ) between subdirectory names, and inserting spaces in names.

For more information, see **/Worksheet Global Default Update**, **/File List**, **/File Retrieve**, *and* **/File Save**.

File Admin Reservation   /FAR

RELEASE
2.2

Purpose

Controls the reservation status of a file. If more than one person has access to a file in a network, /File Admin Reservation controls how the file is shared and who can change and save the file.

Reminders

- On a multiuser system, more than one person can look at the same file simultaneously, but only one person can save changes. The person who can save changes has the file reservation.

- By default, the first person who retrieves or opens the file gets the reservation.

Procedures

1. Type **/far**

2. Choose one of the following commands:

Menu Item	Description
Get	Gets the reservation for the current file so that you can save changes. For this option to be operable, no other users can already have the reservation.

Release	Releases the reservation for the current file so that others can save changes.

Important Cue

If you do not have the file reservation, the indicator RO (for "read only") appears on the status line at the bottom of the screen.

Caution

If you do not have the file reservation, do not make changes: you will not be able to save them.

For more information, see Chapter 7.

File Admin Table   /FAT

Purpose

Creates a table of disk files that includes the files' sizes and the dates and times the files were last modified.

Creates a list of files linked to the current file.

Reminder

Place the cell pointer in a blank area of the worksheet before you use /fat.

Procedures

1. Type **/fat**

2. Choose one of the following commands:

Menu Item	Description
Worksheet	Enters a table of worksheet (.WK*) files
Print	Enters a table of .PRN files
Graph	Enters a table of .PIC graph files
Other	Enters a table of all files in the current drive and directory
Linked	Enters a table of files linked by formulas to the current file

Important Cues

- You may need to change some of the column widths in the table to see the complete display of table information.

- The date and time information appears as serial numbers until the cells are assigned particular **D**ate and **T**ime formats.

Caution

If you do not have enough blank space for the table, information in the table will overwrite information in the worksheet.

For more information, see Chapter 7.

File Admin Link-Refresh   */FAL*

RELEASE
2.2

Purpose

Recalculates, in the current file, formulas that depend on data in files on disk. This command ensures that your formulas reflect the most current data.

Procedures

1. Type **/fal**

For more information, see Chapter 7.

Print Commands /P

These commands print worksheet contents as values or formulas.

Use /pp to send output to the printer; use /pf to send output (as an ASCII file) to disk.

The following menu map shows the **/P**rint commands. **N**one, a command new with Release 2.2, is highlighted.

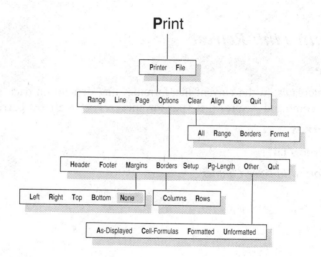

Print Printer /PP

Purpose

Prints worksheet contents (values or formulas) to the printer.

Reminders

- Before you print, check the lower right corner of the screen to see whether the CALC indicator is displayed. If it is, press Calc (F9) and wait until the WAIT indicator stops flashing before you proceed with the **/P**rint commands.

- Graphs cannot be printed from the **P**rint menu. Use the PrintGraph program or (if you are using Release 2.2) Allways to print graphs.

- Before you issue /pp, move the cell pointer to the upper left corner of the range to be printed.

Procedures

1. Type **/pp**

2. Select **R**ange.

3. Type the range address, highlight the range, or enter a range name to specify the range to be printed.

4. Select from the other print options explained in the **/P**rint commands section.

5. Select **A**lign to align the printer and the top of the paper.

6. Select **G**o.

Important Cues

- You can use 1-2-3's **/P**rint commands to set formats for your reports. Use commands from **/P**rint Printer Options to control formats for printing.

- Print an ASCII text file to disk by using **/P**rint File. Most popular software programs, including word processing and database programs, can import ASCII text files.

Cautions

- Because 1-2-3 keeps track of the number of printed lines, the program's line count may be incorrect if you adjust the paper manually. Adjusting the page by hand could cause the information to be printed off to one side or could leave blank spaces in the middle of the page.

- Printers often retain the last control code specified. To cancel the control code, turn off the printer, wait 15 seconds, and turn the printer back on. You also can correct the problem by inserting a reset printer control code at the beginning of every setup string. Using the setup string is less demanding to the printer's electronics.

For more information, see /Print File, /Print [Printer, File] Range, and Chapter 8.

Print File   /PF

Purpose

Prints worksheet contents as an ASCII text file to disk.

ASCII text files are a common means of transferring data to and from different software packages.

Reminders

- Before you print the file, check the lower right corner of the screen to see whether the CALC indicator is displayed. If it is, press Calc (F9) and wait until the WAIT indicator stops flashing before you proceed with the **/Print** commands.

- Before you issue /pf, it is a good practice to move the cell pointer to the upper left corner of the range to be printed.

Procedures

1. Type **/pf**

2. Respond to the following screen prompt:

   Enter name of text file:

   Limit the file name to eight characters (don't use spaces). 1-2-3 automatically gives the file name a .PRN extension.

3. Select **R**ange.

4. Type the range address, highlight the range, or use a range name to specify the range to be printed to disk. Press Enter.

5. Select **O**ptions **M**argins. Set the top, left, and bottom margins to zero; set the right margin to 240. If you're using Release 2.2, select **N**one to eliminate margins.

6. Select **O**ther **U**nformatted to remove headers, footers, and page breaks. (These print options can cause extra work in reformatting when the file is imported by another program.)

7. Select **G**o from the second-level **P**rint menu.

Important Cues

- To see an ASCII text file on-screen, return to the operating system. At the operating-system prompt, type the command **TYPE**, press the space bar, and type the path name and the name of the ASCII text file you want to review. For example, after the prompt (C>), you could enter

   TYPE C:\123\BUDGET\VARIANCE.PRN

   Press Ctrl-S to stop the data from scrolling off the screen. Press the space bar to continue scrolling.

- Before you print the file to disk, make sure that the columns are wide enough to display all the data. If a column is too narrow, values are changed to asterisks, and labels are truncated.

- Refer to your word processor's documentation for instructions on importing ASCII files.

Cautions

- Different database programs accept data in different formats; check to see in what form dates are imported and whether the receiving program accepts blank cells. Be sure to prepare your 1-2-3 file accordingly before printing to an ASCII file. As a general rule, remove numeric formats and align labels to the left before you print the data to disk.

- If the right margin setting is too narrow, data may be truncated when the file is printed to disk.

For more information, see /Print Printer, /Print [Printer, File] Range, and Chapter 8.

Print [Printer, File] Range   /PPR or /PFR

Purpose

Defines the area of the worksheet to be printed.

Reminders

- Check the lower right corner of the screen to see whether the CALC indicator is displayed. If it is, press Calc (F9) and wait until the WAIT indicator stops flashing before you proceed with the /Print commands.

- Graphs cannot be printed from the Print menus. Use the PrintGraph program or (if you are using Release 2.2) Allways to print graphs.

- Before you print, move the cell pointer to the upper left corner of the range to be printed.

Procedures

1. Type **/pp** to print directly to the printer; type **/pf** to print to disk. Specify a file name.

2. Select **R**ange.

3. Type the range address, highlight the range, or enter an assigned range name to specify the range to be printed.

4. Press Enter.

Important Cues

- If you save the file, **/P**rint [**P, F**] **R**ange "remembers" the last print range used, which means that you can reprint the specified worksheet portion without reentering the range. To change the existing print range, press Esc when 1-2-3 displays the print range. Move the cell pointer to the upper left corner of the area you want to print; type a period (.) to anchor that corner of the print range. Next, move the cell pointer to the lower right corner of the print range and press Enter.

- To display the current print range, select **/Print Printer Range**. The second line of the control panel displays the current range address, and the specified range is highlighted on the screen.

- To display each corner of the range, press the period key (.). Each time you press the period key, the next corner is displayed.

- Use **/Print [P, F] Options Borders** to print a specified worksheet row or column at the top or side of every printed page. Use this technique, for example, when you want to print database field names at the top of every page.

- Use **/Worksheet Page** to insert mandatory page breaks in a range.

- After a range has been printed, 1-2-3 does not advance the paper to the top of the next page. Instead, 1-2-3 waits for you to print another range. To advance the paper, use **/Print Printer Page**.

- If the print range is wider than the distance between the left and right margins, the remaining characters are printed on the following page (if printed to paper) or in the rows below the data (if printed to disk).

Caution

Data outside the highlighted area will not be printed. If text in column I spreads across columns J and K, for example, you must include columns J and K in the print range. Figure P.1 shows in rows 3 to 10 the incorrect way to highlight text. The unhighlighted text in rows 8 and 9 will not be printed. All the text highlighted in the figure P.1 is stored in column B. To highlight this material correctly for printing, use the range B3..G10.

Fig. P.1.
The incorrect way to highlight text.

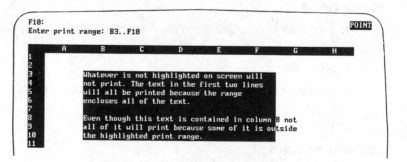

For more information, see **/Worksheet Page**, **/Print Printer**, **/Print File**, *and Chapter 8.*

Print [Printer, File] Line   /PPL or /PFL

Purpose

/Print **Printer** Line controls printer paper handling from within 1-2-3 by advancing the paper one line. If the printhead is at the bottom of a page, the printhead moves to the top of the next page.

/Print **File** Line puts a blank line in a .PRN file.

Reminder

Remember that you cannot print graphs from the **Print** menu. Use the Print-Graph program or (if you are using Release 2.2) Allways to print graphs.

Procedures

1. Type **/pp** (or **/pf**)

2. Select **Line** to advance the paper one line or to insert a blank line in a file. Repeat the keystroke (or press Enter) as many times as necessary to advance the paper to the desired position.

Important Cue

Use this command to insert a blank line between printed ranges. You can get paper out of alignment with 1-2-3's internal line count if you change the position of paper in a printer manually (either by turning the platen knob or by pressing the printer's line feed button). Blank lines in the middle of your printed output can signify that the printer and 1-2-3 are out of alignment. To realign the paper and reset 1-2-3, turn off the printer and roll the paper until the top of a page is aligned with the printhead. Then turn on the printer again and use **/Print Printer Align** to reset 1-2-3.

Print [Printer, File] Page   /PPP or /PFP

Purpose

/Print **Printer** Page controls the paper feed from within 1-2-3 by moving the paper to the bottom of the page and printing any footer and then by advancing the paper farther until the printhead is at the top of the next page.

/Print **File** Page provides a footer and blank lines for a .PRN file.

Reminders

- All **/Print** commands apply when output is printed directly to paper or to a disk file.

- Use **/Worksheet Page** to create a page break in a worksheet. When you print the worksheet, a new page will begin at the page break.

Procedures

1. Type **/pp** (or **/pf**)

2. Select **P**age to advance to the next page and print the footer at the bottom of the page.

Important Cue

If the top of the paper is not in line with the printhead when the paper is advanced, manually move the paper into position and reset 1-2-3 with **/P**rint **P**rinter **A**lign.

Cautions

- The length of the printed page may not match the length of the paper. Check the paper-length settings with **/P**rint **P**rinter **O**ptions **P**g-Length. This problem also occurs when the page-length setting does not match the number-of-lines-per-inch setting. Use **/P**rint **P**rinter **O**ptions **S**etup to change the number of lines per inch to be printed.

- The paper in the printer can get out of alignment if you manually advance the paper to the top of the next page. To realign the paper and reset 1-2-3, turn off the printer and roll the paper until the top of a page is aligned with the printhead. Then turn on the printer again and use **/P**rint **P**rinter **A**lign to reset 1-2-3.

Print [Printer, File] Options Header   /PPOH or /PFOH

Purpose

Prints a header below the top margin on each page. Use the **H**eader option to print page numbers and dates in the heading. Two blank lines are inserted after the header.

Reminders

- Use **/P**rint [**P**, **F**] **O**ptions **B**orders to print column headings above data.

- A header uses the three lines below the top margin.

Procedures

1. Type **/ppo** to print to paper; type **/pfo** to print to disk.

2. Select **H**eader.

3. Type a header as wide as the margin and paper widths allow. The header can be up to 240 characters wide.

4. Press Enter.

Important Cues

- The date and page number can be printed automatically in a header. Enter an "at" sign (@) where you want the date to appear; enter a number sign (#) where you want the page number. The # causes page numbering to begin with 1 and increase by 1 sequentially.

- If the header text is contained in a spreadsheet cell, you can refer to that cell in the header by preceding the cell coordinate with a backslash—for example, type **\A1** for a header contained in cell A1.

  RELEASE
  2.2

- Break the header into as many as three centered segments by entering a vertical bar (|) between segments. For example, to print at page 21 a three-segment header that uses the computer's internal date of October 30, 1989, enter the following:

  @|**Hill and Dale Landscaping**|**Page #**

  The header appears as this:

  ```
  30-Oct-89   Hill and Dale Landscaping    Page 21
  ```

- To print a single page with a page number higher than 1, omit the # and specify the page number.

- Use **/P**rint [**P, F**] **O**ptions **B**orders **R**ows to select worksheet rows that will be printed above the data on each page. The **B**orders command is especially useful for printing database column headings above the data on each page.

- Print an extra header line at the top of the first printed page by using a "false" setup string, which consists of the Escape code followed by your text. For EPSON-compatible printers, an example of such a string is

  ```
  \027"This is a second line."
  ```

- Depending on the first letter in the header, the printer may read the letter as part of the setup string. The printer may thus begin printing in a different mode. If, for example, you wanted to type the phrase **Enter new page** after the Escape code, your printer may interpret the E as the code for enhanced mode. To solve this problem, enclose the header in quotation marks.

- In Release 2.2, the current header is displayed in the Print Settings sheet. This sheet is displayed when you choose **/P**rint [Printer, File].

  RELEASE
  2.2

Caution

Headers longer than margin settings print on the following page.

For more information, see /Print [Printer, File] Options Margins, /Print [Printer, File] Options Borders, and /Print [Printer, File] Options Setup.

Print [Printer, File] Options Footer   */PPOF or /PFOF*

Purpose

Prints a footer above the bottom margin of each page.

Reminders

- Use **/Print [P, F] O**ptions **F**ooter to print, for example, a title, department heading, or identifier. Footers can be used to print page numbers and dates automatically.

- Footers print above the bottom margin. Two blank lines automatically separate the text from the footer.

Procedures

1. Type **/ppo** to print to paper; type **/pfo** to print to disk.

2. Select **F**ooter.

3. You can type a footer that is as wide as the margin and paper widths allow. The footer can be up to 240 characters wide.

4. Press Enter.

Important Cues

RELEASE
2.2

- The footer will not print on the last page (or on the first page if the range is less than a page) unless you choose the **/P**rint **P**rinter **P**age command to feed the paper out.

- The date and page number can be printed automatically in the footer. Enter in the header an "at" sign (@) where you want the date to appear and a number sign (#) where you want the page number. The # causes page numbering to begin with 1 and increase by 1 sequentially.

RELEASE
2.2

- If the footer text is contained in a worksheet cell, you can refer to that cell in the footer by preceding the cell coordinate with a backslash—for example, type **\A1** for a footer contained in cell A1.

- Break the footer into as many as three centered segments by entering a vertical bar (|). To print at page 21 a three-segment footer with a system date of October 30, 1989, for example, enter the following:

  @|Hill and Dale Landscaping|Page #

  The footer appears as this:

  ```
  30-Oct-89  Hill and Dale Landscaping  Page 21
  ```

- Placing one vertical bar to the left of header data centers the data; including no vertical bars left-justifies the data; placing two vertical bars to the left of header data right-justifies the data. To right-justify the page number, enter this:

  ‖**Page #**

- To print a single page whose page number is higher than 1, omit the # and specify the page number.

- In Release 2.2, the current footer is displayed in the Print Settings sheet, which is displayed when you choose **/**Print [**Printer**, **File**].

Footers longer than margin settings will be printed on the following page.

RELEASE

2.2

For more information, see **/Print [Printer, File] Options Header,** **/Print [Printer, File] Options Margins,** **/Print [Printer, File] Options Borders,** *and* **/Print [Printer, File] Options Setup.**

Print [Printer, File] Options Margins /PPOM or /PFOM

Purpose

Changes the left, right, top, and bottom margins. Use /ppom and /pfom to adjust the appearance of the printed page by changing the size of the printed area.

Reminders

- Determine whether you need to use printer setup strings to change the number of characters per inch or lines per inch printed by the printer.

- Turn the printer off and on to reposition the printhead to the zero position. Adjust the paper so that the left edge aligns with the printhead at the zero position. If you always align the paper at this position, printed margins will be consistent.

Procedures

1. Type **/ppo** to print to paper; type **/pfo** to print to disk.

2. Select Margins. Specify margins from these options:

Menu Item	Description
Left	Sets 0 to 240 characters. If you are printing to disk, set to 0.
Right	Sets greater than the left margin but not larger than 240. If you are printing to disk, set to 240.
Top	Sets 0 to 32 lines. If you are printing to disk, set to 0.

Bottom	Sets 0 to 32 lines. If you are printing to disk, set to 0.
None	Clears all margin settings; sets the left, top, and bottom margins to 0 and the right margin to 240

RELEASE
2.2

Important Cues

- If you change print pitch by using printer setup strings, be sure to change the right, top, and bottom margins. For example, if you use a printer setup string to print in compressed mode on 8-inch paper, reset the right margin from 74 to approximately 130.

- Most printers print at 10 characters per horizontal inch and 6 lines per vertical inch. Standard 8 1/2-by-11-inch paper is 85 characters wide and 66 lines long.

RELEASE
2.2

- When you want to print to disk, remember that you should set the left margin to 0 and the right margin to 240. These settings remove blank spaces on the left side of each row. Setting the right margin to 240 ensures that the maximum number of characters per row will be printed to disk. If you are using Release 2.2, select **/Print File Options Margins None** to set these margins.

- Before printing to disk, select **/Print [Printer, File] Options Other Unformat-ted** to remove page breaks, headers, and footers. Page breaks, headers, and footers will confuse data transfer to a database. If you are importing the file to a word processor, use the word processor to insert margins, page breaks, headers, and footers.

RELEASE
2.2

- In Release 2.2, the current margins are displayed in the Print Settings sheet. This sheet is displayed when you choose **/Print [Printer, File]**.

Caution

If the line length is too short for the characters in a printed line, the additional characters are printed on the following line or page. To get a full-width print, use a condensed print setup string.

For more information, see **/Print File**, **/Print [Printer, File] Options Setup**, *and Chapter 8.*

Print [Printer, File] Options Borders   /PPOB or /PFOB

Purpose

Prints row or column headings from the worksheet on every page of the printout.

Use /ppob and /pfob to print database field names as column headings at the top of each printed page.

Reminders

- Before you issue /ppob or /pfob, move the cell pointer to the leftmost column or to the topmost row that you want to use as a header.

- In addition to the border rows you select, only the columns included in the print range will be printed.

- Similarly, in addition to the border columns you select, only the rows included in the print range will be printed.

Procedures

1. Type **/ppob** to print to paper; type **/pfob** to print to disk.

2. Select from these menu items:

Menu Item	Description
Columns	Prints the selected columns at the left side of each page
Rows	Prints the selected rows at the top of each page

3. Press Esc to remove the current range. Move the cell pointer to the top row of the rows you want to use as a border or to the leftmost column you want to use. Press the period key (.) to anchor the first corner of the border. Then move the cell pointer, highlighting down for more rows or to the right for more columns.

4. Press Enter.

Important Cues

- Including borders is useful when you want to print multiple pages. If you want to print sections of a wide worksheet, you can further condense the columns by using **/W**orksheet Column **H**ide to hide blank or unnecessary columns.

- In Release 2.2, the current border ranges are displayed in the Print Settings sheet. This sheet is displayed when you choose **/P**rint [**Printer, File**].

RELEASE
2.2

Cautions

- If you include in the print range the rows or columns specified as borders, the rows or columns will be printed twice.

- When you use **/P**rint [**P, F**] **O**ptions **B**orders **C**olumns or **R**ows and press Enter, the cell pointer's current location becomes a border automatically. To clear the border selection, use **/P**rint [**P, F**] **C**lear **B**orders.

Print [Printer, File] Options Setup /PPOS or /PFOS

Purpose

Controls, from within 1-2-3, the advanced printing features offered by some printers.

Advanced printing features include different character sets, different-sized characters, bold characters, near-letter-quality print, and proportional spacing. Printer control codes entered in setup strings apply to the entire print range.

Reminders

- Your printer manual contains lists of printer setup codes (also known as *printer control codes* or *escape codes*). These codes may be shown two ways: as a decimal ASCII number representing a keyboard character, or as the Esc key followed by a character.

- 1-2-3 setup strings include decimal number codes (entered as three-digit numbers) preceded by a backslash (\ ). For example, the EPSON printer control code for condensed print is 15. The corresponding 1-2-3 setup string is \015.

- Some codes start with the Esc character, followed by other characters. Because the Esc character cannot be typed in the setup string, the ASCII decimal number for Esc (27) is used instead. For example, the EPSON printer code for emphasized print is Esc "E". In the 1-2-3 setup string, enter Esc "E" as \027E.

- Some printers retain previous control codes. Before sending a new code to the printer, clear the previous codes by turning your printer off and then on. You also can send the printer a reset code (\027@ for EPSON-compatible printers). Put the reset code in front of the new code you send. For example, the 1-2-3 printer setup string that resets previous codes and switches to emphasized printing mode is \027@\027E.

Procedures

1. Type **/ppos** or **/pfos**

2. Enter the setup string. If a setup string has already been entered, press Esc to clear the string. Each string must begin with a backslash (\ ). Upper- or lowercase letters must be typed as shown in your printer's manual.

3. Press Enter.

Important Cues

RELEASE
2.2

- In Release 2.2, many special print features are available with the add-in program Allways. This program enables you to change fonts, add lines and shading, and specify the page orientation—without having to enter setup strings.

- Setup strings can be up to 39 characters long. You may be able to create longer setup strings by following these steps:

  1. Enter the first setup string and print only one line of the print range.

  2. Realign the paper to the next top of form.

  3. Clear the previous setup string and enter the remaining setup string. Print the complete print range.

  The printer will "remember" the first string and combine it with the second string. Do not use a printer reset code before you enter the second string.

- If you change character size, change the right margin setting with /Print [Printer, File] Options Margins Right.

- You cannot combine some character sets or print modes. Your printer manual may list combinations that will work for your printer.

- Use embedded setup strings in the print range to change printing features by row. Move the cell pointer to the leftmost cell in the print range row where you want the printing to change. Insert a row with /Worksheet Insert Row. Type two vertical bars and then type the appropriate setup string. Note that only one vertical bar displays.

- When reading setup strings from the printer manual, don't confuse zero (0) with the letter O, or one (1) with the letter l.

- If you get the same several nonsense characters at the top of every printed page, you probably have those nonsense characters in your setup string.

- In Release 2.2, the current setup string is displayed in the Print Settings sheet. This sheet is displayed when you choose /Print [Printer, File].

RELEASE 2.2

Caution

Some printers retain the most recent printer control code. Clear the last code by turning off the printer for approximately five seconds or by preceding each setup string with the printer reset code. The reset code for EPSON-compatible printers is \027@.

For more information, see /Print [Printer, File] Options Margins and Chapter 8.

Print [Printer, File] Options Pg-Length /PPOP or /PFOP

Purpose

Specifies the number of lines per page.

The page-length setting and the top- and bottom-margin settings determine the height of the page's printed area. These settings also indicate where the printer should advance the paper to allow for continuous-feed paper perforations.

Reminders

- Check the size of the paper you are using.

- Check whether the setup string you are using changes the number of lines printed per inch.

- Check the number of lines your printer can print on a page. Laser printers cannot print on the top half-inch and bottom half-inch of the page.

Procedures

1. Type **/ppop** to print to paper; type **/pfop** to print to disk.

2. Enter the number of lines per page if that number is different from the number shown. The page length can be 1 to 100 lines.

3. Press Enter.

Important Cues

- Most printers print 6 lines per inch unless the ratio is changed with a setup string (printer control code). At 6 lines per inch, 11-inch paper has 66 lines, and 14-inch paper has 84 lines.

- The actual number of printable lines on the default 66-line page is 56. The top and bottom margins take up 4 lines, and 6 lines are reserved for the header and footer, regardless of whether you use them.

- Use **/W**orksheet **G**lobal **D**efault **P**rinter **Pg**-Length to change your default page length to 60 if you are using a laser printer.

- In Release 2.2, the current page length is displayed in the Print Settings sheet. This sheet is displayed when you choose **/P**rint [**P**rinter, **F**ile].

- To print short page lengths, increase the top and bottom margins; do not change the page length.

For more information, see **/Print [Printer, File] Options Margins** *and* **/Print [Printer, File] Options Setup**.

RELEASE
2.2

RELEASE
2.2

Print [Printer, File] Options Other   /PPOO or /PFOO

Purpose

Selects the form and formatting in which cells print.

Worksheet contents can be printed as displayed on-screen or as formulas. You can print either option with or without formatting features.

Reminders

- **A**s-Displayed (the default setting) is used with **F**ormatted for printing reports and data.

- Use Cell-Formulas with Formatted to show formulas and cell contents. (Cell-Formulas is often used for documentation.)

- To print to disk the data to be used in a word processor or database, choose As-Displayed with Unformatted. If you are printing to disk (creating an ASCII file to export to a word processor or database), set the left, top, and bottom margins to 0 and the right margin to 240.

Procedures

1. Type **/ppoo** to print to paper; type **/pfoo** to print to disk.

2. Select the type of print from these options:

Menu Item	Description
As-Displayed	Prints the range as displayed on-screen. This is the default setting.
Cell-Formulas	Prints the formula, label, or value contents of each cell on one line of the printout. Contents match information that appears in the control panel: address, protection status, cell format, formula or value, and annotation.

3. The Options menu reappears. Select Other again and choose the type of formatting from these options:

Menu Item	Description
Formatted	Prints with page breaks, headers, and footers. This default setting is normally used for printing to paper.
Unformatted	Prints without page breaks, headers, or footers. This setting is normally used for printing to disk.

4. Select Quit to exit from Options.

Important Cues

- Use Cell-Formulas to print documentation that shows the formulas and cell settings used to create the worksheet.

  The following are examples of codes that may appear in a Cell-Formulas listing:

Code	Meaning
PR	Cell protected with a /Worksheet Global Protection Enable command
U	Cell unprotected with a /Range Unprot command

F2	Fixed format to 2 decimal places, set with a **/R**ange **F**ormat **F**ixed command
C2	Currency format to 2 decimal places, set with a **/R**ange **F**ormat **C**urrency command
W10	Width of 10 characters

- Include with an archival copy of the formulas a printout of the **A**s-Displayed worksheet and a list of range names and associated addresses. **/R**ange **N**ame **T**able will automatically create a table of range name addresses.

- You usually should select **U**nformatted for printing to disk. Headers, footers, and page breaks can be added more easily with a word processor than with 1-2-3. Also, use **U**nformatted on files to be imported to databases. Databases expect to receive ASCII-file data in a consistent order, and headers and footers can disrupt that order.

RELEASE
2.2
- In Release 2.2, the current print format is displayed in the Print Settings sheet. This sheet is displayed when you choose **/P**rint [**P**rinter, **F**ile].

*For more information, see **/Print [Printer, File] Options Margins**.*

Print [Printer, File] Clear   /PPC or /PFC

Purpose

Clears print settings and options—the current print range, borders, headers, and footers—and resets all formats (margins, page length, and setup strings) to default settings.

Reminders

- The Clear option enables you to cancel all or some previous print settings quickly.

- This option is the only way to clear borders after they have been set.

Procedures

1. Type **/ppc** (or **/pfc**)

2. Choose one of the following:

Menu Item	Description
All	Clears all print options and resets all formats and setup strings to their defaults
Range	Clears only the print range specification
Borders	Cancels only columns and rows specified as borders

Format   Resets only the margins, page length, and setup
                                string formats to the default settings

Important Cue

Use the /ppc and /pfc commands in macros to cancel earlier print settings or to reestablish default settings you have specified. For example, use the **W**orksheet **G**lobal **D**efault **P**rinter menu to create as default settings the settings you use most often for margins, the page length, and the setup string. Be sure to use **/W**orksheet **G**lobal **D**efault **U**pdate to update the configuration file to make these settings the default settings for future sessions. Then when you place a **/P**rint **P**rinter **C**lear **A**ll command at the beginning of a macro (or use the command interactively), the default settings you specify will be entered automatically.

Caution

In 1-2-3, print parameters remain in effect until you give different instructions. If you want to provide a new set of parameters, use **/P**rint **P**rinter **C**lear **A**ll to ensure that you are starting from the default parameters. To change the print parameters stored with the worksheet on disk, remember to save the worksheet (use the **/F**ile **S**ave command) to disk.

Print [Printer, File] Align   */PPA or /PFA*

Purpose

Resets 1-2-3's internal line and page counter.

Reminders

- Use this command only after you have manually aligned the printhead with the top of a sheet of printer paper.

- Check the lower right corner of the screen to see whether the CALC indicator is displayed. If it is, press the Calc (F9) key, and the WAIT indicator will appear at the top of the screen. When the WAIT indicator stops flashing, proceed with the **/P**rint command.

- Remember that all **P**rint menu commands apply when output is printed directly to paper or to a disk file.

Procedures

1. Position the printer paper so that the top of a page is aligned with the printhead.

2. Type **/pp** (or **/pf**)

3. Select **A**lign to set the internal line counter to 1 and to synchronize 1-2-3 with the printer.

Cautions

- Printed pages may contain gaps (blank lines) if you do not use this command.

- Because **Align** resets the page counter, page numbers may be wrong if you use the command before a print session is completed.

For more information, see Chapter 8.

Graph Commands /G

/Graph commands control the graph's appearance and specify worksheet ranges to be used as graph data.

Store multiple graphs with /Graph Name and display them at a later time. To print a graph, use /Graph Save to create a .PIC file that you can later print with PrintGraph or (if you're using Release 2.2) Allways.

RELEASE 2.2

The following menu map shows the /Graph commands. Commands new with Release 2.2 are highlighted.

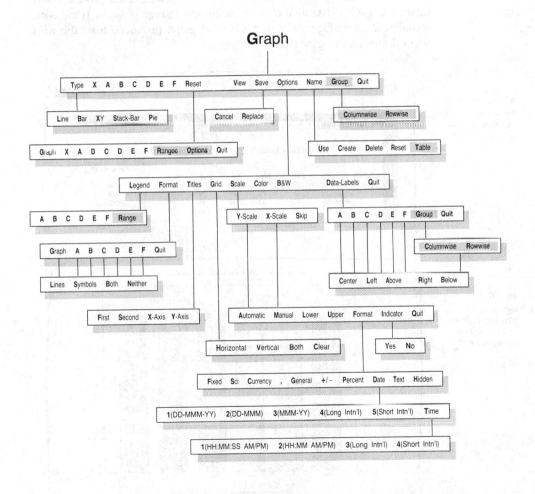

Graph Type /GT

Purpose

Selects from among the 1-2-3 graph types: line, bar, XY, stack-bar, and pie. Each type of graph is best suited for displaying and analyzing a specific type of data.

Reminders

- Before you can create a graph, you must have created a worksheet that has the same number of cells in each x- and y-axis range, similar to the one in figure G.1. Each *y* data item must be in the same range position as the corresponding *x* value. Figure G.2 shows the bar graph produced from the worksheet displayed in figure G.1.

Fig. G.1.
Worksheet with the same number of cells in each x- and y-axis range.

Fig. G.2.
Bar graph produced from the worksheet in figure G.1.

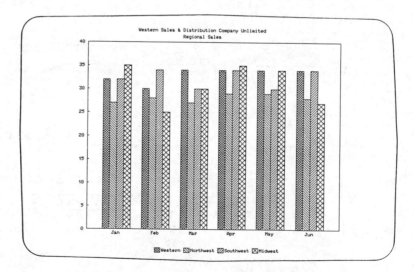

- Except for pie graphs, graphs can have on the y-axis as many as six different series of data. The **Graph** menu choices **A** through **F** are used to highlight the data series. The pie graph accepts data from only the A range.

Procedures

1. Type **/gt**

2. Select the type of graph from the following options:

Menu Item	*Description*
Line	Usually depicts a continuous series of data. The change frequently occurs over time.
Bar	Usually displays discrete data series. The x-axis often represents time.
XY	Graphs data sets of *x* and *y* data; good for plotting clusters of data. (Unlike line graphs with labels on the x-axis and data on the y-axis, XY graphs have data on both axes.) Each *x* value can have between one and six *y* values.
Stack-Bar (Stacked-Bar in Release 2.01)	Shows how proportions change within the whole. A bar can have as many as six portions.
Pie	Shows how the whole is divided into component portions. Uses only the A range to contain the values of each portion. The X range is used to label the pie wedges. 1-2-3 automatically calculates each portion's percentage from the A values.

3. After you make your selection, the **Graph** menu reappears.

4. If you have already highlighted the X range and ranges A through F to indicate the data to graph, select **View**. If you are beginning the graph, see **/Graph X A B C D E F** in this section.

Important Cues

- With 1-2-3, you can build graphs interactively. After selecting **/Graph Type** and at least one x- and y-axis range, select **View** to see the graph as it is currently defined.

- When you save the worksheet to disk, you also save the most recently specified graph type and other graph settings.

- You can shade a pie graph's wedges with eight different shadings. You can even extract wedges from the pie. Use the B range to define the shade of a pie graph wedge and to extract the wedge from the pie. (To learn how to shade the pie graph, see **/Graph X A B C D E F** in this section.)

- To print a graph, use the PrintGraph program or Release 2.2's Allways add-in.

For more information, see **/Graph X A B C D E F** *and Chapter 10.*

Graph X A B C D E F   /GX, /GA through /GF

Purpose

Specifies the worksheet ranges containing x-axis and y-axis data or labels.

Reminders

- The x-axis is the graph's horizontal (bottom) axis. The y-axis is the graph's vertical (left) axis. The labels or data assigned to the x-axis and the six possible sets of y-axis data (A through F) must have the same number of cells. To ensure that the x-axis and y-axis have an equal number of elements, place all the labels and data on adjacent rows.

- Pie graph ranges are different from those of other graph types. Pie graphs use only the A range for data. (The B range contains code numbers to control shading and the extraction of wedges from the pie.)

Procedures

1. Type **/g**

2. From the following options, select the ranges for x- or y-axis data or labels to be entered:

Menu Item	Description
X	Enters x-axis label range. These are labels such as Jan, Feb, Mar, and so on. Creates labels for pie graph wedges and line, bar, and stack-bar graphs (x-axis data range for XY graphs).
A	Enters first y-axis data range—the only data range used by a pie graph.
B	Enters second y-axis data range; enters pie graph shading values and extraction codes. (For more information, see this section's "Important Cues.")
C to F	Enters third through sixth data ranges

3. Indicate the data range by entering the range address, entering a range name, or highlighting the range. If the data range has already been entered, press Esc and enter a new range.

4. Press Enter.

Important Cues

- To ease the task of keeping track of graph data and labels, put the data and labels in labeled rows.

- You do not need to change the **Graph** menu settings when you change or update the data in the ranges. **/Graph** remembers all the settings.

- When all graph ranges are in consecutive rows and columns, use the **/Graph Group** command (Release 2.2 only) to specify all graph ranges at once.

- Use **/Graph Reset Graph** to clear all graph settings. Use **/Graph Reset** [**X** through **F**] to clear individual ranges and their associated settings.

- 1-2-3 automatically updates graphs when you input new data in the worksheet (for new data or labels in the x- and y-axis ranges). Once you have set the graphs with the **/Graph** commands, you can view new graphs from the worksheet by pressing Graph (F10). If the computer beeps and no graph appears, you have not defined that graph, or your computer does not have graphics capability.

- Pie graphs do not use the x- and y-axis title options, grids, or scales.

- Pie graphs are limited because they often have too many elements in the A range, a situation that causes wedges to be small and labels to overlap. The A range is the only data range needed for pie graphs. Enter wedge labels in the X range, as you would for line graphs.

- Use the B range to enter the numeric codes that control the color or black-and-white patterns in each wedge. On color monitors, the eight shades appear as eight different colors. Add 100 to a shading code to extract one or more wedges from the pie.

- In Release 2.2, the current graph ranges are displayed in the Graph Settings sheet.

Caution

If your graph has missing data or if the *y* values do not match the corresponding *x* positions, check to ensure that the x- and y-axis ranges have the same number of elements. The values in the *y* ranges (A through F) graph the corresponding x-range cells.

For more information, see **/Graph Type** *and Chapter 10.*

Graph Reset /GR

Purpose

Cancels all or some of a graph's settings so that you can either create a new graph or exclude from a new graph one or more data ranges from the old graph.

Reminder

The **G**raph option of this command (see "Procedures") enables you to reset all graph parameters quickly.

Procedures

1. Type **/gr**

2. Choose one of the following:

Menu Item	Description
Graph	Resets all graph parameters but does not alter a graph named with **/G**raph **N**ame **C**reate. Use this option if you want to exclude all preceding graph parameters from the new graph.
X	Resets the X range and removes the labels (but not on XY graphs)
A through F	Resets a designated range and corresponding labels so that these are not displayed in the new graph
Ranges	Resets all data ranges and all data labels
Options	Resets all settings defined by **/G**raph **O**ptions
Quit	Returns you to the **G**raph menu

RELEASE
2.2

Important Cue

Take advantage of 1-2-3's capability to remember all the parameters of a named graph until you use **/G**raph **R**eset. Use existing parameters of the named graph as a guide for creating a new graph. You may need to suppress only a few settings to create your new graph. After you are satisfied with a view of the new graph, use **/G**raph **N**ame **C**reate to save it.

Caution

If you use the name of a named graph for a new graph, the new named graph will replace the first graph, which will be lost.

For more information, see Chapter 10.

Graph View */GV*

Purpose

Displays a graph on-screen.

Reminders

- What is displayed depends on the system hardware and the system configuration.

- On a nongraphics screen, no graph displays; the computer simply beeps. Nevertheless, you can use **/Graph Save** to save the graph and then print it with the PrintGraph program or Release 2.2's Allways add-in.

- If your system has a graphics card and either a monochrome display or a color monitor, you can see a graph instead of the worksheet on the screen after you select **View**. You must select **/Graph Options Color** to see the graph in color.

- If you have a Hercules Graphics Card or a COMPAQ Video Adapter for your monochrome display, a graph will take the place of the worksheet on that screen.

- If 1-2-3 and your system are configured to use two monitors, you can see the worksheet on one screen and the graph on the other.

RELEASE

2.2

Procedures

1. Select **View** from the **Graph** menu when you are ready to see the graph you have created. The graph must be defined before you can view it.

2. Press any key to return to the **Graph** menu.

3. Select **Quit** to return to the worksheet and READY mode.

Important Cues

- You can use **/Graph View** to redraw the graph, but an easier way is to press Graph (F10) while you are in READY mode. Graph (F10) is the equivalent of **/Graph View**, but the function key enables you to view a graph after you make a change in the worksheet, without your having to return to the **Graph** menu. (Graph [F10] does not function while the **Graph** menu is visible.) If your system doesn't have two monitors and graphics cards for each, you can use Graph (F10) to toggle back and forth between the worksheet and the graph. You can therefore use Graph (F10) to do rapid "what if" analysis with graphics.

- If you want to create a series of graphs and view the series, you must use **/Graph Name** to name each graph. You can then easily create a macro that will display a whole series of graphs automatically.

• If the screen is blank after you select View, make certain that you have defined the graph adequately, that your system has graphics capability, and that 1-2-3 was installed for your particular graphics device(s). Press any key to return to the Graph menu. Then select Quit to return to the worksheet.

For more information, see Chapter 10.

Graph Save   /GS

Purpose

Saves the graph so that it can be printed with PrintGraph or Release 2.2's Allways.

/Graph Save saves a graph version that can be viewed or printed from Print-Graph or Allways. You cannot, however, edit these graph files.

Use /Graph Name Create and /File Save to save the graph's settings with the worksheet so that you can view multiple graphs.

Reminders

• Select /Graph View or press Graph (F10) to review the graph. Ensure that the graph has the correct scaling, labels, and titles.

• Check the screen's lower right corner for a CALC indicator. If CALC appears and the worksheet is still visible, press Calc (F9) to update all worksheet values before you save the graph.

• If you need to return to this graph later, use /Graph Name Create to save the graph settings; then use /File Save to save the worksheet to disk.

Procedures

1. Type /g

2. Select Save.

3. Enter a new file name, or use the right- or left-arrow key to highlight a name already on the menu bar. If you choose a name already on the menu bar, the new graph file overwrites the old graph file.

4. Press Enter.

Important Cues

• Saved graphs have .PIC file extensions. Other software programs also use .PIC file extensions, but 1-2-3 graph files are rarely compatible with other software.

• DOS file-name rules apply when you name graph files. Names must be no longer than eight characters (letters, numbers, or underlines [_]). Never use a space or a period in a file name.

- To save the file to a different drive and directory, change the current directory with **/File** Directory, or enter the drive and directory before the graph name (for example, **C:\123\cards\print.pic**).
- Use PrintGraph to view saved graphs before you print them.

Caution

If you need to save graph settings and the worksheet's graph display, name the graph with **/Graph Name Create** and then use **/File Save** to save the file. **/Graph Save** saves information used only to print the graph. Files saved with **/Graph Save** cannot be edited from the worksheet, from PrintGraph, or from Allways.

*For more information, see **/Graph Name** and **/File Save**.*

Graph Options Legend   /GOL

Purpose

Specifies descriptions to link shadings or colors on the graph to specific y-axis data ranges.

Legends indicate which line, bar, or point belongs to a specific y-axis data range.

Y-axis data is entered in ranges A, B, C, D, E, and F. Legend titles for each range also are assigned by A, B, C, D, E, and F. Figure G.3 shows, at the bottom of the bar graph, legends relating shading patterns to the division names Western, Northwest, Southwest, and Midwest.

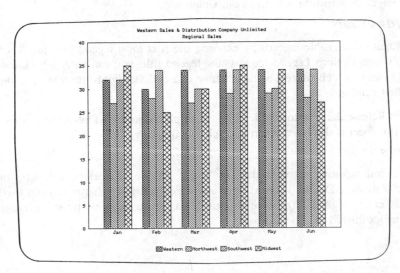

Fig. G.3. Legends relating shading patterns to division names.

Reminder

As you create a graph, write on paper a list of the legend titles you want to associate with each data range (ranges A through F). If you have already created the graph, you can reenter the A-through-F data ranges to see the associated legend ranges. To enter the legends, follow the steps outlined in the following section.

Procedures

1. Type **/go**

2. Select **Legend**.

3. Select from one of the following:

Menu Item	Description
A	Creates a legend for y-axis range A
B	Creates a legend for y-axis range B
C	Creates a legend for y-axis range C
D	Creates a legend for y-axis range D
E	Creates a legend for y-axis range E
F	Creates a legend for y-axis range F
Range	Assigns a legend to all ranges

RELEASE
2.2

4. If you chose **A** through **F**, enter the text for the legend. If you chose **Range**, specify the range containing the legends.

   Entering new legends overwrites previously entered legends. Press Esc to erase the current legend. To keep a legend as it appears, press Enter.

5. Press Enter, and 1-2-3 returns you to the **O**ptions menu.

6. Select **Q**uit to return to the main **G**raph menu.

Important Cues

- Create changeable legends by entering the text for a legend in cells. When **/G**raph **O**ptions **L**egend requests the legend title, you can enter a backslash (\) and the cell address or range name of a cell that holds the text. (See the first caution.)

RELEASE
2.2

- In Release 2.2, the current legends are displayed in the Graph Settings sheet. The sheet is displayed when you select **/G**raph.

Cautions

- If you relocate graphed data by using **/M**ove, **/W**orksheet **I**nsert, or **/W**orksheet **D**elete, 1-2-3 will not adjust cell addresses that have been used to create legends. To solve this problem, create legends by using range names instead of cell addresses.

- In Release 2.01, if a legend title is too long to fit the allocated space, the legend will push other legends to the right and off the screen. Adjust legend lengths so that they all fit on-screen. If you have several legends, you may have to abbreviate them. Release 2.2 will place legends on several rows if they don't fit.

For more information, see **/Range Name**, **/Graph X A B C D E F**, *and Chapter 10.*

Graph Options Format   /GOF

Purpose

Selects the symbols and lines that identify and connect data points.

Some line and XY graphs present information better if the data is linked with data points or if the data is represented by a series of data points linked with a solid line. Use **/Graph Options Format** to select the type of data points used for each data range (symbols, lines, or both).

Reminders

- Time-related data is usually best represented by a continuous series of related data. Trends and slopes are more obvious when they are represented with lines rather than a cluster of data points.

- Data-point clusters representing multiple readings around different x-axis values are likely candidates for symbols instead of lines. Symbols better reflect groupings. The symbol for each y-axis range is unique so that you can keep data separated.

Procedures

1. Type **/gof**

2. Select the data ranges to be formatted:

Menu Item	Description
Graph	Selects a format for the entire graph
A to **F**	Selects a format for y-axis data points

3. Select the data point type:

Menu Item	Description
Lines	Connects data points with a line
Symbols	Encloses each data point in a symbol. Different ranges have different symbols. Symbols is most commonly used with XY graphs.

Both	Connects data points with a line and marks the data point
Neither	Selects neither lines nor symbols. Use **/Graph Options Data-Labels** to "float" labels or data within the graph.

Important Cues

- Figure G.4 is an illustrative worksheet, and figure G.5 shows the corresponding line graph. The A and D data ranges, Western and Midwest, are each plotted with a line. The B and C data ranges, Northwest and Southwest, are each plotted with a particular symbol.

Fig. G.4.
Sample worksheet for the line graph.

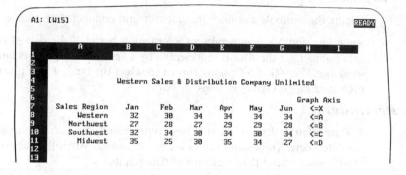

Fig. G.5.
A and D ranges plotted with lines, and B and C ranges plotted with symbols.

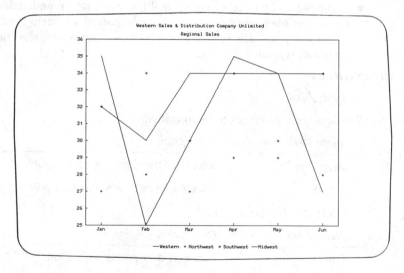

- If you are plotting a regression analysis trend line (**/Data Regression**), set the data points as symbols only and the regression's calculated *y* values as a line. This arrangement highlights the trend as a straight line through a swarm of data points.

- In Release 2.2, the current format is displayed in the Graph Settings sheet. The sheet is displayed when you select /Graph.

Cautions

- Do not misrepresent data by connecting unrelated data points with lines. If each *x,y* data pair is an independent event, unrelated by a series, do not connect the data points with a line.

- Lines do not connect data points in the left-to-right order in which the points appear on the graph. Lines instead connect the data points in the order in which they are entered in the ranges (first data point entered in the range, second data point entered in the range, and so on). If your XY line graphs are a confusing jumble of crossed lines, you must sort the data in x-axis order by arranging each *x,y* data pair in ascending, or descending, x-axis order within the worksheet range. Be sure to sort the y-axis data with the corresponding x-axis data.

For more information, see Chapter 10.

Graph Options Titles   /GOT

Purpose

Adds to the graph one or two headings, and to each axis a single title.

To enhance the reader's understanding of measurement units used in the graph, use x- and y-axis titles.

Reminder

You must know the measurement units used in the x-axis and y-axis. 1-2-3 automatically scales graphs to fit accordingly and displays the scaling factor (for example, thousands) along each axis.

Procedures

1. Type **/got**

2. Select the title to be entered:

Menu Item	Description
First	Centers the top heading of a graph
Second	Centers a second heading of a graph
X-Axis	Centers a title below the x-axis
Y-Axis	Centers a title to the left of the y-axis

3. Type a title up to 39 characters in length. Use cell contents for a title by entering first a backslash (\) and then the cell address. If a title already exists, press Esc to cancel the title, or press Enter to accept it.

4. Press Enter.

Important Cues

- In PrintGraph and Allways, characters in the first line of a heading are larger than those in other heading lines. The second line and axis titles can be printed in a font or style different from that of the first heading.

- In Release 2.2, the current titles are displayed in the Graph Settings sheet. The sheet is displayed when you select /Graph.

- Create changeable titles by putting text in cells. When /Graph Options Title requests text, enter a backslash (\) followed by the cell address or range name of the cell holding the text.

Cautions

- You can lose titles and headings contained in cell addresses if you move the cell contents with /Move, /Worksheet Insert, or /Worksheet Delete. Using range names instead of cell addresses solves this problem.

- 1-2-3 may display on-screen more characters than PrintGraph can print. This discrepancy is related to the font (character type) used and the number of characters in the title. Refer to Chapter 11.

For more information, see Chapter 10.

Graph Options Grid   /GOG

Purpose

Overlays a grid on a graph to enhance readability. The grid lines can be horizontal, vertical, or both.

Reminders

- Before you add a grid, create a graph to view.
- Grid lines cannot be used with pie graphs.

Procedures

1. Type /gog

2. Select the type of grid from the following options:

Menu Item	Description
Horizontal	Draws horizontal grid lines over the current graph from each major y-axis division
Vertical	Draws vertical grid lines over the current graph from each major x-axis division
Both	Draws both horizontal and vertical grid lines
Clear	Removes all grid lines

Important Cues

- Select grid lines that run in a direction that will enhance the presentation of data.

- Use grid lines sparingly. Inappropriate grid lines can make some line and XY graphs confusing.

- Use /Graph Options Scale to change the graph's scale, thereby changing the number of grid lines shown on the graph. Note that although this technique changes the number of grid lines, it also magnifies or reduces the graph's proportion.

- Some data-point graphs are more accurate if you use data labels. Use /Graph Options Data-Labels to create data labels that display precise numbers next to the point on the graph.

- In Release 2.2, the current grid setting is displayed in the Graph Settings sheet. The sheet is displayed when you select /Graph.

RELEASE
2.2

For more information, see /Graph Options Scale, /Graph Options Data-Labels, and Chapter 10.

Graph Options Scale /GOS

Purpose

Varies the scale along the x- and y-axes.

Options within this command include the following:

- Making changes manually to the upper- or lower-axis end points.

- Choosing formats for numeric display. (Options are identical to those in /Worksheet Global Format or /Range Format.)

- Improving the display of overlapping x-axis labels by skipping every specified occurrence, such as every second or third label.

Use /Graph Options Scale to change the axes' end points manually, thereby expanding or contracting the graph scale. Changing the end points expands or contracts the visible portion of the graph.

Use /Graph Options Scale to format numbers and dates that appear on the axes. These formats are the same as /Range Format options.

Reminder

First create and view the graph. Notice which portions of the graph you want to view and which beginning and ending numbers you should use for the new X-scale or Y-scale. Also notice whether the x-axis labels overlap or seem crowded. You can thin the x-axis tick marks by using /Graph Options Scale Skip.

Procedures

1. Type /gos

2. Select from the following options the axis or skip frequency to be changed:

Menu Item	Description
Y Scale	Changes the y-axis scale or format
X Scale	Changes the x-axis scale or format
Skip	Changes the frequency with which x-axis labels display

3. If you selected **Y** Scale or **X** Scale, choose from the following:

Menu Item	Description
Automatic	Automatically scales the graph (based on the values in the data range) to fill the screen; default (normal) selection
Manual	Overrides automatic scaling with scaling you have selected
Lower	When a Manual scale is selected, enters the lowest number for axis. Values may be rounded.
Upper	When a Manual scale is selected, enters the highest number for axis. Values may be rounded.
Format	Selects the formatting type and decimal display from the following options (see /Range Format for descriptions of these options):

Fixed	+/−
Sci (Scientific in Release 2.01)	Percent
Currency	Date
,	Text
General	Hidden

Indicator	Displays or suppresses the magnitude indicator (thousands, millions, and so on)
Quit	Leaves this menu and returns to the Options menu

4. If you choose Skip, you must enter a number to indicate the intervals at which the x-axis labels will appear. If you enter the number 2, for example, then the 1st, 3rd, and 5th x-axis labels will appear. X-axis tick-mark spacing, which appears for an XY graph, cannot be controlled from the menu.

Important Cues

- Selecting a scale inside the minimum and maximum data points creates a graph that magnifies an area within the data.

- If data points have grossly different magnitudes, you may not be able to see all the data; some ranges will be too large for the graph, and others will be too small. As an alternative, create multiple graphs, or manually rescale the graph for different data magnitudes.

- If you are comparing graphs, you may find it helpful to manually scale all the graphs the same way in order to make the visual comparisons of size and trends easier.

- In bar graphs, 1-2-3 ensures that zero (the point of origin) always appears on the graph.

- If y-axis data is greater than 1,000, non-pie graphs automatically convert the numbers to decimals and add the label "Thousands" on the graph's left.

- If possible, Release 2.2 will stagger the x-axis labels so that they don't overlap.

RELEASE
2.2

- In Release 2.2, the current scale settings are displayed in the Graph Settings sheet. The sheet is displayed when you select /Graph.

RELEASE
2.2

Caution

You must select Manual in order for the Upper and Lower settings to work.

For more information, see **/Graph Options Grid** *and Chapter 10.*

Graph Options [Color, B&W]   /GOC or /GOB

Purpose

/**G**raph **O**ptions **C**olor displays graph data in one of three colors on black if you have a color monitor; the command prints the saved graph in color if supported by your printer.

/**G**raph **O**ptions **B&W** displays graph data on a single-color screen (white, amber, or green on black) and prints as displayed.

Reminders

- The default setting assumes that color-capable equipment is not in use.

- The color assignment for the A through F data series is as follows:

Option	Color
A and D	White
B and E	Red
C and F	Blue

Procedures

To set the color option, do the following:

1. Type /**goc**

To set the B&W option, do the following:

1. Type /**gob**

Important Cues

- If you want to see color displayed for a graph with only one data series, specify the B, C, E, or F options to indicate the range. (The pie graph is the only type for which its single, permitted data series must be put in under the A option.)

- If you want to view the graph screen display in color but cannot print in color, restore the B&W option before executing /**G**raph **S**ave.

- In Release 2.2, the Graph Settings sheet indicates whether color is being used or not. The sheet is displayed when you select /**G**raph.

RELEASE

2.2

Caution

In the default B&W setting, the bar and stack-bar graphs differentiate among data series by displaying slant lines that vary in angle and spacing. If you save a graph in color but print on a noncolor printer, all bars will be solid black, and any corresponding legends will be black. Necessary differentiation among data series will be lost.

For more information, see Chapters 10 and 11.

Graph Options Data-Labels   */GOD*

Purpose

Labels graph points from data contained in cells.

Graph labels can be numeric values that enhance the graph's accuracy, or text labels that describe specific graph points.

Reminders

- First create the graph. Then view the graph and note future label locations that correspond to data they represent. Figure G.6 shows three ranges: the X range, the A range, and A-range labels.

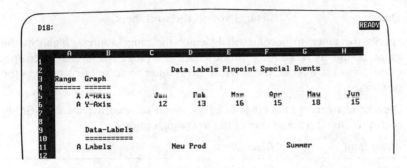

Fig. G.6.
Using X and A ranges to plan the A-range labels.

- Enter labels in an order corresponding to the order of the data-entry points they describe. Move to the first cell of the label range.

- Figure G.7 shows the resulting graph with labels over data points. Note that you do not have to enter a label for every data point.

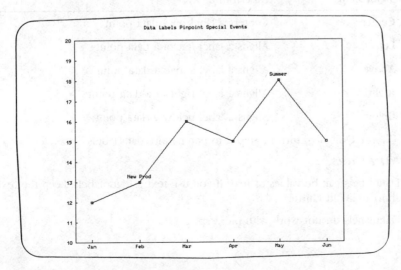

Fig. G.7.
The resulting graph with labels over data points.

Procedures

To label graph points by using labels or values contained in cells, follow these steps:

1. Type **/god**

2. From the following options, select the data range that you want to label:

Menu Item	Description
A through **F**	Enters the label range for the associated data ranges
Group	Enters at one time all the label ranges that describe associated data ranges
Quit	Returns you to the worksheet

3. Specify the range to become labels: enter the range address, highlight the range, or use its range name if one exists. If a range has already been specified, press Esc to erase the range, or press Enter to accept that range as the new range.

4. Press Enter to accept the range of labels. If you selected Release 2.2's **G**roup option in Step 2, choose one of the following options:

Menu Item	Description
Columnwise	Uses columns as data label ranges
Rowwise	Uses rows as data label ranges

5. From the following options, select the data label location relative to the corresponding data points.

Menu Item	Description
Center	Centers a label on a data point
Left	Aligns a label left of a data point
Above	Aligns a label above a data point
Right	Aligns a label right of a data point
Below	Aligns a label below a data point

6. Choose **Q**uit or return to Step 2 to enter more data labels.

Important Cues

- Data labels can be values or text. If you use text as data labels, keep the text short to avoid clutter.

- Data labels do not work with pie graphs.

- In Release 2.2, the current data label ranges are displayed in the Graph Settings sheet. The sheet is displayed when you select /Graph.

- Position "floating" labels anywhere on a graph by associating a set of data labels with data that will be plotted on the graph. To create floating labels, follow these steps:

  1. Set up two ranges that have the same number of cell locations and data points on the graph.

  2. In one range, enter floating labels in the left-to-right order in which you want them to appear in the graph.

  3. In the other range, enter the elevation of the y-axis labels. If the floating labels are to be positioned exactly where you want them, the cells in the elevation and label ranges must parallel actual data points in the x-axis and y-axis.

  4. Use /Graph F to enter the elevations for the F data range.

  5. Use /Graph Options Data-Labels F to specify the label range, and press Enter.

  6. Press Enter and select Center to center the labels on the data points.

  7. To keep the F range data from plotting, use /Graph Options Format F Neither (invisible).

For more information, see Chapter 10.

Graph Name   */GN*

Purpose

Stores graph settings for later use with the same worksheet.

Because 1-2-3 enables only one graph to be active at a time, use /Graph Name to name graphs and store their settings with the corresponding worksheets. To reproduce a stored graph, recall the graph and graph settings by name.

Reminder

Before you can name a graph, you must create one that you can view.

Procedures

1. Type **/gn**

2. From these options, select the activity to name the file:

Menu Item	Description
Use	Retrieves previous graph settings with a saved graph name
Create	Creates for the currently defined graph a name of up to 15 characters. Make sure that no graph currently has the same name, because identical names will overwrite graph contents. You are not given a chance to cancel the entry.
Delete	Removes the settings and name for the graph name chosen from the menu. Be sure that you have the correct name; you are not given the option to cancel.
Reset	Erases all graph names and their settings. You are not given a chance to cancel this command; however, if you have saved your worksheet, you can return to it.
Table	Creates a table of graph names and types

RELEASE
2.2

3. Enter the name of the previously created graph to view (**Use**), assign a name to the current graph (**Create**), or choose the name of the graph to be erased (**Delete**). Either type the name or select the name from the menu.

4. Press Enter.

Important Cues

- Using **/Graph Name** is the only way to store and recall graphs for later use with the same worksheet. **/Graph Save** saves graphs as .PIC files, which you can later print with PrintGraph or Allways.

- Graphs recalled by **/Graph Name Use** reflect changed data within the graph ranges.

- Create a slide-show effect by naming several graphs and recalling them in succession with a macro that controls **/Graph Name Use**.

- Remember that graph names can be as long as 15 characters.

RELEASE
2.2

- The graph name table is not dynamic. When you create, revise, or delete graphs, you must create a new table.

Cautions

- You can recall graphs in later work sessions only if you have first saved the graph settings with **/Graph Name Create** and then saved the worksheet with **/File Save**. Even in the same work session, you cannot return to a previous graph unless you have saved the graph settings with **/Graph Name Create**.

RELEASE
2.2

- Be sure to specify a blank area in the worksheet for the destination of your graph name table.
- Respect the power of **/Graph Name Reset**. It deletes not only all graph names in the current worksheet but also all graph parameters. The graph has no "Yes/No" confirmation step; once you press R for **Reset**, all graphs are gone.

For more information, see **/File Save**, **/File Retrieve**, *and Chapter 10.*

RELEASE
2.2

Graph Group /GG

Purpose

Quickly selects the data ranges for a graph, X and A through F, when data is in adjacent rows and when columns are in consecutive order.

Designing worksheets with the **/Graph Group** command in mind can save you time later.

Reminder

Delete any blank rows or columns in the data area, or they will be entered as data ranges containing zero values.

Procedures

1. Type **/gg**

2. Specify the range containing X and A-F data values. The rows or columns must be adjacent and in the order X, A, B, C, and so on. If the range has already been entered, press Esc and enter a new range.

3. Select **C**olumnwise if the data ranges are in columns; select **R**owwise if the data ranges are in rows.

Important Cues

- Use **/Graph Options Legend Range** to specify legends all at once.
- If you discover that your data area was not set up properly (you may have included blank rows or columns, for example) or that you indicated the wrong group range, you can cancel the current ranges and start over by using the **/Graph Reset Ranges** command.

Cautions

- 1-2-3 can graph only up to six data ranges. If you select Columnwise and indicate a range including more than seven columns (the X range plus six data ranges), the additional columns will be ignored. Likewise, if you select Rowwise and indicate a range including more than seven rows, the additional rows will be ignored.

- If you don't include the x-axis headings in your group range, the first column or row in the range will be used as your X range (even if they are values).

*For more information, see **/Graph X A B C D E F** and Chapter 10.*

PrintGraph Commands

Printgraph commands print graphs that have been saved from the worksheet through **/G**raph **S**ave. PrintGraph is a supplemental 1-2-3 utility available through the Lotus Access System menu.

To access instructions to print a graph, select **P**rintGraph from the 1-2-3 Access System, or type **PGRAPH** at the operating-system prompt. Recall that you can access the operating-system prompt by selecting **/S**ystem. The PrintGraph utility must be in the default disk and directory. The first Print-Graph menu should appear.

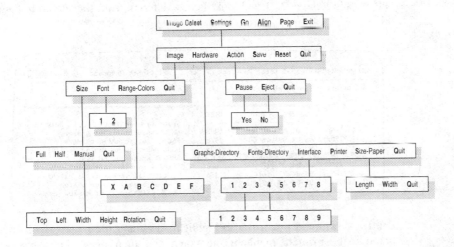

PrintGraph Image-Select

PI

Purpose

Selects .PIC (graph) files to be printed or viewed. Use PrintGraph **I**mage-Select to select multiple files that will be printed in sequence.

Reminders

- Use the worksheet to create and save a graph. When you save the graph and its settings to disk from the worksheet, the file name will have a .PIC extension. (For more information on creating and saving graphs, see the Graph section.)

- Remember that you can use **PrintGraph Image-Select** to view graphs from within PrintGraph, but you cannot change graphs in PrintGraph. Use Print-Graph only to print previously saved graphs.

- Use **PrintGraph Settings Hardware Graphs-Directory** to access the directory in which the .PIC files are located.

Procedures

1. Select **Image-Select** from PrintGraph's menu. You will see a list of the current directory's .PIC files with their respective sizes and creation dates. Previously selected graph files are marked with a number sign (#) to the left of the file names, as shown in figure PG.1. (A screen showing a sample list of .PIC files in Release 2.01 will look slightly different from the screen in figure PG.1.)

Fig. PG.1.
PrintGraph's
list of .PIC files.

```
 _____
|  Copyright 1986, 1989 Lotus Development Corp.  All Rights Reserved. V2.2  [POINT]
|
|  Select graphs to print
|
|
|    GRAPH FILE  DATE     TIME    SIZE
|    ------------------------------------        Space bar marks or unmarks selection
|  # BILLINGS    08-04-89 15:59   1478           ENTER selects marked graphs
|    DEXTEMP      08-04-89 16:00   1478           ESC exits, ignoring changes
|    FIGG4        07-28-89 17:45   9759           HOME moves to beginning of list
|  # GRWTHLN      08-04-89 16:00   1478           END moves to end of list
|    INVESTCM     08-04-89 16:00   1478           ↑ and ↓ move highlight
|    RATIOS       08-04-89 16:01   1478             List will scroll if highlight
|    SURVEY       08-04-89 16:01   1478             moved beyond top or bottom
|                                                GRAPH (F10) previews marked graph
|_____
```

2. Use the down- and up-arrows to highlight the graph file names. To mark a graph to be printed, highlight the graph and then press the space bar. Selected files will be marked with a #. Remove # markings by highlighting the graph file name and again pressing the space bar.

3. To preview the graph on-screen, highlight the file name and press Graph (F10). Press any key to return to the **Image-Select** menu.

4. Press Enter to return to the PrintGraph menu. The graphs marked with # will print when you select **Go**.

5. The selected graph file names will appear on the left side of PrintGraph's main screen. Graphs print in the order selected.

Important Cues

- If you preview a graph on-screen, it will not look the same as the printed graph or the graph viewed from within the worksheet. PrintGraph's preview graphs use BLOCK1 characters and are not on the same scale as printed graphs. This preview function serves only as a reminder of which graph belongs to which file name.

- Previewing graphs from PrintGraph is possible only if you have hardware capable of graphics and if those capabilities are installed for 1-2-3.

For more information, see **/Graph Save** *and Chapter 11.*

PrintGraph Settings Image Size   *PSIS*

Purpose

Controls the location of the graph on the printed page, including the graph's size and its rotation.

The **Full** and **Half** settings automatically control graph location and rotation.

Reminders

- Settings selected from **P**rintGraph **S**ettings **I**mage **S**ize control the printed appearance of graphs selected with **I**mage-Select.

- If you want to print more than one graph per page, draw a thumbnail sketch of how the graphs should be arranged on the page and what their size and rotation should be.

Procedures

1. Select **S**ettings **I**mage **S**ize from PrintGraph's menu.

2. From the following options, select the location/rotation of the graph(s) to be printed:

Menu Item	Description
Full	Prints large graphs on 8 1/2-by-11-inch paper. Automatically sets rotation to 90 degrees to position the bottom of the graph on the paper's right edge.
Half	Prints half-sized graphs to fit two graphs per page. Rotation is automatically set to 0 degrees to position the graph upright.
Manual	Manually sets graph proportions, locations, and rotation

3. If in Step 2 you selected **F**ull or **H**alf, skip to Step 5.

4. If in Step 2 you selected **M**anual, enter the proportions, location, and rotation for your graph from these options:

Menu Item	Description
Top	Sets the margin in inches at the paper's top
Left	Sets the margin between the paper's left edge and the graph
Width	Sets the distance across the graph, measured across the direction of the paper feed
Height	Sets the graph's height, measured along the direction of the paper feed
Rotation	Sets counterclockwise the degrees of rotation. 90 degrees puts the bottom of the graph on the paper's right edge.

5. Choose **Q**uit or press Esc to return to the Settings Image menu.

Important Cues

- To print additional graphs on a single page, roll the paper backward to align the paper's serrations with the top of the printer's strike plate. Select **A**lign to reset the top of form. Use **S**ettings **I**mage **S**ize **M**anual to adjust graph locations, sizes, and rotations so that graphs will not overlap.

- Any changes to the graph's location, size, or rotation will override any **F**ull or **H**alf selections you may have made and will shift **S**ettings **I**mage **S**ize to **M**anual.

- If you selected **F**ull or **H**alf, the graph will print automatically with the same proportions as the on-screen graph (a ratio of 1.385 along the x-axis to 1 along the y-axis). If you set the graph size manually, you can change these proportions. To maintain on-screen proportions, divide the desired x-axis length by 1.385 to get the appropriate y-axis setting.

- To rotate the graph and maintain on-screen proportions, use the **H**eight or **W**idth entry-area options to enter the x- and y-axis lengths as calculated in the previous cue. The options are the following:

Menu Item	Rotation	Enter Length of
Height	0	Graph's y-axis
Width		Graph's x-axis
Height	90	Graph's x-axis
Width		Graph's y-axis

Height	180	Graph's y-axis
Width		Graph's x-axis
Height	270	Graph's x-axis
Width		Graph's y-axis

Caution

Graphs rotated at angles other than right angles will be distorted.

For more information, see Chapter 11.

PrintGraph Settings Image Font   PSIF

Purpose

Determines which fonts (print styles) are used for alphanumeric characters in a printed graph. With this command, you can use one font for the title and another font for legends, other titles, and scale numbers.

Procedures

1. Access the main PrintGraph menu. The status of current PrintGraph settings appears below the double line.

2. Note the path to the Fonts Directory under HARDWARE SETTINGS (HARD-WARE SETUP in Release 2.01). If the path is not accurate, select **S**ettings **H**ardware **F**onts-Directory to specify the directory in which the .FNT (font) files are located. Press Enter and then either choose **Q**uit or press Esc to return to PrintGraph's Settings menu.

3. Note whether the default setting for font 1 and font 2 is BLOCK1. If you do not want to alter the default setting, proceed no further with this command. If you want to change one or both fonts, continue with the following steps.

4. Select **I**mage Font.

5. Choose one of the following:

Menu Item	Description
1	Specifies the print style for the top center title
2	Specifies the print style for other titles and legends

The screen displays the following list of font options:

BLOCK1
BLOCK2
BOLD
FORUM

ITALIC1
ITALIC2
LOTUS
ROMAN1
ROMAN2
SCRIPT1
SCRIPT2

The BLOCK1 default setting is preceded by the # marker and is highlighted. (The marker is not visible if you elect to specify font 2 before you choose font 1. See the "Important Cues" section.)

A number after a font name is an indication of print darkness. A font whose name ends with 2 has darker print than a font whose name ends with 1. Darker fonts are more evident on high-resolution printers and plotters.

6. To choose a different font, use the down-arrow, up-arrow, Home, or End keys to point to the font you want.

7. Press the space bar to move the # marker to the desired font. Note that at this point the space bar is a toggle: repeatedly pressing the space bar turns the marker on and off.

8. Press Enter to select the font, or press Esc if you want 1-2-3 to ignore your action and to exit from the font menu.

9. Repeat Steps 5 through 8 if you want to select another font.

Important Cues

- If you first select menu item **1** in Step 5, the font selection you make affects both font 1 and font 2. You can, however, select menu item **2** before you choose **1**. Selecting menu item **2** lets you make font 2 different from font 1. To choose font **2**, simply move the pointer to the desired font and press Enter. Once you have altered font 2—and until you end the PrintGraph session or unless you use **R**eset to replace current, unsaved settings with the default settings stored in the PGRAPH.CNF file—you can make a change to font 1 without affecting font 2.

- For best results with a dot-matrix printer, use the BLOCK fonts and avoid the ITALIC and SCRIPT fonts. If you have a high-density dot-matrix printer, you should be able to use the BOLD, FORUM, and ROMAN fonts with good results.

- The lower portion of the status screen should show the selected fonts.

- Use **P**rintGraph **S**ettings **S**ave to make the **P**rintGraph **S**ettings specifications the default in the PGRAPH.CNF file.

Cautions

- If you have a two-disk system, then while you are using the PrintGraph program, do not remove from the system the disk containing the font files.

- You cannot specify a print style unless the directory that stores the font instructions has been correctly specified.

PrintGraph Settings Image Range-Colors   *PSIR*

Purpose

Assigns available colors to specified graph ranges for printing.

Reminder

Before you can use **Range-Colors**, you must select a printer or plotter with Settings Hardware Printer.

Procedures

1. Select **Settings** from PrintGraph's menu.

2. If you have not yet designated a printer or plotter, select **Hardware Printer**. After you make your selection and press Esc, choose **Image Range-Colors**.

   If you have already designated a printer or plotter, select **Image Range-Colors**. The **Range Colors** menu displays the colors available on your system. Ranges X and A through F will display only black if your system cannot print in color. If your system can print in color, use the right- and left-arrow keys and the Enter key to choose a range and its color.

   The color of range X is the color of the graph itself, including the grid, scale numbers, and x- and y axis labels. The color for each range from A through F is for each graphed data series and corresponding legend.

3. After you have assigned a color to one range, select another range and assign it a different color. Repeat this process until you have assigned a unique color to each range.

4. Select **Quit** or press Esc to leave the **Range Colors** menu.

Caution

Before you can specify range colors, you must have a color-graphics printer or plotter that has been correctly installed. To install your printer or plotter, choose Install from the 1-2-3 Access System menu and follow the instructions for establishing applicable printer or plotter driver sets. Use **Settings Hardware Interface** and **Settings Hardware Printer** to specify the current printer or plotter configuration.

PrintGraph Settings Action *PSA*

Purpose

Causes the printer to pause or stop between graphs.

Procedures

1. Select **S**ettings **A**ction from PrintGraph's menu.

2. Select **P**ause **Y**es to make the printer pause between graphs so that you can choose other print options or change the paper.

   Or select **E**ject **Y**es to print one graph per page by making the printer advance continuous-feed paper automatically to the next page after a graph is printed.

Important Cues

- If you choose **P**ause **Y**es, the computer will pause during printing and beep as a signal for you to change printer or plotter settings, insert a new sheet of paper, or change plotter pens. To make the printing resume, press the space bar.

- If you select **P**ause **N**o (the default setting), PrintGraph will print graphs without pausing.

- If you choose **E**ject **N**o (the default setting), PrintGraph will print a second graph on a page if the page is long enough. If the page is not long enough, PrintGraph advances the paper to the top of the next page.

- Use **S**ettings **H**ardware **S**ize-**P**aper to alter the page length.

Cautions

- **S**ettings **A**ction **P**ause affects a printer differently in a network: the printing pauses, but PrintGraph gives no signal at the network device.

- Be sure to use **S**ettings **A**ction **P**ause **Y**es if your printer does not use continuous-feed paper or have an automatic sheet feeder.

PrintGraph Settings Hardware *PSH*

Purpose

Defines for PrintGraph which directories contain graphs and fonts, determines the type(s) of printer(s) to be used and how they connect to the PC, and specifies the paper size.

Figure PG.2 shows PrintGraph's Settings Hardware menu. The selections you make from this menu are displayed under the title HARDWARE SETTINGS. (If you are using Release 2.01, you will see the title HARDWARE SETUP instead and note other slight differences between your screen and figure PG.2.)

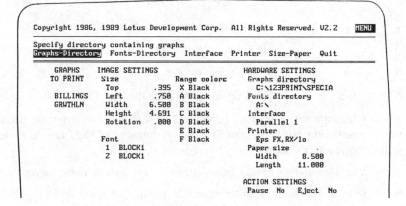

Fig. PG.2.
PrintGraph's
Settings
Hardware
menu.

Reminders

- Use 1-2-3's main Install program (described in 1-2-3's reference manual) to install the printers and plotters to be used to print or plot graphs. You can install more than one printer and/or plotter at a time. PrintGraph cannot communicate to the printer or plotter until you install the printer or plotter with 1-2-3's main Install program.

- If you are using a printer or plotter connected to a serial port, check the printer's or plotter's manual to find the recommended baud rate (transmission rate).

Procedures

To change the directory containing the font or graph files, follow these steps:

1. Select Settings Hardware from PrintGraph's menu.

2. From the following options, select the directory to be changed:

Menu Item	Description
Graphs-Directory	Changes directory where .PIC files are located (for example, C:\123\RESULTS)
Fonts-Directory	Changes directory where font (.FNT) files are located (for example, C:\123)

To change your PC's interface (hardware connection) used to communicate to the printer or plotter, follow these steps:

1. Select Settings Hardware from PrintGraph's menu.

2. Select **Interface**.

3. From the following options, select the interface that connects your printer or plotter to your PC:

Setting	Device
1	First parallel printer (most printers)
2	First serial printer (most plotters)
3	Second parallel printer
4	Second serial printer
5 through **8**	The DOS devices LPT1: through LPT4:

4. If you selected a serial interface (options 2 or 4 in Step 3), enter the baud rate (transmission rate). You can find the recommended baud rate in your printer's or plotter's manual.

To select which printer or plotter installation to use, follow these steps:

1. Select **Settings Hardware** from PrintGraph's menu.

2. Select **Printer**.

3. Use the down- and up-arrow keys to highlight the printer or plotter installation option to be selected. Some installation options may be listed more than once. If you use a printer or plotter with duplicate installation options, experiment with the duplicate listings: they offer different print intensities and resolution.

4. Once you have highlighted your selection, press the space bar to mark your choice with a # sign. To remove the # sign, highlight the choice and press the space bar again.

5. Press Enter to return to the **Settings Hardware** menu.

To select a different page size, follow these steps:

1. Select **Settings Hardware** from PrintGraph's menu.

2. Select **Size-Paper**.

3. Enter separately (in inches) the new paper size for **Length** and **Width**.

4. Press Enter and then select **Quit** to return to the **Settings Hardware** menu.

5. Use the printer's internal control switches (DIP switches) to change the form-length (paper-length) setting. Your printer's manual will describe these miniature switches and their settings.

Important Cue

If **Settings Hardware Printer** does not list an installation option for your printer, select a similar but earlier printer model from the same manufacturer. Also, check with your printer's dealer and Lotus Development Corporation to obtain disks containing additional hardware installation options.

Caution

1-2-3 expects printers to communicate transmitted data according to a certain protocol. Most printers and plotters will already be set to send data according to this protocol. The following are PrintGraph's transmission settings:

Data bits	8
Stop bits	1 (2 for 110 baud)
Parity	None

For more information, see Chapter 11.

PrintGraph Go, Align, and Page   PG, PA, PP

Purpose

Activates the printing process, specifies the printhead position as the top of the page, and advances the paper one page at a time, respectively.

Procedures

1. Check the status area of the PrintGraph screen to verify that the graphs selected have the correct image, hardware, and action settings necessary for the current printing.

2. Make sure that the printer has enough paper for the print job.

3. Position the printhead to the desired top-of-page position and make sure that the printer is on-line.

4. Select one or more of the following options:

Menu Item	Description
Go	Activates the printing operation
Align	Makes the current printhead position the top-of-form position
Page	Advances the paper one page when a key is pressed

Important Cues

- When you use **PrintGraph Align**, PrintGraph inserts a form feed at the end of every page.

- If you want to change the page length specified when the printer was installed, select Install from the Access System menu.

For more information, see Chapter 11.

Data Commands /D

A *database* is an organized collection of information. In 1-2-3, a database is stored in a specific area of rows and columns. Each row of the database is called a *record*. Within a row, each cell is a *field*. Each field must have a unique label, called the *field name*, entered at the top of the column. 1-2-3 needs this field name to search for specific information.

Choosing /**D**ata from the main menu makes the database commands available. The /**D**ata commands enable you to perform three functions: database selection and maintenance, data analysis, and data manipulation. The following map shows you how to access each of these commands.

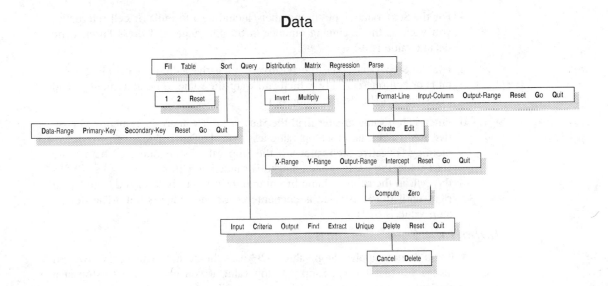

Data Fill /DF

Purpose

Fills a specified range with a series of equally incremented numbers, dates, times, or percentages.

Use **/Data Fill** to create date or numeric rows or columns, headings for depreciation tables, sensitivity analyses, data tables, or databases.

Reminder

Before you issue **/Data Fill**, move the cell pointer to the upper left corner of the range you want to fill.

Procedures

1. Type **/df**

2. Define the range to be filled: type the address (such as B23..D46), type a preset range name, or anchor one corner of the range (by typing a period) and move the cell pointer to the opposite corner or opposite end of the range.

3. Press Enter.

4. For the Start value, type the number (including a formula or cell reference) you want as the beginning number in the fill range, and press Enter. (The default value is 0.)

5. For the Step value, type the positive or negative number (including a formula or cell reference) by which you want the value to be incremented, and press Enter. (The default value is 1.)

6. Enter a Stop value greater than the Start value if you are incrementing (positive Step value). Enter a Stop value less than the Start value if you are decrementing (negative Step value). If the Stop value is encountered before the Start value, the **/Data Fill** command is cancelled without any results. /df fills the cells in the range column-by-column from top to bottom and from left to right until the Stop value is encountered or the range is full. (The default Stop value is 8191.)

Important Cues

- If you do not supply a Stop value, 1-2-3 uses the default, which may give you results you don't want. Supply a Stop value if you want 1-2-3 to stop at a particular value before the entire range is filled.

- Use **/Data Fill** to fill a range of numbers in descending order. Enter a positive or negative Start value and enter a negative Step value. The Stop value must be less than the Start value, even if the Stop value is a negative number.

- Formulas, @functions, or cell references can be used with **/Data Fill**. For example, to create a range of dates from January 1, 1989, to December 31, 1989, select /df, specify a range (A1..A365), enter the formula @DATE(89,1,1) as the Start value, enter a Step value of 1, and enter the formula @DATE(89,12,31) as the Stop value. Use **/Range Format Date** to display the results in **Date** format.

- Use /df to create an index numbering system for database entries. Add blank rows at the end of the database for future entries; insert a column to store the index numbers. Specify this column as the range in the /df command; enter a Step value of 1. You can then sort the database on any column and return to the original order by sorting on the index column.

- Use data tables to change the input values in a formula so that you can see how the output changes. If the input values vary by constant amounts, use /df to create an input column or row for the data table.

Cautions

- Numbers generated by /Data Fill are written over previous entries in the fill range.

- If the Stop value is not large enough, a partial fill occurs. If the Stop value is smaller than the Start value, /df won't even start. Remember that if your increment is negative, the Stop value must be less than the Start value.

*For more information, see /**Data Table** and Chapter 12.*

Data Table 1   /DT1

Purpose

Generates a table composed of one varying input value and the result from multiple formulas.

/Data Table 1 is useful for generating "what if" models that show the results of changing a single variable.

Reminders

- /Data Table 1 is used to show how changes in one variable affect the output from one or more formulas.

- Formulas in /dt1 can include @functions.

- To change two variables in a single formula, use /Data Table 2.

- Before executing /dt1, enter data and formulas as though you are solving for a single solution (see cells B4..C8 in fig. D.1).

- In the leftmost column of the table, enter the numbers or text that will be used as the replacement for the first variable (Input 1). In the second blank cell in the top row of the data table, type the address of the cell containing the formula. Enter additional formulas to the right on the same row. The upper left corner of the /Data Table 1 area (C11 in fig. D.1) remains blank.

- Display the cell addresses of the formulas at the top of the table by using /Range Format Text. You may need to widen the columns if you want to see entire formulas.

Fig. D.1.
/Data Table 1:
Solving with
single inputs.

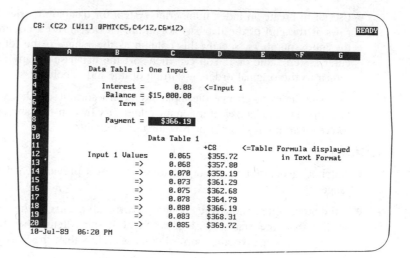

Procedures

1. Type **/dt1**

2. Enter the table range so that it includes the Input 1 values or text in the leftmost column and the formulas in the top row. If a range has been previously specified, press Esc and define the range: type the address, type a range name, or highlight the range.

3. Press Enter.

4. Enter the address for Input 1 by moving the cell pointer to the cell in which the first input values will be substituted. In figure D.1, the values from C12 to C20 will be substituted into C4. Press Enter.

5. 1-2-3 then substitutes an Input 1 value into the designated cell and recalculates each formula at the top of the data table. After each substitution, the results are displayed in the data table. In figure D.1, the variable input for interest (.080) produces a monthly payment of $366.19. With **/Data Table 1**, you can see how "sensitive" the monthly payments are to variations in the interest rate.

Important Cues

● Make the formulas in the top row of the data table area easier to understand by using **/Range Name Create** to change address locations (such as C4) into descriptive text (such as Interest). **/Range Format Text** displays formulas as text although the formulas still execute correctly.

- After you designate range and input values, you can enter new variables in the table and recalculate a new table by pressing Table (F8). You cannot recalculate a data table the same way you recalculate a worksheet—by setting Global Recalculation to Automatic, by pressing Calc (F9), or by placing {CALC} in a macro.

- If input values vary by a constant amount, create them by using /Data Fill.

Caution

The data table will write over existing information in the data table range.

For more information, see **/Data Fill** *and Chapter 12.*

Data Table 2   /DT2

Purpose

Generates a table composed of two input variables and their effect on a single formula.

/Data Table 2 is useful for generating "what if" models that show how changes in two variables affect the output of one formula.

Reminders

- Formulas in /Data Table 2 can include @functions.

- If you have to change a single input and see its result on many formulas, use /Data Table 1.

- Before executing /Data Table 2, enter data and formulas as though you were solving for a single solution (see cells B4..C8 in fig. D.2).

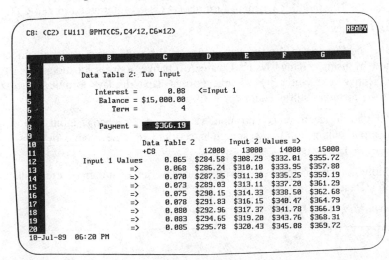

Fig. D.2.
/Data Table 2:
Solving with
two inputs and
a single
formula.

- In the leftmost column of the table, enter the numbers or text that will be used by the first variable, Input 1 (C12..C20 in fig. D.2). In the top row of the table, enter the numbers or text to be used by the second variable, Input 2 (D11..G11). In the blank cell (C11) in the upper left corner of the table, type the address of the cell containing the formula (+ C8).

- Make the cell address in the upper left corner of the table visible by using /Range Format Text. You may need to widen the columns if you want to see all of the formula.

Procedures

1. Type /dt2

2. Enter the table range so that it includes the Input 1 values in the leftmost column and the Input 2 values as the top row. If a range has been previously specified, press Esc and define the range: type the address, type an assigned range name, or highlight the range.

3. Press Enter.

4. Enter the address for Input 1 (C4) by moving the cell pointer to the cell in which the first input values will be substituted. In figure D.2, the values from C12 to C20 will be substituted in C4 as the interest amount. Press Enter.

5. Enter the address for Input 2 (C5) by moving the cell pointer to the cell in which the second input values will be substituted. In the example, the values from D11 to G11 will be substituted in C5 as the principal amount. Press Enter.

6. 1-2-3 then substitutes Input 1 and Input 2 and recalculates the formula in C8. After each combination of substitutions, the formula in C8 calculates a new answer and displays it in the grid. In the example, the variable inputs for interest (.080) and balance ($15,000) produce a monthly payment of $366.19. The monthly payment formula (+ C8) is referenced in cell C11.

Important Cues

- Make the formula in the top left corner of the table range easier to understand by using /Range Name Create to change address locations (C4) to descriptive text (Interest). /Range Format Text displays formulas as text, but the formulas still execute correctly.

- After you designate range and input values, you can change input values in the input column and row and then recalculate a new table by pressing Table (F8).

- If input values are to be an evenly spaced series of numbers, create them with /Data Fill.

For more information, see /Data Fill and Chapter 12.

Data Sort *IDS*

Purpose

Sorts the database in ascending or descending order, according to the entries in one or two columns.

Reminders

- Sorting can be done on one or two fields (columns). The first sort field is called the **P**rimary-Key; the second is the **S**econdary-Key. Either key can be sorted in ascending or descending order.

- Save a copy of the worksheet with **/F**ile **S**ave before sorting. Save to a different name to preserve your original file.

- If, after sorting, you want to return to records (rows) that are in a specific order, insert a column and use **/D**ata **F**ill to fill the column with index numbers. Re-sort on the index numbers to return to the original order.

Procedures

1. Type **/ds**

   In Release 2.2, a Sort Settings sheet displays when you select **/D**ata **S**ort so that you can see your current settings (data range, primary key, and secondary key) at a glance.

2. Select **D**ata-Range.

3. Highlight the data range to be sorted. It must include every field (column) in the database but does not have to include every record (row). Only records in the specified range will be sorted, however. Do not include the field labels at the top of the database, or the labels will be sorted with the data. Enter the range: type the address, type a range name, or highlight the range.

4. Press Enter.

5. Select **P**rimary-Key.

6. Move the cell pointer to the column of the database that will be the **P**rimary-Key; then press Enter.

7. Specify ascending or descending order by entering **A** or **D**.

8. Select **S**econdary-Key if you want to sort the database on a second field within a primary sort key. Move the cell pointer to the column of the database that will be the **S**econdary-Key and then press Enter.

9. Specify ascending or descending order by selecting **A** or **D**.

10. Select **G**o.

RELEASE
2.2

Important Cues

- Select **Q**uit to return to READY mode at any time. Select **R**eset to clear previous **P**rimary-Key, **S**econdary-Key, and **D**ata-Range settings.

- Sort settings are saved with the worksheet. When you enter the **D**ata-Range, **P**rimary-Key, or **S**econdary-Key options, you can accept the current range setting by pressing Enter.

- During the Install process, you can change the order in which 1-2-3 sorts characters. The three sort precedences are ASCII, Numbers First, and Numbers Last. In the Numbers First format, labels beginning with numbers are sorted before alphabetic labels. The reverse is true for Numbers Last.

- In ASCII, uppercase letters are sorted before lowercase; in Numbers First and Numbers Last, the case of characters is ignored. In all three collating sequences, values are sorted last.

Cautions

- If you sort a database without including the full width of records, the sorted portion will be split from the nonsorted portion. Putting the records back together may be nearly impossible. If you saved the worksheet before sorting, you can retrieve the original file.

- Do not include blank rows or the data labels at the top of the database when you highlight the **D**ata-Range. Blank rows sort to the top or bottom of the database in ascending or descending order, and the data labels are sorted into the body of the database.

- Formulas in a sorted database may not be accurate because sorting switches rows to new locations. If the addresses do not use absolute and relative addressing correctly, the formulas in sorted records will change. As a rule, use a relative address in a formula when the address refers to a cell in the same row. If the address refers to a cell outside the database, use an absolute address.

For more information, see **/Data Fill** *and Chapter 12.*

Data Query Input   /DQI

Purpose

Specifies a range of data records to be searched.

Reminders

- You must indicate an input range before you use the Find, Extract, Unique, or Delete command from the **D**ata **Q**uery menu.

- The input range can be the entire database or a part of it.

- The input range must include the field names.

Procedures

1. Type **/dqi**

2. At the Enter Input range: prompt, specify the range of data records you want searched. Either type the range address or move the cell pointer to highlight the range. Be sure to include in the range the field names at the top of the range and portions of the records that may be off the screen.

3. If the input range specification is acceptable, press Enter. If you want to change the range specification, press Esc to clear the current specification, define or highlight the new range, and press Enter.

4. If you want to proceed to define the criteria range, select **Criteria** (**Criterion** in Release 2.01); or if you want to go to READY mode, select **Q**uit to leave the **D**ata **Q**uery command menu.

    In Release 2.2, a Query Settings sheet displays when you select **/D**ata **Q**uery so that you can see your current database ranges (input, criteria, and output) at a glance.

RELEASE

2.2

Caution

Redefine the input range if you add one or more rows to the bottom of the range, add one or more columns before or after the range, or delete the first column or the last row or column of the range. A defined input range will be adjusted automatically if you insert or delete rows or columns within the range.

For more information, see Chapter 12.

Data Query Criteria   /DQC

Purpose

Specifies which records are to be found in a search. (In Release 2.01, the command is **/D**ata **Q**uery **C**riterion.)

Reminders

- You must indicate a criteria range before you use the **F**ind, **E**xtract, **U**nique, or **D**elete options of the **/D**ata **Q**uery command.

- A criteria range can have as many as 32 fields.

- You do not need to include in the criteria and output ranges all the field names in the database. If you do include all the field names, however, you won't have to alter the criteria range to apply a criterion to a new field.

- The first row of the criteria range must contain field names that exactly match the field names of the database, including capitalization.

- The row below the first row of the criteria range contains the search criteria.

- You can use more than one criterion for a search.

- More than one row can contain criteria, but no row in the criteria range should be blank.

- Criteria can be numbers, labels, or formulas. Numbers and labels must be positioned directly below the field name to which they correspond.

- Criteria labels can contain wild-card characters. An asterisk (*) stands for any group of characters; a question mark (?) represents a single character.

- A tilde (~) before a label excludes that label from a search.

- Criteria can contain logical operators (<, <=, >, >=, <>).

- You can use #AND#, #NOT#, or #OR# to create compound logical formulas as criteria.

- Criteria on the same row of the criteria range are treated as if they were linked by #AND# for every condition to be met. Criteria on separate rows are treated as if they were linked by #OR# for any condition to be met.

Procedures

1. If the worksheet is in READY mode, type **/dqc**. If you have just defined the input range, and the **Data Query** command menu is visible, select **C**riteria.

2. At the Enter Criteria range: prompt, specify or highlight the range that will contain field names and criteria. The range should contain at least two rows: the first row for field names from the top row of the database you want searched, and the second row for the criteria you specify. Allow two or more rows for criteria if you use them to specify #OR# conditions.

3. If the range specification is acceptable, press Enter.

4. If you want to change the range specification, press Esc to clear the current specification, define or highlight the new range, and press Enter.

Important Cues

- The field names at the top of the criteria range must exactly match those of at the top of the database input range. The names can be entered in a different order, but the spelling, upper- and lowercase combinations, and label prefixes must match. The easiest way to create exact criteria range field names is to use **/C**opy.

- Use wild cards in the criteria if you are unsure of the spelling or want to find data that may have been misspelled. 1-2-3 will search only for exact matches for the characters in the criteria range.

- You can place the criteria range in the data-entry portion of the worksheet and use a split screen to view the criteria and output ranges simultaneously.

- Database @functions use input and criteria ranges.

- In Release 2.2, a Query Settings sheet displays when you select /**D**ata **Q**uery so that you can see your current database ranges (input, criteria, and output) at a glance.

RELEASE
2.2

Cautions

- Including a blank row in the criteria range causes all records to be found, retrieved, or deleted with **Q**uery commands.

- If you alter the number of rows in a defined criteria range, you need to redefine the range to reflect the change.

For more information, see Chapter 12.

Data Query Output   /DQO

Purpose

Assigns a location for the display of records found in a search.

Reminders

- You must indicate an output range before you use the Extract and Unique options of the /**D**ata **Q**uery command. The **F**ind and **D**elete options do not use an output range.

- Like the criteria range, an output range can have as many as 32 fields.

- Locate the output range so that there is nothing below its columns. Locate the output range so that it will not overlap the input or criteria ranges. Output will be written over data in the output range.

- You can limit the output range by specifying the size of the (multiple-row) range. Or you can ensure that the output range is unlimited in size if you specify the range as the single row of field names. That way, the results of the search can be listed in the unlimited area below the field names.

Procedures

1. If the worksheet is in READY mode, type /**dqo**. If you have just defined the criteria range, and the **D**ata **Q**uery command menu is visible, select **O**utput.

2. At the Enter Output range: prompt, specify or highlight the range that will contain field names and the results of a search.

3. If the range specification is acceptable, press Enter.

4. If you want to change the range specification, press Esc to clear the current specification, define or highlight the new range, and press Enter.

Important Cue

In Release 2.2, a Query Settings sheet displays when you select **/D**ata **Q**uery so that you can see your current database ranges (input, criteria, and output) at a glance.

Caution

If you specify the row of field names as a single-row output range and use **/D**ata **Q**uery **E**xtract, matching records will be listed below the output range. Any information in the cells in the row-and-column path directly below the output range to the bottom of the worksheet is erased. If you want to preserve any information in those cells, specify the output range as a multiple-row range. That way, cells below the last row of the output range will not be affected by any results of a search.

For more information, see Chapter 12.

Data Query Find   /DQF

Purpose

Finds records in the database that meet conditions you have set.

Reminders

- **/D**ata **Q**uery **F**ind moves the cell pointer to the first cell of the first record that meets the specifications in the criteria range. By pressing the up-arrow or down-arrow key, you can display previous or succeeding records that meet the criteria. Using /dqf can be the best way to access a record in a database quickly for editing or viewing purposes.

- You must define a 1-2-3 database complete with input and criteria ranges.

Procedures

1. Type **/dq**

2. Select **I**nput.

3. Move the cell pointer to highlight the input range you want searched. Include in the highlighted range all the field names, records, and fields you want searched. Make sure that you include input areas that may be off the screen. When you have highlighted the correct range, press Enter. If you want to change an existing range, press Esc, highlight a new range, and press Enter.

4. Select Criteria (Criterion in Release 2.01).

5. Highlight the criteria range. Include only the field names and the rows below the field names that include criteria. Including a blank row in the criteria range causes all records to be retrieved.

6. Select Find.

7. The cell pointer highlights the first record that meets the criteria. You will hear a beep if no record in the input range meets the criteria.

8. Press the up- or down-arrow key to move to the next record that meets the criteria. Pressing the Home or End key finds the first or last record that meets the criteria.

9. You can edit contents within a record by moving the cell pointer right or left with the arrow keys. When the cell pointer highlights the cell you want to edit, press the Edit (F2) key and edit the cell contents. Press Enter when you have finished editing.

10. Return to the Data Query menu by pressing Enter or Esc when you are not in EDIT mode.

Important Cues

- After you have entered the /Data Query commands and ranges, you can repeat the operation from READY mode simply by changing the criteria and pressing the Query (F7) key.

- /Data Query Find remembers the last input and criteria range used from the Query menu. You do not have to enter the input and criteria range if they are the same as those used by the previous database command. With Release 2.2, you can check the current ranges by looking at the Query Settings sheet when you select /Data Query. With Release 2.01, check the ranges by selecting Input or Criterion; then press Enter to accept the range, or Esc to clear the previous range so that you can specify a new one.

- Use wild cards (* or ?) in the criteria if you are unsure of the spelling or if you want to find data that may have been misspelled. 1-2-3 will find only exact matches for the characters in the criteria range.

- Before you delete records with /Data Query Delete, use /Data Query Find to display the records that will be deleted.

- The field names at the top of the criteria range must match those at the top of the database input range. The names can be entered in a different order, but the spelling and upper- and lowercase combinations must match. The easiest way to create criteria labels is to use /Copy.

- Make sure that you use /**R**ange Erase to erase previous criteria from the criteria range. If you enter a space and press Enter to clear a cell, /**D**ata Query will try to find a space.

For more information, see Chapter 12.

Data Query Extract   /DQE

Purpose

Copies to the output range of the worksheet those records that meet conditions set in the criteria range.

Reminders

- /**D**ata Query Extract copies records from the input range that match specifications entered in the criteria range; the command places the output under field names (see row 17 in Fig. D.3) in the output range.

Fig. D.3.
/*Data Query*
Extract:
Extracted data
in an output
range.

```
A16: 'Output Range                                           MENU
Input  Criteria  Output  Find  Extract  Unique  Delete  Reset  Quit
Copy all records that match criteria to output range
┌───────────────────── Query Settings ─────────────────────┐
│    Input range:      A8..E13                              │
│                                                           │
│    Criteria range:   A4..E5                               │
│                                                           │
│    Output range:     A17..E17                             │
└───────────────────────────────────────────────────────────┘
 7    Input Range (Database)
 8    ID CODE  DESCRIPTION                   QUANT    COST    TOTAL $
 9    C132     Chair, Buldavaian design          3  $326.23   $978.69
10    D154     Desk, Last of the mahogany        1 $3,500.00 $3,500.00
11    C325     Chair, Fine Corinthian leather    1  $500.65   $500.65
12    T546     Table, Round (Antique)            1 $4,650.00 $4,650.00
13    C223     Chair, Futura five-wheeler w/power 2  $635.00 $1,270.00
14
15
16    Output Range
17    ID CODE  DESCRIPTION                   QUANT    COST    TOTAL $
18    C325     Chair, Fine Corinthian leather    1  $500.65   $500.65
19    C223     Chair, Futura five-wheeler w/power 2  $635.00 $1,270.00
20
```

- You must define a 1-2-3 database complete with input, output, and criteria ranges. The output range must have field names entered exactly as they appear at the top of each database column.

- Choose an output range in a blank area of the worksheet. You can limit the output range to a specified number of rows, or you can give the output range an unlimited number of rows. Be careful, however, if you choose the "unlimited" method. All cells below the output range are erased, which means that any data below that point will be lost.

Procedures

1. Type **/dq**

2. Select **I**nput.

3. Highlight the database to be used in the search operation. Include in the highlighted range all the field names, records, and fields you want searched. If the existing range is acceptable, press Enter. If you want to change the existing range, press Esc and highlight a new range. Press Enter after highlighting the input range.

4. Select **C**riteria (Criterion in Release 2.01).

5. Highlight the criteria range. Include only the field names and the rows below the field names that include criteria. Including a blank row causes all records to be extracted.

6. Select **O**utput.

7. Highlight the output range. Be sure to highlight the field names as the first row in the output range. Highlight additional rows in the output range depending on whether you want the output range to be limited or unlimited.

8. Select **E**xtract. Records that match the specifications entered in the criteria range will be copied to the output range.

9. Select **Q**uit to return to the worksheet.

Important Cues

- If there is not enough room in the output range, 1-2-3 will beep, and an error message will appear. To get out of the error, press Esc and create a larger output range, or limit your criteria to a smaller segment of data.

- After entering new criteria in the criteria range, press the Query (F7) key to repeat the most recent query.

- **/D**ata **Q**uery **E**xtract remembers the last input, criteria, and output ranges used from the Query menu. You do not have to enter the ranges if they are the same as the previous ranges. With Release 2.2, you can check the current ranges by looking at the Query Settings sheet when you select **/D**ata **Q**uery. With Release 2.01, check the current ranges by selecting Input, Criterion, or Output; then press Enter to accept the ranges, or Esc to clear the previous range so that you can specify a new one.

- Select the **R**eset command to clear all range settings.

- Use **/W**orksheet **W**indow to see the input, criteria, and output ranges on one screen. Move the cell pointer between windows by pressing Window (F6).

- Use the * and ? wild cards to extract groups of similar records.

RELEASE
2.2

- You can enter the field names in the output range in any order you want; use this feature to reorganize the database field structure or to print selected fields in reports.

- /Data Query Unique works the same way as /Data Query Extract, but /Data Query Unique extracts only unique records that meet the criteria.

- Field labels in the criteria range must exactly match the field labels in the database, including capitalization.

Caution

If you select only the field names as the output range, you are given an unlimited amount of rows for the extracted report, but existing contents below the output field names are erased.

For more information, see **/Data Query Find**, **/Data Query Unique**, *and Chapter 12.*

Data Query Unique   /DQU

Purpose

Copies to the output range of the worksheet unique records that meet conditions set in the criteria.

Reminders

- Copies records from the input range that match specifications entered in the criteria range to the output range. If multiple records with the same criteria exist, only one record is copied to the output range.

- You must define the input, output, and criteria ranges before using /Data Query Unique.

Procedures

1. Type **/dq**

2. Select **I**nput.

3. Highlight the database you want to use in the search operation. Include in the highlighted range all the field names, records, and fields you want searched. If the existing range is acceptable, press Enter. If you want to change the existing range, press Esc and highlight a new range. Press Enter after highlighting the input range.

4. Select Criteria (Criterion in Release 2.01).

5. Highlight the criteria range. Include only the field names and the rows below the field names that include criteria. Including a blank row causes all records to be retrieved.

6. Select **O**utput.

7. Highlight the output range. Highlight the field names as the first row in the output range. You may or may not highlight additional rows in the output range, depending on whether you want the output range to be limited or unlimited.

8. Select **U**nique. Nonduplicate records that match the criteria range will be copied to the output range. If duplicate records are found, only one record is copied.

9. Select **Q**uit to return to the worksheet.

Important Cues

- If there is not enough room in the output range, 1-2-3 will beep, and an error message will appear. To get out of the error, press Esc and create a larger output range, or limit your criteria to a smaller segment of data.

- To extract all records from the database, both duplicate and unique, use **/D**ata **Q**uery **E**xtract.

- After entering new criteria in the criteria range or copying new headings into the output range, press the Query (F7) key to repeat the most recent query.

- **/D**ata **Q**uery **U**nique remembers the last input, criteria, and output ranges used from the Query menu. You do not have to enter the ranges if they are the same as the previous ranges. With Release 2.2, you can check the current ranges by looking at the Query Settings sheet when you select **/D**ata **Q**uery. With Release 2.01, check the current ranges by selecting Input, Criterion, or Output; then press Enter to accept the ranges, or Esc to clear the previous range so that you can specify a new one.

- Select **R**eset to clear all range settings.

- Use **/W**orksheet **W**indow to see the input, criteria, and output ranges on one screen. Move the cell pointer between windows with Window (F6).

- Make sure that you use **/R**ange **E**rase to remove previous criteria. If you enter a space in the criteria range, 1-2-3 will search for records that have a blank space in that field.

RELEASE

2.2

Cautions

- As with other **/D**ata **Q**uery commands, the field names in the criteria range must match the field names in the database, including capitalization.

- If you select only the field names as the output range, you are given an unlimited number of rows for the extracted report, but existing contents below the output field names will be erased.

*For more information, see **/Data Query Find**, **/Data Query Extract**, and Chapter 12.*

Data Query Delete /DQD

Purpose

Removes from the input range any records that meet conditions in the criteria range.

Reminders

- Use **/D**ata **Q**uery **D**elete to "clean up" your database; remove records that are not current or that have been extracted to another worksheet.

- You must define a 1-2-3 database complete with input and criteria ranges.

- Create a backup file before using /dqd. If data is incorrectly deleted, a copy of the original worksheet will thus be intact.

Procedures

1. Type **/dq**

2. Select **I**nput.

3. Highlight the database from which you want to remove records. Include in the highlighted range all the field names, records, and fields you want to delete. If the existing range is acceptable, press Enter. If you want to change the existing range, press Esc and highlight a new range. Press Enter after highlighting the input range.

4. Select **C**riteria (**C**riterion in Release 2.01).

5. Highlight the criteria range.

6. Select **D**elete.

7. You will be asked whether you want to delete the records. Select **C**ancel to stop the command or **D**elete to remove the records from the input range.

8. Use **/F**ile **S**ave to save the worksheet under a new file name. Do not save the worksheet to the same file name. Doing so will replace the original database with the database from which records have been deleted.

Important Cues

- After entering new criteria, press the Query (F7) key to repeat the most recent query.

- To check which records will be deleted, select **/D**ata **Q**uery **F**ind after you have entered the input and criteria ranges. Use the up- and down-arrow keys to display the records that meet the criteria.

- Another method of checking the records marked for deletion is to use **/D**ata **Q**uery **E**xtract to make a copy of the records. Check this copy against the records you want to delete.

- You do not have to enter the input and criteria ranges if they are the same for the next deletion. With Release 2.2, you can check the current ranges by looking at the Query Settings sheet when you select /Data Query. With Release 2.01, check the current ranges by selecting Input or Criterion; then press Enter to accept the ranges, or Esc to cancel the previous range so that you can specify a new one.

- Create a "rolling" database that stores only current records and removes old records to archive files. Use /Data Query Extract to extract old records from the file; save them to another worksheet by using /File Xtract. Then use /Data Query Delete to remove the old records from the database file.

Cautions

- As with other /Data Query commands, the field labels in the criteria range must match the field labels in the database. The labels can appear in a different order, but the spelling and cases must match. The easiest and safest method of creating criteria labels is to use /Copy.

- You can inadvertently delete more than you want with /Data Query Delete, particularly if a row in the criteria range is empty when you execute /dqd. Make sure that your criteria range is set up correctly before you use this command.

- Deleted records cannot be recovered (undeleted). Make a copy of the original worksheet before deleting records and save the copy until you are sure the /Data Query Delete operation worked properly.

For more information, see /Data Query Find, /Data Query Extract, and Chapter 12.

Data Distribution   /DD

Purpose

Creates a frequency distribution showing how often specific data occurs in a database.

Using data from a local consumer survey, for example, you can have /Data Distribution determine how income is distributed. After you set up income brackets as a bin, /dd will show how many people's incomes fall within each bin. Figure D.4 shows an example of this type of distribution. The contents of column E (text values) were entered manually.

Fig. D.4.
Example of
/Data
Distribution.

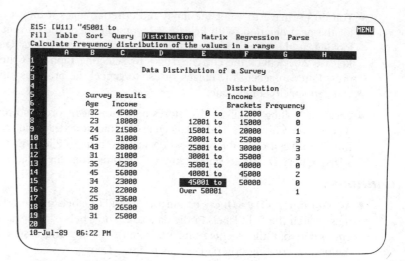

```
E15: [W11] "45001 to                                              MENU
Fill  Table  Sort  Query  Distribution  Matrix  Regression  Parse
Calculate frequency distribution of the values in a range
      A      B      C       D        E          F        G        H
1
2                          Data Distribution of a Survey
3
4                                          Distribution
5              Survey Results              Income
6              Age    Income               Brackets Frequency
7               32    45000          0 to  12000        0
8               23    18000      12001 to  15000        0
9               24    21500      15001 to  20000        1
10              45    31000      20001 to  25000        3
11              43    28000      25001 to  30000        3
12              31    31000      30001 to  35000        3
13              35    42300      35001 to  40000        0
14              45    56000      40001 to  45000        2
15              34    23000      45001 to  50000        0
16              28    22000      Over 50001             1
17              25    33600
18              30    26500
19              31    25000
20
10-Jul-89  06:22 PM
```

Reminders

- **/D**ata **D**istribution works only on numeric values.

- Data must be arranged in a *value range*: a column, row, or rectangular range.

- You must move the cell pointer to a worksheet portion that has two adjacent blank columns. In the left column, enter the highest value for each entry in the bin range. Enter these bin values in ascending order.

Procedures

1. Type **/dd**

2. Enter the value range, which contains the data being analyzed. If an existing range appears, you can accept it by pressing Enter. To indicate a new range, press Esc and enter a new range by typing the address of the range, typing an assigned range name, or highlighting the range. The value range in figure D.4 is C7..C19.

3. Press Enter.

4. Enter the bin range: type the range address, type a range name, or highlight the range. The bin range in figure D.4 is F7..F15.

5. Press Enter.

6. The frequency distribution appears in the column to the right of the bin range. In figure D.4, the distribution appears in G7..G16. Note that the frequency column extends one row beyond the bin range. The last frequency value is the number of values that are greater than the last bin value.

Important Cues

- Use /Data Fill to create a bin range with evenly distributed bins.

- You can find distribution patterns of subgroups in your database by first using /Data Query Extract to create a select database. Use /Data Distribution to find distribution in the subgroup.

- You can make data distribution tables easier to read by including a text column at the left of the bin range.

- Use @DCOUNT with /Data Table 1 to determine the data distribution for text in a database. Enter down the left column of the data table the text being counted. The input cell is the cell in the criteria range into which you would manually insert text. The @DCOUNT function should be placed in the top row of the data table area.

- Use the /Graph commands to create bar and line graphs that display the data distributions.

- Use @DCOUNT if you need to count items that match more than one criterion. (/Data Distribution uses the bin as the only criterion.) Insert criteria in the criteria range by using /Data Table 1 or /Data Table 2.

Cautions

- Text labels and blanks in the values range are ignored in the value range. Cells containing ERR and NA are counted in the first or last bin.

- /Data Distribution overwrites any cell contents that previously existed in the frequency column.

For more information, see Chapter 12.

Data Matrix   /DM

Purpose

Multiplies column-and-row matrices of cells. Inverts columns and rows in square matrices.

Reminder

/Data Matrix, a specialized mathematical command, enables you to solve simultaneous linear equations and manipulate the results.

Procedures

To invert a matrix, follow these steps:

1. Type /dm

2. Choose **Invert**. You can invert a nonsingular square matrix of up to 90 rows and 90 columns.

3. Enter the range address or range name of the range you want to invert.

4. Type or highlight an output range to hold the inverted solution matrix. You can indicate or point to only the upper left corner of the output range. You can locate the output range anywhere on the worksheet, including on top of the matrix you are inverting.

5. Press Enter.

To multiply matrices, follow these steps:

1. Type **/dm**

2. Choose **Multiply**. You can multiply two rectangular matrices together in accordance with the rules of matrix algebra.

3. Enter the range address or range name of the first range to multiply. The number of columns of the first range must equal the number of rows of the second range. Again, the maximum size of the matrix is 90 rows by 90 columns.

4. Enter the range address or range name of the second range to multiply.

5. Enter an output range to hold the multiplied solution matrix. You can type or point to only the upper left corner of the output range, and then press Enter. The resulting matrix has the same number of rows as the first matrix, and the same number of columns as the second.

Caution

The output matrix overwrites existing cell contents.

For more information, see Chapter 12.

Data Regression   */DR*

Purpose

Finds trends in data.

/Data **R**egression uses multiple-regression analysis to calculate the "best straight line" relating a single dependent Y value to a single independent X value. You can have as many as 16 independent variables for each dependent Y value.

Reminders

- **/D**ata **R**egression measures the dependency of dependent values to independent. The measure of this dependency is displayed as R Squared. The closer R Squared is to one, the greater the dependency.

- A completed regression analysis produces the constant and X coefficients so that you can predict new values of Y from a given X. The following equation calculates Y values:

    Y = Constant + Coeff. of X1 * X1 + Coeff. of X2 * X2 + Coeff. of X3 * X3 + . . .

- If there is a single X for each Y, the formula is the familiar formula for a straight line:

    Y = Constant + Coeff. of X1 * X1

- The Constant term is the location where the best-fit line intersects the y-axis. Figure D.5 shows a worksheet containing sets of X and Y data in the range B5..C10. Plot the X values in C5..C10 against the Y calculated values to see the trend line.

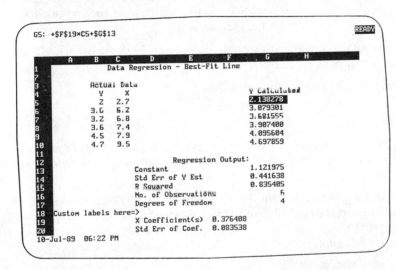

Fig. D.5.
The worksheet with single X and Y inputs.

- Enter your sets of X data and Y data in columns that have an equal number of rows. You can have as many rows of data as will fit in memory. The X data must be in matching order with the Y data and must be in adjacent columns. In figure D.5, the X and Y data is in B4..C10.

- The output area must be at least nine rows in length and two columns wider than the number of sets of X values (no less than four columns wide).

Procedures

1. Type **/dr**

2. Select **X**-Range.

3. Highlight the X range (C5..C10), making sure that the highlighting includes all the rows and columns of X data.

4. Select **Y**-Range.

5. Highlight all rows in the Y range (B5..B10).

6. Select **I**ntercept.

7. Select one of the following:

Menu Item	Description
Compute	Calculates the best-fit equation. The y-axis intercept finds its own value.
Zero	Calculates the best-fit equation but forces the equation to cross the y-axis at zero when all X values are zero.

8. Select **O**utput-Range and enter the cell address of the upper left corner of the output range (D12).

9. Select **G**o to calculate the regression.

Important Cues

- Between the Degrees of Freedom row and the X Coefficient(s) row, you can enter a row of coefficient labels that will not be overwritten by the output range.

- To create a best-fit straight line from the results of **/D**ata **R**egression, execute /dr, sort the original X and Y data in ascending order by using X data as the primary sort field (so that the graph will plot correctly), and then enter the following formula in the top cell of the calculated Y column:

  Ycalc = Xvalue * Coeff. of X1 + Constant

  Copy this formula down a column to produce all the calculated Y values for each real X value. Use the **/G**raph commands to generate an XY graph where the X range for the graph is the real X value. The A graph range is the original Y data, and the B graph range is the calculated Y data.

Caution

/Data **R**egression produces the warning Cannot Invert Matrix if one set of X values is proportional to another set of X values. Two sets of X values are proportional when one set can be multiplied by a constant to produce the second set.

For more information, see **/Graph** *commands and Chapter 12.*

Data Parse *   /DP*

Purpose

Separates the long labels resulting from /File Import into discrete text and numeric cell entries.

The separated text and numbers are placed in individual cells in a row of an output range.

Reminders

- Import the data with /File Import Text. Each record from the file appears as a long label in a single cell in a column of labels in the worksheet.

- The long label resulting from /File Import Text may appear to be entries in more than one cell; however, the long label is located in the single cell at the far left.

- If the file you are importing includes numbers surrounded by spaces and text within quotation marks, use /File Import Numbers. This command automatically separates numbers and text in quotation marks into separate cells.

- Find in the worksheet a clear area to which the parsed data can be copied, and then note the cell addresses of the corners. Move the cell pointer to the first cell in the column you want to parse.

- /Data Parse separates the long label by using the rules displayed in the format line. You can edit the format line if you want the data to be separated in a different way.

- Move the cell pointer to the first cell in the row where you want to begin parsing.

Procedures

1. Type **/dp**

2. Select Format-Line.

3. Select Create. A format line is inserted at the cell pointer, and the row of data moves down. This format line shows 1-2-3's "best guess" at how the data in the cell pointer should be separated.

4. If you want to change the rules displayed by 1-2-3, select Edit from the Format-Line menu. Edit the format line and press Enter.

5. If the imported data is in different formats, such as an uneven number of items or a mixture of field names and numbers, you will need to create additional format lines. Enter these lines at the row where the data format changed. Create additional format lines by selecting Quit and repeating the procedure.

6. Select Input-Column.

7. Specify the column containing the format line and the data it will format. Do not highlight the columns to the right that appear to contain data but do not. Press Enter.

8. Select **O**utput-Range.

9. Move the cell pointer to the upper left corner of the range to receive the parsed data and press Enter.

10. Select **G**o.

Important Cues

- Figure D.6 shows two format lines generated automatically by 1-2-3. The first format line is for the field names; the second is for the data. The initial format lines will separate inventory items that have a blank in the name. The asterisk (*) followed by an L shows where 1-2-3 "thinks" that a new field should begin.

Fig. D.6.
Format lines
for /Data
Parse.

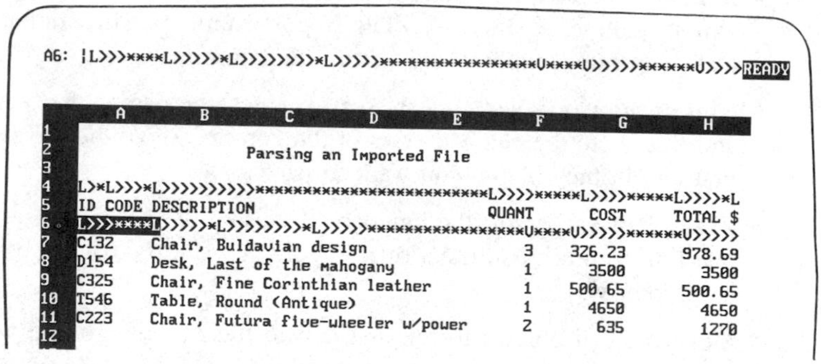

- Use symbols to indicate the first character of a label (L), value (V), date (D), or time (T). You also can choose to skip a character (S), specify additional characters of the same type (>), or add a blank space (*) if the data is longer than the > symbols indicate.

- Editing keys can be used on the format line to change the parsing rules. In addition, you can use the up- and down-arrow, PgDn, and PgUp keys to scroll the information on-screen. Use this method to see whether the format line has assigned enough space for each piece of data being parsed.

RELEASE
2.2

- In Release 2.2, a Parse Settings sheet displays the current input column and output range when you select **/D**ata **P**arse.

Caution

The output range should be blank. Parsed data writes over any information previously in the output range.

For more information, see **/File Import** *and Chapter 12.*

System, Add-In, and Quit Commands

The following menu map shows the **/Add-In** commands. Commands new with Release 2.2 are highlighted.

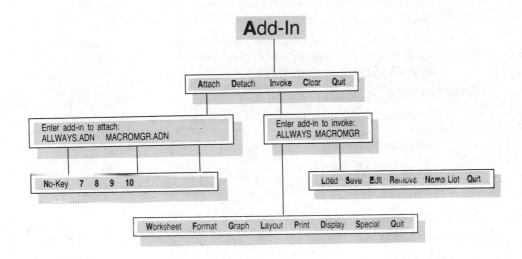

System /S

Purpose

Leaves the current worksheet, exits from 1-2-3 temporarily so that you can run operating-system commands, and returns you to 1-2-3 and the worksheet.

Reminders

- Be certain that the programs you run from within 1-2-3 can fit in your computer's available memory.
- If you want to run an external operating-system command, be sure that the command is available on your disk drive or is on the path for a hard disk system.

Procedures

1. Type **/s**

2. Type the operating-system commands or program names you want to run.

3. When you have finished running a program, return to the operating system.

4. Return to 1-2-3 from the operating-system prompt by typing **EXIT**.

Important Cues

- If COMMAND.COM is not available on disk, the message Cannot invoke DOS appears when you enter **/S**. If the message appears, press Esc, insert a disk containing the COMMAND.COM file, and retype **/S**. To return to 1-2-3, you must reinsert the System disk, type **EXIT**, and press Enter.

- For a complete discussion of the various operating-system commands, see *Using PC DOS*, 3rd Edition; *MS-DOS User's Guide*, 3rd Edition; or *Using OS/2*, all published by Que Corporation.

Caution

The operating-system file, COMMAND.COM, must be copied onto your 1-2-3 System disk before the /System command will work. On a hard disk, the COMMAND.COM file should be at the root directory (\).

For more information, see Chapter 4.

Add-In Attach   /AA

Purpose

Loads an add-in applications program into memory. Add-in applications are programs that work along with 1-2-3 to extend its capabilities. Release 2.2 comes with two add-in programs: Allways and the Macro Library Manager.

Assigns a function key (for example, Alt-F7) that you can use to invoke the add-in each time you want to use it.

Reminders

- Make sure that the add-in program is in your default 1-2-3 directory. Add-in programs have the extension .ADN. The Allways add-in, for example, is ALLWAYS.ADN; the Macro Library Manager is MACROMGR.ADN. For more details, refer to the documentation for your add-in program.

- You may not have enough memory to attach an add-in unless you remove other memory-resident programs (such as SideKick) or detach other add-ins.

Procedures

1. Type **/aa**

2. Highlight the add-in name from the list of .ADN files displayed. Press Enter.

3. Select one of the following:

Menu Item	Description
No-Key	Does not assign the add-in to a function key. The add-in must be invoked with /Add-In Invoke.
7	Assigns the add-in to Alt-F7
8	Assigns the add-in to Alt-F8
9	Assigns the add-in to Alt-F9
10	Assigns the add-in to Alt-F10

Important Cues

- You can invoke an add-in by using the function key you assigned to the add-in when you attached it or by using the /Add-In Invoke command.

- If you want an add-in to attach automatically each time you start 1-2-3, use /Worksheet Global Default Other Add-In Set. Be sure to use /Worksheet Global Default Update to save the setting.

- When you don't have enough memory to attach an add-in, you will get a Memory Full error message. If any other add-ins are attached, you can use /Add-In Detach to remove them from memory, allowing room for the other add-in. You also can exit from 1-2-3 and free up memory by removing any other memory-resident programs you may be using.

Add-In Invoke   /AI

Purpose

Activates an add-in program that you have previously attached.

Use this command whenever you want to use the commands or functions in the add-in program.

Reminder

If you used /Worksheet Global Default Other Add-In Set to attach the add-in automatically, the add-in must be attached either with /Add-In Attach or automatically when 1-2-3 is loaded.

Procedures

If you did not assign a function key to the add-in, do the following:

1. Type /ai

2. Highlight the add-in from the list of attached add-ins. Press Enter.

Refer to the add-in's documentation for specific instructions on using the add-in.

If you assigned a function key to the add-in, do the following:

1. Press Alt and the function key (F7-F10) you assigned to the add-in when you attached it. If you assigned the add-in to the F7 function key, for example, press Alt-F7 to invoke the add-in.

Refer to the add-in's documentation for specific instructions on using the add-in.

Important Cue

You can automatically attach and invoke the add-in by using /**W**orksheet **G**lobal **D**efault **O**ther **A**dd-In **S**et. Choose **Y**es in response to the prompt `Automatically invoke this add-in whenever you start 1-2-3?` Be sure to use /**W**orksheet **G**lobal **D**efault **U**pdate to save the setting.

RELEASE

2.2

Add-In [Detach, Clear]   /AD or /AC

Purpose

Removes add-ins from memory so that you have more memory available for your spreadsheet or other add-ins.

Reminder

If you used /**W**orksheet **G**lobal **D**efault **O**ther **A**dd-In **S**et to attach the add-in automatically, the add-in must be attached either with /**A**dd-In **A**ttach or automatically when 1-2-3 is loaded.

Procedures

To remove an add-in from memory, do the following:

1. Type /**ad**

2. Highlight the add-in from the displayed list of attached add-ins. Press Enter.

3. Select **Q**uit to leave the **A**dd-In menu.

To remove all add-ins from memory, do the following:

1. Type /**ac**

2. Select **Q**uit to leave the **A**dd-In menu.

Important Cue

The /**Add-In D**etach and /**Add-In C**lear commands remove the applications from memory during the current work session only. If you have an auto-attach add-in that you no longer want to attach automatically, use the /**Worksheet Global Default Other Add-In C**ancel command. Be sure to use /**Worksheet Global Default U**pdate to save the setting.

Quit /Q

Purpose

Leaves 1-2-3 for the current work session and returns you to the operating system.

Reminder

Make sure that you have saved the current worksheet and graph before exiting from 1-2-3.

Procedures

1. Type /**q**

2. Select **Yes** to quit 1-2-3 and return to the operating system or the Access System. Select **No** to return to 1-2-3 and the current worksheet.

3. In Release 2.2, if you haven't saved worksheet changes, another No/Yes menu appears. Select **No** if you want to cancel the /**Q**uit command so that you can save your worksheet. Select **Yes** to quit without saving.

4. If you started 1-2-3 from the Access System menu, you will be returned to it. From the Access System menu, choose Exit to leave 1-2-3. If you started 1-2-3 by typing **123**, you will be returned to the operating system.

RELEASE
2.2

Important Cue

Use COPY or DISKCOPY to create a backup of important files. To guard against data loss, be sure to make backup copies regularly and keep a weekly archival backup copy at a separate location. In most cases, your computer can be replaced, but your data and worksheets cannot.

Caution

Worksheets not saved with /**File S**ave or /**File X**tract are lost when you exit from 1-2-3.

For more information, see /***File Save*** *and* /***File Xtract***.

Allways Commands

Allways is an add-in program included with Release 2.2 (Release 2.01 users can buy the program separately). This "spreadsheet publishing" program, which works in conjunction with 1-2-3, enables you to produce professional-looking reports. In addition, Allways enables you to print graphs along with your worksheets—all without leaving 1-2-3.

Allways Menu Map

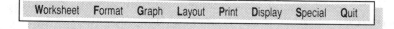

| Worksheet | Format | Graph | Layout | Print | Display | Special | Quit |

RELEASE
2.2

Allways Attach   */AA*

Purpose

Makes available a variety of fonts, lines, and shadings for use in printed reports. A report printed with Allways can look much more professional than one printed with 1-2-3. Figure AW.1 illustrates some of the formatting features you can use with Allways: lines, boxes, shading, fonts, underlining, and boldface.

Fig. AW.1.
A worksheet
formatted with
Allways.

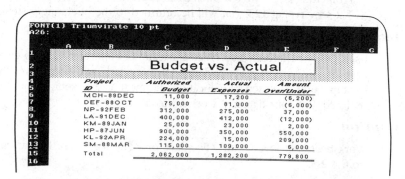

/Allways Attach also prints graphs without your having to exit from 1-2-3 and includes 1-2-3 graphs with reports.

Reminders

- Use the AWSETUP program to install Allways.

- Allways is an add-in program supplied with Release 2.2. (Users of Release 2.01 can buy Allways separately.) As with any add-in, Allways must be attached before it be invoked. You can have Allways attach automatically whenever you load 1-2-3, or you can attach the add-in when you need to use it.

Procedures

1. Type **/aa** (or if you are using Release 2.01's Add-In Manager, press Alt-F10 and choose **A**ttach).

2. Highlight ALLWAYS.ADN and press Enter.

3. Select one of the following:

Menu Item	Description
No-Key	Does not assign Allways to a function key. Allways must be invoked with **/A**dd-In **I**nvoke.
7	Assigns Allways to Alt-F7
8	Assigns Allways to Alt-F8
9	Assigns Allways to Alt-F9
10	Assigns Allways to Alt-F10

Note: With Release 2.01's Add-In Manager, you cannot use Alt-F10 to invoke an add-in.

Important Cues

- You can invoke Allways with the function key you assigned to it when you attached it, or you can invoke Allways with **/A**dd-In **I**nvoke. (If you are using Release 2.01's Add-In Manager, press Alt-F10 and then choose **I**nvoke.)

- If you don't have enough memory to attach the Allways add-in, you will get a `Memory Full` error message. If any other add-ins are attached, you can use **/A**dd-In **D**etach (in Release 2.01's Add-In Manager, press Alt-F10 and choose **D**etach) to remove them from memory, allowing room for the Allways add-in. You also can exit from 1-2-3 and free up memory by removing any other memory-resident programs you may be using.

- To quit Allways and go back to 1-2-3, choose **Q**uit from the Allways menu (Release 2.01 users should choose **1**23 from the Allways menu) or press Esc when the ALLWAYS indicator appears in the upper right corner of the screen.

- Use **/W**orksheet **G**lobal **D**efault **O**ther Add-In **S**et to attach Allways automatically when 1-2-3 is loaded. (If you are using Release 2.01's Add-In Manager, press Alt-F10 and then choose **S**etup Set.)

Caution

Do not detach Allways before saving the worksheet; if you do, your formatting will be lost.

Worksheet Column Set-Width and Worksheet Row Set-Height /WCS and /WRS

Purpose

Precisely adjusts the width of the worksheet columns and the height of the worksheet rows. Always enables column widths to be set in tenths of an inch and row heights to be set in point sizes. Because you can use different font sizes in a worksheet and see the sizes on-screen, you may discover that you need to change the width of a column or the height of a row.

Reminder

Place the cell pointer on the first row or column to be set. To change more than one adjacent column or row, press the period (.) key to anchor one corner of the range and then use the arrow keys to highlight the number of rows or columns.

Procedures

To change the width of a column, do the following:

1. Type **/wcs**

2. Type the new column width or press the right- and left-arrow keys to adjust the width one character at a time. To adjust the width one-tenth of a character at a time, press Ctrl and the right- or left-arrow key.

3. Press Enter.

To change the height of a row, do the following:

1. Type **/wrs**

2. Type the new row height in points or press the up- and down-arrow keys to adjust the point size one increment at a time.

3. Press Enter.

Important Cues

- To return to the original 1-2-3 column widths after adjusting column widths in Allways, use the **/**Worksheet Column **R**eset-Width command. (In Release 2.01, Allways uses **R**eset instead of **R**eset-Width.)

- The default row height setting is **Auto**. Allways automatically calculates the appropriate row height necessary for the font size you have chosen. The row height of a large font size, for example, is taller than that of a tiny font size.

- You can create a thick vertical line by shading a column with **/Format Shade** and then narrowing the column width. To create a thick horizontal line, shade a row and then narrow the row height.

Worksheet Page   /WP

Purpose

Changes where Allways creates a page break. You can tell Allways at which row or column to start a new page.

Reminders

- To see where the current page breaks are, use **/Print Range Set** to define the area to be printed. A dashed line indicates where the page breaks are located.

- Place the cell pointer on the first row or column of the new page.

Procedures

To set a row page break, do the following:

1. Type **/wpr**

2. Position the pointer on the first row of the new page (if you haven't already) and press Enter.

To set a column page break, do the following:

1. Type **/wpc**

2. Position the pointer on the first column of the new page (if you haven't already) and press Enter. A dashed line appears to the left of the specified column to indicate the new page break.

Important Cue

To remove a page break, place the cell pointer on the first row or column of the page and select **/Worksheet Page Delete**.

Format Font   */FF*

Purpose

Selects the font for a range of cells. The font consists of a typeface (for example, Times Roman), a point size, and sometimes an attribute (for example, heavy or italic).

Reminders

- Place the cell pointer on the first cell you want to format.

- If you want to choose a font from a laser cartridge, use the **/P**rint Configuration **C**artridge command to select the cartridge to use.

- The fonts available to choose from depend on your printer; Allways can print any font your printer is capable of printing.

- Allways includes three soft fonts: Courier, Times, and Triumvirate. If you have a dot-matrix printer, Allways uses your printer's graphics mode. If you have a laser printer, these fonts are automatically downloaded to your printer when you use them. Your printer may not have enough memory for larger fonts.

- Each worksheet can use eight different fonts. These eight fonts are stored in a "font set."

- Each worksheet can have its own font set. These font sets can be named and saved in font libraries, which you can use in other worksheets.

Procedures

To choose a font from the current font set, do the following:

1. Type **/ff**

2. Highlight the font or type the number (**1-8**) that appears next to the font.

3. Make sure that **U**se is highlighted in the menu. Press Enter.

4. Indicate the range by highlighting or by typing. Press Enter.

To use a font not in the current font set, do the following:

1. Type **/ff**

2. Specify the font to be replaced: highlight it or type the number (**1-8**) that appears next to the font. (Choose a font you don't need in the current worksheet.)

3. Select **R**eplace.

4. A list appears of all the fonts your printer can use. Highlight the font you want to add, or type the number next to the font. Press Enter.

5. Highlight the point size and press Enter.

6. If you want to use this new font, select Use and highlight the range for the font. Press Enter.

To save the current font set in a library, do the following:

1. Type **/ff**

2. Select Library **S**ave.

3. Type a file name of as many as eight characters and press Enter. The file is saved under the extension .AFS.

To use a font library, do the following:

1. Type **/ff**

2. Select Library **R**etrieve.

3. Allways displays a list of library files (.AFS extension). Highlight the name and press Enter. The eight fonts saved in this library display in the font box. Any of these fonts can now be used in the worksheet.

Important Cues

- Before choosing the **/F**ormat Font command, you can select the range to format. To preselect the range, place the cell pointer on the first cell to format, press the period (.) key to anchor one corner of the range, and then place the cell pointer on the last cell to format. When you use **/F**ormat Font, the range you have selected will be the default range to format.

- To choose a font in the current font set, you can use a "quick" key rather than the menu. First, select the range to format. Then press Alt and the desired font number.

- Create font libraries for combinations of fonts that you are likely to use in other worksheets.

- If you change the font size of a paragraph of text, you may find that the text requires more or fewer columns than it originally did. To respace the text, use the **/S**pecial Justify command. This command is similar to 1-2-3's **/R**ange Justify command, which "wordwraps" text within the range you define.

Caution

Your laser printer may not have enough memory to download soft fonts that have a large point size. If you get an Out of memory error message when you print, you need to specify a different-sized font or use an internal or cartridge font.

Format [Bold, Underline, Color]   */FB, /FU, or /FC*

Purpose

Boldfaces, single-underlines, or double-underlines a range of cells. The titles in figure AW.2 are boldfaced, the last number in each column is single-underlined, and the final totals are double-underlined.

Fig. AW.2.
A worksheet formatted with boldface, single-, and double-underline.

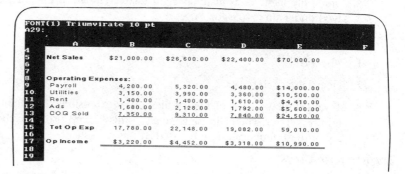

Changes the color of a range of cells (assuming that you have a color printer).

Reminder

Place the cell pointer on the first cell you want to format.

Procedures

To boldface a range, do the following:

1. Type **/fb**

2. Select **S**et.

3. Indicate the range by highlighting or typing. Press Enter.

To underline a range, do the following:

1. Type **/fu**

2. Select one of the following:

Menu Item	Description
Single	Places a single underline under the range
Double	Places a double underline under the range

3. Indicate the range by highlighting or typing. Press Enter.

To add color to a range, do the following:

1. Type **/fc**

2. Highlight the color or type the number (**1-8**) that appears next to the color. Press Enter.

3. Indicate the range by highlighting or by typing. Press Enter.

Important Cues

● Before choosing the /**F**ormat command, you can select the range to format. To preselect the range, place the cell pointer on the first cell to format, press the period (**.**) key to anchor one corner of the range, and then place the cell pointer on the last cell to format. When you use the /**F**ormat command, the range you have selected will be the default range.

● Another way to boldface a range is to use a "quick" key rather than the menu. First, select the range to format. Then press Alt-B. (Note: If the cell is already boldfaced, Alt-B cancels the boldface.)

● You also can underline by using a "quick" key: Alt-U. The first time you press Alt-U, the range will be single-underlined. The second time, it will be double-underlined; the third time, the underlining will be cleared.

● To cancel boldfacing from a cell or a range, use /**F**ormat **B**old **C**lear. To cancel underlining, use /**F**ormat **U**nderline **C**lear.

Format Lines   /FL

Purpose

Draws horizontal or vertical lines; creates boxes around individual cells or an outline around a range of cells.

Reminder

Place the cell pointer in the upper left corner of the range you want to draw a line around.

Procedures

1. Type /**fl**

2. Select one of the following:

Menu Item	Description
Outline	Draws lines around the entire range, forming a single box
Left	Draws a line at the left side of each selected cell in the range
Right	Draws a line at the right side of each selected cell in the range

Top	Draws a line above each selected cell in the range
Bottom	Draws a line below each selected cell in the range
All	Draws lines around each selected cell in the range so that each cell is boxed (the same as choosing **L**eft, **R**ight, **T**op, and **B**ottom)

3. Indicate the range by highlighting or by typing. Press Enter.

Important Cues

- Before choosing the /**F**ormat command, you can select the range to format. To preselect the range, place the cell pointer on the first cell to format, press the period (.) to anchor one corner of the range, and then place the cell pointer on the last cell to format. When you use the /**F**ormat command, the range you have selected will be the default range.

- The "quick" key for drawing lines is Alt-L. The first time you press Alt-L, the range is outlined. The second time, the range will be boxed, and the third time all lines will be cleared.

- To remove lines, use /**F**ormat Lines Clear.

- To change the darkness of lines before you print, use /**L**ayout **O**ptions Line-Weight (LineWeight in Release 2.01). Choose among **N**ormal, **L**ight, and **H**eavy.

- If you need thicker vertical lines, shade a column with /**F**ormat **S**hade and then narrow the column width. To create thick horizontal lines, shade a row and then narrow the row height.

Format Shade /FS

Purpose

Highlights important areas on the printed spreadsheet. The column headings in figure AW.3 stand out because of their light background shading.

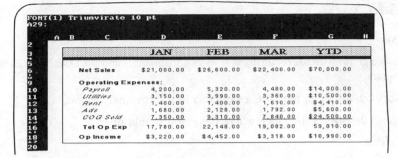

Fig. AW.3. Headings emphasized with light and solid shades.

Creates thick horizontal and vertical lines. The thick line underneath the column headings in figure AW.3 was created with a solid shade on a narrow row.

Reminder

Place the cell pointer in the upper left corner of the range you want to shade.

Procedures

1. Type **/fs**

2. Select one of the following:

Menu Item	Description
Light	Uses the lightest shading available
Dark	Uses a darker shading
Solid	Shades the range a solid black

3. Indicate the range by highlighting or by typing. Press Enter.

Important Cues

- Before choosing the **/F**ormat Shade command, you can select the range to format. To preselect the range, place the cell pointer on the first cell to format, press the period (.) to anchor the corner of the range, and then place the cell pointer on the last cell to format. When you use the **/F**ormat Shade command, the range you have selected will be the default range.

- The "quick" key for shading is Alt-S. The first time you press Alt-S, the range becomes lightly shaded. The second time, the shading becomes dark; the third time, the range is shaded solid. The fourth time you press Alt-S, all shading is cleared.

- To remove shading, use **/F**ormat Shade Clear.

Graph Add /GA

Purpose

Prints a graph without requiring you to exit from 1-2-3 and load the PrintGraph program.

Places a 1-2-3 graph file (.PIC extension) in a spreadsheet report.

Defines the size of the range where the graph should print.

Reminders

- Create the graph in 1-2-3 and save it to a .PIC file by using 1-2-3's /Graph Save command.

- To print the graph in the middle of a report, insert rows or columns where you want the graph to appear.

- Place the cell pointer in the upper left corner of the area where you want the graph to appear in the report.

Procedures

1. Type /ga

2. Highlight the name of the graph from the displayed list of .PIC files. Press Enter.

3. Type or highlight the range where you want the graph to appear. This range defines the size of the graph, so be sure to indicate the width (number of columns) and height (number of rows) of the graph. Press Enter. A hatching pattern appears in the range.

Important Cues

- To see the actual graph, rather than the hatching pattern, on the screen, use the /Display Graphs Yes command.

- To eliminate a graph from the spreadsheet report, use /Graph Remove.

- To change the size of the graph range after you have added the graph, use /Graph Settings Range.

- Use the /Format Lines command to place an outline border around the graph after you have added it. Use /Format Shade to shade the background of the graph.

- With Allways, you can have up to 20 graphs per worksheet.

- To adjust the graph range precisely, you can change the row heights and column widths of the graph range by using the /Worksheet Row and /Worksheet Column commands.

- Use the **/**Graph **G**oto command to move the pointer to a particular graph you have added. This command is useful when you have many graphs in a large spreadsheet.

Caution

Be sure not to define the graph range so that it includes cells containing data; the graph range should include blank cells only.

Graph Settings

/GS

RELEASE
2.2

Purpose

Defines the print fonts for the text in the graph; defines the colors for the graph ranges. Places more white space around the graph and changes the graph's range.

Figure AW.4 shows the **Graph Settings** menu along with the Graph Settings sheet where the current options are displayed.

```
GRAPH(1) A:\AWFIG9.PIC                                      MENU
PIC-File  Fonts  Scale  Colors  Range  Margins  Default  Quit
Replace a graph in the worksheet with a different graph file

   .PIC file: A:\AWFIG9.PIC

   Fonts                          Range: A1..A1
     1: LOTUS        Scale: x 1.00
     0: ITALIC1      Scale: y 1.00

   Colors                         Margins (in inches)
     X: Black                          Left:   0.00
     A: Blue                          Right:   0.00
     B: Black                           Top:   0.00
     C: Black                        Bottom:   0.00
     D: Black
     E: Black
     F: Black

17
18
```

*Fig. AW.4.
The Graph
Settings sheet.*

Reminders

- Allways uses the fonts supplied with 1-2-3's PrintGraph program, so be sure that you have copied the PrintGraph disk to your 1-2-3 subdirectory. The font files have the extension .FNT.

- Use Allways' **/**Graph **A**dd command to insert the graph.

- Place the cell pointer anywhere within the graph range.

Procedures

To change the graph fonts, do the following:

1. Type **/gs**

2. If the cell pointer was not in the graph range, you will be asked to select a graph from a list of graphs you have added to the spreadsheet. Highlight the .PIC file name and press Enter.

3. Choose Fonts.

4. Select one of the following:

Menu Item	Description
1	Specifies the font for the top center title
2	Specifies the font for other titles and legends

5. Highlight the desired font from the displayed list. These are the fonts that come with 1-2-3's PrintGraph program. You also may type the number (**1-11**) that appears next to the font. Press Enter.

To set the font scaling factor (that is, relative size), do the following:

1. Type **/gs**

2. If the cell pointer was not in the graph range, you will be asked to select a graph from a list of graphs you have added to the spreadsheet. Highlight the .PIC file name and press Enter.

3. Choose Scale.

4. Select one of the following:

Menu Item	Description
1	Specifies the scaling factor for the first font (top center title)
2	Specifies the scaling factor for the second font (other titles and legends)

5. Type a number between .5 and 3, inclusive (1 is the default; .5 makes the font half the default size; 3 makes the font three times the default size). Press Enter.

To assign colors to graph data ranges, do the following:

1. Type **/gs**

2. If the cell pointer was not in the graph range, you will be asked to select a graph from a list of graphs you have added to the spreadsheet. Highlight the .PIC file name and press Enter.

3. Choose Colors.

4. Specify a range (**X**, **A**, **B**, **C**, **D**, **E**, or **F**).

5. Highlight the appropriate color from the displayed list, or type the number (**1-8**) that appears next to the color. Press Enter.

To change the graph range, do the following:

1. Type **/gs**

2. If the cell pointer was not in the graph range, you will be asked to select a graph from a list of graphs you have added to the spreadsheet. Highlight the .PIC file name and press Enter.

3. Choose **R**ange. The current graph range is highlighted on the screen.

4. Type the new range, or move the cell pointer and highlight the new range. Before specifying the new range, you can press Esc or Backspace to cancel the current range. Press Enter.

To change the margins around the graph, do the following:

1. Type **/gs**

2. If the cell pointer was not in the graph range, you will be asked to select a graph from a list of graphs you have added to the worksheet. Highlight the .PIC file name and press Enter.

3. Choose **M**argins.

4. Select one of the following:

Menu Item	Description
Left	Designates the left margin, the amount of space between the left edge of the graph range and the beginning of the graph
Right	Designates the right margin, the amount of space between the graph and the right side of the graph range
Top	Designates the top margin, the amount of space between the upper edge of the graph range and the top of the graph
Bottom	Designates the bottom margin, the amount of space between the graph and the bottom of the graph range

5. To specify the size (in inches) of the margin, type a number between 0 and 9.99, inclusive. The default is 0. Press Enter.

Important Cues

- To return the graph settings to their default values, choose **/Graph Settings Default Restore**. To permanently change the default settings, use **/Graph Settings Default Update**. The current settings will be stored as the default.

- You will see an error message if your font files (.FNT files) are not in the 1-2-3 program directory. If you haven't copied these files from the Print-Graph disk, do so. If the files are located in a different subdirectory, use the /Graph FontDirectory command to specify where the .FNT files are.

RELEASE
2.2

Layout PageSize and Layout Margins   */LP and /LM*

Purpose

Defines the size of paper (for example, letter, legal, or custom). Specifies the margins around the page.

Reminder

Attach and invoke the Allways add-in.

Procedures

To define the page size, do the following:

1. Type **/lp**

2. Highlight the page size from the displayed list, or type the number next to the page size. Press Enter.

3. If you chose **Custom**, you will be asked to enter the page width and page length in inches.

To set the margins, do the following:

1. Type **/lm**

2. Specify margins from these options:

Menu Item	Description
Left	Designates the left margin, the amount of space between the left edge of the paper and the printed worksheet
Right	Designates the right margin, the amount of space between the printed worksheet and the right edge of paper
Top	Designates the top margin, the amount of space between the top of the paper and the printed worksheet
Bottom	Designates the bottom margin, the amount of space between the printed worksheet and the bottom of the paper

3. Type a number between 0 and 99.99 inches, inclusive (default is 1.00). Press Enter.

Important Cues

- Allways' **/Layout Margins** command is similar to 1-2-3's **/Print Printer Options Margins** command. You should be aware, however, of several differences. In 1-2-3 the right and left margins are entered in characters, and the top and bottom margins refer to the number of lines; in Allways all the margins are entered in inches. Furthermore, the right margin in Allways is the space between the printed worksheet and the right edge of the page; in 1-2-3 the right margin is the number of characters that will print on the line.

- The margins you enter in 1-2-3's print options are not transferred into Allways.

- To specify landscape (sideways) mode on a laser printer, use the **/Print Configuration Orientation** command.

- To save the page layout settings, use the **/Layout Library Save** command and assign the settings a name (which will be given the extension .ALS). You can then retrieve the settings with other worksheets.

Layout Titles and Layout Borders   /LT and /LB

RELEASE
2.2

Purpose

/Layout Titles prints a one-line title at the top or bottom of every page. This title is called a *header* or *footer*, respectively.

/Layout Borders prints a worksheet range (rows or columns) on every page. This range consists of cells that contain text to be used as a title called a *border*.

Reminder

Attach and invoke the Allways add-in.

Procedures

To specify headers and footers, do the following:

1. Type **/lt**

2. Choose from the following:

Menu Item	Description
Header	Designates a one-line title that prints at the top of each page
Footer	Designates a one-line title that prints at the bottom of each page

3. Type a title of as many as 240 characters. Press Enter.

To print column or row headings on each page, do the following:

1. Type **/lb**

2. Choose from the following:

Menu Item	Description
Top	Instructs Allways to print worksheet row(s) at the top of each page
Left	Instructs Allways to print worksheet column(s) at the left side of each page
Bottom	Instructs Allways to print worksheet row(s) at the bottom of each page

3. Move the cell pointer to the row or column to be used as a border. If the border has multiple rows or columns, press the period (**.**) key to anchor one corner of the range. Highlight the additional rows or columns. Press Enter.

Important Cues

- When specifying a border range, you need to include only one cell in the row for the top and bottom borders or one cell in the column for the left border. In other words, you do not need to highlight all the cells in the border.

- Just as in 1-2-3, the date and page number can be printed automatically in the header or footer. Enter an "at" sign (@) where you want the date to appear and a number sign (#) where you want the page number to appear.

- Break the header or footer into as many as three centered segments by entering a vertical bar (|).

- Allways' **/L**ayout **T**itles command is the equivalent of 1-2-3's **/P**rint Printer **O**ptions [Header, Footer] commands. Similarly, Allways' **/L**ayout **B**orders command is the same as 1-2-3's **/P**rint Printer **O**ptions **B**orders command.

- The headers, footers, and borders you enter in 1-2-3's print options are not transferred into Allways.

- To cancel headers or footers, use the **/L**ayout **T**itles **C**lear command. To cancel borders, use the **/L**ayout **B**orders **C**lear command.

- To save the page layout settings, use the **/L**ayout **L**ibrary **S**ave command and assign the settings a name (which will be given the extension .ALS). You can then retrieve the settings with other spreadsheets.

Caution

If you include in the print range the rows or columns specified as borders, the rows or columns will be printed twice.

Layout Options   */LO*

Purpose

Places a grid on the worksheet and changes the weight of lines created with /Format Line.

Reminder

Attach and invoke the Allways add-in.

Procedures

To change the weight of a line, do the following:

1. Type **/lol**

2. Choose one of the following weights:

Menu Item	Description
Normal	Selects the standard density of a line created with **/Format Line**
Light	Sets the density of a line created with **/Format Line** to about half that of the Normal setting
Heavy	Sets the density of a line created with **/Format Line** to about double that of the Normal setting

3. Select **Quit Quit** to return to Allways.

To set a grid on the worksheet, do the following:

1. Type **/log**

2. Select **Yes** to turn on the grid; select **No** to shut off the grid.

3. Select **Quit Quit** to return to Allways.

Important Cues

- If the densities of the lines are not heavy enough, you may set columns and rows to a suitable width and set the shading of those cells by using /Format Shade Solid.

- Use /Layout Options Grid Yes rather than /Format Lines All. With the former command, each cell is outlined with a dotted pattern. This grid stands out much less than lines.

- The grid covers every cell on the worksheet, whereas /Format Lines covers only specified ranges.

Layout Library   /LL

Purpose

Enables you to make different settings and store each in a file of its own—a library—for easy recall.

Reminders

- Attach and invoke the Allways add-in.

- In the Layout menu, make all necessary changes pertaining to such things as page size, margins, borders, options, and titles.

Procedures

To save a library file, do the following:

1. Type **/lls**

2. Either select from the list one of the current library files to save to or type a new library file name; press Enter.

3. If you selected a file name from the menu, choose whether to Cancel the command or Replace the existing library file with a new library file.

4. Select Quit to return to Allways.

To retrieve a library file, do the following:

1. Type **/llr**

2. Either select from the list one of the current library files to retrieve or type a new library file name; press Enter.

3. Select Quit to return to Allways.

To erase a library file, do the following:

1. Type **/lle**

2. Select a library file from the list or type a file name to erase; press Enter.

3. Select Quit to return to Allways.

Important Cues

- When saving a file, you may select one of the names that are listed or type a new name and press Enter.

- When retrieving a library file, you may select one of the names listed or type a new name and press Enter.

Caution

When selecting Erase, make sure that the file you choose to erase is the one you want to erase. You are not prompted to verify your choice.

Layout Update   /LU

Purpose

Replaces the current layout settings with the default settings or makes the current settings the default settings.

Reminder

Attach and invoke the Allways add-in.

Procedures

To return to the default layout settings, do the following:

1. Type **/ld**

2. Select **R**estore.

3. Select **Q**uit to return to Allways.

To make the current layout settings the default, do the following:

1. Type **/ld**

2. Select Update.

3. Select **Q**uit to return to Allways.

Important Cues

- Make sure that all layout settings are correct before selecting **/L**ayout **D**efault **U**pdate.

- Selecting **/L**ayout **D**efault **R**estore replaces all the current layout settings with the default settings. If you want to save the current settings, select **/L**ayout **L**ibrary **S**ave before restoring the defaults.

Print   /P

Purpose

Prints the worksheet and/or graph that you have formatted with Allways. Specifies what you want to print.

Reminders

- Format the worksheet as you like; specify layout options.

- Make sure that Allways is configured with the correct printer information. You can use the **/P**rint **C**onfiguration command to check or change the current settings for **P**rinter, **I**nterface, **C**artridge, **O**rientation, **R**esolution, and **B**in. (The options available differ depending on which printer you have.)

- Place the cell pointer in the upper right corner of the range to be printed.

Procedures

1. Type **/p**

2. Select **R**ange Set.

3. Specify the range to be printed: type the range address or highlight the range. Press Enter.

4. Choose **S**ettings and select from the following (if necessary):

Menu Item	Description
Begin	Requests the number of the first page to print
End	Requests the number of the last page to print
First	Requests the first page number to be inserted into a header or footer
Copies	Requests the total number of copies to be printed
Wait	Pauses the printer for single-sheet feeding

5. Enter the requested response, according to the option selected in the preceding step.

6. Press Esc to go back to the preceding menu.

7. Select **G**o to begin printing.

Important Cues

- Allways' **/P**rint **R**ange command is the equivalent of 1-2-3's **/P**rint **P**rinter **R**ange command. 1-2-3's print range, however, is not transferred to Allways.

- The **/P**rint **R**ange command puts dashed lines around each page in the print range. If you don't like where the page breaks are, use **/W**orksheet **P**age to set new page breaks before you print.

- You can specify 1-2-3 range names for your print ranges in Allways. When prompted for the print range, type the range name or press the Name (F3) key to choose from a list of names.

- You can select the range to print before choosing the **/P**rint **R**ange command. To preselect the range, place the cell pointer on the first cell to print, press the period (.) to anchor one corner of the range, and then place the cell pointer on the last cell to print. When you use the **/P**rint **R**ange command, Allways automatically fills in the selected range.

- Use **/P**rint **S**ettings **C**lear to return the print settings to their defaults.

Caution

Your laser printer may not have enough memory to download soft fonts that have a large point size. If you get an Out of memory error message when you print, you need to specify a different-sized font or use an internal or cartridge font.

Print File   /PF

RELEASE
2.2

Purpose

Enables Allways to capture printing in a file.

Reminder

Use /fr in 1-2-3 to retrieve the worksheet to print.

Procedures

1. Type **/pf**

2. Select from the list or type the name of the file to contain the printed information.

3. Specify the range to print either by pointing or typing the range.

Important Cue

The /pf command prints a worksheet to a file in the same manner as if the worksheet were printed to the printer. From a DOS prompt, type **COPY /b** *filename*.**PRN PRN**, where *filename* is the name you typed or selected when Allways asked for a name. The file will be printed on a printer as if it were being printed from Allways.

Display   /D

RELEASE
2.2

Purpose

Sets the characteristics of the screen. You can set the colors of the screen's foreground and background, for example. You also can display the worksheet in **G**raphics mode ("what you see is what you get") or in **T**ext mode (like the display in 1-2-3).

Changes the size of the characters on-screen. You can reduce the characters so that you can see more of the worksheet at once on the screen, or you can magnify them to see small fonts more clearly. Figures AW.5 and AW.6 show the same worksheet at two different magnifications: "tiny" and "large."

Fig. AW.5.
A worksheet
zoomed at
the "tiny"
magnification
level.

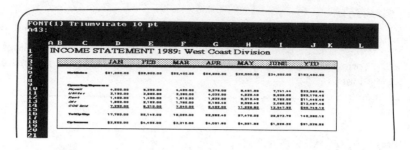

Fig. AW.6.
A worksheet
zoomed at
the "large"
magnification
size.

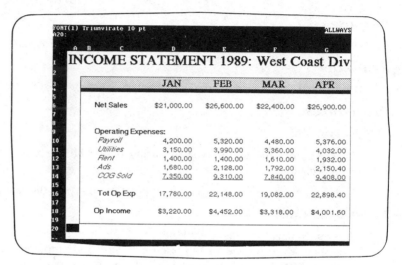

Turns on or off the display of graphs that have been added to the worksheet.

Reminder

The /Display commands do not affect the report printout; they simply change how the worksheet looks on the screen.

Procedures

1. Type **/d**

2. Select one of the following:

Menu Item	Description
Mode	Provides the options **G**raphics and **T**ext mode
Zoom	Provides the options **T**iny, **S**mall, **N**ormal, **L**arge, and **H**uge for character display. Figure AW.5 is an example of "tiny"; figure AW.6 is an example of "large."

Graphs	Enables you to choose whether to show graphs on the screen
Colors	Provides the options **Background**, **Foreground**, and **Highlight**, for which you select colors (assuming that you have a color monitor)

3. Enter the requested response, according to the option selected in the preceding step.

Important Cues

- "Quick" keys are available for some of the display commands:

    Reduce (F4): reduces the display

    Enlarge (Shift-F4): enlarges the display

    Display (F6): switches between **Graphics** and **Text** mode

    Graph (F10): turns the display of graphs on and off

- The **/Display Graphs Yes** command displays the actual graph, rather than the hatching pattern, on the screen. However, you will notice a delay whenever the screen redraws.

- In **Graphics** mode, the formatting displayed on-screen looks much as it does when printed. You must have a graphics monitor to see text in **Graphics** mode.

- You cannot see formatting on-screen in **Text** mode. The control panel, however, displays the formatting instructions for the current cell. The **Zoom** feature also does not work in **Text** mode.

Special Copy and Special Import /SC and /SI

RELEASE
2.2

Purpose

/Special Copy applies the same formatting information contained in one cell or range of cells to another cell or range. The formatting that is copied includes the font, boldfacing, underlining, shading, color, and lines. Use Allways' **Copy** command to save time in formatting.

/Special Import applies to all the formatting information contained in another worksheet on disk. The formatting that is imported includes the individual cell formats, the font set, layout, print range, and graphs. Use this command to format a worksheet that is laid out identically to an existing worksheet you have already formatted.

Reminders

- Save the file in 1-2-3 before copying or importing formats; if you make a mistake when defining the ranges, or if you get unexpected results, you can retrieve the file with its original formatting.

- Allways' /Special Copy and /Special Import commands do not copy data—only the formatting instructions. If you want to copy data, use 1-2-3's /Copy and /File Combine commands.

Procedures

To copy cell formats, do the following:

1. Type **/sc**

2. By highlighting or typing, indicate the range containing the format you are copying. Press Enter.

3. Indicate the range you are copying the format to. Press Enter. This range is now formatted identically to the original range.

To import a format, do the following:

1. Type **/si**

2. Enter the name of the file containing the format you want to copy. Press Enter. The current file now is formatted identically to the original file.

Important Cues

- Use the /Special Move command to move imported cell formats that do not match the current file exactly.

- Another command on the Special menu is Justify. This command is similar to 1-2-3's /Range Justify command, which "wordwraps" text within the range you define. If you change the font size of a paragraph of text, you may find that the text requires more or fewer columns than it originally did. The /Special Justify command respaces the text.

Caution

1-2-3's Undo command does not work in Allways. If you don't like the results of importing the formats from another file, you cannot reverse the operation. The only way to get rid of the new formats is to retrieve the original file (assuming that you saved it before importing).

Macro Library Manager Commands

The Macro Library Manager is an add-in program included with Release 2.2 (Release 2.01 users can buy the program separately). This program, which works in conjunction with 1-2-3, enables you to use your macros in any worksheet without having to store them in each file. Because the macros are in RAM but not in the worksheet, you don't need to worry about accidentally deleting them when you delete rows or columns in the worksheet.

```
Load  Save  Edit  Remove  Name-List  Quit
```

Macro Library Attach   /AA

Purpose

Makes your macros available for use in any worksheet, without your having to store them in each worksheet. The macros are in memory (RAM).

Having macros available in this way saves worksheet space and spares you the time and trouble of copying and renaming "generic" macros in every file. This arrangement also prevents the accidental deletion of macros that are in the same file as the worksheet.

Reminder

The Macro Library Manager (MLM) is an add-in program supplied with Release 2.2. As with any add-in, the MLM must be attached before it can be invoked. You can have the MLM attach automatically whenever you load 1-2-3, or you can attach it when you need to use it.

Procedures

1. Type **/aa** (in Release 2.01 with the Add-In Manager installed, press Alt-F10).

2. Highlight MACROMGR.ADN and press Enter.

3. Select one of the following:

Menu Item	Description
No-Key	Does not assign the MLM add-in to a function key. The add-in must be invoked with /Add-In Invoke.
7	Assigns the MLM add-in to Alt-F7
8	Assigns the MLM add-in to Alt-F8
9	Assigns the MLM add-in to Alt-F9
10	Assigns the MLM add-in to Alt-F10

(Note: In Release 2.01, you cannot select 10.)

Important Cues

- You can invoke an add-in by using the function key you assigned to the add-in when you attached it or by using /Add-In Invoke. In Release 2.01, use Alt-F10 Invoke.

- If you don't have enough memory to attach the MLM add-in, you will get a Memory Full error message. If any other add-ins are attached, you can use /Add-In Detach (in Release 2.01, use Alt-F10 Detach) to remove them from memory, allowing room for the MLM add-in. You also can exit from 1-2-3 and free up memory by removing any other memory-resident programs you may be using.

- Use /Worksheet Global Default Other Add-In Set to attach the MLM add-in automatically when 1-2-3 is loaded. If you use the Release 2.01 Add-In Manager, use Alt-F10 Setup Set.

Macro Library Save

Purpose

Moves the macros in your worksheet into a macro library file and into memory (RAM).

Reminders

- If you used /Worksheet Global Default Other Add-In Set (or Alt-F10 Setup Set in Release 2.01) to attach the MLM add-in automatically, the MLM must be attached either with /Add-In Attach (Alt-F10 Attach in Release 2.01) or automatically when 1-2-3 is loaded.

- Create and name your macros in the current worksheet. Place the cell pointer on the first macro.

Procedures

1. Press Alt and the function key (F7-F10) you assigned to the MLM add-in when you attached it. If you assigned the add-in to the F7 function key, for example, press Alt-F7 to invoke the add-in. The Macro Library Manager menu displays.

   If you did not assign a function key combination, type **/ai** and highlight MACROMGR.ADN from the list of attached add-ins. Press Enter. The Macro Library Manager menu displays.

2. Select Save.

3. Type a name for the library and press Enter. 1-2-3 automatically assigns the extension .MLB.

4. Specify the range containing all the macros. Press Enter.

5. Select **No** if you don't want to assign a password to the file. Select **Yes** if you want to password-protect the library.

6. If you selected **Yes** to assign a password, type the password and press Enter.

Important Cues

- The MLM's **S**ave command loads the library into memory so that you can use the macros with any worksheet you work with.

- A macro library can contain as many as 16,376 cells.

- If you assign a password to the macro library, you (or anyone else) must enter a password before the library can be edited. You do not need to know the password to load the library or to list the macro names in the library

- To add additional macros to an existing library, first copy the existing macros to the current worksheet by using the MLM's **E**dit command. Then use the MLM's **S**ave command to move all macros (old and new) into the same library. Choose **Yes** to overwrite the existing file.

- The MLM's **S**ave command moves the macro names, as well as the keystrokes, out of the current worksheet and into the macro library. (You thus don't need to delete the range names from the current worksheet.)

Caution

If you forget the library's password, you will not be able to look at the contents of, or make any changes in, the library. Passwords are case-sensitive, so remember the exact combination of upper- and lowercase letters you typed when assigning the password.

Macro Library Load

Purpose

Makes the macros in a library accessible in any worksheet.

Reminders

- If you used **/W**orksheet **G**lobal **D**efault **O**ther **A**dd-In **S**et (or **A**lt-F10 **S**etup **S**et in the Release 2.01 Add-In Manager) to attach the MLM add-in automatically, the Macro Library Manager (MLM) add-in must be attached either with **/A**dd-In **A**ttach (**A**lt-F0 **A**ttach in Release 2.01) or automatically when 1-2-3 is loaded.

- Before using **/M**acro **L**ibrary **L**oad, you must create and name a macro library with the MLM's **S**ave command.

Procedures

1. Press Alt and the function key (F7-F10) you assigned to the MLM add-in when you attached it. If you assigned the add-in to the F7 function key, for example, press Alt-F7 to invoke the add-in. The Macro Library Manager menu displays.

   If you did not assign a function key combination, type **/ai** (in Release 2.01, press Alt-F10 and choose **I**nvoke) and highlight MACROMGR.ADN from the list of attached add-ins. Press Enter.

2. Select **L**oad.

3. Highlight the name of the macro library to load from the list of .MLB files. Press Enter.

4. Select **Q**uit. The macros are in memory, available for use in the current worksheet or any other worksheets you create or retrieve.

Important Cues

- If you can't remember the names of the macros in the library, use the MLM's **N**ame-List command to copy the names into the current worksheet. To see the keystrokes associated with the names, use the MLM's **E**dit command.

- You can load as many as 10 macro libraries at once.

- The library remains loaded until you remove it from memory through the MLM's **R**emove command, detach the MLM add-in, or exit from 1-2-3.

Caution

If you load too many macro libraries into memory at once, you will have less space available for your worksheets, and you may run out of memory. Load only the library or libraries you truly need, and remove them after use.

Macro Library Edit

Purpose

Enables you to look at and modify the contents of a macro library; adds new macros to an existing macro library.

Reminders

- If you used /Worksheet Global Default Other Add-In Set (Alt-F10 Setup Set in the Release 2.01 Add-In Manager) to attach the MLM add-in automatically, the MLM add-in must be attached either with /Add-In Attach (Alt-F10 Attach in Release 2.01) or automatically when 1-2-3 is loaded.

- Before using /Macro Library Edit, you must create and name a macro library with the MLM's Save command.

- Place the cell pointer in a blank area where you want the macros to copy.

Procedures

1. Press Alt and the function key (F7-F10) you assigned to the MLM add-in when you attached it. If you assigned the add-in to the F7 function key, for example, press Alt-F7 to invoke the add-in. The Macro Library Manager menu displays.

   If you did not assign a function key combination, type /ai (press Alt-F10 and choose Invoke in Release 2.01) and select MACROMGR.ADN from the list of attached add-ins. Press Enter.

2. Select Edit.

3. Highlight the name of the macro library to edit. Press Enter.

4. If the macro library is password-protected, a prompt requesting the password appears. Enter the password and press Enter.

5. Select one of the following:

Menu Item	Description
Ignore	If the library contains any of the same macro names as in the worksheet, the duplicate names in the library are ignored.
Overwrite	If the library contains any of the same macro names as in the worksheet, the duplicate names in the library overwrite those in the worksheet.

6. Specify the upper left corner of where the macros will copy into the worksheet and press Enter. The macro keystrokes appear in the worksheet.

   Make any desired changes or additions to the library and resave.

Important Cue

To add additional macros to a library, first copy the existing macros into the current worksheet with the MLM's Edit command. Then use the MLM's Save command to move all macros (old and new) into the same library. Choose Yes to overwrite the existing file.

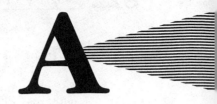

Installing 1-2-3 Release 2.2

Installing 1-2-3 Release 2.2 on your computer is a three-step process. First, you run the initialization program to record your name and company name on the 1-2-3 System disk. Second, you copy the 1-2-3 disks onto your hard disk; if you don't have a hard disk, you need to make working copies of the 1-2-3 disks. Third, you run the INSTALL.EXE program to configure 1-2-3 to your hardware setup.

Noting System Requirements

Before you install 1-2-3 Release 2.2, make sure that your system meets the following hardware and software requirements:

- Is an IBM or compatible computer

- Has one floppy-disk drive and a hard disk or has two double-sided floppy-disk drives (either double- or high-density). The drives can be 5 1/4 inches or 3 1/2 inches in size.

- Has a hard disk and at least one double-sided drive, if you want to use Allways

- Has a monochrome or color monitor and an EGA, VGA, CGA, or Hercules standard display adapter for graphics

- Has at least 320K RAM (512K for Allways)

- Uses DOS V2.0 or higher

The 1-2-3 Disks

To accommodate the two standard sizes of disk drives, Lotus delivers 1-2-3 with two different sets of disks: (1) twelve 5 1/4-inch disks, and (2) six 3 1/2-inch disks. The files contained on the two sets of disks are exactly the same, but the files are divided among the disks somewhat differently.

The 1-2-3 Disks for 5 1/4-Inch Drives

The 1-2-3 package includes twelve 5 1/4-inch disks. Make sure that you have the following disks before proceeding with the installation:

> System disk
> Help disk
> PrintGraph disk
> Translate disk
> Install disk
> Install Library disk
> Sample Files disk
> Allways Setup disk
> Allways disks 2-5

The most important of these disks, the System disk, contains all the 1-2-3 operations except two: the commands for printing graphs and the on-line help system. Printing graphs requires the use of the separate PrintGraph disk, and the Help disk contains 1-2-3's extensive context-sensitive help system.

The Translate disk contains the TRANS.COM program, which is used to convert data to and from 1-2-3 and other software programs (such as dBASE and Symphony).

The Install disk contains the INSTALL.EXE program; the Install Library disk holds all the hardware drivers used to set up 1-2-3 for your system. *Drivers*, briefly, are programs that 1-2-3 uses to control your hardware. Different drivers, for example, are used to control a color monitor and a monochrome monitor.

The Sample Files disk contains the worksheet files discussed in 1-2-3's Tutorial, Quick Start, and Sample Applications manuals.

Also included in the set of disks for 5 1/4-inch drives are five disks for the Allways spreadsheet publishing add-in program. The installation of Allways is covered in the section "Installing Allways" at the end of this appendix. For now, skip to the section "Step 1: Initializing the System Disk."

The 1-2-3 Disks for 3 1/2-Inch Drives

The 1-2-3 package includes six 3 1/2-inch disks. Make sure that you have the following disks before proceeding with the installation:

System/Help and PrintGraph disk
Translate and Sample Files disk
Install and Install Library disk
Allways Setup disk
Allways disks 2 and 3

The System/Help and PrintGraph disk contains all the 1-2-3 operations, including the help facility and the program for printing graphs. The Install and Install Library disk contains the INSTALL.EXE program, which you use to tailor 1-2-3 to your computer system. This disk also holds the library of drivers that you use with the INSTALL.EXE program to set up 1-2-3 for your system. As mentioned in the preceding section, *drivers* are programs that 1-2-3 uses to control your hardware. Different drivers, for example, are used to control a color monitor and a monochrome monitor.

The Translate program disk is used to convert data to and from 1-2-3 and other software programs (such as dBASE and Symphony) along with the sample worksheet files discussed in 1-2-3's Tutorial, Quick Start, and Sample Applications manuals.

Also included in the set of disks for 3 1/2-inch drives are three disks for the Allways spreadsheet publishing add-in program. The installation of Allways is covered in the section "Installing Allways" at the end of this appendix. For now, proceed to the next section, "Step 1: Initializing the System Disk."

Step 1: Initializing the System Disk

Once you have confirmed that you have all the necessary disks, you will initialize the disk containing the System files. Initializing this disk is necessary before you install Release 2.2. Copies of the uninitialized System disk will not initialize and therefore can't be used to install Release 2.2. You should complete this initialization step before copying any files from the System disk to your hard disk. In this step, use only the *original* System disk when the instructions call for the System disk. The System disk must not be write-protected when you attempt to initialize it. Ensure that the write-protect notch on the 5 1/4-inch disk is not covered or that the plastic shutter covers the write-protect opening on the 3 1/2-inch disk.

The initialization program, INIT.EXE, prompts you for your name and company's name. This information is written to the System disk and becomes a permanent record. The initialization program can be run to completion once. You can't change the name and company name by running INIT.EXE again. Although the initialization program's operation is simple, you will want to review your entries for errors before you answer the confirmation prompts. If you are initializing the System disk on behalf of a company, you may want to establish the appropriate name and company name with a supervisor before proceeding. The name and company name will be displayed as part of the start-up banner.

You can stop the initialization program without completing the initialization by pressing Crtl-Break. If you have stopped the initialization program, you may run it again. The program may be stopped and then run any number of times. Once the initialization program has run to completion, however, it cannot be run again.

Once the System disk is initialized, you may use copies of it to install Release 2.2. All copies will contain the initialized name and company name. As a precaution, write-protect the master System disk after you have initialized it.

Note: The instructions for this step assume that you will be using drive A to initialize the master System disk. If you will be using another drive (such as drive B), then be sure to substitute that drive's letter where the instructions use A.

To initialize the program, do the following:

1. Turn on your computer and wait for the DOS prompt to appear.

2. Insert into drive A the 5 1/4-inch System disk or the 3 1/2-inch System/Help and PrintGraph disk.

3. Make drive A the current drive by typing **a:**. Press Enter. The A> prompt should display.

4. Type **init** and press Enter. The copyright screen appears, and you are prompted to press Enter to continue or Ctrl-Break to quit without initializing. Press Enter to proceed.

5. Read the on-screen explanation of initialization and press Enter to proceed.

6. You are then prompted to enter your name. Type your first and last name and press Enter.

7. Press Y and press Enter to confirm your selection. If you made a typing mistake, press N and press Enter to reenter your name. Pressing Ctrl-Break stops the initialization.

8. You are prompted for your company name. Type your company's name and press Enter. If you don't have a company name, type your name again. Pressing Ctrl-Break stops the initialization.

9. Press Y and press Enter to confirm your selection. If you made a typing mistake, press N and press Enter to reenter the name.

10. A screen summarizing your licensing information (product, release, serial number, your name, your company's name) appears. Press Enter if everything is correct and you want to complete the initialization process and make your entries permanent. Press Ctrl-Break to cancel.

11. When prompted, press Enter to end the initialization program and return to DOS.

You are now ready to copy all the 1-2-3 disks to your hard disk or to make backup copies for a floppy-disk-based system.

Step 2: Copying the 1-2-3 Disks

Owners of hard disks should copy all the 1-2-3 disks to the hard drive. If Release 2.2 is the first version of 1-2-3 that you have installed on your hard disk, proceed to the section "Copying the 1-2-3 Disks to a Hard Disk." If you are upgrading to Release 2.2 from Release 1A, 2.0, or 2.01 and want to copy the new version to your hard disk, refer to the next section, "Upgrading to Release 2.2."

If you don't have a hard disk, make backup copies of each of the 1-2-3 disks; you will work with the backup copies instead of the master disks. That way, should you damage one of the backup disks in any way, you can use the master disk to make a replacement copy. To back up your master disks, refer to "Backing Up the 1-2-3 Disks."

Upgrading to Release 2.2

Lotus recommends that users upgrading to Release 2.2 from earlier releases create a different directory for the new version. If you plan to follow their recommendation, you can go immediately to the steps in the next section, "Copying the 1-2-3 Disks to a Hard Disk."

If you want to use the same subdirectory you had for your earlier release of 1-2-3, or if you want to erase all the files in the old subdirectory, you need to follow these basic steps:

1. If you have any worksheet files in your 1-2-3 program subdirectory, copy them to another subdirectory.

2. If you have been running 1-2-3 *without* the System disk in drive A when you load the program, you should remove the copy-protected files from your hard disk. You can skip this step if you have Release

1A or if you never transferred the copy-protected files to your hard disk on Release 2.0 or 2.01. To remove copy protection, do the following:

    a. In Release 2.0, change to your 1-2-3 subdirectory and run the COPYOFF.COM program.

    b. In Release 2.01, change to your 1-2-3 subdirectory and start the INSTALL.EXE program. Select Advanced Options and then choose Remove 1-2-3 from a Hard Disk.

3. You can now erase all the files in the 1-2-3 program subdirectory.

Proceed to the next section to find out how to copy the new version to your hard disk. (You can skip Step 1 because you already have a 1-2-3 subdirectory.)

Copying the 1-2-3 Disks to a Hard Disk

The following steps are required to copy the 1-2-3 disks onto your hard disk so that all the 1-2-3 programs can be started from the hard disk. These instructions assume that your hard disk is formatted, that DOS is installed, and that drive C is your default drive. You should write-protect your master 1-2-3 disks by covering the write-protect notch (on 5 1/4-inch disks) or opening the write-protect window (on 3 1/2-inch disks).

1. Create a subdirectory to hold the 1-2-3 files. To create a subdirectory of the root directory, use DOS's "make directory" (MD) command. Type **md \123** and press Enter, for example, to create a subdirectory named 123.

2. Make this subdirectory the current directory by using DOS's "change directory" (CD) command. If you named the subdirectory 123, type **cd \123** and press Enter.

3. Copy the contents of each 1-2-3 master disk onto the hard disk, following this procedure:

    a. Place one of the master disks into the drive:

5 1/4-inch	*3 1/2-inch*
System disk	System/Help and PrintGraph disk
Help disk	Translate and Sample Files disk
PrintGraph disk	Install and Install Library disk
Translate disk	
Install disk	
Install Library disk	
Sample Files disk	

b. Type **copy a:*.*** and press Enter. (If you're installing from drive B, type **copy b:*.*** and press Enter.) DOS recognizes that you want the files copied to the current directory—C:\123. Note: Do not copy files from any of the Allways disks at this time.

c. When the copying is complete, remove the master disk from drive A and repeat Steps 3a through 3c for each master disk.

Put all the master disks in a safe place and proceed to "Step 3: Running the INSTALL.EXE Program."

Backing Up the 1-2-3 Disks

Before making backup copies, you should become familiar with your computer's disk operating system. For specific explanations of formatting disks and copying files, refer to Que's books *Using PC DOS*, 3rd Edition, or *MS-DOS User's Guide*, 3rd Edition; or check your system's manual. Use the following steps to create backup copies of the 1-2-3 disks:

1. Format seven blank 5 1/4-inch disks or three 3 1/2-inch disks, using the DOS FORMAT.COM program. Format another disk with the /S option to make a DOS System disk (for example, FORMAT B:/S). This disk will be your 1-2-3 System disk, which can be used to start the computer and 1-2-3. Be sure to label the disk formatted with the /S specifier as the System disk in the next step.

2. Label the blank disks as follows:

5 1/4-inch	3 1/2-inch
System disk	System/Help and PrintGraph disk
Help disk	Translate and Sample Files disk
PrintGraph disk	Install and Install Library disk
Translate disk	
Install disk	
Install Library disk	
Sample Files disk	

3. Copy each 1-2-3 master disk onto the appropriate formatted blank disk as follows:

a. Place, in turn, each master 1-2-3 disk into drive A and the formatted disk labeled with the same name into drive B.

b. At the A> prompt, type **copy a:*.* b:** and press Enter.

c. After all files have been copied from the master disk onto the formatted disk, remove the master disk from drive A and the backup copy from drive B.

d. Follow Steps 3a through 3c for each of the master disks.

Put your master disks away in a safe place and proceed to "Step 3: Running the INSTALL.EXE Program."

Step 3: Running the INSTALL.EXE Program

At this point, you could load 1-2-3 and create and save spreadsheets. You would not, however, be able to display graphs or print anything until you run the INSTALL.EXE program.

Installing driver programs tailors 1-2-3 to your particular system. The drivers are small programs that reside in the driver library on the Install Library disk.

The driver files store information about your computer system, such as information about the display(s), printer(s), and plotter. You can create one or many driver files, depending on your needs. For example, if you want to run 1-2-3 on an IBM PC with a color monitor and also run 1-2-3 on a COMPAQ with a monochrome monitor, creating two separate driver files will enable you to run 1-2-3 on either computer whenever you like.

When you make your driver selection, carefully review the options. Whether your system can display graphs and display in color depends on a number of factors: the type of monitor(s) you have, the type of video adapter card(s) (whether it will produce only text or also graphics and color), and the number of colors displayed.

Before you run the INSTALL.EXE program, prepare a list of your equipment. When you run INSTALL.EXE, you will first need to indicate to 1-2-3 what screen display hardware you have—for example, VGA, EGA, CGA, or Hercules.

Second, you will need to indicate to the program what kind of text printer(s) you have. You can specify more than one printer at installation and then select the particular one you want to use from within 1-2-3.

Third, 1-2-3 will ask you to indicate the graphics printer(s) or plotter(s) you will be using. Again, if you specify several graphics printers during installation, you can later select the appropriate one from within 1-2-3. Note that the same printer can be installed as both the text printer and the graphics printer.

If you do not have a hard disk, keep in mind that multiple drivers take up space on your 1-2-3 disk. If disk space is a problem, keep the list of printers to a minimum or store your additional driver files on a separate disk. When you want to use another driver, place the System disk containing your usual driver set (123.SET) into drive A and the disk containing your other drivers into drive B. At the A> prompt, type

123 B:name

where **name** is the name of the particular driver set you want to use. 1-2-3 will then load onto your computer, using the specified driver.

The following steps explain how to install drivers. By pressing F1 when the program is running, you can access detailed, context-sensitive help.

Hard Disk Systems

1. Make sure that your 123 subdirectory is current by typing **cd \123**. If you have given the 123 subdirectory a different name, type **cd ** followed by your subdirectory's name.

2. Type **install** and press Enter. When instructed, press Enter to begin the INSTALL.EXE program.

3. When the main Install menu appears, select First-Time Installation. Then create your driver set by following the step-by-step instructions that appear on your computer screen.

4. If you are creating only one driver set, answer no to the question "Do you want to name your driver set?" The INSTALL.EXE program will then use the default driver name, 123.SET. If you are creating two or more driver sets, you must name each driver. For example, if the driver set contained a color graphics monitor, you could name the driver set COLOR.SET.

5 1/4-Inch Disk Systems

1. Insert the Install disk into drive A.

2. Type **a:** and press Enter to go to drive A.

3. Type **install** and press Enter. When instructed, press Enter to begin the INSTALL.EXE program.

4. When 1-2-3 prompts you to do so, replace the Install disk with the Install Library disk. Then, when prompted, replace the Install Library disk with the System disk.

5. When the main Install menu appears, select First-Time Installation. Then create your driver set by following the step-by-step instructions that appear on your screen.

6. If you are creating only one driver set, answer no to the question "Do you want to name your driver set?" The INSTALL.EXE program will then use the default driver name, 123.SET. If you are creating multiple driver sets, you must name each driver. For example, if the

driver set contained a color graphics monitor, you could name the driver set COLOR.SET. After answering the driver set question, press Enter to continue.

7. When prompted, insert the Install Library disk into drive A and follow the screen prompts for saving your driver set on the System, PrintGraph, and Translate disks.

8. Follow the on-screen instructions for exiting from the INSTALL.EXE program.

3 1/2-Inch Disk Systems

1. Insert the Install and Install Library disk into drive A.

2. Type **a:** and press Enter to go to drive A.

3. Type **install** and press Enter. When instructed, press Enter to begin the INSTALL.EXE program.

4. When prompted, replace the Install and Install Library disk with the System/Help and PrintGraph disk.

5. When the main Install menu appears, select First-Time Installation. Then create your driver set by following the step-by-step instructions that appear on your screen.

6. If you are creating only one driver set, answer no to the question "Do you want to name your driver set?" The INSTALL.EXE program will then use the default driver name 123.SET. If you are creating two or more driver sets, you must name each driver. For example, if the driver set contained a color graphics monitor, you could name the driver set COLOR.SET.

7. When prompted, insert the Install and Install Library disk into drive A and follow the screen prompts for saving your driver set on the System/Help and PrintGraph disk and the Translate and Sample Files disk.

8. Follow the on-screen instructions for exiting from the INSTALL.EXE program.

Changing the Driver Set

If you need to make changes or corrections to your existing driver set(s), enter the INSTALL.EXE program and select the Change Selected Equipment option; then follow the on-screen options. To save your modifications, you must choose the Save Changes option.

Installing Allways

Allways is a spreadsheet publishing add-in program that comes with Release 2.2. The AWSETUP program on the Allways Setup disk automates the entire installation process. The program creates a subdirectory of 123 called Allways, copies all the Allways disks, and runs an installation program so that you can specify the type of hardware you have.

Before proceeding with the Allways installation, you must have the following:

- 1-2-3 installed according to the steps outlined earlier
- A hard disk
- At least 512K RAM
- The Allways Setup disk and the Allways disks. You should have disks numbered 2-5 on 5 1/4-inch disks. On 3 1/2-inch disks, you should have disks 2 and 3.

Follow these steps to copy and install the Allways program:

1. Turn on your computer and wait until the DOS prompt displays.
2. Place the Allways Setup disk in drive A.
3. Type **a:** and press Enter to switch to drive A.
4. Type **awsetup** and press Enter.
5. When the main menu appears, select First-Time Installation. Then install Allways by following the step-by-step instructions that appear on your computer screen.

B

Summary of 1-2-3
Release 2.2 Features

To say 1-2-3 is a powerful, popular program is an understatement. Many users have tested the boundaries of 1-2-3, beyond the applications for which the program was designed. Despite the usefulness of 1-2-3, many users have thought, "if only 1-2-3 had . . . ." Consider the new features of 1-2-3 Release 2.2 and decide for yourself whether the program has what you always wished it had.

This appendix lists the enhancements and new features of 1-2-3 Release 2.2. The enhancements and new features are presented in table form, which indicates what is an enhancement to a Release 2.01 feature and what is actually a new feature. If a check mark appears in both the Release 2.0/2.01 and Release 2.2 columns, the associated feature is *enhanced*. If a check mark appears only in the Release 2.2 column, the feature is *new*. Listed with each enhancement are the keystrokes used to activate the enhancement, if keystrokes are applicable.

The changes and enhancements in this list are arranged in the following order: /Worksheet, /Range, /File, /Print, /Graph, @Functions, Macros, Screen Appearance, Keyboard Control, Memory Usage, General, and Networking.

Enhancement or New Feature	Release 2.0/2.01	Release 2.2
/Worksheet		
Store negative number with minus sign or in parentheses in Currency or comma (,) format—/wgoin.		✔
Replace a zero cell entry with a label—/wgzl.		✔
Replace clock at lower left of screen with file name—/wgdocf.		✔
Shut off 1-2-3's beep—/wgdob.		✔
Enable or disable automatic macros—/wgda.		✔
Enable up to eight add-ins to be attached and invoked automatically—/wgdoas.	✔	✔
Change the width of a range of columns—/wcc.		✔
Recover erased information using Undo—/wgdou.		✔
/Range		
Search a range for a string in formulas, labels, or both; optionally replace the search string with another string—/rs.		✔
/File		
Protect files from being overwritten when 1-2-3 is used on a local-area network—/far.	✔	✔
Create a backup copy of a worksheet any time it could be replaced—/fsb, /fxf, or /fxv.		✔
Refresh links to other worksheets—/fal.		✔
List all files on disk linked to the current worksheet—/fll.		✔
Create a table in the worksheet of files on disk—/fat.		✔
/Print		
Set margins to none—/p[p,f]omn.	✔	✔
Print documents using the Allways spreadsheet publishing add-in.	✔	✔

Enhancement or New Feature	Release 2.0/2.01	Release 2.2

/Graph

Print a graph without leaving 1-2-3 using the Allways add-in. | ✔ | ✔

Create a table in the current file of named graphs—/gnt. | | ✔

Set all graph ranges at once with data either Columnwise or Rowwise—/gg[*range*][c,r]. | | ✔

Reset all ranges selected or reset all options selected—/grr or /gro. | | ✔

Set data-labels for all ranges at once—/godg. | | ✔

Set legends for all ranges at once—/golr. | | ✔

Create a table in the worksheet of all graph names—/gnt. | | ✔

@Functions

Test for the existence of an add-in application—@ISAPP("name"). | | ✔

Test for the existence of an add-in function—@ISAAF("name"). | | ✔

Macros

Macro Commands

Shut off and restore the worksheet borders—{BORDERSOFF} or {FRAMEOFF} and {BORDERSON} or {FRAMEON}. | | ✔

Display and eliminate a graph on the screen—{GRAPHON} and {GRAPHOFF}. | | ✔

Change the mode indicator to display a label as long as the width of the screen—{INDICATE}. | ✔ | ✔

Shut off display in the panel, and clear the control panel and status line—{PANELOFF}. | ✔ | ✔

Turn on and shut off the display of settings sheets while in macro control—{WINDOWSON} and {WINDOWSOFF}. | ✔ | ✔

Call the operating system while 1-2-3 remains in memory—{SYSTEM}. | | ✔

Enhancement or New Feature	*Release 2.0/2.01*	*Release 2.2*
Macro Key Names		
Activate help—{HELP}.		✔
Move the cell pointer up, down, left, or right—{U}, {D}, {L}, or {R}.	✔	✔
General Macro Features		
Record keystrokes to create a macro—/wl and Alt-F5.		✔
Store macros in memory but outside the worksheet—Macro Library Manager.		✔
Run a macro with names other than / and a letter—Alt-F3.		✔
Use STEP mode to debug macros—Alt-F2.	✔	✔
Screen Appearance		
Display either the current file name or date and time in the lower left corner of the screen.		✔
Keyboard Control		
Start an add-in application—Alt-F7, Alt-F8, Alt-F9, and Alt-F10.	✔	✔
Use the Learn feature to place keystrokes into a range on the worksheet to build a macro—Alt-F5.		✔
Memory Usage		
Use up to 4MB of LIM 4.0 or LIM 3.2 expanded memory with DOS.	✔	✔
General		
Minimum recalculation is used so that only formulas affected by a changed cell are recalculated.		✔
Use add-in applications—/a.	✔	✔
Use values from worksheets stored on disk—file linking.		✔
Retrieve a worksheet when you start 1-2-3.		✔
Undo the last change to the worksheet—Alt-F4.		✔

Enhancement or New Feature	Release 2.0/2.01	Release 2.2
View all settings on a settings sheet when you select certain menus.		✔
Networking		
Share data files on a LAN.	✔	✔
Protect a file read from a LAN from being updated by multiple users at the same time.		✔

Index

This index begins with nonalphabetical entries, including listings of 1-2-3 commands and functions. Following this, you will find alphabetical entries.

1-2-3 Functions

B

C

D

G

Using Lotus Magellan

by David Gobel

The ultimate book on Lotus' new file management software! Covers Magellan's file viewing capability and shows how to edit and print files, organize data, index files, use "fuzzy searching," work with macros, and set up Magellan for network use.

Order #980
$21.95 USA
0-88022-448-7, 400 pp.

MS-DOS QuickStart

Developed by Que Corporation

The visual approach to learning MS-DOS! Illustrations help you become familiar with your operating system. This step-by-step guide is perfect for all beginning users of DOS and covers through DOS Version 4.0!

Order #872
$21.95 USA
0-88022-388-X, 313 pp.

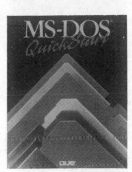

1-2-3 Database Techniques

by Dick Andersen and Bill Weil

Concepts and techniques to help you create complex 1-2-3 database applications! With an emphasis on Release 3 features, this book introduces database fundamentals, compares 1-2-3 with traditional database programs, offers numerous application tips, and discusses add-in programs.

Order #835
$22.95 USA
0-88022-346-4, 450 pp.

1-2-3 Release 2.2 QuickStart

Developed by Que Corporation

Que's popular graphics approach makes it easy to get up and running with Lotus 1-2-3 Release 2.2! More than 100 two-page illustrations explain the program's basics for worksheets, reports, graphs, databases, and macros. This book actually shows you step-by-step how to get maximum 1-2-3 results fast! Also covers Release 2.01.

Order #1041
$19.95 USA
0-88022-502-5, 450 pp.

1-2-3 Tips, Tricks, and Traps, 3rd Edition

by Dick Andersen

Covering all releases of Lotus 1-2-3—including 2.2 and 3—this updated Que classic presents hundreds of tips and techniques! Covers three-dimensional spreadsheet capabilities, new graphics features, macros, and database enhancements. An excellent reference for 1-2-3 power users!

Order #963
$22.95 USA
0-88022-416-9, 550 pp.

Upgrading to 1-2-3 Release 3

Developed by Que Corporation

Upgrading to 1-2-3 Release 3 helps Release 2.01 users make the transition quickly and easily. This practical text covers all the features new to Release 3, including multiple worksheet and file capabilities, enhanced graphics, and new database functions. A perfect resource for getting started with Release 3!

Order #1018
$14.95 USA
0-88022-491-6, 400 pp.

Using Paradox 3

by Walter Bruce

Using Paradox 3 is the complete guide to Borland's unique database management program. This comprehensive text for beginning and inter-meditate users explores how to record a sequence of commands as an easy-to-use script, the program's multiuser capabilities, and the Paradox Application Language.

Order #859
$22.95 USA
0-88022-362-6, 450 pp.

1-2-3 Release 2.2 Quick Reference

Developed by Que Corporation

Gain instant access to the essential features of Lotus 1-2-3 Release 2.2! *1-2-3 Release 2.2 Quick Reference* is a handy resource for the most important commands and functions of this powerful spreadsheet software—in a compact, portable format!

Order #1042
$7.95 USA
0-88022-503-3, 160 pp.

Using Ventura Publisher, 2nd Edition

by Diane Burns, S. Venit, and Linda Mercer

Dozens of detailed example documents are presented in this classic combination of tutorial and reference material. The text highlights the new features of Ventura Publisher 2.0, including the powerful Professional Extension!

Order #940
$24.95 USA
0-88022-406-1, 800 pp.

dBASE IV Handbook, 3rd Edition

by George T. Chou, Ph.D.

Beginning users will progress step-by-step from basic database concepts to advanced dBASE features, and experienced dBASE users will appreciate the information on the powerful features of dBASE IV. Also includes Quick Start tutorials.

Order #852
$23.95 USA
0-88022-380-4, 600 pp.

Using Harvard Graphics

by Steve Sagman and Jane Graver Sandlar

This well-written text presents both program basics and presentation fundamentals to create bar, pie, line, and other types of informative graphs. Helps you put a professional polish on all your business presentations.

Order #941
$24.95 USA
0-88022-407-X, 550 pp.

1-2-3 Macro Library, 3rd Edition

Developed by Que Corporation

Includes companion disk! From simple keystroke macros to complex macro programs, *1-2-3 Macro Library*, 3rd Edition, helps you automate spreadsheet applications. Also teaches you how to develop sophisticated macro programs for database and financial applications.

Order #962
$39.95 USA
0-88022-418-5, 600 pp.
Available 4th Quarter

Using Computers in Business

by Joel Shore

This text covers all aspects of business computerization, including a thorough analysis of benefits, costs, alternatives, and common problems. Also discusses how to budget for computerization, how to shop for the right hardware and software, and how to allow for expansions and upgrades.

Order #1020
$24.95 USA
0-88022-470-3, 450 pp.

Using Professional Write

by Katherine Murray

Quick Start tutorials introduce word processing basics and helps you progress to advanced skills with this top-selling executive word processing program. Also contains a section on macros, easy-to-follow examples and printing tips. Using Professional Write with other programs also is discussed.

Order #1027
$19.95 USA
0-88022-490-8, 400 pp.

Using WordPerfect 5

by Charles O. Stewart III, et al.

The #1 best-selling word processing book! Introduces WordPerfect basics and helps you learn to use macros, styles, and other advanced features. Also includes Quick Start tutorials, a tear-out command reference card, and an introduction to WordPerfect 5 for 4.2 users.

Order #843
$24.95 USA
0-88022-351-0, 867 pp.

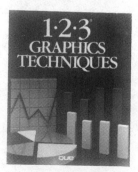

1-2-3 Graphics Techniques

by Dick Andersen

1-2-3 Graphics Techniques presents the most effective methods for analyzing spreadsheet data with 1-2-3 graphs! This practical text fully explains graph commands and provides useful techniques for customizing graphs and producing high-quality printouts. Packed with examples!

Order #1066
$22.95 USA
0-88022-515-7, 450 pp.
Available 4th Quarter

Managing Your Hard Disk, 2nd Edition
by Don Berliner

Learn how to organize your programs and data on a hard disk! This practical guide presents detailed information on DOS 3.3, IBM's PS/2 hardware, and the newest application and utility software!

Order #837
$22.95 USA
0-88022-348-0, 600 pp.

Networking IBM PCs, 2nd Edition
by Michael Durr

Explore the critical issues of networking in this easy-to-understand text! You'll learn the advantages of local area networks, security concerns, hardware considerations, mainframe access techniques, and tips on efficient management.

Order #71
$19.95 USA
0-88022-271-9, 202 pp.

Upgrading and Repairing PCs
by Scott Mueller

A comprehensive resource to personal computer upgrade, repair, maintenance, and troubleshooting. Covers all types of IBM computers and compatibles—from the original PC to the PS/2 models. A runaway best-seller.

Order #882
$27.95 USA
0-88022-395-2, 724 pp.

1-2-3 Release 2.2 Business Applications
Developed by Que Corporation

Book and disk set! Combining ready-to-run business applications with an easy-to-follow, illustrated text, *1-2-3 Release 2.2 Business Applications* demonstrates successful strategies for building spreadsheet and database applications. Guaranteed to improve your efficiency!

Order #1065
$39.95 USA
0-88022-516-5, 550 pp.

More Computer Knowledge from Que

Free Catalog!

Mail us this registration form today, and we'll send you a free catalog featuring Que's complete line of best-selling books.

Name of Book _____

Name _____

Title _____

Phone (___) _____

Company _____

Address _____

City _____

State _____ ZIP _____

Please check the appropriate answers:

1. Where did you buy your Que book?
   - ☐ Bookstore (name: _____)
   - ☐ Computer store (name: _____)
   - ☐ Catalog (name: _____)
   - ☐ Direct from Que
   - ☐ Other: _____

2. How many computer books do you buy a year?
   - ☐ 1 or less
   - ☐ 2-5
   - ☐ 6-10
   - ☐ More than 10

3. How many Que books do you own?
   - ☐ 1
   - ☐ 2-5
   - ☐ 6-10
   - ☐ More than 10

4. How long have you been using this software?
   - ☐ Less than 6 months
   - ☐ 6 months to 1 year
   - ☐ 1-3 years
   - ☐ More than 3 years

5. What influenced your purchase of this Que book?
   - ☐ Personal recommendation
   - ☐ Advertisement
   - ☐ In-store display
   - ☐ Price
   - ☐ Que catalog
   - ☐ Que mailing
   - ☐ Que's reputation
   - ☐ Other:

6. How would you rate the overall content of the book?
   - ☐ Very good
   - ☐ Good
   - ☐ Satisfactory
   - ☐ Poor

7. What do you like *best* about this Que book?

   _____
   _____

8. What do you like *least* about this Que book?

   _____
   _____

9. Did you buy this book with your personal funds?
   - ☐ Yes   ☐ No

10. Please feel free to list any other comments you may have about this Que book.

   _____
   _____
   _____

que

Order Your Que Books Today!

Name _____

Title _____

Company _____

City _____

State _____ ZIP _____

Phone No. (___) _____

Method of Payment.

Check ☐   (Please enclose in envelope.)

Charge My: VISA ☐   MasterCard ☐

American Express ☐

Charge # _____

Expiration Date _____

Order No.	Title	Qty.	Price	Total

You can **FAX** your order to **1-317-573-2583**. Or call **1-800-428-5331, ext. ORDR** to order direct.

Please add $2.50 per title for shipping and handling.

Subtotal	
Shipping & Handling	
Total	

que

Here's a tiny sample of the kinds of articles you'll read in every issue of *Absolute Reference*:

Discover the incredible power of macros—shortcuts for hundreds of applications and subroutines.
- A macro for formatting text
- Monitoring preset database conditions with a macro
- Three ways to design macro menus
- Building macros with string formulas
- Having fun with the marching macro
- Using the ROWs macro
- Generating a macro for tracking elapsed time

New applications and new solutions—every issue gives you novel ways to harness 1-2-3 and Symphony
- Creating customized menus for your spreadsheets
- How to use criteria to unlock your spreadsheet program's data management power
- Using spreadsheets to monitor investments
- Improving profits with more effective sales forecasts
- An easy way to calculate year-to-date performance
- Using /Data Fill to streamline counting and range filling

Extend your uses—and your command—of spreadsheets
- Printing spreadsheets sideways can help sell your ideas
- How to add goal-seeking capabilities to your spreadsheet

- Hiding columns to create custom worksheet printouts
- Lay out your spreadsheet for optimum memory management
- Toward an "intelligent" spreadsheet
- A quick way to erase extraneous zeros

Techniques for avoiding pitfalls and repairing the damage when disaster occurs
- Preventing and trapping errors in your worksheet
- How to create an auditable spreadsheet
- Pinpointing specific errors in your spreadsheets
- Ways to avoid failing formulas
- Catching common debugging and data-entry errors
- Detecting data-entry errors
- Protecting worksheets from accidental (or deliberate) destruction
- Avoiding disaster with the /System command

Objective product reviews—we accept *no advertising*, so you can trust our editors' outspoken opinions
- Metro Desktop Manager
- Freelance Plus
- Informix
- 4Word, InWord, Write-in
- Spreadsheet Analyst
- 101 macros for 1-2-3

Mail this card today!